Toward a Livable Life

Toward a Livable Life

A 21st Century Agenda for Social Work

EDITED BY MARK ROBERT RANK
Herbert S. Hadley Professor of Social Welfare
Washington University
St. Louis, Missouri

Oxford University Press is a department of the University of Oxford. It furthers
the University's objective of excellence in research, scholarship, and education
by publishing worldwide. Oxford is a registered trade mark of Oxford University
Press in the UK and certain other countries.

Published in the United States of America by Oxford University Press
198 Madison Avenue, New York, NY 10016, United States of America.

© Oxford University Press 2020

All rights reserved. No part of this publication may be reproduced, stored in
a retrieval system, or transmitted, in any form or by any means, without the
prior permission in writing of Oxford University Press, or as expressly permitted
by law, by license, or under terms agreed with the appropriate reproduction
rights organization. Inquiries concerning reproduction outside the scope of the
above should be sent to the Rights Department, Oxford University Press, at the
address above.

You must not circulate this work in any other form
and you must impose this same condition on any acquirer.

CIP data is on file at the Library of Congress
ISBN 978–0–19–069105–9

1 3 5 7 9 8 6 4 2

Printed by Integrated Books International, United States of America

CONTENTS

Acknowledgments vii
Contributors ix

1. Introduction 1
   MARK ROBERT RANK

2. Tackling the Social Determinants of Ill Health 16
   DARRELL L. HUDSON, SARAH GEHLERT, AND SHANTA PANDEY

3. Alleviating Poverty 45
   MARK ROBERT RANK

4. Confronting Stigma, Discrimination, and Social Exclusion 70
   VANESSA D. FABBRE, ELENI GAVERAS, ANNA GOLDFARB SHABSIN,
   JANELLE GIBSON, AND MARK ROBERT RANK

5. Reducing Cumulative Inequality 94
   MARK ROBERT RANK

6. Developing Financial Assets for Lower-Income Households 114
   STEPHEN ROLL, MICHAL GRINSTEIN-WEISS, JOSEPH STEENSMA,
   AND ANNA DERUYTER

7. Preventing Child Maltreatment 152
   MELISSA JONSON-REID, BRETT DRAKE, PATRICIA L. KOHL, AND
   WENDY F. AUSLANDER

8. Fostering Civic Engagement Across the Life Course 193
   VETTA L. SANDERS THOMPSON AND GENA GUNN MCCLENDEN

9. Building Healthy, Diverse, and Thriving Communities 211
   CAROLYN LESOROGOL, ANA A. BAUMANN, AMY EYLER, MOLLY W. METZGER,
   RODRIGO S. REIS, AND RACHEL G. TABAK

10. Achieving Environmental Justice 232

LISA REYES MASON

11. Engaging Older Adults 253

SOJUNG PARK AND NANCY MORROW-HOWELL

12. Generating Effective Demand and Use of Social Services 276

MELISSA JONSON-REID, MATTHEW W. KREUTER, EDWARD F. LAWLOR,
DAVID A. PATTERSON SILVER WOLF, AND VETTA L. SANDERS THOMPSON

13. Designing and Implementing Policy and Program Innovations 311

BARRY ROSENBERG, PATRICK J. FOWLER, AND ROSS C. BROWNSON

14. Leveraging Big Data Analytics and Informatics 337

DEREK S. BROWN, BRETT DRAKE, PATRICK J. FOWLER, JENINE K.
HARRIS, AND KIMBERLY J. JOHNSON

15. Looking Back, Looking Ahead 357

EDWARD F. LAWLOR, MARY M. MCKAY, SHANTI K. KHINDUKA,
AND MARK ROBERT RANK

Index 367

ACKNOWLEDGMENTS

One of the delightful consequences of working on a project such as this is becoming familiar with your colleagues' ideas and scholarship. During the course of the past several years, I have been fortunate in getting the chance to learn much about the research that takes place in the offices, classrooms, and hallways of the George Warren Brown School of Social Work at Washington University in St. Louis. Our faculty's dedication and creativity to understanding and making this world a better place has been personally inspiring. First and foremost, this book is a tribute to the groundbreaking work of these scholars.

Next, the project would not have been possible without the vision and energy of Gautam Yadama. Gautam was instrumental in getting this work off the ground, and he laid the intellectual foundation for the book to be built upon. Although he has since become the Dean of the School of Social Work at Boston College, his footprint upon the ideas in this book is large indeed.

Our school has been fortunate over the years to have been guided by truly outstanding leadership. I have had the personal pleasure of serving under three deans during my tenure at Washington University—Shanti Khinduka, Edward Lawlor, and Mary McKay. Each of them in their own way have encouraged and inspired their faculty to reach for new heights. They have created an environment that welcomes innovation and impact. The success of the school is in no small part the result of their stellar leadership.

I should also point out something unusual about Washington University and its School of Social Work. As I talk to faculty members around the country, they sometimes complain about the perceived second-class status of their school or department in the eyes of their higher administration. Fortunately, at Washington University that has never been the case. From our Chancellor on down, the school has been enthusiastically supported as a crowning achievement of the university. This point of pride is yet another reason for the school's success over the years.

It has been said that we are able to gain greater understanding of the world only by "standing on the shoulders of giants." I have come to fully appreciate this saying through working on this project. Our social work founders and pioneers have laid a strong foundation on which we can build and extend their insights and discoveries. To all who have walked and paved the path, a heartfelt note of appreciation.

Finally, a last tip of the hat to our outstanding editor at Oxford, Dana Bliss. Dana has provided the encouragement and guidance throughout this project that has been so important to its fruition. His insights and knowledge regarding the field of social work have proven to be an invaluable asset for this book.

Many thanks to one and all!

CONTRIBUTORS

Wendy F. Auslander
Barbara A. Bailey Professor
Social Work
George Warren Brown School
of Social Work, Washington
University in St. Louis
St. Louis, MO, USA

Ana A. Baumann
Research Assistant Professor
George Warren Brown School
of Social Work, Washington
University in St. Louis
St. Louis, MO, USA

Ross C. Brownson
Steven H. and Susan U. Lipstein
Distinguished Professor
George Warren Brown School
of Social Work, Washington
University in St. Louis
St. Louis, MO, USA

Derek S. Brown
Associate Professor
George Warren Brown School
of Social Work, Washington
University in St. Louis
St. Louis, MO, USA

Anna deRuyter
Business Development
Professional Writer
Centene Corporation
St. Louis, MO, USA

Brett Drake
Professor
George Warren Brown School
of Social Work, Washington
University in St. Louis
St. Louis, MO, USA

Amy Eyler
Associate Professor
George Warren Brown School
of Social Work, Washington
University in St. Louis
St. Louis, MO, USA

Vanessa D. Fabbre
Assistant Professor, George Warren
Brown School of Social Work
Washington University in St. Louis
St. Louis, MO, USA

Patrick J. Fowler
Associate Professor, George Warren
Brown School of Social Work
Washington University in St. Louis
St. Louis, MO, USA

Eleni Gaveras
PhD Student
George Warren Brown School of
Social Work
Washington University in St. Louis
St. Louis, MO, USA

Sarah Gehlert
Dean
College of Social Work, University of
South Carolina
Columbia, SC, USA

Janelle Gibson
Senior Lecturer
George Warren Brown School
of Social Work, Washington
University in St. Louis
St. Louis, MO, USA

Michal Grinstein-Weiss
Shanti K. Khinduka Distinguished
Professor
George Warren Brown School
of Social Work, Washington
University in St. Louis
St. Louis, MO, USA

Jenine K. Harris
Associate Professor
George Warren Brown School
of Social Work, Washington
University in St. Louis
St. Louis, MO, USA

Darrell L. Hudson
Associate Professor
George Warren Brown School
of Social Work, Washington
University in St. Louis
St. Louis, MO, USA

Kimberly J. Johnson
Associate Professor
George Warren Brown School
of Social Work, Washington
University in St. Louis
St. Louis, MO, USA

Melissa Jonson-Reid
Ralph and Muriel Pumphrey
Professor of Social Work Research
George Warren Brown School
of Social Work, Washington
University in St. Louis
St. Louis, MO, USA

Shanti K. Khinduka
George Warren Brown Distinguished
Professor Emeritus
George Warren Brown School
of Social Work, Washington
University in St. Louis
St. Louis, MO, USA

Patricia L. Kohl
Associate Professor, George Warren
Brown School of Social Work
Washington University in St. Louis
St. Louis, MO, USA

Matthew W. Kreuter
Kahn Family Professor of
Public Health
George Warren Brown School
of Social Work, Washington
University in St. Louis
St. Louis, MO, USA

Edward F. Lawlor
William E. Gordon Distinguished
Professor Emeritus
George Warren Brown School
of Social Work, Washington
University in St. Louis
St. Louis, MO, USA

CONTRIBUTORS

Carolyn Lesorogol
Professor
George Warren Brown School
  of Social Work, Washington
  University in St. Louis
St. Louis, MO, USA

Lisa Reyes Mason
Associate Professor
College of Social Work, University of
  Tennessee, Knoxville
Knoxville, TN, USA

Gena Gunn McClenden
Center for Social Development
  Director of Voter Access and
  Engagement, Financial Capability
  and Asset Building Initiatives
George Warren Brown School
  of Social Work, Washington
  University in St. Louis
St. Louis, MO, USA

Mary M. McKay
Neidorff Family and Centene
  Corporation Dean
George Warren Brown School
  of Social Work, Washington
  University in St. Louis
St. Louis, MO, USA

Molly W. Metzger
Senior Lecturer
George Warren Brown School
  of Social Work, Washington
  University in St. Louis
St. Louis, MO, USA

Nancy Morrow-Howell
Betty Bofinger Distinguished
  Professor Social Policy
George Warren Brown School
  of Social Work, Washington
  University in St. Louis
St. Louis, MO, USA

Shanta Pandey
Professor
School of Social Work, Boston
  College
Boston, MA, USA

Sojung Park
Assistant Professor
George Warren Brown School
  of Social Work, Washington
  University in St. Louis
St. Louis, MO, USA

Mark Robert Rank
Herbert S. Hadley Professor of Social
  Welfare
George Warren Brown School
  of Social Work, Washington
  University in St. Louis
St. Louis, MO, USA

Rodrigo S. Reis
Professor
George Warren Brown School
  of Social Work, Washington
  University in St. Louis
St. Louis, MO, USA

Stephen Roll
Research Assistant Professor
George Warren Brown School
  of Social Work, Washington
  University in St. Louis
St. Louis, MO, USA

Barry Rosenberg
Professor of Practice
George Warren Brown School
  of Social Work, Washington
  University in St. Louis
St. Louis, MO, USA

Anna Goldfarb Shabsin
Teaching Professor
George Warren Brown School
of Social Work, Washington
University in St. Louis
St. Louis, MO, USA

Joseph Steensma
Professor of Practice
George Warren Brown School
of Social Work, Washington
University in St. Louis
St. Louis, MO, USA

Rachel G. Tabak
Research Associate Professor
George Warren Brown School
of Social Work, Washington
University in St. Louis
St. Louis, MO, USA

Vetta L. Sanders Thompson
E. Desmond Lee Professor of Racial
and Ethnic Diversity
George Warren Brown School
of Social Work, Washington
University in St. Louis
St. Louis, MO, USA

David A. Patterson Silver Wolf
Associate Professor
George Warren Brown School
of Social Work, Washington
University in St. Louis
St. Louis, MO, USA

1

Introduction

MARK ROBERT RANK

The profession of social work has historically confronted many of society's most vexing social problems and challenges. Beginning at the end of the 19th and early 20th centuries, social work arose to confront the challenges of poverty and the destructive conditions surrounding such deprivation. Throughout the 20th century, social work expanded its scope to tackle a variety of conditions that have diminished the quality of life. These included racial disparities, mental illness, child abuse, community disorganization, and many others.

As we have entered the 21st century, there is a renewed call for the profession to once again commit itself to addressing the most pressing problems of our times. This has led to recent discussions in the field regarding the goals and aspirations that social work as a profession should commit itself to.

In this book, we will explore a number of these critical issues confronting the field. To do so, we have recruited a wide range of social work scholars and practitioners associated with the George Warren Brown School of Social Work at Washington University in St. Louis. However, before we begin this examination, a bit of background is first in order.

Several years ago our school initiated a dialogue that explored what might be some of the overarching goals of social work in the years ahead. While we readily admitted that we could not speak for the profession as a whole, we did feel that we had an important voice to lend to the discussion. After a series of conversations and deliberations, we arrived at the core idea that, in our estimation, the primary concern of social work should be to ensure that every individual is able to live what we have termed a "livable life."

A livable life can be thought of as one in which individuals are able to reach their full potential and capacity. To do so, certain conditions must be met. For example, a reasonable degree of economic security needs to be present in individuals' lives. This entails having the necessary supports and resources to take care of basic needs (e.g., shelter, nutrition, safety, health, education), which ultimately puts individuals in a better position to have the opportunity to develop their own and their children's full potential.

From our vantage point, it appeared that the goal of a livable life was becoming harder to achieve in the United States over the past decades. Greater numbers of individuals and families were struggling to reach a decent standard of living. Mounting pressures upon such families and individuals could be readily found throughout society. In short, the ability to lead a livable life was beyond the grasp for growing numbers of Americans.

This led to a further round of discussions focusing on the barriers and challenges that individuals faced in their quest to lead such a life. At the same time, the field of social work was initiating preliminary conversations regarding the "grand challenges" that social work might be facing in the years ahead. The emphasis upon grand challenges began in the professions of engineering and global health nearly 20 years ago and has since spread to many other disciplines, including social work. As a leading school of social work and knowledge builder in the field, we believed that our community could offer much in terms of helping to shape the profession's approach in defining and addressing the grand challenges.

The result of these conversations and deliberations is the book that appears before you now. Brown School faculty organized themselves into different teams to take on what we felt were the most pressing problems facing the profession and its clientele.

Tying the book together is that each of these separate challenges undercuts individuals from achieving a livable life. As we argue throughout, achieving such a life must be the ultimate goal of social work in the 21st century. Whether the focus is upon the individual, the family, the community, or the society at large, striving toward conditions in which all members of these groups can reach their full potential is paramount.

Our book examines the challenges for social work largely within the context of the United States. However, at various points throughout the chapters we reflect on the international dimension of these social issues as well. Our expertise largely falls within the domestic arena, but we feel that it is also important to be cognizant of the international scope of many of these social problems and challenges.

We begin this chapter by exploring the uniqueness of the field of social work and the guiding principles that have helped inform its understanding of the world around us. Next, we turn to an examination of the concept of livable lives. Here we will go into some detail exploring the meaning of this concept and its relevancy to social work. Finally, we conclude our discussion by outlining the overall structure of the book and the specific chapters that lie ahead.

Introduction

The Social Work Approach

Since its inception, the field of social work has been referred to as "the helping profession." Over the decades, social workers have been educated and trained to confront many of society's most intractable problems and to provide help and assistance to those on the receiving end of such problems. As noted earlier, these have included poverty, discrimination, family disorganization, and a host of other economic and societal ills. In addition, social workers have been charged with addressing the root causes of these problems and, by doing so, working toward alleviating them in the first place.

In its early days, the field was closely aligned with the discipline of sociology. While sociology was viewed as providing a theoretical and research foundation for understanding various issues and problems, social work was seen as having a more applied and action-oriented approach toward these problems. Taken together, the two disciplines attempted to provide a holistic approach to many of the social problems addressed. However, as the decades passed, the two fields eventually went their own ways. Universities found that their joint departments of sociology and social work were splitting off and creating separate departments and schools, particularly during the 1920s and 1930s.

While social work continued to borrow sociological insights throughout its development, it turned to other social sciences as well, such as psychology, to inform its research and practice. Much of the clinical emphasis in social work has been built upon various theories and frameworks found within psychology and psychiatry. In addition, social welfare policy analysis has often been influenced by the methodologies and techniques found within the field of economics.

In short, social work has greatly benefited from the insights of a wide variety of academic fields. However, this has also raised the question of what precisely is unique about social work's approach for understanding and addressing social problems. Clearly one of the strengths of the profession has been its ability to draw from a wide range of fields to inform both its research and practice. Yet at the same time, this eclecticism has resulted in questions regarding the distinctiveness of the "social work" approach in understanding and improving the world around us.

We argue that today's social work is, indeed, unique in the way in which it seeks to understand and impact society at large and that there are a handful of distinctive characteristics that have largely defined the profession since its onset. They represent the essence of the social work approach. Specifically, three overriding principles epitomize the social work approach to understanding and attempting to rectify various harmful conditions for human development.

Social Justice

First, the profession has long been driven by the underlying value of social justice. Social work is not a value neutral profession, rather, it seeks to build a more socially just world than the one that we currently have. In fact, much of the original impetus behind the field was to "right" the glaring "wrongs" that social reformers were observing at the end of the 19th and beginning of the 20th centuries. For example, Jane Addams actively confronted the economic and social injustices that many immigrants and new arrivals faced. Such social reform is inherently built upon the value of social justice.

To commemorate the 100th anniversary of the establishment of the National Council of Social Work (NASW), the academic journal, *Social Service Review*, published a special issue assessing the current state of the field. Its editor, Mark Courtney, noted, "Perhaps the most consistent theme that appears throughout this special issue is the significance to all areas of social work practice of social work's focus on achieving social justice" (2018: 495). The pursuit of social justice has been and remains a strongly embedded value that clearly defines the profession.

Of course, the question naturally arises as to what exactly is meant by "social justice." We would argue that the discussion of social justice in social work has largely revolved around two premises. First, there is the belief that everyone is entitled to certain basic human rights. These would include having access to sufficient food, shelter, health care, quality education, safe neighborhoods, a means of earning a living, and many others (e.g., see the United Nation's [2015] Universal Declaration of Human Rights). A socially just society ensures that all of its members are entitled to and able to access such necessities.

A second component of social justice emphasized in social work, and related to the first, has been the goal of leveling the playing field in order for every individual to be able to reach their full potential and capacity. Consequently, social work has emphasized the importance of reducing and eliminating the barriers that prevent such a goal. These have included poverty and economic destitution, racial and gender discrimination, economic exploitation, political power structures, and many others.

The profession has historically committed itself to reducing such barriers so that all individuals have a real opportunity at succeeding and thriving in life. This, we argue, has been a cornerstone of how social work has implemented the value of social justice. Of course, there are many other values that underlie social work practice as well, with the social work code of ethics delineating many of these. But behind each of these principles lies the central value of social justice.

In fact, the very notion of social work as a helping profession implies a social justice stance. The concept of "helping" signifies that we have a collective responsibility to each other and that through such help we begin to create a more humane and just society. While some have shied away from the term "helping," it is, in reality, an active and engaged concept, focusing on the rights and concerns of all.

The emphasis upon social justice also allows us to distinguish the social work approach from the more value-neutral position of the various social science disciplines that social work has often drawn from. The topics that social workers study are strongly influenced by social justice concerns. Whether they be economic inequality, racial differences in incarceration rates, causes of child maltreatment, or dozens of other topics, the concern and emphasis is that by understanding these problems better, we are in a stronger position to eliminate these barriers and thereby create a better world. As Heidi Allen and colleagues note,

> the intense research and practice focus on poverty that characterizes the profession derives directly from its commitment to social justice. Social work scholars not only seek to understand the nature and causes of poverty but also have a professional mission to reduce poverty. Most students enroll in social work programs because they share this commitment to social justice and believe that training at our schools will equip them with tools to achieve that mission. (2018: 534)

Clearly then, the pursuit of social justice is a first hallmark of the social work approach.

Person-in-Environment

A second key feature of the social work approach is the importance of understanding social problems through the lens of the person-in-environment perspective. From its early origins, social workers have understood that the individual problems they were observing and wrestling with were often the result of the wider environments in which individuals and families found themselves. Such environments included the economic, social, political, and physical structures within communities. Social workers have been taught and trained over the decades to recognize the importance of these systems and the impact that they have upon those within their boundaries. The profession thus seeks to locate individual actions and behaviors within the wider environmental context.

This perspective has also been referred to as the ecological approach. Deriving from systems theory and environmental studies, it places an individual within a set of broader contexts. The result is that social work by its very nature is interdisciplinary. As Allen points out, "leading social work scholar are not siloed—they work in interdisciplinary research teams or, at the least, draw on insights from other disciplines" (2018: 535). Consequently, social work places individual problems and concerns within wider environmental structures.

Take the case of poverty. The most common approach for understanding poverty within an American context has been through the lens of individual failure. Survey research has repeatedly demonstrated that the majority of citizens and policymakers explain poverty as the result of individual failings (Eppard, Rank, and Bullock, 2020). These include not working hard enough, poor decision-making, lack of skills and talent, and so on. As a result, the poverty stricken need to address their own shortcomings to succeed and escape impoverishment.

In contrast, the social worker using a person-in-environment or ecological perspective seeks to locate an individual's poverty within the context of the broader environments in which they reside. Consequently, what are the economic conditions and job opportunities available within the community? Have there been patterns of hiring discrimination in the past? What is the quality of the educational system in the community? Is the social safety net adequate to prevent poverty in the first place? How has the physical environment impacted the individual's well-being? All of these questions and more would naturally arise when one begins placing personal problems within the context of the person-in-environment perspective.

In addition, this perspective also recognizes the power of individuals and groups to impact their wider environments. Consequently, the person-in-environment perspective is not simply a one-directional process. As Mary Kondrat notes, it "incorporates the notion that there is a reciprocity to the person–environment relationship, such that the individual can impact the various elements of the environment, just as the environment can exert a conducive or inhibiting influence on the individual" (2008: 348).

An example of such a reciprocal process is the struggle for living wages across the United States. As a result of stagnate economic conditions and low-wage jobs, organizing efforts have occurred across many communities to fight for an increase in the minimum wage. These organizing efforts have resulted in successes and gains in many localities and states, resulting in higher minimum wages. However, some have argued that these higher minimum wages may then have the effect of employers hiring fewer workers because they feel they can no longer hire as many employees at the higher wage. This, in turn, may then impact the job opportunities available to individual workers.

This example illustrates the reciprocal process that can occur when employing the person-in-environment perspective. Such an approach provides a much deeper understanding into the dynamics of why particular problems exist and how they might be addressed. This then represents a second hallmark of the social work approach for understanding and addressing social problems. As Kondrat concludes in her review, "to date, the principle that social work practice is characterized by a person-in-environment perspective seems to have stood the test of time" (2008: 352).

Evidence Based

A third key principle that has guided social work scholarship has been the emphasis upon evidence-based research, practice, and evaluation. Policy and practice approaches to social problems are best viewed as informed by well-constructed research designs that result in solid evidence. This evidence, in turn, should guide policy and practice approaches to such social problems.

The recent emphasis upon evidence-based practice began approximately 20 years ago in the field of medicine but quickly moved to social work as well. However, it should be noted that social work scholars and practitioners were writing about and utilizing evidence-based research for decades. For example, the work of Seebohm Rowntree in England at the beginning of the 20th century employed innovative research techniques that uncovered the prevalence of poverty across the life course. This, in turn, helped to alert practitioners in the field to the increased likelihood of poverty and economic destitution at particular stages of adulthood.

Similarly, the work of one of the key founders of social work, Mary Richmond, was instrumental in advocating for an evidence-based model. As Jeanne Marsh and Mary Bunn note,

> Mary Richmond is best known for her approach to casework, which outlined a formalized and scientific approach for direct practitioners in order to understand individuals' problems. While there are many criticisms of Richmond's model, particularly for the ways in which it emphasizes the authority and expertise of the worker and adaptation to social problems, her emphasis on defining rigorous and scientific practice methods continues to be a critical component of direct practice models today and foreshadows professional concerns with evidence-based practice in contemporary social work. (2018: 658)

During the profession's more recent development, there has also been an emphasis upon what is known as "best practices." Again, the idea is that both clinical and policy work should be informed and guided by a rigorous body of scientific research.

There is also a recognition that such research can comprise a wide variety of methodologies, including quantitative, qualitative, and mixed methods. This recognition reflects the fact that the social realities that social workers are confronting are often multidimensional. In many ways, social work has been well positioned to employ a mixed-methods approach for uncovering the patterns, causes, and consequences of social problems. Such an approach can often expose the various layers of understanding behind a particular problem or issue.

To be sure, social work has been criticized in the past for straying from these three overall principles that we have been discussing. For example, Harry Specht and Mark Courtney (1994) have argued that as a result of the push for professionalization, social work has largely abandoned its social justice perspective along with its focus on community. Conversely, those on the right have accused the profession of being driven by political correctness to the exclusion of facts and evidence.

Nevertheless, we would argue that the profession has been largely guided by these three overriding themes: (a) Social work is informed by the values of making the world a more socially just and fair place; (b) social work seeks to understand the world through the lens of the person-in-environment; and (c) social work examines, measures, evaluates, and impacts this world by evidence-based research and practice. Through researchers and practitioners engaging and emphasizing these themes, the profession seeks to achieve the goal that all members of society are able to live a livable life.

The Goal of a Livable Life

Background

Since the early 1970s, the United States has experienced growing income and wealth inequality. Nearly all of the economic gains over the last 50 years have been concentrated in the upper one-fifth of the income and wealth distributions, particularly in the upper 5 and 1 percent. Many Americans have been hard at work over the past five decades, only to find themselves falling further behind financially.

For example, median earnings of men working full-time in 1973, adjusted for inflation, stood at $55,317. By 2017, their earnings had fallen to $52,146 (U.S. Census Bureau, 2018). In other words, the typical male worker in the United States has actually lost ground over this time in terms of their real wages. In the United States today, 40 percent of jobs are considered low wage, that is, paying less than $16.00 an hour (U.S. Census Bureau, 2018).

In addition, many of these jobs have failed to provide essential benefits. Most notably, adequate and affordable health insurance through one's job has become increasingly harder to come by. Furthermore, rising numbers of Americans are working part-time jobs but would rather be working a full-time job.

Accompanying this wage stagnation has been a growing tide of individual economic risk and vulnerability. Job security has weakened, income volatility has increased, and the level of consumer debt has reached historically record levels. This increased economic vulnerability has led to social strains within families and communities.

Health is an area of particular concern. Notwithstanding significant advances and expenditures in the field of medicine, the United States lags behind the rest of the world with respect to health status. A Commonwealth Fund study (Schneider et al., 2017) finds that the quality of the American health care system ranks low in comparison to other industrialized countries. A further study has found that life expectancy has actually dropped for white males between the ages of 45 and 54 (Case and Deaton, 2015). In addition, many disadvantaged populations struggle to live healthy and productive lives due to disparities in access and delivery of medical care. Individuals with low incomes and education, or people of color, often face exceptional challenges in maintaining health and are less likely to have quality medical care.

At the same time, other aspects of the social safety net have been eroded, resulting in middle- and lower-income families facing retrenchments in social and economic protections. Cutbacks have occurred in a wide range of social programs. During this same period, public policy has exacerbated inequalities by generating large income tax cuts for the wealthy, along with highly regressive asset building subsidies for homeownership, retirement savings plans, and other social programs. Middle- and lower-income families benefit little or not at all from these massive asset building subsidies. Given this background, the ability to live a livable life has become severely strained. But what exactly is a livable life, and what conditions need to be present to achieve it?

The Meaning of a Livable Life

During the past two millenniums, there have been many attempts to delineate what comprises a fulfilling life. For Aristotle, the key to a fulfilling and satisfying life was to develop your true promise and potential. As Edith Hall writes in her book, *Aristotle's Way*, "Aristotle has more recently been reclassified as belonging to the category of utopian thinker because his works on ethics and politics assume that creating circumstances in which humans can flourish, achieve their full potential and be happy, was the goal of human life" (2018: 50). Hall goes on to note, "A universal commitment to the full realization of human potential in the Aristotelian sense just might solve the problems today facing the human race" (41).

More recent attempts at defining a fulfilling life have included Abraham Maslov's "hierarchy of needs," Amartya Sen's "capabilities perspective," "the second generation of rights" detailed in the United Nation's (2018) Universal Declaration of Human Rights, and the "concept of decency" found among many social justice advocacy organizations.

Keeping these important statements in mind, we can define a livable life as one in which an individual is able to thrive and develop in a healthy manner across their lifetime to reach their full potential. Psychological research has demonstrated that within each of us lies a variety of talents, skills, abilities, and aptitudes. In addition, we possess a wide set of personality characteristics that help us to lead fulfilling lives. A livable life is one in which these characteristics are able to flourish. As a result, the individual is able to feel a sense of purpose and fulfillment throughout their life, as well as a sense of agency and control. President John F. Kennedy summed this up succinctly in describing happiness as "the full use of your powers along lines of excellence in a life affording scope."

Of course, these abilities and aptitudes will vary widely across a population. The meaning of a livable life acknowledges and, in fact, celebrates this. The goal of a livable life is to ensure that each individual is able to fully develop their own talents and abilities. Such abilities will vary from individual to individual, but the important point is that these abilities are allowed to flourish. The well-known quote from Dr. Martin Luther King exemplifies this:

> If a man is called to be a street sweeper, he should sweep streets even as a Michelangelo painted, or Beethoven composed music or Shakespeare wrote poetry. He should sweep streets so well that all the hosts of heaven and earth will pause to say, "Here lived a great street sweeper who did his job well."

The concept of a livable life also overlaps with the social work value of empowerment. Social work has traditionally emphasized the goal of empowering its clientele such that they are able to exert agency over their lives. Within a livable life, the individual is, in fact, able to exert such agency over their life. Being able to both feel and actually be in control of one's destiny has been shown to be an important component of overall psychological well-being.

Also closely connected to the concept of a livable life is Amartya Sen's discussion of capabilities. According to Sen, fostering human capabilities allows "people to lead the lives they have reason to value and to enhance the real choices they have" (1999: 293). Sen notes that the goal of social policy should be to ensure that individuals are able to develop their capabilities fully to lead such lives. As he writes, if expanding human freedom enables individuals

> to live the kind of lives that people have reason to value, then the role of economic growth in expanding these opportunities has to be integrated into that more foundational understanding of the process of development as the expansion of human capability to lead more worthwhile and more free lives (1999: 295)

Martha Nussbaum (1995) further observes that these capabilities include a wide range of attributes, including good physical and mental health, strong emotional development, creativity, a developed sense of morality, and many others.

A livable life is therefore one in which individuals can flourish in their development, exert agency over their lives, and, as a result, reach their full potential. In discussing the role of social work and social justice, Michael Reisch notes,

> At its best, social work stands for the creation of a society in which people, individually and in community, can live decent lives and realize their full human potential. This requires us to advocate for the elimination of those policies that diminish people's sense of control over their lives and drain finite resources from basic human needs. Simultaneously, we need to work for the expansion of those programs that enable people to exercise personal freedom by removing the fear of economic and physical calamity from their lives and making them feel like integral and valued parts of society. (2002: 351)

Barriers to a Livable Life

Unfortunately, many Americans as well as people around the globe have been unable to achieve a livable life. As noted earlier, the goal of a livable life appears to have become more elusive over the past decades as a result of numerous barriers. In many ways, these barriers represent the challenges confronting social work today and in the future. We might think of these barriers as falling broadly within the economic, social, political, and physical environments of society.

Perhaps most apparent would be economic insecurity, vulnerability, and poverty. As demonstrated in previous work (Rank, 2004), such conditions stunt human development, particularly for children. Conditions of economic destitution lead to increased stress and anxiety, resulting in both physical and mental health problems.

In addition, poverty and a lack of income impacts many other aspects of life that prevent people from living a livable life. For example, Sen defines poverty as a lack of freedom. In many European countries, poverty is referred to as social exclusion or social disenfranchisement. Clearly then, these conditions undermine people's ability to experience a fulfilling life.

Turning to the social environment, a myriad of barriers prevent a livable life. These include various forms of stigma and discrimination, dysfunctional family dynamics, poor-quality educational systems, cultural norms and patterns of violence, and many more. These social barriers can be found from the micro to the macro levels of society.

Barriers to achieving a livable life can be found at the political level as well. These often take the forms of various policies, programs, and laws at the federal, state, and local levels. Policies and legislation that exacerbate current inequalities quickly come to mind. They include regressive tax cuts at the top of the income distribution, criminal justice legislation targeted at minorities, current immigration policy, and recent Supreme Court decisions aimed at restricting campaign finance reform efforts. All of these exert a detrimental impact on the quality of life for many Americans.

Finally, the physical environment can also have a profound impact upon achieving a livable life. The research on environmental justice has demonstrated that those with lower incomes and people of color are much more likely to be exposed to environmental toxins. Likewise, such individuals face a greater risk of encountering various forms of violence in their communities. Within an international context, global warming and climate change are likely to disproportionally affect the world's lower-income populations in a negative manner. All of these environmental impacts result in serious barriers for achieving a livable life.

And, of course, the economic, social, political, and physical barriers to a livable life are often interconnected. For example, environmental degradation may lead to a worsening of economic opportunities, which, in turn, creates communities mired by social problems, resulting in punitive legislation aimed at reducing crime. Clearly then, the barriers found within the economic, social, political, and physical environments are closely interconnected.

Our chapters in the pages that follow address many of these barriers. As we have argued, they undercut the ability of individuals and families to grow and develop in settings that provide the necessary nourishment for a healthy life. They represent many of the key challenges that social work will face in the years to come. In short, they prevent human beings from achieving a livable life.

Organization

Our book is organized around ten key areas that we feel the profession of social work must focus on to allow individuals and families to lead livable lives. These include tackling the root socioeconomic determinants of ill health; alleviating poverty; confronting stigma/discrimination/social exclusion; reducing cumulative inequality; developing financial and tangible assets for lower- and moderate-income populations; preventing child maltreatment; fostering civic engagement across the life course; building healthy, diverse, and thriving communities; achieving environmental justice; and engaging older adults.

Beyond these ten, three additional initiatives are felt to be important in helping the profession achieve a livable life for all: generating effective demand and use of social services, designing and implementing policy and program innovations, and leveraging big data analytics and informatics.

Our book concludes with a final chapter written by three of the most recent deans serving the George Warren Brown School of Social Work. Their experience with the school stretches from the mid-1970s to the present time, representing nearly 50 years of experience. They were asked to apply their collective wisdom to gaze backward at the lessons learned over the previous decades and to look forward to the promises and challenges that lie ahead.

Taken together, *Toward a Livable Life* provides an in-depth exploration into this collection of social work challenges. As we noted at the beginning of this chapter, we have enlisted a wide range of faculty in the George Warren Brown School of Social Work at Washington University to help shape and write the individual chapters addressing each of these topics. Within the school itself, faculty fall within the disciplines of social work, public health, and social policy. In addition, these faculty have been trained in a wide array of fields. They are uniformly at the cutting edges of their particular areas of expertise and represent a wealth of experience and knowledge that we are fortunate to draw upon.

Authors were charged with addressing several basic questions within their individual chapters: (1) What are the dynamics and scope of the problem; (2) why is it important to confront the problem, and how will alleviating the problem facilitate a livable life; (3) how can we understand the reasons behind the problem; and (4) in what ways can we address and potentially solve the problem? By framing the chapters around these questions, a degree of consistency and coherence is achieved across topics.

Authors were also asked to reflect on their topic areas from both a national and an international perspective. Although the primary focus is upon the United

States, contributors were encouraged to utilize international research and examples as well. Consequently, many chapters touch upon domestic and international aspects of their respective topics. Converging trends across the globe in urbanization, aging, economic inequality, and other societal patterns are an underlying motivation for addressing both domestic and international aspects of our social work topical areas. The international dimension allows the reader a comparative sense of the nature, the extent, and the depth of the problem.

Such a consideration is rooted in the notion that these obstacles are impediments to a livable life not only in the United States but also in many other societies. A solution or an innovation in one corner of the globe should be available to the profession of social work in another part of the globe. Effective interventions to complex problems are leveraged by integrating knowledge from different disciplines and from the experience of communities and practitioners around the world. The goal in examining domestic and international aspects of each of the topics is to begin a dialogue among educators, practitioners, and researchers to search for solutions and knowledge transfer—not just from the United States to other countries but also in the reverse direction to spur new social work practice here in the United States.

Finally, it is our deep hope that this book sparks an engaging discussion among social work researchers, practitioners, and students, as well as inspiring future social workers beginning the journey of making this world a better place to live. The challenges and problems facing everyday Americans and those around the world are great. It certainly does not take our book to tell you that. But we also believe that this is a very exciting time to be a social worker. We are living in a period of great change, and with such change comes the possibilities of many opportunities. The field of social work is well positioned to be an active and important player in helping to shape the trajectory of this change. As Martin Luther King observed, "let us realize that the arc of the moral universe is long, but it bends towards justice." Social workers have traditionally been on the right side of history, with many of the issues social workers have fought for coming to fruition.

However, the future is now upon us. Social workers have both great opportunities and responsibilities for improving the living conditions of individuals, families, communities, and societies. The goal of striving for all to experience a livable life is one that is worthy of the profession in the 21st century. The challenges and barriers to such a life are daunting, but not insurmountable. It is time to focus our energy on such a mission. It is time to roll up our sleeves and get to work.

References

Allen, H., I. Garfinkel, and J. Waldfogel. 2018. "Social Policy Research in Social Work in the Twenty-First Century: The State of Scholarship and the Profession; What Is Promising, and What Needs to Be Done." *Social Service Review*, 92, 504–547.

Case, A., and A. Deaton. 2015. "Rising Morbidity and Mortality in Midlife Among White Non-Hispanic Americans in the 21st Century." *PNAS*, 112, 15078–15083.

Courtney, M. E. 2018. "Whither American Social Work in Its Second Century?" *Social Service Review*, 92, 487–503.

Eppard, L. M., M. R. Rank, and H. Bullock. 2020. *Rugged Individualism and the Misunderstanding of American Inequality*. Bethlehem, PA: Lehigh University Press.

Hall, E. 2018. *Aristotle's Way: How Ancient Wisdom Can Change Your Life*. New York: Penguin Press.

Kondrat, M. E. 2008. "Person-in-Environment." *Encyclopedia of Social Work*. 20th ed. Edited by T. Mizrahi and. L. Davis. New York: Oxford University Press, pp. 348–354.

Marsh, J. C., and M. Bunn. 2018. "Social Work's Contribution to Direct Practice with Individuals, Families, and Groups: An Institutionalist Perspective." *Social Service Review*, 92, 647–692.

Nussbaum, M. C. 1995. *Poetic Justice: The Literary Imagination and Public Life*. Boston: Beacon Press.

Rank, M. R. 2004. *One Nation, Underprivileged: Why American Poverty Affects Us All*. New York: Oxford University Press.

Reisch, M. 2002. "Defining Social Justice in a Socially Unjust World." *Families in Society*, 83, 343–352.

Schneider, E. C., D. O. Sarnak, D. Squires, A. Shah, and M. M. Doty. 2017. *Mirror, Mirror 2017: International Comparison Reflects Flaws and Opportunities for Better U.S. Health Care*. Report prepared for The Commonwealth Fund, July 2017.

Sen, A. 1999. *Development as Freedom*. New York: Knopf.

Specht, H., and M. Courtney. 1994. *Unfaithful Angels: How Social Has Abandoned Its Mission*. New York: Free Press.

United Nations. 2015. *Universal Declaration of Human Rights*. New York: United Nations.

U.S. Census Bureau. 2018. *Income and Poverty in the United States: 2017* (Report No. P60-263). Washington DC: U.S. Government Printing Office.

2

Tackling the Social Determinants of Ill Health

DARRELL L. HUDSON, SARAH GEHLERT, AND SHANTA PANDEY

Good health is a cornerstone for a livable life. It allows individuals the opportunity to grow and reach their fullest potential. It is a key ingredient for succeeding at school, at work, at home, and many other facets of life. Conversely, poor health can transform an individual from "normal" to "patient" in an instant (Rose, 2001). Social work practitioners frequently face situations in which individuals are debilitated by chronic health conditions and by mental health symptoms that affect interpersonal functioning. In the face of stressful, ongoing health problems, little else may matter to individuals and their families because such conditions often require total focus. Good health is therefore foundational and linked to many social and economic outcomes associated with a livable life.

Health affects the social and economic trajectories of individuals from an early age. For instance, chronic diseases such as asthma and epilepsy have a negative effect on children's educational performance and attainment because children who miss school due to these conditions will likely fall behind their peers (Dowd, Zajacova, and Aiello, 2009; Johnson and Schoeni, 2011). Likewise, without the consumption of key nutrients, individuals lack the energy to perform the tasks expected of them and are at risk of various diseases and deleterious health conditions in addition to developmental and cognitive problems (Barker, 1997; Dowd et al., 2009; Scholte, van den Berg, and Lindeboom, 2012). It is also the case that in developing countries a lack of clean water, sanitation, hygiene, and living conditions mean that over 1 billion adults and children are chronically infected with parasitic worms that increase the risk of impaired physical and cognitive development (Andrews, Bogoch, and Utzinger, 2017; Clarke et al., 2017).

Chronic exposure to social stressors, such as those related to poverty, is not only associated with poor health outcomes across the life course, but also with decreased ability to learn and remember information. This, in turn, affects an individual's ability to secure the education and training that could improve their overall life chances (McEwen, 2003a; Seeman et al., 2010; Shonkoff and Garner, 2012; Tse et al., 2012). This overall process is what is known as "cumulative disadvantage" and is discussed at length in Chapter 5 of this volume. Cumulative disadvantage with respect to health disparities begins at an early age and progresses through the later years of life.

Social workers have traditionally focused on treating distress and health problems as they arise. Yet increasingly social workers have turned to preventing ill health at the individual, family, community, and population levels. This emphasis on prevention has begun to infuse social work curricula, along with an emphasis upon health at the macro level. Over time, the field has moved from being labeled "hospital social work," to "medical social work," to "health social work," reflecting this shift to the community level (Gehlert, 2011). Issues of health are likely to increase in importance in the years ahead.

The goals of this chapter are to illustrate why addressing the social determinants of health are critical to the achievement of livable lives, to illustrate the fundamental dynamics and nature of social determinants of health, and to recommend future directions for research, practice, and policy related to improving livable lives. In addition, we discuss how social determinants of health shape the built environment and fuel disparities in health through access to resources such as healthy food options, safe and hygienic places to recreate, and health services.

Health as a Cornerstone of a Livable Life

Preamble to the Constitution of the World Health Organization as adopted by the International HealthConference, New York, 19–22 June, 1946; signed on 22 July 1946 by the representatives of 61 States,

> a state of complete physical, mental and social well-being and not merely the absence of disease or infirmity. The enjoyment of the highest attainable standard of health is one of the fundamental rights of every human being without distinction of race, religion, political belief, economic or social condition.

Further, it implies that the "health of all peoples" is contingent upon the cooperation of individuals and states, along with the government's ability for effectively addressing the social determinants of health and people's access to health-related knowledge. Health is therefore foundational and is inextricably linked with the social and economic factors related to an individual's ability to lead a livable life.

It is not enough to simply implore individuals to eat a healthier diet or to engage in more physical activity. Rather, improving population-level health and reducing and eliminating racial/ethnic and socioeconomic health disparities are built upon addressing the social determinants of health at multiple levels.

In addition to the role of social determinants of health upon livable lives, it is also critical to note that good health is not equally distributed in society. There are wide inequalities in health across race/ethnicity, socioeconomic status, gender, sexual orientation, and immigration status. These inequalities are not only important for individual lives, but also for society at large—reducing such inequalities increases economic productivity, reduces healthcare costs, and lowers the spread of disease (McLaughlin and Rank, 2018; Wilkinson, 2005; Wilkinson and Pickett, 2011).

Defining Social Determinants of Health

Although the term "social determinants of health" is widely used, much more progress is still needed for truly addressing the social determinants that drive health. To this end, the WHO established the Commission on Social Determinants of Health (CSDH) in March 2005, completing its report in July 2008 (CSDH, 2008). Using data from multiple countries, the report demonstrated the strong relationship between societal factors and health outcomes. Consistent with Amartya Sen's prior writings on human capabilities (discussed in Chapter 1 of this volume), the report determined that the high burden of illness and poor life chances are largely the result of the "conditions in which people are born, grow, live, work, and age" (CSDH, 2008: 26). It concluded that a wide range of economic and political circumstances, including poverty and unfair economic arrangements, contributed to poor health outcomes. Social determinants of health were also critical. These included race and ethnicity, social context, and place-based resources such as schools, access to quality food outlets, and safe spaces to recreate.

In addition, it was argued that health helps drive economic and social well-being. Consequently, there is a reciprocal relationship between health and socioeconomic security. Good health helps to foster economic well-being, and this economic well-being, in turn, further amplifies an individual's overall physical and mental well-being.

Social determinants of health are especially challenging to address because they affect multiple disease outcomes and fuel racial/ethnic and socioeconomic disparities in health. Subsequently, researchers have implored the field to consider health in all policies developed, ranging from zoning and housing, to education and workforce development, to effectively addressing the social determinants of health. For those living in poverty, addressing the social determinants of health means ensuring safe neighborhoods that allow physical activity and interpersonal affiliation that combat undesired isolation and the lack of healthful foods. Health social workers frequently work with community organizations to ensure that this occurs.

Social determinants that influence desired outcomes (such as employment, financial capabilities, school quality, and the safety and well-being of family members and friends) often get in the way of health maintenance behaviors like monitoring blood pressure or getting regular health screenings. Medical professionals frequently note that individual patients are deeply concerned about their jobs, family responsibilities, and the health and well-being of their loved ones (Fiscella et al., 2002; Fiscella and Franks, 1997). These are the issues that people care deeply about, sometimes above their own health.

These "competing demands" at the individual level help explain why individuals might not seek regular medical treatment or obtain preventative screenings for diseases such as cancer, cardiovascular disease, and diabetes. However, it is not merely individual choice that explains health disparities. In fact, many of the social and economic determinants affecting health are beyond individual control, especially for persons of lower socioeconomic status who must often expend energy locating food and shelter for themselves and their families. Yet even individuals who have sufficient resources may perceive the costs associated with maintaining a healthy lifestyle (such as the cost of fresh produce, learning how to prepare a healthy meal, or growing accustomed to the tastes or portion size of a new dish) as outweighing the benefits associated with changing health behaviors (Ajzen, 2011; Montano and Kasprzk, 2008). Additionally, the stress of being marginalized as a result of race and ethnicity, gender, or sexual orientation can also preclude one's concerns about personal health (Braveman, Egerter, and Williams, 2011; Gee and Ford, 2011).

Socioeconomic status also plays a key role in determining whether individuals seek medical care. Opportunities for health care through state Medicaid programs are shrinking, and many hospitals and clinics in rural and inner city neighborhoods have closed over the past years. Individuals living in poverty often perceive the costs associated with health care as more stressful than knowing their actual disease status (Hudson et al., 2018; Phillips, Mayer, and Aday, 2000).

How Health Disparities Affect Livable Lives

The National Institutes of Health defines disparities in health as differences in the incidence, prevalence, mortality, and burden of diseases and other adverse health conditions that exist among specific population groups in the United States. These groups include nonwhite, rural, low-income, and other underserved populations such as sexual minorities and immigrant groups. Population-level disparities in health are considered mutable rather than naturally occurring. Consequently, health disparities are avoidable and largely driven by policies and practices that systematically place socially and economically disadvantaged groups at a further disadvantage concerning their health (Braveman, 2006).

The CSDH adopted a conceptual framework postulating that health inequities are largely the result of three factors: (1) socioeconomic and political context including governance, policy, cultural and societal norms and values; (2) social position including education, occupation, income, gender, race and ethnicity; and (3) access to health care systems (CSDH, 2008). In this framework, these three structural drivers determine health inequity. They affect multiple disease outcomes across the developmental life span. Recent research supports the notion of transgenerational effects of poverty and its sequelae on health (Adler and Stewart, 2010; Johnson and Schoeni, 2011; Wickrama, Conger, and Abraham, 2005).

Social determinants of health are critical in the development of preventative health efforts because they affect multiple disease outcomes, often disproportionately affecting population groups that are the most socially and economically disadvantaged. In the United States, social and economic factors drive racial/ethnic disparities in health because they often shape the resources that are protective of health such as access to healthy food outlets and health care (Borrell et al., 2013; LaVeist and Wallace, 2000; LaVeist et al., 2011; Link and Phelan, 1995). Simply put, people with greater resources maintain better health behaviors. Those with more education and income are more likely to join gyms and seek other healthful recreational activities. In particular, studies support the notion that disparities in health outcomes have widened by educational attainment. Those with higher levels of education are more likely than others to pursue healthy lifestyles and behavior, use preventive care promptly, and benefit from advances in medical innovation (Goldman and Smith, 2011; Jemal et al., 2008; Olshansky et al., 2012). At the same time, greater resources such as higher income and social capital can be used to avoid proximal and distal causes of disease and premature death. Drugs and other treatments not covered by insurance are outside the means for many individuals and families.

Likewise, high levels of racial residential segregation in the United States constrain health-promoting resources, such as access to fresh produce, safe places to recreate, and easy access to preventative health care. Not only are there fewer outlets for healthy, affordable food, but also a preponderance of fast food restaurants as well as stores that largely sell calorie-dense products that contain little nutritional value. The locations of what is known as "food deserts" occurs predominately in low-income, non-white neighborhoods. The U.S. Department of Agriculture defines these areas as places where a full-service grocery store or supermarket is more than a mile away in urban localities or ten miles away in rural communities.

Although public health campaigns urge physical activity, persons living in neighborhoods with high rates of crime are often forced inside and resigned to sedentary activities rather than being able to walk, jog, or ride bicycles in their neighborhoods (Diez, Roux, and Mair, 2010). The risks in poorer neighborhoods are characterized by high levels of poverty and community violence, which in turn weaken the levels of neighborhood trust and organization (Balfour and Kaplan, 2002; Cattell, 2001; Stoddard et al., 2011).

To address health disparities, health equity must be the goal. The concept of health equity implies that everyone is able to attain the best health possible and should not be disadvantaged because of their social position or other socially determined circumstances. This is consistent with the concept of livable lives discussed in the introductory chapter, in which the goal is for all to be able to reach their full potential.

Margaret Whitehead and colleagues have argued that health equity involves creating opportunities and removing barriers for achieving the fullest health potential for all people (Whitehead, Dahlgren, and Gilson, 2001). Health equity, according to the U.S. Department of Health and Human Services (DHHS), is the attainment of the highest level of health for all people. Due to the existence of inequalities, not all Americans can achieve optimal health (DHHS, 2010). Therefore, a growing body of research has made a persuasive argument that health is a human right, and everyone should have the right to obtain the highest level of health in their society (Brudney, 2016; Castillo et al., 2017; Chapman, 2015; Christopher and Caruso, 2015; Dauda and Dierickx, 2012; Friedman et al., 2013; Gostin et al., 2016; Hunt, 2016; Rumbold et al., 2017; Saunders et al., 2010; Tasioulas and Vayena, 2015). The concept that health is a human rights issue requires looking at health equity through a social justice lens which, as discussed in Chapter 1 of this volume, is a hallmark of the social work approach.

By addressing the social determinants of health, it is possible to simultaneously improve health at the individual level as well as at the community and societal levels. Addressing social determinants of health is critical for preventing poor health outcomes and making it possible for populations to lead livable lives.

This is not to say that addressing broad, population-level social factors is easy. It is undoubtedly more straightforward for a social worker to change an individual's behavior than to change the existing structural barriers. Yet, change at the neighborhood, community, and national levels is consistent with the Code of Ethics of the National Association of Social Workers (2017). In fact, if social workers do not address change at the macro level, we may simply be blaming the victim for their ill health (Piven and Cloward, 1978).

Social determinants of health affect well-being through a number of pathways and mechanisms. These factors are easily observed in different neighborhoods and communities across the country and the world. Place-based resources such as schools, access to quality food outlets, and safe spaces to recreate are critical to all aspects of health. In the journal, *Health Affairs*, its 2014 policy brief on social determinants of health concluded with five major categories of health determinants—genetics, behavior, social circumstances, environmental and physical influences, and medical care (Health Policy Brief: The Relative Contribution of Multiple Determinants to Health Outcomes, 2014). It emphasized the importance of examining multiple determinants of health and the interactions between those determinants as well. In addition, it notes the need to examine the multiple levels that influence health, ranging from the intrapersonal to the societal level.

An alternative way of thinking about social determinants of health is as "fundamental causes." Bruce Link and Jo Phelan (1995) describe fundamental causes of health as resources that can be used to avoid risks or minimize causes, affect multiple health outcomes over time, and impact different health outcomes when risk profiles change. If interventions focus on risk factors for specific diseases and conditions without addressing the fundamental causes of health, diseases and conditions eventually shift to the most vulnerable populations, populations lacking socioeconomic resources or power. Leonard Syme (2008) argues that people in the most vulnerable groups will eventually replace those who are considered most at risk no matter what the actual risk factors for a disease or condition.

What Are the Underlying Causes of Social Determinants of Health?

Social determinants of health are closely intertwined. Examples of demographic and social determinants of health include socioeconomic status, gender, tradition/cultural practices, race/ethnicity, immigration status, and sexual orientation. These are important factors because they can increase or decrease the risk of marginalization. For instance, women are often compensated for work at a lower rate than men (Mullings, 2002; Seng et al., 2012). Similarly, members of racial/ethnic minorities are more likely to be discriminated against in various settings (Hudson et al., 2015; Hicken et al., 2013; Lewis et al., 2012). In the discussion that follows, we use a social determinants of health lens to explain how some of these social determinants of health—gender, tradition/culture, race, and discriminatory practices—are associated with health, not only because gender and racial/ethnic minorities receive different treatment within health care settings, but also because gender and race/ethnicity are intertwined with socioeconomic status, neighborhood context, and social disadvantage.

Socioeconomic Status

As discussed in Chapter 5 of this volume, one of the strongest and most consistent finding in health research has been the positive relationship between socioeconomic status and health. Beginning with the groundbreaking results from the Whitehall studies in England during the 1960s and 1970s, a consistent finding in epidemiology has been the relationship between health and socioeconomic status. The lower the socioeconomic status (and particularly poverty), the more powerful are the detrimental effects upon health. Conversely, the higher the socioeconomic status, the greater the positive impact on health.

This relationship is consistent across a wide range of health outcomes. In fact, some scholars describe socioeconomic status as a "fundamental cause" of health and well-being (Link and Phelan, 1995). Fundamental causes are defined as resources that allow individuals to avoid risks or minimize causes of disease, that affect multiple health outcomes over time, and that influence health outcomes even when risk profiles change (Phelan, Link, and Tehranifar, 2010). The manner in which socioeconomic status affects health and fuels socioeconomic health inequities is fairly straightforward. For instance, individuals earning higher incomes can afford to purchase homes in safer, more organized neighborhoods in which health-producing resources such as high-quality schools, grocery stores, and safe places to recreate are readily available. Over the life course, access (or lack of access) to such resources not only perpetuates the socioeconomic standing and stability of individuals and their families, but also promotes socioeconomic health inequalities that people with lower levels of income and assets disproportionately bear (Link and Phelan, 1995).

Similarly, most Americans have employer-based health insurance, and therefore healthcare access is overwhelmingly dependent on securing and maintaining employment that provides health insurance as a benefit (Kaiser Family Foundation, 2018). There are currently 28 million Americans without health insurance coverage (Kaiser Family Foundation, 2018). These individuals often cannot obtain preventative health screenings and checkups because of a lack of affordable healthcare services. People also delay or avoid treatment for health problems, exacerbating the severity and impact of health conditions, which might have been mitigated with timely treatment (Kaiser Family Foundation,

2018). Indeed, some Americans perceive the cost associated with health care as a greater stressor than the diagnosis itself (Hudson et al., 2018).

Another critical way that socioeconomic status affects health is through the stress process. Researchers have developed different concepts for describing how stressful experiences, such as financial strain, get "under the skin" in affecting different disease pathways (Geronimus et al., 2006, 2016; Hertzman and Boyce, 2010; Krieger, 2001a). Krieger describes this process as embodiment—the process in which humans incorporate the world we live in, including societal and environmental factors, into our bodies (Krieger, 2001b, 2001a). The process of embodiment presents another health challenge for the poverty stricken as many will face substantial disadvantage early in life, which can then negatively affect their health throughout the life course. Several researchers have even worked to determine whether there is an intergenerational transmission of trauma and stress that negatively influences population health (Walters et al., 2011). The long-term effects of socioeconomic status on health are deeply entrenched and difficult to erase. Some of these mechanisms are discussed in further detail in the following discussion.

Gender

Approximately, 289,000 women died in 2010 as a result of birth-related complications. These deaths were concentrated in low- and middle-income countries of sub-Saharan Africa and Southern Asia (United Nations [UN], 2015). A pregnant woman in Nepal has a seven times higher risk of dying due to birth-related complications than her counterpart in the United States (Pandey et al., 2017). Home delivery is the norm in Nepal, India, and Bangladesh and is safe when the pregnancy and birth are normal. However, this age-old tradition of delivery in the comfort of one's own home quickly turns fatal when women develop complications. A systematic analysis of 23 studies from 115 countries comprising 60,799 maternal deaths between 2003 and 2009 found that hemorrhage was the leading cause of maternal death resulting in 37 percent of all deaths in northern Africa, 30 percent in southern Asia, and 27 percent worldwide (Say et al., 2017). Safe strategies of transporting women who develop complications to health facilities are unavailable for many rural women in these countries, which contributes to health inequity.

The decision to use a health facility for delivery involves a complex set of intra-household, community, and structural factors that health professionals alone cannot address (Pandey et al., 2017). Health professionals may advise pregnant women to seek an institution for delivery; when labor begins, however, these women will need family or community members to rapidly transport them to the health institution at that critical time. Social workers who work within the community and understand the cultural nuances can partner with health professionals to improve women's access to maternal and child health.

To achieve health equity, it is essential that health institutions treat all patients with dignity and respect irrespective of their social position. If women from marginalized backgrounds experience discrimination at the health institutions, they may avoid returning for future use of health services. Several studies have shown women's unequal access to health services based on social class, caste, and living arrangement (Bhanderi and Kannan, 2010; Iyengar et al., 2009; Kesterton et al., 2010; Nair, Ariana, and Webster, 2012). For instance, in Uttar Pradesh, India, women's caste determined their likelihood of using contraceptives, antenatal care, and institutional delivery (Sanneving et al., 2013; Saroha, Altarac, and Sibley, 2008).

One of the core competencies of social work professionals is advancing human rights and social and economic justice. Social workers are trained to analyze and understand different forms of social discrimination and injustice. In partnership with health professionals they can understand, challenge, and find solutions to problems rooted in discriminatory social norms and inequalities. They have the skills to advocate for equal access to services regardless of caste or ethnicity and can facilitate equal access to health services. In Nepal, the UN Population Fund (UNFPA) now has social workers on staff who are engaged in the design and implementation of community interventions that increase women's access to contraceptives and help to end violence against women of reproductive age.

Tradition/Culture

A third social determinant of health is rooted in tradition and culture. Specifically, the practice of girl child marriage has produced adverse health consequences for women. Although child marriage is on the decline globally, there are still approximately 14 million girls under the age of 18 married annually (UNFPA, 2012). This practice is concentrated in developing countries, with 50 to 70 percent of girls being married before age 18 in particular Asian countries (Hampton, 2010; Nour, 2009; Pandey, 2017; Raj, 2010). As a part of this tradition, many of these girls are forced into marriage (Kopelman, 2016; McFarlane et al., 2016; Sabbe et al., 2013; Salvi, 2009). Women who married as children are at a much higher risk for intimate partner violence and maternal mortality (Babu and Kar, 2010; Hampton, 2010; Koenig et al., 2006; Lloyd and Mensch, 2008; Nour, 2006, 2009; Pandey, 2016; Raj, 2010; Raj et al., 2010; Speizer and Pearson, 2011).

It will be difficult to attain health equity without addressing child marriage. While many countries now have national laws prohibiting child marriage of girls, cultural practices continue (Pandey, 2017). We need to understand the root causes behind this practice and begin exploring ways for eliminating child marriage. In many of these countries, governments do not maintain vital registration of births and marriage. This makes it very difficult to implement the law. Nevertheless, social workers can influence governments in these countries, encouraging them to collect vital statistics on all children and therefore making it is easier to implement child marriage prohibition laws (Pandey et al., 2017). With social workers on staff, the UNFPA-Nepal has begun working with local priests and astrologers to stop child marriage in the far-western region of the country. Social workers can also simultaneously work with multiple layers of local communities (organize girls, boys, their parents, local priests, and community members) to defend child rights and help delay the marriage of girls until they attain legal age (Pandey et al., 2017).

Race/Ethnicity

Mervyn Susser asserts that "states of health do not exist in a vacuum apart from people. People form societies, and any study of the attributes of people is also a study of the manifestations of the form, the structure, and the processes of social forces" (1973, p. 6). Understanding how humans organize themselves, particularly around a social hierarchy, is important in our understanding of racial/ethnic health inequalities. Stress derived from low social status and poorer health has been thoroughly documented in the literature (Adler et al., 1994, 2008; Kwate and Meyer, 2011; Marmot et al., 1991; Meyer, Schwartz, and Frost, 2008).

The process of racial categorization and racism clearly illustrate the effects of social stratification on health disparities in the United States. Racial categorization is a foundational stratification factor in the United States. Indeed, data on race were collected during the inaugural U.S. Census in 1790. The United States remains highly stratified by race. This stratification is manifest at multiple levels, from interpersonal prejudice and stereotypes to laws and practices that determined which racial/ethnic groups were eligible for bank loans and inclusion in reformative social and economic policies. Researchers have documented that racism, measured at multiple levels, has negative effects on the overall health and well-being of people of color (Jones, 2000). Building on Powell's (2008) framework, Gee and Ford define structural racism as "the macro-level systems, social forces, institutions, ideologies, and processes that interact with one another to generate and reinforce inequities among racial and ethnic groups" (2011: 3). They further argue that structural racism "emphasizes the most influential socioecologic levels at which racism may affect racial and ethnic health inequities" (3). For instance, high levels of racial residential segregation in the United States constrain the health-promoting resources available in neighborhoods that are predominantly composed of racial/ethnic minority groups (Jackson, Knight, and Rafferty, 2010; LaVeist et al., 2011; Mezuk et al., 2013). Similarly, racial sentencing disparities within the criminal justice system disproportionately affect the African American community (Gee and Ford, 2011; Western and Wildeman, 2009).

Racial residential segregation is one of the most prominent contemporary manifestations of structural racism. Neighborhoods provide the scaffolding for a livable life—access to healthy foods, healthcare, safety, and quality education, to name a few. However, segregation, fueled by racist policies and practices, constrains the resources and life possibilities for many people of color (Charles, Dinwiddie, and Massey, 2004; Williams and Collins, 2001). For instance, while health behaviors are critical for longevity and quality of life, segregation ensures that many people of color live in environments that are incongruent with recommendations from health professionals for changing behavior (Gottlieb, Sandel, and Adler, 2013). Further, people have formidable competing demands such as employment, financial distress, school quality, and the safety and well-being of family members and friends that take priority over maintaining normative blood pressure levels or getting regular health screenings (Gottlieb et al., 2013). Effective prevention efforts must take into account the multidimensional nature of health and wellness. Fortunately, researchers and practitioners are starting to link the social and economic factors in which people are embedded in within their health care interactions (Braveman, Egerter, and Williams, 2011).

Intended/Unintended Consequences of Social Policies and Practices

Social determinants of health, felt in the lives of individuals who have a poorer quality of life and/or truncated life expectancies, are fueled by policies and practices. The New Deal policies and programs that aimed at alleviating the impact of the Great Depression of 1929 provided a prominent, comprehensive set of policies geared at improving the lives of individuals and thereby increased the overall prosperity and access to the American Dream. One such New Deal era policy was low-interest home loans. Low-interest, federally backed housing loans instituted during the New Deal era allowed a much larger proportion of Americans to buy homes since it reduced the down payment to about 20 percent of the final price (Katznelson, 2005). The Homeowners' Loan Act of 1933 established Home Owners Loan Corporation (HOLC) to help refinance nonfarm home mortgages that were at risk of foreclosure. Essentially, the HOLC bought underwater mortgages from banks and issued new long-term (15 years) amortized home mortgage loans to homeowners.

Before the New Deal era, home buyers had to save a much larger proportion of the total home cost as a down payment and needed to pay off the entire loan within three to five years. However, people of color were systematically denied these low-interest home loans because of redlining practices used by mortgage companies. Banks redlined neighborhoods that were predominantly minority, refusing to lend to homebuyers in these neighborhoods (Conley, 1999; Oliver and Shapiro, 2006). Furthermore, Federal Housing Authority loans were used widely in the suburbs of major American cities. The result of this was the depopulation of many central cities, stripping the central cities of employment opportunities and investments in new residential and commercial developments, along with straining the capacity of city services (Farley et al., 1994; Oliver and Shapiro, 2006).

Such discriminatory practices have a direct impact on individuals and populations, not only in the number and quality of health-promoting resources people can access, but also in their financial capabilities. For instance, home equity comprises a large proportion of the wealth that Americans hold (Conley, 1999; Oliver and Shapiro, 2006). In spite of the government's prompt response at mitigating the impact of the Great Depression on homeownership, certain sections of the society remained marginalized and did not benefit to the same extent as those living in suburban areas.

Systematic racism in policies and practices continue to affect the housing sector today. Homes located in predominantly white neighborhoods are, on average, worth substantially more than homes in predominately African American neighborhoods (Adelman, 2004; Alba and Logan, 1993; Charles, Dinwiddie, and Massey, 2004). The result of this is that in 2017, the net worth for whites versus blacks was approximately ten to one.

Stress

Another important consideration for understanding the social determinants of health is stress. Humans are hardwired to handle stress, allowing us to adapt to changes in the environment and avoid threats (McEwen, 2003b). However, stress, like good health, is not equally distributed (Meyer et al., 2008). While everyone experiences stress in their daily life, the types of stressors, chronicity, and duration of stress varies greatly. The resources people have, whether financial or social, help tremendously when stressors arise in our day-to-day lives. Sarah Gehlert and colleagues (2008) have linked the presence of environmental stressors to physiological stress hormone changes in African Americans resulting in higher breast cancer mortality rates than whites.

Increasingly, researchers are interested in understanding how stress, particularly chronic stress, "gets under the skin," resulting in disease (Kemeny and Schedlowski, 2007; Seeman et al., 2010). Chronic stress exposure has both short- and long-term effects on health. For instance, Krieger describes how psychosocial stressors "embody" themselves over time—a process in which the society is biologically incorporated into individuals bodies (Krieger, 2001b). Bruce McEwen describes allostatic load as the "wear and tear" on the body that occurs and is exacerbated with greater exposure to chronic stress (McEwen, 2003b). Developed by Geronimus and colleagues (2006), weathering is the notion that people under chronic stress experience accumulated disadvantage and accelerated aging over the life course. These different theoretical frameworks and models delineate the pathways between the experience of social stress and the development of poor health.

Social work scholars such as Michael Spencer and Leopoldo Cabassa have worked with community stakeholders to devise culturally appropriate health behavior change efforts aimed at altering diet. For instance, the Detroit REACH project has worked with Hispanic community members to devise health messages for individuals with diabetes. These interventions, aimed at social change within communities, resulted in changes in biology such as a small but statistically significant reduction in hemoglobin A1c, which is tied to negative outcomes in diabetes. Social interventions can indeed reduce health disparities by changing biology (Spencer et al., 2011, 2013). The Department of Social Work at Mt. Sinai Hospital in New York City now employees over 600 health social workers, many of whom work in communities rather than traditional hospital settings. Both Michigan and New York are currently leading efforts to standardize training and certification of community health workers.

The effects of chronic stress exposure accumulated over the life course can cascade into cellular level dysregulation. Examples of this include shortened telomere length, increased levels of inflammatory markers, and decreases in immune system functioning (Geronimus et al., 2006; Kemeny and Schedlowski, 2007; Link and Phelan, 2002; Seeman et al., 2010). For instance, it is hypothesized that chronic stress negatively affects telomeres, which then affect how cells age as they cap and protect the end of our chromosomes (Buwalda, 2001; Kemeny and Schedlowski, 2007). Additionally, stress has a negative effect on immune system functioning, which may cause chronically stressed individuals to be more susceptible to infections and disease (Link and Phelan, 2002; McEwen, 2003a). Evidence from the field of psychoneuroimmunology also indicates that dysregulation due to chronic stress leads to inflammation, which in turn is a key factor in the development of cardiovascular disease, the leading cause of death in the United States (Borrell et al., 2010; Kershaw et al., 2016; McEwen, 2004).

Social Context Effect on Health

The social context, particularly the neighborhoods in which people reside, has a profound effect on health disparities between racial/ethnic groups in the United States. Social context not only shapes the social norms and health behaviors of individuals from an early stage in life, but context also influences the stressors, coping resources, and other factors affecting individuals (Diez Roux and Mair, 2010; Jackson et al., 2010; Link and Phelan, 1995). People are embedded within social networks and may adhere to social norms that do not promote the lifestyle changes that public health and health care professionals would like to see (Bandura, 2001, 2004).

For example, people often interact with others through food and therefore important social and cultural considerations must be considered when developing programs and policies geared toward improving dietary practices. Asking individuals to change their health behavior is often asking them to make substantial changes to their participation in social networks. Additionally, social norms may influence the likelihood of abstaining from foods that public health professionals might consider unhealthy (Bandura, 2001; Jackson et al., 2010; Rose, 2001). If an individual is part of a family that holds regular dinners, with calorie-dense foods as part of the menu, it may be difficult to ask someone to refrain from indulging in the food their family has prepared, not only because individuals are being asked to deny themselves foods they have grown to love, but also because refraining from the foods may be interpreted as a negative or offensive behavior on the part of the family members who have prepared the food.

This is where the right to health as a human right dialogue clashes with health as a shared responsibility (Acharya, 2016). People may ignore self-care because of the preference for food they grew up eating or because of limited alternatives. Given such realities, some suggest that institutions should play a role in guiding people's choices (Brudney, 2016). Along this line, several cities (i.e., New York City) and countries (i.e., Mexico's soda tax) have begun banning or increasing taxes on some food items that are considered unhealthy (Halpin et al., 2010; Jacobson and Brownell, 2000).

Environmental factors such as a preponderance of fast food restaurants and liquor stores over full-service grocery stores in predominantly African American neighborhoods decrease the adoption of healthy behaviors as well (Jackson et al., 2010; LaVeist and Wallace, 2000). Using data drawn from the Baltimore Epidemiologic Catchment Area study, Mezuk and colleagues (2011) found that poor health behaviors provided an effective means of coping with the stress of social disadvantage and mitigating the negative effects of stress on depression. Specifically, as stress exposure increased, African Americans who engaged in poor health behaviors actually had a lower risk of depression. This finding indicates that coping with poor health behaviors could provide temporary psychological relief from exposure to chronic stress and social disadvantage. However, in the long term, adoption of poor health behaviors comes at the risk of physical health problems.

There is no doubt that health is strongly influenced by individual choices such as maintaining a proper diet, getting adequate levels of exercise, and seeking preventative health care. However, the social determinants of health, such as where people live and the resources embedded in their neighborhoods, are beyond the control of individuals. Understanding the role of social determinants of health in livable lives allows one to envision a way to facilitate health at the micro level by removing barriers at the macro level to encourage positive health behaviors.

How Can We Address Social Determinants of Health?

The CSDH report recommends that U.S. states do the following in addressing social determinants of health: (1) improve the conditions of daily life, that is, the social and economic conditions in which people are born, grow, live, work, and age; (2) address structural inequalities of power, money, and resources; and (3) evaluate interventions, expand the knowledge base, and raise public awareness about the social determinants of health. Importantly, the CSDH charges states with identifying and using evidence-based practices for promoting and attaining health equity within one generation (Commission on Social Determinants of Health, 2008). It is not enough to simply implore individuals to eat a healthier diet or exercise more. Reducing disparities in health and improving the overall health of the entire population requires that social determinants of health must be addressed. Effectively addressing the social determinants of health requires upstream, complex solutions. These solutions are difficult to bring about because they require multisector approaches and, often, tremendous cost, including the state's commitment and expenditure of political capital.

In terms of improving economic conditions for lower-income households, scholars (Kim et al., 2015; Sherraden et al., 2016) have developed and implemented Child Development Accounts (CDAs), as a way of building asset accumulation for such households (see Chapter 6 of this volume for a more extended discussion). It has been demonstrated that even low levels of savings among individuals can foster asset accumulation over the long-term development. Oklahoma has adopted this approach and implemented universal CDAs (SEED for Oklahoma Kids), and research has demonstrated that families participating in SEED OK are more likely to open a college savings account for their children and make greater contributions compared to control group families (Nam et al., 2013). These modest investments are associated with greater educational expectations among parents who participated in SEED OK (Kim et al., 2015). Other scholars have argued that the implementation of "baby bonds" can help reduce racial inequalities in wealth (Hamilton and Darity, 2010). Hamilton and Darity propose that the United States could use the scaffolding provided by CDAs to scaled up CDAs to infuse $50,000 to $60,000 for children in the lowest wealth quartiles. They argue that this magnitude of investment would be critical for addressing deeply entrenched, historical racial wealth inequalities. This kind of progressive infusion of financial resources could be transformative for many poor American families and would likely improve the overall health and well-being of the entire country.

At the international level, the Conditional Cash Transfer (CCT) policy intervention has consistently shown positive results in improving social and health outcomes. The CCT was originally introduced in Mexico in the 1990s. Since then many countries in Africa, Asia, and Latin America have introduced their own version of the CCT program. In Latin American countries, cash is transferred to poor pregnant women and those with young, school-aged children, if they meet the program requirements—using preventive health services, attending health education sessions, and ensuring the enrollment of school-age children. Studies show that the CCT programs in Latin American countries have empowered women and have improved children's health, nutrition and education (Department for International Development, 2011; Lagarde, Haines, and Palmer, 2007, 2009). Similarly, in Bangladesh, their pilot voucher program significantly increased the use of antenatal, delivery, and postnatal care with qualified providers (Nguyen et al., 2012). It is imperative that researches and practitioners from various disciplines work together in order to ensure healthy lives for all.

Effectively addressing social determinants of health also requires the development of stronger social theory for identifying the social and economic root causes of disease, as well as gaining a better understanding in how different levels and systems can be intervened to address disparities in health. Considering multiple levels will help provide solutions at the individual, family, community, organization, and policy level. For example, the cross-level effects of individual and neighborhood socioeconomic status are significantly related to mortality.

Social work professionals face the difficult task of developing effective interventions and policies to encourage healthy lifestyles for individuals. As a result of work obligations and family responsibilities, they often do not have the time or energy bandwidth to take on lifestyle changes that could extend their lives and improve their quality of life. Members of vulnerable populations are both the hardest to reach and yet are most in need of intervention and information. Social work educators must do a better job of equipping students for meeting these challenges by providing real-world examples inside and outside of classrooms that are focused on the application of classroom knowledge toward the crafting of solutions. Additionally, effective community partnerships can be developed that are beneficial to students as well as serving the needs of community agencies and organizations.

Social determinants of health are also integral to individuals' access to resources, and they affect multiple disease outcomes through different mechanisms. Understanding the nature of upstream determinants is best achieved through partnerships with community stakeholders. Community-engaged and community-based participatory research approaches, which combine research and social change, have proved useful in devising and testing the effectiveness of interventions in areas such as church-based diabetes prevention. Likewise, involving stakeholders helps to ensure that interventions are "owned" by community members and thus are more likely to be sustained across time.

Addressing the social determinants of health requires multisector and multilevel solutions, but partnerships are needed as well. Partnerships can effectively craft solutions aimed at reducing racial health disparities (Gehlert et al., 2014). Due to the various factors that may impede individuals from reaching their optimal level of health, collaborating with nontraditional partners outside of the health care arena is imperative. Health starts before entering the health care system—our homes, schools, work places, neighborhoods, and communities. Therefore, multiple partners are needed to address health disparities and reduce inequalities to achieve health equity.

Organizations like PolicyLink, headquartered in Oakland, California, have lead the way and have developed multisector strategies aimed at improving the economic, social, and health status of various neighborhoods. PolicyLink provides a set of equity tools on its website, including an equitable development toolkit that centers on the development of communities of opportunity that will lead to equitable outcomes (www.policylink.org). PolicyLink also has a number of opportunities to highlight the innovative work in different communities across the country through their Equity Summits and regular webinars.

The Robert Wood Johnson Foundation is devoted to establishing a "culture of health." This culture of health is characterized by good health and well-being across sociodemographic factors like race/ethnicity and place (www.rwjf.org). To achieve this culture of health, the foundation has developed an action plan in which health equity is at the center. The plan calls for including opportunities for individuals and families to make health choices and forging multisector collaborations with government, business, individuals, and organizations working together to build healthy communities. To this end, the foundation uses the Culture of Health Prize for highlighting and elevating the work that different communities across the United States are doing to achieve health equity.

Additionally, the factors that allow people to thrive in the face of adversity must be considered. Despite the facts and figures about racial/ethnic disparities in health, many individuals can survive and thrive. Developing a clear understanding of assets embedded in neighborhoods that might be considered socially or economically disadvantaged is important. For instance, social connectedness is considered a major factor in the risk and resilience of individuals and communities (Cattell, 2001). The social networks and the social support that people offer each other is critical for buffering against stress and for providing an avenue for pooling resources (Krause, 2006; Link and Phelan, 1995). Government social services may not meet the needs of disadvantaged communities, and informal networks are often the lifelines that individuals rely upon within their networks. Fostering the organic social networks that exist within communities strengthens the levels of trust, feelings of safety, collective efficacy, and norms of reciprocity within neighborhoods (House, 2002; Leventhal and Brooks-Gunn, 2000; Rose, 2001; Sampson, Raudenbush, and Earls, 1997). Furthermore, providing linkages between communities and other sectors such as business and policymakers can empower communities to advocate for the resources that communities need for individuals to thrive (Israel et al., 2006; Israel et al., 1994). Again, this requires the development of social theory to guide the exploration of resiliency factors, the examination of multiple levels of influence on health, and addressing the practical challenges of connecting with key stakeholders across different sectors.

Healthy People 2020 aims at informing and improving health policies and practices on the national, state, and local levels. In addition, it works to increase public, individual, and community awareness of the prevention of chronic disease, morbidity, disability, and premature death. Health care access through affordable health insurance coverage is a health policy approach that has linked individuals to quality prevention and treatment services.

The Affordable Care Act (ACA) has increased health care access for individuals who may be low-income and uninsured (Koh and Sebelius, 2010). In addition, the ACA has also helped expand nonprofit health organizations' community benefit programs. The ACA now requires health care organizations to provide community needs assessments and health improvement plans, guiding these organizations to invest in the communities they serve beyond providing charity care. It is in the nation's best interest to encourage a healthy population by investing in communities.

The provision of evidence-based care is also important for reducing health disparities. Access to and quality of care delivered by health professionals is critical in the prevention and detection of disease. Providers and their staff can adopt up-to-date evidence-based clinical practice guidelines for promoting healthy behaviors. Clinicians should be aware of the economic barriers many individuals face in health care and provide education and referrals for prescription subsidizing programs or Medicaid/Medicare-covered treatment options for their patients (Gottlieb, Sandel, and Adler, 2013).

Examples of public policies that have been implemented at local and state levels include the taxation of tobacco and low-nutrient foods (e.g., soft drinks) and mandated food labeling. Similarly, tobacco use policies have regulated access to tobacco products, banned tobacco advertisement and sponsorships, and regulated exposure to environmental tobacco smoke (e.g., workplace, restaurants, public transportation, and public spaces; Jacobson and Brownell, 2000). Urban planning initiatives, such as the installation of walk and cycling paths as well as appropriate lighting, have improved the built environments and have increased physical activity in communities (Halpin et al., 2010). Other examples of local and state policies are zoning laws that regulate the location of fast food establishments and providing healthy foods in public school cafeterias.

At the global level, the WHO has developed the Framework Convention on Tobacco Control (FCTC), which seeks to engage developing countries in evidence-based strategies for reducing tobacco use (WHO, 2003). In 2015, the UN adopted 17 Sustainable Development Goals (SDGs) of which goal three (SDG-3) ensures healthy lives and promotes well-being at all ages by 2030 (UN, 2015). The UN has recommended its member nations to find solutions and focus on eliminating health inequities, including avoidable maternal and child mortalities. Most member nations now have public polices for curbing tobacco use, child marriage, and violence against women. For example, Nepal's Tobacco Control and Regulatory Act passed in 2011 abides by the vast majority of the FCTC articles including prohibiting the sale of tobacco products to pregnant women and children under 18 years of age (Ministry of Health and Population, 2012). Private foundations, such as the Bill and Melinda Gates Foundation are focused not only on finding solutions to vaccinate all children and eradicate diseases such as polio and malaria but are also increasingly realizing the value of addressing social determinants of health to close the gaps in health outcomes. The Gates Foundation recently committed $80 million for promoting women and girls' empowerment, closing gender gaps, and helping low-and-middle-income countries attain the UN Sustainable Development Goals.

While the efforts reviewed here are not exhaustive, they provide insight into a multilevel public health approach for reducing health disparities and increasing health and wellness. Designing prevention and intervention programs should consider the target population, target behavior, and the social, political, environmental context. It is also critical to consider the assets of individuals and communities. Gaining more information about the protective factors that individuals possess will be important for designing interventions at multiple levels. The insights from individuals who have resilience in challenging social environments can provide ways to foster those assets and learn lessons that can inspire innovative solutions (Walsh, 1996, 2016). The deliberate consideration of these factors leads to culturally tailored health programs, which public health research has identified as the most effective approach for health promotion (Kreuter et al., 2005; Sanders Thompson, 2009).

Relatedly, it is also necessary to incorporate the social determinants of health lens into the development of science policy, particularly national research funding priorities. As mentioned before, the priorities of individuals and communities are often misaligned with the priorities of health professionals. Similarly, the funding priorities of agencies like the National Institutes of Health can be misaligned with the needs of communities (Syme, 2008). For instance, it is often the case that when working with a community, the priorities of the community of concern center on social determinants of health such as economic opportunities, school quality, and safety rather than a specific disease or condition. Consequently, in the development of programs geared toward addressing health disparities, it is often the case that the intervention efforts frequently do not meet the needs that community members have identified.

Social work educators should focus on factors at all levels of influence, from the biological to the societal. Human problems that produce ill health are multifaceted. We must prepare a work force that can take a broad and integrated approach to these problems. Pairing social advocacy with research and practice holds promise for making significant and meaningful change in population health. By doing so, we ensure that many more individuals are able to achieve a livable life.

References

Acharya, G. 2016. "The Right to Health is a Fundamental Human Right but Better Health is a Shared Responsibility." *Acta Obstetricia et Gynecologica Scandinavica*, 95, 1203–1204.

Adelman, R. 2004. "Neighborhood Opportunities, Race, and Class: The Black Middle Class and Residential Segregation." *City and Community*, 3, 43–63.

Adler, N. E., T. Boyce, M. A. Chesney, S. Cohen, S. Folkman, R. L. Kahn, and S. L. Syme. 1994. "Socioeconomic Status and Health: The Challenge of the Gradient." *The American Psychologist*, 49, 15–24.

Adler, N., A. Singh-Manoux, J. Schwartz, J. Stewart, K. Matthews, and M. G. Marmot. 2008. "Social Status and Health: A Comparison of British Civil Servants in Whitehall-II with European- and African-Americans in CARDIA." *Social Science and Medicine*, 66, 1034–1045.

Adler, N. E., and J. Stewart. 2010. "Health Disparities Across the Lifespan: Meaning, Methods, and Mechanisms." *Annals of the New York Academy of Sciences*, 1186, 5–23.

Ajzen, I. 2011. "Theory of Planned Behavior." *Handbook Theory Social Psychology*, 1, 438.

Alba, R. D., and J. R. Logan. 1993. "Minority Proximity to Whites in Suburbs: An Individual-Level Analysis of Segregation." *The American Journal of Sociology*, 98, 1388–1427.

Andrews, J. R., J. Bogoch, and J. Utzinger. 2017. "The Benefits of Mass Deworming on Health Outcomes: New Evidence Synthesis, the Debate Persists." *Lancet Global Health*, 5, e4–e5.

Babu, B. V., and S. K. Kar. 2010. "Domestic Violence in Eastern India: Factors Associated with Victimization and Perpetration." *The Royal Society for Public Health*, 124, 136–148.

Balfour, J. L., and G. A. Kaplan. 2002. "Neighborhood Environment and Loss of Physical Function in Older Adults: Evidence from the Alameda County Study." *American Journal of Epidemiology*, 155, 507–515.

Bandura, A. 2001. "Social Cognitive Theory: An Agentic Perspective." *Annual Review of Psychology*, 52, 1–26.

Bandura, A. 2004. "Health Promotion by Social Cognitive Means." *Health Education and Behavior*, 31, 143–164.

Barker, D. P. 1997. "Fetal Nutrition and Cardiovascular Disease in Later Life." *British Medical Bulletin*, 53, 96–108.

Bhanderi, M. N., and S. Kannan. 2010. "Untreated Reproductive Morbidities Among Never Married Women of Slums of Rajkot City, Gujarat: The Role of Class, Distance, Provider Attitudes, and Perceived Quality of Care." *Journal Urban Health*, 87, 254–263.

Borrell, L. N., A. V. Diez Roux, D. R. Jacobs, S. Shea, S. Jackson, S. Shrager, and R. S. Blumenthal. 2010. "Perceived Racial/Ethnic Discrimination, Smoking and Alcohol Consumption in the Multi-Ethnic Study of Atherosclerosis (MESA)." *Preventive Medicine*, 51, 307–312.

Borrell, L. N., C. I. Kiefe, A. V. Diez-Roux, D. R. Williams, and P. Gordon-Larsen. 2013. "Racial Discrimination, Racial/Ethnic Segregation, and Health Behaviors in the CARDIA Study." *Ethnicity and Health*, 18, 227–243.

Braveman, P. 2006. "Health Disparities and Health Equity: Concepts and Measurement." *Annual Review of Public Health*, 124, 167–194.

Braveman, P., S. Egerter, and D. R. Williams. 2011. "The Social Determinants of Health: Coming of Age." *Annual Review of Public Health*, 32, 381–398.

Brudney, D. 2016. "Is Health Care a Human Right?" *Theoretical Medicine and Bioethics*, 37, 249–257.

Buwalda, B. W., M. Blom, J. M. Koolhaas, and G. van Dijk. 2001. "Behavioral and Physiological Responses to Stress are Affected by High-Fat Feeding in Male Rats." *Physiology and Behavior*, 73, 371–377.

Castillo, C. M., V. Garrafa, T. Cunha, and F. Hellmann. 2017. "Access to Health Care as a Human Right in International Policy: Critical Reflections and Contemporary Challenges." *Ciencia & Saude Coletiva*, 22, 2151–2160.

Cattell, V. 2001. "Poor People, Poor Places, and Poor Health: The Mediating Role of Social Networks and Social Capital." *Social Science Medicine*, 52, 1501.

Chapman, A. 2015. "The Foundations of a Human Right to Health: Human Rights and Bioethics in Dialogue." *Health and Human Rights Journal*, 17, E6–E18.

Charles, C. Z., G. Dinwiddie, and D. S. Massey. 2004. "The Continuing Consequences of Segregation: Family Stress and College Academic Performance." *Social Science Quarterly*, 85, 1353–1373.

Christopher, A. S., and D. Caruso, D. 2015. "Promoting Health as a Human Right in the Post-ACA United States." *AMA Journal of Ethics*, 17, 958–965.

Clarke, N. E., A. C. Clements, S. A. Doi, D. Wang, S. J. Campbell, D. Gray, and S. V. Nery. 2017. "Differential Effect of Mass Deworming and Targeted Deworming for Soil-Transmitted Helminth Control in Children: A Systematic Review and Meta-Analysis." *The Lancet*, 389, 287–297.

Commission on Social Determinants of Health. 2008. *Closing the Gap in a Generation: Health Equity Through Action on the Social Determinants of Health.* Final Report of the Commission on Social Determinants of Health. World Health Organization. Retrieved from https://apps.who.int/iris/handle/10665/43943.Conley, D. 1999. *Being Black, Living in the Red.* Berkeley, CA: University of California Press.

Dauda, B., and K. Dierickx. 2012. "Health, Human Right, and Health Inequalities: Alternative Concepts in Placing Health Research as Justice for Global Health." *American Journal of Bioethics,* 12, 42–44.

Diez Roux, A. V., and C. Mair. 2010. "Neighborhoods and Health." *Annals of the New York Academy of Sciences,* 1186, 125–45.

Dowd, J. B., A. Zajacova, and A. Aiello. 2009. "Early Origins of Health Disparities: Burden of Infection, Health, and Socioeconomic Status in U.S. Children." *Social Science and Medicine,* 68, 699–707.

Farley, R., C. Steeh, M. Krysan, T. Jackson, and K. Reeves. 1994. "Stereotypes and Segregation: Neighborhoods in the Detroit Area." *The American Journal of Sociology,* 100, 750–780.

Fiscella, K., and P. Franks. 1997. "Does Psychological Distress Contribute to Racial and Socioeconomic Disparities in Mortality?" *Social Science and Medicine,* 45, 1805–1809.

Fiscella, K., P. Franks, M. P. Doescher, and B. G. Saver. 2002. "Disparities in Health Care by Race, Ethnicity, and Language Among the Insured: Findings from a National Sample." *Medical Care,* 45, 52–59.

Fox Piven, F., and R. Cloward. 1978. *Poor People's Movements: Why They Succeed, How They Fail.* New York: Vintage Books.

Friedman, E. A., J. Dasgupta, A. E. Yamin, and L. O. Gostin. 2013. "Realizing the Right to Health Through a Framework Convention on Global Health? A Health and Human Rights Special Issue." *Health and Human Right Journal,* 15, E1–E4.

Gee, G. C., and C. L. Ford. 2011. "Structural Racism and Health Inequalities." *Du Bois Review: Social Science Research on Race,* 8, 115–132.

Gehlert, S. 2011. "Chicago Team Explores Links of Environment and Biology." *Health Affairs,* 30, 1902–1903.

Gehlert, S. O. M. Fayanju, S. Jackson, S. Kenkel, I. McCullough, C. Oliver, and M. Sanford. 2014. "A Method for Achieving Reciprocity of Funding in Community-Based Participatory Research." *Progress in Community Health Partnerships: Research, Education, and Action,* 8, 861–570.

Gehlert, S., D. Sohmer, T. Sacks, C. Mininger, M. McClintock, and O. Olopade. 2008. "Targeting Health Disparities: A Model Linking Upstream Determinants to Downstream Interventions." *Health Affairs (Project Hope),* 27(2), 339–349. doi:10.1377/hlthaff.27.2.339.

Geronimus, A. T., M. Hicken, D. Keene, and J. Bound. 2006. " 'Weathering' and Age Patterns of Allostatic Load Scores Among Blacks and Whites in the United States." *American Journal of Public Health,* 96, 826–833.

Geronimus, A. T., S. A. James, M. Destin, L. A. Graham, M. Hatzenbuehler, M. Murphy, J. P. Thompson. 2016. "Jedi Public Health: Co-Creating an Identity-Safe Culture to Promote Health Equity." *SSM – Population Health,* 2, 105–116.

Goldman, D., and J. P. Smith. 2011. "The Increasing Value of Education to Health." *Social Science and Medicine,* 72, 1728–1737.

Gostin, L. O., E. A. Friedman, P. Buss, M. Chowdhury, A. Grover, and M. Heywood, 2016. "The Next WHO Director-General's Highest Priority: A Global Treaty on the Human Right to Health." *Lancet Global Health,* 4, e890–e892.

Gottlieb, L., M. Sandel, and N. E Adler. 2013. "Collecting and Applying Data on Social Determinants of Health in Health Care Settings." *JAMA Internal Medicine,* 173, 1017–1020.

Halpin, H. A., M. M. Morales-Suarez-Varela, and J. M. Martin-Moreno. 2010. "Chronic Disease Prevention and the New Public Health." *Public Health Reviews,* 32, 120–154.

Hamilton, D., and W. Darity. 2010. "Can 'Baby Bonds' Eliminate the Racial Wealth Gap in Putative Post-Racial America?" *The Review of Black Political Economy,* 37, 207–216.

Hampton, T. 2010. "Child Marriage Threatens Girls' Health." *JAMA*, 304, 509–510.

Halpin, H. A., M. M Morales-Suarez-Varela, and J. M. Martin-Moreno. 2010. "Chronic Disease Prevention and the New Public Health." *Public Health Reviews*, 32, 120–154.

Hertzman, C., and T. Boyce. 2010. "How Experience Gets Under the Skin to Create Gradients in Developmental Health." *Annual Review of Public Health*, 31, 329–347.

Hicken, M. T., H. Lee, J. Ailshire, S. A. Burgard, and D. R. Williams. 2013. "Every Shut Eye, Ain't Sleep": The Role of Racism-Related Vigilance in Racial/Ethnic Disparities in Sleep Difficulty." *Race and Social Problems*, 5(2), 100–112. doi:10.1007/s12552-013-9095-9

House, J. S. 2002. "Understanding Social Factors and Inequalities in Health: 20th Century Progress and 21st Century Prospects." *Journal of Health and Social Behavior*, 43, 125–142.

Hudson, D. L., J. Eaton, A. Banks, W. Sewell, and H. Neighbors. 2018. "'Down in the Sewers': Perceptions of Depression and Depression Care Among African American Men." *American Journal of Men's Health*, 12, 126–137. https://doi.org/10.1177/1557988316654864

Hudson, D. L., H. W. Neighbors, A. T. Geronimus, and J. S. Jackson. 2015. "Racial Discrimination, John Henryism, and Depression Among African Americans." *Journal of Black Psychology*, 43, 221–243.

Hunt, P. 2016. "Interpreting the International Right to Health in a Human Rights-Based Approach to Health." *Health Human Rights Journal*, 18, 109–130.

Israel, B. A., B. Checkoway, A. Schulz, and M. Zimmerman. 1994. "Health Education and Community Empowerment: Conceptualizing and Measuring Perceptions of Individual, Organizational, and Community Control." *Health Education Quarterly*, 21, 149–170.

Israel, B. A., A. J. Schulz, L. Estrada-Martinez, S. N. Zenk, E. Viruell-Fuentes, A. M. Villarruel, and C. Stokes. 2006. "Engaging Urban Residents in Assessing Neighborhood Environments and their Implications for Health." *Journal of Urban Health*, 83, 23–539.

Iyengar, S. D., K. Iyengar, V. Suhalka, and K. Agarwal. 2009. "Comparison of Domiciliary and Institutional Delivery-Care Practices in Rural Rajasthan, India." *Journal of Health, Population, and Nutrition*, 27, 303–312.

Jackson, J. S., K. M. Knight, and J. A. Rafferty. 2010. "Race and Unhealthy Behaviors: Chronic Stress, the HPA Axis, and Physical and Mental Health Disparities over the Life Course." *American Journal of Public Health*, 100, 933–939.

Jacobson, M. F., and K. D. Brownell. 2000. "Small Taxes on Soft Drinks and Snack Foods to Promote Health." *American Journal of Public Health*, 90, 854–857.

Jemal, A., E. Ward, R. N. Anderson, T. Murray, and M. J. Thun. 2008. "Widening of Socioeconomic Inequalities in U.S. Death Rates 1993–2001." *PLoS One*, 3, e2181.

Johnson, R. C., and R. F. Schoeni. 2011. "Early-Life Origins of Adult Disease: National Longitudinal Population-Based Study of the United States." *American Journal of Public Health*, 101, 2317–24.

Jones, C. P. 2000. "Levels of Racism: A Theoretic Framework and a Gardener's Tale." *American Journal of Public Health*, 90, 1212–1215.

Kaiser Family Foundation. 2018. *Key Facts About the Uninsured Population*. Washington, DC: Kaiser Family Foundation.

Katznelson, I. 2005. *When Affirmative Action Was White: An Untold Story of Racial Inequality in Twentieth Century America*. New York: W. W. Norton.

Kemeny, M. E., and M. Schedlowski. 2007. "Understanding the Interaction Between Psychosocial Stress and Immune-Related Diseases: A Stepwise Progression." *Brain, Behavior, and Immunity*, 21, 1009–1018.

Kershaw, K. N., T. T. Lewis, A. V. Diez Roux, N. S. Jenny, K. Liu, F. J. Penedo, and M. R. Carnethon. 2016. "Self-Reported Experiences of Discrimination and Inflammation Among Men and Women: The Multi-Ethnic Study of Atherosclerosis." *Health Psychology*, 35, 343–350.

Kim, Y., M. Sherraden, J. Huang, and M. Clancy. 2015. "Child Development Accounts and Parental Educational Expectations for Young Children: Early Evidence from a Statewide Social Experiment." *Social Service Review*, 89, 99–137.

Kesterton, A. J., J. Cleland, A. Sloggett, and C. Ronsmans. 2010. "Institutional Delivery in Rural India: the Relative Importance of Accessibility and Economic Status." *BMC Pregnancy Childbirth*, 10, 1–9.

Koenig, M. A., R. Stephenson, S. Ahmed, S. J. Jejeebhoy, and J. Campball. 2006. "Individual and Contextual Determinants of Domestic Violence in North India." *American Journal of Public Health*, 96, 132–137.

Koh, H. K., and K. G. Sebelius. 2010. "Promoting Prevention Through the Affordable Care Act" *New England Journal of Medicine*, 363, 1296–1299.

Kopelman, L. M. 2016. "The Forced Marriage of Minors: A Neglected Form of Child Abuse." *American Society of Law, Medicine and Ethics*, 44, 173–181.

Krause, N. 2006. "Neighborhood Deterioration, Social Skills, and Social Relationships in Late Life." *International Journal of Aging and Human Development*, 62, 185–207.

Kreuter, M. W., C. Sugg-Skinner, C. L. Holt, E. M. Clark, D. Haire-Joshu, Q. Fu, A. C. Booker, K. Steger-May, and D. Bucholz. 2005. "Cultural Tailoring for Mammography and Fruit and Vegetable Intake Among Low-Income African-American Women in Urban Public Health Centers." *Preventive Medicine*, 41, 53–62.

Krieger, N. 2001a. "A Glossary for Social Epidemiology." *Journal of Epidemiology and Community Health*, 55, 693–700.

Krieger, N. 2001b. "Theories for Social Epidemiology in the 21st Century: An Ecosocial Perspective." *International Journal of Epidemiology*, 55, 668–677.

KKwate, N. A., and I. H. Meyer. 2011. "On Sticks and Stones and Broken Bones" *Du Bois Review: Social Science Research on Race*, 8, 191–198.

Lagarde, M., A. Haines, and N. Palmer. 2007. "Conditional Cash Transfers for Improving Uptake of Health Interventions in Low-and Middle-Income Countries: A Systematic Review." *JAMA*, 298, 1900–1910.

Lagarde, M., A. Haines, and N. Palmer. 2009. "The Impact of Conditional Cash Transfers on Health Outcomes and Use of Health Services in Low and Middle Income Countries." *Cochrane Database of Systematic Reviews*, 4, 1–50.

LaVeist, T., K. Pollack, R. Thorpe, R. Fesahazion, and D. Gaskin. 2011. "Place, Not Race: Disparities Dissipate in Southwest Baltimore When Blacks and Whites Live Under Similar Conditions." *Health Affairs*, 30, 1880–1887.

LaVeist, T. A., and J. M. Wallace. 2000. "Health Risk and Inequitable Distribution of Liquor Stores in African American Neighborhood." *Social Science and Medicine*, 51, 613–617.

Leventhal, T., and J. Brooks-Gunn. 2000. "The Neighborhoods They Live in: The Effects of Neighborhood Residence on Child and Adolescent Outcomes." *Psychological Bulletin*, 126, 309–337.

Lewis, T. T., F. M. Yang, E. A. Jacobs, and G. Fitchett. 2012. "Racial/Ethnic Differences in Responses to the Everyday Discrimination Scale: A Differential Item Functioning Analysis." *American Journal of Epidemiology*, 175, 391–401.

Link, B. G., and J. C. Phelan. 1995. "Social Conditions as Fundamental Causes of Disease." *Journal of Health and Social Behavior*, Special No, 80–94.

Link, B. G., and J. C. Phelan. 2002. "McKeown and the Idea That Social Conditions are Fundamental Causes of Disease." *American Journal of Public Health*, 92, 730–732.

Lloyd, C. B., and B. S. Mensch. 2008. "Marriage and Childbirth as Factors in Dropping Out From School: An Analysis of DHS Data from Sub-Saharan Africa." *Population Studies*, 62, 1–13.

Marmot, M. G., S. Stansfeld, C. Patel, F. North, J. Head, I. White, E. Brunner, A. Feeney, M. G. Mrmot, G. Davey Smith. 1991. "Health Inequalities Among British Civil Servants: The Whitehall II Study." *The Lancet*, 337, 1387–1393.

McEwen, B. S. 2003a. "Early Life Influences on Life-Long Patterns of Behavior and Health." *Mental Retardation and Developmental Disabilities Research Reviews*, 9, 149–154.

McEwen, B. S. 2003b. "Interacting Mediators of Allostasis and Allostatic Load: Towards an Understanding of Resilience in Aging." *Metabolism: Clinical and Experimental*, 52, 10–16.

McEwen, B. S. 2004. "Protection and Damage from Acute and Chronic Stress: Allostasis and Allostatic Overload and Relevance to the Pathophysiology of Psychiatric Disorders." *Annals of the New York Academy of Sciences*, 1032, 1–7.

McFarlane, J., A. Nava, H. Gilroy, and J. Maddoux. 2016. "Child Brides, Forced Marriage, and Partner Violence in America: Tip of an Iceberg Revealed." *Obstetrics and Gynecology*, 127, 706–713.

McLaughlin, M., and Mark R. Rank. 2018. "Estimating the Economic Cost of Childhood Poverty in the United States." *Social Work Research*, 42(2), 73–83. https://doi.org/10.1093/swr/svy007

Meyer, I. H., S. Schwartz, and D. M. Frost. 2008. "Social Patterning of Stress and Coping: Does Disadvantaged Social Statuses Confer More Stress and Fewer Coping Resources?" *Social Science and Medicine*, 67, 368–379.

Mezuk, B., C. M. Abdou, D. Hudson, K. N. Kershaw, J. A. Rafferty, H. Lee, J. S. Jackson. 2013. "'White Box' Epidemiology and the Social Neuroscience of Health Behaviors: The Environmental Affordances Model." *Society and Mental Health*, 3, 1–22.

Mezuk, B., J. A. Rafferty, K. N. Kershaw, D. Hudson, C. M. Abdou, H. Lee, and J. S. Jackson. 2011. "Reconsidering the Role of Social Disadvantage in Physical and Mental Health: Stressful Life Events, Health Behaviors, Race, and Depression." *American Journal of Epidemiology*, 172, 1238–1249.

Ministry of Health and Population. 2012. *Brief profile on tobacco control in Nepal*. Ministry of Health and Population, Government of Nepal.

Montano, D., and D. Kasprzk. 2008. "The Theory of Reasoned Action, Theory of Planned Behavior and the Integrated Behavioral Model." *Health Behavior and Health Education: Theory, Research and Practice*. Edited by K. M. Glanz, B. K. Rimer, and K. Viswanath. San Francisco: Jossey-Bass, pp. 67–96.

Mullings, L. 2002. "The Sojourner Syndrome: Race, Class, and Gender in Health and Illness." *Voices*, 6, 32–36.

Nair, M., P. Ariana, and P. Webster. 2012. "What Influences the Decision to Undergo Institutional Delivery by Skilled Birth Attendants? A Cohort Study in Rural Andhra Pradesh, India." *Rural Remote Health*, 12, 2311.

Nam, Y., Y. Kim, M. Clancy, R. Zager, and M. Sherraden, 2013. "Do Child Development Accounts Promote Account Holding, Saving, and Asset Accumulation for Children's Future? Evidence from a Statewide Randomized Experiment." *Journal of Policy Analysis and Management*, 32, 6–33.

National Association of Social Workers. 2017. "Code of Ethics." Retrieved from https://www.socialworkers.org/About/Ethics/Code-of-Ethics/Code-of-Ethics-English.

Nguyen, H. T., L. Hatt, M. Islam, N. L. Sloan, J. Chowdhury, J. O. Schmidt, A. Hossain, and H. Wang. 2012. "Encouraging Maternal Health Service Utilization: An Evaluation of the Bangladesh Voucher Program." *Social Science Medicine*, 74, 989–996.

Nour, N. M. 2006. "Health Consequences of Child Marriage in Africa." *Emerging Infectious Disease*, 12, 1644–1649.

Nour, N. M. 2009. "Child Marriage: A Silent Health and Human Rights Issue." *Reviews in Obstetrics and Gynecology*, 2, 51–56.

Oliver, M. L., and T. M. Shapiro. 2006. "Forced Marriage, Forced Sex: the Perils of Childhood for Girls." *Black Wealth/White Wealth*. Edited by M. Ouattara, P. Sen, and M. Thomson. New York: Routledge, pp. 27–33.

Olshansky, S. J., T. Antonucci, L. Berkman, R. H. Binstock, A. Boersch-Supan, J. T. Cacioppo, B. A. Carnes, L. L. Carstensen, L. P. Fried, D. P. Goldman, J. Jackson, M. Kohli, J. Rother, Y. Zheng, and J. Rowe. 2012. "Differences in Life Expectancy Due to Race and Educational Differences Are Widening, and Many May Not Catch Up." *Health Affairs*, 31, 1803–1813.

Pandey, S. 2016. "Physical or Sexual Violence Against Women of Child Bearing Age Within Marriage in Nepal: Prevalence, Causes, and Prevention Strategies." *International Social Work*, 59, 803–820.

Pandey, S. 2017. "Persistent Nature of Child Marriage Among Women Even When It Is Illegal: The Case of Nepal." *Children and Youth Services Review*, 73, 242–247.

Pandey, S., Y. B. Karki, V. Murugan, and A. Mathur. 2017. "Mothers' Risk for Experiencing Neonatal and Under-Five Child Deaths in Nepal: The Role of Empowerment." *Global Social Welfare*, 4, 105–115.

Phelan, J. C., B. G. Link, and P. Tehranifar. 2010. "Social Conditions as Fundamental Causes of Health Inequalities: Theory, Evidence, and Policy Implications." *Journal of Health and Social Behavior*, 51(1_suppl), S28–S40. https://doi.org/10.1177/0022146510383498

Phillips, K.A., M. L. Mayer, and L. A. Aday. 2000. "Barriers to Care Among Racial/Ethnic Groups Under Managed Care." *Health Affairs*, 19, 65–75.

Raj, A. 2010. "When the Mother Is a Child: The Impact of Child Marriage on the Health and Human Rights of Girls." *Archives of Disease in Childhood*, 95, 931–935.

Raj, A., N. Saggurti, M. Winter, A. Labonte, M. R. Decker, D. Balaiah, J. G Silverman. 2010. "The Effect of Maternal Child Marriage on Morbidity and Mortality of Children Under 5 in India: Cross Sectional Study of a Nationally Representative Sample." *BMJ*, 340, b4258.

Rose, G. 2001. "Sick Individuals and Sick Populations." *International Journal of Epidemiology*, 30, 427–432.

Rumbold, B., R. Baker, O. Ferraz, S. Hawkes, C. Krubiner, P. Littlejohns, O. F. Norheim, T. Pegram, A. Rid, S. Venkatapuram, A. Voorhoeve, D. Wang, A. Weale, J. Wilson, A. E. Yamin and, P. Hunt. 2017. "Universal Health Coverage, Priority Setting, and the Human Right to Health." *Lancet*, 390, 712–714.

Sabbe, A., H. Oulami, W. Zekraoui, H. Hikmat, M. Temmerman, and Leye, E. 2013. "Determinants of Child and Forced Marriage in Morocco: Stakeholder Perspectives on Health, Policies and Human Rights." *BMC International Health Human Rights*, 13, 43.

Salvi, V. 2009. "Child Marriage in India: A Tradition with Alarming Implications." *Lancet*, 373, 1826–1827.

Sampson, R. J., S. W. Raudenbush, and F. Earls. 1997. "Neighborhoods and Violent Crime: A Multilevel Study of Collective Efficacy." *Science*, 277, 918–924.

Sanders Thompson, V. L. 2009. "Cultural Context and Modification of Behavior Change Theory." *Health Education and Behavior*, 36, 156S–160S.

Sanneving, L., N. Trygg, D. Saxena, D. Mavalankar, and S. Thomsen. 2013. "Inequity in India: The Case of Maternal and Reproductive Health." *Global Health Action*, 6, 1–31.

Saroha, E., M. Altarac, and L. M. Sibley. 2008. "Caste and Maternal Health Care Service Use Among Rural Hindu Women in Maitha, Uttar Pradesh, India." *Journal of Midwifery and Women's Health*, 53, e41–e47.

Saunders, A., T. Schiff, K. Rieth, S. Yamada, G. G. Maskarinec, and S. Riklon. 2010. "Health as a Human Right: Who Is Eligible?" *Hawaii Medical Journal*, 69, 4–6.

Say, L., D. Chou, A. Gemmill, Ö Tunçalp, A. B. Moller, J. Daniels, A. M. Gülmezoglu, M. Temmerman, and L. Alkema. 2017. "Global Causes of Maternal Death: A WHO Systematic Analysis." *The Lancet Global Health*, 2, e323–e333.

Scholte, R., G. J. van den Berg, and M. Lindeboom. 2012. "Long-Run Effects of Gestation During the Dutch Hunger Winter Famine on Labor Market and Hospitalization Outcomes." *SSRN Electronic Journal*, 6307, 1–35.

Seeman, T., E. Epel, T. Gruenewald, A. Karlamangla, and B. S. McEwen. 2010. "Socio-Economic Differentials in Peripheral Biology: Cumulative Allostatic Load." *Annals of the New York Academy of Sciences*, 1186, 223–239.

Seng, J. S., W. D. Lopez, M. Sperlich, L. Hamama, and C. D. Reed Meldrum. 2012. "Marginalized Identities, Discrimination Burden, and Mental Health: Empirical Exploration of an Interpersonal-Level Approach to Modeling Intersectionality." *Social Science and Medicine*, 75, 2437–2445.

Sherraden, M., Clancy, M., and Y. Nam. 2016. "Universal and Progressive Child Development Accounts." *Urban Education*, 53, 806–833.

Shonkoff, J. P., and A. S. Garner. 2012. "The Lifelong Effects of Early Childhood Adversity and Toxic Stress." *Pediatrics*, 129, e232–e246.

Speizer, I. S., and E. Pearson. 2011. "Association Between Early Marriage and Intimate Partner Violence in India: A Focus on Youth from Bihar and Rajasthan." *Journal of Interpersonal Violence,* 26, 1963–1981.

Spencer, M. S., J. Hawkins, N. R. Espitia, B. Sinco, T. Jennings, C. Lewis, G. Palmisano, and E. Kieffer. 2013. "Influence of a Community Health Worker Intervention on Mental Health Outcomes among Low-Income Latino and African American Adults with Type 2 Diabetes." *Race and Social Problems,* 5, 137–146.

Spencer, M. S., A. M. Rosland, E. C. Kieffer, B. R. Sinco, M. Valerio, G. Palmisano, and M. Heisler. 2011. "Effectiveness of a Community Health Worker Intervention Among African American and Latino Adults with Type 2 Diabetes: A Randomized Controlled Trial." *American Journal of Public Health,* 101, 2253–2260.

Stoddard, S. A., S. J. Henly, R. E. Sieving, and J. Bolland. 2011. "Social Connections, Trajectories of Hopelessness, and Serious Violence in Impoverished Urban Youth." *Journal of Youth and Adolescence,* 40, 278–295.

Susser, M. 1973. *Causal Thinking in the Health Sciences: Concepts and Strategies of Epidemiology.* New York: Oxford University Press.

Syme, S. L. 2008. "Reducing Racial and Social-Class Inequalities In Health: The Need for a New Approach. Health Affairs." *Human Behavior,* 27, 456–459.

Tasioulas, J., and E. Vayena. 2015. "Getting Human Rights Right in Global Health Policy." *Lancet,* 385, e42–e44.

The Relative Contribution of Multiple Determinants to Health. 2014. Health Affairs Health Policy Brief, August 21. doi:10.1377/hpb20140821.404487

Tse, A. C., J. W. Rich-Edwards, K. Koenen, and R. J. Wright. 2012. "Cumulative Stress and Maternal Prenatal Corticotropin-Releasing Hormone in an Urban U.S. Cohort." *Psychoneuroendocrinology,* 37, 970–979.

United Nations. 2015. *Global Strategy for Women's, Children's and Adolescents' Health, 2016–2030.* New York: United Nations.

United Nations Population Fund. 2012. "Marrying Too Young: End Child Marriage." Retrieved from https://www.unfpa.org/sites/default/files/pub-pdf/MarryingTooYoung.pdf. United Nations.

U.S. Department of Health and Human Services. 2010. "Healthy People 2020." Retrieved from https://www.healthypeople.gov/2020/about/foundation-health-measures/Disparities

Walsh, F. 1996. "The Concept of Family Resilience: Crisis and Challenge." *Family Process,* 35, 261–281.

Walsh, F. 2016. *Strengthening Family Resilience.* New York: Guilford Press.

Walters, K. L., S. A. Mohammed, T. Evans-Campbell, R. E. Beltrán, D. H. Chae, and B. Duran. 2011. "Bodies Don't Tell Stories, They Tell Histories: Embodiment of Historical Trauma Among American Indians and Alaska Natives." *DuBois Review,* 1, 179–189.

Western, B., and C. Wildeman. 2009. "The Black Family and Mass Incarceration." *The Annals of the American Academy of Political and Social Science,* 621, 221–242.

Whitehead, M., G. Dahlgren, and L. Gilson. 2001. "Developing the Policy Response to Inequities in Health: A Global Perspective." *Challenging Inequities in Health Care: From Ethics to Action.* Edited by T. Evans, M. Whitehead, F. Diderichesen, A. Bhuiya, and M. Wirth. New York: Oxford University Press, pp. 309–322.

Wickrama, K. A. S., R. D. Conger, and W. T. Abraham. 2005. "Early Adversity and Later Health: The Intergenerational Transmission of Adversity through Mental Disorder and Physical Illness." *The Journals of Gerontology. Series B, Psychological Sciences and Social Sciences,* 60, 125–129.

Wilkinson, R. G. 2005. *The Impact of Inequality: How to Make Sick Societies Healthier.* New York: New Press.

Wilkinson, R., and K. Pickett. 2011. *The Spirit Level: Why Greater Equality Makes Societies Stronger.* New York: Bloomsbury.

Williams, D. R., and C. Collins. 2001. "Racial Residential Segregation: A Fundamental Cause of Racial Disparities in Health." *Public Health Reports*, 116, 404–416.

Williams, D. R., M. V. Costa, A. O. Odunlami, and S. A. Mohammed. 2008. "Moving Upstream: How Interventions That Address the Social Determinants of Health Can Improve Health and Reduce Disparities." *Journal of Public Health Management and Practice*, 14, S8–S17.

3

Alleviating Poverty

MARK ROBERT RANK

As discussed in the introductory chapter, the roots of social work began at the turn of the 20th century largely in response to the widespread conditions of poverty and economic destitution. Throughout the decades, poverty has remained an issue of primary concern for the profession. Many of the problems examined in this book are attenuated by the destructive influence of poverty. Whether the challenge is reducing health disparities, promoting civic engagement, developing assets for underserved populations, or countless others, poverty represents a sizeable obstacle preventing the realization of these goals.

Consequently, the subject of poverty has been of central importance to the profession of social work. In fact, it could be argued that addressing poverty lies at the heart of what the profession stands for. As Barbara Simon notes, the original twin missions of social work were "those of relieving the misery of the most desperate among us and of building a more just and humane social order" (1994: 23). This mission rings true today as well. The National Association of Social Work's Code of Ethics begins by stating, "The primary mission of the social work profession is to enhance human well-being and help meet the basic human needs of all people, with particular attention to the needs and empowerment of people who are vulnerable, oppressed, and living in poverty" (2017: 1). Likewise, the Council on Social Work Education's Curriculum Policy Statement declares that the purpose of the social work profession is "actualized through its quest for social and economic justice, the prevention of conditions that limit human rights, the elimination of poverty, and the enhancement of the quality of life for all persons, locally and globally" (2015: 5).

Social work has placed a heavy emphasis on alleviating poverty for at least two reasons. First, poverty has been viewed as undermining the concept of a just society. In an affluent nation such as the United States, it appears patently unfair that not only are many left out of such prosperity, but that they also live in debilitating economic conditions. As discussed in the introductory chapter, one of the hallmarks of the profession has been its emphasis upon the importance of striving to create a more socially just world. Both domestically and internationally, poverty is a significant obstacle for achieving such a world.

Second, as previous noted, social workers have long understood that poverty underlies many of the problems and issues that they confront on a daily basis. Whether the discussion revolves around racial or gender inequalities, family stress, child welfare, economic development, or a host of other topics, research indicates that poverty is intricately connected to each of these subjects. The alleviation of poverty is therefore perceived to be essential in striving toward the enhancement of well-being and helping to "meet the basic human needs of all people" (National Association of Social Workers, 2017: 1). As a result, the profession has historically engaged in research, practice, organizing, and advocacy on the local, state, and federal levels with respect to poverty alleviation.

Furthermore, it is clear that the overall aspiration of a livable life is seriously undermined by poverty (Hick and Burchardt, 2016). As will be discussed throughout this chapter, poverty damages both the development and well-being of individuals, families, and communities. In addition, it represents a significant cost to society as a whole. The alleviation of poverty is therefore a major step toward enabling more individuals and families to achieve a livable life.

The chapter is organized into four sections, beginning with a discussion of the widespread nature of poverty, particularly in the United States. Next, the impact of poverty upon the realization of livable lives is explored. Third, the mechanisms driving and perpetuating poverty are examined. Finally, strategies designed to alleviate poverty are reviewed.

The Scope of Poverty

We begin with the question of how much poverty is there? There are a variety of ways to both define and measure poverty (see Kus, Nolan, and Whelan, 2016; Smeeding, 2016). In the United States, poverty is officially defined and measured as falling below a minimum threshold of annual income. In 2018 this ranged from $12,784 for a one person household, to $25,701 for a family of four, to $51,393 for a household of nine or more (U.S. Census Bureau, 2019a). Consequently, a household of four whose annual income in 2017 fell below $25,701 would be counted as officially in poverty for the year. The idea behind a poverty line is that those falling below such a level are assumed to have great difficulty purchasing the essential goods and services necessary for a minimally decent existence. These would include food, housing, clothing, transportation, and so on.

In using this measure, the U.S. poverty rate for 2018 stood at 11.8 percent. This represented 38.1 million individuals, or approximately one out of eight Americans. If we raise the poverty line by 25 percent, we find that 51.7 million Americans fell under this level, representing 16.0 percent of the population. It should be noted that at whatever point a poverty line is drawn, such an amount represents poverty at its most opulent level—impoverished individuals fall to varying degrees below such a line. For example, of the 38.1 million people who fell below the official poverty line in 2018, 45 percent fell below one-half of the poverty line, or what is referred to as extreme poverty.

Over the past 50 years, the overall rate of poverty has varied between approximately 11 and 15 percent. It has tended to increase during periods of economic recession and has decreased during stronger economic times. For some groups, such as the elderly, poverty rates have declined substantially over this period of time. For other groups, such as children, rates of poverty have increased.

We also have considerable data on who is more likely to experience poverty in any given year. Individuals with characteristics that put them at a disadvantage in the labor market are at a heightened risk of poverty. Consequently, those with less education, having a disability, single-parent families, nonwhites, women, children, young adults, and those residing in inner cities or remote rural areas all have elevated risks of poverty (U.S. Census Bureau, 2019a). Each of these characteristics place individuals at a disadvantage in the competition for good jobs and opportunities.

An alternative measure of poverty, widely used internationally, is to define poverty as falling below one-half of a country's median household income. Consequently, if the overall median income for a country was $60,000 (which was roughly the case for the United States in 2018) than those falling below $30,000 would be counted as in poverty. This measure is often used when making cross-national comparisons of poverty. For 2016, the poverty rate in the United States using such a relative measure of poverty was 17.8 percent (Organisation for Economic Cooperation and Development [OECD], 2019). In contrast, most high-economy OECD countries had much lower rates of poverty. For example, the Scandinavian and Benelux countries tend to have relative poverty rates in the range of 5 to 10 percent, while the United States rates of poverty tend to fall between 15 to 20 percent from year to year.

Yet another way of measuring the scope of poverty is to apply a life course perspective. Here the question is not how many Americans fall into poverty in any given year, but how many experience poverty across a much wider period of time. In using this approach, Mark Rank and colleagues have shown that the risk of poverty during adulthood is quite high. Depending upon how poverty and the period of time are defined, over half of the U.S. population will be poor at some point.

For example, 51 percent of the U.S. population between the ages of 25 and 60 will experience at least one year of poverty (defined as below 150 percent of the official poverty line). However, if we take a somewhat more expansive view of poverty, this percentage becomes even higher. Consequently, 79 percent of Americans between the ages of 25 and 60 will experience one year of either poverty, using a safety net program, or being unemployed (Rank, Hirschl, and Foster, 2014). The reason why these percentages are so high is that across long periods of time, events are much more likely to occur that can throw individuals and families into poverty (e.g., losing a job, families splitting up, health emergencies).

A further life course analysis using a relative measure of poverty showed similar patterns (Rank and Hirschl, 2015). Between the ages of 25 and 60, 61.8 percent of the U.S. population experienced at least one year below the 20th percentile of the income distribution, while 42.1 percent experienced at least one year below the 10th percentile.

The conclusion from this life course work is that poverty is an event that will strike the majority of Americans at some point in their lives. What is particularly troubling about this are the negative ramifications of poverty upon individual, family, and community well-being. We now turn to a discussion of several such ramifications.

Poverty as a Barrier to a Livable Life

Although there are many experiences associated with poverty, in earlier work I have argued that three in particular capture the essence of the experience of poverty (Rank, 2004). Each of these, in turn, seriously undermines the ability of individuals and families to experience a livable life. They include (1) having to do without as a result of making significant compromises regarding the daily necessities in life; (2) enduring elevated levels of stress as a result of such insufficiencies; and (3) experiencing a stunting of one's development and potential as a result of impoverishment.

Doing Without

By its very definition, poverty represents a lack or absence of essential resources. Webster defines poverty in three complimentary ways: "1. the state or condition of having little or no money, goods, or means of support; 2. deficiency of necessary or desirable ingredients, qualities, etc.; 3. scantiness; insufficiency." The experience of poverty is epitomized by having to do without.

Alleviating Poverty

This having to do without includes insufficiencies and compromises involving basic resources such as food, clothing, shelter, health care, and transportation (Kus, Nolan, and Whelan, 2016). It also entails not having additional items and services that many of us take for granted, from the convenience of writing a check to the small pleasure of going out for lunch. In short, poverty embodies a "deficiency of necessary or desirable ingredients" that most individuals in fact have.

Particularly harmful is that living in poverty often means having to do without a sufficiently balanced diet and adequate intake of calories (Barrett and Lentz, 2016). Several large-scale studies have indicated that those in poverty routinely have bouts of hunger, undernutrition, or a detrimental altering of the diet at some point during the month (Coleman-Jensen et al., 2018). This risk affects both children and adults (Food Research and Action Center, 2018).

A second key area where families in poverty often have to do without is good health. One of the most consistent findings in epidemiology is that the quality of an individual's health is negatively affected by lower socioeconomic status, particularly impoverishment (see Chapter 2 of this volume). Poverty is associated with a host of health risks, including elevated rates of heart disease, diabetes, hypertension, cancer, infant mortality, mental illness, undernutrition, lead poisoning, asthma, dental problems, and a variety of other ailments and diseases (Angel, 2016). The result is a death rate for the poverty stricken approximately three times higher than that for the affluent (Pappas et al., 1993). As Nancy Leidenfrost notes in her review of the literature, "Health disparities between the poor and those with higher incomes are almost universal for all dimensions of health" (1993: 1).

Furthermore, poverty often exerts a negative effect upon children's health status, which in turn impacts upon their well-being as adults. According to Bradley Schiller,

> a child born to a poverty-stricken mother is likely to be undernourished both before and after birth. Furthermore, the child is less likely to receive proper postnatal care, to be immunized against disease, or even to have his or her eyes and teeth examined. As a result, the child is likely to grow up prone to illness and poverty, and in the most insidious of cases, be impaired by organic brain damage. (2008: 136)

Although Medicaid, Medicare, and the Affordable Care Act have helped to increase the poor's access to health care in the United States, nevertheless when use of health services is compared to need for services, low-income households have the lowest rate (Angel, 2016). For instance, a number of the poor have no insurance whatsoever (16.3 percent), and when insurance is carried, it is often restrictive in terms of what is covered (U.S. Census Bureau, 2019b).

Just as good health is often comprised as a result of poverty, so too is living in a safe and decent neighborhood. Although it is true that most of the poor do not live in neighborhoods that are characterized as impoverished inner city areas, poverty nevertheless limits the choices available in terms of the overall quality of life in a neighborhood (Pattillo and Robinson, 2016). In addition, racial discrimination in the housing market further restricts the options available to minorities, particularly African Americans (Desmond, 2016; Massey, 2016).

Being confined to a low-income neighborhood, when coupled with lack of transportation, often results in the poor paying more and spending more time acquiring basic necessities (Caplovitz, 1963; Dunbar, 1988; Edin and Lein, 1997). It is a bitter irony that those with the least amount of resources, often wind up paying the most for basic goods and services, from financial services to the cost of healthy food.

What is also readily apparent is that a lack of financial resources creates a situation where hard choices must be made between necessities. This involves compromises in juggling the need for food, clothing, shelter, utilities, and so on. The well-known "heat or eat" dilemma has been reported repeatedly in research studies, where the poverty stricken must choose between which basic need will take priority (Bhattacharya et al., 2003).

In short, living in poverty is epitomized by struggling to acquire and at times forgoing the daily necessities and resources that most of us take for granted. It is the humiliation of having to do without and the bitter taste of being left out of the simple pleasure of life. Clearly, this undermines the ability to lead a livable life.

The Stressful Weight of Poverty

A consequence of the previously discussed struggles is that impoverishment puts a heavy weight upon the shoulders of those who walk in its ranks. The burden of poverty is routinely a heavy load that individuals must carry. In essence, poverty acts to amplify the daily stress found in everyday life and its relationships (Abramsky, 2013; Desmond, 2016; Edin and Shaefer, 2015). Each of us throughout our lives have sets of problems and anxieties to deal with. For example, we often struggle to successfully navigate our way across various relationships with spouses, children, friends, co-workers, and so on. What poverty does is to intensify the stress and tension within the individual and, by extension, to their relationships.

Take the marital relationship. Research has consistently found that poverty and lower income is associated with a greater risk of separation and divorce, as well as spousal and child violence (see Chapter 7 of this volume). What can often happen is that unemployment precipitates a fall into poverty which results in a tremendous strain upon a marriage. Research has indeed shown that the impact of unemployment upon marital relationships is quite deleterious (Edin and Shaefer, 2015). Yet when blended with poverty, it creates a particularly destructive combination.

In many ways, the stress of poverty is even greater for single-parent families. For these women, there is no partner to turn to provide a helping hand during the routine crises and struggles outlined earlier. Furthermore, most single heads of households work at two full-time jobs (within the labor force and at home). The result is often stress, frustration, and exhaustion, which in turn influences the caring and raising of children (Gibson-Davis, 2016).

Consequently, because of the financial strains that individuals in poverty experience, considerable mental stress and anguish are ever present. As epidemiological research has demonstrated, such stress results in worse health and stunted development.

Stunted Growth

The result of having to do without, combined with the stress of living in poverty, often produces a stunting of growth. An obvious analogy is to that of a tree. If one denies a tree the proper nutrients, while at the same time creating stressful environmental conditions, the result is that it will fail to develop to its full potential. Often there will be a noticeable stunting of growth and deformity of its trunk and branches.

So it is with individuals in poverty. A lack of proper food, shelter, education, and other essential resources, coupled with the stress of impoverishment, results in stunted individual development. Sometimes this stunting is visibly apparent; often times it lies underneath the surface. In addition, the longer the duration of poverty and the greater the depth of poverty, the greater the negative effects will generally be. The ability for a child to reach his or her potential can be severely stunted as a result of poverty.

These negative impacts occur in a wide variety of areas, but are perhaps most salient in the stunting effects upon young children's physical and mental growth. Research has indicated that poor infants and young children in the United States are much more likely to have lower levels of physical and mental growth (as measured in a variety of ways) when compared to their nonpoor counterparts (McLoyd, Jocson, and Williams, 2016).

Furthermore, both the duration and depth of poverty intensify these negative outcomes. In their research on poverty's effects upon young children's cognitive and verbal ability and early school achievement, Judith Smith and colleagues report, "Duration of poverty has very negative effects on children's IQ, verbal ability, and achievement scores. Children who lived in persistently poor families scored 6–9 points lower on the various assessments than children who were never poor. In addition, the negative effects of persistent poverty seem to get stronger as the child gets older" (1997: 164). They also found that "the effects of family poverty varied dramatically depending on whether a family was very poor (family income below 50 percent of the poverty level), poor, or near poor. Children in the very poor group had scores 7–12 points lower than did children in the near-poor group" (164).

Likewise, in a study which looked at the impact of the duration of poverty upon children's mental health, Jane McLeod and Michael Shanahan found that "the length of time spent in poverty is an important predictor of children's mental health, even after current poverty status is taken into account. As the length of time spent in poverty increases, so too do children's feelings of unhappiness, anxiety, and dependence" (1993: 360).

As children grow older, and if they continue to reside in poverty, the disadvantages of growing up poor multiply. These include attending inferior schools (Hanaum and Xie, 2016), coping with the various problems associated with disadvantaged neighborhoods (Wilson, 2016), residing in less educationally stimulating home environments (Mayer, 1997), having health needs left unattended to (Rylko and Farmer, 2016), and a host of other disadvantages.

The disadvantages of poverty continue to multiply for adolescents. Consequently, by the time they reach their early 20s they are often at a significant disadvantage in terms of their ability to compete effectively within the labor market, which in turn increases their risk of experiencing poverty as adults (Fox, Torche, and Waldfogel, 2016). This intergenerational process is explored in much greater detail in Chapter 5 of this volume.

As adults age, the stunting effects of poverty become less pronounced but are nevertheless still quite real. These include negative impacts upon physical and mental health, worker productivity, civic participation, and other aspects of life.

Suffice it to say that a third bitter taste of poverty involves not being to achieve the full development of one's potential and one's children's potential. This is perhaps the most painful pill to swallow. It is poverty's knack of being able to undercut the capabilities that are found in all of us. It is not an exaggeration to call this a tragedy, for that is precisely what the loss of such human potential is.

The Economic Cost of Poverty

As we have just discussed, poverty exerts a heavy toll upon those who fall within its ranks. Yet what we have too often failed to recognize is that poverty places enormous economic, social, and psychological costs upon the nonpoor as well. These costs affect us both individually and as a nation. Nevertheless, we have been slow to recognize such costs. Too often the attitude has been, "I don't see how I'm affected, so why should I worry about it?"

Yet the issues that many Americans are in fact deeply concerned about, such as crime, access and affordability of health care, or worker productivity, to name but a few, are directly affected and exasperated by the condition of poverty. As a result, the general public winds up paying a heavy price for allowing poverty to walk in our midst. A report by the Children's Defense Fund on the costs of childhood poverty made this strikingly clear.

> The children who suffer poverty's effects are not its only victims. When children do not succeed as adults, all of society pays the price: businesses are able to find fewer good workers, consumers pay more for their goods, hospitals and health insurers spend more treating preventable illnesses, teachers spend more time on remediation and special education, private citizens feel less safe on the streets, governors hire more prison guards, mayors must pay to shelter homeless families, judges must hear more criminal, domestic, and other cases, taxpayers pay for problems that could have been prevented, fire and medical workers must respond to emergencies that never should have happened, and funeral directors must bury children who never should have died. (Sherman, 1994: 99)

This sense of a broad awareness into the costs of poverty can be referred to as enlightened self-interest. In other words, by becoming aware of the various costs associated with poverty or, conversely, the various benefits associated with the reduction of poverty, we begin to realize that it is in our own self-interest to combat the condition of poverty.

This awareness is often accomplished through education since such connections are frequently not self-evident. The case of poverty is a good example. For most Americans, poverty is seen as an individualized condition that impacts exclusively upon that person, their family, and perhaps their neighborhood. Rarely do we conceptualize a stranger's poverty as having a direct or indirect effect upon our own well-being. By becoming aware of such impacts through informed knowledge, we begin to understand that reducing poverty is very much in our enlightened self-interest.

Yet the ability to estimate the magnitude of the costs surrounding an issue such as poverty is exceedingly complex. Arriving at a dollar amount and claiming precision is difficult at best. Although countless studies have demonstrated that the costs of poverty to society are both real and consequential, it is extremely hard to factor in all the nuances and relevant components that affect society.

Nevertheless, several attempts have been made to estimate the overall cost of poverty (Holzer et al., 2008), most recently by McLaughlin and Rank (2018). In their analysis, the authors estimated the effect of childhood poverty upon the loss of economic productivity, increased health and crime costs, and increased costs as a result of child homelessness and maltreatment. By using cost-measurement analysis, they calculated that the annual aggregate cost of U.S. child poverty was $1.0298 trillion, representing 28 percent of the entire federal budget for 2015. In addition, they found that for every dollar spent on reducing childhood poverty, the country would save at least $7 (and up to $12) with respect to the economic costs of poverty.

The bottom line is that poverty, particularly childhood poverty, represents a significant economic burden to the United States. This is largely because living in poverty stunts the growth and undermines the potential of children. As Martin Ravallion has noted, "Children growing up in poorer families tend to suffer greater human development gaps, with lasting consequences for their adult lives" (2016: 595). Impoverished children grow up with fewer skills and are less able to contribute to the economy. They are more likely to engage in crime and experience more frequent health care problems. These costs are ultimately borne not only by the children themselves, but by the wider society as well.

Understanding the Mechanisms Behind Poverty

Given the costs and suffering associated with poverty, the question must be asked, Why does poverty occur? In this section we argue that American poverty is largely the result of failings at the economic and the political levels, rather than at the individual level (Rank, 1994; 2004; Rank, Hirschl, and Foster, 2014).

It has certainly been the case that within the United States the emphasis has been on individual inadequacies as the major reason for poverty. That is, people are often viewed as not motivated enough, not working hard enough, have failed to acquire enough skills and education, or have just made bad decisions in their lives. These are the behaviors and attributes that are seen as leading people into poverty as well as keeping them in poverty (Gilens, 1999; Hunt and Bullock, 2016). And in fact this is the manner in which we have tended to understand most social problems in this country, that is, as individual pathology (O'Connor, 2016).

In contrast, the argument made here is that the fundamental problem of poverty lies in the fact that there are simply not enough viable opportunities for all. While it is certainly true that particular individual shortcomings, such as the lack of education or skills, helps to explain who is more likely to be left out in the competition to locate and secure good opportunities, it cannot explain why there is a shortage of such opportunities in the first place. To answer that

Alleviating Poverty

question we must turn to the inability of the economic and political structures to provide the supports and opportunities necessary to lift all Americans out of poverty.

The most obvious example of this is the mismatch between the number of decent-paying jobs versus the pool of labor in search of such jobs. Over the past 45 years, the U.S. economy has been producing more and more low-paying jobs, part-time jobs, and jobs that are lacking in benefits. It is estimated that approximately 40 percent of all jobs in the United States for 2018 were low paying, that is, paying less than $16 an hour (Gould, 2019). And of course, beyond these low-paying jobs, there are millions of Americans who are unemployed at any point in time.

For example, during the past 40 years, U.S. monthly unemployment rates have averaged between 4 and 10 percent (U.S. Bureau of Labor Statistics, 2019). These percentages represent individuals who are out of work but are actively looking for employment. It does not include discouraged workers who have given up looking for work, or individuals who are working part-time but want to be working full-time. Furthermore, it is important to note that the unemployment rate represents how many individuals are unemployed at a given month in time. If instead we focus on the likelihood of experiencing a spell of unemployment at some point across the entire period of one year, the numbers and percentages are much higher. For example, in 2017, the average number of Americans unemployed in any given month was approximately 7 million, representing an unemployment rate of 4.4 percent. However, 15.6 million Americans experienced unemployment at some point during 2017, which translated into an annual unemployment rate of 8.6 percent (U.S. Bureau of Labor Statistics, 2018).

Beyond the lack of good paying jobs, the United States has also failed to offer the types of universal coverage for child care, health care, and affordable housing that most other developed countries routinely provide. The result has been an increasing number of families at risk of economic vulnerability and poverty.

The way that I have illustrated this situation is through the analogy of musical chairs. Picture a game of musical chairs in which there are ten players but only eight chairs available at any point in time. Who is more likely to lose out at this game? Those more likely to lose out will tend to have characteristics that put them at a disadvantage in terms of competing for the available chairs (such as less agility, not as much speed, a bad position when the music stops, and so on). We can point to these reasons for why the two individuals lost out in the game.

However, given that the game is structured in a way such that two players are bound to lose, these individual attributes only explain who in particular loses out, not why there are losers in the first place. Ultimately, those two people have lost out because there were not enough chairs for everyone who was playing the game.

The critical mistake that has been made in the past is that we have equated the question of who loses out at the game with the question of why the game produces losers in the first place. They are, in fact, distinct and separate questions. So while characteristics such as deficiencies in skills or education, or being in a single parent family, help to explain who in the population is at a heightened risk of encountering poverty, the fact that poverty exists in the first place results not from these characteristics, but rather from a failure of the economic and political structures to provide enough decent opportunities and supports in society.

By focusing solely upon individual characteristics, such as education, we can shuffle people up or down in terms of their being more likely to land a job with good earnings, but we are still going to have somebody lose out if there are not enough decent paying jobs to go around.

In short, we are playing a large scale version of musical chairs in which there are many more players than there are chairs.

The recognition of this dynamic represents a fundamental shift in thinking from the past. It helps to explain why the social policies of the last four decades have largely been ineffective in reducing the rates of poverty. We have focused our attention and resources on either altering the incentives and disincentives for those playing the game through various welfare reform measures, or in a very limited way, upgrading their skills and ability to compete in the game through various job training programs, while at the same time we have left the structure of the game untouched.

When the overall rates of poverty do in fact go up or down, they do so primarily as a result of changes on the structural level that increase or decrease the number of available chairs. In particular, the performance of the economy has been historically important. Why? Because when the economy is expanding, more opportunities (or chairs in this analogy) are available for the competing pool of labor and their families. The reverse occurs when the economy slows down and contracts, as we saw with the Great Recession of 2008. To explain the rise and fall of poverty by the rising or falling levels of individual inadequacies or motivation makes little sense. Rather, an increase or decrease in poverty has everything to do with improving or deteriorating economic conditions.

Likewise, changes in various social supports and the social safety net can make a significant difference in terms of how well families are able to avoid poverty or near poverty. When such supports were increased through the War on Poverty initiatives in the 1960s, along with the strong economy, poverty rates declined significantly. Likewise, when Social Security benefits were expanded during the 1960s and 1970s, the elderly's poverty rates sharply declined. Conversely, when social supports have been weakened and eroded, as in the case of children's programs over the past 40 years, their rates of poverty have gone up.

The recognition of poverty as a structural failing also makes it quite clear why the United States has such high rates of poverty compared to other high economy OECD countries. These rates have nothing to do with Americans being less motivated or hard working than those in other countries, but with the fact that our economy has been producing millions of low-wage jobs in the face of global competition and that our social policies have done relatively little to economically support families compared to other industrialized countries.

From this perspective then, one of the keys to addressing poverty is to increase the labor market opportunities and social supports available to American households. By doing so, we are able to provide more chairs for those playing the game. We now turn to a discussion of several of these strategies

Strategies to Alleviate Poverty

Given the structural analysis of poverty just discussed, what might be the implications in terms of strategies to reduce poverty. Although many policies and initiatives exist, we limit our discussion to three. These include (1) ensuring the availability of jobs that will economically support a household; (2) providing an effective social safety net that also incorporates key social and public goods; and (3) building lower-income individual and community assets. Each are discussed in the following text.

Ensuring the Availability of Decent Paying Jobs

Essential to any overall strategy to reduce poverty within both the United States and other countries are policies that will increase the availability of jobs that can support a family above the poverty line. As Bradley Schiller notes, "jobs—in abundance and of good quality—are the most needed and most permanent solution to the poverty problem" (2008: 296).

The problem of not enough jobs has played itself out somewhat differently within an American versus a European context. Within the United States, the economy over the past 40 years has done quite well in terms of creating new jobs. The problem is that many of these jobs are low paying and/or lacking in basic benefits such as health care. The result has been that although unemployment rates have been relatively low in the United States (often averaging between 4 and 6 percent), working full-time does not ensure that a family will be lifted out of poverty or near poverty. For example, Smeeding and colleagues (2001) found that 25 percent of all American full-time workers could be classified as being in low-wage work (defined as earning less the 65 percent of the national median for full-time jobs). This was by far the highest percentage of the developed countries analyzed, with the overall average falling at 12 percent.

In contrast, the European economies have been more sluggish in terms of creating new jobs over the past 40 years, resulting in unemployment rates much higher than in the United States. In addition, workers have remained out of work for longer periods of time. However, for those who are employed, employees are generally paid more and have greater benefits than their American counterparts, resulting in substantially lower rates of poverty (Alesina and Glaeser, 2004).

What then can be done to address the related problems of jobs that do not pay enough to support a family and not enough jobs in the first place? Two broad initiatives would appear essential. The first is transforming the existing job base so that it will support a family (which is particularly relevant within an American context). The second is the creation of enough jobs to employ all who are in need of work (which is particularly relevant within a European context).

Within the context of the United States, one might begin with the following benchmark—individuals who are employed full-time throughout the year (defined as working 35 hours per week over a 50 week period) should be able to generate earnings that will enable them to lift a family of three above the poverty threshold. Such a family might include a married couple with one child, a one-parent household with two children, or a three-generation household of mother, grandmother, and son. The 2017 poverty threshold for a family of three in the United States was set at $19,515. Consequently, to lift such a family above the poverty line, an individual needs to be earning $11.15 an hour.

There are at least two specific ways of accomplishing this. One is to raise the minimum wage to a level that will support a family above the poverty line and then index it to inflation so that it will continue to lift such a family over the poverty line in the future. A second approach is to provide a tax credit (such as the Earned Income Tax Credit [EITC]) that supplements workers' wages so that their total income for the year lifts them above the poverty line.

The minimum wage in the United States went into effect in October 1938 at an initial level of $0.25 an hour. The basic concept was that no employee should fall below a certain wage floor. There was an underlying value that workers should receive a fair wage for a fair day's work. However, unlike Social Security, the minimum wage has never been indexed to inflation; changes in the minimum wage must come through congressional legislation. Years often go by before Congress acts to adjust the minimum wage upward, causing it to lag behind the rising cost of living. The current minimum wage in the United States stands at $7.25 an hour, a rate that went into effect in July 2009. An individual working full-time during the year (50 weeks at 35 hours per week) would earn a total of $12,688, far short of the $19,515 needed to lift a family of three above the poverty line.

Alleviating Poverty   59

As noted, to lift such a family above the poverty line, an individual needs to be earning at least $11.15 per hour. Consequently, what is needed is to raise the minimum wage to approximately $12.00 per hour and then index the minimum wage each year to the rate of inflation to hold its purchasing power. The phase-in period to raise the minimum wage to $12.00 per hour might take place over several years to spread out the increase. Indeed, many states currently have a minimum wage much higher than the federal minimum wage.

The positive impact of tying the minimum wage to the poverty level for a family of three and then indexing it to the rate of inflation would be substantial. First, it would establish a reasonable floor below which no full-time worker would fall. Second, it would allow such a worker to support a family of three above the official poverty line. Third, it would reinforce the value that Americans have consistently attached to work. Fourth, it would remove the political wrangling from the minimum wage debate. Fifth, it would address in a limited way the increasing inequities between CEOs who earn 300 or 400 times what their average paid workers earn.

A second approach for supplementing and raising the earnings of low-income workers is through the tax structure, specifically through the use of tax credits. The primary example of such a credit in the U.S. is the EITC. The EITC was enacted in 1975 and underwent a significant expansion during the 1990s. In fact, it currently represents the largest cash antipoverty program in the United States and is frequently considered one of the more innovative American economic policy ideas (see Ventry, 2002, for a historical and political background of the EITC).

The program is designed to provide a refundable tax credit to low-income workers, with the vast majority going to households with children. In 2018, a family with one child could qualify for the EITC if its earned income was below $40,320 (or $46,010 for married couples), while a family with three or more children could qualify if its household income was under $49,194 (or $54,884 for married couples). The maximum credit for a one-child family was $3,461; the benefit rose to $6,431 for a family with three or more children. The credit is normally received in a lump-sum payment as part of an overall tax refund for the previous year. Since it is a refundable credit, families receive the payment even if they do not owe any taxes.

The goals of the EITC are to deliver economic relief at the low end of the earnings distribution and to furnish a strong work incentive. An individual cannot qualify for the EITC without earned income, and the impact is particularly strong at the lower levels. For example, for a head of household with one child that was earning $7.50 an hour (and her total earnings were under $10,000), the EITC would effectively raise her wage by an additional $3.00 an hour, to $10.50 an hour.

The program thus provides a significant supplement to low earners as well as an incentive to work. In 2016, it was estimated that 28 million Americans benefited from the EITC and that it pulled approximately 5.8 million individuals above the poverty line who otherwise would have fallen into poverty (Center on Budget and Policy Priorities, 2018). For families that remain in poverty, the EITC has helped to reduce the distance between their household income and the poverty line. It has also enabled families to purchase particular resources that can improve their economic and social mobility (e.g., school tuition, a car, or a new residence) or to meet daily expenses (Meyer and Holtz-Eakin, 2002).

To make the EITC even more effective, its benefits should be expanded so that they provide greater assistance to low-income workers without children. The vast majority of the EITC benefits go to families with children. Yet there is no compelling reason why such benefits should not also be provided for individuals without children. Further research also needs to be done to examine the feasibility of receiving the EITC throughout the year, rather than as lump sum during the tax season (although many families do prefer this way of receiving the EITC). Third, some households that qualify for the EITC fail to claim and take advantage of the tax credit. Better educating tax filers about the benefits of the EITC appears warranted. Fourth, state EITC programs should be encouraged as an additional antipoverty component on top of the federal EITC benefits. Finally, consideration should also be given to modestly increasing the size of the credits currently given to families (although, as mentioned, considerable expansion occurred in the early 1990s and the federal program may currently be close to its optimal size; for example, see Liebman, 2002).

The policy of an expanded EITC, in conjunction with the raising and indexing of the minimum to the level of a living wage, would substantially help working men and women in the United States who, in spite of their efforts, are unable to get themselves and their families out of poverty or near-poverty. In addition, such policies begin to address (although in a very limited way) the increasing inequalities and perceived unfairness of American income distribution and wage structure.

In terms of the problem of producing enough jobs (which affects the European Union to a greater extent than the United States), in many ways this is a much more difficult task than supplementing and raising the wages of existing jobs. Nevertheless, it is essential that a sufficient number of jobs be available to meet the demands of the existing labor pool.

Various labor demand policies have the potential to generate a more robust rate of job growth. Several approaches can be taken. First, economic policy should seek in broad way to stimulate job growth. These would include fiscal policies such as increasing government expenditures, enhancing tax incentives for investment, or enacting consumer tax cuts. Monetary policy can provide a stimulus by making access to credit easier and cheaper (Schiller, 2008).

A second approach is to provide targeted wage subsidies to employers to stimulate job creation. Although the details of such programs can vary considerably, the basic concept is that an employer receives a monetary subsidy for creating a position and/or hiring an individual (often from a targeted population) that the employer might not have hired without such an incentive. This approach could be aimed at businesses and industries that are potential employers of individuals from lower-income or lower-skill backgrounds.

A third strategy for creating jobs is through public service employment. As Ellwood and Welty (2000) note in their review of the effectiveness of public service employment programs, if done carefully and judiciously, they can help increase employment without displacing other workers, and they can produce genuinely valuable output. Such an approach appears particularly pertinent for those out of work for long periods of time.

Taken as a whole, an overall strategy for reducing poverty in the OECD countries must begin with a set of policies that will increase the availability of jobs that can economically support families above the poverty threshold. To a large extent, poverty in the industrialized nations is the result of not having a job, or having a job that is not able to viably support a family. Policies must address these shortcomings within the high-economy free market societies.

Providing an Effective Social Safety Net and Access to Key Social Goods

A second general strategy for reducing poverty within many countries (particularly the United States) is the existence of an effective social safety net along with providing access to key social and public goods such as health care, a quality education, child care, and affordable housing.

No matter how strong economic growth may be, some individuals and families will invariably fall between the cracks. Whether through the loss of a job, a sudden disability, or some other unanticipated event, there are times and situations in people's lives when a social safety net is needed. In developed countries, this has taken the form of various programs and policies encompassed under the social welfare state, while in developing countries the role of the social safety net has more typically been fulfilled by the extended family.

Hyman Minsky (1986) points out that free-market economies are prone to periods of instability, such as periodic recessions and economic downturns. Safety net programs help to serve as automatic stabilizers for the economy during these periods. That is, they grow during times of need and diminish during more prosperous times. For example, as rates of unemployment rise, more individuals draw on unemployment insurance to weather the temporary economic problems caused by the lack of jobs. As economic conditions improve, more people are able to find jobs and so no longer need unemployment insurance. In this fashion, safety net programs help to automatically stabilize the instability inherent within the economy.

A social safety net is therefore important in assisting individuals and families during times of need and in alleviating the economic instability associated with recessionary periods. One of the reasons that the U.S. rate of poverty is so high, and the Scandinavian nations are so low, is a result of differences in the extent and depth of their social safety nets. Compared to other Western industrialized countries, the United States devotes far fewer resources to programs aimed at assisting the economically vulnerable (Alesina and Glaeser, 2004; Brady, Blome, and Kleider, 2016; Lee and Koo, 2016; OECD, 1999). In fact, the United States allocates a smaller proportion of its GDP to social welfare programs than virtually any other industrialized country (Lee and Koo, 2016). As Charles Noble writes, "the U.S. welfare state is striking precisely because it is so limited in scope and ambition" (1997: 3).

In contrast, most European countries provide a wide range of universal social and insurance programs that largely prevent families from falling into poverty. These include substantial family or children's allowances, which are designed to transfer cash assistance to families with children. Unemployment assistance is far more generous in these countries than in the United States, often providing support for more than a year following the loss of a job. Furthermore, health coverage is routinely provided, along with considerable support for child care.

The result of these social policy differences is that they substantially reduce the extent of poverty in Europe and Canada, while U.S. social policy exerts only a small impact upon poverty reduction. As Rebecca Blank notes,

> the national choice in the United States to provide relatively less generous transfers to low-income families has meant higher relative poverty rates in the country. While low-income families in the United States work more than in many other countries, they are not able to make up for lower governmental income support relative to their European counterparts. (1997: 141–142).

Consequently, a key reason behind why the United States has such high levels of poverty is a result of the nature and scope of its social safety net. The Scandinavian countries are able to lift a significant percentage of their economically vulnerable above the threshold of poverty through governmental transfer and assistance policies. In contrast, the United States provides substantially less support through its social safety net, resulting in poverty rates that are currently among the highest in the industrialized world. In summarizing this research, Jurgen Kohl notes,

> If there is a common pattern behind the bewildering variety of rates and risk of poverty in the advanced Western countries, it is perhaps this: Differences in the extent and the relative risks of poverty reflect the differing capabilities and/or willingness of welfare states to cope with social risks and problems by means of social policy programmes. . . . Cross-national comparisons provide examples that adequate social programmes can contain the poverty risk of vulnerable groups and, thereby, the extent of poverty in society in general. (1995: 272)

In addition to providing a social safety net, it is also critical that governments make available easy and affordable access to several key social and public goods. In particular, a quality education, health care, affordable housing, and child care are vital in building and maintaining healthy and productive citizens and families. Each of these deserve a chapter in their own right.

The European countries provide far greater access and coverage to health care, affordable housing, and child care than does the United States (although it is also true that the social welfare states in many of these countries have been under increasing retrenchment pressure; Korpi: 2003). All of them provide some form of national health care. In addition, many provide accessible, affordable, and good quality child care and subsidized housing. European countries also do not tend to display the wide fluctuations in educational quality that American children are subjected to at the primary and secondary levels.

The result is that these policies have the effect of mitigating the harshness of poverty and economic vulnerability. In addition, there is a belief that there are certain social and public goods that all individuals have a right to and that making such resources accessible results in more productive citizens and societies in both the short and the long run. As stated in the European Union Council's communication to the Nice European Council,

> the European social model, with its developed systems of social protection, must underpin the transformation to the knowledge economy. People are Europe's main asset and should be the focal point of the Union's policies. Investing in people and developing an active and dynamic welfare state will be crucial both to Europe's place in the knowledge economy and for ensuring that the emergence of this new

economy does not compound the existing social problems of unemployment, social exclusion and poverty. (Esping-Andersen, 2002: 18).

Providing easy and affordable access to these vital social and public goods is essential to any overall strategy of alleviating poverty.

Building Assets

Social policies are frequently designed to alleviate the current conditions of poverty. Indeed, the strategies of creating work and providing a social safety net are each aimed at improving the current economic conditions of individuals and families. This is understandable, given that poverty affects children and adults in the here and now.

Yet approaches to poverty alleviation must also pay attention to longer-term processes and solutions. In particular, the accumulation of assets is crucial, both across the individual life course and within the communities in which families reside. The acquisition of such assets allows families to more effectively function and, for our purposes, to reduce their risk of poverty. These assets enable households to ride out periods of economic vulnerability. They also allow for the growth and strengthening of individual and family development. Assets build a stake in the future that income by itself often cannot provide. Unfortunately, the opportunities to acquire such assets have often been in short supply for lower-income families.

However, as discussed extensively in Chapter 6 of this volume, there are many evolving initiatives designed to increase the asset holdings of these households. The rising tide of Child Development Accounts is one such policy. As described in Chapter 6 of this volume, these accounts are designed to build the savings of children such that they can be used for educational or other expenses when they turn 18. They are generally started with an initial deposit by the government and then later deposits by parents are frequently matched by state governments. These programs are found in a majority of U.S. states as well as in a number of other countries. An example of a country that has invested heavily in the concept of asset building has been that of Singapore, with its Central Provident Fund (CPF). Introduced in 1955, the CPF is a mandatory pension fund in which its members are able to use their savings for housing, medical expenses, and education.

Just as individuals thrive with the acquisition and development of assets, so too do communities. Poor neighborhoods are often characterized by their lack of strong community assets, such as quality schools, decent housing, adequate infrastructure, economic opportunities, and available jobs. These, in turn, affect the life chances of residents in such communities.

Strengthening the major institutions found within lower-income communities is vital because they have the power to improve the quality of life, foster the accumulation of human capital, and increase the overall opportunities for community residents. Among such institutions are schools, businesses and industries, lending establishments, community centers, and so on. A wide range of strategies can be used to strengthen these institutions to meet the needs of the community. Creating greater equity in funding across school districts, attracting businesses in lower-income communities, opening up the lending practices of banks and savings and loans to people in economically depressed areas—all would provide substantial benefits.

Some of the techniques and policies for arriving at such goals would include community development strategies, grassroots organizing techniques, neighborhood movements such as the rise of community development corporations, and tax incentive policies targeted at businesses that choose to locate in a specified impoverished area (see Chapter 9 of this volume). Strengthening the resources and assets of economically vulnerable communities is vital, in conjunction with individual and family asset building, to an overall poverty reduction strategy.

Conclusion

Since its beginnings, the profession of social work has emphasized the importance and critical need to alleviate poverty. The deplorable conditions of poverty and destitution at the end of the 19th and beginning of the 20th centuries led social reformers to shine a light on these conditions. Jacob Riis's book *How the Other Half Lives*, documented the wretched conditions of tenement dwellers in an area known as "the Bend" in New York City during the 1880s. Riis used his vast knowledge as a police reporter to chronicle the situations that impoverished families found themselves languishing in. Equally important, Riis relied upon the relatively new technology of photography to visually document the conditions he wrote so provocatively about. Looking at his photographs today, they continue to stand as a powerful statement against the horrific conditions he had found in the city of New York.

At the same time, other groundbreaking work helped to further uncover and address these conditions. The efforts of Jane Addams and the establishment of Hull House in 1889 was instrumental in drawing attention to the importance of providing children and adults with a venue for self-development through the settlement house movement. Other efforts soon followed that emphasized the importance of alleviating the destructive conditions of poverty and economic destitution and of providing opportunities for individuals to achieve a livable life.

At various points throughout the 20th century and now the 21st century, the profession of social work has emphasized the injustice of poverty, both domestically and internationally. Consequently, social workers have understood the importance of addressing the human ramifications of poverty. Less well understood, however, has been the importance of confronting the root causes of poverty. As we have argued in this chapter, these causes are primarily the result of failings at the structural level. They imply that social work must advocate and lobby for policies that can alter the economic and social structures that perpetuate poverty. Social workers are in an ideal position to share their on-the-ground insights and knowledge with community leaders, public policy experts, and state and federal legislators.

As we look into the future, the problem of poverty is unlikely to disappear any time soon. However, various social movements such as Occupy Wall Street, Black Lives Matter, and the Fight for 15 have shown the power of organizing around issues of economic inequality and poverty. As these conditions continue to plague us in the years ahead, social work must join hands with those who are waging social justice battles both in the United States and around the globe. These efforts represent vital and encouraging steps along the way to a world in which all are able to achieve a livable life.

References

Abramsky, S. 2013. *The American Way of Poverty: How the Other Half Still Lives*. New York: Nation Books.

Alesina, A., and E. L. Glaeser. 2004. *Fighting Poverty in the US and Europe: A World of Difference*. Oxford, UK: Oxford University Press.

Angel, R. J. 2016. "Social Class, Poverty, and the Unequal Burden of Illness." *The Oxford Handbook of the Social Science of Poverty*. Edited by D. Brady and L. M. Burton. New York: Oxford University Press, pp. 660–683.

Barrett, C. B., and E. C. Lentz. 2016. "Hunger and Food Insecurity." *The Oxford Handbook of the Social Science of Poverty*. Edited by D. Brady and L. M. Burton. New York: Oxford University Press, pp. 117–140.

Bhattacharya, J., T. DeLeire, S. Haider, and J. Currie. 2003. "Heat or Eat? Cold-Weather Shocks and Nutrition in Poor American Families." *American Journal of Public Health*, 93, 1149–1154.

Blank, R. M. 1997. *It Takes a Nation: A New Agenda for Fighting Poverty*. Princeton, NJ: Princeton University Press.

Brady, D., A. Blome, and H. Kleider. 2016. "How Politics and Institutions Shape Poverty and Inequality." *The Oxford Handbook of the Social Science of Poverty*. Edited by D. Brady and L. M. Burton. New York: Oxford University Press, pp. 117–140.

Caplovitz, D. 1963. *The Poor Pay More: Consumer Practices of Low-Income Families*. Glencoe, IL: Free Press.

Center on Budget and Policy Priorities. 2018, April. "Policy Basics: The Earned Income Tax Credit."

Coleman-Jensen A., M. P. Rabbitt, C. A. Gregory, and A. Singh. 2018. *Household Food Security in the United States in 2017*, ERR-256. U.S. Department of Agriculture, Economic Research Service.

Council on Social Work Education. 2015. *Educational Policy and Accreditation Standards for Baccalaureate and Master's Social Work Programs*. Commission on Accreditation, Commission on Educational Policy.

Desmond, M. 2016. *Evicted: Poverty and Profit in the American City*. New York: Broadway Books.

Dunbar, L. 1988. *The Common Interest: How Our Social-Welfare Policies Don't Work, and What We Can Do about Them*. New York: Pantheon.

Edin, K. J., and L. Lein. 1997. *Making Ends Meet: How Single Mothers Survive Welfare and Low-Wge Work*. New York: Russell Sage Foundation.

Edin, K. J., and H. L. Shaefer. 2015. *$2.00 a Day: Living on Almost Nothing in America*. Boston: Mariner Books.

Ellwood, D. T., and E. D. Welty, 2000. "Public Service Employment and Mandatory Work: A Policy Whose Time Has Come and Gone and Come Again?" *Finding Jobs: Work and Welfare Reform*. Edited by D. E. Card and R. M. Blank. New York: Russell Sage Foundation, pp. 299–372.

Esping-Andersen, G. 2002. *Why We Need a New Welfare State*. Oxford, UK: Oxford University Press.

Food Research and Action Center. 2018, August. Food Hardship in America: A Look at National, Regional, State, and Metropolitan Statistical Area Data on Household Struggles with Hunger. Food Research and Action Center Report.

Fox, L., F. Torche, and J. Waldfogel. 2016. "How Politics and Institutions Shape Poverty and Inequality." *The Oxford Handbook of the Social Science of Poverty*. Edited by D. Brady and L. M. Burton. New York: Oxford University Press, pp. 117–140.

Gibson-Davis, C. M. 2016. "Single and Cohabiting Parents and Poverty." *The Oxford Handbook of the Social Science of Poverty*. Edited by D. Brady and L. M. Burton. New York: Oxford University Press, pp. 21–46.

Gilens, M. 1999. *Why Americans Hate Welfare: Race, Media, and the Politics of Antipoverty Policy*. Chicago: University of Chicago Press.

Gould, E. 2019. "The State of Working America Wages 2018." Economic Policy Institute, Washington, DC.

Hannum, E., and Y. Xie. 2016. "Education." *The Oxford Handbook of the Social Science of Poverty*. Edited by D. Brady and L. M. Burton. New York: Oxford University Press, pp. 462–485.

Hick, R., and T. Burchardt. 2016. "Capability Deprivation." *The Oxford Handbook of the Social Science of Poverty*. Edited by D. Brady and L. M. Burton. New York: Oxford University Press, pp. 75–92.

Holzer, H., D. Schanzenbach, G. Duncan, and J. Ludwig. 2008. "The Economic Costs of Childhood Poverty in the United States." *Journal of Children and Poverty*, 14, 41–61.

Hunt, M. O., and H. E. Bullock. 2016. "Ideologies and Beliefs about Poverty." *The Oxford Handbook of the Social Science of Poverty*. Edited by D. Brady and L. M. Burton. New York: Oxford University Press, pp. 93–116.

Kohl, J. 1995. "The European Community: Diverse Images of Poverty." *Poverty: A Global Review*. Edited by E. Oyen, S. M. Miller, and S. A. Samad. Oslo: Scandinavian University Press, pp. 251–286.

Korpi, W. 2003. "Welfare-State Regress in Western Europe: Politics, Institutions, Globalization, and Europeanization." *Annual Review of Sociology*, 29, 589–609.

Kus, B., B. Nolan, and C. T. Whelan. 2016. "Material Derivation and Consumption." *The Oxford Handbook of the Social Science of Poverty*. Edited by D. Brady and L. M. Burton. New York: Oxford University Press, pp. 577–601.

Lee, C. S., and I. H. Koo. 2016. "The Welfare States and Poverty." *The Oxford Handbook of the Social Science of Poverty*. Edited by D. Brady and L. M. Burton. New York: Oxford University Press, pp. 709–732.

Liebman, J. B. 2002. "The Optimal Design of the Earned Income Tax Credit." *Making Work Pay: The Earned Income Tax Credit and Its Impact on American Families.* Edited by B. D. Meyer and D. Holtz-Eakin. New York: Russell Sage Foundation, pp. 196–234.

Massey, D. S. 2016. "Segregation and the Perpetuation of Disadvantage." *The Oxford Handbook of the Social Science of Poverty.* Edited by D. Brady and L. M. Burton. New York: Oxford University Press, pp. 369–394.

Mayer, S. E. 1997. *What Money Can't Buy: Family Income and Children's Life Chances.* Cambridge, MA: Harvard University Press.

McLaughlin, M., and M. R. Rank. 2018. "Estimating the Economic Cost of Childhood Poverty in the United States." *Social Work Research,* 42, 73–83.

McLeod, J. D., and M. J. Shanahan, 1993. "Poverty, Parenting, and Children's Mental Health." *American Sociological Review,* 58, 351–366.

McLoyd, V. C., and R. M. Jocson. 2016. "Linking Poverty and Children's Development: Concepts, Models, and Debates." *The Oxford Handbook of the Social Science of Poverty.* Edited by D. Brady and L. M. Burton. New York: Oxford University Press, pp. 141–165.

Meyer, B. D., and D. Holtz-Eakin, 2002. *Making Work Pay: The Earned Income Tax Credit and Is Impact on America's Families.* New York: Russell Sage Foundation.

Minsky, H. P. 1986. *Stabilizing an Unstable Economy.* New Haven, CN: Yale University Press.

National Association of Social Workers. 2017. *Code of Ethics.* Washington DC: NASW Press.

Noble, C. 1997. *Welfare as We Knew It: A Political History of the American Welfare State.* New York: Oxford University Press.

O'Connor, A. 2016. "Poverty Knowledge and the History of Poverty Research." *The Oxford Handbook of the Social Science of Poverty.* Edited by D. Brady and L. M. Burton. New York: Oxford University Press, pp. 169–192.

Organisation for Economic Cooperation and Development. 1999. *Social Expenditure Database 1980-1996.* Paris: Organisation for Economic Cooperation and Development.

Organisatioh for Economic Cooperation and Development. 2019. "Poverty Rate (Indicator)." Retrieved from https://www.doi.org/10.1787/0fe1315d-en

Pappas, G., et al. 1993. "The Increasing Dispairty in Mortality between Socioeconomic Groups in the United States, 1960 and 1986." *New England Journal of Medicine,* 329, 103–115.

Pattillo, M., and J. N. Robinson. 2016. "Poor Neighborhoods in the Metropolis." *The Oxford Handbook of the Social Science of Poverty.* Edited by D. Brady and L. M. Burton. New York: Oxford University Press, pp. 341–368.

Rank, M. R. 1994. *Living on the Edge: The Realities of Welfare in America.* New York: Columbia University Press.

Rank, M. R. 2004. *One Nation, Underprivileged: Why American Poverty Affects Us All.* New York: Oxford University Press.

Rank, M. R., and T. A. Hirschl. 2015. "The Likelihood of Experiencing Relative Poverty over the Life Course." *PLoS One,* 10, e0116370.

Rank, M. R., T. A. Hirschl, and K. A. Foster. 2014. *Chasing the American Dream: Understanding What Shapes Our Fortunes.* New York: Oxford University Press.

Ravallion, M. 2016. *The Economics of Poverty.* New York: Oxford University Press.

Rylko-Bauer, B., and P. Farmer. 2016. "Structural Violence, Poverty and Social Suffering." *The Oxford Handbook of the Social Science of Poverty.* Edited by D. Brady and L. M. Burton. New York: Oxford University Press, pp. 47–74.

Schiller, B. R. 2008. *The Economics of Poverty and Discrimination.* Upper Saddle River, NJ: Prentice Hall.

Sherman, A. 1994. *Wasting America's Future: The Children's Defense Fund Report on the Costs of Child Poverty.* Boston: Beacon Press.

Simon, B. L. 1994. *The Empowerment Tradition in American Social Work: A History.* New York: Columbia University Press.

Smeeding, T. M. 2016. "Poverty Measurement." *The Oxford Handbook of the Social Science of Poverty.* Edited by D. Brady and L. M. Burton. New York: Oxford University Press, pp. 21–46.

Smeeding, T. M., L. Rainwater, and G. Burtless. 2001. "U.S. Poverty in a Cross-National Context." *Understanding Poverty*. Edited by S. H. Danziger and R. H. Haveman. Cambridge, MA: Harvard University Press, pp. 162–189.

Smith, J. R., J. Brooks-Gunn, and P. K. Klebanov. 1997. "Consequences of Living in Poverty for Young Children's Cognitive and Verbal Ability and Early School Achievement." *Consequences of Growing Up Poor*. Edited by G. J. Duncan and J. Brooks-Gunn. New York: Russell Sage Foundation, pp. 132–189.

U.S. Bureau of Labor Statistics. 2018, December 14. "Work Experience of the Population (Annual) News Release."

U.S. Bureau of Labor Statistics. 2019. Historical Data on Unemployment.

U.S. Census Bureau. 2019a. *Health Insurance Coverage in the United States: 2018*. Report Number P60-267. Washington DC: U.S. Government Printing Office.

U.S. Census Bureau. 2019b. *Income and Poverty in the United States: 2018*. Report Number P60-266. Washington DC: U.S. Government Printing Office.

Ventry, D. J. 2002. "The Collision of Tax and Welfare Politics: The Political History of the Earned Income Tax Credits." *Making Work Pay: The Earned Income Tax Credit and Its Impact on American Families*. Edited by B. D. Meyer and D. Holtz-Eakin. New York: Russell Sage Foundation, pp. 15–66.

Wilson, W. J. 2016. "Urban Poverty, Race, and Space." *The Oxford Handbook of the Social Science of Poverty*. Edited by D. Brady and L. M. Burton. New York: Oxford University Press, pp. 394–413.

4

Confronting Stigma, Discrimination, and Social Exclusion

VANESSA D. FABBRE, ELENI GAVERAS, ANNA GOLDFARB SHABSIN, JANELLE GIBSON, AND MARK R. RANK

Social workers are concerned by the ways in which social, economic, and political forces generate injustice in our society and how this injustice impacts the well-being of individuals, families, communities, and society as a whole. This concern has fueled a profession that seeks to confront these issues simultaneously and on multiple levels. Stigma, discrimination, and social exclusion are thought to be key forces that perpetuate injustice and human suffering and impede people from experiencing a livable life marked by opportunity and wellness. Many of the groups and clientele that social workers engage with suffer from the effects of stigma, discrimination, and/or social exclusion. Thus, social workers seek to make sense of these forces with the aim of preventing or interrupting these barriers to well-being.

This chapter presents and discusses several overlapping perspectives on stigma, discrimination, and social exclusion and uses empirical evidence to outline their effects on human well-being, especially for people from oppressed groups. We frame this presentation and discussion with respect to the concept of "defensive othering," which has previously been used to describe coping mechanisms for members of oppressed groups, but which we believe can be applied even more broadly to members of dominant groups to explain how stigma, discrimination, and social exclusion function on multiple levels in society. We conclude by linking this expanded concept of defensive othering to critical reflectivity and structural social work that can be used to confront these forces in society and promote social justice.

Conceptualizing Stigma, Discrimination, and Social Exclusion

There is a rich and multidisciplinary scholarly literature on the nature and impact of stigma, discrimination, and social exclusion on human well-being, with global contributions from scholars in the humanities, social sciences, and biomedical sciences. As discussed in Chapter 1 of this volume, social workers often draw from multiple theoretical traditions and disciplinary orientations to social life and, thus, are well positioned to synthesize and utilize contributions from this robust literature.

Conceptualizations of Stigma

Erving Goffman's (1963) work, *Stigma: Notes on the Management of Spoiled Identity*, is often seen as the foundation of contemporary conceptualizations of stigma. Goffman is said to have described stigma as a "process where the reaction of others spoils a normal identity" (Nettleton, 2006: 95), meaning that stigma is a relational dynamic through which people's otherwise "neutral" characteristics or identities are devalued in the eyes of others, thereby lowering their social status. This inherently relational aspect to stigma means that stigmatized people are often aware that others devalue them and therefore may anticipate a stigmatizing encounter before one happens (Pescosolido and Martin, 2015). Frequently this creates a vicious circle of stigmatizing encounters leading to self-imposed social withdrawal or isolation, which in turn leads to further stigmatizing misconceptions and marginalization (Link and Phelan, 2014). Bruce Link and Jo Phelan (2001) have also defined stigma as the "co-occurrence of its components—labeling, stereotyping, separation, status loss, and discrimination" and further indicate that "for stigmatization to occur, power must be exercised" (p. 363). Their emphasis on power in this process also points toward the ways in which stigmatization is used to maintain social hierarchies.

Recent conceptualizations of stigma are increasingly drawing attention to multiple levels of this phenomenon, whereby stigma occurs both in the surrounding environment and is also internalized within the individual (Corrigan and Watson, 2002; Bockting, 2014; Corrigan and Fong, 2014; Link & Phelan, 2014; White-Hughto, Reisner, and Panchankis, 2015). For social workers, this multilevel perspective aligns well with the profession's commitment to addressing injustices broadly in society, but also in supporting the well-being of individuals, families, and communities that are most negatively impacted by these injustices. Drawing upon two models commonly used in social work, the social cognitive model and the socio-ecological model, these conceptualizations of stigma align with the social work perspective of viewing the person-in-environment as discussed in the introductory chapter.

The social cognitive model is based in Albert Bandura's (1999) social learning theory, which posits that human behavior is determined by a combination of environmental factors (social norms and the ability to enforce these norms), personal factors (individual attitudes), and behaviors (individual agency, self-efficacy, and action) that interact with each other. Bandura suggests that through observational learning and personal cognitive mediation of environment, people act and react to their social systems, and, in turn, these actions influence their social environment. Further, stigma theory drawing upon this social cognitive model conceptualizes stigma into two forms—public stigma and self-stigma. Public stigma is the devaluation of a characteristic or identity that is worth less than others while self-stigma is the internalization of this societal norm (Corrigan, 1998; Corrigan and Watson, 2002). Actions that result from public stigma include distancing and acts of discrimination, while actions resulting from self-stigma include social isolation and withdrawal from social services (Corrigan and Watson, 2002).

Recent expansions on this conceptualization of stigma also utilize the socio-ecological model. Urie Bronfenbrenner's (1994) ecological model suggests that any understanding of human development must consider the microsystem (family, friends, and peers), ecosystem (school environment, community, and parent's work), and macrosystem (society, policy and laws). Based on this socio-ecological model, White-Hughto, Reisner, and Panchakis have articulated a multilevel model of stigma with individual, interpersonal, and structural levels. At the individual level, stigma is conceptualized as "the feelings people hold about themselves or the beliefs they perceive others to hold about them [which] may shape future behavior such as the anticipation and avoidance of discrimination" (2015: 223). At the interpersonal level, stigma refers to "direct or enacted forms of stigma" such verbal harassment, physical violence, and sexual assault, from people known to an individual (223). Structural level stigma refers to "the societal norms and institutional policies that constrain access to resources" (223), which impacts experiences for individuals, but also the degree to which entire groups of people experience barriers to well-being.

These approaches to conceptualizing stigma have also traditionally focused on the impact of singular stigmatized or marginalized identities and have not yet fully accounted for intersectional identities (Hatzenbuehler, Phelan, and Link, 2013). In addition, studies of stigmatization have traditionally focused on identities that can be "concealed," such as persons living with HIV, persons living with mental illness, and some sexual and gender minorities (Phelan, Link, and Dovidio, 2008; Bockting, 2014; Pescosolido and Martin, 2015; Hatzenbuehler, Phelan, and Link, 2013; White-Hughto, Reisner, and Panchakis, 2015). Stigma scholars now argue that conceptualizations of stigma must account for intersectional identities that were previously studied as separate constructs in different populations and use research to understand the complicated ways in which people with overlapping stigmatized identities, or a mix of stigmatized and nonstigmatized identities, navigate the social world (Hatzenbuehler, Phelan, and Link, 2013; Pescosolido and Martin, 2016; Oexle and Corrigan, 2018). In addition, recent scholarship on stigma calls for more attention to the ways in which stigmatized individuals and groups exert agency in the face of constraining social forces (Bandura, 2001; Fabbre and Gaveras, 2019).

Conceptualizations of Discrimination

Doman Lum defines discrimination as the behavioral response by an advantaged group (who receives advantages and is dominant and powerful) that is unfavorable toward a targeted group (who lacks power and privilege) (2004). Often, stigmatized characteristics and identities are used to justify discrimination, even though many are immutable or unchangeable. Thus, the nature of discrimination is shaped by stigmatizing beliefs, which also reflect a society comprised of dominant and subordinate groups. Furthermore, the process of stigmatization is closely linked to the notion of prejudice, originally conceptualized and articulated by Gordon Allport, who described ethnic prejudice as "an antipathy based upon a faulty and inflexible generalization that may be felt or expressed" (1954: 9). Further, "it may be directed toward a group as a whole, or toward an individual because he is a member of that group" (9). Thus, stigma and prejudice both shape the nature of discrimination and often provide motivation or rationalization for its enactment.

In their comparison of stigma and prejudice constructs used in scholarly research, Phelan, Link and Dovodio (2008) argue that the separate scholarly literatures that have developed around stigma versus prejudice have obscured the overlapping nature of both and have hampered researchers' ability to understand these social processes in ways that lead to meaningful interventions. Further, they argue that most differences between stigma and prejudice are only matters of focus and emphasis. For example, they argue that conceptualizations of prejudice often focus on issues of race and ethnicity (following Allport's original notion) and that stigma focuses more on "deviant" behaviors, disease, and disability. However, the overlapping nature of these processes necessitates a joint conceptualization, especially given their role in shaping and facilitating discrimination against oppressed groups in society. In this regard, Phelan and colleagues

(2008) argue that stigma and prejudice serve three main functions in the efforts of members of dominant groups to maintain social hierarchies: (1) exploitation and domination, or what they call "keeping people down;" (2) norm enforcement, or what they call "keeping people in;" and 3) disease avoidance, or what they call "keeping people away." Discrimination could thus be conceptualized as the actions people take, both individually and collectively, to achieve these aims.

Discrimination can be carried out in many ways, from small perceived slights, to public acts of violence (White-Hughto, Reinser, and Pachankis, 2015), to systematic social exclusion of entire groups (Link and Phelan, 2014). Thus, multiple conceptual domains are needed to make sense of these actions. In this vein, Link and Phelan (2001, 2014) identify four mechanisms of discriminatory actions. Direct *person-to-person discrimination*, perhaps the most well-known, is an openly expressed statement against another person based on a prejudicial attitude or stereotype (Link and Phelan, 2014). *Structural discrimination* can be explicit or implicit and manifests in social policies, laws, institutional practices, and public opinion (Link and Phelan, 2014). Often, structural discrimination leads to a reduction or unfair distribution of social resources, along societal lines of who is perceived as "deserving" or "undeserving" of public resources such as safe housing, education, and health care (Hatzenbuehler and Link, 2014). *Interaction discrimination* is conceptualized as the often implicit actions that are carried out when a member of a dominant group interacts with someone deemed less powerful, which can include acting with uncertainty, superiority, or even with "excessive kindness" (Link and Phelan, 2014: 25). *Discrimination operating through a stigmatized person* is when individual awareness about both real and perceived threats manifests in less self-assurance, stress, and self-imposed social isolation and exclusion (Link and Phelan, 2014).

Conceptualizations of Social Exclusion

Social exclusion has been conceptualized as the act of distancing a person or group seen as less desirable in society and preventing them from engaging in meaningful activities, thus reinforcing their status as undesirable (Morgan et al., 2007). While similar to stigma, social exclusion utilizes stigma and stigmatizing beliefs to structure how different groups co-exist in society (Levitas et al., 2007; Morgan et al., 2007). Much of the early work on social exclusion stems from a European context, often from studies that explore questions of integration and exclusion of ethnic-minority immigrants (Cantor-Graae and Selten, 2005; Morgan and Hutchinson, 2010). This work has led to a multidimensional conceptualization of social exclusion, which, somewhat like a multilevel conceptualization of stigma, emphasizes distinct but overlapping domains of exclusion for oppressed groups whose social status and opportunities are limited by the beliefs and actions of dominant groups.

This multidimensional conceptualization has been articulated through the Bristol Social Exclusion Matrix (Levitas et al., 2007), which is used to assess the kinds of social exclusion that different groups of people experience in the following areas: (1) resources (material, economic, and social, along with access to public and private services); (2) participation (economic, social, cultural, and educational); and (3) quality of life (health and well-being, living environment, and exposure to crime, harm, and criminalization (10). According to this matrix, the more dimensions that apply to an individual or population, the greater the degree of social exclusion. Ruth Levitas and colleagues (2007) posit that the number of dimensions that apply to an individual or population indicates the degree to which they are excluded from mainstream social life and provide insight into areas of potential intervention to promote inclusion.

If social exclusion is conceptualized as a means of preventing people from engaging in activities that are meaningful to them in society (Morgan et al., 2007), then this becomes a powerful force that impedes the pursuit of livable lives. In this way, social exclusion is a key mechanism through which people's unique capabilities are hampered, misdirected, and diminished within a social structure that benefits dominant groups. Here, Amartya Sen's (2000) notion of "capability depreciation" and its emphasis on the relational nature of exclusion echoes the nature of stigma and discrimination in that these are, at their core, relational modes of controlling people's choices, opportunities and freedom. The goals of exclusionary social norms, laws, and policies are thus aimed (whether consciously or unconsciously) at giving dominant groups the power to reify stigmatization and codify discrimination in ways that maintain the status quo. For members of stigmatized groups, these social processes shape experiences of daily life, potential for growth and development, and the direction of life course trajectories.

An Expanded Conceptualization of Defensive Othering

The mutually constituting nature of stigma, discrimination, and social exclusion calls for an overarching approach to thinking about these oppressive social forces. The foundation for our expanded conceptualization of defensive othering is the notion of *stigma power,* which draws attention to how stigma is used to exploit, control, or exclude others, often in hidden or misrecognized ways. Drawing upon Pierre Bourdieu's (1987, 1990) work on symbolic power, or the capacity of powerful groups to impose a legitimized vision of the social world on others, Link and Phelan argue that stigma is used at multiple levels to keep people "down, in, and away" (2001: 24). To reflect on how the exertion of power is used to achieve these aims, Link and Phelan suggest considering the following questions:

1. Do the people who might stigmatize have the power to ensure that the human difference they recognize and label is broadly defined in the culture?
2. Do the people who might confer stigma have the power to ensure that the culture recognizes and deeply accepts the stereotypes they connect to the labeled differences?
3. Do the people who stigmatize have the power to separate "us" from "them" and to have the designation stick? And do those who might confer stigma control access to major life domains like educational institutions, jobs, housing, and health care in order to put really consequential teeth into the distinctions they draw? (2001: 376).

Answers to these questions draw attention to the ways in which stigma, discrimination, and social exclusion function as a means of maintaining social hierarchies and controlling opportunities for individuals and groups to develop their capabilities and lead livable lives. Further, any threats (real or perceived) to a dominant group's ability to exert stigma power in these ways are likely to trigger defensiveness and increased efforts to maintain the status quo if it benefits this group.

Defensive othering was first conceptualized by Jean Miller (1976) as a means of capturing the process through which members of oppressed groups exert power and status over members of their own or other oppressed groups. This process is thought to be carried out in response to threatening stigmatizing attitudes and beliefs held by dominant groups, often coupled with negative stereotypes, which motivate people to elevate their own status with respect to a "lower" group (Johnson, 2006). This process is also thought to serve as a coping function in response to their own experiences of stigmatization and oppression. Michael Schwalbe and colleagues have articulated defensive othering as the process of "accepting the legitimacy of a devalued identity imposed by the dominant group, but then saying, in effect, 'there are indeed Others to whom this applies, but it does not apply to me'" (2000: 425). This process is conceived as identity work that may help some stigmatized people to be affirmed by members of dominant groups, but which ultimately reifies stigmatizing attitudes, beliefs, and stereotypes.

Matthew Ezzell (2009) has used the concept of defensive othering to illuminate the ways in which female rugby players negotiate identity dilemmas as a subordinate group in a male-defined sport. To respond to sexist and homophobic stigma aimed at female rugby players in general, some women emphasize their fulfillment of heteronormative expectations while stigmatizing other players who are "butch" or "dykes" and break gender norms; this defensive response serves to situate them higher in a social hierarchy determined by the dominant heterosexual male group. In addition, Anima Adjepong (2017) found that this process is inherently intersectional, often relying on race-based stigma and stereotypes to bolster this form of social positioning and dominance in the sport. Similarly, Amy McClure found that people from two religiously marginalized groups in the U.S. Bible Belt (nonbelievers and pagans) used defensive othering to manage threats of discrediting stereotypes (e.g., the "militant atheist" and the "hedonistic pagan") to "defend against stigma and moral indictment" (2017: 340). Defensive othering as a concept has also been used to understand the identity work of homeless men (Snow and Anderson, 2001), the social positioning of residents in overcrowded rental units in Shanghai (Liang, 2018), and how some women exert power and control over other women in the pornography industry (Paul, 2005).

While defensive othering has been used to conceptualize the cognition and actions of members of oppressed groups as a means of coping with stigma threats from dominant groups, we theorize that the notion of perceiving a threat and feeling compelled to defend one's status also applies to members of dominant groups. This process may or may not be conscious, but would serve to distance people in privileged positions in society from those whose existence might challenge taken-for-granted aspects of the social order and whose potential agency might threaten society's structures. Thus, the notion of privilege plays an important role in this expanded conceptualization of defensive othering. As Peggy McIntosh's now-famous metaphor of the "invisible and weightless knapsack" suggests, privilege is experienced both through unearned entitlements in society and a sense of conferred dominance over others (1989: 10). Since privilege is not necessarily something that members of dominant groups choose for themselves (being instead generated by society's structures and systems; Johnson, 2006), we theorize that this puts people in positions where they are likely to feel defensive when their status and identities are challenged.

One way to visualize the effects of the invisible or unfelt forces of privilege is to picture a bicyclist who is cycling with the wind. When this occurs, they are able to cycle much faster and yet do not feel the wind at all. It is only when the cyclist turns into the wind that they experience and must confront its real force. When members of dominant groups, either consciously or unconsciously, sense that oppressed groups challenge or threaten their taken-for-granted status (e.g., cycling with the wind), we theorize that they protect themselves and create social distance from these groups by leveraging stigmatizing attitudes, beliefs, and stereotypes against others.

Thus, we see stigma power, as articulated by Link and Phelan, as emphasizing the exertion of power and dominance in maintaining an unequal society and an expanded conceptualization of defensive othering as emphasizing the threat perceived by those in positions of power and dominance. Taken together, we think of defensive othering as the process through which members of dominant groups exert stigma power and reinforce oppressive forces in society. In addition, if we view livable lives as achieved through the direct ability to access the rights, resources, services, and systems that make life worth living for everyone, and we understand that we all hold intersecting identities (both stigmatized and not), then many people are at risk for experiencing the effects of defensive othering at some point in their lives.

Defensive Othering and Livable Lives

The combination of stigma, discrimination, and social exclusion, what we conceive of as defensive othering from members of both dominant and oppressed groups, has profound and lasting impacts on people's ability to lead livable lives. These impacts are felt at the individual level, but also by groups and communities, in ways that are both contemporaneous and historical. We approach our empirical considerations of defensive othering and livable lives with respect to Abraham Maslow's (1968) theory that human beings are motivated toward personal growth, based on a sense of belonging, which requires that basic needs be met in ways that promote self-actualization. Further, we acknowledge that what it means to live a livable life is often context driven and culturally shaped. Thus, our empirical examples of the impacts of defensive othering are best used as sensitizing forms of knowledge that facilitate further investigation into the full meaning of livability in diverse people's lives. We focus our discussion of the impacts of defensive othering on two essential aspects of livability in contemporary American society—physical and mental health and economic well-being.

Physical and Mental Health

Stigma, and the discrimination and social exclusion that it fuels, are thought to have negative impacts on opportunities and capabilities for people from oppressed groups across multiple domains in areas such as housing, employment, and physical and mental health (Link and Phelan, 2001; Hatzenbueler, 2011). In the areas of physical and mental health, scholars now argue that stigma be viewed as a fundamental cause of disease that generates and perpetuates heath inequalities. Hatzenbueler, Phelan, and Link (2013) make this argument for stigma as a social determinant of health by identifying several empirical effects of stigmatization that mediate the relationship between peoples' identities or characteristics and their health status. These mediators are (1) access to tangible resources (e.g., financial, employment, wages, housing); (2) social isolation and social support; (3) psychological responses to stigma (e.g., emotional regulation strategies that contribute to reduced adaptive coping skills including suppression, rumination, smoking, drinking, and overeating); and (4) stress (caused by external events that lead to internalization and expectation of rejection causing heightened levels of hypervigilance and stress). Stigma magnifies the mediating factors that have a negative effect on health and decreases protective factors such as financial resources and social support. In this way, stigmatization (as a key component of defensive othering) fuels multiple pathways that lead to poor health, which impedes people's ability to lead livable lives.

A key process connecting defensive othering to mental health is how these forces are internalized by individuals and groups, such that they shape the intrapsychological cognitions and emotions that influence identity development and mental well-being. To understand internalization processes, it is helpful to identity two forms of stigma that are thought to influence them. First, enacted stigma refers to the real lived experiences of stigmatizing encounters with other people in the social world, while felt stigma refers to the fear or perception that a discriminatory event is about to happen (Bockting, 2014). For example, enacted stigma surrounding how serious psychiatric symptoms such as suicidal ideation and psychosis are responded to by others can cause felt stigma that leads to withdrawal from mental health services by people experiencing these symptoms. In fact, enacted and felt stigma have been shown to increase mental health symptom severity such as depressive episodes, psychosis symptoms, and suicidal ideation (Lysaker et al., 2007; Yanos et al., 2008; Ben Zeev et al., 2012; Oexle et al., 2017). Or, in the case of people whose identities are stigmatized in society, such as transgender adults, harsh and stigmatizing punishments for gender transgressions in childhood lead to internalized shame and fear as well as avoidance of accessing health care and social services later in life (Fabbre, 2017a; Fabbre and Gaveras, 2019). In this case, these forms of enacted and felt stigma are also associated with substance use problems and suicidal ideation throughout the life course (Fabbre and Gaveras, 2019).

Racism, as a form of defensive othering, provides another powerful example of the ways in which enacted and felt stigma influence health. Johnson, Pate, and Givens (2010) draw attention to the ways that racism devalues and dehumanizes the identities of African American men, which is experienced in both enacted and felt ways. For those living in poor neighborhoods and communities, exposure to community violence further enforces this dehumanization (Johnson, Pate, and Givens, 2000). These factors, often compounded with trauma, lead to shame and anxiety surrounding the internalization of a perceived "lesser" identity in society, which Johnson, Pate, and Givens argue manifests in externalizing emotions such as anger that impair one's capabilities and well-being. Substantial race-based health inequalities have been observed when it comes to receipt of physical and mental health services for persons living with serious mental illness. During psychosocial assessments, African Americans are more likely to be diagnosed with schizophrenia or increased symptom severity when compared to people of other races (Schwarz and Blankenship, 2014; Oluwoye et al., 2018), and there is evidence this is due to health care provider bias rather than any real difference in occurrence across groups (Schwarz and Blankenship, 2014; Oluwoye et al., 2018). In this case, we interpret "health care provider bias" as a form of defensive othering though which professionals in positions of power are unconsciously threatened by African American patients' experiences and world views and thus seek to distance themselves from their patients' realities by stigmatizing their mental health symptomatology. In this vein, a mixed-methods study of the primary care experiences of Hispanic people living with mental illness identified the combined experience of stigma and discrimination based on race, culture, and perceived linguistic ability and its impact on service utilization (Cabassa et al., 2014). In addition, findings in this study indicate that due to stigma about one's combined mental health and minority status, physical health complaints were ignored or brushed aside by primary health care providers. However, patients did not feel stigmatized when they sensed they had a strong personal relationship with a provider and that that provider took a genuine interest in their life.

Stigma that is experienced early in life and in relation to family and peer ties often has devasting effects later in life. For example, transgender adults report strikingly high rates of childhood maltreatment by family members (Factor and Rothblum, 2007; Rotondi et al., 2011a, 2011b) and bullying by peers (Stotzer, 2009). In some families, transgender children have been found to experience higher rates of physical, verbal, and sexual assault than their cisgender siblings (Factor and Rothblum, 2007). The damaging effects to health stemming from child maltreatment, such as heart disease and posttraumatic stress disorder, has been well documented (Felitti et al., 1998). Lack of family support (Simons et al., 2013) and abandonment by family have been found to have damaging effects on well-being, including the often devastating experience of homelessness that also increases risks of exposure to trauma, extreme poverty, and subsequent mental health problems (Koken, Bimbi, and Parsons, 2009). These forms of enacted stigma often lead to felt stigma, which has also been shown to delay coming out for transgender people until older adulthood (Fabbre, 2014; Gagne and Tewksbury, 1998). Transgender people who carry the effects of childhood stigma also commonly experience stigmatizing interactions with health care providers who are supposed to care for them (Poteat, German, and Kerrigan, 2013; Snelgrove et al., 2012). These experiences come in the form of treatment refusal or verbal harassment in health care settings and have been shown to significantly impact poor emotional well-being (Reisner, 2014, 2015). These empirical findings point toward the ways in which defensive othering that is experienced at any point in the life course can have lasting effects.

We have provided several examples of defensive othering in the form of enacted and felt stigma, often with respect to interpersonal dynamics. However, the collective forces of stigmatization, discrimination, and social exclusion also function at the structural level of society. In this regard, the notion of structural stigma is helpful for illuminating these functions. Structural stigma constitutes the "societal-level conditions, cultural norms, and institutional policies that constrain opportunities, resources, and well-being of the stigmatized" (Hatzenbuehler and Link, 2014: 2). This constraining function depends on the exertion of power by dominant groups, which we think makes defensive othering, as an overarching concept, relevant at the structural level. For example, Hatzenbuehler and colleagues (2009, 2010) found that living in states with discriminatory policies toward sexual minorities increased their risk of psychiatric problems such as mood disorders, posttraumatic stress disorder, and anxiety. Sexual minorities' physical health is also impacted by coping with these structural stressors and manifests in behaviors like tobacco and alcohol use that are thought to increase cardiovascular disease (Hatzenbuehler, Slopen and McLaughlin, 2014). Further, sexual minority youth who live in areas with high levels of prejudice towards sexual minorities are 20 percent more likely to attempt suicide than their sexual minority peers living in low prejudice areas, even when controlling for individual-level risk factors such as binge drinking, peer victimization, and exposure to physical abuse (Hatzenbuehler, 2011). However, defensive othering at the structural level is not static. For example, researchers using longitudinal methods found a significant reduction in depression, anxiety, and suicide attempts among sexual minorities after the passage of state-level marriage equality acts in the 2000s (Hatzenbuehler, Keyes, and Hasin, 2009).

Economic Well-Being

A second key area of livability revolves around economic well-being. As discussed in Chapter 3 of this volume, poverty and economic insecurity seriously undermine an individual's ability to lead a livable life. Beyond material hardship, residing in poverty and economic need are also highly stigmatized conditions in the United States. In addition, those in poverty are routinely excluded from mainstream society and, at times, discriminated against by those with greater economic status.

Within the American context, poverty and the use of safety net programs are highly stigmatized. Survey research has repeatedly demonstrated that the common understanding of poverty is primarily as an individual and moral failing (Eppard, Rank, and Bullock, 2020; Gilens, 1999). Consequently, the poor are often perceived to be lazy, unmotivated, and making bad decisions in life. This perspective goes back hundreds of years. For example, the English Poor Laws at the beginning of the 17th century made the distinction between the deserving and the undeserving poor. Those deserving of compassion and assistance were seen as experiencing poverty through no fault of their own and constituted a small percentage of the poor, such as widows, young children, and the disabled. On the other hand, the majority of the poor were viewed as able-bodied individuals who were simply "not working hard enough" to get themselves out of poverty and therefore undeserving of help.

Consistent with this perspective, U.S. poverty is primarily viewed as a sign of individual and moral failure. The cultural narrative that America represents a "land of opportunity" where hard work and skill lead to upward mobility and a good life rationalizes the belief that those who have not done so have only themselves to blame. This notion of individual failure permeates how poverty is understood in the United States. We interpret this longstanding individualistic view of poverty and poor people as a ubiquitous form of defensive othering in the United States that both *defends* the status of those who benefit from our economic system and *others* who are most vulnerable to it.

Considerable social research has shown that these stigmatizing attitudes are deeply experienced by those in poverty (Abramksy, 2013; Edin and Shaefer, 2015). For example, Mark Rank (1994) found in his book, *Living on the Edge: The Realities of Welfare in America,* that those in poverty and receiving public assistance programs encounter stigma and disdain from others on a routine basis. These experiences ranged from using the Supplemental Nutrition Assistance Program (or food stamps) at the grocery store to feelings of being constantly watched and scrutinized. For example, a 29-year-old mother describes her acute awareness of being sized up by frontline workers in the medical field:

> Some receptionists turn off the friendliness when they see Medical Assistance. Sometimes I catch them looking at me, maybe if I have on a necklace or something. I don't think I look like the stereotypical welfare mother, and I see them scrutinizing me and thinking it over. It's pretty subtle. (Rank, 1994: 139)

In a further example of defensive othering, Rank found that welfare recipients were careful to distinguish their own circumstances from that of the perceived "typical welfare recipient." Consequently, when asked why they had turned to welfare assistance, most cited events that had happened that were largely beyond their control—being laid off of a job, health emergencies, or families splitting up. In contrast, when asked why most welfare recipients were receiving assistance, stereotypes surrounding welfare prevailed—individuals were lazy, unmotivated, addicted to drugs or alcohol, and so on. This distancing of oneself from the predominate stigmatized image of the "typical" welfare recipient is found for many other stigmatized groups as well. This distancing reiterates Schwalbe's argument that defense othering incorporates the process of "accepting the legitimacy of a devalued identity imposed by the dominant group, but then saying, in effect, 'there are indeed Others to whom this applies, but it does not apply to me'" (Schwalbe et al., 2000: 425).

Stigmatizing experiences like this have been shown to permeate the existence of Americans living in poverty (Desmond, 2016; Hays, 2003; Seccombe, 1999). Further, this stigmatization is systematically linked to the social exclusion of the poor from mainstream society. In Europe, for example, poverty is often viewed as serving an inherently exclusionary function and is referred to as a form of social deprivation. In the United States, this form of exclusion leads to a wide range of troubling outcomes, such as lower rates of voting and less engagement in community affairs by the poor or a lack of concern for lower-income populations by government legislators. As discussed in Chapter 3 of this volume, much of the human meaning of poverty revolves around notions of deprivation and exclusion. Further, Amartya Sen's (1999) argument that poverty constitutes both a lack of freedom and a barrier to achieving the full development of one's capabilities demonstrates how economic well-being is fundamentally linked to defensive othering that maintains social hierarchies in a capitalist society.

Finally, considerable research indicates that those in poverty suffer from various forms of discrimination. These include being more likely to be convicted and sentenced to longer periods of time for specific criminal offenses (Reiman, 2004), job and housing market discrimination (Desmond, 2016; Feagin, 2014), paying more for basic goods (Caplovitz, 1963), and experiencing stifling rates of borrowing and credit (Caskey, 1994). Taken together, defensive othering in the form of stigmatization, discrimination, and exclusion of those living in poverty has a detrimental impact upon the health and well-being of those most vulnerable. This impact is literally a matter of life and death, as those in the upper 5 percent of the income distribution in the United States can expect to live approximately nine years longer than those in the bottom 10 percent (Jencks, 2002).

Furthermore, as Mark Rank has argued in earlier work (2004, 2011, 2014), the result of stigma, discrimination, and social exclusion that surrounds issues of poverty and the social safety net results in an implicit acceptance of the status quo of high poverty within the context of U.S. material wealth. Furthermore, we theorize that this acceptance of high economic inequality is actually maintained and bolstered by defensive othering, which uses stigma, discrimination, and exclusion to distance and disparage people living in poverty from those who benefit from this material wealth. This process of defensive othering is largely unconscious and made invisible by the widespread belief in American society that poverty is an individual and moral failing. Thus, federal and state governments bear little responsibility for alleviating such conditions and challenging the status quo. In fact, a long-running theme from conservatives has been that by helping those in poverty, government programs actually worsen the problem by making individuals increasingly dependent. This point was successfully argued by Ronald Reagan during his presidency, who declared, "We fought a war on poverty, and poverty won," and it has remained a strong theme for conservatives ever since.

By understanding the ways in which defensive othering serves to maintain economic inequality and perpetuate poverty, we gain insight into the formidable challenges to upward mobility that people living in poverty face. We also gain greater insight into why the United States has such elevated rates of poverty and inequality compared to other high economy countries. These rates are largely the result of an extremely weak social safety net coupled with a lack of universal benefits such as health care, child care, and affordable low-income housing. A key reason for these lack of supports stems from the defensiveness of economically privileged groups and the social distance they generate from those who are most negatively impacted by America's economic structure.

Critical Reflectivity and Structural Social Work

While social workers seek to interrupt forces like defensive othering and its stigmatizing, discriminating, and exclusionary functions, they may also perpetuate these injustices unknowingly. Despite their good intentions, American social workers are socialized within the same structure that facilitates defensive othering, and many also benefit from some of the privileges that this structure affords members of dominant groups. Thus, social workers should rigorously examine their own social positions in society while simultaneously engaging in practice that challenges oppression and promotes liberation for all. This is an ambitious but necessary aim for the profession, especially with respect to its history. While social workers in the United States have long sought to improve living conditions and opportunities for members of vulnerable groups, they have also, at times, shown more concern for their own professional status than social change (Ehrenreich, 1985). This historical knowledge can and should be used as a catalyst for re-envisioning social work practice in the 21st century.

In her seminal work on practitioner self-awareness, *Who Is the "Self" in Self-Aware: Professional Self-Awareness from a Critical Theory Perspective*, Mary Kondrat (1999) argues for a critical approach to self-awareness for social workers who wish to interrupt structural forces in society. She argues that social workers have too often relied on forms of self-awareness that do not fully situate the self in society's larger social, economic and political forces. For example, many social workers strive to articulate their own feelings about work with clients, or seek feedback from peers on the nature of their practice, but fall short of critically examining how they may (often unconsciously) reinforce oppressive social norms that hurt the clients and communities with which they work. For example, some social workers, despite being consciously affirming of lesbian, gay, bisexual, transgender, and queer people, unknowingly continue to promote gender conformity and transphobia in their work. Consider the following case scenario based on a real clinical encounter outlined by Vanessa Fabbre in her article, *Queer Aging: Implications for Social Work Practice with LGBTQ Older Adults*:

> Cara is a White, cisgender, lesbian-identified woman in her late 50s who generally presents herself in an androgynous manner (e.g. she does not wear make-up, wears her hair cropped short, and wears gender neutral clothing). Cara shares with her new therapist that she often startles other women in public bathrooms and that this experience is upsetting and anxiety provoking for her. The therapist then suggests that she might consider wearing earrings to avoid being mistaken for a man. Cara, put off by this suggestion, questions the therapist's competency for working with LGBTQ older adults and terminates the relationship shortly thereafter. (2017b: 74)

In this clinical encounter, the therapist has good intentions and is likely using a solution-focused orientation to their work. Indeed, wearing earrings would probably solve the client's "problem" fairly easily. However, the point at which the therapist suggests that the client alter their gender presentation, the therapist is at once both product of and producer of heteronormativity in society. By framing this issue as one of individual choice in gender expression, rather than confronting heteronormative social forces that stigmatize gender nonconforming people, the therapist misses an opportunity to link "macro" and "micro" forces and promote a liberatory therapeutic experience for this client.

If social workers are to confront stigma, discrimination, and social exclusion, they must rigorously examine the ways in which their own thoughts, feelings, behaviors, and professional priorities might serve to reinforce these very targets of their efforts. This is challenging and difficult work and requires a structural orientation to social work practice.

Bob Mullaly, a Canadian social work scholar and educator, offers such an orientation to social work practice that is aimed at addressing structural injustice in contemporary neo-liberal societies. In what he calls the *new structural social work*, Mullaly (2007) outlines the ways in which capitalist political economies fuel longstanding social marginalization and oppression, drawing attention to how social workers have, at times, lost sight of addressing these causes of human suffering. For example, Mullaly argues that some social workers have unwittingly engaged in "blaming the victim" with respect to vulnerable groups by engaging in the following process of social scientific/social welfare practice described by William Ryan: First, social scientists and social welfare advocates identify a problem (e.g., poverty); they then study those affected by the problem and discover how they are different from the rest of society (e.g. ethnographic research in poor neighborhoods); they define these differences, which are in fact the effects of injustice and discrimination, as the causes of the problem (e.g. culture of poverty theory); and then they promote an intervention to "correct" these differences by changing the people affected by the problem (e.g., mixed-income housing initiatives) (1976, as cited in Mullaly, 2007: 232). This process of blaming the victim is problematic because it distracts social workers from addressing the root causes of human suffering while also perpetuating oppressive norms and social structures.

Mullaly's view of structural social work has two aims: to alleviate the negative effects on people of an exploitative and alienating social order (in other words, to offer relief), and transform the conditions and social structures that cause these negative effects (2007: 245).

To achieve these aims, Mullaly argues for a twofold approach to structural social work practice: radical humanism and radical structuralism. Radical humanism is based on the recognition that casework or clinical work can be emancipatory, as opposed to oppressive, and that consciousness-raising at the micro level is necessary for structural change. Practicing radical humanism means approaching interpersonal work with individuals and groups in a contextual way and making sense of problems not as solely idiosyncratic and unique to individuals but as linked to structural forces in society. This involves intensive listening, self-awareness, and approaching relationships with the goal of empowering people. It also requires consciousness-raising and normalization of how people's seemingly individual-level struggles may be caused by larger social, economic, and political forces in society. These relationships must be dialogical, meaning that power is shared as much as possible, that social workers are transparent about their motivations and actions, and that practice decisions are made in a mutual way. At all points in a relationship with a client or community, social workers practicing radical humanism strive to use critical reflectivity to situate themselves and their work with respect to social structure, with the aim of engaging in therapeutic relationships that explicitly push back on oppressive norms, institutions, laws, and policies.

Radical humanism offers a way of conceptualizing practice "*within the system*" (Mullaly, 2007: 288), meaning it offers a means of promoting change for social workers who may be working in traditional clinical practice or within many of the institutions that are thought to serve oppressive functions. However, there are limits to this work, and social work as a profession should promote alternative ways to change oppressive structures. Mullaly offers many concrete examples of doing this: by developing alternative services and organizations to provide human care services (e.g., feminist health care collectives), building and joining coalitions and social movements (i.e., Black Lives Matter), supporting unions, developing radical professional associations (like the rank-and-file movement of the 1930s), engaging in electoral politics, and looking for ways to revitalize the public sector that is under attack by both neo-conservatives and neo-liberals.

In these ways, social workers can engage in radical structuralism and push for change "*outside the system*" (Mullaly, 2007: 331). Mullaly also argues that an essential point in this orientation to social work practice is, in fact, that it constitutes more than just practice but a way of life. The final element to pursuing radical humanism and radical structuralism is examining one's own social positions and actions in society and being intentional about changing the ways in which these perpetuate an oppressive social order. This means reflecting on how one makes, spends and saves money; where one lives; how one's actions impact the natural environment; and what needs to be done to align a radical social work practice with one's personal life. This is an ongoing challenge and one that is best carried out collectively, harnessing the power generated by a justice-oriented social work profession.

Conclusion

Stigma, discrimination, and social exclusion are powerful social forces that both stem from and reinforce social structure in American society. This structure facilitates livability for those from dominant groups but impedes livability for those whose characteristics, experiences, identities, practices, and values pose threats to this order. To understand these forces in society, their deleterious effects, and potential interventions, social workers must engage with conceptual and empirical knowledge in ways that lead to action.

Conceptually, stigma is the process through which the characteristics and identities of some individuals and groups are devalued in society and is expressed at multiple levels—individual, interpersonal, and structural (White-Hughto, Reisner, and Panchakis, 2015). Phelan and Link (2001) argue that stigmatization serves to "keep people down, in, and away," which leads to our conceptualization of discrimination as the actions people take, both individually and collectively, to achieve these aims. Further, discrimination is carried out through multiple mechanisms—direct person-to-person interactions where stigma and prejudice are overtly expressed; structurally through policies, laws, institutions and public opinion; interactionally through implicit and even unconscious actions; and, perhaps most damaging, through the ways in which discriminatory norms are internalized by stigmatized people and can lead to self-imposed social isolation (Link and Phelan, 2014). Thus, stigma and discrimination have inherently exclusionary functions, which are emphasized in conceptualizations of social exclusion and capability depreciation. In this regard, Morgan and colleagues (2007) conceptualize social exclusion as the act of "distancing" a person or group seen as less desirable in society and preventing them from engaging in meaning activities, which takes place through limiting people's access to society's resources, participation in social life, and quality of life (Levitas et al., 2007). These limitations are thought to depreciate one's capability to achieve a life driven by one's values and aspirations, which inherently limits freedom (Sen, 2000). This lack of freedom is especially hypocritical in the United States, which espouses itself as a free society.

The relational aspects of stigma, discrimination, and social exclusion suggest that these processes reflect the psychology of both individuals and groups. In this regard, we theorize that the act of defensive othering, previously used to capture the ways in which members of oppressed groups stigmatize and oppress others (Schwalbe et al., 2000), may also apply when members of dominant groups use stigmatization and discrimination to keep people "down, in, and away" (Link and Phelan, 2001: 24). This expanded conceptualization of defensive othering emphasizes the threat that subordinate groups pose to a social order that confers privilege and advantage to some and posits that even those at the top of a social hierarchy may feel defensive and sense the need to actively defend their status and world view by stigmatizing, discriminating against, and excluding others from social life. An expanded conceptualization of defensive othering thus draws our attention to the processes that, in part, promote inequality and injustice.

For social workers who care about the well-being of vulnerable and oppressed people, there is a growing body of useful evidence that illuminates the relationship between stigma, discrimination, and social exclusion and livable lives, especially in the domains of physical and mental health and economic well-being. In terms of health, research on the impacts of stigmatization now strongly supports the claim that stigma is a fundamental cause of ill health and population-based health disparities (Hatzenbuehler, Phelan, and Link, 2013). One of the most detrimental connections between stigma and health may be the ways in which it is internalized, often leading to major threats to livability such as substance abuse and suicidal behavior (Fabbre and Gaveras, 2019). These processes often stem from early life experiences and have implications for well-being at all stages of the life course. Similar to the areas of physical and mental health, economic well-being reflects the power of defensive othering to shape lives and livability. In the United States, we theorize that the cultural narrative that poverty is caused by individual and moral failings is a powerful and persistent form of defensive othering that fuels the implementation of laws and policies that perpetuate economic inequality and injustice. This is felt especially by those Americans struggling to survive on low incomes and without a robust social safety net to facilitate access to safe and affordable housing, high-quality health care, and nutritious food.

The pervasiveness and persistence of what we conceptualize as defensive othering in our society necessitates critical reflectivity and structurally oriented practice as social workers prepare for action in a new century. Social workers, just like all people, are both products of and producers of our social structure, which requires high levels of self-awareness and a structural perspective to illuminate and interrupt. Further, heightened self-awareness coupled with a structural perspective holds the potential to move the profession beyond traditional macro and micro orientations to practice and strengthen efforts to confront social forces such stigma, discrimination, and social exclusion. By engaging in a rigorous process of critical reflectivity, practicing radical humanism, and working both within and outside oppressive systems, 21st-century social workers have the capability to promote social justice and livable lives for all.

References

Abramsky, S. 2013. *The American Way of Poverty: How the Other Half Still Lives.* New York: Nation Books.

Adjepong, A. 2017. "'We're, like, a Cute Rugby Team': How Whiteness and Heterosexuality Shape Women's Sense of Belonging in Rugby." *International Review for the Sociology of Sport,* 52, 209–222.

Allport, G. 1954. *The Nature of Prejudice.* Cambridge: Perseus Books.

Anderson, L. and D. A. Snow. 2001. "Inequality and the Self: Exploring Connections from an Interactionist Perspective." *Symbolic Interaction,* 24, 395–406.

Bandura, A. 1999. "A Social Cognitive Theory of Personality." *Handbook of Personality*. Edited by L. Pervin and O. John. New York: Guildford Press, pp. 154–196.

Bandura, A. 2001. "Social Cognitive Theory: An Agentic Perspective." *Annual Review of Psychology*, 52, 1–26.

Ben-Zeev, D., R. Frounfelker, S. B. Morris, and P. W. Corrigan. 2012. "Predictors of Self-Stigma in Schizophrenia: New Insights Using Mobile Technologies." *Journal of Dual Diagnosis*, 8, 305–314.

Bockting, W. 2014. "The Impact of Stigma on Transgender Identity Development and Mental Health." *Gender Dysphoria and Disorders of Sex Development: Progress in Care and Knowledge.* Edited by B. Kreukels, T. D. Steensma, and A. De Vries. New York: Springer, pp. 319–330.

Bourdieu, P. 1987. "What Makes a Social Class? On the Theoretical and Practical Existence of Groups." *Berkeley Journal of Sociology*, 32, 1–17.

Bourdieu, P. 1990. *The Logic of Practice*. Stanford, CA: Stanford University Press.

Bronfenbrenner, U. 1994. "Ecological Models of Human Development." *Readings on the Development of Children*. Edited by M. Gauvian and M. Cole. New York: Freeman, pp. 37–43.

Cabassa, L. J., and A. Gomes. 2014. "Primary Health Care Experiences of Hispanics with Serious Mental Illness: A Mixed-Methods Study." *Administration and Policy in Mental Health*, 41, 724–736.

Cantor-Graae, E., and J. Selten. 2005. "Schizophrenia and Migration: A Meta-Analysis and Review." *The American Journal of Psychiatry*, 62, 12–24.

Caplovitz, D. 1963. *The Poor Pay More: Consumer Practices of Low-Income Families*. Glencoe, IL: Free Press.

Caskey, J. P. 1994. *Fringe Banking: Check-Cashing Outlets, Pawnshops, and the Poor*. New York: Russell Sage Foundation.

Corrigan, P. W. 1998. "The Impact of Stigma on Severe Mental Illness." *Cognitive and Behavioral Practice*, 5, 201–222.

Corrigan, P. W., and M. W. M. Fong. 2014. "Competing Perspectives on Erasing the Stigma of Illness: What Says the Dodo Bird?" *Social Science & Medicine*, 103, 110–117.

Corrigan, P. W., and A. C. Watson. 2002. "The Paradox of Self-Stigma and Mental Illness." *Clinical Psychology: Science and Practice*, 9, 35–53.

Desmond, M. 2016. *Evicted: Poverty and Profit in the American City*. New York: Broadway Books.

Edin, K. J., and H. L. Shaefer. 2015. *$2.00 a Day: Living on Almost Nothing in America*. New York: Houghton Mifflin Harcourt.

Ehrenreich, J. 1985. *The Altruistic Imagination: A History of Social Work and Social Policy in the United States*. Ithaca, NY: Cornell University Press.

Eppard, L. M., M. R. Rank, and H. Bullock. 2020. *Rugged Individualism and the Misunderstanding of American Inequality*. Bethlehem, PA: Lehigh University Press.

Ezzell, M. B. 2009. "Barbie Dolls" on the Pitch: Identity Work, Defensive Othering, and Inequality in Women's Rugby." *Social Problems*, 56, 111–131.

Fabbre, V. D. 2014. "Gender Transitions in Later Life: The Significance of Time in Queer Aging." *Journal of Gerontological Social Work*, 57, 161–175.

Fabbre, V. D. 2017a. "Agency and Social Forces in the Life Course: The Case of Gender Transitions in Later Life." *Journal of Gerontology: Social Sciences*, 72, 479–487.

Fabbre, V. D. 2017b. "Queer Aging: Implications for Social Work Practice with LGBTQ Older Adults." *Social Work*, 62, 73–76.

Fabbre, V. D., and E. Gaveras. 2019. "The Manifestation of Multi-Level Stigma in the Lived Experiences of Transgender and Gender Nonconforming (TGNC) Older Adults." Unpublished manuscript.

Factor, R. J., and E. D. Rothblum. 2007. "A Study of Transgender Adults and Their Non-Transgender Siblings on Demographic Characteristics, Social Support, and Experiences of Violence." *Journal of LGBT Health Research*, 3, 11–30.

Goffman, E. (1963). *Stigma: Notes on the management of spoiled identity*. Englewood Cliffs, NJ: Prentice-Hall.

Feagin, J. R. 2014. *Racist America: Roots, Current Realities, and Future Reparations*. New York: Routledge.

Felitti, F., J. Vincent, M. Anda, F. Robert, D. Nordenberg, D. P. Williamson, F. David, M. Spitz, M. Alison, V. Edwards, M. Marks, and S. James. 1998. "Relationship of Childhood Abuse and Household Dysfunction to Many of the Leading Causes of Death in Adults: The Adverse Childhood Experiences (ACE) Study." *American Journal of Preventive Medicine*, 14, 245–258.

Gagne, P., and R. Tewksbury. 1998. "Conformity Pressures and Gender Resistance Among Transgendered Individuals." *Social Problems*, 45, 81–101.

Gilens, M. 1999. *Why Americans Hate Welfare: Race Media, and the Politics of Antipoverty Policy*. Chicago: University of Chicago Press.

Hatzenbuehler, M. L. 2011. "The Social Environment and Suicide Attempts in Lesbian, Gay, and Bisexual Youth." *Pediatrics*, 127, 896–903.

Hatzenbuehler, M. L., K. M. Keyes, and D. S. Hasin. 2009. "State-Level Policies and Psychiatric Morbidity in Lesbian, Gay, and Bisexual Populations." *American Journal of Public Health*, 99, 2275–2281.

Hatzenbuehler, M. L., and B. G. Link. 2014. "Introduction to the Special Issue on Structural Stigma and Health." *Social Science and Medicine*, 103, 1–6.

Hatzenbuehler, M. L., K. A. McLaughlin, K. M. Keyes, and D. S. Hasin. 2010. "The Impact of Institutional Discrimination on Psychiatric Disorders in Lesbian, Gay, and Bisexual Populations: A Prospective Study." *American Journal of Public Health*, 100, 452–459.

Hatzenbuehler, M. L., J. C. Phelan, and B. G. Link. 2013. "Stigma as a Fundamental Cause of Population Health Inequalities." *American Journal of Public Health*, 103, 813–821.

Hatzenbuehler, M. L., N. Slopen, and K. A. McLaughlin. 2014. "Stressful Life Events, Sexual Orientation, and Cardiometabolic Risk Among Young Adults in the United States." *Health Psychology*, 33, 1185–1194.

Hays, S. 2003. *Flat Broke with Children: Women in the Age of Welfare Reform*. New York: Oxford University Press.

Jencks, C. 2002. "Does Inequality Matter?" *Daedalus*, 131, 49–65.

Johnson, A. 2006. *Power, Privilege, and Difference*. St. Louis, MO: McGraw-Hill Higher Education.

Johnson, W., D. J. Pate, and J. Givens. 2010. *Big Boys Don't Cry, Black Boys Don't Feel: The Intersection of Shame and Worry on Community Violence and the Social Construction of Masculinity among Urban African American Males—The Case of Derrion Albert*. Berkeley: University of California Press.

Koken, J. A., D, S. Bimbi, and J. T. Parsons. 2009. "Experiences of Familial Acceptance–Rejection Among Transwomen of Color." *Journal of Family Psychology*, 23, 853–860.

Kondrat, M. E. 1999. "Who Is the Self in Self-Aware?" *Social Service Review*, 73, 451–477.

Levitas, R., C. Pantazis, E. Fahmy, D. Gordon, E. Lldoy, and D. Patsois. 2007. *The Multi-Dimensional Analysis of Social Exclusion*. Bristol, UK: University of Bristol.

Liang, L. 2018. "No Room for Respectability: Boundary Work in Interaction at a Shanghai Rental." *Symbolic Interaction*, 41, 185–209.

Link, B. G., and J. C. Phelan. 2001. "Conceptualizing Stigma." *Annual Review of Sociology*, 27, 363–385.

Link, B. G., and J. C. Phelan. 2014. "Stigma Power." *Social Science & Medicine*, 103, 24–32.

Lum, D. 2004. *Social Work Practice and People of Color: A Process Stage Approach*. Belmont, CA: Brooks Cole.

Lysaker, P. H., D. Roe, and P. T. Yanos. 2007. "Toward Understanding the Insight Paradox: Internalized Stigma Moderates the Association Between Insight and Social Functioning, Hope, and Self-Esteem Among People with Schizophrenia Spectrum Disorders." *Schizophrenia Bulletin*, 33, 192–199.

Maslow, A. H. 1968. *Toward a Psychology of Being*. New York: D. Van Nostrand Company.

McClure, A. 2017. "Becoming a Parent Changes Everything: How Nonbeliever and Pagan Parents Manage Stigma in the U.S. Bible Belt." *Qualitative Sociology*, 40, 331–352.

McIntosh, P. 1989. *White Privilege: Unpacking the Invisible Knapsack*. Peace and Freedom.

Miller, J. B. 1976. *Toward a New Psychology of Women*. Boston: Beacon Press.

Morgan, C., T. Burns, R. Fizpatrick, V. Pinfold, and S. Priebe. 2007. "Social Exclusion and Mental Health." *The British Journal of Psychiatry*, 191, 477–483.

Morgan, C., and G. Hutchinson. 2010. "The Social Determinants of Psychosis in Migrant and Ethnic Minority Populations: A Public Health Tragedy." *Psychological Medicine*, 40, 705–709.

Mullaly, B. 2007. *The New Structural Social Work*. 3rd ed. Don Mills, ON: Oxford University Press.

Nettleton, S. 2006. *The Sociology of Health and Illness*. Cambridge, Polity Press.

Oexle, N., and P. W. Corrigan. 2018. "Understanding Mental Illness Stigma Toward Persons with Multiple Stigmatized Conditions: Implications of Intersectionality Theory." *Psychiatric Services*, 69, 587–589.

Oexle, N., N. Rusch, S. Viering, C. Wyss, E. Seifritz, Z. Xu, and W. Kawohl. 2017. "Self-Stigma and Suicidality: A Longitudinal Study." *European Archives of Psychiatry and Clinical Neuroscience*, 267, 359–361.

Oluwoye, O., B. Stiles, M. Monroe-DeVita, L. Chwastiak, and J. McClellan. 2018. "Racial-Ethnic Disparities in First-Episode Psychosis Treatment Outcomes from the RAISE-ETP Study." *Psychiatric Services*, 69, 1138–1145

Paul, P. 2005. *Pornified: How Pornography Is Damaging Our Lives, Our Relationships, and Our Families*. New York: Henry Holt.

Pescosolido, B. A., and J. K. Martin. 2015. "The Stigma Complex." *Annual Review of Sociology*, 41, 87–116.

Phelan, J. C., B. G. Link, and J. F. Dovidio. 2008. "Stigma and Prejudice: One Animal or Two?" *Social Science & Medicine*, 67, 358–367.

Poteat, T., D. German, and D. Kerrigan. 2013. "Managing Uncertainty: A Grounded Theory of Stigma in Transgender Health Care Encounters." *Social Science & Medicine*, 84, 22–29.

Rank, M. R. 1994. *Living on the Edge: The Realities of Welfare in America*. New York: Columbia University Press.

Rank, M. R. 2004. *One Nation, Underprivileged: Why American Poverty Affects Us All*. New York: Oxford University Press.

Rank, M. R. 2011. "Rethinking American Poverty." *Contexts*, 10, 16–21.

Rank, M. R., T. A. Hirschl, and K. A. Foster. 2014. *Chasing the American Dream: Understanding What Shapes Our Fortunes*. New York: Oxford University Press.

Reiman, J. 2004. *The Rich Get Richer and the Poor Get Prison: Ideology, Class, and Criminal Justice*. Boston: Allyn and Bacon.

Reisner, S. L., K. J. Conron, L. A. Tardiff, S. Jarvi, A. R. Gordon, and S. B. Austin. 2014. "Monitoring the Health of Transgender and Other Gender Minority Populations: Validity of Natal Sex and Gender Identity Survey Items in a U.S. National Cohort of Young Adults." *BMC Public Health*, 14, 1224.

Reisner, S. L., E. E. Dunham, K. J. Heflin, J. Coffey-Esquivel, and S. Cahill. 2015. "Legal Protections in Public Accommodations Settings: A Critical Public Health Issue for Transgender and Gender-Nonconforming People." *The Milbank Quarterly*, 93, 484–515.

Rotondi, N. K., G. R. Bauer, K. Scanlon, M. Kaay, R. Travers, and A. Travers. 2011a. "Prevalence of and Risk and Protective Factors for Depression in Female-to-Male Transgender Ontarians: Trans PULSE Project." *Canadian Journal of Community Mental Health*, 30, 135–155.

Rotondi, N. K., G. R. Bauer, R. Travers, A. Travers, K. Scanlon and M. Kaay. 2011b. "Depression in Male-to-Female Transgender Ontarians: Results from the Trans PULSE Project." *Canadian Journal of Community Mental Health,* 30, 113–133.

Schwalbe, M., D. Holden, D. Schrock, S. Godwin, S. Thompson, and M. Wolkomir. 2000. "Generic Processes in the Reproduction of Inequality: An Interactionist Analysis." *Social Forces*, 79, 419–452.

Schwartz, R. C., and D. M. Blankenship. 2014. "Racial Disparities in Psychotic Disorder Diagnosis: A Review of Empirical Literature." *World Journal of Psychiatry*, 4, 130–140.

Seccombe, K. 1999. *So You Think I Drive a Cadillac? Welfare Recipients' Perspective on the System and Its Reform.* Needham Heights, MA: Allyn and Bacon.

Sen, A. 1999. *Development as Freedom.* New York: Knopf.

Sen, A. 2000. "Social Exclusion: Concept, Application, and Scrutiny." Social Development Papers No. 1: Office of Environment and Social Development, Asian Development Bank.

Simons, L., S. M. Schrager, L. F. Clark, M. Belzer, and J. Olson. 2013. "Parental Support and Mental Health Among Transgender Adolescents." *The Journal of Adolescent Health,* 53, 791–793.

Snelgrove, J. W., A. M. Jasudavisius, B. W. Rowe, E. M. Head, and G. R. Bauer. 2012. "'Completely Out-At-Sea' with 'Two-Gender Medicine': A Qualitative Analysis of Physician-Side Barriers to Providing Healthcare for Transgender Patients." *BMC Health Services Research,* 12, 110.

Stotzer, R. L. 2009. "Violence Against Transgender People: A Review of United States Data." *Aggression and Violent Behavior,* 14, 170–179.

White Hughto, J. M., S. L. Reisner, and J. E. Pachankis. 2015. "Transgender Stigma and Health: A Critical Review of Stigma Determinants, Mechanisms, and Interventions." *Social Science and Medicine,* 147, 222–231.

Yanos, P. T., D. Roe, K. Markus, and P. H. Lysaker. 2008. "Pathways Between Internalized Stigma and Outcomes Related to Recovery in Schizophrenia Spectrum Disorders." *Psychiatric Services,* 59, 1437–1442.

5

Reducing Cumulative Inequality

MARK ROBERT RANK

Perhaps the quintessential American board game is that of Monopoly. The objective of the game is to acquire properties, build houses and hotels, collect rent, make money, and eventually put the other players out of business. The rules themselves are straightforward. Normally, each player is given $1,500 at the start of the game. The playing field is in effect level, with each of the players' outcomes determined by the roll of the dice and by their own skills and judgments.

This notion of a level playing field is largely the way that we like to imagine the economic race in America is run. Each individual's outcome is determined by their own skill and effort and by taking advantage of what happens along the road of life. Our belief in equality of opportunity as a nation underlies this principle.

However, let us now imagine a modified game of Monopoly, in which the players start out with quite different advantages and disadvantages, much as they do in life. Player 1 begins with $5,000 and several Monopoly properties on which houses have already been built. Player 2 starts out with the standard $1,500 and no properties. Finally, Player 3 begins the game with only $250.

The question becomes who will be the winners and losers in this modified game of Monopoly? Both luck and skill are still involved, and the rules of the game remain the same, but given the differing sets of resources and assets that each player begins with, these become much less important in predicting the game's outcome. Certainly, it is possible for Player 1, with $5,000 to lose, and for Player 3, with $250, to win, but that is unlikely given the unequal allocation of money at the start of the game. Moreover, while Player 3 may win in any individual game, over the course of hundreds of games, the odds are that Player 1 will win considerably more often, even if Player 3 is much luckier and more skilled.

In addition, the way each of the three individuals are able to play the game will vary considerably. Player 1 is able to take greater chances and risks. If he or she makes several tactical mistakes, these probably will not matter much in the larger scheme of things. If Player 3 makes one such mistake, it may very well result in disaster. Player 1 will also be easily able to purchase properties and houses that Player 3 is largely locked out of, causing the rich to get richer and the poor to get poorer. These assets, in turn, will generate further income later in the game for Player 1 and in all likelihood will result in the bankrupting of Players 2 and 3.

Consequently, given the initial advantages or disadvantages at the start of the game, they result in additional advantages or disadvantages as the games progresses. These, in turn, will then lead to further advantages or disadvantages, and so the process goes.

This analogy illustrates the concept that Americans are not beginning their lives at the same starting point (see Rank, 1994, 2004; Rank, Hirschl, and Foster, 2014). But it also illustrates the cumulative process that compounds advantages or disadvantages over time. Differences in parental incomes and resources exert a major influence over children's ability to acquire valuable skills and education. These differences in human capital will, in turn, strongly influence how well children compete in the labor market, and therefore help to determine the extent of their economic success during the course of their lives.

In this chapter we explore this major barrier and determinant of a livable life—cumulative inequality. The argument is that as a result of the position one starts in life, particular advantages or disadvantages may be present. These initial advantages or disadvantages can then result in further advantages or disadvantages, producing a cumulative process in which inequalities are widened across the life course. This perspective has been used to understand various inequities and how they can multiply throughout a lifetime.

One of the earliest discussions addressing this topic was an analysis of scientific productivity by the sociologist Robert Merton. Merton (1968) argued that early recognition, placement, and advantage in the career of a young scientist often led to exponential gains and rewards over time, which, in turn, further solidified the status and reputation of the scientist. Scientists who did not experience these key early advantages (although they were often as capable) generally saw their careers stall and plateau. Merton described cumulative advantage as "the way in which initial comparative advantage of trained capacity, structural location, and available resources make for successive increments of advantages such that the gaps between the haves and the have-nots . . . widen" (1988: 606). Merton referred to this process as the Matthew Effect in science. Since Merton's initial discussions, this concept has been applied in a wide array of subjects, including differences in schooling, work and career opportunities, and overall health status (DiPrete and Eirich, 2006; Ermisch, Jantti, and Smeeding, 2012; Katz et al., 2005).

Of course, a much more familiar example of cumulative inequality is found in the classic 1939 song, *God Bless the Child*, written by Billie Holiday and Arthur Herzog Jr. The well-known verse goes, "Them that's got shall get, them that's not shall lose. So the Bible said, and it still is news." The dynamic of cumulative inequality has been observed and commented upon over a very long period of time.

We begin by outlining some of the more apparent ways in which cumulative inequality operates across the life course. Within these examples, we focus on two major fault lines in American society that are particularly poignant in illustrating cumulative advantage and disadvantage—class and race. These two factors exert a profound influence on people's life chances, and we examine how these factors play out across the life course. They allow some individuals to achieve a livable life while preventing many others from doing so. We then turn to why we should be concerned about this dynamic and, finally, what can be done to reduce such inequality.

The Process and Dynamics of Cumulative Inequality
The Geography of Disadvantage

We begin our exploration of cumulative inequality with a look at the types of neighborhoods that children grow up in, specifically with respect to race and income. The neighborhood a child is raised in can have a profound impact upon that child's future well-being and life chances, and the neighborhood one is brought up in is highly dependent upon a child's class and race. Growing up in a high poverty neighborhood can be particularly detrimental, whereas growing up in an affluent neighborhood often carries significant advantages (see Chapter 9 of this volume for a further discussion of neighborhood effects).

Over the past 30 years, researchers have focused on the economic well-being of the neighborhoods that individuals reside in as one way in which to describe and understand the nature of American poverty. The argument is that neighborhoods mired in poverty detrimentally affect all who reside in such communities, and are particularly harmful to children. For example, Paul Jargowsky poses the question, "Why should we be concerned with the spatial organization of poverty?" His answer is the following:

> The concentration of poor families and children in high-poverty ghettos, barrios, and slums magnifies the problems faced by the poor. Concentrations of poor people lead to a concentration of the so-cial ills that cause or are caused by poverty. Poor children in these

neighborhoods not only lack basic necessities in their own homes, but also they must contend with a hostile environment that holds many temptations and few positive role models. Equally important, school districts and attendance zones are generally organized geographically, so that the residential concentration of the poor frequently results in low-performing schools. (2003: 2)

Research indicates that even after controlling for individual income and race, children's well-being in high poverty neighborhoods suffers in many ways (Brooks-Gunn, Duncan, and Aber, 1997; Evans, 2004, 2006; Leventhal and Brooks-Gunn, 2000; Pattillo and Robinson, 2016). For example, Margery Turner and Deborah Kaye found that, independent of individual characteristics, "as a neighborhood's poverty rate rises, so too does the likelihood of negative behavior among young children, of being expelled from school, of negative school engagement, of lack of involvement in activities, of not being read to or taken on outings, of living in a family with no full-time workers, and of having a caretaker who is aggravated or in poor mental health" (2006: 20).

This neighborhood context of poverty has been particularly significant in the seminal work of William Julius Wilson (1987, 1996, 2009), Douglas Massey (2007, 2016; Massey and Denton, 1993), and Robert Sampson (Sampson et al., 1997; Sampson and Morenoff, 2006). Their research has shown that children growing up in high poverty neighborhoods suffer from many disadvantages as a result of geographical residence. In addition, the children impacted by these negative effects are often children of color due to the long-established patterns of residential racial segregation in American cities (Charles, 2003; Farley, 2008; Fischer, 2003; Wilson, 2016).

The opposite is generally true for children growing up in middle-class or affluent neighborhoods. Here we often find an environment that is likely to facilitate individual growth and development. Such neighborhoods are characterized by good schools, low crime, plentiful recreational facilities, quality housing, and so on. The result is a strong foundation upon which children are able to develop their potential.

In addition, research has indicated that there has been a rise in residential segregation on the basis of income over the last 30 years (Reardon and Bischoff, 2011). Douglas Massey discussed this growing trend in his often quoted 1995 presidential address to the Population Association of America entitled, "The Age of Extremes: Concentrated Affluence and Poverty in the Twenty First Century" (Massey, 1996). Massey noted that the separation of the haves from the have-nots was becoming wider and would likely continue to do so into the future. Consequently, growing up in high poverty neighborhoods is a significant disadvantage and represents a starting point for cumulative disadvantage, just as growing up in an affluent neighborhood is a significant advantage.

As troubling as these findings are with respect to the racial/ethnic divide in neighborhood poverty, what is perhaps more troubling is evidence indicating that mobility out of such neighborhoods, particularly for racial minorities, is limited. Lincoln Quillian (2003) has shown that for black residents living in high poverty census tracts (40 percent or more poverty), nearly 50 percent were still residing in a high poverty census tract 10 years later. Even more disturbing, Patrick Sharkey (2008) found that 72 percent of black children growing up in the poorest quarter of American neighborhoods remained in the poorest quarter of neighborhoods as adults. Consequently, the effects of neighborhood poverty upon children of color are typically prolonged and long lasting.

Furthermore, because black homeowners are more likely to buy homes later than whites and to purchase homes in lower-income neighborhoods, the amount of home equity that they have built up is substantially less than in the white population. The result is that in 2016, overall median net worth for whites was $171,000, whereas for blacks it was $17,600 (Federal Reserve Bank, 2017). This ten to one difference in wealth then has a further cumulative effect on the life chances and well-being of children.

The work of Raj Chetty and colleagues has also demonstrated the profound effect of the neighborhood one is raised in upon future life chances (Chetty and Hendren, 2018; Chetty et al., 2017). Chetty has shown that there are wide differences in upward mobility depending on the neighborhood in which one is raised in. Children growing up in disadvantaged neighborhoods are much less likely to experience economic upward mobility than children growing up in economically thriving neighborhoods, even after taking into account individual socioeconomic and demographic differences.

In addition, children raised in neighborhoods marked by high poverty are much more likely to encounter a variety of environmental health hazards (see Chapter 10 of this volume). These include elevated exposure to various toxic pollutants, greater likelihood of being victimized by crime and violence, higher arrest rates, increased risk of substance abuse, greater exposure to sexually transmitted diseases, and so on (Drake and Rank, 2009). All of these can detrimentally affect a child's health, which, in turn, can have a profound impact upon that child's health and economic well-being as an adult (Case and Paxson, 2006).

Similarly, as we will discuss in the next section, children living in high poverty neighborhoods are quite likely to be attending educationally inferior neighborhood schools. Financing for public schools in the United States is largely drawn from local property tax revenues, resulting in poorer districts having a much smaller tax base to draw upon than wealthier districts. As Steven Durlauf notes, "despite the existence of state and federal programs to assist less affluent school districts, the role of local public finance in education produces large disparities in educational expenditure across school districts" (2006: 146). The result is that schools in low income neighborhoods often find that their "teachers are frequently underpaid and over stressed, the physical facilities may be severely deteriorated and outdated, class sizes are often quite large, as well as many other disadvantages" (Rank, 2004: 207). Such schools have been shown to produce lower levels of academic achievement among children than if those same children were attending schools with less poverty and more educational resources (Leventhal and Brooks-Gunn, 2000). In addition, research has shown that the socioeconomic status of one's classmates has an important influence on a child's educational achievement, independent of that child's individual economic background (Kahlenberg, 2002).

Finally, as noted earlier, substantial ethnographic and empirical research has indicated that friends and peers who are impoverished can exert a negative influence upon fostering a range of counterproductive attitudes and behaviors among children and adolescents. These include lower academic aspirations and achievement, greater likelihood of teenage pregnancy, increased chances of engaging in illegal activities, and so on (Durlauf 2001, 2006). The result of all this is that such children carry with them a significant disadvantage as they move through the educational system and into the labor market.

Schools and Education

Travel to any U.S. city and you are likely to observe a similar pattern over and over again. Begin your trip with a drive out to an affluent suburb. The schools you encounter there are likely to be impressive with respect to their physical facilities, the quality of their instruction, and the depth of their curriculum. Next, turn the car around and drive into a poor neighborhood, perhaps in the central city, and there you are likely to see quite the opposite—decaying schools, demoralized faculty, and districts facing a loss of accreditation. Finally, take a much further drive out into the remote countryside and you may discover a school district with the fewest resources of all.

Right outside the door of my home such patterns can be easily found. Within a ten-minute drive is a highly regarded public high school in an affluent school district. In that district, the average amount of money spent per pupil is around $16,000. The education that students receive is among the best in the nation's public schools. Drive a few minutes further, and you may notice a private high school that could very well be mistaken for a small university campus. There the spending per pupil averages out to $30,000. The quality and options of courses offered to students is almost unlimited. Finally, travel 20 minutes in the opposite direction and you will reach a high school that is literally falling apart, where the average money spent per pupil is around $9,000. The school district has lost its accreditation, and its students are nearly all poor and children of color.

In each of these different schools we find American children, all in the same metropolitan area, yet it is clear that some are entitled to a first-rate education, while others are not. To say that these children are experiencing equality of opportunity or a level playing field is simply absurd. Rather, cumulative inequality is clearly operating within the system of education that we have in the United States. Where one lives and the size of one's parent's pocketbook largely determine the quality of education that children will receive. Over three decades ago, Jonathan Kozal referred to this situation as the "savage inequalities" of America.

Unfortunately, it is as true today, if not more so, than it was 25 years ago. A report by the U.S. Department of Education begins with the following statement, "While some young Americans—most of them white and affluent—are getting a truly world-class education, those who attend school in high poverty neighborhoods are getting an education that more closely approximates schools in developing countries" (2013: 12).

One reason for this is the way that public education is funded in this county. The United States is one of the very few industrialized countries where the bulk of funding for public schools comes from state and local tax dollars rather than from the federal government. In particular, the overall value of real estate in a school district is a key determinant of the amount of resources that district will have available. Consequently, children living in lower-income neighborhoods tend to be enrolled in schools with far fewer resources and a lower quality of instruction than children living in well to do neighborhoods (Hannum and Xie, 2016).

In their book, *The American Dream and the Public Schools,* Jennifer Hochschild and Nathan Scovronick note,

> School district boundaries help to provide such an advantage when they follow neighborhood lines that separate wealthy children from those who are poor and often nonwhite; school financing schemes have this effect when they are based on local property value and thereby create or maintain a privileged competitive position for wealthier children at the expense of the others. Tracking provides advantages when the best teachers or the most resources are devoted to a high track disproportionately filled with wealthier students. (2003: 12–13)

Research also indicates that since the mid-1970s, schools have actually become more segregated on the basis of race and income. For example, in the 2002–2003 school year, 73 percent of black students nationally were attending schools in which 50 percent or more of their fellow students were minorities, while 38 percent of black students were in schools in which 90 percent or more of their fellow students were minorities. The comparable percentages for Latino students were 77 percent and 38 percent (Orfield and Lee, 2005). Schools that are predominately minority are also highly skewed in the direction of poverty and low income (Orfield and Lee, 2005). Rather than reducing the differences and disadvantages that some children face, the structure of schooling in the United States further increases and exacerbates those differences. As Hochschild and Scovronick state,

> Public schools are essential to make the American dream work, but schools are also the arena in which many Americans first fail. Failure there almost certainly guarantees failure from then on. In the dream, failure results from lack of individual merit and effort; in reality, failure in school too closely tracks structures of racial and class inequality. Schools too often reinforce rather than contend against the intergenerational paradox at the heart of the American dream. (2003: 5)

The intergenerational paradox that Hochschild and Scovronick refer to is that "inequalities in family wealth are a major cause of inequality in schooling, and inequalities of schooling do much to reinforce inequalities of wealth among families in the next generation – that is the intergenerational paradox" (2003: 23). Indeed, research has shown that the amount of education and wealth of parents is highly correlated with the educational levels achieved by their children (Ermisch, Jantti, and Smeeding, 2012; Shapiro, 2004).

The cumulative advantages and disadvantages at the K through 12 level, become further extended into the likelihood of graduating from high school and then completing a college degree. Children from wealthier families are often able to attend top-flight private universities, children from middle-class backgrounds frequently enroll at public universities, while children from lower-class backgrounds will probably not continue on to college at all, or if they do, are likely to attend a community or two-year college. As Daniel McMurrer and Isabel Sawhill note, "Family background has a significant and increasing effect on who goes to college, where, and for how long. With the reward for going to college greater than ever, and family background now a stronger influence over who reaps those rewards, the United States is at risk of becoming more class stratified in coming decades" (1998: 69).

In summarizing the research on education, neighborhood, and income, Greg Duncan and Richard Marmame state, "As the incomes of affluent and poor American families have diverged over the past three decades, so too has the educational performance of the children in these families. Test score differences between rich and poor children are much larger now than thirty years ago, as are differences in rates of college attendance and college graduation" (2011: 15). Unfortunately, it appears that we may be moving even further afield of a level playing surface when it comes to education.

Jobs and Careers

The process of cumulative advantage and disadvantage continues on after one's formal education is completed. The amount and quality of education that an individual receives are key determinants in locating and attaining a well-paying job and profession, or conversely, working at a dead-end, low-paying job, or no job at all. As Arne Kalleberg writes, "Although educational attainment cannot guarantee a good job, higher levels of education make acquiring a better job more likely, and the lack of education is certainly a major disadvantage in the new labor market (2011: 80).

A simple way of observing this is with the latest U.S. Census numbers on median income by level of education for those over the age of 25. In 2018, median income was $25,318 for those with less than nine years of education; $25,280 for those with some amount of high school; $35,016 for high school graduates; $37,811 for those with some college; $57,105 for college graduates; and $70,241 for those with a master's degree (U.S. Bureau of the Census, 2019). From these figures it is quite easy to see that greater levels of education translates into greater levels of income.

The relationship between education and the risk of poverty is just as strong. For individuals who have not completed high school, their overall rate of poverty in 2018 was 25.9 percent; 12.7 percent for high school graduates; 8.4 percent for those with some college; and 4.4 percent for college graduates (U.S. Bureau of the Census, 2019). Consequently, the cumulative advantage or disadvantage of being able to acquire various levels of education is directly related to earnings in the prime working years.

Furthermore, the quality and type of job that one works at is also highly dependent upon the quantity and quality of one's education. Those who fail to graduate from high school are often locked into a series of dead-end, less stable jobs throughout their working career (Smith, 2016). On the other hand, those with a college or advanced degree are much more likely to find themselves in a well-paying and rewarding professional career that includes various benefits. Consequently, the cumulative advantages and disadvantages that begin with childhood and neighborhood, continue through adolescence and early adulthood with educational differences and are then further extended into the prime working years through occupational sorting.

Kalleberg argues that these educational and skill differences have become even more important in today's economy. As he writes,

> [D]ifferences in education and skill levels increasingly separate those workers who have good jobs from those who have bad jobs. . . . While more-educated and higher-skilled workers may not necessarily have more job security with a particular employer, their more marketable skills enhance their labor market security, which, in turn, generally provides them with higher earnings, greater control over their jobs, higher intrinsic rewards, and better-quality jobs overall. (2011: 181)

For African Americans and other minorities, a series of subtle and not so subtle acts of discrimination in the job market serve to intensify the effect of cumulative disadvantage. Such acts of discrimination have been demonstrated in a multitude of court cases and research studies (Feagin, 2010). One of the best known of the recent analyses was conducted by two economists, Marianne Bertrand and Sendhil Mullainathan (2003). The researchers sent out similar resumes to various job ads in Chicago and Boston. The one difference was that some of the resumes had "white-sounding" names, while the others had "black-sounding names." Even though the resumes were virtually identical, the white-sounding name resumes were 50 percent more likely to be contacted by the employer than the black-sounding name resumes. This and many other studies have clearly shown that discrimination on the basis of race and ethnicity is alive and well in the job market and consequently influences the process of cumulative inequality.

Health Disparities

A further cumulative advantage and disadvantage that stems from these prior processes is the combined effect that educational background and current socioeconomic status have upon overall health and well-being (see Chapter 2 of this volume). Beginning with the groundbreaking results from the Whitehall studies in England during the 1960s and 1970s, one of the most consistent findings in epidemiology has been the strong relationship between health and socioeconomic status. The lower the socioeconomic status (and particularly poverty), the more significant are the detrimental effects upon health (Angel, 2016; Leidenfrost, 1993; Pappas et al., 1993). Conversely, the higher the socioeconomic status, the greater the positive impact on health. This relationship has been replicated in hundreds of studies over the years (Wilkinson and Pickett, 2009). In addition, race has been found to have an additional independent effect upon health status.

African Americans, Hispanics, and Native Americans are more likely to suffer from various health problems, even after taking into account socioeconomic status, than are whites (Wilkinson, 2005).

The process begins early. Research has demonstrated that the physical and mental well-being of children is strongly affected by socioeconomic status. Children living in lower socioeconomic status households are more likely to experience a range of health problems than children in higher socioeconomic status households (Schiller, 2008). Perhaps most insidious is that children in lower-income households are much more likely to be exposed to lead poisoning.

Poverty and low income are further associated with a host of health risks across the adulthood years, from elevated rates of heart disease to significant dental problems (Rank, 2004). The result is a much higher death rate and shortened life expectancy (Geronimus et al., 2001). For example, Americans in the top 5 percent of the income distribution can expect to live approximately nine years longer than those in the bottom 10 percent (Jencks, 2002). Moreover, in many metropolitan areas, differences in residency based upon zip code may produce a difference in life expectancy of up to 25 years.

Older Adults

As a result of the dynamics of cumulative inequality across the life course, by the time individuals have reached retirement, these differences are often magnified, leaving many groups in dire financial and emotional straits. Take the case of retirement savings. The amount one is able to accrue in a retirement account is largely dependent upon the types of occupations that one has been employed in across a career. Individuals in good-paying jobs with generous benefits are often able to build a 401(k) account with a matching dollar amount from their employer. In other cases (although this has been in sharp decline) individuals might be able to work toward a pension, resulting in a guaranteed monthly income during their retirement.

In addition, the amount that one eventually receives from Social Security is largely dependent on the amount contributed across the working years. Individuals in higher-paying jobs will have had greater deductions and therefore will receive more in Social Security when they retire.

On the other hand, those with fewer years of education and skills will generally find themselves in lower-paying jobs across the working years. As a result, they are less likely to have an adequate retirement savings plan or pension and have undoubtedly contributed much less into Social Security than their more fortunate counterparts. The result is that for a sizeable percentage of the population, very little in assets and savings is waiting for them when they reach retirement (Federal Reserve Bank, 2018). To illustrate, it is estimated that 21 percent of the retired population in 2018 have retirement savings less than $5,000 (Transamerica Center for Retirement Studies, 2018).

In this fashion, the process of cumulative inequality plays out in the final years. A history of cumulative advantage or disadvantage affects the extent to which individuals will be able to enjoy the later stages of life. Cumulative disadvantage produces a final indignity in the lives of those who must face its full impact.

Why Care?

The issue of cumulative inequality and its solutions have perplexed philosophers for centuries. This dynamic has long been recognized as a primary reason for inequalities throughout life. For example, the concept of the Jubilee year from the Old Testament reflected this. According to the verses of Leviticus, after every 50 years, all property, land, and property rights were to be reallocated along with the forgiving of debts. Philosophers and theologians since ancient times have been concerned and debated the fairness and possible remedies to cumulative inequality.

There are many reasons why we should be concerned about cumulative inequality in our current age. To start, it significantly undermines the idea of a level playing field that social workers have strived for in their research, practice, and policy work. As noted in the introductory chapter, the concept of social justice is frequently interpreted as having a society where the playing field is level, and, as a result, individuals are able to reach their potential.

This is closely tied to the historical emphasis in the United States upon the importance of equality of opportunity. The premise is that all should be entitled to certain basic opportunities that allow individuals to get ahead in life. These include a quality education, open access to the job and housing markets, and so on. For America to live up to its moniker of the "land of opportunity," these conditions must be met.

The existence of cumulative disadvantage clearly undermines these core values. It prevents individuals from being able to achieve their full potential, while at the same time it undermines the belief in equality of opportunity. Both of these erode the ability of individuals and families to truly lead a livable life.

However, just as important is a powerful argument rooted in economics. By allowing a significant portion of the population to be undervalued and underinvested in, all of society pays the price. Consequently, it is in each of our own self-interests to be concerned and proactive in addressing this dynamic. This sense of a broad awareness of the costs of cumulative inequality can be referred to as enlightened self-interest. That is, by becoming aware of the various costs associated with cumulative inequality or, conversely, the various benefits associated with the reduction of cumulative inequality, we begin to realize that it is in our own self-interest to confront this problem.

In a recent analysis, Michael McLaughlin and Mark Rank (2018) attempted to place a dollar value on the cost of this dynamic (also discussed in Chapter 3 of this volume). They focused on measuring the long-term economic costs of childhood poverty in the United States. These long-term costs included worse health, lower economic productivity, and higher costs associated with crime. All of these can be understood within the framework of cumulative disadvantage. Children growing up in poverty experience a variety of disadvantages, resulting in greater numbers of health problems, being less economically productive during their working careers, and more likely to engage in crime.

While cumulative disadvantage clearly bears a heavy burden upon the individual, this research indicated that it also bears a burden upon society as a whole. McLaughlin and Rank (2018) estimated that the annual aggregate cost of childhood poverty was slightly over $1 trillion. To put this into perspective, the total federal budget for 2015 was $3.7 trillion. Consequently, the annual cost of childhood poverty represented 28 percent of the entire budget for 2015. In addition, the authors estimated that for every dollar spent on reducing childhood poverty, the country would save at least $7 with respect to the cumulative costs of poverty.

This research is but one of a series of analyses that have demonstrated that in the long run, prevention on the front end of a problem is a much more cost-effective policy than attempting to address the repercussions of a problem on the back end. Policy work has long showed the advantages of being proactive when it comes to issues such as poverty and health. The same is clearly true with respect to cumulative inequality. In the long run, it is in all of our self-interests to address the root causes of cumulative inequality.

Addressing Cumulative Inequality

How then do we open up the avenues of opportunity to all Americans such that we reduce some of the insidious effects of cumulative inequality? Obviously, it is impossible to eliminate all such advantages and disadvantages. Nevertheless, we can move to temper their most glaring effects and therefore begin to level the playing field.

The first and most obvious solution is to ensure that every child in the United States receives the resources that they need to thrive. This begins at pregnancy with good medical care and nutrition for the mother. It continues at birth with quality health care and resources for infants and toddlers.

Once again, research has shown that these policies save money in the long run. For example, for every dollar spent on children's nutrition programs, it is estimated that $3 to $4 are saved in future health care costs. Gosta Esping-Andersen in reviewing this research notes, "Here we arrive at a crucial finding of recent research: very early child investments matter most. What happens in the earliest years, especially in the preschool ages, is decisive for children's subsequent school success, and the effects persist into adulthood" (2007: 25).

Second, high-quality and affordable child care that is accessible to all parents is essential. The United States is one of the few developed countries that does not provide this type of child care to all of its children. We can learn much from countries such as France and Sweden, which have led the way in providing quality and affordable child care to all (Collins, 2019).

Next, a first-class education is essential. This would begin with pre-K programs through elementary, middle, and high school. It is simply wrong and shortsighted not to ensure such a policy. As we discussed earlier, the vast differences in the quality of education are largely the result of the way schooling is funded in the United States. Local property taxes provide the bulk of the funding, which results in wide discrepancies in the resources and quality of instruction across school districts. Creative and innovative ideas for changing the funding schemes of public schools are necessary (U.S. Department of Education, 2013).

Beyond K through 12, access to college, community college, and technical and trade schools should be made more available and affordable, especially to lower-income youth. These provide the skills and training necessary to compete in today's changing economy. Government assistance programs such as Pell grants are essential for opening up higher education to disadvantaged young adults.

One strategy that can make higher education more affordable, particularly for lower-income children, is that of Children's Development Accounts (see Chapter 6 of this volume). This idea has been gaining traction in various parts of the world and is designed to provide an initial governmental sum of money at a child's birth that can be used for education. As the child ages, the parents are expected to put in amounts of funds, which are then matched by the government. The matching and funding is more generous for lower-income children than for middle-income children. When children reach college age, they are then able to tap into this source of income to support their college education costs (Elliot and Sherraden, 2013).

The investment in children's health, education, and skills is a wise investment. It is also fundamental to ensuring that more children are able to compete fairly and achieve the American Dream. By doing so we create a virtuous cycle where our population is more innovative and skilled, which in turn creates more opportunities and quality jobs in the future.

Connected to this is the importance of reinvesting and reinvigorating poverty stricken and economically depressed neighborhoods (see Chapter 9 of this volume). As we have shown, the quality of a neighborhood that a child experiences can have a profound influence upon shaping their life course. The authors in Chapter 9 of this volume provide us with many excellent ideas and proposals for building healthy, diverse, and thriving communities.

Reducing and eliminating patterns of adult racial discrimination is also a key area of policy intervention with respect to opening up the avenues of opportunity and alleviating the impact of cumulative disadvantage. Substantial research has demonstrated that such discrimination continues in both the labor market and housing market. Targeting and reducing the lingering patterns of discrimination found in both the occupational structure and housing market is essential. Vigilant enforcement of fair housing laws and antidiscrimination policies in the work place are essential for breaking down decades of discriminatory practices (Stainback and Tomaskovic-Devey, 2012).

Finally, we can do much to bolster the wages and benefits of those who are working at low-wage jobs. At least three basic strategies should be adopted to strengthen their working conditions (also see Chapter 3 of this volume). First, the minimum wage should be raised and indexed each year to the rate of inflation. Because raising the minimum wage is dependent upon passage of Congress, it tends to be many years before it is increased. Raising the minimum wage to a livable wage, and then indexing it to the Consumer Price Index, would allow for a much more reasonable floor that full-time workers would not fall below. The minimum wage, as it stands today, is inadequate to pull a family of three out of poverty if there is only one wage earner working full time. This is a situation that can and should be corrected.

A second approach is to supplement the wages of those at the bottom of the income distribution through the tax structure. The primary program to accomplish this is the Earned Income Tax Credit (EITC). The EITC provides a refundable tax credit primarily to families with children who are working but earning below a certain income level. This provides an important source of income and hence greater economic security to these families. It is designed to both encourage work and to provide needed income to those who are working at jobs whose pay is inadequate. One of the problems with the EITC, however, is that it does very little to help single individuals without children who are working. The EITC should be expanded so that it provides assistance to both families with and without children.

A third key strategy for assisting those in low-wage jobs has been the recent health care reforms, which are a step in the right direction with respect to all workers being able to have health care coverage. This has long been a serious problem and is partially corrected with the full implementation of the Affordable Care Act in 2014. Consequently, those who are working at low-wage jobs should be able to obtain health care coverage at a reasonable cost.

With all of these proposals comes the key question of how do we pay for them? We would argue that it is time for a serious discussion regarding changing both the current tax rates and our budget priorities. The United States currently has among the lowest tax rates for high-income earners among the group of OECD countries. In addition, the United States spends far more on defense spending and national security than any other country in the world. Although it has been politically unpopular to discuss raising taxes, it is time to seriously consider tax restructuring and particularly raising personal and corporate taxes on the higher end. Up until Ronald Reagan's election in 1980, tax rates at the top of the income distribution were considerably higher, well over 80 percent. There is no need to return to such rates, but some reasonable increase is clearly warranted.

Likewise, we need to reassess our budget and spending priorities. The issue of investing in the human capital of all of our future citizens must be given a very high priority. As we continue to engage and complete within a global economy, it is vitally important that we invest in our most valuable resource— our children. We simply do not have the luxury of neglecting and harming significant portions of our population. This is clearly a matter of both national security and social justice. As such, this must become one of our highest priorities.

Conclusion

We began this chapter with the analogy of an altered game of Monopoly representing the process of cumulative inequality. Rather than everyone starting the game with a similar set of resources, Americans in fact have access to a widely different set of opportunities and advantages, which, in turn, leads to further advantages or disadvantages. In particular, class and race are fundamental dividing lines in American society. They also represent significant dividing lines in many other countries as well.

The process begins with the financial resources of parents and the neighborhood a child is raised in. This then affects the quality of schooling a child receives, which then influences the type of job and career that they acquire and work at. All of these, in turn, can affect the quality of health an individual experiences, along with how well one is prepared for the retirement years.

We should note that these cumulative patterns of inequality have only accentuated over recent times. The three players in our Monopoly analogy are now starting at even more disparate levels of initial resources than in our example. Levels of income and wealth inequality are at an all-time high. Not since the Gilded Age have we seen such extreme levels of inequality (Saaz, 2019). The top 1 percent of the population currently hold 46 percent of the country's entire financial wealth, while the bottom 60 percent of the population hold less than 1 percent of such wealth (Wolff, 2017). These wide discrepancies in assets have greatly accentuated the process of cumulative inequality.

Or take the distance between an average worker's salary and that of an average CEO of an S&P 500 Index company. In 1980, the average CEO earned around 42 times what the average worker earned. By 2017, this distance had ballooned to 361 times (Executive Paywatch, 2018). Furthermore, an average worker today is much less likely to have the benefits that they might have had 40 or 50 years ago. Health insurance, pensions, sick leave, job security, and many other benefits have been increasingly harder to come by (Hacker, 2006).

These macro-economic changes have accentuated the impact of cumulative inequality upon the course of individuals' lives. Within the United States, there has always been a clear distinction made between equality of opportunity versus equality of outcome. The belief has been that inequalities of outcomes are acceptable as long as equality of opportunities exists. However, what we have failed to recognize is that inequality of outcomes produce inequality of opportunities. This is the process that we have been discussing in this chapter. The wide economic differences in where children are starting life, leads to widely varying opportunities as they grow and develop. These, in turn, profoundly affect the trajectory of their life course.

As we strive toward the goal of a livable life for all, it is imperative that we alter this path of widening inequality. Social workers have a vital role to play in addressing these inequities. Through their practice and research, social workers see this process play out on a daily basis. They must use their clinical, organizing, and policy skills to effectively intervene in the process. Grassroots efforts around the country and world have shown that such efforts can indeed have an impact. To give but one example, the Fight for 15 has been successful in both raising the awareness around the struggles of low-wage workers and in spearheading various state and city initiatives around the country to raise the minimum wage.

A livable life is one in which there is a real promise of personal growth and progress in the future. It is one in which each individual is able to reach their full potential. Largely because of cumulative inequality, this is too often an illusion for too many. The time has come to address this glaring obstacle preventing millions from experiencing a livable life.

References

Angel, R. J. 2016. "Social Class, Poverty, and the Unequal Burden of Illness." *The Oxford Handbook of the Social Science of Poverty.* Edited by D. Brady and L. M. Burton. New York: Oxford University Press, pp. 660–683.

Bertrand, M., and S. Mullainathan. 2003. "Are Emily and Greg More Employable Than Lakisha and Jamal? A Field Experiment on Labor Market Discrimination." NBER Working Paper Series, Working Paper 9873, National Bureau of Economic Research.

Brooks-Gunn, J., G. J. Duncan, and J. L. Aber. 1997. *Neighborhood Poverty: Context and Consequences for Children.* New York: Russell Sage Foundation.

Case, A., and C. Paxson. 2006. "Children's Health and Social Mobility." *Future of Children,* 16, 151–173.

Charles, C. Z. 2003. "The Dynamics of Racial Residential Segregation." *Annual Review of Sociology,* 29, 167–207.

Chetty, R., D. Grusky, M. Hell, N. Hendren, R. Manduca, and J. Narang. 2017. "The Fading American Dream: Trends in Absolute Income Mobility Since 1940." *Science,* 356, 398–406.

Chetty, R., and N. Hendren. 2018. "The Impacts of Neighborhoods on Intergenerational Mobility II: County-Level Estimates." *The Quarterly Journal of Economics,* 133, 1163–1228.

Collins, C. 2019. *Making Motherhood Work: How Women Manage Careers and Caregiving.* Princeton, NJ: Princeton University Press.

DiPrete, T. A., and G. M. Eirich. 2006. "Cumulative Advantage as a Mechanism for Inequality: A Review of Theoretical and Empirical Developments." *Annual Review of Sociology,* 32, 271–297.

Drake, B., and M. R. Rank. 2009. "The Racial Divide Among American Children in Poverty: Reassessing the Importance of Neighborhood." *Children and Youth Services Review,* 31, 1264–1271.

Duncan, G. J., and R. J. Marmame. 2011. *Whither Opportunity? Rising Inequality, Schools, and Children's Life Chances.* New York: Russell Sage Foundation.

Durlauf, S. N. 2001. "The Membership Theory of Poverty: The Role of Group Affiliations in Determining Socioeconomic Status." *Understanding Poverty.* Edited by S. H. Danziger and R. H. Haveman. New York: Russell Sage Foundation, pp. 392–416.

Durlauf, S. N. 2006. "Groups, Social Influences, and Inequality." *Poverty Traps.* Edited by S. Bowles, S. N. Durlauf, and K. Hoff. New York: Russell Sage Foundation, pp. 141–175.

Elliot, W., and M. Sherraden. 2013. "Assets and Educational Achievement: Theory and Evidence." *Economics of Education Review,* 33, 1–7.

Ermish, J., M. Jantti, and T. Smeeding. 2012. *From Parents to Children: The Intergenerational Transmission of Advantage.* New York: Russell Sage Foundation.

Esping-Andersen, G. 2007. "Equal Opportunities and the Welfare State." *Contexts,* 6, 23–27.

Evans, G. W. 2004. "The Environment of Childhood Poverty." *American Psychologist,* 59, 77–92.

Evans, G. W. 2006. "Child Development and the Physical Environment." *Annual Review of Psychology,* 57, 423–451.

Executive Paywatch. 2018. "Executive Paywatch Report for 2017." AFL/CIO.

Farley, J. E. 2008. "Even Whiter Than We Thought: What Median Residential Exposure Indices Reveal About While Neighborhood Contact with African Americans' in US Metropolitan Areas." *Social Science Research,* 37, 604–623.

Feagin, J. R. 2010. *Racist America: Roots, Current Realities, and Future Reparations.* New York: Routledge.

Federal Reserve Bank. 2017. "Recent Trends in Wealth-Holding by Race and Ethnicity: Evidence from the Survey of Consumer Finances." FEDS Notes, Sept. 27, 2017

Federal Reserve Bank. 2018. *Report on the Economic Well-Being of U.S. Households in 2017.* Washington DC: Board of Governors of the Federal Reserve System.

Fischer, M. J. 2003. "The Relative Importance of Income and Race in Determining Residential Outcomes in U.S. Urban Areas, 1970–2000. *Urban Affairs Review*, 38, 669–696.

Geronimus, A. T., J. Bound, T. A. Waldmann, C. G. Colen, and D. Steffick. 2001. "Inequality in Life Expectancy, Functional Status, and Active Life Expectancy across Selected Black and White Populations in the United States." *Demography*, 38, 227–251.

Hacker, J. S. 2006. *The Great Risk Shift*. New York: Oxford University Press.

Hannum, E., and Y. Xie. 2016. "Education." *The Oxford Handbook of the Social Science of Poverty*. Edited by D. Brady and L. M. Burton. New York: Oxford University Press, pp. 462–485.

Hochschild, J., and N. Scovronick. 2003. *The American Dream and the Public Schools*. New York: Oxford University Press.

Jargowsky, P. A. 2003. "Stunning Progress, Hidden Problems: The Dramatic Decline of Concentrated Poverty in the 1990's." *The Living Cities Census Series*, May 2003, The Brookings Institution.

Jencks, C. 2002. "Does Inequality Matter?" *Daedalus*, 131, 49–65.

Kahlenberg, R. D. 2002. "Economic School Integration: An Update." Century Foundation Issue Brief Series, Century Foundation, New York.

Kalleberg, A. L. 2011. *Good Jobs, Bad Jobs: The Rise of Polarized and Precarious Employment Systems in the United States, 1970s to 2000s*. New York: Russell Sage Foundation.

Katz, M. B., M. J. Stern, and J. J. Fadler. 2005. "The New African American Inequality." *Journal of American History*, 92, 75–108.

Leidenfrost, N. B. 1993. "An Examination of the Impact of Poverty on Health." Report prepared for the Extension Service, U.S. Department of Agriculture.

Leventhal, T. and J. Brooks-Gunn. 2000. "The Neighborhoods They Live In: The Effects of Neighborhood Residence on Child and Adolescent Outcomes." *Psychological Bulletin*, 126, 309–337.

Massey, D. S. 1996. "The Age of Extremes: Concentrated Affluence and Poverty in the Twenty-First Century." *Demography*, 33, 395–412.

Massey, D. S. 2007. *Categorically Unequal: The American Stratification System*. New York: Russell Sage Foundation.

Massey, D. S. 2016. "Segregation and the Perpetuation of Disadvantage." *The Oxford Handbook of the Social Science of Poverty*. Edited by D. Brady and L. M. Burton. New York: Oxford University Press, pp. 369–394.

Massey, D. S., and N. A. Denton. 1993. *American Apartheid: Segregation and the Making of the Underclass*. Cambridge, MA: Harvard University Press.

McLaughlin, M., and M. R. Rank. 2018. "Estimating the Economic Cost of Childhood Poverty in the United States." *Social Work Research*, 42, 73–83.

McMurrer, D. P., and I. V. Sawhill. 1998. *Getting Ahead: Economic and Social Mobility in America*. Washington, DC: Urban Institute Press.

Merton, R. K. 1968. "The Matthew Effect in Science: The Reward and Communication System of Science." *Science*, 199, 55–63

Merton, R. K. 1988. "The Matthew Effect in Science, II: Cumulative Advantage and the Symbolism of Intellectual Property." *ISIS*, 79, 606–623.

Orfield, G., and C. Lee. 2005. "Why Segregation Matters: Poverty and Educational Inequality." The Civil Rights Project, Harvard University.

Pappas G., S. Queen, W. Hadden, and G. Fisher. 1993. "The Increasing Disparity in Mortality Between Socioeconomic Groups in the United States, 1960 and 1986." *New England Journal of Medicine*, 329, 103–109.

Pattillo, M., and J. N. Robinson. 2016. "Poor Neighborhoods in the Metropolis." *The Oxford Handbook of the Social Science of Poverty*. Edited by D. Brady and L. M. Burton. New York: Oxford University Press, pp. 341–368.

Quillian, L. 2003. "How Long Are Exposures to Poor Neighborhoods? The Long-Term Dynamics of Entry and Exit from Poor Neighborhoods." *Population Research and Policy Review*, 22, 221–249.

Rank, M. R. 1994. *Living on the Edge: The Realities of Welfare in America.* New York: Columbia University Press.

Rank, M. R. 2004. *One Nation, Underprivileged: Why American Poverty Affects Us All.* New York: Oxford University Press.

Rank, M. R., T. A. Hirschl, and K. A. Foster. 2014. *Chasing the American Dream: Understanding What Shapes Our Fortunes.* New York: Oxford University Press.

Reardon, S. F., and K. Bischoff. 2011. "Income Inequality and Income Segregation." *American Journal of Sociology*, 116, 1092–1153

Saez, E. 2019, March 2. "Striking It Richer: The Evolution of Top Incomes in the United States (Updated with 2017 Final Estimates)."

Sampson, R. J., and J. D. Morenoff. 2006. "Spatial Dynamics, Social Processes, and the Persistence of Poverty in Chicago Neighborhoods." Edited by S. Bowles, S. N. Durlauf, and K. Hoff. New York: Russell Sage Foundation, pp. 176–203.

Sampson, R. J, S. W. Raudenbush, and F. Earls. 1997. "Neighborhoods and Violent Crime: A Multilevel Study of Collective Efficacy." *Science*, 227, 918–924.

Schiller, B. R. 2008. *The Economics of Poverty and Discrimination, Tenth Edition.* Upper Saddle River, NJ: Prentice Hall.

Shapiro, T. M. 2004. *The Hidden Cost of Being African American: How Wealth Perpetuates Inequality.* New York: Oxford University Press.

Sharkey, P. 2008. "The Intergenerational Transmission of Context." *American Journal of Sociology*, 113, 931–969.

Smith, S. S. 2016. "Job-Finding among the Poor: Do Social Ties Matter?" *The Oxford Handbook of the Social Science of Poverty.* Edited by D. Brady and L. M. Burton. New York: Oxford University Press, pp. 438–461.

Stainback, K., and D. Tomaskovic-Devey. 2012. *Documenting Desegregation: Racial and Gender Segregation in Private-Sector Employment Since the Civil Rights Act.* New York: Russell Sage Foundation.

Transamerica Center for Retirement Studies. 2018, December. "A Precarious Existence: How Today's Retirees are Financially Faring in Retirement."

Turner, J. A., and D. R. Kaye. 2006. "How Does Family Well-Being Vary Across Different Types of Neighborhoods?" *Low-Income Working Families Series*, Paper 6, The Urban Institute.

U.S. Census Bureau. 2019. *Income and Poverty in the United States: 2018* (Report Number P60-266). Washington DC: U.S. Government Printing Office.

U.S. Department of Education, Equity and Excellence Commission. 2013. *For Each and Every Child: A Strategy for Education Equity and Excellence.* Washington, DC: Education Publications Center.

Wilkinson, R. 2005. *The Impact of Inequality: How to Make Sick Societies Healthier.* New York: The New Press.

Wilkinson, R., and K. Pickett. 2009. *The Spirit Level: Why Greater Equality Makes Societies Stronger.* New York: Bloomsbury Press.

Wilson, W. J. 1987. *The Truly Disadvantaged: The Inner City, the Underclass, and Public Policy.* Chicago: University of Chicago Press.

Wilson, W. J. 1996. *When Work Disappears: The World of the New Urban Poor.* New York: Alfred A. Knopf.

Wilson, W. J. 2009. *More Than Just Race: Being Black and Poor in the Inner City.* New York: W. W. Norton.

Wilson, W. J. 2016. "Urban Poverty, Race, and Space." *The Oxford Handbook of the Social Science of Poverty.* Edited by D. Brady and L. M. Burton. New York: Oxford University Press, pp. 394–413.

Wolff, E. N. 2017. "Household Wealth Trends in the United States, 1962 to 2016: Has Middle Class Wealth Recovered?" National Bureau of Economic Research, Working Paper 24085.

6

Developing Financial Assets for Lower-Income Households

STEPHEN ROLL, MICHAL GRINSTEIN-WEISS, JOSEPH STEENSMA, AND ANNA DERUYTER

Issues surrounding economic equity have been an almost constant source of public discussion in the United States. U.S. policymakers, researchers, social workers, and other practitioners in the fields of financial capability and social welfare have shared an ongoing concern about the rising tide of economic inequality. Since the beginning of the 20th century, economic inequality has motivated the birth of the labor movement, the New Deal response to the Great Depression, the Great Society programs of the 1960s, legislation to increase the minimum wage, and, most recently, the Occupy Wall Street movement and the rise of populist political candidates. While each of these policy shifts and movements have had a number of motivating factors underlying them, they were nevertheless driven in part by the feeling that the structure of the economy was fundamentally unfair and that the American promise of equality of opportunity was not being met.

These modern feelings of economic discontent are borne out by the evidence. As discussed in Chapter 5 of this volume, inequality has returned to levels found prior to the Great Depression, with 1 percent of Americans currently holding approximately one-third of the net worth in the country (Piketty, 2014). At the same time, children are increasingly less economically mobile than their parents, evidenced by the fact that 90 percent of children born in 1940 earned more than their parents, while only 50 percent of those born in the 1980s did so (Chetty et al., 2017). Additionally, a distressingly high proportion of Americans lack even small amounts of emergency savings, to say nothing of the ability to save for those traditional signifiers of the American Dream such as taking on a home mortgage or pursuing a college education without a large debt burden.

If we want to move toward a society where the opportunity to build a livable life is available for the entire population, these issues demand responses and solutions. While economic inequality is a multifaceted problem driven by a complex array of factors, this chapter focuses specifically on the problem of asset inequality and covers many of its motivating causes and impacts, as well as promising approaches to address the challenge of building assets for the entire population. Building assets in poorer households and communities has the potential to markedly improve people's lives, and this chapter aims to illustrate that.

Our focus is therefore threefold. First, we demonstrate the importance of promoting asset building in lower-income households by detailing many of the financial and nonfinancial benefits of assets. Next, we discuss the economic, institutional, and policy factors underlying the disparities observed in asset holding among U.S. households, as well as exploring these disparities across different populations. Finally, we provide an overview of the landscape of asset-building efforts at both the policy and program level and discuss the ways that research and practice can further address low levels of asset holding in lower-income populations.

The Importance of Assets in Building Livable Lives

When thinking about the role that assets play in facilitating a livable life, it is useful to first understand what we mean when we discuss assets. At its most basic, an asset is simply anything a person owns that has some financial value. This includes financial assets like cash, money in bank accounts, and stocks, but it also includes nonfinancial assets like the equity built up in a home, the sale value of a car, and the value of any other property a person holds. Broader definitions of assets may include the investments a person makes in building their skills (i.e., human capital) or the relationships they can leverage as a means of achieving some goal (i.e., social capital). These more general concepts of assets are important in understanding the welfare of individuals and communities. However, when we discuss building assets in this chapter, we are referring specifically to those assets that have a direct, tangible value—a household's emergency savings, the money they have set aside for a college education, the equity in a home, and so on. As our chapter will show, ownership of these types of assets have substantial implications for a household's well-being, and yet there are massive disparities across the U.S. population in both the ownership of these assets and the ability to build them up.

So what is the relationship between assets and a livable life? How does someone's assets (their savings, their homes, and their investments) allow them to reach their full potential? In thinking about this, it is perhaps easier to consider the question from the opposite perspective: How does a lack of assets prevent someone from reaching their full potential? Consider first the case of someone who, like large swaths of the U.S. population, lacks enough assets to easily cover a modest emergency (Board of Governors of the Federal Reserve System, 2016). Assuming they are employed, this person is likely living paycheck to paycheck and covering their basic needs, but is ultimately exposed to constant economic and environmental risks. A health emergency, the loss of a job, an unexpected reduction in hours, or even their car breaking down could lead to a person falling into poverty or taking on high-cost debt just to make ends meet. These financial risks may be accompanied by constant stress from having to balance tight budgets and finding ways to cope when the unexpected happens. Given the exposure of many Americans to economic volatility, it is not surprising that financial concerns have consistently been the largest source of stress for U.S. households and that low-income Americans in particular report higher levels of overall stress than higher-income households (Anderson et al., 2015).

Outside of the exposure to unexpected shocks and the stress of managing tight budgets, a subsistence-level, paycheck-to-paycheck existence almost by definition precludes people from pursuing any of their goals that require substantial amounts of money. Down payment requirements on a mortgage may prevent them from buying a home, rental deposit requirements may prevent them from moving to a better neighborhood, the costs of car maintenance may prevent them from taking a job not accessible by walking or public transit, and the rising cost of tuition may prevent them (or their children) from pursuing higher education unless they want to take on large amounts of debt. Of course, this does not include those niceties that enhance a person's life—vacations, new clothes, nights out, gifts during the holidays, and so on.

In short, assets provide stability in a person's life, and this stability provides a foundation that allows households to better work toward their short- and long-term goals. This has implications for every stage of a person's life. A family's assets can govern the neighborhoods they live in, the schools their children go to, their ability to borrow to make other investments, the debt they have to take on for college, and their level of comfort in retirement. Taking up the challenge of building assets for everyone allows us to move beyond simply providing policy and program solutions that enable people to subsist in their given economic condition. It not only allows us to address one of the most striking disparities in America today, but it also enables us to help poor households build a foundation from which they can start their own business, get the training they need for the job they want, move to a better neighborhood, or give their children the best education they can. Consequently, building assets in poor and economically insecure households not only provides the potential to help these households move out of poverty, but it also helps them to reach their fullest potential. To illustrate the fundamental role of assets in promoting a livable life, let us trace several of the primary financial and nonfinancial benefits of asset accumulation.

The Financial Benefits of Asset Accumulation

Developing the assets of low-income populations can directly address the problems of poverty in many ways, including buffering households against emergencies, providing enough money to make purchases that can help move people out of poverty (such as a car to travel to a better job), building home equity, providing access to higher education, allowing for a comfortable retirement, and enabling families to transfer wealth across generations.

Protecting Against Financial Emergencies and Meeting Basic Needs

At their most basic, assets can function as a way of allowing households to meet their essential needs in the event of an unexpected financial obligation or shock. Research demonstrates that the average cost of a financial emergency is between $1,500 and $2,000 (Collins and Gjertson, 2013; Searle and Köppe, 2014), which can throw an individual living on the financial edge into poverty (or exacerbate existing levels of poverty) if they do not have sufficient reserves to weather this level of expense. It is hard to overstate the importance of this role for assets in supporting a livable life. Having access to enough emergency savings in the event of a job loss, a health crisis, or even an unexpected automobile repair may be the deciding factor between being evicted, losing a job because of lost access to transportation, forgoing essential medical care, paying bills late and losing access to low-cost credit, or being able to afford enough food for a family. As important as having this minimal level of assets may be, lower-income U.S. households still struggle to meet this threshold. A 2009 study demonstrated that only half of U.S. households thought they could come up with $2,000 within 30 days if needed, while less than a quarter of those with incomes below $20,000 could come up with this amount (Collins and Gjertson, 2013).

In addition to buffering households against shocks, even relatively small amounts of assets may play a substantial role in addressing poverty and helping households build a better life. For example, having enough money in savings to cover a few missed work hours may allow individuals to interview for better or higher-paying jobs. Likewise, having enough money to cover a security deposit on a rented apartment may allow an individual to move to a part of town with more job opportunities. Savings can also be used to pay for the necessary purchases that often facilitate pursuing higher-income jobs, including clothes suitable for job interviews or a vehicle to travel to and from a relatively distant job. Thus, even as we often think of poverty alleviation or economic mobility as something purchased through large investments like college, a home, or starting a business, even modest improvements in asset levels may substantially help families avoid or emerge from poverty and improve their overall prospects.

Homeownership

The relationships between assets, homeownership, and financial security is complex. While homeownership has long been considered an integral component of the American Dream, the housing market collapse of 2007 provided a striking demonstration of the risks of homeownership. After the collapse, the percentage of low-income households with "underwater" mortgages, or mortgages where individuals owed more than the house was worth, functionally doubled (Carter and Gottschalck, 2011). Yet despite the risks, homeownership is still an integral component of building wealth in the United States. Home equity makes up a substantial portion of wealth for Americans, accounting for approximately half of the total wealth held by American households (Iacoviello, 2011).

There is, of course, a direct and reciprocal link between homeownership and asset building. First, building assets over time leads to the increased likelihood of meeting down payment requirements on a home. Although down payments often range from 3 to 20 percent of the principal, meeting even the low end of this range may be a challenge for many lower-income households. As previously noted, lower-income households struggle to save $2,000 for an emergency. Even if these households qualified for a federal program requiring only a 3.5 percent down payment on a $100,000 house, their down payment on the home would still be $3,500 (and may be accompanied by a requirement to pay for mortgage insurance). For many lower-income households, meeting this threshold would be a challenge and, if met, would likely wipe out their emergency savings. However, once aspiring home buyers meet this threshold, a house becomes a tool in and of itself for building assets, as mortgage payments directly build an individual's equity in their home in ways that rent payments do not. Thus, assets facilitate a home purchase, and a home purchase, in turn, facilitates asset growth.

The development of home equity appears to have benefits for homeowners generally, as demonstrated in a study looking at short-term outcomes for homeowners compared to renters. It found that lower-income homeowners had increased net worth, assets, and nonhousing net worth compared to those renting (Grinstein-Weiss et al., 2013). This equity, which is valuable in and of itself, can also further facilitate financial security across the life cycle by providing access to credit. Home equity lines of credit can then allow homeowners to borrow money at low rates if they need to finance essential purchases or cover unexpected shortfalls, while reverse mortgages allow older homeowners to turn their home equity into a stream of payments that can supplement their retirement income. Although neither of these options is in any way riskless, they do provide lower-income homeowners with an expended set of financial tools that, when used appropriately, can enhance their overall well-being.

Educational Attainment

In the United States, where the funding available to a school district is directly connected to the assets held by the people in that school district (via the property tax mechanism of funding schools) and where the costs of higher education are continually rising, assets and education are inextricably linked. Empirical research validates this link and supports the common observation that parental wealth is associated with the likelihood of their child attending college (Hotz, Rasmussen, and Wiemers, 2016). It is worth noting the importance of this observation to understanding the disparities in building livable lives across the population. Attending college is not simply a mechanism to increase future earnings potential. It is also a way of pursuing passions, learning about new fields and topics, living in a different environment, and building an upwardly mobile social network. For those children who come from poor families, their access to each of these benefits is severely diminished through their reduced likelihood of attending college; not only do they face lower lifetime earnings on average, but they have fewer opportunities to explore the different options in building their future life.

While an increased likelihood of attending college is an advantage in and of itself, having wealthier parents (or parents who can afford to put aside money in a college fund) also facilitates the avoidance of student debt burdens for both parents and their children. For individuals who cannot rely on their parents to finance their education, their options are to either not attend college at all or to take on student loans. As college becomes ever more essential to getting a high-paying job, more individuals than ever are opting to take on student loan debt to finance their college expenses. In 2019, student loan debt surpassed $1.6 trillion (Board of Governors of the Federal Reserve System, 2019), and the greatest burden of student loan debt tends to fall on those in the lowest fifth of the income spectrum (Fry, 2012). This likely puts them in a less suitable position to build wealth after college and may make them less willing (or able) to take on additional debt to even finish school, thus directly impacting their long-term earnings and wealth potential (Center on Assets, Education, and Inclusion, 2016). Moreover, this inequity in access to equally affordable education for lower-income populations compared to higher-income populations, and the outcomes related to it, further perpetuates the cycle of poverty and ultimately contributes to observed wealth disparities. Recent research has captured this relationship, finding that for lower-income households, simply having student debt was associated with an increased likelihood of skipping bills, rent, and medical care, as well as overdrawing bank accounts and being unable to purchase food. This relationship held even when accounting for the factors that motivate households to take on student debt (Despard et al., 2016).

While assets at the family or the individual level facilitate the pursuit of higher education, building assets at the community level may enhance educational outcomes at a more formative stage of development. During the early years of a child's education, the characteristics of the local tax base in the district where the child goes to public school play a significant role in the quality of education and experience that child has (Poterba, 1997). Public schools in the United States are funded in large part by property taxes. Consequently, in areas with high property values, schools receive more funding and likely provide much better educational outcomes (graduation rates, college attendance, etc.) than neighborhoods with low property values (as discussed in Chapter 5 of this volume). In this way, the educational benefits of assets are intertwined with increased levels of homeownership facilitated by assets, as areas with higher rates of homeownership tend to have higher property values (Rohe and Stewart, 1996).

Retirement and Intergenerational Wealth Transfers

Building assets is also an integral part of allowing households to live comfortably in their later years and possibly leaving an inheritance that helps support their children. The advent of Social Security in the United States and the subsequent expansions of its benefits have dramatically lowered the rate of elder poverty (Engelhardt and Gruber, 2004), but there remains a large gap between people's retirement needs and their actual retirement savings. For example, over half of American households near retirement (age 55 and above) lacked any retirement savings and almost a third lacked both retirement savings and access to a pension, likely forcing them to rely solely on the benefits provided by Social Security (U.S. Government Accountability Office, 2015). Even households with savings only have enough to provide approximately $310 in income per month (U.S. Government Accountability Office, 2015), which is unlikely to finance a comfortable lifestyle in retirement. When this lack of retirement savings is considered at the national level, the size of the gap between our needs and our assets is striking. One estimate put this gap at between $6.8 and $14 trillion (Rhee, 2013). While the overall U.S. population finds it difficult to save for retirement, the problem is exacerbated in low-income households. A 2015 survey, for example, found that over half of households with under $40,000 in yearly income had no retirement savings (Board of Governors of the Federal Reserve System, 2016), and a later survey found that fewer than 40 percent of Americans feel as though their retirement is on track (Board of Governors of the Federal Reserve System, 2018).

Inasmuch as Social Security may prevent starvation or extreme hardship among its beneficiaries, it is worth considering what a "livable" retirement might look like. Rather than a person's twilight years being occupied with delicate budget management, an austere lifestyle, and a reliance on children for financial resources and support, a livable retirement might include trips to locations not yet visited, using newfound leisure time to pursue new or existing hobbies, and buying gifts for grandchildren. To be able to do these things freely and comfortably, a person will generally require more money than that provided by Social Security, and therefore building assets in long-term savings vehicles over the course of one's working life is essential to maintaining a livable life in the postwork years.

Beyond retirement, building assets for the whole population is an important component in improving the welfare of families across generations. Intergenerational transfers of wealth are a significant contributor to the perpetuation and growth of that wealth; these transfers can help young families buy homes, pay for college, or save for their own eventual retirement. This also represents another benefit of promoting homeownership as well, as the home is a large asset that can be transferred to children by their parents. Yet while parents handing down wealth to their children may facilitate economic opportunity and mobility, this also contributes to the growth of economic inequality. For example, one study demonstrated that nearly 50 percent of parents in the top wealth quintile made at least one educational-related transfer to their children to help with their school, and the transfer amount per child averaged approximately $20,000 (Hotz, Rasmussen, and Wiemers, 2016). This is compared to only 33 percent in the second wealth quintile and only 18 percent in the lowest. Similar patterns are observed for wealth transfers related to homeownership. Since these intergenerational transfers contribute substantially to the perpetuation of economic inequality, the benefits of these transfers also speak to the opportunities inherent in building assets within poorer communities. If successful, asset-building efforts within these communities may continue to pay dividends for the children and grandchildren of the beneficiaries of these efforts.

Nonmonetary Benefits of Assets

While the financial benefits of asset building are clear and are in many ways intuitive, there is an emerging body of research examining the nonfinancial benefits. These include the benefits to perceptions, decision-making, and mental and physical health as well. This research speaks to the pervasive way in which assets impact people's lives and contribute to their overall well-being.

Building Expectations and an Orientation to the Future

One of the primary nonfinancial impacts of holding assets relates to the changing expectations about the future and the "future orientation" of the individual (Sherraden, 1990; Sherraden, 1991; Shobe and Page-Adams, 2001). The future orientation of an individual is the degree to which that individual plans and invests in the future, rather than focusing on short-term or day-to-day obligations. A future orientation is in many ways necessary for long-term financial security, as it requires planning for retirement and structuring one's life and finances to pursue training, education, and job opportunities. However, for many cash-strapped households, such an orientation is neither likely nor perhaps even desirable. In a case where a household's expenses exceed its income, it becomes necessary to focus on daily obligations like looking for work, finding ways to cut costs, increasing the hours worked, or finding sources of short-term credit. For lower-income households who may not be as cash-strapped but still struggle to save, their orientation may be toward focusing on the next week or month as they save for necessary expenses (such as back-to-school clothes for their children or high utility bills in the winter).

By providing a buffer against short-term financial concerns and emergencies and making long-term investments more attainable, assets facilitate the expectations that someone can build a livable life. For example, many lower-income households may operate with the knowledge that higher education is unaffordable and out of reach, and their behaviors conform to that expectation. Yet if this expectation changes and the possibility of college becomes present and real for households, their orientation to thinking and planning for the future has been demonstrated to change to fit this new perception (Sherraden, 1991; Shobe and Page-Adams, 2001). When the possibility of college attendance is introduced to children and their families early on, they have been shown to make categorically different choices related to education as a result of framing their thinking toward the future and its possibilities. By giving parents hope that their children can attend college in the future, they subsequently develop higher expectations for them (Beverly, Elliott, and Sherraden, 2013; Huang et al., 2014). This body of research indicates that even modest access to assets can facilitate more optimistic expectations of the future. These expectations, in turn, can translate into real behaviors oriented toward improving one's financial future and their long-term prospects.

Avoiding a Scarcity Mindset

Beyond facilitating expectations, access to assets (or a lack thereof) can influence the way we make decisions. Research in the field of wealth and poverty has looked into the impact of financial scarcity on decision-making. Behavioral researchers argue that operating under a condition of scarcity can lead to a phenomenon called "tunneling," in which an individual focuses on immediate and urgent concerns to the exclusion of other less pressing but still important concerns (Mullainathan and Shafir, 2013). It is easy to imagine the consequences of tunneling in low-income individuals. For example, they might become so focused on keeping their children fed and paying the electricity bill that they forget to pay a credit card bill, despite the fact that a delinquent payment will lead to higher borrowing costs down the road. Or perhaps they had their hours cut at their job and are so concerned with making ends meet this month that they take out a payday loan without fully considering its long-term costs, leading to more hardship down the road. This mindset can be particularly insidious when it comes to taking on debt, as the benefits of taking on debt (i.e., being able to make a purchase or cover an expense quickly) are immediate and tangible while the costs are incurred in the future and diffused over time. Tunneling can thus lead people into cycles of debt, while assets, by giving people more flexibility to manage their expenses, can help avoid the mindset that leads to tunneling.

Further, when resources are scarce, a decision to purchase one thing can often mean forgoing another important purchase. Every substantial financial decision thus requires considering the trade-offs involved in the purchase (Shah, Shafir, and Mullainathan, 2015). This fact is one of the key elements that separates the realities of the poor from the realities of the more affluent. An affluent person can fill up their gas tank without worrying about overdrawing their bank account, or buy new clothes for their growing children without thinking about the implications for their food budget over the coming weeks. Poorer households, by contrast, must often think about what they have to give up to make even small purchases. This is exemplified in the "heat or eat" dilemma often faced by the poverty stricken as mentioned in Chapter 3 of this volume.

Due in part to the need to constantly consider trade-offs, living in poverty has been shown to reduce cognitive ability. Attempting to function under persistent income constraints leads to the increased use of mental resources, which leaves less resources for other tasks (Mani et al., 2013). However, this phenomenon is not simply an issue of managing stress or cognitive strain. The pressure to constantly think about short-term needs and trade-offs necessarily crowds out thinking about long-term goals such as looking for better employment, saving for college, or any number of other financial aspirations (Mullainathan and Shafir, 2013).

Physical and Mental Health

It is difficult to imagine a livable life that is not accompanied by good physical and mental health (see Chapter 2 of this volume), and here too access to assets plays a role. The body of research supporting the relationship between stress and health is deep (Carr and Umberson, 2013) and demonstrates that stress significantly impacts both physical and mental health. Financial stress is not excluded from this relationship and can also lead to physical and mental health challenges over the course of one's life. As mentioned earlier, without a stable income and a strong asset base to weather fluctuations in income and expenses, financial stress is a common occurrence (Anderson et al., 2015). This is intuitive—money is one of our most fundamental concerns, and a consistent inability to make ends meet either due to income constraints or volatility in income and expenses is likely going to be a source of persistent and acute stress.

Financial stress is not limited to lower-income households, as relatively affluent families can also suffer from huge expenses like health emergencies or from unsustainable spending habits driving them deep into debt. Yet there is likely something different about the ongoing financial strain experienced by lower-income households and the strain experienced by relatively affluent households, as affluent households can often discharge their debts (via bankruptcy) or translate their existing assets into sources of credit (e.g., by borrowing against their home equity). Lower-income households, by contrast, may face more structural constraints in which their incomes simply do not cover their expenses or are insufficient to facilitate saving and therefore face persistent and unavoidable shortfalls in funds. Nor can many borrow against homes they do not own or afford the fees required to declare bankruptcy and emerge from debt (Gross, Notowidigdo, and Wang, 2014). These persistent shortfalls and structural constraints have real consequences for the mental health of those experiencing them. One study demonstrated that those in the lowest wealth quintile were three times more likely to experience psychological distress compared to those in the highest wealth quintile (Carter et al., 2009).

Over time, chronic stress can lead to exhaustion and an inability of the body to defend itself against illness and disease effectively. Outcomes such as diabetes and high blood pressure can result from this (Carter et al., 2009). The risks of physical and mental strains are likely compounded for lower-income households, as they may not have the health insurance coverage (which is its own source of stress) required to adequately address these issues and, even if they do have health insurance, may not be able to afford to miss work due to health problems. By providing a buffer against the unexpected, and giving families some financial breathing room, assets can potentially reduce stress and are thus a likely facilitator of positive health outcomes (Roll, Taylor, and Grinstein-Weiss, 2016).

The Asset Problem and Its Underlying Causes

In the prior section, we made a case for the pervasive influence that assets have on many different aspects of our lives, impacting everything from our day-to-day finances to our long-term life outcomes to the ways in which we make decisions. Yet despite the fact that access to even basic levels of assets can potentially have a large impact on a person's life, there are large disparities in people's access to assets. In the modern U.S. economy, wealth inequality is the most extreme it has been since the lead-up to the Great Depression in the 1930s (Saez and Zucman, 2016). While inequality is not necessarily a problem in itself (i.e., if the population's wealth and well-being is improving overall), this growth in inequality has been accompanied by persistently low savings rates among those in the bottom 90th percentile of U.S. wealth holding. The factors driving this increasing wealth disparity and the persistently low rates of savings are complex. They involve historical factors that prevented many groups (particularly racial minority groups) from independently building wealth for generations, structural factors that lead to low levels of wage growth, institutional factors that make building savings and accessing cheap credit easier for the wealthy relative to the poor, and a policy structure that actively discourages savings in low-income households.

The fact that this large disparity exists and is particularly pronounced across historically disenfranchised groups, particularly racial minorities, adds a moral component to the economic need to develop assets for the whole population: If assets are integral to a livable life, then this large disparity means that we are excluding entire swaths of the population from building this type of life, and we are doing so in a way that exacerbates historical inequities.

This section focuses on understanding the factors that lead to this disparity in asset-building opportunities. Specifically, it explores the ways that the structure of our economy, our institutions, and our policies present barriers to building wealth in U.S. lower-income households. Understanding these factors and overcoming the barriers to asset building will not immediately alleviate the large wealth discrepancy we observe in the U.S. population, but addressing these issues will help ensure that everyone is on a more equal footing when it comes to building assets, achieving their life goals, and reaching their full potential.

Economic Barriers to Asset Building

One of the primary factors driving the low levels of savings and wealth accumulation seen in lower-income households is, unsurprisingly, the problem of limited cash flow. While turning income into assets relies on a number of behavioral and institutional factors (such as a willingness to save income and the availability of investment products), the simple fact is that households with incomes at or below a minimum sustainable level will have difficulty saving at all. While the link between low incomes and low savings levels is in many ways obvious, what is particularly concerning about this issue is the stagnation of income growth over the last two decades. When adjusting for price inflation, the real median household income in the United States has been roughly flat since 1999 (U.S. Bureau of the Census, 2017). Stagnant incomes have a number of troubling implications for savings levels in the United States. Without a broad-based increase in incomes there is no fundamental reason to expect that households will be better able to build savings in the future than they are today, absent other substantial policy interventions or cultural shifts in our approach to consumption and savings decisions.

Many lower-income households in the United States live paycheck to paycheck and often struggle to afford basic necessities. When one's income is entirely consumed by the need to make rent, afford food, pay for gas, and purchase clothing for children, there is simply not enough financial slack to build up even a modest amount of emergency savings to buffer against financial shocks. Given that many lower-income households lack the ability to save for short-term concerns like income or expense shocks, it is of course even more unlikely that they will be able to save for long-term investments that can enhance their financial security and overall quality of life such as attending college or covering a down payment on a home. For example, looking at four-year public institutions, only 34 percent of low-income, first-generation students earned bachelor's degrees within a six-year time frame, compared to 66 percent of their peers (Engle and Tinto, 2008). Additionally, these students were nearly four times more likely to leave higher education after the first year than students who were middle- or high-income with parents who attended college. This disparity extends to homeownership as well. As of 2015, households in the bottom quintile of income had a homeownership rate 46 percentage points lower than those in the top quintile (Prosperity Now, 2017c).

Beyond low incomes precluding longer-term investments like college and homeownership, households with severe income constraints struggle even to save minimal amounts of money. Having little to no savings can also make affording and bouncing back from unforeseen financial expenses challenging, which is pervasive among the poor. A nationally representative survey from 2010 revealed that only half of U.S. households had savings equivalent to 75 percent of one month's income-a level defined as adequate to buffer against an emergency. Fewer than 40 percent of households below the poverty line met this threshold (Key, 2014). Even more troubling is that almost half of U.S. households could not easily manage an emergency costing only $400 (Board of Governors of the Federal Reserve System, 2016). The problem of limited savings has real, tangible impacts on household welfare and has been associated with increases in a household's vulnerability to material hardship such as going without basic necessities such as food, medical and dental care, and utilities (Babiarz and Robb, 2014; Collins and Gjertson, 2013; Mckernan, Ratcliffe, and Vinopal, 2009; Sherraden and Sherraden, 2000).

Exacerbating the previously discussed issues is the level of exposure lower-income households have to economic fluctuations. Taking the Great Recession of 2008 as an example, we can see how economic shocks are disproportionately felt by the most financially insecure households. Although the Great Recession impacted the wealth of a large majority of Americans (more than 50 percent of families lost at least a quarter of their wealth between 2007 and 2011, while a quarter of families lost at least 75 percent of their wealth) lower-income households, along with less-educated and minority populations, were hit the hardest (Pfeffer, Danziger, and Schoeni, 2013). These findings, when considered jointly with the previously discussed research on lower-income households' vulnerability to shocks, show that poorer households are extremely exposed to both personal emergencies and broader economic shocks.

Institutional Barriers to Asset Building

Beyond the fundamental issue of limited cash flows leading to limited savings, lower-income populations face other substantial financial challenges that contribute to a difficulty in saving money. Indeed, even if a lower-income household manages to get their finances to a point where they can save money, they may still experience a number of institutional barriers that either limit their ability to safely build assets or expose them to high levels of risk from taking on debt. These institutional factors include a lack of access to affordable mainstream banking services; a need to rely on alternative financial services such as high-cost payday or title loans; the use of other high-cost debt such as private student loans, high-cost credit cards, and predatory mortgages; and a lack of access to secure investment options that allow their money to grow, such as employer-sponsored retirement accounts like a 401(k). Additionally, building assets in lower-income populations is made more difficult because many aspects of the U.S. tax system only focus on incentivizing saving for more affluent households. Furthermore, the U.S. social service system actively disincentivizes saving in low-income households. Each of the institutional barriers is examined in the following discussion.

Access to Affordable Mainstream Banking Services

Relative to the general population, a high number of lower-income households are either "unbanked," meaning they do not have either a checking or a savings account in a financial institution, or "underbanked," meaning they may have a checking or savings account but still rely on financial services outside of the mainstream banking system such as payday lenders (Federal Deposit Insurance Corporation, 2018). Bank account ownership is in many ways a key component of building assets, as it affords households many financial resources and opportunities such as having a secure way to pay bills, directly depositing paychecks into bank accounts, accumulating savings, accessing and building credit at affordable rates, and earning interest on assets (Birkenmaier and Fu, 2015; Federal Deposit Insurance Corporation, 2018; Hogarth, Anguelov, and Lee, 2005; Robbins, 2013). Research has linked bank account ownership with overall financial well-being. Being unbanked has been associated with higher levels of material hardship including going without basic goods and services such as food, housing, clothing, medical care, lower financial security including experiencing fluctuations in income, the inability to cover unexpected expenses, and feeling worried or anxious about finances (Beverly, 2001; Collins and Gjertson, 2013; Lee and Kim, 2016). These experiences impact a household's ability to build wealth over their lifetime (Barr, 2010). Despite the benefits of being banked, 7 percent of U.S. households are unbanked and 20 percent are underbanked, leading them to rely on high-cost loan providers like those explored in the next section, which can serve immediate financial needs but be detrimental to long-term financial health (Federal Deposit Insurance Corporation, 2018).

The Lack of Mainstream Credit Access and the Use of Alternative Financial Services

In the absence of a sufficient level of assets to maintain day-to-day expenses and offset income or expense shocks, households may turn to high-cost, short-term credit as a means of coping with their financial needs. This is particularly true if households do not have access to lower-cost sources of credit like credit cards, which is the case for many lower-income households (Barr, 2004; Despard et al., 2015). Sources of mainstream credit, including credit cards, can provide a way of managing expenses and buffering against shocks by allowing households to borrow against a preset credit limit and pay down their debt in installments. While credit cards are not riskless financial management tools, they can provide a reliable and effective means of smoothing a household's finances even as households with limited or poor credit histories may pay high interest rates on these cards.

Although it is possible for cash-constrained households to get into debt trouble through the use of credit cards, the risks of relying on mainstream credit to manage finances are much less pronounced than those involved in relying on many alternative financial services. Common types of alternative financial services include payday loans, which are essentially cash advances to be repaid when the borrower receives their next paycheck, and auto title loans, which are loans that use the title to the borrower's vehicle as collateral. These loans, which can carry triple-digit interest rates after accounting for all the costs and fees associated with their use (Consumer Financial Protection Bureau, 2013), can potentially trap households in cycles of debt and further exacerbate the strain experienced by financially insecure households (Birkenmaier and Tyuse, 2005).

Despite the high costs and riskiness of these loans, they appear to perform necessary functions in the financial lives of lower-income households. Recent research on payday loan usage finds that the vast majority of these households use payday loans to either cover essential expenses like rent or food or to manage some unexpected emergency (Davison et al., 2017). Further, lower-income households who rely on payday loans also report being turned down for mainstream credit at dramatically higher rates than lower-income households who did not report payday loan use, indicating that these households are turning to high-cost sources of credit because they have few other options.

Payday loans and other alternative financial services have grown into a major industry in the United States. It is estimated that today these services process over $300 billion in transactions annually and that over a fifth of all U.S. households have used one in the last year (Bradley et al., 2009; Federal Deposit Insurance Corporation, 2018). In a study looking specifically at lower-income households, 39 percent had used an alternative financial service in the prior 12 months (Despard et al., 2015). In a sense, the growth of this industry can be seen as both a cause and effect of the asset problem in the United States. In the absence of emergency savings and access to mainstream credit, many households have no choice but to rely on services like payday lenders to make ends meet, yet easy access to high-cost short-term loans can also burden households with exorbitant fees and interest payments that further limit their ability to save any money.

However, even if lower-income households do qualify for mainstream sources of credit like credit cards, home loans, or student loans, they may end up paying higher rates on their debt than upper income households. Although income is not a factor in determining an individual's credit score (the score given to consumers that is basically a measure of the risk that they will default on a loan and partially determines the interest paid on their loans), there is nevertheless a strong correlation between income and credit scores. For example, about 60 percent of people living in lower-income neighborhoods have poor or fair credit compared to only around 40 percent of the general population. Put differently, substantially fewer than half of people in lower-income neighborhoods have "good" credit scores and are thus more likely to pay higher interest on a wide array of loans, further constraining their income and the potential for them to set aside money for their financial goals.

Unequal Access to Long-Term Investment Options

While lower-income households face a relative lack of access to products that can provide them with secure ways of building short-term savings or affordable ways of taking on short-term debt, they also face unequal access to long-term investment products like retirement accounts. Americans often save for retirement through plans offered by their employers. Historically, many employers provided pension plans, in which they paid a specific monthly amount to retired employees. However, access to pensions has declined over the years (Wiatrowski, 2012) and retirement savings in the United States has shifted to plans in which employees make contributions to fund their own retirement, such as 401(k) plans. Most Americans have access to employer-sponsored retirement programs, even as they may not actually participate in these plans, but many people still work for employers that do not offer retirement plans. In 2017, 35 percent of American employees were not offered any sort of retirement plan, and this number was substantially higher (around 60 percent) for part-time employees (Pew Charitable Trusts, 2017). This lack of access to employer-sponsored retirement accounts for the disparity in retirement savings between lower-income households and the rest of the population (Board of Governors of the Federal Reserve System, 2016).

The Racial Wealth Gap

A discussion of the institutional factors underlying disparities in assets across the population would be incomplete without an examination of how the wealth gap manifests in terms of race. Many institutional arrangements, like those outlined already in this section, have the potential to depress asset building for lower-income households generally, but the unique history of racial minorities in the United States has led to acute disparities in asset holdings by race. The difference in wealth accumulation across racial groups is striking. Research using the Panel Study of Income Dynamics has found that the median level of wealth was around $18,100 in black households, $33,600 in Hispanic households, and $122,900 in white non-Hispanic households (McKernan et al., 2014). This massive gap is not adequately explained by job attainment, as research by Melvin Oliver and Thomas Shapiro has found stark differences in net assets for blacks and whites at varying levels of professional statuses. After splitting professional status up into five categories (upper-white-collar, lower-white-collar, upper-blue-collar, lower-blue-collar, and the self-employed) results showed that only upper-white-collar blacks had a positive net asset amount (Oliver and Shapiro, 1997). Some of this gap is certainly due to historical factors and institutional arrangements that prevented black households from accumulating wealth in the past. Hamilton and Darity (2010) review a number of these motivating factors, citing systematic abuses and property destruction against black individuals by both governments and white communities, redlining and other housing discrimination, and dramatically lower rates of loan approval for black applicants in comparison to white ones, even when accounting for income. This historical and institutional discrimination has manifested in lower rates of wealth transfers across generations in minority households; less wealth accumulation in the past leads to fewer wealth transfers in the present. Research has helped quantify the intergenerational component of the racial wealth gap, finding that black families receive about $5,000 less in large gifts or inheritances over an average two-year period (McKernan et al., 2013).

While the gap in overall wealth between races is remarkable, perhaps an even more pressing concern is the racial discrepancy in the minimal financial resources needed to weather short-term emergencies. The nationally-representative Survey of Household Economics and Decision-Making, for example, asked respondents if they could completely pay within a month's time for an emergency expense of $400 using cash or a credit card. Among low-income respondents, only 20 percent of black non-Hispanic households could meet this expense compared to 40 percent of white non-Hispanic households (Board of Governors of the Federal Reserve System, 2016). In other words, low-income white households were twice as likely to be able to manage a minor emergency than low-income black households. This difference persists (though is less pronounced) across other income levels. This short-term savings gap and the long-term asset accumulation gap as previously outlined are likely intertwined. The Institute on Assets and Social Policy has calculated that each dollar increase in income for white households corresponds to an increase of $5.19 in wealth over time, while a dollar increase in income for black households only corresponds to an increase of $0.69 in wealth over time (Shapiro, Meschede, and Osoro, 2013). The authors attribute this to black households needing all their income to manage day-to-day expenses and save for emergencies (rather than investing their money) and to long-term patterns of discrimination in job and benefit access.

Policies That Serve as Barriers to Wealth Building
for Low-Income Populations

While there are many social policies in place that provide measurable assistance to lower-income households in the form of food, housing, health care, and financial support, these policies are almost entirely focused on providing additional income, reducing essential costs, or maintaining an appropriate level of consumption in a household. Other than perhaps the Earned Income Tax Credit (EITC), most major welfare policies targeted at low-income households are not oriented toward facilitating saving and in some cases can actively discourage saving. This is one of the biggest differences between the aims of government assistance to the poor and government assistance to the relatively well-off. Asset building is actively promoted through policies like the mortgage interest deduction and the preferential tax treatment of certain retirement savings accounts, yet these policies are predominately accessible to middle- and upper-income families leaving lower-income families behind. For example, lower-income households are often excluded from government benefits around retirement savings due to the fact that many households' primary form of retirement saving is in employer-based retirement savings accounts, which (as noted earlier) are predominately available to more affluent households.

By contrast, programs like the Supplemental Nutrition Assistance Program (SNAP, or "food stamps") and Temporary Assistance for Needy Families (TANF, or what is typically thought of as "welfare") have historically limited the amount of assets potential beneficiaries could have to qualify for the program. While many states have eliminated asset requirements, and the asset limits on Medicaid have been largely eliminated at the federal level, 16 states still have asset limits for SNAP and 42 states (and the District of Columbia) still have asset limits for TANF (Prosperity Now, 2017b). Such limits are a substantial disincentive for lower-income households to save and may even disincentivize them from opening a bank account out of fear of their finances being monitored and jeopardizing their benefits (Neuberger, Greenstein, and Orszag, 2006; O'Brien, 2008).

What Will Be Required to Advance
Asset-Building Solutions

Having discussed the benefits of holding assets and the factors leading to low levels of asset accumulation in lower-income households, we now turn to potential solutions. Adequately addressing wealth disparities in the United States to promote a livable life for everyone is no small task. This is, to put it mildly, a very contentious topic. Wealth itself has long held moral connotations for the public, as wealth is often associated with behaviors perceived as virtuous (e.g., thrift, sacrifice, business acumen, and hard work). Issues of wealth disparities are also enmeshed in other polarizing issues in the United States, including racial equity and equality of opportunity across socioeconomic strata. To give a sense of the scope of the challenge, the last major reversal of the growth in wealth disparities between the rich and the poor required a major global economic depression and a world war (Piketty, 2014; Saez and Zucman, 2016). As the challenge is complex and multifaceted, so too must be the resources we bring to bear to address it. Effectively promoting inclusive asset building will require innovations in research, practice, and policy.

A First Step: Reframing the Understanding of Inequality

Most policymakers and practitioners tend to use income as the primary metric to understand poverty and inequality. Efforts to redress economic inequality have thus typically focused on policies intended to provide income support or those that maintain a minimum level of consumption. These efforts are, of course, important and have the potential to substantially impact the levels of poverty and general economic hardship in the United States. For example, raising the minimum wage from its current level of $7.25 an hour is a common proposal to address stagnant incomes for those on the lower end of the income spectrum. Even though only 2.7 percent of hourly paid workers are paid at the exact minimum wage, a federally mandated raising of the income floor may lead to more broad-based wage increases for U.S. households as firms move to make their wages competitive with a higher minimum. Higher wages may translate to less financial constraint on average and, by extension, increased ability to save; evidence also indicates that higher minimum wages have a minimal impact on hiring practices (Card and Krueger, 2015).

Other common proposals to address poverty and inequality center around welfare programs like TANF (which provides time-limited cash support for low-income families with children), the SNAP, and Social Security, which all provide essential components of the American social safety net. However, while these policies are absolutely essential to supporting impoverished or economically vulnerable families, they ultimately serve as a sort of economic stopgap measure intended to soften the burdens of poverty without alleviating its root causes (see Chapters 3 and 5 of this volume for a further discussion on the root causes of poverty).

While concepts of income and wealth are related, and a discussion of income and wages is crucial to understanding the issues related to economic vulnerability and inequality, the asset-based perspective taken in this chapter offers a distinct measure to describe the social problems associated with poverty. This perspective presents a unique array of tools that can be employed to increase upward social mobility for individuals and communities. Shifting our focus to include asset accumulation measures for problem assessment and solution development is thus critical in developing policies and programs that address the full scope of financial issues rather than just the subset of issues directly concerned with income and consumption (Sherraden, 1991).

One of the primary arguments in favor of an asset perspective compared to an income focus is that assets can impact households' long-term perspectives and thinking compared to income that is much more transactional, fleeting, and short term. By reconceptualizing the issue to emphasize assets, policies can begin to help lower-income households develop a critical kind of financial security that not only provides direct financial stability through buffering households against emergencies and facilitating investment, but may also reorient their entire perspective and generate long-term and persistent benefits for both individuals and their communities. As policies and programs take the asset needs of lower-income households into consideration, we may see households more consistently finding their way out of poverty and investing in themselves instead of living paycheck to paycheck and always one or two financial emergencies away from insolvency (Shapiro, 2001; Sherraden, 1991).

In short, while the income perspective is essential, it ultimately only speaks to a part of the fundamental problem of economic inequality. Income and consumption tools like those historically favored by policymakers can help keep families fed, clothed, and housed, but they are likely not as effective in giving households a way out of the subsistence living that defines impoverishment. Income and consumption support do not build human capital, grow over time, create investment in communities, or allow individuals to build toward their financial goals. Assets do, and their importance must be recognized at all levels of the social and political system, from the legislators in federal and state governments to the social workers embedded in these communities.

Understanding the Landscape of Wealth-Building Policies and Programs

Once the perception of economic inequality expands to include both income and assets, the range of policies for which researchers, policymakers, and practitioners can advocate expands as well. To understand how the policy discussion around asset building has evolved, this section outlines some of the primary asset-building policies that have emerged on national, state, and local policy agendas in recent years.

Child Development Accounts

Child Development Accounts (CDAs) are one of the most promising avenues for building wealth in lower-income populations. CDA programs have been adopted in a majority of American states and in a number of other countries. Although the scope and structure of these programs vary between states and countries, the fundamental idea behind CDAs is that children are provided (often at birth) with a savings account that is "seeded" with an initial deposit. For example, the Harold Alfond College Challenge (a CDA program in Maine) provides $500 to every baby born as a resident of Maine (Harold Alfond College Challenge, 2017). These programs often have other features intended to promote asset building or financial security, including financial education components, matched savings incentives, or restrictions on how funds can be used to promote using the funds for investments like college or a down payment on a home.

While the growth in CDA programs is encouraging, and research into the impacts of CDA programs has found positive effects of providing CDAs to families (e.g. Clancy et al., 2006; Employment and Social Development Canada, 2015; Zager et al., 2010), CDA programs in the United States remain hindered by the patchwork nature of the array of programs. At the time of writing, 19 states do not offer CDAs (Ain and Newville, 2017), and those states that do offer CDAs provide relatively modest financial support. U.S. policymakers have proposed a policy to universalize a CDA-type account—the ASPIRE Act was intended to provide every child born in America with an account worth $500 at birth and provided additional funds for households with incomes below the national median (King, 2010). Universalizing the receipt of CDAs is an important first step in strengthening CDA policy, but the modest contribution amounts still limit the ability of CDAs to address the types of extreme wealth inequality outlined earlier in the chapter. International CDAs, however, provide an example of the potential of these programs in addressing issues of economic inequality. The recently introduced CDA program in Israel, for example, provides every Israeli child with a 50 shekel (about $14) deposit every month that can be placed in an array of investment accounts and includes the opportunity for Israeli households to make additional contributions (Grinstein-Weiss et al., 2019). This program thus has the potential, even at its most conservative, to provide well over $3,000 to children turning 18; an amount that can quintuple if parents choose to invest in accounts with higher interest rates and save the money until their children turn 21.

Individual Development Accounts

Individual Development Accounts (IDAs) are similar to CDAs but instead focus on low-income households generally rather than children specifically. IDAs are intended in part to address a core discrepancy in asset-building policy in the United States—most of the asset-building policies in the United States target higher-income households who can afford a mortgage or retirement account contribution (Sherraden, 1991). Eighty four percent of the federal asset-building budget benefits households making more than $80,000 a year, while 0.04 percent of asset-building expenditures go to households making $19,000 or less (Woo, Rademacher, and Meier, 2010). IDAs seek to rectify this imbalance by providing low-income households with the types of savings incentives provided to higher-income households.

IDAs have several core components. Participants are lower-income; the money saved by the participant is partially or fully matched; the savings are restricted and can only be used for purposes like education, housing, or starting a small business; and participants must often complete financial education courses. Unlike CDAs, IDAs are not typically run at larger scales like a state or a city but instead are usually sponsored by organizations such as nonprofit social service agencies. The accounts provided in IDA programs are housed within a traditional financial institution like a bank or credit union, thus allowing for increased financial access for lower-income populations.

Research shows that access to IDAs has a number of benefits to households, including increased homeownership rates and educational attainment (Leckie, Dowie, and Gyorfi-Dyke, 2008; Mills et al., 2008). A recent randomized, controlled trial of the federally supported Assets for Independence IDA program found a number of positive results: IDA program participants increased their median liquid assets held and experienced substantially lower rates of hardships relating to their utilities, their housing, or their health (Mills et al., 2016). These households were also less likely to use certain alternative financial services and reported increased confidence in their ability to handle normal expenses. It is thus encouraging that IDAs have been widely adopted at the community level. In fact, over a thousand IDA programs with tens of thousands of IDA

Developing Financial Assets 137

participants have been created over the years (Prosperity Now, 2017a). Many of these programs are supported by public expenditures, most prominently through the aforementioned Assets for Independence program administered through the U.S. Department of Health and Human Services. While the number of IDA programs is large and IDAs continue to be a popular service, expanding the reach and support of IDA programs should remain a key focus in addressing issues of unequal wealth access in the United States.

Tax Policies to Promote Asset Building

While programs like CDAs and IDAs are encouraging, they are currently limited in scope. As previously noted, tax policy in many ways encourages wealth inequality in the United States through financing asset-building policies that primarily benefit the already well-off. However, tax policy can also be used to promote asset building among lower-income populations. Changes to tax policy can affect large swaths of the U.S. population and are thus an encouraging avenue to pursue asset-building reforms. Two proposals are designed to support lower-income saving—the Financial Security Credit and the Rainy Day EITC.

The Financial Security Credit is a proposed change to the tax code that incentivizes the type of savings accessible to lower-income households. This credit offers up to $500 in additional funds for households that save in a wide variety of savings vehicles ranging from retirement accounts to basic savings accounts (H.R. 4236, 2015). This differentiates the Financial Security Credit from other tax policies like the Saver's Credit, which only incentivize retirement savings. By linking this credit to tax filing (and offering the ability to directly open savings accounts at tax time, something not currently allowed under U.S. regulations), this credit incentivizes savings at the point where lower-income families are often receiving large financial windfalls from the tax refund and are thus more likely to be able to save their money.

The Rainy Day EITC proposal builds off the fact that the EITC is one of the most substantial antipoverty policies in the United States, lifting around 6.5 million people (and 3.3 million children) out of poverty by providing a lump-sum cash transfer to wage-earning lower-income households when they file their taxes (Center on Budget and Policy Priorities, 2016). The EITC plays a substantial role in providing financial security to working lower-income households, but the one-time payment structure of the policy may make it difficult to save— receiving a large payout early in the year may lead to those funds being exhausted and thus unable to buffer against any emergencies later in the year. The Rainy Day EITC proposal addresses this by allowing households to defer part of their EITC payment (20 percent) for six months and to also receive a 50 percent match for doing so (Levin, 2015). For example, a household receiving a $2,500 EITC would receive $2,000 at tax time and $750 six months later for a total of $2,750. This proposal would allow households to better distribute their tax credits across the year and directly incentivizes savings.

Universal Retirement Accounts

The previously described programs and policies are intended to help build assets to protect households against emergencies in the short term and to increase the accessibility of investments like higher education or homeownership in early or later adulthood. However, they do not directly address the issue of providing substantial assets in retirement. As previously noted, Americans in general do not have enough assets to support themselves in retirement, and this problem is especially acute for lower-income households. While higher-income Americans typically have access to tax-preferred retirement savings vehicles like the 401(k) through their employers, these retirement programs are not available to many lower-income households.

The myRA program, a Federal program that was implemented in 2016 but discontinued soon thereafter, was one effort aimed at rectifying this discrepancy by offering a free retirement account to any U.S. household that is not tied to any employer. MyRA had many elements that would benefit lower-income households. For instance, it had no withdrawal penalties and thus allowed funds to be used to manage any emergencies, it had a very simple structure (there was only one investment choice), it was relatively easy to navigate for households who may have never managed a retirement account before, and there was no minimum amount required to open or maintain an account (U.S. Department of the Treasury, 2017). Although myRA represented a potential means of addressing the lack of retirement savings among lower-income households, the take-up of the program was low. Only approximately 20,000 people signed up for a myRA at the end of its first year (Lobosco, 2016). This low enrollment combined with the relatively modest returns offered by myRA (the interest rate on myRA investments was substantially lower than what is typically available through other investment funds) meant that myRA could only be a partial solution to the lack of retirement savings among lower-income households.

While myRA was ended by the federal government in 2017, the idea of a universal retirement savings account still has potential to help build long-term savings for the entire population. Another option proposed by the Brookings Institution would be to tie retirement savings accounts to individuals rather than to employers (Friedman, 2015). Such an approach would ensure that access to the benefits of having retirement accounts was afforded to all households and not just those working in a certain class of jobs and would also provide a way for the government to directly incentivize employers to offer a retirement plan through the use of tax credits. A policy like this has the potential to generate tens of billions of dollars in additional savings contributions, with lower-income households benefiting substantially more under the proposed system than under the current one.

Using Research to Enhance the Impact of Programs and Policies

Since the work on building assets in lower-income households began in earnest in the early 1990s, research on the role that assets play in the lives of lower-income households has grown steadily. Although this growth in interest is welcome, there is still much work to be done in both understanding how to effectively design policies and programs to help build assets in lower-income households.

The decentralized and diverse nature of asset-building interventions is both a challenge and an opportunity in understanding the efficacy of these programs. Many asset-building programs are run by single organizations like nonprofit social service agencies or credit unions, and, as such, these programs have a limited reach and scalability. Moreover, the nature of the organizations implementing these programs makes rigorous impact evaluations a challenge, as social service agencies may be hesitant to restrict the number of people offered asset-building programs to create a control group for a randomized, controlled trial. However, the diffuse landscape of asset-building programs also means there is ample room for flexibility and creativity in the design and evaluation of these programs, as well as a continual need for pilot tests to assess the efficacy of asset-building interventions.

As an example, consider CDA programs in the United States. There are dozens of these programs offered in dozens of states, and these programs have different structures in terms of funding sources, administration, requirements, payments, and supplemental program offerings. In general, the evidence shows that CDAs are effective in improving savings behaviors and promoting long-term investments like higher education. However, what we do not categorically know is how best to optimize these programs. There remains a wide array of outstanding questions. Is financial education an effective way of encouraging enhanced engagement with CDAs or with the ways in which CDA funds are used? What is the relationship between varying levels of initial seed deposits into the CDAs and outcomes? What is the optimal matched savings rate to promote parents making additional deposits into the accounts? Are matched savings or lotteries more effective at driving savings behaviors? What is the ideal place to enroll parents and children in CDAs (e.g., hospitals, schools, banks, etc.)? Can financial capability initiatives targeted at parents increase the efficacy of CDAs for children?

Every one of these questions can be answered to some extent through experimental research, and the fact that CDA programs are themselves wrestling with these issues means that there are a host of different venues in which research on CDAs can play an important role in optimizing the programs. This is not unique to CDAs. Emergency savings programs, which are often implemented by nonprofits or credit unions seeking to address the lack of liquid assets in their populations, and tax-time savings programs like those implemented at Volunteer Income Tax Assistance sites are often very diverse in both the structure of the program and in the populations they serve. Similarly, many of the questions on how to optimize CDAs can be applied to the optimization of IDAs as well. In a sense, this has been a hidden benefit of the lack of federal support for lower-income asset-building policies. As states, cities, and organizations have stepped in to fill the gap, they have also created the sort of diverse program array that is ideal for researchers interested in improving asset-building interventions.

Although there are many promising opportunities for research on asset-building interventions, the type of research conducted is important. This is particularly true if the ultimate goal of this work is robust and universal programs and policies aimed at addressing issues of wealth inequality. Advocates for large, asset-building programs for the poor will likely face strong opposition to their enactment and implementation, and so arguing for these policies requires strong evidence of the sort provided by randomized, controlled trials conducted in the field. This is particularly true as many financial capability interventions are acutely vulnerable to self-selection issues (Meier and Sprenger, 2013). For example, a nonexperimental evaluation of a financial education program (i.e., an evaluation without a control group who did not receive financial education) might show that participants' savings behaviors improved after the program, but this may simply be attributable to the fact that people who selected to enroll into the program were also motivated to improve their savings and these improvements would have happened with or without the financial education program. Randomized, controlled trials allow us to isolate the effects of the program and confidently make assertions about what works and what does not in asset-building initiatives.

Beyond running experimental evaluations, it is also important to look at the impacts of asset-building interventions over time. Although some asset-building initiatives like those focused on building emergency savings may be appropriate to evaluate over shorter time frames, many programs like CDAs and IDAs are concerned with asset building over long periods of a person's life. As such, the field of asset building sorely needs more work assessing the impacts of these programs over extended time frames. Currently, there are only a handful of experimental analyses of asset-building initiatives over time, including the American Dream Demonstration (Grinstein-Weiss et al., 2012), SEED OK (Huang et al., 2014), and the Refund to Savings Initiative (Roll et al., 2019). Asset-building research should also seek to understand how access to different types of assets interact with each other over time. For example, there is currently very limited understanding of the ways in which interventions that build emergency savings (such as the Refund to Savings Initiative) may lead to enhanced development of long-term assets over time. It is possible that buffering lower-income households against shocks in the short term allows them the necessary space to save for home improvements, a down payment on a house, or additional education.

Reforming Policies and Advocating for Programs to Spread the Wealth

This chapter has outlined the various ways in which public policy fails to facilitate saving in lower-income populations while promoting saving in more affluent households and has proposed several specific policies to address this issue including the Financial Security Credit and the Rainy Day EITC proposal. Although one of the biggest explicit barriers to promoting saving in lower-income households has been recently rectified (i.e., asset limits for Medicaid recipients), there remains much work to be done in reforming policy to create enhanced opportunities for lower-income households.

Irrespective of specific policies on wealth building, a fundamental challenge to promoting lower-income savings at the policy level stems from misguided perceptions about lower-income households and the role of the government in supporting asset growth. This perspective views TANF cash transfers and SNAP support as "welfare," while policies like the mortgage interest deduction, the tax-preferred treatment of 401(k)s, and the low tax rates on capital gains are not perceived similarly. It is also this perspective that views the poor as being unable or unwilling to save their money, despite considerable evidence to the contrary (Schreiner and Sherraden, 2007).

This issue is not something that can be easily solved with a new policy or additional public funding of existing programs. It requires a new understanding of the financial lives of the poor that cuts against entrenched American views that hold that poverty is something that can just be overcome with hard work and sacrifice and that the poor are simply too impecunious or impulsive to save. However, there are many intermediate steps we can take to make policy more conducive to asset building in lower-income populations, even as we work to overhaul entrenched and harmful perspectives surrounding the economic lives of the poor. The first step should be the easing or elimination of asset limits to qualify for the TANF or SNAP programs. While there is some logic to creating limitations on assets to qualify for social welfare programs (providing food stamps to wealthy households serves no public interest), the current structure of asset limits likely causes more harm than good. For example, more than half of U.S. states impose TANF asset limits of somewhere between $1,000 and $2,500, and the vast majority of states restrict participation to those with assets of less than $9,000 (Pew Charitable Trusts, 2016). These limitations put our policy structures and American social values at cross purposes. On the one hand, our political rhetoric tends to hold that social welfare programs should be temporary and people should pull themselves out of poverty through hard work and responsible money management, while on the other hand, we force people to draw down (or never build up) the very assets that can protect them from future financial emergencies or allow them to save toward investments that can pull them out of poverty. In essence, our social welfare programs may alleviate the impacts of poverty in the short term while increasing the likelihood of continued impoverishment in the long term.

Beyond simply easing the asset limitations to access subsistence programs, the United States should shift also some of its focus away from wealth-building policies that cater to higher-income households, and any new federal and state asset-building policies should be developed with special attention to enabling asset building for lower-income households. Building assets for all people in the United States will necessitate programs that are progressive and universal, begin early in life, and are streamlined (Beverly et al., 2008). The program type that most obviously fits this bill is CDAs. Some states have made modest CDAs available to every child born within that state, but the benefits provided by these programs are likely too small to adequately address the massive and growing wealth gap in the United States. A CDA program that was supported by the federal government and made available to every child born in the United States, similar to what Israel has recently implemented, would by contrast have the potential to be generous enough to address these wealth disparities. This would be particularly true if the program were given a progressive structure as this would help provide redress to the historical factors that have prevented many communities in the United States from building their wealth across time.

Emerging Solutions

While robust, universal, progressive wealth-building policies are perhaps the ideal way of addressing the wealth disparity, such policies and programs often have to wait a long time for their political moment to emerge. Rather than waiting for the next key political moment to make broad, systemic changes, there are many exciting and encouraging solutions to asset building in lower-income households emerging from the public and private sectors today. Many of these are quite new and represent key avenues for future research and program development.

The Expansion of Employer-Based Financial Wellness Programs

These programs, which have multiplied substantially in recent years, involve employers providing some level of financial services to their employees. These programs are extremely varied. They can range from one-off seminars providing financial education, to in-depth financial management tools, to access to financial coaches, to employer-sponsored small dollar loan programs that provide short-term loans from employers to employees in the case of a financial need, offering better terms than other sources of short-term credit like payday lenders.

Building Savings into Existing Payment Streams

Banks, nonprofits, cities, and private organizations have experimented with ways to help people build savings as they meet existing payment obligations. The basic idea behind these programs is that people have a wide variety of necessary payments they have to make as part of their continual financial obligations, and by shifting a portion of these payments into savings, it is possible to help individuals improve their asset levels. There are several examples of these programs. Credit builder loans are small loans given to help the borrower build their credit history and their savings levels at the same time. The borrower's monthly payments are used to pay down the loan balance and are automatically shifted into a savings account that the borrower gets access to after the loan is repaid. Other possibilities include tying the development of emergency savings levels into payment obligations like child support payments (U.S. Department of Health and Human Services, 2016), debt management plans operated by credit counseling agencies (Heisler and Lutter, 2015), or rent payments (Emple, 2013).

Behavioral Economics Interventions

Behavioral economics approaches seek to understand how biases in individual decision-making can lead to suboptimal decisions and then develop interventions to address those biases. They have in many ways revolutionized our approach to designing financial capability programs. There have been too many behavioral interventions to cover here, but some notable examples include the Save More Tomorrow program, which allows employees to commit to dedicating a portion of their future income increases to their retirement account (Thaler and Benartzi, 2004), the aforementioned Refund to Savings Initiative, which changes the way tax refund allocation choices are structure to promote the saving of the refund (Grinstein-Weiss et al., 2015), and the shift of retirement savings contributions from an opt-in to an opt-out structure (Madrian and Shea, 2001). Through relatively modest changes in the way decisions are structured, each of these programs have led to striking changes in financial behaviors.

Financial Capability Apps

As smartphones become fairly ubiquitous in households across the income spectrum, an entire cottage industry of apps has emerged to help smartphone users meet their financial goals. An in-depth exploration of these apps, their advantages, and their drawbacks is not possible here, but many of these apps show promise in helping households build their short- and long-term savings by functionally automating savings behaviors and using behavioral techniques or algorithms to make the process of saving relatively painless. The Qapital app, for example, "punishes" households by saving a set amount when a household spends money on a guilty pleasure. It also incentivizes thrifty spending behavior by directly linking this behavior with progress toward tailored financial goals. The Digit app tracks a person's spending habits and moves money into a savings account if the app determines the user can afford it. The Acorns app will round-up every purchase made to the nearest dollar and deposit the excess in an investment account. For example, a $3.25 coffee purchase would translate into $0.75 invested.

While the continued development of these apps is both exciting and encouraging, they are unlikely to substantially address the savings needs of lower-income households. Families whose incomes are almost entirely spent on essential expenses cannot afford to have an average of $0.50 per purchase sent to an investment account or to have excess money taken out of their accounts when they "splurge" on a special purchase. However, other apps do have the potential to improve lower-income households' financial capability without imposing additional constraints on their finances. The Mint app, for example, contains an array of features that make financial management easier and more automatic. It creates highly detailed budgets automatically based on past spending behavior, provides alerts when users are approaching or exceeding their budget limits, provides payment reminders, and links a wide variety of accounts (e.g., bank accounts, credit cards, retirement accounts, etc.) so they can all be summarized on a single screen. For households who operate continually under conditions of scarcity and face all the associated behavioral and cognitive risks of scarcity (Mullainathan and Shafir, 2013), a tool that automates budgeting and provides prompts to guide behavior may help nudge households toward better financial outcomes while imposing few opportunity costs.

Conclusion

It takes more than money to make a life livable. This chapter has viewed the issue of promoting livable lives through a largely financial lens, but a well-ordered balance sheet by itself is not sufficient for someone to live a fulfilling life. To do this, individuals need access to good health care, strong educational options for themselves and their children, the ability to live in a community that suits their needs, a reasonable certainty that their lives will not be derailed by an unexpected emergency, and so on. However, while many of the components of a livable life encompass much more than financial concerns, finances in many ways dictate our relationship to these components. If a person has enough in savings that they can forgo a day of work, they may be more likely to go see a doctor for essential care. If a family is able to set aside a little money each month for a college fund, their child may be more willing to pursue higher education. If a household can save enough for the first and last months' rent, they can afford to make the security deposit on an apartment in a safer neighborhood and better schools.

The relationship between finances and life outcomes is in many ways intuitive. What is not intuitive is how to solve the issue of the massive and increasing wealth disparities observed in the United States as well as the issue of the widespread lack of emergency savings to protect against an unexpected financial shock. This challenge is complex, and while it is possible to imagine a number of simple solutions to facets of the issue (an increased minimum wage, free college tuition, or universal child development accounts), these solutions are likely to face serious political barriers and will only address elements of the asset problem.

As the problem is complex, so too must be the solutions. They must involve a deeper understanding among frontline workers in nonprofits and social welfare agencies about the need to promote savings in their lower-income populations and the available policy and program options to do so. They must involve the continued innovation of programs that make savings easier and more automatic, either at the employer level or through the development of apps or other technologies. They must also involve changes to policy. Cities, states, and the federal government should continue to adopt, support, and expand proven savings programs including IDAs and CDAs, and federal policymakers should also consider both implementing positive wealth policies like the Rainy Day EITC policy and further weakening the asset limits attached to welfare programs.

Researchers too must continue to generate new ideas on how to promote asset building in lower-income communities and further build out the number of randomized, controlled trials evaluating asset-building programs and their long-term impacts. More effort must also be made to establish an economic case for robust asset-building initiatives. While many behavioral economics-oriented interventions are cheap and low-touch, often involving simple changes to a decision environment (such as switching decisions from an opt-in structure to an opt-out structure), programs like IDAs, CDAs, EITC expansions, or universal savings account programs cost money to implement, administer, and support. Researchers must make the case for the economic benefits of these programs. For example, CDAs may generate an increased tax base through promoting college attendance and, therefore, driving higher employment and wages. IDAs may promote improved property values through providing savings for down payments on homes or small business investments. EITC expansions may help families better weather financial emergencies and prevent them from taking on high-cost debt or losing a job because they cannot fix a car or treat an illness. Further, all of these programs have the potential to help families emerge from poverty in ways that income- and consumption-based policies like SNAP and TANF do not. The arguments are there to be made, but they must be made convincingly and with the best available evidence.

These programs and others like them are not a panacea to all our social and economic ills. Our proverbs are replete with all the things money cannot buy such as love, happiness, or friendship. Moreover, a major limitation of many asset-building policies and programs is that they cannot help the extremely poor. Most asset-building initiatives require some degree of contribution from their beneficiaries, and the most impoverished members of our society almost certainly cannot afford to set aside their limited incomes for either short- or long-term savings purposes. However, what asset-building programs can do is to promote stability and flexibility among a large swath of the U.S. population that sorely needs it. By expanding the focus of wealth-building policies and programs to include lower-income and less affluent households, these efforts seek to provide such households with the same type of economic foundation to build their lives that middle- and upper-income households have long had. Of course, we have a long way to go in ensuring that the poor have the same opportunity for a livable life as their wealthier counterparts, but given the severity of the asset problem in the United States, even small steps in the right direction may help substantial numbers of people build lives more aligned with their goals and potential.

Developing Financial Assets 147

References

Ain, J., and D. Newville. 2017. "Expanding Educational Opportunity through Savings." CFED Federal Policy Brief. Retrieved from: https://prosperitynow.org/files/PDFs/expanding_educational_opportunity_through_savings.pdf

Anderson, N. B., C. D. Belar, S. J. Breckler, K. C. Nordal, D. W. Ballard, L. F. Bufka, and K. Wiggins. 2015. *Stress in America: Paying with our Health.* Washington, DC: American Psychological Association.

Babiarz, P., and C. A. Robb. 2014. "Financial Literacy and Emergency Saving." *Journal of Family and Economic Issues,* 35, 40–50.

Barr, M. S. 2004. "Banking the Poor." *Yale Journal on Regulation,* 21, 121.

Barr, M. S. 2010. *And Banking for All?* Darby, PA: Diane Publishing.

Beverly, S. G. 2001. "Measures of Material Hardship: Rationale and Recommendations." *Journal of Poverty,* 5, 23–41.

Beverly, S. G., W. Elliott, and M. Sherraden. 2013. "Child Development Accounts and College Success: Accounts, Assets, Expectations, and Achievements." *CSD Perspective,* 13, 27.

Beverly, S., M. Sherraden, M., R. Cramer, T. Williams Shanks, Y. Nam, and M. Zhan. 2008. "Determinants of Asset Holdings." *Asset Building and Low-Income Families.* Edited by S. M. McKernan and M. Sherraden. Washington, DC: Urban Institute Press, pp. 89–151.

Birkenmaier, J., and Q. Fu. 2015. "The Association of Alternative Financial Services Usage and Financial Access: Evidence from the National Financial Capability Study." *Journal of Family and Economic Issues,* 37, 1–11.

Birkenmaier, J., and S. W. Tyuse. 2005. "Affordable Financial Services and Credit for the Poor: The Foundation of Asset Building." *Journal of Community Practice,* 13, 69–85.

Board of Governors of the Federal Reserve System. 2016. "Report on the Economic Well-Being of U.S. Households in 2015." Retrieved from http://www.federalreserve.gov/2015-report-economic-well-being-us-households -201605.pdf

Board of Governors of the Federal Reserve System. 2018. "Report on the Economic Well-Being of U.S. Households in 2017." Retrieved from https://www.federalreserve.gov/publications/files/2017-report-economic-well-being-us-households-201805.pdf

Board of Governors of the Federal Reserve System. 2019. "Student Loans Owned and Securitized, Outstanding." Retrieved from https://fred.stlouisfed.org/series/SLOAS

Bradley, C., S. Burhouse, H. Gratton, and R. A. Miller. 2009. "Alternative Financial Services: A Primer." *FDIC Quarterly,* 3, 39–47.

Card, D., and A. B. Krueger. 2015. *Myth and Measurement: The New Economics of the Minimum Wage.* Princeton, NJ: Princeton University Press.

Carr, D., and D. Umberson. 2013. "The Social Psychology of Stress, Health, and Coping." *Handbook of Social Psychology.* Edited by J. DeLamater and A. Ward. Netherlands: Springer, pp. 465–487.

Carter, K. N., T. Blakely, S. Collings, F. I. Gunasekara, and K. Richardson. 2009. "What Is the Association Between Wealth and Mental Health?" *Journal of Epidemiology and Community Health,* 63, 221–226.

Carter, G. R., and A. O. Gottschalck. 2011. "Drowning in Debt: Housing and Households with Underwater Mortgages." U.S. Census Bureau American Housing Survey Working Paper. Washington, DC: U.S. Census Bureau.

Center on Assets, Education, and Inclusion. 2016. "How Student Debt Is Helping to Increase the Wealth Gap and Reduce the Return on a Degree: Are Children's Savings Accounts (CSAs) a Viable Alternative?" AEDI Brief. Retrieved from https://pdfs.semanticscholar.org/88f3/16ee960476f20ac32f78052dc35ac2345973.pdf

Center on Budget and Policy Priorities. 2016. "The Earned Income Tax Credit. Policy Basics." Retrieved from https://www.cbpp.org/sites/default/files/atoms/files/policybasics-eitc.pdf

Chetty, R., D. Grusky, M. Hell, N. Hendren, R. Manduca, and J. Narang. 2017. "The Fading American Dream: Trends in Absolute Income Mobility Since 1940." *Science*, 356, 398–406.

Clancy, M., C. K. Han, L. R. Mason, and M. Sherraden. 2006. "Inclusion in College Savings Plans: Program Features and Savings." *Proceedings, Annual Conference on Taxation and Minutes of the Annual Meeting of the National Tax Association*, 99, 385–393.

Collins, J. M., and L. Gjertson. 2013. "Emergency Savings for Low-Income Consumers." *Focus*, 30, 12–17.

Consumer Financial Protection Bureau. 2013. "Payday Loans and Deposit Advance Products: A White Paper of Initial Data Findings." Retrieved from https://files.consumerfinance.gov/f/201304_cfpb_payday-dap-whitepaper.pdf

Davison, G., S. Roll, S. Taylor, and M. Grinstein-Weiss. 2017. "Financial Necessity or Financial Nightmare? The Experience of Payday Loan Use in Low-Income Households." CSD Research Brief. St. Louis, MO: Washington University, Center for Social Development.

Despard, M. R., D. C. Perantie, L. Luo, J. Oliphant, and M. Grinstein-Weiss. 2015. "Use of Alternative Financial Services Among Low- and Moderate-Income Households: Findings from a Large-Scale National Household Financial Survey." CSD Research Brief No. 15-57. St. Louis, MO: Washington University, Center for Social Development.

Despard, M. R., D. Perantie, S. Taylor, M. Grinstein-Weiss, T. Friedline, and R. Raghavan. 2016. "Student Debt and Hardship: Evidence from a Large Sample of Low- and Moderate-Income Households." *Children and Youth Services Review*, 70, 8–18.

Emple, H. 2013. "Asset-Oriented Rental Assistance: Next Generation Reforms for HUD's Family Self-Sufficiency Program." New America Foundation.

Employment and Social Development Canada. 2015. "2014 CESP Annual Statistical Review." Retrieved from https://www.canada.ca/en/employment-social-development/services/student-financial-aid/education-savings/reports/2014-statistical-review.html

Engle, J., and V. Tinto. 2008. "Moving Beyond Access: College Success for Low-Income, First-Generation Students." Pell Institute for the Study of Opportunity in Higher Education.

Engelhardt, G. V., and J. Gruber. 2004. "Social Security and the Evolution of Elderly Poverty." No. w10466. National Bureau of Economic Research.

Federal Deposit Insurance Corporation. 2018. "2017 FDIC National Survey of Unbanked and Underbanked Households." Washington, DC: FDIC.

Financial Security Credit Act of 2015, H.R. 4236, 114th Congress. 2015.

Friedman, J. N. 2015. "Building on What Works: A Proposal to Modernize Retirement Savings." Discussion Paper 2015-06. The Hamilton Project.

Fry, R. 2012. "A Record One-in-Five Households Now Owe Student Loan Debt." Pew Research Center. September 26.

Grinstein-Weiss, M., C. Key, S. Guo, Y. H. Yeo, and K. Holub. 2013. "Homeownership and Wealth Among Low-and Moderate-Income Households." *Housing Policy Debate*, 23, 259–279.

Grinstein-Weiss, M., O. Kondratjeva, S. P. Roll, O. Pinto, and G. Gottlieb. 2019. "The Saving for Every Child Program in Israel: An Overview of a Universal Asset-Building Policy." *Asia Pacific Journal of Social Work and Development*, 29, 20–33.

Grinstein-Weiss, M., D. C. Perantie, B. D. Russell, K. Comer, S. H. Taylor, L. Luo, C. Key, and D. Ariely. 2015. "Refund to Savings 2013: Comprehensive Report on a Large-Scale Tax-Time Saving Program." CSD Research Report 15-06. St. Louis, MO: Washington University, Center for Social Development.

Grinstein-Weiss, M., M. Sherraden, W. Rohe, W. G. Gale, M. Schreiner, and C. Key. 2012. "Long-Term Follow-Up of Individual Development Accounts: Evidence from the Add Experiment." SSRN Working Paper No. 2096408.

Gross, T., M. J. Notowidigdo, and J. Wang. 2014. "Liquidity Constraints and Consumer Bankruptcy: Evidence from Tax Rebates." *Review of Economics and Statistics*, 96, 431–443.

Hamilton, D., and W. Darity. 2010. "Can 'Baby Bonds' Eliminate the Racial Wealth Gap in Putative Post-Racial America?" *The Review of Black Political Economy*, 37, 207–216.

Harold Alfond College Challenge. 2017. "$500 Alfond Grant for Your Baby's Future!" Retrieved from https://www.500forbaby.org/

Heisler, K., and S. Lutter. 2015. "Incorporating Savings into the Debt Management Plan." *A Fragile Balance*. Edited by J. M. Collins. New York: Palgrave Macmillan, pp. 193–200.

Hogarth, J. M., C. E. Anguelov, and J. Lee. 2005. "Who Has a Bank Account? Exploring Changes over Time, 1989–2001." *The Journal of Family and Economic Issues*, 26, 7–30.

Hotz, V. J., J. Rasmussen, and E. Wiemers. 2016. "Intergenerational Transmission of Inequality: Parental Wealth and the Financing of Children's College and Home Buying." Paper presented to Society of Labor Economists, Seattle.

Huang, J., M. Sherraden, Y. Kim, and M. Clancy. 2014. "Effects of Child Development Accounts on Early Social-Emotional Development: An Experimental Test." *JAMA Pediatrics*, 168, 265–271.

Iacoviello, M. 2011. "Housing Wealth and Consumption." International Finance Discussion Papers 1027. Board of Governors of the Federal Reserve System.

Key, C. 2014. "The Finances of Typical Households After the Great Recession." *The Assets Perspective: The Rise of Asset Building and Its Impact on Social Policy*. Edited by R. Cramer and T. R. Williams Shanks. New York: Palgrave Macmillan, pp. 33–65.

King, J. 2010. "ASPIRE Act Introduced in the House." *New America*. Retrieved from: https://www.newamerica.org/asset-building/the-ladder/aspire-act-introduced-in-the-house/

Leckie, N., M. Dowie, and C. Gyorfi-Dyke. 2008. "Learning to Save, Saving to Learn: Early Impacts of the Learn $ave Individual Development Accounts Project." Social Research and Demonstration Corporation.

Lee, J. M., and K. T. Kim. 2016. "Assessing Financial Security of Low-Income Households in the United States." *Journal of Poverty*, 20, 296–315.

Levin, E. 2015. "Rainy Day EITC: A New Idea to Boost Financial Security for Low-Wage Workers." *Prosperity Now Blog*. Retrieved from: https://prosperitynow.org/blog/rainy-day-eitc-new-idea-boost-financial-security-low-wage-workers

Lobosco, K. 2016. "After One Year, 20,000 People Are Saving for Retirement with Obama's myRA." *CNN Money*. Retrieved from http://money.cnn.com/2016/12/16/retirement/obama-myra-retirement-saving/

Madrian, B. C., and D. F. Shea. 2001. "The Power of Suggestion: Inertia in 401 (k) Participation and Savings Behavior." *The Quarterly Journal of Economics*, 116, 1149–1187.

Mani, A., S. Mullainathan, E. Shafir, and J. Zhao. 2013. "Poverty Impedes Cognitive Function." *Science*, 341, 976–980.

McKernan, S. M., C. Ratcliffe, M. Simms, and S. Zhang. 2014. "Do Racial Disparities in Private Transfers Help Explain the Racial Wealth Gap? New Evidence from Longitudinal Data." *Demography*, 51, 949–974.

McKernan, S. M., C. Ratcliffe, E. Steuerle, and S. Zhang. 2013. "Less than Equal: Racial Disparities in Wealth Accumulation." Washington, DC: Urban Institute.

McKernan, S. M., C. Ratcliffe, and K. Vinopal. 2009. "Do Assets Help Families Cope with Adverse Events?" Washington, DC: Urban Institute.

Meier, S., and C. D. Sprenger. 2013. "Discounting Financial Literacy: Time Preferences and Participation in Financial Education Programs." *Journal of Economic Behavior & Organization*, 95, 159–174.

Mills, G., W. G. Gale, R. Patterson, G. V. Engelhardt, M. D. Eriksen, and E. Apostolov. 2008. "Effects of Individual Development Accounts on Asset Purchases and Saving Behavior: Evidence from a Controlled Experiment." *Journal of Public Economics*, 92, 1509–1530.

Mills, G., S. McKernan, C. Ratcliffe, S. Edelstein, M. Pergamit, B. Braga, H. Hahn, and S. Elkin. 2016. "Building Savings for Success: Early Impacts from the Assets for Independence Program Randomized Evaluation." OPRE Report #2016-59. The Urban Institute and the Office of Planning, Research and Evaluation.

Mullainathan, S., and E. Shafir. 2013. *Scarcity: Why Having Too Little Means So Much*. New York: Macmillan.

Neuberger, Z., R. Greenstein, and P. Orszag. 2006. "Barriers to Saving." Communities and Banking Series. Boston: Federal Reserve Bank of Boston.

O'Brien, R. 2008. "Ineligible to Save? Asset Limits and the Saving Behavior of Welfare Recipients." *Journal of Community Practice*, 16, 183–199.

Oliver, M. L., and T. M. Shapiro. 1997. *Black Wealth/White Wealth*. New York: Routledge.

Pew Charitable Trusts. 2016. "A Look at Access to Employer-Based Retirement Plans and Participation in the States." Retrieved from http://www.pewtrusts.org/en/research-and-analysis/reports/2016/01/a-look-at-access-to-employer-based-retirement-plans-and-participation-in-the-states

Pew Charitable Trusts. 2016. "Do Limits on Family Assets Affect Participation in, Costs of TANF?" Issue Brief. Retrieved from http://www.pewtrusts.org/en/research-and-analysis/issue-briefs/2016/07/do-limits-on-family-assets-affect-participation-in-costs-of-tanf

Pew Charitable Trusts. 2017. "Retirement Plan Access and Participation Across Generations." Issue Brief. Retrieved from https://www.pewtrusts.org/-/media/assets/2017/02/ret_retirement_plan_access_and_participation_across_generations.pdf

Pfeffer, F. T., S. Danziger, and R. F. Schoeni. 2013. "Wealth Disparities Before and After the Great Recession." *The Annals of the American Academy of Political and Social Science*, 650, 98–123.

Piketty, T. 2014. *Capital in the 21st Century*. Cambridge, MA: Harvard University Press.

Poterba, J. M. 1997. "Demographic Structure and the Political Economy of Public Education." *Journal of Policy Analysis and Management*, 16, 48–66.

Prosperity Now. 2017a. "Everything You Need to Know About Individual Development Accounts (IDAs)." Retrieved from https://prosperitynow.org/everything-you-need-know-about-individual-development-accounts-idas

Prosperity Now. 2017b. "Prosperity Now Scorecard: Asset Limits in Public Benefit Programs." Retrieved from http://scorecard.prosperitynow.org/data-by-issue#finance/policy/asset-limits-in-public-benefit-programs

Prosperity Now. 2017c. "Prosperity Now Scorecard: Homeownership by Income." Retrieved from http://scorecard.prosperitynow.org/data-by-issue#housing/outcome/homeownership-by-income

Rhee, N. 2013. *The Retirement Savings Crisis*. Washington, DC: National Institute on Retirement Security.

Robbins, E. 2013. "Banking the Unbanked: A Mechanism for Improving the Financial Security of Low-Income Individuals." *Policy Perspectives*, 20, 85–91.

Rohe, W. M., and L. S. Stewart. 1996. "Homeownership and Neighborhood Stability." *Housing Policy Debate*, 7, 37–81.

Roll, S. P., G. Davison, M. Grinstein-Weiss, M. R. Despard, and S. Bufe. 2018. "Refund to Savings 2015–2016: Field Experiments to Promote Tax-Time Saving in Low- and Moderate-Income Households." CSD Research Report No. 18-28. St. Louis, MO: Washington University, Center for Social Development.

Roll, S. P., B. D. Russell, D. C. Perantie, and M. Grinstein-Weiss. 2019. "Encouraging Tax Time Savings with a Low Touch, Large Scale Intervention: Evidence from the Refund to Savings Experiment." *Journal of Consumer Affairs*, 53, 87–125.

Roll, S. P., S. H. Taylor, and M. Grinstein-Weiss. 2016. "Financial Anxiety in Low- and Moderate-Income Households: Findings from the Household Financial Survey." CSD Research Brief No. 16-42. St. Louis, MO: Washington University, Center for Social Development.

Saez, E., and G. Zucman. 2016. "Wealth Inequality in the United States Since 1913: Evidence from Capitalized Income Tax Data." *The Quarterly Journal of Economics*, 131, 519–578.

Schreiner, M., and M. Sherraden. 2007. *Can the Poor Save?: Saving and Asset Building in Individual Development Accounts*. New York: Transaction Publishers.

Searle, B. A., and S. Köppe. 2014. "Assets, Saving and Wealth, and Poverty: A Review of Evidence." Final Report to the Joseph Rowntree Foundation. Personal Finance Research Centre.

Shah, A. K., E. Shafir, and S. Mullainathan. 2015. "Scarcity Frames Value." *Psychological Science*, 26, 402–412.

Shapiro, T N. 2001. "The Importance of Assets: The Benefits of Spreading Asset Ownership." *Assets for the Poor: The Benefits of Spreading Asset Ownership*. Edited by T. N. Shapiro and E. Wolff. New York: Russell Sage Foundation, pp. 11–33.

Shapiro, T. N. T. Meschede, and S. Osoro. 2013. "The Roots of the Widening Racial Wealth Gap: Explaining the Black–White Economic Divide." Institute on Assets and Social Policy Research and Policy Brief. Waltham, MA: Brandeis University.

Sherraden, M. 1990. "Stakeholding: Notes on a Theory of Welfare Based on Assets." *Social Service Review*, 64, 580–601.

Sherraden, M. 1991. *Assets and the Poor: A New American Welfare Policy*. New York: M. E. Sharpe.

Sherraden, M., and M. Sherraden. 2000. "Asset Building: Integrating Research, Education and Practice." *Advances in Social Work*, 1, 61–77.

Shobe, M. and D. Page-Adams. 2001. "Assets, Future Orientation, and Well-Being: Exploring and Extending Sherraden's Framework." *Journal of Sociology and Social Welfare*, 28, 109–128.

Thaler, R. H., and S. Benartzi. 2004. "Save More Tomorrow: Using Behavioral Economics to Increase Employee Saving." *Journal of Political Economy*, 112, S164–S187.

U.S. Bureau of the Census. 2017. "Real Median Household Income in the United States." Retrieved from https://fred.stlouisfed.org/series/MEHOINUSA672N

U.S. Department of Health and Human Services, Office of Child Support Enforcement. 2016. "Building Assets for Fathers and Families (BAFF) Demonstration Grant." (Financial Capability Fact Sheet #1). Retrieved from:https://www.acf.hhs.gov/sites/default/files/programs/css/baff_grant_financial_apability_fact_sheet_1.pdf

U.S. Department of the Treasury. 2017. "About myRA." Retrieved from https://myra.gov/about/

U.S. Government Accountability Office. 2015. "Retirement Security: Most Households Approaching Retirement Have Low Savings." GAO-15-419. Report to the Ranking Member, Subcommittee on Primary Health and Retirement Security, Committee on Health, Education, Labor, and Pensions, U.S. Senate. Washington, DC: U.S. Government Accountability Office.

Wiatrowski, W. J. 2012. "The Last Private Industry Pension Plans: A Visual Essay." *Monthly Labor Review*, 135, 3.

Woo, B., I. Rademachaer, and J. Meier. 2010. "Upside Down: The $400 Billion Federal Asset-Building Budget." CFED Report.

Zager, R., Y. Kim, Y. Nam, M. Clancy, and M. Sherraden. 2010. "The SEED for Oklahoma Kids Experiment: Initial Account Opening and Savings." CSD Research Brief 10–41.

7

Preventing Child Maltreatment

MELISSA JONSON-REID, BRETT DRAKE, PATRICIA L. KOHL,
AND WENDY F. AUSLANDER

The widespread prevalence and detrimental impact of child abuse and neglect
(maltreatment) is an issue of critical importance for the profession of social
work. Although data and research on child maltreatment are more common
in Western industrialized countries, it is nevertheless recognized as a global
problem with sizeable short and long-term costs to individuals and societies
(Fang et al., 2012, 2015; Gilbert et al., 2009; World Health Organization
[WHO], 2016). As a result of its destructive influence upon behavioral, cognitive, health, and personal development, prevention of maltreatment is foundational for a livable life.

What Do We Mean by Child Maltreatment?

There is considerable debate about the best means of defining maltreatment, illustrated by significant variation across both research and policy analyses. For
example, WHO defines maltreatment in the following way:

> Child maltreatment is the abuse and neglect that occurs to children
> under 18 years of age. It includes all types of physical and/or emotional
> ill-treatment, sexual abuse, neglect, negligence and commercial or other
> exploitation, which results in actual or potential harm to the child's
> health, survival, development or dignity in the context of a relationship
> of responsibility, trust or power. Exposure to intimate partner violence
> is also sometimes included as a form of child maltreatment. (2016)

In contrast, federal law in the United States takes a more limited view that
includes "any recent act or failure to act on the part of a parent or caretaker

which results in serious physical or emotional harm, sexual abuse or exploitation . . . or presents an imminent risk of serious harm" (Child Abuse Prevention and Treatment Act, 2010). States are often left to further decide what types of actions or inaction to include to guide intervention by child protection. For example, in Georgia there is no provision to report emotional abuse but in Missouri there is, while in Oregon exposure to domestic violence may be considered maltreatment but not in Missouri (Child Welfare Information Gateway, n.d.). In the United States, child maltreatment is limited to actions or inactions by parent figures or others in caregiving roles (e.g., biological, step, foster parents, other kin guardians, or substitute caregivers such as child care workers). In contrast, the international community often broadens the meaning of who can commit maltreatment to include violence by strangers (WHO, 2016).

Of course, researchers are not necessarily limited to policy definitions. The Centers for Disease Control and Prevention (CDC) includes the words "harm, potential for harm, or threat of harm" in their definition of maltreatment. CDC guidelines encourage researchers to include physical abuse, sexual abuse, psychological abuse, and specific forms of neglect. Neglect may include physical neglect, emotional neglect, medical and dental neglect, educational neglect, inadequate supervision, and exposure to violent environments (Leeb et al., 2008).

There are also a variety of scales and measures used for capturing maltreatment in terms of retrospective recall by children, parents, or sentinel reports (maltreatment risk typically reported by parents, administrative data or case file review; Drake and Jonson-Reid, 2018a). And certainly within the general public there remains a significant debate as to how to define maltreatment, such as when corporal punishment should be considered physical abuse (Ateah and Durrant, 2005; Frechette, Zoratti, and Romano, 2015). Cultural variation in parenting norms may also influence what the public perceives as abusive or neglectful (Calheiros et al., 2016; Klevens et al., 2019; Nadan, Spilsbury, and Korbin, 2015).

Prevalence

Given this variation in definitions, it is not surprising that there is also considerable variation in our understanding of overall prevalence. U.S. estimates of officially reported cases of child maltreatment provide an annual incidence rate of 3.2 in100 children with reports screened in for investigation or assessment and a lifetime estimate of one in three by age 17 (Kim et al., 2016; U.S. Department of Health and Human Services [DHHS], 2019). Self-report estimates of prevalence prior to age 18 range from 38 to 41 percent depending on the form of maltreatment (Finkelhor et al., 2015; Hussey, Chang, and Kotch, 2006).

Although maltreatment is recognized as an international concern, the availability of data across countries and the methodological rigor of data collection varies considerably. A recent study of maltreatment in the United Kingdom provided a lifetime estimate of 24.5 percent of children experiencing some form of maltreatment by age 18 (Radford et al., 2013). This was similar to the rate of 31 percent reported in a recent study of maltreatment in Germany (Witt et al., 2017). Three recent meta-analyses of maltreatment across multiple countries found a combined average prevalence estimate of 22.6 percent for physical abuse (Stoltenborgh et al., 2013), 12.7 percent for sexual abuse (Stoltenborgh et al., 2011), and 18.4 percent for neglect (Stoltenborgh et al., 2013). However, these meta-analyses do not provide an overall combined estimate and the authors note that there were only 16 studies available that included child neglect.

Several other recent international studies have focused on the prevalence of physical abuse. A meta-analysis of studies specific to physical abuse in China found a lifetime prevalence rate of 36.6 percent (Ji and Finkelhor, 2015). A more recent survey in South Korea reported a combined rate of 25.3 percent for physical and psychological maltreatment (Ahn et al., 2017). A prevalence rate of over 40 percent was found for moderate levels of physical abuse within the past month among African and transitional countries (Akmatov, 2010).

Less is known about prevalence among indigenous populations, immigrants, sexual minority youth, children with disabilities, and other cultural subpopulations (Detlaff, Earner, and Phillips, 2009; Euser et al., 2010; Fox, 2003; Friedman et al., 2011; Hibbard et al., 2007; Jones et al., 2012; MacLaurin et al., 2008; O'Donnell et al., 2010; Zhai and Gao, 2009). While some evidence suggests that children with disabilities are at higher risk for maltreatment, there is conflicting evidence in regard to the type of disability and higher or lower risk (Hibbard et al., 2007; Maclean et al., 2017; McDonnell et al., 2018). In regard to race and ethnicity, certain groups appear more or less represented in U.S. official maltreatment counts, but such differences frequently disappear once poverty is taken in account (Putnam-Hornstein et al., 2013). In other cases, there appears to be variation based on nativity rather than poverty (Detlaff et al., 2009). Frequently there are simply too few cases to provide a solid estimate (e.g., many Asian populations, American Indian children, children with disabilities and sexual minority youth; Fox, 2003; Friedman et al., 2011; Hibbard et al., 2007; Zhai and Gao, 2009).

Despite the fact that our understanding of prevalence varies across populations and countries, it is nevertheless clear that child maltreatment is relatively common worldwide. It is also quite clear that child abuse and neglect poses a serious threat to well-being across the lifespan.

How Does Child Maltreatment Impact the Ability to Achieve a Livable Life?

As discussed throughout this book, there are many barriers and challenges preventing individuals and families from experiencing a livable life. However, child maltreatment is particularly pernicious. Childhood can be a time of great joy as well as significant growth and change. It is a time for establishing trust and laying the foundation for strong relationships across a lifetime. It is also a time for establishing the cognitive, self-regulatory, and moral groundwork for supporting a successful transition to the roles and responsibilities necessary for a productive adult life. While some individuals may recover from or exhibit resilience despite abuse or neglect, for others, child maltreatment irreconcilably damages the ability to achieve a livable life.

A significant body of research suggests that the individual and societal costs of maltreatment without effective intervention are substantial. The most recent U.S. estimate of lifetime costs associated with officially reported child abuse and neglect was limited to a single-year cohort, meaning that the lower range for reported children of $272 billion is a significant underestimate (Fang et al., 2012). These economic costs result from higher rates of negative outcomes including lost productivity (Currie and Widom, 2010; Zielinski, 2009), immediate physical injury and death (Gibbs et al., 2013; Spivey et al., 2009; Jonson-Reid, Chance and Drake, 2007; Jonson-Reid, Drake, and Kohl, 2009, 2017), cognitive and educational deficits (Jonson-Reid et al., 2004; Mersky and Topitzes, 2010; Ryan et al., 2018; Scarborough and McCrae, 2010; Stone, 2007), negative health consequences (Duncan et al., 2015; Hussey, Chang, and Kotch, 2006; Felitti et al., 1998; Lanier et al., 2009; Widom et al., 2012), and increased risk of mental health disorders, risky behaviors, criminality, re-victimization, and aggression (Auslander et al., 2002; Auslander et al., 2016; Ben-David et al., 2015; Gerassi, Jonson-Reid and Drake, 2016; Hussey et al., 2006; Jonson-Reid, Kohl and Drake, 2012; Kaplow and Widom, 2007; Mersky and Topitzes, 2010; Renner and Slack, 2006; Turner, Finkelhor, and Ormrod, 2006). Although the majority of outcome research has been done in the United States, available data from other countries suggest that significant costs to individuals and society are common regardless of country of origin (Cromback and Bambonve, 2015; Fang et al., 2015; Gilbert et al., 2009; Kessler et al., 2010; McCarthy et al., 2016; Mbagava, Oburu, and Bakermans-Kranenburg, 2013; Pieterse, 2015).

The multideterminant nature and impact of child abuse and neglect has led to the framing of child maltreatment as a complex and deeply rooted problem (Devaney and Spratt, 2009). For example, the relationship between poverty and child maltreatment is well documented (Drake and Jonson-Reid, 2014; Fowler et al., 2013; Pelton, 2015). Yet clearly, most low-income families do not maltreat their children (Jonson-Reid and Drake, 2018). Research indicates that families at risk of maltreatment face multiple barriers to healthy functioning such as exposure to risks like poverty at the family and community levels, parental mental health or substance abuse problems, and other factors (Holosko et al., 2015; Jonson-Reid and Drake, 2018; Wald, 2014). Further, many children experience chronic maltreatment or other forms of exposure to violence that may compound the deleterious effects of any singular abusive or neglectful experience on the likelihood of achieving a healthy, satisfying, and productive adulthood (Finkelhor et al., 2011; Jonson-Reid, Kohl, and Drake, 2012). A large body of literature has documented that exposure to multiple adverse childhood experiences such as childhood abuse, neglect, and exposure to family violence are leading causes of mental and physical illness in the United States. and internationally (Afifi et al., 2016; Cecil et al., 2017; Duncan et al., 2015; Felitti et al., 1998; Kessler et al., 2010).

Why does maltreatment have such a significant and widespread impact on the life chances of a child? There are many pathways by which abusive or neglectful behaviors may result in harm to developmental processes that allow a child to grow into a healthy and productive adult. Given the multidetermined nature of maltreatment itself, research in this area often relies on an ecological framework, acknowledging the possible impact of risk or protective factors from the individual, to the family, to the community, and to the broader societal policy (Institute of Medicine and National Research Council, 2014). Within this framework a variety of paths have been posited for various outcomes following maltreatment. For example, one explanation for the relationship between child maltreatment and negative health outcomes is that the stress associated with this experience causes lasting neurobiological changes that lead to mental health problems, poor health behaviors, and health outcomes (e.g., Heim et al., 2010; Teicher, Anderson, and Polcari, 2012). Maltreatment and other co-occurring risks can also significantly impact cognitive development as well as educational progress (e.g., Leiter, 2007; Ryan et al., 2018; Stone, 2007), which may then have lasting effects on a child's future socioeconomic status and productivity. Other children may lack the early nurturing relationship that provides the foundation for attachment (De Wolff and Ijzendoorn, 1997), which can cause long-term barriers to healthy relationships and increase the likelihood of risky behaviors in adults (Constantino et al., 2006; Kim and Cicchetti, 2004; Lo, Chan, and Ip, 2017; Oshri et al., 2015). Children also require supervision and protection from threats in their environment. These threats can cause physical injury or exposure to dangers outside the family (e.g., community violence, sexual assault), which may result in significant alterations in development (Jonson-Reid and Drake, 2018; Tillyer, 2015).

At a minimum, a livable life requires the opportunity to achieve positive developmental milestones that allow a child to live a satisfying, healthy, and productive life. The CDC frame the issue by referring to the need of all children to have "safe, secure and nurturing relationships and environments" (2014: 7). This is not dissimilar to the much older idea of Maslow's (1943) hierarchy of needs, which assumes that safety and provision of basic needs and nurturing (love) are foundational to a fulfilled life. The experience of maltreatment threatens some or all of these building blocks, making primary prevention and effective intervention critically important.

Clearly then, child maltreatment represents a significant barrier hindering an individual's chances of experiencing a productive and satisfying adulthood. It can have profound repercussions on an individual's well-being throughout their life. It can damage their development and their ability to form stable and healthy relationships across the life course, which constitute a cornerstone of a livable life.

What Does This Mean for Social Work?

Accepting that child maltreatment is a major threat to an individual experiencing a livable life means advancing practices in the area of surveillance as well as prevention and intervention strategies. Indeed, these two issues are clearly intertwined. Understanding prevalence, risk, and outcomes is key to making the case for intervening but also key to measuring possible improvements over time in relation to policy and practice. This conclusion is echoed in the 2006 WHO report, in conjunction with the International Society for Prevention of Child Abuse and Neglect, that stressed the need for population-based data collection across countries (WHO, 2006).

Social work has a long history of being involved with preventive and intervention approaches to maltreatment and related threats to child and family well-being (Jonson-Reid and Drake, 2018). These efforts over the years, however, have become siloed into professional areas of specialty like child welfare or mental health. This can make continued work toward effective prevention and intervention with such a complex issue difficult. There is often a tension between the role of the social worker in promoting family strengths and strong communities and the role of the social worker in systems like child welfare that intervene after maltreatment occurs. Prevention is increasingly referred to as the domain of public health (Prinz, 2016) although most authors also conclude that any approach taken must include multiple disciplines (Klika, Lee, and Lee, 2018). By contrast, child welfare or the formal response to reported child abuse and neglect is clearly seen as a part of the social work profession (Holosko and Faith, 2015).

Of course, prevention of child maltreatment can be understood to mean many things. First, the "who" and the "when" are unclear. Do we mean intervening with everyone, with a set of at-risk people, or only with people who have already experienced maltreatment? Do we aim to reduce the risk of maltreatment per se or would we like to see gains in other, supporting areas (e.g., family functioning, parental or child well-being). Do we target individual behavior, structural risks like material needs, building community, or all of the above? These answers may guide whether a particular social worker is acting as part of a school, a community development organization, or in policy advocacy. Equally important we might ask, "Who is doing the preventing?" Prevention approaches do exist, but as shown later, this research remains scant and programs difficult to replicate.

While primary prevention is clearly preferable, data indicate that effective intervention to prevent chronic experiences of maltreatment has a significant impact on the risk of long-term outcomes (English et al., 2005; Jaffee and Maikovish-Fong, 2011; Jonson-Reid et al., 2012; Thompson, English, and White, 2016). This suggests that while prevention strategies are being built and tested, equal attention should be paid to families already involved in maltreating behaviors to prevent recurrent abuse and neglect as well as to help ameliorate harm. Here again, although strategies are available, many have yet to be rigorously evaluated across populations and contexts. While several countries have advanced programming around family support across the life span (Pösö, Skivenes, and Hestbæk, 2014), there have been few attempts to replicate approaches across varied cultures and regions (e.g., Chaffin et al., 2012; Howe et al., 2017; Silvosky et al., 2011). Even when an intervention has significant empirical support, we often lack the knowledge and/or resources needed to scale up these approaches (e.g., Fowler et al., 2017; Mikton et al., 2013).

Because of the difficulty in describing the varying support systems and policies internationally, the remainder of the chapter draws on research and practice that is heavily U.S.-centric with hopes that the international study of this phenomenon and policy and program efforts will increase in the future.

What Are the Underlying Factors That Lead to Maltreatment?

An important step in the search for a solution to maltreatment is understanding the modifiable factors that place a child at risk of abuse or neglect. Yet despite decades of research, there are several large gaps that hamper our ability to move

Preventing Child Maltreatment

from discussions of association to cause (Institute of Medicine and National Research Council, 2014). It is not possible to review every key risk and protective factor related to child maltreatment in a single chapter. Consequently, we focus on several of the most important including poverty (at the macro and family levels), caregiver incapacity related to mental health, substance abuse, intimate partner violence, and child vulnerability due to age and disability. These factors are chosen in part because of the well-established associations or co-occurrence with maltreatment as well as their relevance for current intervention practices.

Poverty

Poverty as a factor leading to child maltreatment occurs at both the community and family levels. However, it must first be emphasized that most low-income families do not maltreat their children. Research suggests that poverty either creates stressful conditions that overwhelm a parent's capacity to adequately care for a child or that among poor families there are a subset of families whose socioeconomic condition and poor parenting are related to other underlying causes, such as mental health difficulties or substance abuse (Jonson-Reid and Drake, 2018). We address the first issue, although arguably many of the strategies and potential future directions might apply to both.

Poverty as a risk factor for maltreatment can be thought of geographically in terms of communities (Coulton et al., 2007) as well as at the family level. This first line of work suggests the importance of broader community development (Lothridge et al., 2012). While the idea that neighborhoods may influence maltreatment is not new (e.g., Drake and Pandey, 1996), the mechanisms by which that occurs are not as well articulated (Coulton et al., 2007). There is some evidence that we are seeing very small yet positive reductions in recent household poverty (Fontenot, Semega, and Kollar, 2018). Yet it is unclear at what point such changes may be sufficient to detect population shifts in abuse and this may in part depend on what mechanism is most key to impacting parental behavior.

Some have argued that it is the psychological dimension of a community (i.e., collective efficacy) that is of equal or greater import to parenting than the objective level of resources (Emery, Trung and Wu, 2015; Jaffee et al., 2007). Cohesive and efficacious communities are also believed to provide more informal surveillance and monitoring of children, particularly in relation to the sexual abuse prevention literature (Leclerc, Chiu, and Cale, 2016). On the other hand, other research suggests a role of neighborhood social cohesion for prevention of neglecting but not abusive behaviors (Maguire-Jack and Showalter, 2016). Some argue that this indicates a need for interventions to build a "sense of community" that is broadly supportive of families (Melton, 2014) instead of a more structural economic development approach designed to reduce poverty per se. Much of the work on community-based approaches to child maltreatment prevention focuses on a combination of improving social supports and community efficacy and/or building community-based linkages to services. However, to date, very little rigorous testing of these approaches has occurred (Molner, Beatriz, and Beardslee, 2016).

Other researchers argue that much of the risk conferred by residing in a very low-income community is structural. Disadvantaged communities tend to lack adequate services, healthy foods, and transportation and often have a surplus of less desirable institutions like liquor outlets combined with abandoned homes, broken windows, and vacant lots (Coulton et al., 2007; Freisthler, Byrnes, and Gruenewald, 2009). Physical neighborhood disorder has been linked to intimate partner violence, poor health, and less willingness to report maltreatment (Cohen et al., 2003; Gracia and Herrero, 2007; Kirst et al., 2015). A study using a form of predictive risk modelling at the community level found that while community poverty exerted the strongest effect on predicting substantiated maltreatment, concentration of domestic violence incidents, aggravated assaults, runaway incidents, murders, and drug crimes were also highly predictive (Daley et al., 2016). While neighborhood disorder may increase external risks for children (i.e., safety and crime) and competent parenting is considered a strong buffer for risk related to poverty (Raver and Leadbeater, 1999), some research indicates that increased perception of neighborhood disorder among mothers is associated with lower maternal responsiveness (Lin and Reich, 2016). Structural deficits in community resources not only make it more difficult to parent, but potentially make it more difficult to seek and receive help once maltreatment has occurred (Lothridge, McCroskey and Pecora, 2012).

Poverty is also a key component in the discussion of the overrepresentation of certain racial and ethnic groups among official reports of maltreatment (Jonson-Reid and Drake, 2018; Kim ad Drake, 2017; Pelton, 2015). The overlap between race and poverty at both the family and the community level has its roots in a number of structural and historical injustices (O'Connor, 2001). Not only are African American children more likely to live in lower-income families, they are much more likely to live in high-poverty neighborhoods than their white counterparts (Drake and Rank, 2009). Because poverty places greater strains on parents and because certain groups are more likely to experience family and community level poverty, these becomes powerful explanations for the disproportionate representation of certain minority children among those reported for maltreatment (Pelton, 2015). While some have argued that poverty and/or racial bias leads to heightened surveillance rather than actual heightened risks, empirical data do not support this (Drake et al., 2011; Jonson-Reid et al., 2009;

Drake and Jonson-Reid, 2017). Still others point to the problem that poverty does not appear to have the same impact for Latino or American Indian children despite high levels of poverty. For Latino children, however, researchers have found that this apparent "paradox" does not hold across regions and appears to vary by nativity, with U.S.-born children often overrepresented (Detlaff and Johnson, 2011). For American Indian children, this paradox may reflect issues in national data because of a lack of cross-reporting between tribal child welfare and state child welfare agencies (Kim et al., 2017).

Other researchers have focused on poverty at the family rather than community level. At this level, the stressors imposed by issues such as not being able to meet basic needs or having to work multiple and low-wage jobs with few benefits lead to impaired parenting (Drake and Jonson-Reid, 2014; Slack et al., 2004; Warren and Font. 2015). A recent meta-analysis of the temporal association of family poverty and maltreatment found that cumulative material hardships, income losses, and housing hardship were consistent predictors of maltreatment (Conrad-Heibner and Byram, 2018). Poverty may also exacerbate other factors like early child-rearing or depression that in turn heighten the risk of maltreatment (Jonson-Reid and Drake, 2018). While comparatively little work on addressing material needs to prevent maltreatment has been done, some research indicates that increased employment (Conrad-Heibner and Byram, 2018; Slack et al., 2003), additional child support income (Cancian et al., 2013), and more generous earned income tax credits (Berger et al., 2017) are associated with declines in official maltreatment reported, especially for neglect.

Impaired Caregiver Capacity

The CDC (2014) developed a campaign around the promotion of families that provide safe, stable, and nurturing relationships and environments for children to prevent child maltreatment. This requires caregivers to have the capacity to provide the necessary care, love, and supervision for children. Unfortunately, this is not always the case. Issues of mental health, substance abuse, cognitive delay, intimate partner violence, and social isolation may all impede a person's ability to parent.

Maternal mental health and substance abuse are strongly associated with maltreatment in the literature because they can often impact upon an adult's ability to parent (Dubowitz et al., 2011; Walsh, MacMillan, and Jamieson, 2003; Young, Boles, and Otero, 2007). However, impaired parenting does not always reach the threshold of abuse or neglect. While parenting quality is diminished for most parents with substance abuse or mental health problems, not all parents that have such difficulties go on to abuse or neglect their children (e.g., Neger and Prinz, 2015; Reupert and Mayberry, 2007). We know much less about how maltreating behaviors may develop due to a mental health or substance abuse problem when compared to our understanding of their comorbidity. Only one study was located that attempted to identify the prevalence of maltreating behaviors among women with substance abuse disorders, but the outcome was limited to a self-report of individual neglectful behaviors (Cash and Wilke, 2003). Several studies have noted a relationship between mental health service history and later reports of maltreatment or recurrent maltreatment (Drake, Jonson-Reid, and Sapokaite, 2006; O'Donnell et al., 2015).

There are various ways in which either mental health or substance abuse disorders may increase the risk of maltreatment. Maternal mental health conditions may impede healthy attachment and parenting behaviors in early childhood (Dubber et al., 2015; Muzik and Borovska, 2010) and continue to impact a parent's ability to provide a safe permanent home for their child (Ben David et al., 2015; Kohl, Jonson-Reid, and Drake, 2011). A recent study found that mothers with prior histories of maltreatment as a child were more susceptible to maternal depression, which in turn predicted higher levels of maltreating behaviors toward their own children (Choi et al., 2018). Similarly, substance abuse (often comorbid with other mental health problems) significantly impacts a caregiver's ability to respond to the needs of their child (Seay and Kohl, 2015). Negative impacts on parenting are likely stronger when supportive services are not in place for both the mental health or substance abuse disorders (Neger and Prinz, 2015; Ruepert and Mayberry, 2007). Maternal mental health issues have also been found to be confounded with poverty, which may exert additional impacts on child development (Bouvette-Turcot et al., 2017; Luby, 2015).

Yet another risk factor for maltreatment that may play a confounding role in the relationship of maternal mental health and parenting is the existence of intimate partner violence (McFarlane et al., 2014; Kohl et al., 2005). Intimate partner violence often co-occurs with child maltreatment (Kelleher et al., 2006), leading to a focus on family violence as a significant challenge for social work (Barth and Jonson-Reid, 2017; Barth and Macy, 2018). However, the way in which these issues overlap is not clear. Some have posited that the stress of intimate partner violence may lead to mental health problems in the mother that then increase the risk of maltreating behaviors. On the other hand, Ernest Jouriles and colleagues (2008) in a review of co-occurrence studies found evidence that some violent partners abused both children and mothers Also confounding our understanding of this relationship is that there are typically high rates of other significant risk factors as well (e.g., poverty, substance abuse, etc.; Jones, Gross, and Becker, 2002; Lee, Kotch, and Cox, 2004; Millett, Seay, and Kohl, 2015).

Raising a child is a complex task requiring multiple formal and informal resources across the life course. It is therefore not surprising that social isolation, stress, and lack of parenting skills are associated with maltreatment risk (Berlin, Appleyard, and Carmody, 2014; MacMillan et al., 2009; Rodriguez and Tucker, 2015; Stith et al., 2009). Once again, our understanding of the mechanism by which risk is increased is hampered by several factors. Several studies in this area have looked at the relationship between a "risk for" maltreatment rather than actual abusive or neglectful behaviors (e.g., Rodriguez and Tucker, 2015). Furthermore, the lack of a strong effect of participation in home visiting on child maltreatment (which hypothetically is both a source of social support and parenting skills) calls into question whether these factors in isolation are the prime mechanisms of risk (Jonson-Reid et al., 2018). For example, a study of intergenerational maltreatment found that social support was not a significant protective factor once the researchers controlled for domestic partner violence and community risks (Jaffee et al., 2007). Another recent study found that the availability of social services was associated with decreased relevance of social support in predicting lower levels of child neglect (Negash and Maguire-Jack, 2016). In other words, access to social services may offset deficits in informal social supports.

Child Age and Vulnerability

Given the greater vulnerability to physical and developmental harm and the apparent higher rate of abuse and neglect during the earliest years of life (DeVooght et al., 2011; DHHS, 2019), the maltreatment of very young children (under age 5) is of heightened concern. The care of very young children may be particularly stressful. For example, "shaken baby" behaviors can result in significant brain damage or death and is often related to attempts to stop an infant's crying (e.g., Barr et al., 2009). This stress may be compounded in cases where a mother is ill prepared to parent. One study found that unplanned pregnancy is one of the earliest identifiable risk factors for maltreatment (Guterman 2015). Jessica Bartlett (2014) reported that the following factors were associated with young mothers' risk of infant neglect: median income, low infant birth weight, maternal smoking, maternal childhood history of neglect and positive care, interpersonal violence, and maternal use of mental health services. Similarly, children with seven or more modifiable risk factors noted on birth certificate data (e.g., maternal smoking, lack of prenatal care, birth abnormality, maternal education, young maternal age at birth, multiple children, poverty and lack of father noted) had a very high predicted probability (0.89) of an allegation of maltreatment by age 5 (Putnam-Hornstein and Needell, 2011). The impact of quality child care could be preventive if it provides a respite function and reduces strain related to work for a parent (Ha, Collins and Martino, 2015). However, poverty itself may present a significant barrier to accessing such resources (Klein, 2011).

Raising a child with special needs may also increase parental stress and is often noted as a high risk factor for maltreatment (Svensson, Erickson and Janson, 2013). Similar to intimate partner violence and maltreatment, we know more about the overlap than the causal ordering or possible confounding effects (e.g., Jonson-Reid et al., 2004; Sullivan and Knutson, 2000). For example, low birthweight and birth abnormalities have been found to have a higher risk of a report to child protective services (Putnam-Hornstein and Needell, 2011), but it is not clear if maltreatment was associated with the child's special needs or other parental attributes (Bugental and Happaney 2004; Strathearn et al., 2001; Windham, Rosenberg, and Fuddy, 2004). It is also not clear if all forms of special needs are of an equal risk for abuse or neglect. One study found that behavioral or mental health disorders in very young children predicted maltreatment but not developmental delay (Jaudes and Mackey-Bilaver, 2008). Other studies have partially supported this association but have also found higher risk for certain types of developmental delay (Maclean et al., 2017; McDonnell et al., 2018). A final confound may again be access to services. While the overlap between child disability and child maltreatment is known, studies suggest that at least among families reported to child welfare, access to early childhood intervention programming is low (Jonson-Reid et al., 2004; Silver et al., 2006). However, other studies suggest such services can help remediate delays in children who have already experienced maltreatment (Merritt and Klein, 2015).

It is hard to escape the repeated theme of cumulative or multiple risks throughout much of the literature on child maltreatment. While there is a substantial literature documenting the association of factors at various levels of the ecological framework with maltreatment, often the causal link is unclear or is difficult to disentangle with the co-morbid risks. Additionally, many of the same risk factors that are present in the maltreatment literature are also related to the risk of experiencing other forms of violence (Wilkins et al., 2014). On the one hand, it may be hopeful that spillover effects from addressing one form of violence may help prevent others as well, it also confounds our understanding of whether policy, program, or clinical interventions are optimized to directly impact maltreatment itself. As we will see in our discussion of potential solutions, there remains a great need to advance our understanding of intervention in relation to known risk and protective factors related to maltreatment. Confounding this is a final issue that poses a risk to effective prevention—the lack of a family support system in the United States.

The United States has a number of distinct programs, each serving a portion of the population and each requiring a documented risk status or existing problem to become engaged (the one arguable exception to this is the public school system, which is universal but does not have an explicit family support function). Programs exist to support poor families economically (e.g., Earned

Income Tax Credit, Temporary Assistance for Needy Families) or educationally (Head Start). Some legal structures exist to help particular subgroups of children, such as disabled children (Individuals with Disabilities Education Act). Other state agencies provide services to children with specific problems (the juvenile justice system). Finally, we have the variously (and often misleadingly) named entities tasked with responding to child abuse and neglect (Division of Children and Family Services). Child protection is much like other family programs in that it requires a family to be at risk or in trouble before it can be served. Programs such as Child Protective Services, which respond after the fact, simply do not have a true (primary) prevention role. This role of child protection is similar across many developed countries (Drake and Jonson-Reid, 2015). We are therefore left with something of a conundrum: If it is nobody's job to prevent child abuse before it happens and if it is nobody's job to help families before they get into trouble, how can we expect that things will ever change?

How Can We Address and Potentially Solve the Problem of Child Maltreatment?

A multidetermined problem suggests the need for a multifaceted solution. At the systems level, we must find families that need extra support to prevent abusive or neglecting behaviors from developing, or once problems have occurred, from continuing. This same system needs to be tapped as a resource to evaluate progress in prevention over time. Additionally, in cases that are missed by primary prevention, we need interventions at the child level that will help prevent untoward developmental outcomes. To implement such services, there is a need for a platform(s) delivering the needed resources and services that are accessible by and acceptable to the population. The programs or interventions delivered should be effective, which will require ongoing research as well as a trained workforce. The following section explores current approaches and the related evidence across these areas.

Surveillance for Prevention

An applied "smart" data surveillance system that is in real time and linked to field responses is required for identifying families in need before their situation reaches crisis levels and children are harmed. In the *Social Work Grand Challenges* report, an example of a small-scale use of such a system is discussed—the Birth Match program. This program, which is being implemented in four states, links prior child welfare and criminal records with birth data to identify mothers with histories of serious maltreating behavior. This allows for proactive provision of a voluntary home visit to try to provide the support needed to adequately parent the new infant. The goal is prevention of serious injury and child maltreatment fatalities (Barth et al., 2016; Commission to Eliminate Child Abuse and Neglect Fatalities, 2016). Beyond this, the interest in and use of predictive analytic models has grown in health care (Raghupathi and Raghupathi, 2014) and is increasingly considered for targeting services aimed at early intervention and prevention of maltreatment (Amrit et al., 2017; Daley et al., 2016; Drake and Jonson-Reid, 2018b; Vaithianathan et al., 2013). Linked real time data could also be used to more effectively guide case management and referral processes as well as capture outcome information to then feed back into improved services (Ramsey et al., 2015).

The actual promise of preventive use of cross-sector data or predictive risk models for maltreatment prevention, however, is much greater assuming that it is accompanied by an ethical mandate for prevention and by the ability to deliver resources (Drake and Jonson-Reid, 2017; Keddell, 2014). Such a system can be used for identifying populations or geographical areas at heightened risk to more effectively target preventive resources (Daley et al., 2016; Heimpel, 2016; Putnam-Hornstein et al., 2013). Social work must be engaged in the process of developing data systems that assure the appropriate elements are available for targeting and service (i.e., identifying the appropriate modifiable variables for tracking, building, and enhancing services to meet the need) as well as the evaluation of those services provided (Hebert et al., 2014; Jonson-Reid and Chiang, 2019; Russell, 2015). Child welfare systems are already making use of performance data for feedback to practice at an aggregate level (Lery et al., 2015). Social work researchers are also building data systems used for pinpointing needs (Drake and Jonson-Reid, 2017; Putnam-Hornstein et al. 2013; Putnam-Hornstein, Needell and Rhodes, 2013; Shaw et al., 2013). Beyond potential benefits for service delivery, such a surveillance system built on ongoing linked data would greatly advance the speed at which one could inform local, state, and national policy.

A truly "smart system" must be adaptable and designed as user friendly, which will entail close collaboration between computer scientists, the research community, and the practice community. Integrated data may also provide a means of targeting resources as well as strengthening research, policymaker, agency stakeholder, and community partnerships (e.g., Atherton et al., 2015; Chang et al., 2007). This should be accompanied by a thorough review of existing program fragments and what is known about best practices with empirical support. This process can be applied to develop incremental plans that can then be implemented by policymakers and administrators and continually evaluated by the research community. Here again is a role for technology in the use of simulation, modeling, and monitoring processes. Finally, there is a need for integrating cost–benefit analyses using different approaches (such as the Scandinavian model) or voluntary help-seeking programs into the planning process.

Addressing Poverty

Research on poverty and maltreatment focuses upon family level socioeconomic disadvantage (Berger, 2004; Berger, 2015) as well as material needs (Fowler et al., 2013). The approaches lend themselves to related but not identical avenues of prevention. The former may be more directly linked to enhancing income or preventing income loss (Conrad-Hiebner and Byram, 2018), while the latter may focus more on alleviating the burden of acquiring basic needs such as housing or food (e.g., Fowler et al., 2013). With respect to supportive income, there is very limited yet promising evidence that such approaches may decrease the risk of maltreatment (Berger et al., 2017; Cancian, Yang, and Slack, 2013; Pelton, 2015). The data on provision of material needs are less clear, with some indication that addressing issues like housing may not prevent maltreatment per se but may prevent more serious maltreatment and the need for foster care (Fowler and Chavira, 2014). Material resources may also offset some of the negative impact of maltreatment by enhancing stability and reducing stress associated with uncertain housing. Findings from a recent meta-analysis suggest that the impact of material needs may be associated with the number rather than the specific type of need, suggesting that efforts may require attention to a range of issues to reduce maltreatment (Conrad-Hiebner and Byram, 2018). At least one randomized control trial of a differential response system (an assessment approach compared to traditional investigation with families reported for maltreatment) found some preventive effect, but much of this was attributed to the availability of funds providing material services (assistance with food and clothing, car repair, rent, utilities and other immediate financial needs) that is not a typical part of child welfare intervention (Loman and Siegel, 2015; Pecora et al., 2014).

There are other family or caregiver poverty interventions that may also have relevance for maltreatment prevention but have not been tested directly in this way. These large-scale initiatives include approaches like Individual Development Accounts (Schreiner and Sherraden, 2007) and two-generation educational approaches that seek improvement in parental education levels and employment while providing child care and child education (Chase-Lansdale and Brooks-Gunn, 2014; LaForett and Mendez, 2010). Finally, in a few areas, community level development approaches are being implemented that address disparities in resources in low-income communities to prevent maltreatment both in the United States and internationally. Evaluation of these approaches is just emerging but indicate some promise (Butterfield et al., 2017; McCroskey et al., 2010).

It is critical that social work research is not only guided by an ecological model but that it also integrates measurement of cross-system issues like poverty at both the community and individual levels. It should also assess the degree to which interventions at the individual-/family-based level, community-based level, or both levels have impacts on parenting behavior. Experimental tests of both material needs provision and income enhancement show potential for certain populations, but the research to date cannot provide guidance toward a specific approach. Other programs, like two-generation approaches, could have spillover effects in regard to the prevention of maltreatment as they impact poverty and related conditions. Thus far, however, no such published work is available. Finally, community development approaches may offer promise in offsetting the disparities in resource access that can place families at additional risk. Again, much more work is needed. As various income and poverty initiatives are put forward by the Livable Lives movement in the social work profession (Center for Social Development, 2014), this may provide an opportunity for greater collaboration in relation to measurement of reduction of maltreatment as a possible "unintended or spillover" benefit of these approaches.

Improving Services for Mental Health and Substance Abuse

Identifying research that focuses on parental mental health and/or substance abuse as a means for primary prevention of maltreatment can be difficult, since much of the literature overlaps these two subjects. At least one study suggests that effective intervention promoting resiliency and addressing trauma in one generation may offset the mental health problems that impact parenting in the next generation (Sexton et al., 2015). Other work suggests that mental health treatment addressing issues of emotional regulation and negative affect may show potential in reducing the risk of maltreatment among women with past histories of trauma (Smith et al., 2014). It is not clear how intervention approaches may need to vary by particular mental health disorder, the level of severity of symptoms, or the type of drug in the case of substance abuse.

Arguably the degree of impairment of parenting as well as the risks to the child may vary by the substance used, age of the child, and the presence of another adult caregiver who is not impaired. For example, children of parents using methamphetamine may experience immediate harm as a result of the toxins involved in the manufacture of the drug (Lineberry and Bostwick, 2006). This is not the case for a child living with a parent abusing alcohol.

We know less about the promise of intervening early with substance-abusing women. Thus far, most of the work related to substance abuse and parenting has focused on mothers already involved with child welfare such as family drug courts (Marsh, Smith, and Bruni, 2011). What little work is available in this area again highlights the issues of multiple concurrent risk. Mothers involved in substance abuse treatment who also had contact with child welfare were younger, had more children, were more likely to have histories of abuse themselves, and had greater economic problems (Grella, Hser and Huang, 2006).

The availability of quality evidence-based care for adult mental health that simultaneously attends to parenting has been noted as a global "grand challenge" in maternal child health (Rahman et al., 2013). In reviewing research on substance abuse and maltreatment, Neger and Prinz (2015) point out that while some aspects of addiction (i.e., preoccupation with acquiring the drug) may directly increase risk of maltreatment, there are other risk factors relating to both substance abuse and maltreatment that suggest a need for concurrent treatment. While this call was not raised in social work per se, the elements mentioned in addressing this need include issues quite familiar to social work (e.g., attention to stigma, screening, effective referrals, access, cultural competency, evidence-based care, and retention in services). Typically, adult mental health or substance abuse intervention and parenting and child maltreatment prevention have been largely siloed (Marsh, Smith and Bruni, 2011). One study examined the possible effects of intensive case management with substance dependent parenting women and found that it increased treatment engagement but had no impact on later child welfare involvement (Dauber et al., 2012). In a recent review of integration of substance abuse and parenting, six programs with control groups showed positive impacts on both substance use and parenting, but parenting was typically measured based on self-report of parenting skills or stress, making the impact on maltreating behaviors unclear (Neger and Prinz, 2015). Much more research is needed to assess the effects of mental health and substance abuse treatment combined with, and separate from, parenting intervention as a means to reduce child abuse and neglect. There is a significant gap in our understanding of the effectiveness of addressing these issues with high-quality services before maltreatment begins. This has implications not only for research but also for policy around the funding of these services for adults. For example, if quality adult mental health intervention has a significant impact on maltreatment, this should bolster arguments for increasing access and payment for adult mental health.

Addressing Intimate Partner Violence

Given the overlap of intimate partner violence and child maltreatment, addressing family violence was named part of the grand challenges for social work (American Academy of Social Work and Social Welfare, 2017; Barth and

Jonson-Reid, 2017). Policy innovations aimed at bringing intimate partner violence into the realm of child protection have met with mixed reviews because these approaches have largely focused on increased surveillance rather than careful consideration of the coordination of services to address these risks (Herrenkohl et al., 2015; Jonson-Reid and Drake, 2018). Most models reflect either some type of closer collaboration between the two systems (e.g., Bragg, 2003; Cross et al., 2012), or they develop a new system addressing both (e.g., Humphreys and Absler, 2011), which is arguably more prevention of recurrent maltreatment rather than primary prevention. The empirical testing of such interventions is still in its infancy, but there are several training programs that have shown promise in assisting professionals (Turner et al., 2015). In terms of addressing intimate partner violence as prevention of maltreatment, recommendations include proactive screening in primary care as well as early childhood home visitation. Research on the effectiveness of such approaches, however, has not yet emerged (Jonson-Reid et al., 2016). Furthermore, these preventive approaches have focused solely on intimate partner violence, rather than possible parenting or child maltreatment benefits.

Providing Parenting Support

Another area receiving significant attention has been early childhood interventions. These range from home visitation approaches to quality child care centers/preschool programming. The Maternal, Infant, and Early Childhood Home Visiting Program (MIECHV), established under the Patient Protection and Affordable Care Act of 2010 has strengthened support for home visitation approaches, particularly for those with established empirical support. Some form of home visitation exists in all 50 states although the program models vary widely.

There is evidence to suggest that struggles in parenting are quite common, ranging from uncertainty about how to address a given situation, to physically abusive behaviors (Prinz, 2016). Hypothetically, elements of home visitation such as provision of parenting information and skills, or connection to additional services through referral, could reduce maltreatment risk (Jonson-Reid et al., 2018). While various studies have indicated positive results for child behavior, child development, and injury, the impact of home visitation specifically on the prevention of child abuse and neglect is mixed (Chen and Chan, 2016; Howard and Brooks-Gunn, 2009). In most cases, effect sizes for home visitation programs have been nonexistent or small and/or limited to particular domains like neglectful behavior or risk factor reduction rather than maltreatment per se (Chen and Chan, 2016; Duggan et al., 2004; Peacock et al., 2013). Furthermore, the measurement of maltreatment in these studies has ranged from scales attempting to capture the risk of a future action, to harsh parenting, to actual documentation of maltreatment. For example, the Nurse Family Partnership model, open to first-time mothers enrolled in early prenatal care, has not been successful at reducing maltreatment in early childhood, although the longer-term benefits of the program related to child behavior have been strong (Olds, Eckenrode, and Kitzman, 2005; Zielinski, 2009). While all home visitation programs impart parenting information and skills, it may be that these programs lack content specific for reducing maltreatment like emotional regulation skills (Neger and Prinz, 2015). It is also not clear how frequently families most at risk of maltreatment are engaged in these programs. Therefore, more research is needed regarding the role of home visitation in maltreatment prevention and which models or approaches are most effective with which populations.

It is also unclear as to what extent maltreatment could be reduced if there were broader societal availability of positive parenting information and supports. Parenting is not an easy task even in a well-supported family. Many evidence-based parenting programs (not a part of the home visitation models discussed earlier) were designed primarily to assist parents with child behaviors as compared to preventing abusive or neglectful parenting, although some of the targets of intervention theoretically could also prevent maltreatment (Barlow, 2015). While a few have been explored as maltreatment prevention programs (Prinz, 2016), implementation with families already engaged with child protection to prevent recurrent maltreatment is more common (Chaffin et al., 2011; Webster-Stratton, 2014). Even in the latter case, the number of controlled trials of such approaches is quite small. One of the other challenges related to the increased use of evidence-based parenting programs has been the issue of surveillance and targeting. As these programs tend to be expensive, it is difficult to imagine them as universal. On the other hand, some promising but less well-researched and less expensive approaches are receiving increased attention (e.g., Howe et al., 2017).

It may also be possible to impact maltreatment through larger-scale preventive education efforts (Morrill et al., 2015; Prinz, 2016). Unlike the many avenues and messages for receiving information about diet, for example, there is no similar large-scale preventive education effort for parenting. There are several international examples of countries that have made a concerted effort to ban corporal punishment, resulting in altered public practices (Durrant, 1999) and some relatively small scale studies of preventive approaches engaging health practitioners in the dissemination of positive parenting approaches (Hornor, 2015). A multilevel parenting program called Triple P (Sanders, Markie-Dadds, and Turner, 2003) has a population level preventive component, but such approaches require increased research attention for assessing their effectiveness and their relative acceptability across differing populations, as well as the feasibility and sustainability of large-scale implementation. The use of technology for disseminating parenting information is another exciting possibility that requires further research (Breitenstein, Gross, and Christophersen, 2014).

Although child care programs do not always provide parenting training, the impact of quality child care could be preventive if it provides a respite function and reduces parents' work related strain (Ha, Collins, and Martino, 2015). Much of the research on quality child care, however, has focused on the benefits to a maltreated child's development as compared to prevention of maltreatment itself (Moore, Armsden, and Gogerty, 1998; Howes et al., 1998; Merritt and Klein, 2015). Some attention has been paid to the coordination of early childhood care and child welfare to facilitate the participation in quality child care for families already in contact with child protection (Meloy, Lipscomb, and Baron, 2015). However, the outcome of such efforts is not known. Although the profession of social work has not been a key player in the provision of child care services, it has played an active role in supportive intervention for children with special needs and advocating for family support.

Finally, there are a variety of early parenting intervention approaches, from home visiting, to child care, to evidence-based parenting groups. Thus far, there is little indication that any of these approaches alone are sufficient for significantly impacting the rate of maltreatment. However, that does not mean these efforts are not critical. In other words, it is possible that we consider the idea of necessary but insufficient. This turns the focus from searching for the magic bullet to (1) comparing the relative benefit and feasibility of implementation of various approaches with different populations and (2) better understanding what package of additional services or resources is needed to increase and sustain the magnitude of the effects.

Addressing Child Trauma

While primary prevention is always favorable, addressing the needs of maltreated children until such a time that our prevention efforts improve is both a critical aspect of helping them achieve livable lives as well as a moral imperative. Several of the parenting programs alluded to previously were initially designed to address child behavior problems and to promote healthy development. If they can be implemented with families that already have histories of maltreatment, or who are at very high risk of such behaviors, these may hold promise for promoting positive developmental outcomes even if their effects on maltreatment per se are not strong (e.g., Eckenrode et al., 2001; Reynolds, Mathieson, and Topitzes, 2009; Petra and Kohl, 2010). Additionally, there are an increasing number of promising and evidence-based intervention approaches for children designed to ameliorate the negative impact of abuse and neglect (Bartlett et al., 2018; Hamilton-Giachritsis, 2016).

Several evidence-based approaches that incorporate a cognitive behavioral approach exist for children who have experienced trauma (see California Evidence-Based Clearinghouse, https://www.cebc4cw.org/). Increasingly, there has been recognition of the need for trauma-informed and trauma-focused interventions for children in the child welfare system (e.g., Bartlett et al., 2016). However, strong evidence demonstrating the effectiveness of such interventions in this population is limited (Bartlett et al., 2016; Goldman et al., 2013; Kessler, Gira, and Poertner, 2005; Maher et al., 2009). Recent work indicates several promising interventions adapted for child welfare-involved youth (Auslander et al., 2017; Bartlett et al., 2018; Child Welfare Information Gateway, 2015), and the positive effects of a trauma-informed system on children's well-being (Murphy et al., 2017). Social work, with its integrative and multidisciplinary approach to training and research, is uniquely positioned to reduce harm and prevent future risk in this population.

Creating a Complete Child Protection/Family Support System

One of the many questions that must be addressed related to the prevention of maltreatment is, Who will deliver the services? Currently, the child protection system in the United States (as well as in many other countries) is set up to provide an initial emergency response and provides little in the way of services until things are sufficiently serious to warrant intensive intervention or foster care (Drake and Jonson-Reid, 2015; Jonson-Reid and Drake, 2018). Arguably this was not done by design but rather as a result of addressing the immediate concerns for child safety without a funding stream or a plan. This has led to simultaneous calls to dismantle what exists and redirect the funds toward something else (e.g., Melton, 2005) along with calls for reform and improvements that would increase the provision of services and coordinated care (Jonson-Reid and Drake, 2018). The former is problematic given the amount of funds available for redirection as well as the lack of evidence of another effective delivery system. The latter requires additional funds and political will to invest. The recently enacted Family First Prevention Services Act (2018) appears to be a step in this direction, albeit more focused on preventing entry into foster care than preventing initial child maltreatment.

Given the complexity surrounding the needs of families at risk of maltreatment, as well as the current nature of funding and location of services in various sectors, a completed system is necessarily going to be a network of interoperable services. Examples and opportunities for movement in this area are increasing. Collaborations between child protection agencies, family support, and home visitation have grown substantially since the increase in funding for home visitation was initiated through the Affordable Care Act (Schmitt et al., 2015). The Family First Act (2018) includes coverage for mental health, substance abuse, and in-home parenting skills delivered under a trauma-informed organizational structure (Alliance for Strong Families and Communities, 2018). Building system components through collaboration with community stakeholders to assure congruence between the goals of safety and permanency and the needs of the families also shows promise as an approach for moving child welfare systems in the direction of preventive activities (Lorthridge et al., 2012). All of these approaches are heavily reliant on collaboration across agencies, communities, and disciplines, as well as between the levels of policy, management, and practice. Policy innovations are being made across systems that reduce barriers to resources like child care and health services, which may improve family resilience (Klevens et al., 2015); however, much work remains to be done in the implementation and evaluation of these approaches.

While smart surveillance was described in terms of targeting and prevalence, linked data systems have promise for understanding how services and risk factors across sectors of social work intervention impact outcomes (e.g., Jonson-Reid et al., 2009; Meloy, Lipscomb, and Baron, 2015). Such systems may also assist social workers in meeting administrative reporting needs in a less time intensive way (Jonson-Reid and Drake, 2016) and improve the coordination and evaluation of services across systems (Hebert et al., 2014; Jonson-Reid and Chiang, 2019). Tracking rates of reported maltreatment in a given geography through such a system may also be one of the most feasible means of assessing the impact of large-scale community-based preventive interventions (Lothridge et al., 2012; Prinz, 2016).

Professionalism

Professionalism and linkage to the broader ethics of social work practice is critical for practitioners in the field. Parents that have contact with child welfare mention competence, sensitivity, and knowledge as traits in workers that they value (Dawson and Berry, 2002; Jonson-Reid and Drake, 2018). As a field, however, many of the prevention programs (such as home visitation programs) and child welfare systems in several states, depend on a paraprofessional or bachelor's degree in any field (not specific to social work). Working with families involved in child protection is fraught with difficult and pressured decisions that are often made in difficult contextual experiences. Turnover in the field is high, with greater training, higher pay, and increased support among co-workers associated with longer retention (DePanfilis and Zlotnik, 2008). Many argue that there is a strong need for attention to professionalism in the child welfare workforce—specifically the need for social work expertise (Barth, Lee, and Horodowicz, 2017; Scannapieco, Hegar, and Connell-Carrick, 2012). Holosko and Faith (2015) highlight how bachelor's and master's degrees in social work align with various child protection positions from screening, to provision of services, to families. We would argue that ideally such professional education highlights a broad preparation for child protection work that includes advocacy for social justice needs of the population (D'Andrade et al., 2017; McLaughlin, Gray, and Wilson, 2015; Lothridge et al., 2012), adequate funding for prevention and early intervention related to the various factors that place families at risk for maltreatment (Fong, 2017; McLaughlin and Jonson-Reid, 2017; Mersky, Topitzes, and Blair, 2017), and preparation for prescribed roles, including use of data within existing organizations (Holosko and Faith, 2015; Naccarato, 2010).

Preparing the Research Pipeline

Throughout our discussion on protective factors and possible solutions, significant gaps in research are evident. This problem gained national recognition in the report on child maltreatment by the Institute of Medicine and National Research Council, which stated,

> To be productive, high-quality scientific research requires a sophisticated infrastructure. Research on child abuse and neglect is especially complex, involving diverse independent service systems, multiple professions, ethical issues that are particularly complicated, and levels of outcome analysis ranging from the individual child to national statistics. Moreover, the building of a national research infrastructure designed to adequately address the problem of child abuse and neglect will require a dedicated and trained cadre of researchers with expertise that spans the many domains associated with research in this field and the supports necessary to sustain high-quality, methodologically sound research endeavors. (2013: 9)

Social work schools within research universities have an obvious leadership role to play.

Faculty at the George Warren Brown School of Social Work have been actively engaged in building this pipeline for several years. For example, the second year of a five-year training institute was recently completed to "prepare a new cadre of skilled investigators dedicated to engaging in child abuse and neglect research" (Jonson-Reid and Widom, 2016). Other schools employ an integrated approach to child welfare training that spans the range from master's level education to doctoral-level research combined with evaluation opportunities such as the Center for Child Welfare Excellence at the Silberman School of Social Work at Hunter College. Other schools of social work have specialized centers that provide training opportunities in research specific to child welfare such as the Center on Child Welfare Policy and Practice at the University of Wisconsin, the Children and Family Research Center at the University of Illinois, and the Center for Innovation in Child Maltreatment Policy, Research and Training at Washington University. Still others have partnerships with semi-independent research organizations as is the case with Chapin Hall and the University of Chicago or specialized research projects that include partnerships with state child welfare organizations as in the California Child Welfare Indicators Project at the University of California, Berkeley School of Social Welfare.

Doctoral students must also be trained to systematically evaluate evidence-based interventions in relation to reviewing existing literature as well as being able to develop intervention studies (Auslander et al., 2012). Methodologically, there are opportunities in social work research related to fully leveraging how analyses focused on an issue like poverty may cross-inform efforts in prevention. This work can help us understand spillover effects between important social issues that may lead to more optimistic appraisals of prevention efforts. Additionally, students must be prepared to take full advantage of the opportunities for increased access to and advanced analyses of so-call big data or integrated data systems to inform child maltreatment prevention as well as child welfare intervention (Jonson-Reid and Drake, 2016; Naccarato, 2010; Putnam et al., 2013). This includes exposure to data sciences and programming as well as advanced approaches to mining such data such as machine-learning approaches (Schwartz et al., 2017). For a further discussion of big data, readers should turn to Chapter 14 in this volume.

Students should also be exposed to the latest analytic approaches that can address the inherent complexity in studies of maltreatment, particularly as the availability of techniques to allow for such modeling has increased exponentially (e.g., Freisthler et al., 2005; Hovmand, Jonson-Reid, and Drake, 2007; Guo and Frazer, 2014; Hu and Puddy, 2010; Lawrence, Rosanbalm, and Dodge, 2011; Luke, 2005; Ratner, 2012). For example the Social Systems Dynamics Lab at Washington University has been engaged in a number of projects applying cutting edge systems dynamic approaches to family violence. These projects frequently employ PhD students who have greatly benefited from their exposure to this technique (Hovmand, 2013).

Conclusion

Many years ago, Abraham Maslow proposed a hierarchy of needs common to human beings that were necessary for addressing the higher order behaviors related to livable lives. These included building positive relationships, educational and work achievement, and other adult capacities (Maslow, 1943). According to this model, the meeting of basic needs, safety, and nurturing were foundational for positive development and were the very things that children living with abuse and neglect so often lack. Children who experience abuse and/or neglect are arguably caught at the bottom tiers of Maslow's hierarchy where their basic needs for safety, food, clothing, housing, and nurturing frequently go unmet. Currently, we spend billions of dollars on the negative behavioral, health, and economic consequences of maltreatment that bear witness to its negative impact on achieving a livable life (Fang et al., 2012).

Although there is clearly a range of effective interventions needed to improve resilience and recovery for maltreated children (e.g., Auslander et al., 2017; Leenarts et al., 2013), a more concerted effort to prevent maltreatment must also be a part of creating a world where livable lives are possible for all. As we have seen, despite decades of research there remain significant gaps in our knowledge that hamper the development of effective solutions. This, along with a seeming lack of political will to address many of the related policy and funding issues, helps us understand why despite acceptance of maltreatment as a significant problem, the prevalence of reported cases has not changed over the years (DHHS, 2019). Large reductions in maltreatment will require a truly multidisciplinary and ecological systems approach combining innovations in surveillance, service delivery, intervention, and policy across the multiple issues associated with child abuse and neglect. Having long been engaged in research and practice related to child abuse and neglect, social work is well positioned to take a leadership role in taking this work to the next level. Addressing maltreatment should be a core aspect of any effort to promote social justice and the right of all children to experience a livable life.

References

Afifi, T. O., H. L. MacMillan, M. Boyle, K.Cheung, T. Taillieu, S. Turner, and J. Sareen. 2016. "Child Abuse and Physical Health in Adulthood." *Health Reports*, 27, 10–8.

Ahn, J., B. J. Lee, S. K. Kahng, H. L. Kim, O. K. Hwang, E. J. Lee, H. R. Shin, M. S. Yoo, Y. Cho, Y. S. Yoo, Y. J. Kwak, Y. M. Shin, J. Y. Lim, Y. J. Cho, S. Y. Park, and J. P. Yoo. 2017. "Estimating the Prevalence Rate of Child Physical and Psychological Maltreatment in South Korea." *Child Indicators Research*, 10, 187–203.

Akmatov, M. K. 2010. "Child Abuse in 28 Developing and Transitional Countries-Results from the Multiple Indicator Cluster Surveys." *International Journal of Epidemiology*, 40, 219–227.

Alliance for Strong Families and Communities. 2018. "Family First Prevention Services Act Summary." Families in Society, FEI Behavioral Health. PCG Human Services is co-author with Alliance. https://www.acesconnection.com/g/resource-center/fileSendAction/fcType/0/fcOid/464758151152075082/filePointer/479542389221270598/fodoid/479542389221270594/Family%20First%20Act%202018%20Summary_8-18_v2.pdf

American Academy of Social Work and Social Welfare 2017. "Stop Family Violence. 12 Challenges." Retrieved from http://grandchallengesforsocialwork.org/grand-challenges-initiative/12-challenges/stop-family-violence/

Amrit, C., T. Paauw, R. Aly, and M. Lavric. 2017. "Identifying Child Abuse Through Text Mining and Machine Learning." *Expert Systems with Applications*, 88, 402–418.

Ateah, C., and J. Durrant. 2005. "Maternal Use of Physical Punishment in Response to Child Misbehavior: Implications for Child Abuse Prevention." *Child Abuse and Neglect*, 29, 169–185.

Atherton, I. M., E. Lynch, A. J. Williams, and M. D. Witham. 2015. "Barriers and Solutions to Linking and Using Health and Social Care Data in Scotland." *British Journal of Social Work*, 45, 1614–1622.

Auslander, W., C. Fisher, M. Ollie, and M. Yu. 2012. "Teaching Master's and Doctoral Social Work Students to Systematically Evaluate Evidence-Based Interventions." *Journal of Teaching in Social Work*, 32, 320–341.

Auslander, W.F., H. McGinnis, S. Myers Tlapek, P. Smith, A. Foster, T. Edmond, and J. Dunn. 2016. "Adaptation and Implementation of a Trauma-Focused Cognitive Behavioral Intervention for Adolescent Girls in Child Welfare." *American Journal of Orthopsychiatry*, 87, 206–215.

Auslander, W.F., H. McGinnis, S. Myers Tlapek, P. Smith, A. Foster, T. Edmond, and J. Dunn, 2017. "Adaptation and Implementation of a Trauma-Focused Cognitive Behavioral Intervention for Adolescent Girls in Child Welfare." *American Journal of Orthopsychiatry*, 87, 206–215.

Auslander, W., J. C. McMillen, D. Elze, R. Thompson, M. Jonson-Reid, and A. Stiffman. 2002. "Mental Health Problems and Sexual Abuse Among Youths in Foster Care: Relationship to HIV Risk Behaviors and Intentions." *AIDS and Behavior*, 6, 351–359.

Auslander, W., P. R. Sterzing, J. Threlfall, D. Gerke, and T. Edmond, 2016. "Childhood Abuse and Aggression in Adolescent Girls Involved in Child Welfare: The Role of Depression and Posttraumatic Stress." *Journal of Child and Adolescent Trauma*, 9, 1–10.

Barlow, J. 2015. "Preventing Child Maltreatment and Youth Violence Using Parent Training and Home Visiting Programmes. *The Oxford Textbook of Violence Prevention: Epidemiology, Evidence and Policy*. Edited by P. D. Donnelly and C. L. Ward. Oxford: Oxford University Press, pp. 133–140.

Barr, R. G., F. P. Rivara, M. Barr, P. Cummings, J. Taylor, L. J. Lengua, and E. Meredith-Benitz. 2009. "Effectiveness of Educational Materials Designed to Change Knowledge and Behaviors Regarding Crying and Shaken-Baby Syndrome in Mothers of Newborns: A Randomized, Controlled Trial." *Pediatrics*, 123(3), 972–980.

Barth, R., and M. Jonson-Reid. 2017. "Better Use of Data to Protect Children and Families. A Policy Action to End Family Violence." *Grand Challenges for Social Work Policy Action*, 2–5. http://grandchallengesforsocialwork.org/wp-content/uploads/2017/03/PAS.3.1.pdf

Barth, R. P., B. R. Lee, and M. T. Hodorowicz. 2017. "Equipping the Child Welfare Workforce to Improve the Well-Being of Children." *Journal of Children's Services*, 12, 211–220.

Barth, R. and R. J. Macy. 2018. "Stop Family Violence." *Grand Challenges for Social Work and Society*. Edited by in R. Fong, J. Lubben, and R. Barth. New York: Oxford University Press, pp. 56–80.

Barth, R. P., E. Putnam-Hornstein, T. V. Shaw, and N. S. Dickinson. 2016. "Safe children: Reducing severe and fatal maltreatment (grand challenges for social work initiative working paper no. 17)." Retrieved from American Academy of Social Work & Social Welfare website: http://aaswsw. org/wp-content/uploads/2015/12/WP17-with-cover. pdf.

Bartlett, J. D., B. Barto, J. L. Griffin, J. G. Fraser, H. Hodgdon, and R. Bodian. 2016. "Trauma-Informed Care in the Massachusetts Child Trauma Project." *Child Maltreatment*, 21, 101–112.

Bartlett, J. D., J. L. Griffin, J. Spinazzola, J. G. Fraser, C. R. Noroña, R. Bodian, and B. Barto. 2018. "The Impact of a Statewide Trauma-Informed Care Initiative in Child Welfare on the Well-Being of Children and Youth with Complex Trauma." *Children and Youth Services Review*, 84, 110–117.

Bartlett, J. D., M. Raskin, C. Kotake, K.D. Nearing, and M. A. Easterbrooks. 2014. "An Ecological Analysis of Infant Neglect by Adolescent Mothers." *Child Abuse and Neglect*, 38, 723–734.

Ben-David, V., M. Jonson-Reid, B. Drake, and P. L. Kohl. 2015. "The Association Between Childhood Maltreatment Experiences and the Onset of Maltreatment Perpetration in Young Adulthood Controlling for Proximal and Distal Risk Factors." *Child Abuse and Neglect*, 46, 132–141.

Berger, L. M. 2004. "Income, Family Structure, and Child Maltreatment Risk." *Children and Youth Services Review*, 26, 725–748.

Berger, L. M. 2015. "Economic Resources and Child Maltreatment: Early Results from the Getting Access to Income Now Evaluation." Paper presented at the Society for Social Work and Research 19th Annual Conference: The Social and Behavioral Importance of Increased Longevity. Albuquerque, NM.

Berger, L. M., S. A. Font, K. S. Slack, and J. Waldfogel. 2017. "Income and Child Maltreatment in Unmarried Families: Evidence from the Earned Income Tax Credit." *Review of Economics of the Household*, 15, 1345–1372.

Berlin, L. J., M. Shanahan, and K. A. Carmody. 2014. "Promoting Supportive Parenting in New Mothers with Substance Use Problems: A Pilot Randomized Trial of Residential Treatment Plus an Attachment Based Parenting Program." *Infant Mental Health Journal*, 35, 81–85.

Bouvette-Turcot, A. A., E. Unternaehrer, H. Gaudreau, J. E. Lydon, M. Steiner, M. J. Meaney, and MAVAN Research Team. 2017. "The Joint Contribution of Maternal History of Early Adversity and Adulthood Depression to Socioeconomic Status and Potential Relevance for Offspring Development." *Journal of Affective Disorders*, 207, 26–31.

Bragg, L. 2003. *Child Protection in Families Experiencing Domestic Violence*. Washington, DC: Child Abuse and Neglect User Manual Series.

Breitenstein, S. M., D. Gross, and R. Christophersen. 2014. "Digital Delivery Methods of Parenting Training Interventions: A Systematic Review." *Worldviews on Evidence Based Nursing*, 11, 168–176.

Bugental, D. B., and K. Happaney. 2004. "Predicting Infant Maltreatment in Low-Income Families: The Interactive Effects of Maternal Attributions and Child Status at Birth." *Developmental Psychology*, 40, 234–243.

Butterfield, A. K., J. L. Scherrer, and K. Olcon. 2017. "Addressing Poverty and Child Welfare: The Integrated Community Development and Child Welfare Model of Practice." *International Social Work*, 60, 321–335.

Calheiros, M. M., M. B. Monteiro, J. N. Patrício, and M. Carmona. 2016. "Defining Child Maltreatment Among Lay People and Community Professionals: Exploring Consensus in Ratings of Severity." *Journal of Child and Family Studies*, 25, 2292–2305.

Cancian, M., M. Y. Yang, and K. S. Slack, K. S. 2013. "The Effect of Additional Child Support Income on the Risk of Child Maltreatment." *Social Service Review*, 87, 417–437.

Cash, S. J., and D. J. Wilke. 2003. "An Ecological Model of Maternal Substance Abuse and Child Neglect: Issues, Analyses, and Recommendations." *American Journal of Orthopsychiatry*, 73(4), 392–404.

Cecil, C. A., E. Viding, P. Fearon, D. Glaser, and E. J. Mccrory. 2017. "Disentangling the Mental Health Impact of Childhood Abuse and Neglect." *Child Abuse and Neglect*, 63, 106–119.

CenterforSocialDevelopment,WashingtonUniversity.2014."LivableLivesProjects."Retrievedfrom https://Csd.Wustl.Edu/Ourwork/Thrivingcommunities/Livablelivesinitiative/Pages/ Livablelivesprojectinformation.Aspx

Centers for Disease Control and Prevention. 2014. "Essentials for Childhood: Steps To Create Safe, Stable, Nurturing Relationships and Environments." Retrieved from https://www.cdc.gov/violenceprevention/pdf/essentials_for_childhood_framework.pdf

Chaffin, M., D. Bard, D. S. Bigfoot, and E. J. Maher. 2012. "Is a Structured, Manualized, Evidence-Based Treatment Protocol Culturally Competent and Equivalently Effective Among American Indian Parents in Child Welfare?" *Child Maltreatment*, 17, 242–252.

Chaffin, M., B. Funderbunk, D. Bard, L. V. Valle, and R. Gurwitch. 2011. "A Combined Motivation and Parent–Child Interaction Therapy Package Reduces Child Welfare Recidivism in a Randomized Dismantling Field Trial." *Journal of Consulting and Clinical Psychology*, 79, 84–95.

Chang, Y. J., H. H. Liu, L. D. Chou, Y. W. Chen, and H. Y. Shin. 2007. "A General Architecture of Mobile Social Network Services." *IEEE*, 151–156. https://ieeexplore.ieee.org/abstract/document/4420252

Chase-Lansdale, P. L., and J. Brooks-Gunn. 2014. "Two-Generation Programs in the Twenty-First Century." *Future of Children*, 24, 13–39.

Chen, M., and K. L. Chan. 2016. "Effects of Parenting Programs on Child Maltreatment Prevention a Meta-Analysis." *Trauma, Violence, and Abuse*, 17, 88–104.

Child Abuse Prevention and Treatment Act of 2010, 42 U.S.C. § 3817

Child Welfare Information Gateway. n.d. "State Statutes." Retrieved from https://www.childwelfare.gov/systemwide/laws_policies/statutes/define.cfm

Child Welfare Information Gateway. 2015. Developing a Trauma-Informed Child Welfare System. Retrieved from https://effectivehealthcare.ahrq.gov/ehc/products/298/1422/trauma-interventions-maltreatment-child-executive-130415.pdf

Choi, K. W., R. Houts, L. Arseneault, C. Pariante, K. J. Sikkema, and T. E Moffitt. 2018. "Maternal Depression in the Intergenerational Transmission of Childhood Maltreatment and Its Sequelae: Testing Postpartum Effects in a Longitudinal Birth Cohort." *Development and Psychopathology*, 31, 143–156.

Cohen, D. A., K. Mason, A. Bedimo, R. Scribner, V. Basolo, and T. A. Farley. 2003. "Neighborhood Physical Conditions and Health." *American Journal of Public Health*, 93, 467–471.

Commission to Eliminate Child Abuse and Neglect Fatalities. 2016. *Within Our Reach: A National Strategy to Eliminate Child Abuse and Neglect Fatalities: Final Report 2016*. Washington, DC: Government Printing Office.

Conrad-Hiebner, A., and E. Byram, 2018. "The Temporal Impact of Economic Insecurity on Child Maltreatment: A Systematic Review." *Trauma, Violence, & Abuse*. Online Ahead of Print. https://doi.org/10.1177/1524838018756122

Constantino, J. N., L. M. Chackes, U. G. Wartner, M. Gross, S. L. Brophy, J. Vitale, and A. C. Heath. 2006. "Mental Representations of Attachment in Identical Female Twins With and Without Conduct Problems." *Child Psychiatry and Human Development*, 37, 65–72.

Coulton, C. J., D. S. Crampton, M. Irwin, J. C. Spilsbury, and J. E. Korbin. 2007. How Neighborhoods Influence Child Maltreatment: A Review of the Literature and Alternative Pathways. *Child Abuse & Neglect*, 31(11-12), 1117–1142.

Crombach, A., and M. Bambonyé. 2015. "Intergenerational Violence in Burundi: Experienced Childhood Maltreatment Increases the Risk of Abusive Child Rearing and Intimate Partner Violence." *European Journal of Psychotraumatology*, 6, 26995.

Cross, T. P., B. Mathews, L. Tonmyr, D. Scott, and C. Ouimet. 2012. "Child Welfare Policy and Practice on Children's Exposure to Domestic Violence." *Child Abuse and Neglect*, 36, 210–216.

Current Population Survey. 2016, September. Historical Poverty Tables: People and Families— 1959 to 2015. Retrieved from https://www.census.gov/data/tables/time-series/demo/income-poverty/historical-poverty-people.html

Currie, J., and C. S. Widom. 2010. "Long-Term Consequences of Child Abuse and Neglect on Adult Economic Well-Being." *Child Maltreatment*, 15, 111–120.

Daley, D., M. Bachmann, B. A. Bachmann, C. Pedigo, M. T. Bui, and J. Coffman. 2016. "Risk Terrain Modeling Predicts Child Maltreatment." *Child Abuse & Neglect*, 62, 29–38.

D'andrade, A., J. D. Simon, D. Fabella, L. Castillo, C. Mejia, and D. Shuster. 2017. "The California Linkages Program: Doorway to Housing Support for Child Welfare Involved Parents." *American Journal of Community Psychology*, 60, 125–133.

Dauber, S., C. Neighbors, C. Dasaro, A. Riordan, and J. Morgenstern. 2012. "Impact of Intensive Case Management on Child Welfare System Involvement for Substance-Dependent Parenting Women on Public Assistance." *Children and Youth Services Review*, 34, 1359–1366.

Dawson, K., and M. Berry. 2002. "Engaging Families in Child Welfare Services: An Evidence-Based Approach to Best Practice." *Child Welfare*, 81, 293–317.

Depanfilis, D., and J. L. Zlotnik. 2008. "Retention of Front-Line Staff in Child Welfare: A Systematic Review of Research." *Children and Youth Services Review*, 30, 995–1008.

Dettlaff, A. J., and M. A. Johnson. 2011. "Child Maltreatment Dynamics Among Immigrant and US Born Latino Children: Findings from the National Survey of Child and Adolescent Well-being (NSCAW)." *Children and Youth Services Review*, 33(6), 936–944.

Dettlaff, A. J., I. Earner, and S. D. Phillips. 2009. Latino Children of Immigrants in the Child Welfare System: Prevalence, Characteristics, and Risk." *Children and Youth Services Review*, 31(7), 775–783.

De Wolff, M. S., and M. H. Van Ijzendoorn. 1997. "Sensitivity and Attachment: A Meta-Analysis on Parental Antecedents of Infant Attachment." *Child Development*, 68, 571–591.

Devaney, J., and T. Spratt. 2009. "Child Abuse as a Complex and Wicked Problem: Reflecting on Policy Developments in the United Kingdom in Working with Children and Families with Multiple Problems." *Children and Youth Services Review*, 31, 635–641.

Devooght, K., M. Mccoy-Roth, and M. Freundlich. 2011. "Young and Vulnerable: Children Five and Under Experience High Maltreatment Rates." *Child Trends: Early Childhood Highlights*, 2, 1–20.

Drake, B., and M. Jonson-Reid. 2014. "Poverty and Child Maltreatment." *Handbook of Child Maltreatment. Contemporary Issues in Research and Policy.* Edited by J. Korbin and R. Krugman. New York: Springer.

Drake, B., and M. Jonson-Reid. 2015. "Competing Values and Evidence: How Do We Evaluate Mandated Reporting and CPS Response?" *Mandatory Reporting Laws and Identification of Severe Child Abuse and Neglect.* Edited by B. Mathews and D. Brosss. New York: Springer.

Drake, B., and M. Jonson-Reid. 2017. "Administrative Data and Predictive Risk Modelling in Public Child Welfare: Ethical Issues." White Paper for Los Angeles Children's Data Network.

Drake, B., and M. Jonson-Reid. 2018a. "Defining and Estimating Child Maltreatment." *The APSAC Handbook of Child Maltreatment.* 4th ed. Edited by J. B. Klika and J. Conte. Los Angeles, CA: SAGE.

Drake, B., and M. Jonson-Reid. 2018b. "If We Had a Crystal Ball, Would We Use It?" *Pediatrics*, 141(2), e20173469.

Drake, B., and S. Pandey. 1996. "Understanding the Relationship Between Neighborhood Poverty and Specific Types of Child Maltreatment." *Child Abuse and Neglect*, 20, 1003–1018.

Drake, B., and M. R. Rank. 2009. "The Racial Divide Among American Children in Poverty: Reassessing the Importance of Neighborhood." *Children and Youth Services Review*, 31, 1264–1271.

Drake, B., M. Jonson-Reid, and L. Sapokaite. 2006. "Rereporting of Child Maltreatment: Does Participation in Other Public Sector Services Moderate the Likelihood of a Second Maltreatment Report?." *Child Abuse & Neglect*, 30(11), 1201–1226.

Drake, B., J. M. Jolley, P. Lanier, J. Fluke, R. P. Barth, and M. Jonson-Reid. 2011. "Racial Bias in Child Protection? A Comparison of Competing Explanations Using National Data." *Pediatrics*, 127(3), 471–478.

Dubber, S., C. Reck, M. Müller, and S. Gawlik. 2015. "Postpartum Bonding: The Role of Perinatal Depression, Anxiety and Maternal–Fetal Bonding During Pregnancy." *Archives of Women's Mental Health*, 18(2), 187–195.

Dubowitz, H., J. Kim, M. M. Black, C. Weisbart, J. Semiatin, and L. S. Magder. 2011. "Identifying Children at High Risk for a Child Maltreatment Report." *Child Abuse and Neglect*, 35, 96–104.

Duggan, A., E. Mcfarlane, L. Fuddy, L. Burrell, S. M. Higman, A. Windham, and C. Sia. 2004. "Randomized Trial of a Statewide Home Visiting Program: Impact in Preventing Child Abuse and Neglect." *Child Abuse and Neglect*, 28, 597–622.

Duncan, A. E., W. Auslander, K. Bucholz, D. Hudson, R. Stein, and N. White. 2015. "Relationship Between Abuse and Neglect in Childhood and Diabetes in Adulthood: Differential Effects by Sex, National Longitudinal Study of Adolescent Health." *Prevention of Chronic Disease*, 12, 1–14.

Durrant, J. E. 1999. "Evaluating the Success of Sweden's Corporal Punishment Ban." *Child Abuse and Neglect*, 23, 435–448.

Eckenrode, J., D. Zielinski, E. Smith, L. A. Marcynyszyn, C. R. Henderson Jr, H. Kitzman, R. Cole, J. Powers, and D. L. Olds. 2001. "Child Maltreatment and the Early Onset of Problem Behaviors: Can a Program of Nurse Home Visitation Break the Link?" *Development and Psychopathology*, 13, 873–890.

Emery, C. R., H. N. Trung, and S. Wu. 2015. "Neighborhood Informal Social Control and Child Maltreatment: A Comparison of Protective and Punitive Approaches." *Child Abuse and Neglect*, 41, 158–169.

English, D. J., J. C. Graham, J. Litrownik, M. Everson, and S. I. Bangdiwala. 2005. "Defining Maltreatment Chronicity: Are There Differences in Child Outcomes?" *Child Abuse and Neglect*, 29, 575–595.

Euser, E. M., M. H. Van Ijzendoorn, P. Prinzie, P., and M. J. Bakermans-Kranenburg. 2010. Elevated Child Maltreatment Rates in Immigrant Families and the Role of Socioeconomic Differences. Child Maltreatment, 16, 63–73.

Family First Prevention Services Act of 2018 (H.R. 5456).

Fang, X., D. S. Brown, C. S. Florence, and J. A. Mercy. 2012. "The Economic Burden of Child Maltreatment in the United States and Implications for Prevention." *Child Abuse and Neglect*, 36, 156–165.

Fang, X., D. A. Fry, D. S. Brown, J. A. Mercy, M. P. Dunne, A. R. Butchart, P. S. Corso, K. Maynzyuk, Y. Dzhygyr, Y. Chen, A. McCoy, and D. M. Swales. 2015. "The Burden of Child Maltreatment in the East Asia and Pacific Region." *Child Abuse and Neglect*, 42, 146–162.

Felitti, V. J., R. F. Anda, D. Nordenberg, D. F. Williamson, A. M. Spitz, V. Edwards, M. P. Koss, and J. S. Marks. 1998. "Relationship of Childhood Abuse and Household Dysfunction to Many of the Leading Causes of Death in Adults: The Adverse Childhood Experiences (ACE) Study." *American Journal of Preventive Medicine*, 1, 245–258.

Finkelhor, D., H. A. Turner, S. Hamby, S., and R. Ormrod. 2011. "Polyvictimization: Children's Exposure to Multiple Types of Violence, Crime, and Abuse." *Free Inquiry in Creative Sociology*, 39, 45–63.

Finkelhor D., H. A. Turner, A. Shattuck, and S. L. Hamby, 2015. "Prevalence of Childhood Exposure to Violence, Crime, and Abuse." *JAMA Pediatrics*, 169, 746–754.

Fong, K. 2017. "Child Welfare Involvement and Contexts of Poverty: The Role of Parental Adversities, Social Networks, and Social Services." *Children and Youth Services Review*, 72, 5–13.

Fontenot, K., J. Semega, and M. Kollar. 2018. "U.S. Census Bureau, Current Population Reports, P60-263, Income and Poverty in the United States: 2017." U.S. Government Printing Office: Washington, DC.

Fowler, P. J., and D. Chavira, 2014. "Family Unification Program: Housing Services for Homeless Child Welfare-Involved Families." *Housing Policy Debate*, 24, 802–814.

Fowler, P. J., A. F. Farrell, K. E. Marcal, S. Chung, S., and P. S. Hovmand. 2017. Housing and Child Welfare: Emerging Evidence and Implications for Scaling Up Services." *American Journal of Community Psychology*, 60, 134–144.

Fowler, P. J., D. B. Henry, M. Schoeny, J. Landsverk, D. Chavira, and J. J. Taylor. 2013. "Inadequate Housing Among Families Under Investigation for Child Abuse and Neglect: Prevalence from a National Probability Sample." *American Journal of Community Psychology*, 52(1-2), 106–114.

Fox, K.A. 2003. "Collecting Data on the Abuse and Neglect of American Indian Children." *Child Welfare*, 82, 707–726.

Fréchette, S., M. Zoratti, and E. Romano. 2015. "What Is the Link Between Corporal Punishment and Child Physical Abuse?" *Journal of Family Violence*, 30, 135–148.

Freisthler, B., H. F. Byrnes, and P. J. Gruenewald. 2009. "Alcohol Outlet Density, Parental Monitoring, and Adolescent Deviance: A Multilevel Analysis." *Children and Youth Services Review*, 31(3), 325–330.

Freisthler, B., B. Needell, and P. J. Gruenewald. 2005. "Is the Physical Availability of Alcohol and Illicit Drugs Related to Neighborhood Rates of Child Maltreatment?" *Child Abuse and Neglect*, 29, 1049–1060.

Friedman, M.S., M. P. Marshal, T. E. Guadamuz, C. Wei, C. F. Wong, E. M. Saewyc, and R. Stall. 2011. "A Meta-Analysis of Disparities in Childhood Sexual Abuse, Parental Physical Abuse, and Peer Victimization Among Sexual Minority and Sexual Nonminority Individuals." *American Journal of Public Health*, 101, 1481–1494.

Gerassi, L., M. Jonson-Reid, and B. Drake. 2016. "Sexually Transmitted Infections in a Sample of At-Risk Youth: Roles of Mental Health and Trauma Histories." *Journal of Child and Adolescent Trauma*, 9, 209–216.

Gibbs, D., L. Rojas-Smith, S. Wetterhall, T. Farris, P. G. Schnitzer, R. T. Leeb, and A. E. Crosby. 2013. "Improving Identification of Child Maltreatment Fatalities Through Public Health Surveillance." *Journal of Public Child Welfare*, 7, 1–19.

Gilbert, R., C. S. Widom, K. Browne, D. Fergusson, E. Webb, and S. Janson. 2009. "Burden and Consequences of Child Maltreatment in High-Income Countries." *The Lancet*, 373, 68–81.

Goldman Fraser, J., S. W. Lloyd, R. Murphy, M. Crowson, C. Casanueva, A. Zolotor, M. Coker-Schwimmer, K. Letourneau, A. Gilbert, T. Swinson Evans, K. Crotty, and M. Viswanathan. 2013, April. "Child Exposure to Trauma: Comparative Effectiveness of Interventions Addressing Maltreatment." Comparative Effectiveness Review No. 89. Prepared by the RTI-UNC Evidence-Based Practice Center Under Contract No. 290-2007-10056-I. AHRQ Publication No. 13-EHC002-EF. Rockville, MD: Agency for Healthcare Research and Quality.

Gracia, E., and J. Herrero. 2007. "Perceived Neighborhood Social Disorder and Attitudes Toward Reporting Domestic Violence Against Women. *Journal of Interpersonal Violence*, 22, 737–752

Grella, C. E., Y. I. Hser, and Y. C. Huang. 2006. "Mothers in Substance Abuse Treatment: Differences in Characteristics Based on Involvement with Child Welfare Services." *Child Abuse and Neglect*, 30, 55–73.

Guo, S., and M. W. Fraser. 2014. Propensity Score Analysis: Statistical Methods and Applications. Los Angeles, CA: SAGE.

Guterman, K. 2015. "Unintended Pregnancy as a Predictor of Child Maltreatment." *Child Abuse and Neglect*, 48, 160–169.

Ha, Y., M. E. Collins, and D. Martino. 2015. "Child Care Burden and the Risk of Child Maltreatment Among Low-Income Working Families." *Children and Youth Services Review*, 59, 19–27.

Hamilton- Giachritsis, C. 2016. "What Helps Children and Young People Move Forward Following Child Maltreatment?" *Child Abuse Review*, 25, 83–88.

Hebert, S., W. Bor, C. C. Swenson, and C. Boyle. 2014. "Improving Collaboration: A Qualitative Assessment of Inter-Agency Collaboration Between a Pilot Multisystemic Therapy Child Abuse and Neglect (MST-CAN) Program and a Child Protection Team." *Australasian Psychiatry*, 22, 370–373.

Heim, C., M. Shugart, W. E. Craighead, and C. B. Nemeroff, 2010. "Neurobiological and Psychiatric Consequences of Child Abuse and Neglect." *Developmental Psychobiology*, 52, 671–690.

Heimpel, D. 2016. "An Upstream Approach: Using Data-Driven Home Visiting to Prevent Child Abuse." *The Chronicle for Social Change*. Retrieved from https://chronicleofsocialchange. org/featured/targeting-home-visiting-programs-prevent-child-abuse/20119

Herrenkohl, T. I., D. J. Higgins, M. T. Merrick, and R. T. Leeb. 2015. "Positioning a Public Health Framework at the Intersection of Child Maltreatment and Intimate Partner Violence: Primary Prevention Requires Working Outside Existing Systems." *Child Abuse & Neglect*, 48, 22–28.

Hibbard, R. A., L. W. Desch, and Committee on Child Abuse and Neglect. 2007. "Maltreatment of Children with Disabilities." *Pediatrics*, 119, 1018–1025.

Holosko, M. J., R. Cooper, K. High, A. Loy, and J. Ojo. 2015. "The Process of Intervention with Multiproblem Families: Theoretical and Practical Guidelines." *Evidence-Informed Assessment and Practice in Child Welfare*. Edited by J. S. Wodarski, M. J. Holosko, and M. D. Feit. Cham, Switzerland: Springer, pp. 137–164.

Holosko, M. J., and E. Faith. 2015. "Educating BSW and MSW Social Workers to Practice in Child Welfare Services." *Evidence-Informed Assessment and Practice in Child Welfare*. Edited by J. S. Wodarski, M. J. Holosko, and M. D. Feit. Cham, Switzerland: Springer, pp. 3–25.

Hornor, G. 2015. "Childhood Trauma Exposure and Toxic Stress: What the PNP Needs to Know." *Journal of Pediatric Health Care*, 29, 191–198.

Hovmand, P. 2013. *Community Based System Dynamics*. New York: Springer Science and Business Media.

Hovmand, P., M. Jonson-Reid, and B. Drake. 2007. "Mapping Service Networks." *Journal of Technology and Human Services*, 25, 1–22.

Howard, K. S., and J. Brooks-Gunn. 2009. "The Role of Home-Visiting Programs in Preventing Child Abuse and Neglect." *The Future of Children*, 19, 119–46.

Howe, T. R., M. Knox, E. R. P. Altafim, M. B. M. Linhares, N. Nishizawa, T. J. Fu, A. P. L. Camargo, G. I. R. Ormeno, T. Marques, L. Barrios, and A. I. Pereira. 2017. "International Child Abuse Prevention: Insights from ACT Raising Safe Kids." *Child and Adolescent Mental Health*, 22, 194–200.

Howes, C., C. Rodning, D. C. Galluzzo, and L. Myers. 1988. "Attachment and Child Care: Relationships with Mother and Caregiver." *Early Childhood Research Quarterly*, 3, 403–416.

Hu, X., and R. W. Puddy. 2010. "An Agent-Based Model for Studying Child Maltreatment and Child Maltreatment Prevention." *Advances in Social Computing*. Edited by S-K. Chai J. J. Salerno, and P. L. Mabry. Cham, Switzerland: Springer, pp. 189–198.

Humphreys, C., and D. Absler. 2011. "History Repeating: Child Protection Responses to Domestic Violence." *Child and Family Social Work*, 16, 464–473.

Hussey, J. M., J. J. Chang, and J. B. Kotch. 2006. "Child Maltreatment in the United States: Prevalence, Risk Factors, and Adolescent Health Consequences." *Pediatrics*, 118, 933–942.

Institute of Medicine and National Research Council. 2014. *New Directions In Child Abuse and Neglect Research*. Washington, DC: The National Academies Press.

Jaffee, S. R., A. Caspi, T. E. Moffitt, M. Polo-Tomás, and A. Taylor. 2007. "Individual, Family, and Neighborhood Factors Distinguish Resilient from Non-Resilient Maltreated Children: A Cumulative Stressors Model." *Child Abuse and Neglect*, 31, 231–253.

Jaffee, S. R., and A. K. Maikovich- Fong, A. K. 2011. "Effects of Chronic Maltreatment and Maltreatment Timing on Children's Behavior and Cognitive Abilities." *Journal of Child Psychology and Psychiatry*, 52, 184–194.

Jaudes, P. K., and L. Mackey-Bilaver. 2008. "Do Chronic Conditions Increase Young Children's Risk of Being Maltreated?" *Child Abuse and Neglect*, 32, 671–681.

Ji, K., and D. Finkelhor. 2015. "A Meta-Analysis of Child Physical Abuse Prevalence in China." *Child Abuse and Neglect*, 43, 61–72.

Jones, L. P., E. Gross, and I. Becker. 2002. "The Characteristics of Domestic Violence Victims in a Child Protective Service Caseload." *Families in Society*, 83(4), 405–415.

Jones, L., M. A. Bellis, S. Wood, K. Hughes, E. Mccoy, L. Eckley, G. Bates, C. Mikton, T. Shakespeare, and A. Officer. 2012. "Prevalence and Risk of Violence Against Children with Disabilities: A Systematic Review and Meta-Analysis of Observational Studies." *Lancet*, 380, 899–907.

Jonson-Reid, M, T. Chance, and B. Drake. 2007. "Risk of Death Among Children Reported for Non-Fatal Maltreatment." *Child Maltreatment*, 12, 86–95.

Jonson-Reid, M., and C. Chiang. 2019. Problems in Understanding Program Efficacy in Child Welfare. *Re-Visioning Public Health Approaches for Protecting Children*. Edited by B. Lonne, D. Scott, D. Higgins, and T. Herrenkohl. Cham, Switzerland: Springer, pp. 349–378.

Jonson-Reid, M., and B. Drake. 2018. *After the Cradle Falls: What Child Abuse Is, How We Respond to It, and What You Can Do About It.* New York: Oxford University Press.

Jonson-Reid, M., B. Drake, and P. Kohl. 2009. "Is the Overrepresentation of the Poor in Child Welfare Caseloads Due to Bias or Need?" *Children and Youth Services Review*, 31, 422–427.

Jonson-Reid, M., B. Drake, and P. Kohl. 2017. "Childhood Maltreatment, Public Service System Contact and Preventable Death in Young Adulthood." *Violence and Victims*, 32(1), 93–109. https://www.doi.org/10.1891/0886-6708.VV-D-14-00133

Jonson-Reid, M, B. Drake, J. Kim, S. Porterfield, and L. Han. 2004. "A Prospective Analysis of the Relationship Between Reported Child Maltreatment and Special Education Eligibility Among Poor Children." *Child Maltreatment*, 9, 382–394.

Jonson-Reid, M., B. Drake, J. Constantino, M. Tandon, L. Pons, P. Kohl, S. Roesch, E. Wideman, A. Dunnigan, and W. Auslander. 2018. A Randomized Trial of Home Visitation for Intact Families Reported to Child Protective Services: Feasibility and the Moderating Impact of Prior Report History and Maternal Depression." *Child Maltreatment*, 23, 281–293.

Jonson-Reid, M., T. Edmond, J. Lauritsen, and D. Schneider. 2016. "Violence Prevention: Public Health and Policy." Prevention Policy and Public Health. Edited by A. Eyler, R. Brownson, J. Chriqui, and S. Russell. New York: Oxford University Press.

Jonson-Reid, M., P. L. Kohl, and B. Drake. 2012. "Child and Adult Outcomes of Chronic Child Maltreatment." *Pediatrics*, 129, 839–845.

Jouriles, E., R. Mcdonald, A. Slep, R. Heyman, and E. Garrido. 2008. "Child Abuse in the Context of Domestic Violence: Prevalence, Explanations, and Practice Implications." *Violence and Victims*, 23, 221–235.

Kaplow, J. B., and C. S. Widom, 2007. "Age of Onset of Child Maltreatment Predicts Long-Term Mental Health Outcomes." *Journal of Abnormal Psychology*, 116, 176–187.

Keddell, E. 2014. "The Ethics of Predictive Risk Modelling in the Aotearoa/New Zealand Child Welfare Context: Child Abuse Prevention or Neo-Liberal Tool?" *Critical Social Policy*, 35, 39–88.

Kelleher, K., W. Gardner, J. Coben, R. Barth, J. Edleson, and A. Hazen. 2006. "Co-Occurring Intimate Partner Violence and Child Maltreatment: Local Policies/Practices and Relationships to Child Placement, Family Services and Residence." Department of Justice. Retrieved from https://www.ncjrs.gov/pdffiles1/nij/grants/213503.pdf

Kessler, M., E. Gira, and J. Poertner. 2005. "Moving Best Practice to Evidence-Based Practice in Child Welfare." *Families In Society*, 86, 244–250.

Kessler, R. C., K. A. Mclaughlin, J. G. Green, M. J. Gruber, N. A. Sampson, A. M. Zaslavsky, S. Aguilar-Gaxiola, A. O. Alhamzawi, J. Alonso, M. Angermeyer, C. Benjet, E. Bromet, S. Chatterji, G. de Girolamo, K. Demyttenaere, J. Fayyad, S. Florescu, G. Gal, O. Gureje, J.M. Haro, C. Y. Hu, E. G. Karam, N. Kawakami, S. Lee, J.P. Lépine, J. Ormel, L. Posada-Villa, R. Sagar, A. Tsang, T. B. Ustün, S. Vassilev, M. S. Viana, and D. R. Williams. 2010. "Childhood Adversities and Adult Psychopathology in the WHO World Mental Health Surveys." *The British Journal of Psychiatry*, 197, 378–385.

Kim, H., C. Wildeman, M. Jonson-Reid, and B. Drake. 2016. "Lifetime Prevalence of Child Maltreatment Among US Children." *American Journal of Public Health*, 107, 274–280.

Kim, J., and D. Cicchetti. 2004. "A Longitudinal Study of Child Maltreatment, Mother–Child Relationship Quality and Maladjustment: The Role of Self-Esteem and Social Competence." *Journal of Abnormal Child Psychology*, 32, 341–354.

Kim, H., and B. Drake. 2017. "Duration in Poverty-Related Programs and Number of Child Maltreatment Reports: A Multilevel Negative Binomial Study." *Child Maltreatment*, 22(1), 14–23.

Kirst, M., L. P. Lazgare, Y. J. Zhang, P. O'Campo. 2015. "The Effects of Social Capital and Neighborhood Characteristics on Intimate Partner Violence: A Consideration of Social Resources and Risks." *American Journal of Community Psychology*, 55, 314–325.

Klein, S. 2011. "The Availability of Neighborhood Early Care and Education Resources and the Maltreatment of Young Children." *Child Maltreatment*, 16, 300–311.

Klevens, J., L. M. Kollar, G. Rizzo, G. O'Shea, J. Nguyen, and S. Roby. 2019. "Commonalities and Differences in Social Norms Related to Corporal Punishment Among Black, Latino and White Parents." *Child and Adolescent Social Work Journal*, 36(1), 19–28.

Klika, J. B., S. Lee, and J. Y. Lee. 2018. "Prevention of Child Maltreatment." *The APSAC Handbook on Child Maltreatment*. Edited by J. B. Klika and J. R. Conte. Sage Publications, Inc: Thousand Oaks, CA, pp. 235–251.

Kohl, P. L., R. Barth, A. L. Hazen, and J. A. Landsverk, 2005. "Child Welfare as a Gateway to Domestic Violence Services." *Children and Youth Services Review*, 27, 1203–1221.

Kohl, P., M. Jonson-Reid, and B. Drake, B. 2011. "The Role of Parental Mental Illness in the Safety and Stability of Maltreated Children." *Child Abuse and Neglect*, 35, 309–318.

Laforett, D.R., and J. L. Mendez. 2010. "Parent Involvement, Parental Depression, and Program Satisfaction Among Low-Income Parents Participating in a Two-Generation Early Childhood Education Program." *Early Education and Development*, 21, 517–535.

Lanier, P., M. Jonson-Reid, M. Stahlschmidt, B. Drake, and J. Constantino, 2009. "Child Maltreatment and Pediatric Health Outcomes: A Longitudinal Study of Low-Income Children." *Journal of Pediatric Psychology*, 35, 511–22.

Lawrence, C. N., K. D. Rosanbalm, and K. A. Dodge. 2011. "Multiple Response System: Evaluation of Policy Change in North Carolina's Child Welfare System." *Children and Youth Services Review*, 33, 2355–2365.

Leclerc, B., Y. N. Chiu, and J. Cale. 2016. "Sexual Violence and Abuse Against Children a First Review Through The Lens of Environmental Criminology." *International Journal of Offender Therapy and Comparative Criminology*, 60, 743–765.

Lee, L. C., J. B. Kotch, and C. E. Cox. 2004. "Child Maltreatment in families Experiencing Domestic Violence." *Violence and Victims*, 19(5), 573–591.

Leeb, R. T., L. J. Paulozzi, C. Melanson, T. Simon, and I. 2008. *Child Maltreatment Surveillance: Uniform Definitions for Public Health and Recommended Data Elements*. Vol. 1. Atlanta, GA: Centers for Disease Control.

Leenarts, L. E., J. Diehle, T. A. Doreleijers, E. P. Jansma, and R. J. Lindauer. 2013. "Evidence-Based Treatments for Children with Trauma-Related Psychopathology as a Result of Childhood Maltreatment: A Systematic Review." *European Child and Adolescent Psychiatry*, 22, 269–283.

Leiter, J. 2007. "School Performance Trajectories After the Advent of Reported Maltreatment." *Children and Youth Services Review*, 29, 363–382.

Lery, B., E. Putnam-Hornstein, W. Wiegmann, and B. King. 2015. "Building Analytic Capacity and Statistical Literacy Among Title IV-E MSW Students." *Journal of Public Child Welfare*, 9, 256–276.

Lin, J., and S. M. Reich. 2016. "Mothers' Perceptions of Neighborhood Disorder Are Associated with Children's Home Environment Quality." *Journal of Community Psychology*, 44, 714–728.

Lineberry, T. W., and J. M. Bostwick. 2006. "Methamphetamine Abuse: A Perfect Storm of Complications." *Mayo Clinic Proceedings*, 81, 77–84.

Lo, C. K., K. L. Chan, and P. Ip. 2017. "Insecure Adult Attachment and Child Maltreatment: A Meta-Analysis." *Trauma, Violence, & Abuse*, 20(5), 706–719.

Loman, L. A. and G. L. Siegel. 2015. "Effects of Approach and Services Under Differential Response on Long Term Child Safety and Welfare." *Child Abuse and Neglect*, 39, 86–97.

Lorthridge, J., J. Mccroskey, P. J. Pecora, R. Chambers, and M. Fatemi. 2012. "Strategies for Improving Child Welfare Services for Families of Color: First Findings of a Community-Based Initiative in Los Angeles." *Children and Youth Services Review*, 34, 281–288.

Luby, J. L. 2015. "Poverty's Most Insidious Damage: The Developing Brain." *JAMA Pediatrics*, 169, 810–811.

Luke, D. A. 2005. "Getting the Big Picture in Community Science: Methods That Capture Context." *American Journal of Community Psychology*, 35, 185–200.

Maclaurin, B., N. Trocmé, B. Fallon, C. Blackstock, L. Pitman, and M. Mccormack. 2008. "A Comparison of First Nations and Non-Aboriginal Children Investigated for Maltreatment in Canada In 2003." CECW Information Sheet# 66E.

Maclean, M. J., S. Sims, C. Bower, H. Leonard, F. J. Stanley, and M. O'Donnell. 2017. "Maltreatment Risk Among Children With Disabilities." *Pediatrics*, 139, 1–10.

MacMillan, H. L., C. N. Wathen, J. Barlow, D. M. Fergusson, J. M. Leventhal, and H. N. Taussig. 2009. "Interventions to Prevent Child Maltreatment and Associated Impairment." *The Lancet*, 373(9659), 250–266.

Maguire-Jack, K., and K. Showalter. 2016. "The Protective Effect of Neighborhood Social Cohesion in Child Abuse and Neglect." *Child Abuse & Neglect*, 52, 29–37.

Maher, E. J., L. J. Jackson, P. J. Pecora, D. J. Schultz, A. Chandra, and D. S. Barnes-Broby. 2009. "Overcoming Challenges to Implementing and Evaluating Evidence-Based Interventions in Child Welfare: A Matter of Necessity." *Children and Youth Services Review*, 31, 555–562.

Marsh, J.C., B. D. Smith, and M. Bruni. 2011. "Integrated Substance Abuse and Child Welfare Services for Women: A Progress Review." *Children and Youth Services Review*, 33, 466–472.

Maslow, A. H. 1943. "A Theory of Human Motivation." *Psychological Review*, 50, 370.

Mbagaya, C., P. Oburu, and M. J. Bakermans-Kranenburg. 2013. "Child Physical Abuse and Neglect in Kenya, Zambia and the Netherlands: A Cross-Cultural Comparison of Prevalence, Psychopathological Sequelae and Mediation by PTSS." *International Journal of Psychology*, 48, 95–107.

Mccarthy, M. M., P. Taylor, R. E. Norman, L. Pezzullo, J. Tucci, and C. Goddard. 2016. "The Lifetime Economic and Social Costs of Child Maltreatment in Australia." *Children and Youth Services Review*, 71, 217–226.

Mccroskey, J., T. Franke, C. A. Christie, P. J. Pecora, J. Lorthridge, D. Fleischer, and E. Rosenthal. 2010. "Prevention Initiative Demonstration Project (PIDP): Year Two Evaluation Report." Report prepared for Casey Family Programs.

Mcdonnell, C. G., A. D. Boan, C. C. Bradley, K. D. Seay, J. M. Charles, and L. A. Carpenter. 2018. "Child Maltreatment in Autism Spectrum Disorder and Intellectual Disability: Results from a Population-Based Sample." *Journal of Child Psychology and Psychiatry*, 60, 576–584.

Mcfarlane, J., L. Symes, B. Binder, J. Maddoux, and R. Paulson. 2014. "Maternal–Child Dyads of Functioning: The Intergenerational Impact of Violence Against Women on Children." *Maternal and Child Health Journal*, 18, 2236–2243.

Mclaughlin, A. M., E. Gray, and M. Wilson. 2015. "Child Welfare Workers and Social Justice: Mending the Disconnect." *Children and Youth Services Review*, 59, 177–183.

Meloy, M. E., S. T. Lipscomb, and M. J. Baron. 2015. "Linking State Child Care and Child Welfare Policies and Populations: Implications for Children, Families, and Policymakers." *Children and Youth Services Review*, 57, 30–39.

Melton, G. B. 2005. "Mandated Reporting: A Policy Without Reason." *Child Abuse & Neglect*, 29(1), 9–18.

Melton, G. B. 2014. "Strong Communities for Children: A Community-Wide Approach to Prevention of Child Maltreatment." *Handbook of Child Maltreatment: Contemporary Issues in Research and Policy*. Edited by J. Korbin and R. Krugman. New York: Springer, pp. 329–339.

Merritt, D. H., and S. Klein. 2015. "Do Early Care and Education Services Improve Language Development for Maltreated Children? Evidence from a National Child Welfare Sample." *Child Abuse and Neglect*, 39, 185–196.

Mersky, J. P., and J. Topitzes. 2010. "Comparing Early Adult Outcomes of Maltreated and Non-Maltreated Children: A Prospective Longitudinal Investigation." *Children and Youth Services Review*, 32, 1086–1096.

Mersky, J. P., J. Topitzes, and K. Blair. 2017. "Translating Evidence-Based Treatments into Child Welfare Services Through Community-University Partnerships: A Case Example of Parent–Child Interaction Therapy." *Children and Youth Services Review*, 82, 427–433.

Mikton, C., M. Power, M. Raleva, M. Makoae, M. Al Eissa, I. Cheah, N. Cardia, C. Choo, and M. Almuneef. 2013. "The Assessment of the Readiness of Five Countries to Implement Child Maltreatment Prevention Programs on a Large Scale." *Child Abuse and Neglect*, 37, 1237–1251.

Millett, L. S., K. D. Seay, and P. L. Kohl. 2015. "A National Study of Intimate Partner Violence Risk Among Female Caregivers Involved in the Child Welfare System: The Role of Nativity, Acculturation, and Legal Status." *Children and Youth Services Review*, 48, 60–69.

Molnar, B. E., E. D. Beatriz, and W. R. Beardslee. 2016. "Community-Level Approaches to Child Maltreatment Prevention." *Trauma, Violence, and Abuse*, 17, 387–397.

Moore, E., G. Armsden, and P. L. Gogerty. 1998. "A Twelve-Year Follow-Up Study of Maltreated and At-Risk Children Who Received Early Therapeutic Child Care." *Child Maltreatment*, 3, 3–16.

Morrill, A. C., L. Mcelaney, B. Peixotto, M. Vanvleet, and R. Sege. 2015. "Evaluation of All Babies Cry, a Second Generation Universal Abusive Head Trauma Prevention Program." *Journal of Community Psychology*, 43, 296–314.

Murphy, K., K. A. Moore, Z. Redd, and K. Malm. 2017. "Trauma-Informed Child Welfare Systems and Children's Well-Being: A Longitudinal Evaluation of KVC's Bridging the Way Home Initiative." *Children and Youth Services Review*, 75, 23–34.

Muzik, M., and S. Borovska. 2010. "Perinatal Depression: Implications for Child Mental Health." *Mental Health in Family Medicine*, 7(4), 239–247.

Naccarato, T. 2010. "Child Welfare Informatics: A Proposed Subspecialty for Social Work." *Children and Youth Services Review*, 32, 1729–1734.

Nadan, Y., J. C. Spilsbury, and J. E. Korbin. 2015. "Culture and Context in Understanding Child Maltreatment: Contributions of Intersectionality and Neighborhood-Based Research." *Child Abuse and Neglect*, 41, 40–48.

Negash, T., and K. Maguire-Jack. 2016. "Do Social Services Matter for Child Maltreatment Prevention? Interactions Between Social Support and Parent's Knowledge of Available Local Social Services." *Journal of Family Violence*, 31, 557–565.

Neger, E. N., and R. J. Prinz. 2015. "Interventions to Address Parenting and Parental Substance Abuse: Conceptual and Methodological Considerations." *Clinical Psychology Review*, 39, 71–82.

O'Connor, A. 2001. "Understanding Inequality in the Late Twentieth-Century Metropolis: New Perspectives on the Enduring Racial Divide." *Urban Inequality: Evidence from Four Cities*. Edited by A. O'Connor, L. Bobo, and C. Tilly. New York: Russell Sage, pp. 1–34.

O'Donnell, M., M. J. Maclean, S. Sims, V. A. Morgan, H. Leonard, and F. J. Stanley. 2015. "Maternal Mental Health and Risk of Child Protection Involvement: Mental Health Diagnoses Associated with Increased Risk." *Journal of Epidemiology Community Health*, 69, 1175–1183.

O'Donnell, M., N. Nassar, H. Leonard, P. Jacoby, R. Mathews, Y. Patterson, and F. Stanley. 2010. "Characteristics of Non-Aboriginal and Aboriginal Children and Families with Substantiated Child Maltreatment: A Population-Based Study." *International Journal of Epidemiology*, 39, 921–928.

Olds, D., J. Eckenrode, and H. Kitzman. 2005. "Clarifying the Impact of the Nurse-Family Partnership on Child Maltreatment: Response to Chaffin (2004)." *Child Abuse & Neglect*, 29(3), 229–233.

Oshri, A., T. E. Sutton, J. Clay-Warner, and J. D. Miller. 2015. "Child Maltreatment Types and Risk Behaviors: Associations with Attachment Style and Emotion Regulation Dimensions." *Personality and Individual Differences*, 73, 127–133.

Peacock, S., S. Konrad, E. Watson, D. Nickel, and N. Muhajarine. 2013. "Effectiveness of Home Visiting Programs on Child Outcomes: A Systematic Review." *BMC Public Health*, 13, 17.

Pecora, P. J., D. Sanders, D. Wilson, D. English, A. Puckett, and K. Rudlang-Perman. 2014. "Addressing Common Forms of Child Maltreatment: Evidence-Informed Interventions and Gaps in Current Knowledge." *Child and Family Social Work*, 19, 321–332.

Pelton, L. H. 2015. "The Continuing Role of Material Factors in Child Maltreatment and Placement." *Child Abuse and Neglect*, 4, 130–39.

Petra, M., and P. Kohl. 2010. "Pathways Triple P and the Child Welfare System: A Promising Fit." *Children and Youth Services Review*, 32, 611–618.

Pieterse, D. 2015. "Childhood Maltreatment and Educational Outcomes: Evidence from South Africa." *Health Economics*, 24, 876–894.

Pösö, T., M. Skivenes, and A. D. Hestbæk. 2014. "Child Protection Systems Within the Danish, Finnish and Norwegian Welfare States-Time for a Child Centric Approach?" *European Journal of Social Work*, 17, 475–490.

Prinz, R. J. 2016. "Parenting and Family Support Within a Broad Child Abuse Prevention Strategy: Child Maltreatment Prevention Can Benefit from Public Health Strategies." *Child Abuse and Neglect*, 51, 400–406.

Putnam-Hornstein, E., and B. Needell. 2011. "Predictors of Child Protective Service Contact Between Birth and Age Five: An Examination of California's 2002 Birth Cohort." *Children and Youth Services Review*, 33, 1337–1344.

Putnam-Hornstein, E., B. Needell, and A. E. Rhodes. 2013. "Understanding Risk and Protective Factors for Child Maltreatment: The Value of Integrated, Population-Based Data." *Child Abuse and Neglect*, 37, 116–119.

Putnam-Hornstein, E., J. N. Wood, J. Fluke, A. Yoshioka-Maxwell, and R. P. Berger. 2013. "Preventing Severe and Fatal Child Maltreatment: Making the Case for the Expanded Use and Integration of Data." *Child Welfare*, 92, 59–75.

Radford, L., S. Corral, C. Bradley, and H. L. Fisher. 2013. "The Prevalence and Impact of Child Maltreatment and Other Types of Victimization in the UK: Findings from a Population Survey of Caregivers, Children and Young People and Young Adults." *Child Abuse and Neglect*, 37, 801–813.

Raghupathi, W., and V. Raghupathi. 2014. "Big Data Analytics in Healthcare: Promise and Potential." *Health Information Science and Systems*, 2, 1.

Rahman, A., P. J. Surkan, C. E. Cayetano, P. Rwagatare, and K. E. Dickson. 2013. "Grand Challenges: Integrating Maternal Mental Health Into Maternal and Child Health Programmes." Plos Medicine, 10, 1–7.

Ramsey, A. T., A. Baumann, B. Cooper, and D. A. Patterson. 2015. "Informing the Development of an Electronic Clinical Dashboard in Addiction Services." Poster Presentation at the 8th Annual Conference on the Science of Dissemination and Implementation, Washington, DC.

Ratner, B. 2012. *Statistical and Machine-Learning Data Mining: Techniques for Better Predictive Modeling and Analysis of Big Data*. Boca Raton, FL: CRC Press.

Raver, C. C., and B. J. Leadbeater. 1999. "Mothering Under Pressure: Environmental, Child, and Dyadic Correlates of Maternal Self-Efficacy Among Low-Income Women." *Journal of Family Psychology*, 13(4), 523–534.

Renner, L. M., and K. S. Slack. 2006. "Intimate Partner Violence and Child Maltreatment: Understanding Intra-and Intergenerational Connections." *Child Abuse and Neglect*, 30, 599–617.

Reupert, A., and D. Maybery. 2007. "Families Affected by Parental Mental Illness: A Multiperspective Account of Issues and Interventions." *American Journal of Orthopsychiatry*, 77, 362–369.

Reynolds, A. J., L. C. Mathieson, and J. W. Topitzes. 2009. "Do Early Childhood Interventions Prevent Child Maltreatment? A Review of Research." *Child Maltreatment*, 14, 182–206.

Rodriguez, C., and M. Tucker. 2015. "Predicting Maternal Physical Child Abuse Risk Beyond Distress and Social Support: Additive Role of Cognitive Processes." *Journal of Child and Family Studies*, 24, 1780–1790.

Russell, J. 2015. "Predictive Analytics and Child Protection: Constraints and Opportunities." *Child Abuse and Neglect*, 46, 182–189.

Ryan, J. P., B. A. Jacob, M. Gross, B. E. Perron, A. Moore, and S. Ferguson. 2018. "Early Exposure to Child Maltreatment and Academic Outcomes." *Child Maltreatment*, 23, 365–375.

Sanders, M. R., C. Markie-Dadds, and K. M. T. Turner. 2003. "Theoretical, Scientific and Clinical Foundations of Tripe P-Positive Parenting Program: A Population Approach to the Promotion of Parenting Competence." *Parenting Research and Practice Monographs*, 1–21.

Scannapieco, M. R. Hegar, and K. Connell-Carrick. 2012. "Professionalization in Public Child Welfare: Historical Context and Workplace Outcomes for Social Workers and Non-Social Workers." *Children and Youth Services Review*, 34, 2170–2178.

Scarborough, A. A., and J. S. Mccrae. 2010. "School-Age Special Education Outcomes of Infants and Toddlers Investigated for Maltreatment." *Children and Youth Services Review*, 32, 80–88.

Schmit, S., L. Schott, L. Pavetti, and H. Matthews. 2015. "Effective, Evidence -Based Home Visiting Programs in Every State at Risk If Congress Does Not Extend Funding." *Center on Budget and Policy Priorities*. Retrieved from https://www.cbpp.org/research/effective-evidence-based-home-visiting-programs-in-every-state-at-risk-if-congress-does-not

Schreiner, M., and M. Sherraden. 2007. *Can The Poor Save? Saving and Asset Building in Individual Development Accounts*. New Brunswick, NJ: Taylor & Francis.

Schwartz, I. M., P. York, E. Nowakowski-Sims, and A. Ramos-Hernandez. 2017. "Predictive and Prescriptive Analytics, Machine Learning and Child Welfare Risk Assessment: The Broward County Experience." *Children and Youth Services Review*, 81, 309–320.

Seay, K. D., and P. L. Kohl. 2015. "The Comorbid and Individual Impacts of Maternal Depression and Substance Dependence on Parenting and Child Behavior Problems." *Journal of Family Violence*, 30, 899–910.

Sexton, M. B., L. Hamilton, E. W. Mcginnis, K. L. Rosenblum, and M. Muzik. 2015. "The Roles of Resilience and Childhood Trauma History: Main and Moderating Effects on Postpartum Maternal Mental Health and Functioning." *Journal of Affective Disorders*, 174, 562–568.

Shaw, T.V., R. P. Barth, J. Mattingly, D. Ayer, and S. Berry. 2013. "Child Welfare Birth Match: Timely Use of Child Welfare Administrative Data to Protect Newborns." *Journal of Public Child Welfare*, 7, 217–234.

Silovsky, J. F., D. Bard, M. Chaffin, D. Hecht, L. Burris, A. Owora, L. Beasley, D. Boughty, and J. Lutzker. 2011. "Prevention of Child Maltreatment in High-Risk Rural Families: A Randomized Clinical Trial with Child Welfare Outcomes." *Children and Youth Services Review*, 33, 1435–1444.

Silver, E., A. Heneghan, L. Bauman, and R. Stein. 2006. "The Relationship of Depressive Symptoms to Parenting Competence and Social Support in Inner-City Mothers of Young Children." *Maternal and Child Health Journal*, 10, 105–112.

Slack, K. S., J. L. Holl, B. J. Lee, M. Mcdaniel, L. Altenbernd, and A. B. Stevens. 2003. "Child Protective Intervention in the Context of Welfare Reform: The Effects of Work and Welfare on Maltreatment Reports." *Journal of Policy Analysis and Management*, 22, 517–536.

Slack, K. S., J. L. Holl, M. McDaniel, J. Yoo, and K. Bolger. 2004. "Understanding the Risks of Child Neglect: An Exploration of Poverty and Parenting Characteristics." *Child Maltreatment*, 9(4), 395–408.

Smith, A. L., D. Cross, J. Winkler, T. Jovanovic, and B. Bradley. 2014. "Emotional Dysregulation and Negative Affect Mediate the Relationship Between Maternal History of Child Maltreatment and Maternal Child Abuse Potential." *Journal of Family Violence*, 29, 483–494.

Spivey, M. I., P. G. Schnitzer, R. L. Kruse, P. Slusher, and D. M. Jaffe. 2009. "Association of Injury Visits in Children and Child Maltreatment Reports." *Journal of Emergency Medicine*, 36, 207–214

Stith, S.M., T. Liu, L. C. Davies, E. L. Boykin, M. C. Alder, J. M. Harris, A. Som, M. McPherson, J. E. M. E. G. Dees. 2009. "Risk Factors in Child Maltreatment: A Meta-Analytic Review of the Literature." *Aggression and Violent Behavior*, 14, 13–29.

Stoltenborgh, M., M. J. Bakermans-Kranenburg, and M. H. Van Ijzendoorn. 2013. "The Neglect of Child Neglect: A Meta-Analytic Review of the Prevalence of Neglect." *Social Psychiatry and Psychiatric Epidemiology*, 48, 345–355.

Stoltenborgh, M., M. J. Bakermans-Kranenburg, M. H. Ijzendoorn, and L. R. Alink. 2013. "Cultural-Geographical Differences in the Occurrence of Child Physical Abuse? A Meta-Analysis of Global Prevalence." *International Journal of Psychology*, 48, 81–94.

Stoltenborgh, M., M. H. Van Ijzendoorn, E. M. Euser, and M. J. Bakermans-Kranenburg. 2011. "A Global Perspective on Child Sexual Abuse: Meta-Analysis of Prevalence Around the World." *Child Maltreatment*, 16, 79–101.

Stone, S. 2007. "Child Maltreatment, Out-of-Home Placement and Academic Vulnerability: A Fifteen-Year Review of Evidence and Future Directions." *Children and Youth Services Review*, 29, 139–161.

Strathearn, L., P. Gray, M. O'Callaghan, and D. Wood. 2001. "Childhood Neglect and Cognitive Development in Extremely Low Birth Weight Infants: A Prospective Study." *Pediatrics*, 108, 142–151.

Sullivan, P. M., and J. F. Knutson. 2000. "Maltreatment and Disabilities: A Population-Based Epidemiological Study." *Child Abuse and Neglect*, 24, 1257–1273.

Svensson, B., U. Eriksson, and S. Janson. 2013. "Exploring Risk for Abuse of Children with Chronic Conditions or Disabilities-Parent's Perceptions of Stressors and the Role of Professionals." *Child: Care, Health and Development*, 39, 887–893.

Teicher, M. H., C. M. Anderson, and A. Polcari. 2012. "Childhood Maltreatment Is Associated with Reduced Volume in the Hippocampal Subfields CA3, Dentate Gyrus, and Subiculum." *Proceedings of the National Academy of Sciences*, 109, E563–E572.

Thompson, R., D. J. English, and C. R. White. 2016. "Maltreatment History as Persistent Risk: An Extension of Li and Godinet (2014)." *Children and Youth Services Review*, 64, 117–121.

Tillyer, M. S. 2015. "The Relationship Between Childhood Maltreatment and Adolescent Violent Victimization." *Crime & Delinquency*, 61, 973–995.

Turner, H. A., D. Finkelhor, and R. Ormrod. 2006. "The Effect of Lifetime Victimization on the Mental Health of Children and Adolescents." *Social Science and Medicine*, 62, 13–27.

Turner, W., J. Broad, J. Drinkwater, A. Firth, M. Hester, N. Stanley, E. Szilassy, and G. Feder. 2015. "Interventions to Improve the Response of Professionals to Children Exposed to Domestic Violence and Abuse: A Systematic Review." *Child Abuse Review*, 26(1), 19–39.

U.S. Department of Health and Human Services, Administration for Children and Families, Administration on Children, Youth and Families, Children's Bureau. 2017. *Child Maltreatment 2015–2017*. Washington DC: Author.

Vaithianathan, R., T. Maloney, E. Putnam-Hornstein, E., and N. Jiang. 2013. "Children in the Public Benefit System at Risk of Maltreatment: Identification via Predictive Modeling." *American Journal of Preventive Medicine*, 45, 354–359.

Wald, M. S. 2014. "Beyond Maltreatment: Developing Support for Children in Multiproblem Families." *Handbook of Child Maltreatment*. Edited by J. Korbin and R. Krugman. Dordrecht, Netherlands: Springer, pp. 251–280.

Walsh, C., H. L. Macmillan, and E. Jamieson. 2003. "The Relationship Between Parental Substance Abuse and Child Maltreatment: Findings from the Ontario Health Supplement." *Child Abuse and Neglect*, 27, 1409–1425.

Warren, E. J., and S. A. Font. 2015. "Housing Insecurity, Maternal Stress, and Child Maltreatment: An Application of the Family Stress Model." *Social Service Review*, 89, 9–39.

Webster-Stratton, C. L. 2014. "Incredible Years® Parent and Child Programs for Maltreating Families." *Evidence-Based Approaches for the Treatment of Maltreated Children*. Edited by S. Timmer and A. Urquiza. Dordrecht, the Netherlands: Springer, pp. 81–104.

Widom, C. S., S. J. Czaja, T. Bentley, and M. S. Johnson. 2012. "A Prospective Investigation of Physical Health Outcomes in Abused and Neglected Children: New Findings from a 30-Year Follow-Up." *American Journal of Public Health*, 102, 1135–1144.

Wilkins, N., B. Tsao, M. Hertz, R. Davis, and J. Klevins. 2014. "Connecting the Dots: An Overview of the Links Among Multiple Forms of Violence." Report prepared for the National Center for Injury Prevention and Control, Centers for Disease Control and Prevention.

Windham, A.M., L. Rosenberg, and L. Fuddy. 2004. "Risk of Mother-Reported Child Abuse in the First 3 Years of Life." *Child Abuse and Neglect*, 28, 645–667.

Witt, A., R. C. Brown, P. L. Plener, E. Brähler, and J. M. Fegert. 2017. "Child Maltreatment in Germany: Prevalence Rates in the General Population." *Child and Adolescent Psychiatry and Mental Health*, 11(1), 47.

World Health Organization. 2006. *Preventing Child Maltreatment: A Guide to Taking Action and Generating Evidence*. Geneva, Switzerland: Author.

World Health Organization. 2016. "Child Maltreatment Fact Sheet." https://www.who.int/en/news-room/fact-sheets/detail/child-maltreatment

Young, N. K., S. M. Boles, and C. Otero. 2007. "Parental Substance Use Disorders and Child Maltreatment: Overlap, Gaps, and Opportunities." *Child Maltreatment*, 12, 137–149.

Zhai, F., and Q. Gao. 2009. "Child Maltreatment Among Asian Americans: Characteristics and Explanatory Framework." *Child Maltreatment*, 14, 207–224.

Zielinski, D. S. 2009. "Child Maltreatment and Adult Socioeconomic Well-Being." *Child Abuse and Neglect*, 33, 666.

8

Fostering Civic Engagement Across the Life Course

VETTA L. SANDERS THOMPSON AND GENA GUNN MCCLENDEN

Despite the widespread agreement that civic engagement is important in building the vitality and equity of a society, multiple indicators suggest that civic engagement is declining. This decline is particularly troubling in that the most economically disenfranchised groups in society are also the least engaged in civic affairs. A decline in civic engagement is both a collective concern and responsibility. Changing these dynamics requires a framework for understanding the factors influencing the decline and evidence for policies that may support strategies intended to increase civic engagement. This chapter examines the importance of civic engagement as a component of achieving a livable life. A framework for understanding civic engagement is provided, followed by a review of current research on the importance of civic engagement and public participation for outcomes such as societal decision-making, economic prosperity, community cohesion, and problem-solving. We discuss voting behavior, individual and structural barriers to civic participation, and strategies to overcome these barriers. The historical and future role of social work in civic engagement is highlighted.

The Scope of Engagement and Why It Matters

A discussion of the status and importance of terms as broad as civic engagement and public participation requires a definition of terms. Civic engagement has been conceptualized in many ways. It consists of political and nonpolitical processes to affect, change, or improve the quality of life in communities (Adler and Goggin, 2016) and public problem-solving (Corporation for National and Community Service, 2017). These activities may be formal or informal and include volunteerism through membership in groups and associations, serving on boards and commissions, fundraising for charities, registering voters, working on political campaigns (local, state, and national), and making political campaign contributions. Other involvement includes participating in government meetings, as well as contacting public officials, media, or other concerned members of the community (Battistoni, 2017). Traditionally, civic engagement is thought to involve community dialogue to gain insights into diverse perspectives. These insights are then built upon to develop approaches on which there is consensus. Advocacy for identified issues is achieved through coalition and consensus building, constituency and community outreach, communication, grassroots organizing, and efforts related to organizational development (Adler and Goggin, 2016; Zakus and Lysack, 1998). Ideally, the activities, issues, decisions, and actions supported are informed by data and information that adequately cover and convey relevant history and experience.

Frameworks for civic engagement assume that individuals affected by policies and practices have a right to be involved in the decision-making process (Zakus and Lysack, 1998). The most common framework organizes civic engagement into three basic strategies. The first strategy is individual civic engagement in which an individual demonstrates their involvement through individual responsibility and action (e.g., voting, giving, and volunteerism). The second form of civic engagement is participatory and includes attention to and involvement in community affairs on all levels, such as serving on boards or commissions and working on political campaigns and advisory boards. Finally, there is social justice and advocacy-oriented engagement designed to identify and collectively work toward community change and improvement (Battistoni, 2017). Social justice and advocacy-oriented engagement include organizing to impact laws and policy, as well as block units, beautification boards, and organized protest. This form of engagement speaks to how community participation links to policy and action (Fung, 2006).

To fully understand community participation, frameworks have examined the processes and conditions that support participation, as well as the levels of participation observed (Hung, Sirakaya-Turk, and Ingram, 2011). There are social, economic, and political issues that may influence participation, most notably power imbalances. In addition, the unique characteristics of communities (e.g., longevity, sense of history, identity and attachment to place, and resources) and individual characteristics (e.g., time, knowledge, interest, awareness, confidence, and education) are important to consider. These processes and conditions can be understood as influencing who participates (Fung, 2006). It should be pointed out that community participation takes place along a continuum. Sherry Arnstein (1969) organized this continuum into eight levels, beginning with nonparticipation and extending to participatory strategies giving citizens a voice in decision-making. These levels of participation describe how segments of the community may communicate and engage in decision-making together (Fung, 2006).

The importance of civic engagement has been linked to its ability to strengthen community ties and trust in government among the governed. Robert Putnam (1995) notes that civic engagement provides opportunities for those who are reluctant to interact, for ideas to be examined and refined, and, importantly, to provide opportunities for learning skills critical to a democracy such as running meetings and speaking in public. Citizens who are able to achieve mutually agreed upon goals or resolve mutually agreed upon concerns become more empowered through increased self and collective efficacy, access to expanded social networks, and increased knowledge and understanding of the structural problems affecting society (Putnam, 1995). As a result, they become more effective agents of change (Jones and Wells, 2007; Zakus and Lysack, 1998). Data suggest that from the standpoint of governance, regions with strong civic engagement experience increased social capital and more efficient and innovative policies (Putnam, 1995).

In addition to building and maintaining trust in societal institutions, civic engagement allows members of the society to participate and invest in the decisions made about the care of the world in which we live (Putnam, 1995). If civic engagement enhances social capital, then we can speculate that the tensions among diverse groups observed around the world positions civic engagement as a process for addressing and reducing conflict among groups through opportunities for one on one contact that requires cooperation rather than competition (Taylor and Moghaddam, 1994).

Although civic engagement is essential to a democratic society, many Americans have reduced their participation in public and social affairs, which social scientists suggest results in weakened communal connections and trust in societal institutions (Checkoway, 2001a; Quan-Haase et al., 2002). Social work and its goal of a livable life for all are intimately connected to this issue. Civic engagement allows for all voices in a community to be heard. By doing so, decisions and policies that impact upon individual and community well-being are more likely to reflect the interests of a broad array of the populace. Civic engagement also fosters higher levels of trust in a society, which again helps to facilitate lives of purpose and meaning. This trust is reflective in lower levels of crime, tax evasion, and other counterproductive behaviors that are found in countries with low levels of civic engagement.

Dynamics of and Barriers to Civic Engagement

To effectively address declines in civic engagement and public participation activities, we must examine activities within each domain of engagement and attempt to understand the factors that act as barriers and those that facilitate participation. Across the life course, there are different levels of opportunities available for civic engagement as well as different strategies to positively impact the possibility of engagement. Differences in engagement across age, race/ethnicity, and socioeconomic status are briefly discussed. In short, the data reveal that younger, nonwhite individuals with lower levels of socioeconomic status are least likely to be civically engaged.

Patterns of Civic Engagement

Researchers analyzing civic engagement in the United States have documented declines in voting, attendance at community meetings, gatherings in public places, and involvement in voluntary organizations and civic concerns, as well as declines in positive attitudes toward community life and a sense of obligation to contribute to the health and well-being of the community (Quan-Haase et al., 2002). This decline has been taking place since the 1960s (Putnam, 2000).

Robert Putnam (2000) stated that over a 25-year period there had been a 35 percent decline in attendance at public meetings and an approximately 50 percent decline in participation in clubs and civic organizations. Recent survey data suggest that these trends may be less dramatic. Data from a 2013 Bureau of Labor Statistics report indicated that volunteerism was at its lowest level, 25.4 percent, since data collection began in 2002 (O'Neil, 2014). The survey reported declines in 16 of 20 indicators considered, including decreases in rates of individuals reporting that they volunteered or participated in a community organization, and decreases in levels of trust in public institutions (O'Neil, 2014). However, a Pew survey suggests that civic engagement has increased over their benchmark survey. Data from the 2016 Pew survey were compared to the 2013 CPS Civic Engagement Supplement and indicated that more individuals reported volunteering through organizations (59 percent vs. 25 percent), have worked with a neighbor to solve a problem in the past year (46 percent vs. 8 percent), participated in a school group or community organization in the past (36 percent vs. 13 percent), and participated in a service or civic organization in the past year (15 percent vs. 6 percent). Although the data suggest increased civic engagement, rates of engagement remain discouraging low (Pew Research Center, 2017).

Surveys suggest that the most frequent forms of civic engagement are volunteering and voting (Corporation for National and Community Service, 2010). Individuals who live in cities are less civically engaged than those living in suburbs or rural communities, and veterans are more engaged than nonveterans, as are individuals with strong social connections (Corporation for National and Community Service, 2010).

There are also differences in rates of volunteering by age, gender, education, and social class. Survey data indicate that women volunteer at higher rates than men, 28.4 percent compared to 22.2 percent. Approximately one third of Americans between the ages of 35 and 44 participated in a formal volunteer activity in 2013, which was the highest rate of any age group (O'Neil, 2014). However, older adults between the ages of 65 and 74 provided the most volunteer time. In North America, 40 to 50 percent of older adults formally volunteer to provide diverse health and human services (Gottlieb and Gillespie, 2008). Even adults with young children volunteered at a higher rate than very young adults despite their additional responsibilities. However, age interacts with education to affect young adult reports of civic engagement. Young adults, aged 18 to 24 and enrolled in college, volunteered at a rate of 26.7 percent, which was almost twice the rate of young adults not enrolled in college (O'Neil, 2014). This interaction seems to persist beyond college, as people with college degrees and higher education are more likely to be engaged civically than those without college degrees. African Americans have the highest rate of voting among all racial and ethnic groups in the United States. Voting is the most frequent form of community engagement among mid-life to older adults, but all adults, except those who are 45 to 49, experienced decreases in voting between 2009 and 2012 (AARP, 2012).

A Pew survey that took into account the use of the Internet confirmed many of these findings but also noted other characteristics that influenced the type of civic engagement (Smith et al., 2009). In the Pew survey, individuals under the age of 30 and Hispanic were more likely to report having attended an organized protest within a 12-month period, while individuals who reported living in a suburban community were more likely to have attended a political meeting on local, town, or school affairs. Those between 50 and 60 were more likely to have contacted a government official. Finally, the Pew survey found that gender, age, race, and ethnicity were less significant than differences based on income or education (Smith et al., 2009).

A 2012 Pew survey of civic engagement resulted in similar findings and noted that online, Internet-based engagement (e.g., signing petitions, political donations, texting or emailing government officials, using online strategies to send letters to the editor of magazines or newspapers) was prominent among higher income and better educated individuals. However, activism on social networking sites reduced income and age disparities noted in the rates of civic engagement. Young adults were as civically engaged on social media platforms (e.g., Facebook, Twitter) as older adults, and the same is true for those with lower incomes (Smith, 2013).

Frameworks for understanding community engagement attempt to consider the mechanisms that influence who participates (Fung, 2006). The role of income and education in predicting levels of civic engagement are likely related to two factors among adults younger than 65 years of age. First, civic engagement and public participation require time commitments, a factor theorized to affect who can participate. Better educated individuals are more likely to be employed in careers that provide more scheduling flexibility, leisure time, and disposable income for charitable contributions. Second, education likely exposes adults, including young adults in college, to the skills required for organizing, running meetings, letters to public officials and the media, and so on. Older adults likely provide more volunteer hours because they devote less of their time to full-time employment. Finally, English-speaking individuals and those who are white enjoy an education and income advantage that may affect rates of civic engagement, as well as fewer language barriers.

Using voting, reading newspapers, and following political trends as measures, Watts and Flanagan (2007) reported that political participation has declined among youth. Kahne and Middaugh (2008) suggest that differences in civic engagement rates among parents affect adolescent levels of civic engagement. The differences in family modeling and school-based opportunities may also contribute to variations noted in engagement by race and ethnicity observed in adolescence and continuing into adulthood. Higher income families are more likely to participate in political campaigns, engage in informal community work, contact elected officials, protest, or sit on a board (Kahne and Middaugh, 2008). In addition, these same families are likely to live in communities with schools that have significant resources. Well-funded schools have greater availability of school-based civic learning and service opportunities that promote voting and other forms of civic engagement (Kahne and Middaugh, 2008). We should not be surprised that white students and students attending higher social economic status high schools received more of the school-based civic learning opportunities that promote voting and broader forms of civic engagement than low-income students and students of color (Kahne and Middaugh, 2008).

The declines in and persistently low levels of U.S. civic engagement suggest various questions. Have the factors that influence who is engaged, how they engage, and why they engage, changed? What motivates citizens' desire to participate in governance and community life? What is the proper balance between citizen role, action and activities, voice, and government controlled and determined policies? Should citizens participate in all aspects and final decisions of government activities or only some?

Barriers to Engagement: Structural

Many factors influence civic engagement, and several are important to explore as we attempt to understand declining civic engagement in the United States. Given the importance of voting in a democracy and the declines noted in voting participation, we highlight some of the structural barriers that are encountered among the poor, people of color, those with disabilities, and other marginalized communities.

Many argue that photo identification laws discriminate against racial/ethnic minority and low-income voters because of the time and cost associated with acquiring the form of identification that some states require. Survey estimates of photo identification rates vary, but a 2012 Project Vote Survey indicates that 13 percent of blacks, 10 percent of Hispanics, and only 5 percent of whites lack photo ID (Perez, 2015). Income is also a factor. Twelve percent of adults earning less than $25,000 a year lack a photo ID while only 2 percent of individuals in households earning over $150,000 annual income lack a photo ID. Young adults are very likely to be affected by photo ID requirements for voting, with 15 percent of 17 to 20 year-olds and 11 percent of those 21 to 24 without photo identification (Perez, 2015). A Government Accountability Office (2014) study suggests that strict photo identification laws reduce voter turnout by 2 to 3 percent. Voting times may also favor those who have more autonomy and flexibility in their work schedules, mostly middle- and higher-income workers. While Colorado, Oregon, and Washington have introduced mail voting, the polls in most states open between 6 or 7 AM and close between 6 and 8 PM, with even more variations occurring across counties. Although this may appear a reasonable amount of time to allow voters access to the polls, it does not take into account child care responsibilities, commuting distances, and limited modes of transportation that lower-income voters disproportionally face (Encyclopedia of American Politics, 2017).

In addition, voting and volunteer time may be more difficult for workers on evening and night shifts due to competing sleep requirements and family obligations during voting time periods. With some 24 million workers, these issues should be of concern as less than optimal levels of civic engagement have been noted (Saenz, 2008). The poor are more likely than the nonpoor to engage in shift work and are twice as likely to begin work between 3 and 7 PM. Employees who work more traditional schedules are more educated, have more prestigious occupations, and have higher earnings than those working evenings and nights (Saenz, 2008).

Furthermore, issues such as voting locations, transportation, and travel requirements may have implications for individuals who do not own cars or do not have sufficient disposable income for extra public transportation costs. These issues and concerns are again more likely to affect poor and racial/ethnic minorities. African Americans (National Equity Atlas, 2015) and lower-income households are less likely to own an automobile (Berube et al., 2006). These households have difficulty coming up with the resources needed for a down payment on a car while financing costs are likely higher for them on average due to issues such as credit history and possibly discriminatory treatment (Berube et al., 2006). Finally, impoverished families may lack flexibility in child care arrangements, which can affect willingness to vote, access to town hall meetings, and other political activities.

With respect to voter participation, the tradition of Tuesday voting serves as a barrier due to work and school schedules that employed parents with children must coordinate. While absentee voting and extended hours address some concerns that Tuesday voting raises, they by no means address all of them in the way that weekend or holiday options might allow. Further complicating voter participation is the number of states that do not allow same-day voter registration, have reduced voting hours, and have decreased the number of voting locations. Since 2010, 20 states have implemented new restrictions on voting, and there are now 32 states with some ID requirement to vote (Brennan Center for Justice, 2019). Ten states have developed restrictive voter ID laws, six of these require strict photo IDs, seven states have laws that make it harder for citizens to register, six states cut back on early voting days and hours, and three have made it harder to restore voting rights for those with criminal convictions (Brennan Center for Justice, 2019). Most often discussed is the increasing number of states that require state-issued identification to vote. Cobb et al. (2010) examined an election in which it was anticipated that voter ID laws were unlikely to result in racial differences. Their data provided strong evidence that Hispanic voters and moderate evidence that black voters were asked for identification at higher rates than white voters (Cobb et al., 2010). These discrepancies do not verify voter suppression but are nevertheless red flags when considering the restriction of civic engagement.

Voting is not the only form of civic engagement, and it is worth considering further barriers that can affect other types of civic engagement. These are sometimes forgotten barriers to civic engagement related to the level of inclusiveness in our society. For example, the failure to provide accommodations for individuals with health concerns and/or disabilities can undermine comfort and stimulate mistrust that results in disengagement from community life. Relevant issues include accessible buildings, the availability of interpreters, translated materials, and sensory aids to support communication. Immigration status and primary language affect civic engagement through access to information about institutions and organizations that support and serve the community, which is essential to the trust that supports civic engagement (Seif, 2009). Language not only inhibits access to information but may also affect the ability of immigrants or individuals whose primary language is not the dominant language to freely and fully participate in community and organizational meetings as well as sharing their perspectives with government officials. Language can also affect comprehension of issues under consideration and/or ballot initiatives and votes, discouraging participation.

It is important to further consider access to opportunities for civic engagement through organizations. National Center for Charitable Statistics notes that there are approximately 1.5 million 501(c)(3) organizations, including public charities, private foundations, and other nonprofits registered with the federal government (GrantSpace, 2019). These organizations have the potential to engage a significant number of clients and community members in public policy and social decision-making. However, nonprofits are regulated by the federal government and the restrictions placed on their political activities may discourage efforts to provide opportunities for their followers to engage in the public policy and decision-making process. Jeffrey Berry (2005) discusses how regulatory standards might skew public participation, noting that middle- and upper-income individuals have many organizations that engage and mobilize them. However, nonprofits, churches, and foundations are the organizations most likely to advocate for the poor, immigrants, individuals with disabilities, people of color, and other marginalized constituencies. Unfortunately, federal regulations pertaining to these organizations suppress civic participation by the most disadvantaged in society.

Older adults have barriers to civic engagement that are generally the same as other segments of the population, but often at levels that exceed those of other groups (McBride, 2006). Some older adults lack the financial resources that would allow them to give up employment, and thus they have less time for volunteer activities (McBride, 2006). Older adults also face transportation barriers that affect volunteering, voting, and other civically engaged activities. This occurs for a variety of reasons, including physical limitations and health concerns that affect driving and access to public transportation, as well as the financial constraints that can affect car ownership (McBride, 2006). The rates of health and physical conditions posing barriers to civic engagement are higher among older adults, making this set of barriers much more significant. In addition, older adults in the labor force will face the same shift and time-off constraints upon civic engagement as younger workers.

Knowledge is a variable that has long been recognized as an essential factor in social and civic engagement. Thomas Jefferson noted, "Though [the people] may acquiesce, they cannot approve what they do not understand." For this reason, issues such as education, literacy, and the ability to make use of information, as well as primary language can affect civic engagement. Irwin Rosenstock notes that a "person's beliefs about the availability and effectiveness of various courses of action, and not the objective facts about the effectiveness of action, determine what course he/she will take" (2005: 7). These beliefs are influenced by the descriptive and injunctive norms (perceived approval/disapproval) of the individual's social/referent group, as represented by family, friends, and media sources (Rosenstock, 2005). Thus, individuals consider any number of sources of information that vary in quality, as they make decisions about voting, volunteering, donating funds, or writing to government and other officials. This information and its comprehension may influence how civic activities are valued in light of competing interests such as work, family, and leisure obligations and time commitments.

Knowledge and education may also affect civic engagement, due to a mismatch between citizens' skills, needs, preferences, and expectations, along with information available to guide their decision-making (Hung et al., 2011). Studies of literacy indicate that 14 percent of the population cannot read, and 21 percent of U.S. adults read below the fifth-grade level (U.S. Department of Education, National Center for Education Statistics, 2006). Literacy levels likely affect who feels capable of speaking at community meetings, writing to community and government leaders, or volunteering in the community. The mismatch between the civic information available and that needed by citizens is most often encountered by individuals who are lower income, less well-educated, older, and members of racial and ethnic groups. Literacy and its impact on civic engagement is not only a U.S. factor but a global issue given there are 781 million individuals in the world who cannot read (D'Almeida, 2015).

Awareness is another individual characteristic acknowledged as likely to affect who and how an individual will be civically engaged. News media and entertainment appear to have a positive impact on political and civic engagement. However, those involved in promoting civic engagement should recognize that media sources can be another area of mismatch. Media are accessed differently depending on the issues, advocacy concerns, and community needs (Chang et al., 2004). This issue is made more salient by reported variations in the ways in which individuals from different racial and ethnic groups access news and information relevant to their lives (American Press Institute, 2014). For example, members of underserved communities may trust and value ethnic media pertaining to racial issues but may favor mainstream local media for voting information or local concerns and trade or professional media for information on policies related to work and employment policies.

Attention to these issues may help to address those voters who are registered but do not frequently vote. Many intermittent voters report that they do not know enough about the issues or the candidate to vote (Pew Research Center, 2006). It therefore becomes important to understand the media sources and strategies to provide credible, accurate, and accessible information. Intermittent voters are younger and less likely to be married (Pew Research Center, 2006), which may make it less likely that there is someone in the household who votes regularly or can transmit social norms or concerns that influence them to participate. In addition, these voters are more distrustful of others, further restricting access to information that might encourage voting (Pew Research Center, 2006). Given these characteristics, what social activities, organizations, and media venues can be optimized to stimulate political engagement?

Solutions: Building on What We Know

In this final section, we discuss the historical and future role of social work in promoting civic engagement. Social work has long been at the forefront of civic engagement and can continue to play a vital role promoting civic engagement. Social work's major contribution stems from its long-standing role in nonprofit development and capacity building (McBride, 2008). The social work profession is well positioned to play an important role in strengthening and disseminating the research evidence with respect to civic engagement. In addition, social work's practice orientation can facilitate active engagement in efforts to implement innovative, evidence-based programs that are accessible to diverse communities. Social work's extensive experience in diverse communities is critical for organizations seeking to address barriers to civic engagement that are based on income, education, race/ethnicity, language, younger or older age, physical limitations, and health. Finally, social workers themselves may be called upon to engage more directly as professionals playing a significant role in advocacy and political participation (Rome and Hoechstetter, 2010). The profession's long history in promoting social justice, equality, and self-determination include influencing policy agendas, working on campaigns or in elective offices, and holding elected office (Lane and Pritzker, 2018). Social workers have participated in political efforts such as the Address to the Legislature of New York in 1854 and the Women's March for Equality in Washington in 1913 (Browne-Marshall, 2016). Social workers have also provided leadership for equal access to voting by race with the Voting Rights Act and the Civil Rights Act of the 1960s (Sherraden et al., 2015).

Given this background, we can make efforts toward building the next generation of voter protectors. One example is to re-engage political social work. Researchers Lane and Humphreys define political social work as a

> practice specialization . . . that includes social workers running for or holding office. . . . Social workers that work for elected officeholders are appointed by elected officials or must be confirmed by elected officials and social workers who spend considerable time lobbying elected officials as a volunteer or paid advocates. (2011: 225–226)

Today, social work professionals are hired by social service organizations to establish voter registration drives, develop voter turnout strategies, and build civic engagement activities for clients (Lane and Humphreys, 2011). Other activities for engagement include increasing public awareness regarding new voting laws and developing research agendas to collect data on voter participation policies and barriers that inform the community. Yet another example is infusing political social work as a specialization in social work education programs. A political social work curriculum would uniquely position the social work professional in efforts that support the well-being of people toward a positive political system that empowers individuals and communities (Ostrander et al., 2017).

There are over 400 known social workers who have run for political office at the local, state, or federal elected level (Lane and Humphreys, 2011). Perhaps the most well-known of these social workers has been Barbara Mikulski, the former U.S. senator from Maryland. As Mikulski demonstrated, the elected official with a social work worldview offers a different perspective than the traditional candidate whose professional background is more apt to be in law, business, public policy, or higher education (Lane and Humphreys, 2011; Lawless and Fox, 2005). The National Association of Social Workers (1999) Code of Ethics states that social workers should promote equal access for all people through social and political action. Importantly, social workers bring to the table a somewhat different perspective for viewing social problems than the more traditional backgrounds of legislators.

Social workers can also be engaged in efforts to improve U.S. voter participation by developing policies that remove barriers. For example, Sweden, Germany, and Chile automatically register citizens to vote as soon as they become old enough (DeSilver, 2018). This removes obstacles related to identification, the location of registration sites, and transportation. In Australia, voting is required by law, resulting in voting participation rates approaching 95 percent.

A range of changes in the United States have been proposed, including giving people flexibility in where they vote, making election day a holiday, and designing voting booths and locations that can accommodate the physical challenges of older voters and those with physical limitations. These changes also address structural barriers that transportation and family responsibilities produce. In addition, some have even suggested offering financial incentives for voting. Of course, given our current climate and debates over more restrictive voting laws, the question is how can the political will be mustered (Brennan Center for Justice, 2017)?

Nevertheless, we can use what we have observed and learned from research to improve public participation in community and political life. For example, we know that when students perform service that addresses social issues, compared to performing no service or completing service that is divorced from need or community concerns, they are more likely to express the intention to engage in future service and civic activities (Metz et al., 2003). The results suggest that in addition to assuring that all youth have adequate access to civic engagement opportunities (Kahne and Middaugh, 2008), it is essential to expose students to high-quality government and civics education. Similarly, it is important that service opportunities are available that support skills related to running meetings, developing collaborations and coalitions, and communicating positions and recommendations to others (Metz et al., 2003). Future research might examine whether the outcomes of adolescent service opportunities also results in greater voting registration.

Youth civic engagement efforts may take many forms, including youth-run programs, youth and adult partnerships, and school-based civics projects and programming. There are also adult community-based participatory research programs that might be adapted to support youth engagement and skill development needed for engagement. The Community Research Fellows Training program is a community-based participatory research program effort designed to increase the opportunity and likelihood of civic engagement (D'Agostino et al., 2015). The program enhances the capacity for involvement in health advocacy, research, and interventions through 15 weeks of didactic training for community members in research methods and evidence-based public health, as well as advocacy and policy. Findings to date demonstrate that the training increases awareness of health disparities and increases research knowledge, and program fellows have become involved in community health programs and research activities (D'Agostino et al., 2015; Coats et al., 2015; Komaie et al., 2017). This model has been adapted for youth (Goodman et al., 2018) and may provide a template for increasing skills needed for civic engagement.

Final Thoughts

The pathway to a strong democracy never reaches an endpoint. The struggle is never over, the victory is never complete. Today, communities struggle with issues critical to livable lives. These include living wages and compensation, access to safe and affordable housing, healthy foods and health care when needed, access to clean water and air, and long-term maintenance of planetary health (see Chapter 10 for a further discussion). Attitudes and opinions about national and international policies and actions, as well governmental roles on a day-to-day basis, are very often fueled by where one stands in the social hierarchy and milieu. To bridge the gaps in political and social support for potential solutions to today's problems, what is required is social capital, trust in social and governmental institutions, and strategies for addressing conflict. Civic engagement provides a venue to assure that policies supporting livable lives exist. Civic engagement can be the mechanism through which those who have been socially disenfranchised interact. The result can be new opportunities for citizens and those who govern to achieve mutually agreed upon goals that resolve mutually agreed upon concerns (Putnam, 1995). In addition, civic engagement builds trust in both government and social institutions. This trust, in turn, can lead to healthier and more socially just environments in which lives are lived.

As we attempt to apply knowledge from social and behavioral science, Barry Checkoway (2001b) notes how few researchers recognize the role of and relationship between civic engagement and societal decision-making with respect to these important domains of life and society. This lack of awareness results in missed opportunities to increase community capacity and opportunity for civic engagement. Despite the lack of attention to this area of study, participatory action research and community-based participatory research have grown as alternatives to traditional research and have become essential tools for encouraging stronger civic engagement (Checkoway, 2001a).

The failure of academics and practitioners to fully engage in this area of inquiry may explain the range of issues largely unexamined in this chapter. Although we have objective ways of examining voter turnout, because of the protections afforded citizens by the secret ballot we do not fully understand the motivations that issues and political values play in voter behavior (Gerber et al., 2012). For example, are the same people likely to vote in local, state, and national elections? Are there subgroups more likely to vote based on the election level, candidate, or issue? Does this vary by age, gender, income, or education? If there are such variations, is civic engagement declining or are there fewer candidates and issues that motivate particular portions of the populace? Can the structures that impact civic engagement be changed? Finally, who in the voting public believes and trusts the secret ballot, and how exactly does the promise of a secret ballot affect voter turnout (Gerber et al., 2012)?

Yet if we measure political engagement as voter turnout, we are quite limited in our ability to state with certainty what is happening to engagement across populations. In the case of social engagement, what is the right number and balance of social activities and interactions to understand and fully capture social capital and engagement? Do we equate petition initiatives prevalent on the Internet to voter registration drives? How do we weigh activities that are linked to church attendance, union, or professional membership? While public participation in a range of social, political, and economic issues is very desirable (International Association for Public Participation, 2006), do we have the correct conceptual framework for understanding the phenomena? What are the right measurement and research protocols for assessing where we are? Without these, do we have the evidence needed to understand and articulate the way forward?

All of these questions raise important concerns. The social work tradition of promoting social change and social justice would imply that social workers have an active role to play in facilitating civic engagement, particularly with respect to those who have been disenfranchised and excluded from mainstream society and the corridors of political power. They represent essential voices that have too often not been heard in the various public policy debates and legislation.

As discussed throughout this book, the concept of a livable life incorporates many different components and dimensions that allow individuals to lead a fulfilling life. One such component is civic engagement. It allows individuals to experience a degree of agency in their community life and to have their voices heard in community matters. In addition, policies and programs that affect the lives of millions are shaped by the interests of various constituencies. In a democratic society, it is essential that all members of a society be allowed and encourage to freely participate in the workings of its democracy. It is through such participation that democracy comes alive, empowering its members in the process. Surely, this is an important dimension of a livable life and one that the profession of social work must strive for in the decades ahead.

References

AARP. 2012, December. "Civic Engagement Among Mid-life and Older Adults: Findings from the 2012 Survey on Civic Engagement Research and Strategic Analysis Integrated Value and Strategy."

Adler, R. P., and J. Goggin. 2016. "What Do We Mean by 'Civic Engagement'?" *Journal of Transformative Education*, 3, 236–253.

American Press Institute. 2014. "Race, Ethnicity, and the Use of Social Media for News." Retrieved from https://www.americanpressinstitute.org/publications/reports/survey-research/race-ethnicity-social-media-news/

Arnstein, S. R. 1969. "A Ladder of Citizen Participation." *Journal of the American Institute of Planners*, 35, 216–224.

Battistoni, R. M. 2017. *Civic Engagement Across the Curriculum: A Resource Book for Service-Learning Faculty in All Disciplines*. Sterling, VA: Stylus.

Berry, J. M. 2005. "Nonprofits and Civic Engagement." *Public Administration Review*, 65, 568–578.

Berube, A., E. Deakin, and S. Raphael. 2006. "Socioeconomic Differences in Household Automobile Ownership Rates: Implications for Evacuation Policy." Retrieved from http://socrates.berkeley.edu/~raphael/BerubeDeakenRaphael.pdf

Brennan Center for Justice. 2019. "New Voting Restrictions in America." Retrieved from http://www.brennancenter.org/new-voting-restrictions-america

Browne-Marshall, G. J. 2016. *The Voting Rights War: The NAACP and the Ongoing Struggle for Justice*. New York: Rowman and Littlefield.

Chang, B. L., S. Bakken, S. S. Brown, T. K. Houston, G. L. Kreps, G. L. R. Kukafka, P. Z. Stavri, and P. 2004. "Bridging the Digital Divide: Reaching Vulnerable Populations." *Journal of the American Medical Informatics Association*, 11, 448–457.

Checkoway, B. 2001a. "Renewing the Civic Mission of the American Research University." *The Journal of Higher Education*, 72, 125–147.

Checkoway, B. 2001b. "Strategies for Involving the Faculty in Civic Renewal." *Journal of College and Character*, 2, Article 1.

Coats, J. V., J. D. Stafford, V. Sanders Thompson, B. Johnson Javois, and M. S. Goodman. 2015. "Increasing Research Literacy: The Community Research Fellows Training Program." *Journal of Empirical Research on Human Research Ethics*, 10, 3–12.

Cobb, R. V, D. J. Greiner, and K. Quinn. 2010. "Can Voter ID Laws Be Administered in a Race-Neutral Manner? Evidence from the City of Boston in 2008." *Quarterly Journal of Political Science*, 7, 1–33.

Corporation for National and Community Service. 2010. "Civic Life in America: Key Findings on the Civic Health of the Nation." Retrieved from https://ncoc.org/wp-content/uploads/2015/04/2010AmericaIssueBrief.pdf

Corporation for National and Community Service. 2017. "A Definition of Civic Engagement." Retrieved from https://www.vistacampus.gov/definition-civic-engagement

D'Agostino McGowan, L., J. D. Stafford, V. L. Thompson, B. Johnson-Javois, and M. S. Goodman. 2015. "Quantitative Evaluation of the Community Research Fellows Training Program." *Front Public Health*, 3, 179.

D'Almeida, K. 2015, April 10. "781 Million People Can't Read this Article." *Inter Press Service News Agency*. Retrieved from http://www.ipsnews.net/2015/04/781-million-people-cant-read-this-story/

DeSilver, D. 2018, May 21. "U.S. Trails Most Developed Countries in Voter Turnout." *Pew Research Center Fact Tank*. Retrieved from http://www.pewresearch.org/fact-tank/2018/05/21/u-s-voter-turnout-trails-most-developed-countries/

Encyclopedia of American Politics. 2017. "State Poll Opening and Closing Times." Retrieved from https://ballotpedia.org/State_Poll_Opening_and_Closing_Times_(2016)

Fung, A. 2006. "Varieties of Participation in Complex Governance." *Public Administration Review*, 66, 66–75.

Gerber, A. S., G. A. Huber, D. Doherty, C. M. Dowling, and S. J. Hill. 2012. "The Voting Experience and Beliefs about Ballot Secrecy." Working Paper. Retrieved from http://ddoherty.sites.luc.edu/documents/TheVotingExperience.pdf

Goodman, M. S., E. Gbaje, S. M. Yassin, J. Johnson Dias, K. Gilbert, and V. Thompson. 2018. "Adaptation, Implementation, and Evaluation of a Public Health Research Methods Training for Youth." *Health Equity*, 2, 349–355.

Gottlieb, B. H., and A. A. Gillespie. 2008. "Volunteerism, Health, and Civic Engagement Among Older Adults." *Canadian Journal on Aging/La Revue Canadienne du Vieillissement*, 27, 399–406.

Government Accountability Office. 2014. "Issues Related to State Voter Identification Laws, Report to Congressional Requesters." Retrieved from http://www.gao.gov/assets/670/665966.pdf

GrantSpace. 2019. "How Many Nonprofit Organizations Are There in the US?" Retrieved from https://grantspace.org/resources/knowledge-base/number-of-nonprofits-in-the-u-s/

Hung, K., E. Sirakaya-Turk, and L. J. Ingram. 2011. "Testing the Efficacy of an Integrative Model for Community Participation." *Journal of Travel Research*, 50, 276–288.

International Association for Public Participation. 2006. "IAP2 Core Values." Retrieved from http://www.iap2.org/?page=A4

Jones, L., and K. Wells. 2007. "Strategies for Academic and Clinician Engagement in Community-Participatory Partnered Research." *Journal of American Medical Association*, 297, 407–10.

Kahne, J., and E. Middaugh. 2008. "Democracy for Some: The Civic Opportunity Gap in High School." Circle Working Paper 59. Center for Information and Research on Civic Learning and Engagement (CIRCLE). http://files.eric.ed.gov/fulltext/ED503646.pdf

Komaie, G., C. C. Ekenga, V. L. S. Thompson, and M. S. Goodman. 2017. "Increasing Community Research Capacity to Address Health Disparities: A Qualitative Program Evaluation of the Community Research Fellows Training Program." *Journal of Empirical Research on Human Research Ethics*, 12, 55–66.

Lane, S. R. and N. R. Humphreys. 2011. "Social Workers in Politics: A National Survey of Social Work Candidates and Elected Officials." *Journal of Policy Practice*, 10, 225–244.

Lane, S. R., and S. Pritzker. 2018. *Political Social Work: Using Power to Create Social Change*. Gewerbestrasse, Switzerland: Springer International.

Lawless, J., and R. L. Fox. 2005. *It Takes a Candidate: Why Women Don't Run for Office*. New York: Cambridge University Press.

McBride, A. M. 2006. "Civic Engagement, Older Adults, and Inclusion." *Generations*, 30, 66–71.

McBride, A. M. 2008. "Civic Engagement." *Encyclopedia of Social Work*. Edited by Chief, Cynthia Franklin. New York: Oxford University Press.

Metz, E., J. McLellan, and J. Youniss. 2003. "Types of Voluntary Service and Adolescents' Civic Development." *Journal of Adolescent Research*, 18, 188–203.

National Association of Social Workers. 1999. "NASW's Electoral Political Program." Retrieved from https://www.socialworkers.org/archives/advocacy/electoral/default.asp?back=yes

National Equity Atlas. 2015. "Car Access." Retrieved from https://nationalequityatlas.org/indicators/Car_access

O'Neil, M. 2014, December 17. "Americans' Engagement with Organizations Wanes, Report Says." *The Chronicle of Philanthropy: News and Analysis*. Retrieved from https://www.philanthropy.com/article/Americans-Engagement-With/152055

Ostrander, J., S. R. Lane, J. McClendon, C. Hayes, and T. Rhodes Smith. 2017. "Collective Power to Create Political Change: Increasing the Political Efficacy and Engagement of Social Workers." *Journal of Policy Practice*, 3, 261–275.

Perez, V. M. 2015. "Americans with Photo ID: A Breakdown of Demographic Characteristics." *Project Vote*. Retrieved from http://www.projectvote.org/wp-content/uploads/2015/06/AMERICANS-WITH-PHOTO-ID-Research-Memo-February-2015.pdf

Pew Research Center. 2006. Who Votes, Who Doesn't, and Why: Regular Voters, Intermittent Voters, and Those Who Don't. Retrieved from http://www.people-press.org/2006/10/18/who-votes-who-doesn't-and-why/2/

Pew Research Center. 2017. "Reports of Civic Engagement Higher than in Benchmark Surveys." Retrieved from http://www.pewresearch.org/2017/05/15/what-low-response-rates-mean-for-telephone-surveys/pm-05-15-2017_rddnonresponse-00-07/

Putnam, R. D. 1995. "Tuning In, Tuning Out: The Strange Disappearance of Social Capital in America." *Political Science and Politics*, 28, 664–683.

Putnam, R. D. 2000. *Bowling Alone: America's Declining Social Capital*. New York: Palgrave Macmillan US.

Quan-Haase, A., B. Wellman, J. C. Witte, and K. N. Hampton. 2002. "Capitalizing on the Net: Social Contact, Civic Engagement, and Sense of Community." *The Internet in Everyday Life*. Edited by B. Wellman and C. A. Haythornthwaite. Malden, MA: Blackwell, pp. 291–324.

Rome, S. H., and S. Hoechstetter. 2010. "Social Work and Civic Engagement: The Political Participation of Professional Social Workers." *Journal of Sociology and Social Welfare*, 37, 107–129.

Rosenstock, I. M. 2005. "Why People Use Health Services." *The Milbank Quarterly*, 83, 1–32.

Saenz, R. 2008. "A Demographic Profile of U.S. Workers Around the Clock." *Population Reference Bureau*. Retrieved from http://www.prb.org/Publications/Articles/2008/workingaroundtheclock.aspx

Seif, H. 2009. "The Civic Education and Engagement of Latina/o Immigrant Youth: Challenging Boundaries and Creating Safe Spaces." Research Paper Series on Latino Immigrant Civic Participation, No. 5. www.wilsoncenter.org/migrantparticipation

Sherraden, M., P. Stuart, R. P. Barth, S. Kemp, J. Lubben, J. D. Hawkins, C. Coulton, R. McRoy, K. Walters, L. Healy, B. Angell, K. Mahoney, J. Brekke, Y. Padilla, D. DiNitto, D. Padgett, T. Schroepfer, and R. Catalano. 2014. *Grand accomplishments in social work (Grand Challenges for Social Work Initiative, Working Paper No. 2)*. Baltimore, MD: American Academy of Social Work and Social Welfare.

Smith, A. 2013. "Civic Engagement in the Digital Age: Online and Offline Political Engagement." *Pew Research Center*. Retrieved from http://www.pewinternet.org/2013/04/25/civic-engagement-in-the-digital-age/

Smith, A., K. L. Schlozman, S. Verba, and H. Brady. 2009. "The Current State of Civic Engagement in America." *Pew Research Center*. Retrieved from http://www.pewinternet.org/2009/09/01/the-current-state-of-civic- engagement-in-america/ September 1, 2009

Taylor, D. M., and F. M. Moghaddam. 1994. *Theories of Intergroup relations: International Social Psychological Perspectives*. Westport, CO: Greenwood.

U.S. Department of Education, National Center for Education Statistics. 2006. "1992 National Adult Literacy Survey (NALS) and 2003 National Assessment of Adult Literacy (NAAL), A First Look at the Literacy of America's Adults in the 21st Century; and Supplemental Data." Retrieved from http://nces.ed.gov/naal/Excel/2006470_DataTable.xls

Watts, R. J., and C. Flanagan. 2007. "Pushing the Envelope on Youth Civic Engagement: A Developmental and Liberation Psychology Perspective." *Journal of Community Psychology*, 35, 779–792.

Zakus, J. D., and C. L. Lysack. 1998. "Revisiting Community Participation." *Health Policy and Planning*, 13, 1–12.

9

Building Healthy, Diverse, and Thriving Communities

CAROLYN LESOROGOL, ANA A. BAUMANN, AMY EYLER,
MOLLY W. METZGER, RODRIGO S. REIS, AND RACHEL G. TABAK

An overarching goal of social work is to support and help build communities where every individual has the opportunity to thrive. When thinking about the concept of a livable life, core elements include the ability to provide for one's basic needs such as food, clothing, shelter, and good health. These needs are fundamental to the overall health of a community and, in turn, to the ability of its members to experience livable lives. A thriving community is one where people are able to access and enjoy such basic needs along with opportunities for growth and success. Having the capability to live lives of meaning and purpose, an idea developed by Amartya Sen (1999), is central to thriving communities. Although capabilities often refer to an individual's abilities and potential in order for individuals to thrive, there is also a need to reside in healthy communities. Thriving communities, in turn, require community-level collective action. Acting together, community members provide many of the resources and public goods necessary for livable lives, including infrastructure such as roads, railways and ports, public education, social protection, public spaces, legal systems, and public safety. Individual opportunities rely on individual initiative as well as public/collective action. Thriving communities are places where both are present—where individuals in communities realize their potential due to the supports and resources available to all.

Standing in the way of thriving communities and the possibility of livable lives are the persistent problems of poverty and inequality found in countries around the world. Poverty is symptomatic of failures to realize the conditions for reaching the potential of a thriving community (see Chapter 3 of this volume for an extended discussion of poverty). When significant segments of the population live in poverty, they are often excluded or disadvantaged from being able to access opportunities that develop their capabilities. Collective action to provide public goods may also be weak in such situations, further limiting the availability of needed resources. Poverty and inequality around the world persist in spite (although some argue because) of economic growth, the spread of industrialization, improvements in technology, expansion of education, and access to more health and social services achieved over the last several decades (Escobar, 2015; Dabla-Norris et al., 2015).

In the United States, the poverty rate of 12.3 percent in 2017 has changed very little over the past five decades (U.S. Census Bureau, 2018). The poverty line is set at three times the cost of a minimum food basket (established in 1964 and updated annually to account for inflation). In 2017, the poverty line for a family of four was an annual income of $25,094 (U.S. Census Bureau, 2018). Many have criticized this line as being far below the actual cost of living in the United States (Greenberg, 2009). U.S. poverty rates are higher in urban inner city areas, many rural areas, and increasingly in inner-ring suburbs. They are also disproportionately high among minority populations such as African Americans, Latinos, and American Indians and among people with lower educational attainment (U.S. Census Bureau, 2018).

Globally, poverty is generally defined as the number of people living below $2.00 per person per day. The World Bank estimates that in 2015, 700 million people lived below this threshold of extreme poverty. The highest rates of poverty are concentrated in sub-Saharan Africa and South Asia. Similar to the United States, poverty rates are often highest among minority groups and people living in rural areas or in urban slums (World Bank, 2015; Imai and Maleb, 2015).

As is the case with poverty, inequality is measured in a number of ways. One of the most common measures is what is known as the Gini Index, which estimates the amount of inequality in a nation's overall income distribution. The Gini Index ranges from zero (perfect equality) to 100 (perfect inequality). Current country estimates vary from a low of 21.5 in Finland to a high of 63 in Lesotho (U.S. Central Intelligence Agency, 2014). The U.S. Gini Index is 45 and ranks 40th out of 150 countries ranked.

The United Nations' Inequality Adjusted Human Development Index (HDI) is another way of assessing the effect of inequality on factors considered critical to positive human development. These include life expectancy, expected years of schooling, mean years of schooling, and gross national income per capita. The inequality adjusted index takes into account how each of these dimensions is distributed across a country's population and displays the difference in the HDI. For example, the HDI for the United States in 2015 was 0.92 (ranking 10th highest in the world). However, once adjusted for inequality, it falls to 0.79 (20th highest in the world). Most countries HDI falls when adjusted for inequality, demonstrating the negative impact of inequality on overall well-being (United Nations Development Programme [UNDP], 2016b).

The Multidimensional Poverty Index is another gauge of inequality within countries, measuring the percent of the population that is multidimensionally poor across ten indicators (UNDP, 2016a). This index therefore takes into account many more components of poverty than either the Gini Index or the HDI, including indicators such as household nutrition, child mortality, fuel source, drinking water access, and assets (UNDP, 2016a).

Poverty and inequality create the conditions for unhealthy communities as individuals and families lack the resources and opportunities to meet basic needs for education and health. Without these basics, individuals, families, and entire communities are excluded from developing their full potential to live lives of meaning and purpose (discussed further in Chapters 3 and 5 of this volume). In addition, it is much more difficult for them to thrive. Persistent poverty and inequality are associated with many social problems from basic concerns such as hunger, malnutrition, disease, and early mortality to social marginalization, mental health issues, disempowerment, and hopelessness. These, in turn, can contribute to further problems like crime and social dysfunction. A major challenge for the profession of social work is to find ways of working together with individuals, communities, and policy leaders to tackle the challenges of poverty and inequality in order for communities to flourish.

Underlying Causes of the Problem

Poverty (as measured by income, assets/wealth, or opportunities) stems from complex historical circumstances often characterized by social and political systems that create structural inequalities. As a result, some communities (or individuals and groups within communities) lack access to the facilities and opportunities that would enable them to pursue livable lives (Kabeer 2000, 2016). Amartya Sen (1999) argues that successful development of a society requires that individuals have the substantive freedoms and capabilities that enable them to participate effectively in social, political, and economic activities. All sectors of society play a role in ensuring the five freedoms (economic, political, social, security, and transparency) that Sen outlines as essential to human flourishing. Access to high-quality education and health facilities, for example, enables citizens to gain the knowledge and skills to effectively participate in the economy and to make informed political choices. These facilities include infrastructure such as schools and housing as well as the broader built environment of roads, railways, parks, and public spaces. Sen underscores the value of a free press for promoting government transparency, which facilitates effective social protection policies. For example, famine is much less likely in societies with a free press where problems of hunger are exposed and public action demanded

(Sen, 1981). One study showed that in Uganda, schools that were closer to newspaper outlets in which school funding allocations were published had higher rates of receiving those funds (Reinikka and Svensson, 2011). Stronger citizen voice through multiple channels such as the press, social media, and elections improves transparency and security. Thus, the five freedoms are synergistic in promoting individual capabilities as well as effective collective action for the public good.

Histories of discrimination, colonization, social exclusion, marginalization, and unequal investment hinder the development of these freedoms and capabilities. Evidence for this is found in urban communities in the United States where people of color have endured blatantly racist policies that limited their opportunities in education, employment, home ownership, healthcare access, and many more (Rothstein, 2017). Structural economic changes in the United States, particularly the transformation of the economy from heavy industry to information and services, have disadvantaged people who lack access to high-quality education to prepare them for employment in these fields. Furthermore, when unemployment and poverty become the norm, there are negative effects on social relations and cohesion in communities (Kim et al., 2018; Wilson, 1996).

Around the world, poverty and inequality are sustained by policies that include deep colonial legacies and ongoing postcolonial relationships among countries. Many economies in low- and middle-income countries were shaped by the preferences of colonial regimes such as the reliance on a small number of cash crops or minerals, making them vulnerable to market fluctuations and dependent on aid and imported goods. In addition, colonial political and social institutions created highly unequal social relations and opportunity systems (Mamdani, 1996). These legacies are still felt today and present challenges to creating more inclusive societies where all members have access to the freedoms that Sen outlines. Multidimensional inequalities around the world constitute major challenges to achieving individual well-being for all and the capability to build livable lives (Kabeer, 2016).

In addition to these historical structural factors, poor communities are often subject to shocks, both natural (e.g., drought, flood, earthquake) and man-made (e.g., famine, epidemic) that increase vulnerability and limit their ability to build assets needed to sustain themselves. For example, in low-income countries, rural agricultural systems are very susceptible to climate related shocks and uncertainties (see Chapter 10 of this volume). Farmers must expend scarce resources mitigating or reducing risks that results in lower productivity than would otherwise be expected (Binswanger-Mkhize, 2012). Most low-income countries lack robust social safety nets to cushion farmers from climate risks, thus placing much of the burden on rural households and communities themselves.

Policies and practices related to the built environment also influence the health and well-being of communities. There is an increasing body of evidence that connects community design and the built environment to adverse health outcomes. Noncommunicable diseases such as diabetes, heart disease, cancer, and chronic respiratory conditions can all be influenced by the community in which one resides (see Chapters 2 and 10 of this volume). The links between exposures to macro level (i.e., poor urban design and planning) and micro level (i.e., housing) built environment characteristics increase the likelihood of unhealthy diets, sedentary behavior, and physical inactivity, which then increases the risk of worse health outcomes. Even though these adverse health outcomes can be mitigated by physical activity or healthy eating, communities vary greatly in the ways in which the built environment facilitates or inhibits such healthy behaviors.

For example, in the United States, disparities in chronic diseases exist between rural residents and residents of urban/suburban areas. Mortality rates between 1999 and 2014 from heart disease, cancer, unintentional injury, chronic lower respiratory disease, and stroke were higher in rural than urban areas (Garcia, 2017). Similarly, a cohort study from 2013 examining birth/infant death rates showed that high poverty in rural areas was associated with term-infant mortality even after controlling for maternal sociodemographic, health, and obstetric factors (Mahomaoud et al., 2019). This may be due to disparities in health behaviors, with residents of rural areas more likely to have poorer health behaviors (e.g., tobacco use, diet and exercise, alcohol and drug use, sexual activity). Yet these behaviors may partially reflect the rural built environment, such as a lack of grocery stores, transportation, employment, and other essential amenities (Lutfiyya et al., 2012; Martin et al. 2005; Ward et al., 2015). In addition to disparities in nutrition behaviors, there are also high rates of physical inactivity in rural communities (Parks et al., 2003; Wilcox et al., 2000; Eberhardt and Pamuk, 2004; Martin et al., 2005). Across the country, approximately 50 percent of the U.S. adult population meets the 150 minutes of physical activity recommended per week (Centers for Disease Control, 2018), but these rates are disproportionately lower in rural areas, with the lowest rates in small rural communities with populations under 10,000 (Parks et al., 2003; Fan et al., 2014).

Urban communities, where the economy has been hollowed out by job loss and the exiting of many middle-class families, are often characterized by crumbling infrastructure, unsafe and unhealthy housing stock, and an absence of important products and services such as healthy food, safe facilities for outdoor activity, and financial and health services. All of these factors disadvantage inner-city residents in their ability to lead healthy lives (Pinard et al., 2016; Richardson et al., 2017; Nau et al., 2015).

Globally, the most significant health issues (e.g., chronic diseases, traffic injuries, infectious diseases), have been closely linked to rapid urbanization and aging processes (Beaglehole et al., 2012; Thurlow et al., 2019). With the world's population reaching 10 billion people by 2050, and 75 percent of the population living in urban areas (United Nations Population Fund [UNFPA], 2011), city planning and design have become a high priority in all corners of the world. However, whereas high-income countries experienced rapid urbanization in the first half of the 20th century, the same process is currently occurring in low- and middle-income countries (UNFPA, 2011, 2012). Low- and middle-income nations are in a position to learn from earlier experiences of rapid urbanization and hopefully avoid some of the worst problems associated with it such as the growth of informal settlements and slums, lack of needed infrastructure and services, and a mismatch between population and employment in cities. In addition to rapid urbanization, communities are becoming more diverse due to immigration and migration, creating additional challenges as well as potential opportunities.

Built environments in high-, middle-, and low-income countries share some similarities but also vary greatly. For example, a recent study across 14 cities in ten middle-income and high-income countries on five continents found that residential density, intersection density, number of public transport stops, and number of parks within walking distance were significantly, positively, independently, and linearly related to physical activity (Sallis et al., 2016). These findings suggest that cities across the globe could benefit from improvements in access to public transportation and public open spaces as well as greater connectivity, regardless of their level of economic development. However, there are also marked differences within and between low- and middle-income countries. For instance, in most middle-income countries, density patterns (e.g. residential, street, population) are generally higher than in higher income countries (United Nations Department of Economic and Social Affairs, 2012), and cities tend to be more compact and monocentric (with jobs, cultural opportunities, and activities mainly located in the city center). Additionally, in low- and middle-income countries urban communities rely more often on informal transport services (Gomez et al., 2015), putting them at greater risk of exposure to air pollution and traffic accidents (Gomez et al., 2015). Individuals in low-income countries usually live in less urbanized areas with poor access to job opportunities and services and inadequate sanitation and housing. Hence, the environmental differences between and within low- and middle-income countries also contribute to greater social inequities observed in their communities.

From these examples, it is clear that governments (present and past) have and continue to play an important role in creating and potentially addressing the problems of poverty and inequality. Government has a responsibility of providing essential public goods such as education, health care, security, and infrastructure that are fundamental to the achievement of capabilities. Government policies may promote equal access and opportunities for all social groups or, conversely, discriminate against certain groups with negative implications for capability development. Certainly, government is not alone in bearing responsibility for the underlying causes of these problems. All sectors of society, including the private sector, nonprofit, and civil society organizations and communities, must be engaged in reversing negative trends and building livable lives for the future. Furthermore, the international community has a responsibility to attend to past injustices that have contributed significantly to the current situation. Efforts such as the Sustainable Development Goals reflect the idea that collective action to alleviate global problems must occur globally.

The implication of this analysis is that building livable lives requires addressing several related factors. Structures, policies, and processes can be made more inclusive to provide the freedoms and opportunities needed for individuals to build their capabilities. With access to freedoms and adequate capabilities, individuals and communities can participate in productive activities that are the basis for livelihoods which enable people to stay out of poverty and limit inequality. Strong livelihoods supported by effective infrastructure and services are the basis for thriving communities and livable lives.

Addressing the Problem: Achieving Thriving Communities

Developing policies, programs, and approaches that address the root causes of community poverty and inequality and that build upon the inherent strengths and resilience found in communities are the means for transforming unhealthy communities into places where people can thrive and achieve livable lives. From our prior discussion of underlying causes of poverty and inequality, it is clear that this is a multilevel and multidimensional challenge. In discussing potential solutions, a social ecological approach is helpful, as it describes different levels of influence and the complex interactions among individual characteristics, the social environment, the community, and the policy environment (Bronfenbrenner, 1979). A key principle in this approach is that to effectively influence behaviors interventions should address changes within levels as well as multilevel interactions across the levels. For example, in terms of promoting physical activity for health, a person's self-motivation to walk as a leisure-time physical activity might be enhanced by social support from others but may not be feasible unless their community has safe and well-maintained sidewalks (Baker et al., 2011; Ding et al., 2012). Similarly, a child's academic success will be more likely if they have supportive parents with time to focus on their education and access to a high-quality school ensured by policies that guarantee adequate and equitable educational funding (Muller, 1993). We present in the following discussion a number of examples of promising strategies and programs to illustrate the types of approaches the field of social work might consider in working toward the prospect of thriving communities for all.

The current overarching global framework for eliminating poverty and reducing social disparities are the Sustainable Development Goals, comprising 17 goals adopted by the United Nations in 2016. The goals include "no poverty," "zero hunger," "good health and well-being," and "quality education," all of which align with a basic needs or Sen-influenced approach to building capabilities. Also included are goals of "reduced inequalities," "sustainable cities and communities," "peace, justice and strong institutions," and the final goal, necessary to achieve the rest, "partnerships for the goals." Each goal is accompanied by a number of targets and indicators, but specific strategies, policies, and programs are to be designed by member nations with the broad involvement of interested parties, populations, and stakeholders. This approach recognizes that there is no one-size-fits-all solution to problems this complex and that local context and multiple levels of intervention, such as suggested by the social ecological framework, must be considered in designing programs and policies. Although the Sustainable Development Goals are often considered solely for low- and middle-income countries, we argue that these goals are suitable to the pursuit of thriving communities everywhere, and we provide examples from both the United States as well as other countries to illustrate this point.

Poverty Reduction and Capability Development

A number of promising poverty reduction approaches have been tried at scale over the past few decades. These approaches fit broadly within a social protection framework that emphasizes (to varying degrees depending on the context and policy choices) risk, rights, and needs (Barrientos and Hulme, 2008). These strategies span the levels of the social ecological framework, often focusing on bringing about individual behavior change through policies that create incentives to move individual behavior in directions believed to be positive for building human capital and other capabilities.

For example, a risk perspective to social protection recognizes the role of risk in undermining the ability of people to overcome poverty. Risk management and mitigation approaches focus on the welfare losses sustained when there are market failures. However, they are also concerned with the "moral hazard" problem that providing too much assistance or social protection may reduce incentives for self-help and create dependency. Thus, they focus on the design of policies and programs that provide highly targeted assistance under certain conditions, such as conditional cash transfers that provide cash to households on the condition that they take specific actions such as keeping children in school or taking them for health checks. New forms of micro insurance and index-based insurance also fall into this category of intervention. These policies and programs emphasize the role of beneficiaries in making appropriate choices, drawing on behavioral economics thinking about the power of incentives to shape choice.

The theory behind conditional cash transfers is that investing in human capital development (i.e., through education and health), and thus building capabilities of the next generation, will break the poverty cycle. In some countries, these programs also support the supply of health and education services, recognizing that as demand for services increases, adequate and high-quality service provision become more important (Rawlings and Rubio, 2005). There is considerable evidence from rigorous research studies including randomized control trials that conditional cash transfers are successful in bolstering household consumption, increasing educational attainment, and improving health status among children (Rawlings and Rubio, 2005). However, questions remain regarding their impact on intergenerational poverty reduction and, consequently, more long-term follow-up studies are required to establish the significance of this effect (Molina-Millan et al., 2016). Also, the need for conditionality in these programs has been questioned, and there is growing evidence that unconditional cash transfers are equally effective in boosting consumption and increasing saving and investment at the household level without being as prescriptive and top–down as conditional cash transfers (Hanlon et al., 2010; https://www.hsnp.or.ke/index.php/our-work/measurement-evaluation, n.d.).

Direct cash transfers to support consumption have a long history in the United States through programs such as Aid to Families with Dependent Children (AFDC) and, since welfare reform in 1996, Temporary Assistance for Needy Families (TANF). In the past, these were entitlement programs—if one met the income and other eligibility criteria, one would receive the transfer. Today receipt of case welfare is short term (i.e., five-year lifetime limits on receipt in most states) and conditioned upon recipients actively pursuing employment or employment-related activities such as job training. Unlike conditional cash transfers, contemporary programs do not specifically address children's health and education and thus appear to lack the intergenerational human capital development objective common to conditional cash transfers (Vartanian and McNamara, 2004).

Experiments with index-based agricultural insurance are another risk reduction approach. These systems tie insurance payments to area-wide indices such as vegetation greenness or rainfall rather than individual farm performance. With an accurate index, these are far simpler and cheaper to implement than conventional crop insurance and avoid excessive risk-taking by the insured (Chantarat et al., 2013). Pilot programs with market-based insurance in semi-arid regions in northern Kenya have been relatively successful, although constraints on the ability to pay among poor households has led to a decision by the government to subsidize insurance premiums to help spread the benefits of insurance to more households. During the drought in the region in 2016–2017, substantial payouts from the insurance program were made with the aim of protecting herders from the worst impacts of drought (ILRI, 2017). The intention of such risk reduction approaches to social protection is that poor households will be better able to preserve and build their income and assets, which in turn can enable them to rise out of poverty over time.

Providing productive assets directly to poor households is another approach for supporting households by reducing vulnerability to risk. For rural poor households in low- and middle-income countries, livestock are an important class of assets that contribute in multiple ways to household well-being, particularly by providing food and financial benefits. Animal source foods such as milk, meat, and fish provide critical micro nutrients that are particularly beneficial for young children's development (Iannotti and Lesorogol, 2014). Small livestock such as goats, sheep, chickens, and pigs are an important store of value that can be relatively easily converted to cash for immediate needs such as education or health costs. In addition, in many societies, small livestock are cared for by women. Improving their access to them may have positive effects for their relative standing in the household. A number of programs around the world have experimented with providing small livestock to households. The most rigorous evidence to date regarding the effectiveness of these interventions comes from a randomized control trial in six countries that provided a package of interventions including provision of a productive asset (usually livestock), training, consumption support, coaching through home visits, and encouragement for savings. This intervention showed positive impacts on household consumption, assets, income, physical and mental health, political involvement, and women's empowerment in the treatment group compared to the control group one year after the end of the intervention (Banerjee et al., 2015). Importantly, the intervention was adapted to each of the six country contexts and efforts were made to assess the scalability and cost-effectiveness of the approach with early results indicating good potential for scale-up (Banerjee et al., 2015).

In the United States and several other countries, programs for assisting households to build assets through savings (particularly lower-income households) have shown great potential to increase savings for education, home ownership, and business (see Chapter 6 of this volume). In addition, research indicates that child saving accounts have positive effects on mother's mental health and children's social-emotional development (Beverly et al., 2016). Similar approaches promoting child savings accounts have been tested in a number of low-income countries and have showed the potential for young people to save for their future and, more generally, to engage with financial institutions (YouthSave Initiative, 2015). All of these efforts promoting saving and financial inclusion aim toward the development of human capabilities through building financial capital that can be further applied to productive uses such as education or business development.

Finally, a rights-based approach sees poverty as a violation of basic human rights. Social protection involves extending rights to all people including economic and social rights in addition to political and civic rights (Barrientos and Hulme, 2008). Rights are also connected to ideas of needs and utilities—what people have a right to is usually assumed to be basic needs such as food, health care, shelter, and security. This approach is less concerned about the design and operation of specific programs than in promoting recognition that all citizens should be treated equitably and have access to necessary resources. Programs in this domain have a social justice and equity orientation that is critical of conditionality and the ways that structural disadvantage shapes antipoverty and social protection programs. Putting an emphasis on rights suggests that poverty-reduction efforts should be more inclusive, bottom–up, participatory, and providing processes and tools for communities to challenge structural disadvantage and inequality and to claim their rights from the state and/or other civil society actors (Chambers, 2017; Vermuelen, 2005; Gaventa, 2011). Some recent examples include legal literacy camps where communities learn about their legal rights and how to claim them (Upadhyay, 2005), the use of interactive radio drama to encourage community engagement in developing a biodiversity action plan (Apte, 2005) or improving enforcement of logging regulations by involving local communities in analyzing how current laws are actually enforced and jointly designing and implementing improvements (Kazoora et al., 2005). In each case, community engagement is central to defining the issues to be addressed and the decisions to be taken. Facilitating organizations can assist with information and participatory methodologies, enabling communities to pursue solutions with the potential for improving their living conditions.

Urban Design for Livable Lives: Housing and Built Environment

Interventions aimed at making cities places where communities can thrive will require a comprehensive and multisectoral approach. Although low- and middle-income countries face major challenges, there are several examples of programs and policies that created changes in the built and social environments with positive results on physical activity levels (Sallis et al., 2016; Heath et al., 2012), access to health services (Gomez et al., 2015; Diaz Del Castillo et al., 2011), and social inequalities (Reis et al., 2016; Lemoine et al., 2016; Torres et al., 2013). These interventions are multisectoral (e.g., city planning, transport, education, culture, leisure, environmental sustainability, health) and show potential to be scalable (Reis et al., 2016; Lemoine et al., 2016; Torres et al., 2013). Over the last two decades, several examples of multisectoral programs and policies implemented in low- and middle-income countries have demonstrated positive health and social results. For instance, several cities in Latin America have implemented extensive bus rapid transit systems resulting in lower transport inequities, greater access to public services (i.e., health care) and employment opportunities, and increased physical activity levels (Gomez et al., 2015; Lemoine et al., 2016). Additionally, community-based physical activity programs such as free physical activity classes, re-engineered and beautified public spaces (e.g., small parks and plazas), and access to physical activity equipment, have been associated with increased levels of physical activity (Reis et al., 2010, 2014; Simoes et al., 2017). These have decreased health inequalities by reaching a population at higher risk for inactivity (Siqueira Reis et al., 2013). Additionally, bicycle-share programs (Becerra et al., 2013) and bicycling promotion programs (Sarmiento et al., 2010) have been widely implemented in low- and middle-income countries, although typically in socioeconomically advantaged areas (Sarmiento et al., 2016; Becerra et al., 2013; Sarmiento et al., 2010).

Improvements to urban infrastructure have the potential to enhance health and well-being for city dwellers. However, one critical concern is gentrification. As cities become more livable and appealing, they attract new populations such as younger, upwardly mobile professionals. Health-promoting designs such as walkable and transit-oriented development have been identified as key predictors of increased housing costs, which may in turn displace low-income populations who stand to benefit the most from those sustainable investments (Anguelovski, 2015; Chapple, 2009; Krause and Bitter, 2012).

Toward the goal of development without displacement, several strategies have proven effective in the U.S. context. These strategies include, but are not limited to, community land trusts and inclusionary zoning ordinances (Lubell, 2016). Similar to some of the rights-based approaches mentioned earlier, the community land trust model is premised on the idea that community improvement is most likely to benefit community residents when they have an ownership stake in the neighborhood (Democracy Collaborative, n.d.). In a community land trust, a nonprofit community organization maintains ownership of the land but sells the home built on that land to a low- to moderate-income buyer at a reduced cost. If and when the home owner decides to sell the home, it must remain affordable at a level determined by the community organization. This model has been used effectively to (1) help individual home owners build equity and (2) maintain a permanent stock of affordable housing in a neighborhood that might otherwise be gentrifying.

A promising model for development without displacement that focuses on renters as opposed to home buyers is inclusionary zoning (Jacobus, 2015). Inclusionary zoning laws require housing developers to set aside a certain percentage of housing units for low- to moderate-income households. Inclusionary zoning laws are structured differently in different cities. For instance, they may be mandatory (required of all housing development) or voluntary (tied to special incentives for developers who opt in). Inclusionary zoning laws have been shown to be a positive predictor of stable neighborhood integration with respect to both race and class (Kontakosta, 2014).

Physical Activity and Healthy Eating

In the United States, several key components of community design and built environment influence diet and healthy eating. Dietary choices are impacted by the food retail environment and how much (or little) access residents have to fresh, healthy, affordable food (Al Hasan and Eberth, 2016; Thompson et al., 2019). Additionally, access to fast food and convenience stores can encourage unhealthy eating leading to increased chronic disease risk (Mezuk et al., 2016). Globally, community features such as farmers markets and community gardens are important elements of the food environment, with the potential to promote healthy eating and well-being (Bowen et al., 2015; Egli et al., 2016; Berezowitz et al., 2015; Vibert, 2016). Strategies to improve nutritional behaviors can target environment and policies (Frieden et al., 2010; Glickman et al., 2012; McGuire, 2012); however, the evidence base is derived primarily from studies in suburban and urban settings (Calancie et al., 2015). Promising approaches include increasing availability and affordability of healthy food choices and reducing availability of less healthy foods and beverages in public service venues (e.g., schools, afterschool programs, child care centers, community recreational facilities), as well as limiting advertising of less healthy foods and beverages. For example, schools can implement policies to improve the nutritional quality in school meals and limit the sale of sugar-sweetened beverages by restricting access to vending machines (Khan et al., 2009). A review identifying interventions for healthy eating in rural communities found that such interventions were primarily targeted at increasing access to nutritious foods and decreasing access to unhealthy choices. It may be necessary, however, to incorporate adaptations to address the rural setting such as the long distances in the food supply system, tailoring to the food culture of the local area, and partnering with the local community (Calancie et al., 2015).

Community design and the built environment are also related to physical activity and/or sedentary behavior in many places around the world. Neighborhood walkability has been consistently associated with increased levels of physical activity (Bauman et al., 2012; Sallis et al., 2016). Transportation choices within communities can also enable physical activity. Interconnection between destinations (e.g., shopping, work, education, recreation) are associated with active transportation. People are more likely to use nonmotorized modes of transit if these options exist (Sallis et al.; 2012). Availability of and proximity to recreation facilities are associated with greater physical activity among adults, adolescents, and children. Increasing evidence shows the importance of the built environments (e.g., mixed use development, presence of parks) in supporting physical activity (Frost et al., 2010; Bancroft et al., 2015; Smith et al., 2017), but, again, few rural studies are available (Barnidge et al., 2013). It remains unclear whether the findings from urban areas can be generalized to rural communities due to differences in culture, population densities, physical environment, and other contextual factors (Barnidge et al., 2013; Cleland et al., 2015). The small amount of research focusing on built environment effects in rural settings suggests safety, aesthetics, and the existence of parks, walking trails and recreation centers were positively associated with physical activity among rural residents (Frost et al., 2010). The strategies most commonly used to increase physical activity included improving infrastructure to support walking, increasing opportunities for extracurricular physical activity, and increasing opportunities for activity at school outside of physical education (Umstattd et al., 2016). However, research indicates that interventions aimed at improving nutrition and physical activity through changes to the environment, in rural and urban settings, may be insufficient to change behavior if they are not nested within a multilevel intervention to address healthy eating and activity (Glickman et al., 2012).

Conclusion

Social work has a vital role to play in facilitating the development of thriving communities which are necessary for achieving livable lives for all. Accomplishing these goals will require a multidimensional and multilevel approach that recognizes the complexity of problems such as poverty, inequality, and structural disadvantage. A social ecological approach is helpful in thinking through how individual behaviors are influenced by familial, neighborhood, regional, national, and international contexts. It is insufficient to only consider interventions that focus on individuals without considering these broader levels. Many recent approaches to healthy eating, built environment, and poverty reduction do recognize these connections and endeavor to design policies and programs that act on more than one level. However, there remain significant gaps in knowledge and a need for further research and testing of promising policies and interventions. Innovative methods for including members of poor communities have been developed and utilized, but more could be done to ensure the spread and quality of these participatory methodologies. The values of equity and social justice are foundational to social work as well as to the goal of livable lives. In addition, they undergird many of the strategies discussed here. Working from this foundation, social work practitioners are well-placed to partner with peoples across the globe to build healthy, diverse communities where all can thrive.

Our review of promising approaches and programs underscores the critical role of community in achieving a livable life. Communities are important as a source of ideas, resources, and social support for the kinds of individual opportunities, behaviors, and capabilities necessary for improving one's prospects. For individuals suffering from structural disadvantages, it is particularly important that proactive approaches include the community, because this is the place where policies become programs that potentially create opportunities. There is often a gap between well-intended policies and their translation into workable and effective programs. Furthermore, it is from the community level that organizations implementing social programs can receive feedback on the effectiveness of their interventions and their broader impact. Therefore, community forms a critical node linking individuals to opportunities for building their capabilities, along with organizations seeking to serve the needs of disadvantaged populations.

Social work has had an historical focus on working at the community level, borne out by the realization that individuals' lives will be improved when their community conditions are improved. That is, when people live in places that promote healthy lifestyles, where diversity is found and where opportunities are abundant, they are more likely to make choices that enhance their life chances. Many social workers engage with communities as organizers, running nonprofit social service agencies, or doing rights-based work. In low- and middle-income countries, the field of social work is more closely associated with community development work than with interventions at the individual level (which is more common in high-income countries). Recognizing the vital role of community in the achievement of a livable life through the enhancement of capabilities and within the framework of the Sustainable Development Goals, social workers are well-placed to provide creative solutions that take into account local context, historical factors, and the multiple levels of the social ecological framework in designing, implementing, and evaluating policies and programs that promote opportunities for thriving communities and livable cities for all. Social workers are also instrumental in sharing experiences as well as innovative practices and lessons learned across the globe. It is incumbent upon social work education to equip students with the relevant skills, knowledge, and experiences across regions, countries, economic levels, and cultural differences. With a global perspective and social work tools for working in partnership with communities, social workers can play a vital role in accelerating progress toward livable lives for all.

References

Al Hasan, D. M., and J. M. Eberth. 2016. "An Ecological Analysis of Food Outlet Density and Prevalence of Type II Diabetes in South Carolina Counties." *BMC Public Health*, 16, 10.

Anguelovski, I. 2015. "Healthy Food Stores, Greenlining and Food Gentrification: Contesting New Forms of Privilege, Displacement and Locally Unwanted land Uses in Racially Mixed Neighborhoods." *International Journal of Urban and Regional Research*, 39, 1209–1230.

Apte, T. 2005. "Creating Stakeholder Ownership of Biodiveristy Planning: Lessons from India." *Participatory Learning and Action*, 53, 54–60.

Baker, P. R., D. P. Francis, J. Soares, A. L. Weightman, and C. Foster. 2011. "Community Wide Interventions for Increasing Physical Activity." *Sao Paulo Medical Journal*, 129, 436–437.

Bancroft, C., S. Joshi, A. Rundle, M. Hutson, C. Chong, C. C. Weiss, and G. Lovasi. 2015. "Association of Proximity and Density of Parks and Objectively Measured Physical Activity in the United States: A Systematic Review." *Social Science and Medicine*, 138, 22–30.

Banerjee, A., E. Duflo, N. Goldberg, D. Karlan, R. Osei, W. Parienté, and C. Udry. 2015. "A Multifaceted Program Causes Lasting Progress for the Very Poor: Evidence from Six Countries." *Science*, 348, 6236, 1260799-1-1260799-16.

Barnidge, E. K., C. Radvanyi, K. Duggan, F. Motton, I. Wiggs, E. A. Baker, and R. C. Brownson. 2013. "Understanding and Addressing Barriers to Implementation of Environmental and Policy Interventions to Support Physical Activity and Healthy Eating in Rural Communities." *The Journal of Rural Health*, 29, 97–105.

Barrientos, A., and D. Hulme. 2008. *Social Protection for the Poor and Poorest*. London: Palgrave Macmillan.

Bauman, A. E., R. S. Reis, J. F. Sallis, J. C. Wells, R. J. Loos, and B. W. Martin. 2012. "Correlates of Physical Activity: Why Are Some People Physically Active and Others Not?" *The Lancet*, 380, 258–271.

Beaglehole, R., R. Bonita, R. Horton, M. Ezzati, N. Bhala, M. Amuyunzu-Nyamongo, M., and K. S. Reddy. 2012. "Measuring Progress on NCDs: One Goal and Five Targets." *The Lancet*, 380, 1283–1285.

Becerra, J. M., R. S. Reis, L. D. Frank, F. A. Ramirez-Marrero, B. Welle, E. Arriaga Cordero, and J. Dill. 2013. "Transport and Health: A Look at Three Latin American Cities." *Cadernos de Saúde Pública*, 29, 654–666.

Berezowitz, C. K., A. B. Bontrager Yoder, and D. A. Schoeller. 2015. "School Gardens Enhance Academic Performance and Dietary Outcomes in Children." *Journal of School Health*, 85, 508–518.

Beverly, S. G., M. M. Clancy, and M. Sherraden. 2016. "Universal Accounts at Birth: Results from SEED for Oklahoma Kids." CSD Research Summary No. 16-07. St. Louis, MO: Washington University, Center for Social Development.

Binswanger-Mkhize, H. P. 2012. "Is There too Much Hype about Index-based Agricultural Insurance?" *Journal of Development Studies*, 48, 187–200.

Bowen, W., E. Barrington, and S. Beresford. 2015. "Identifying the Effects of Environmental and Policy Change Interventions on Healthy Eating." *Annual Review Public Health*, 36, 289–306.

Bronfenbrenner, U. 1979. *The Ecology of Human Development.* Cambridge, MA: Harvard University Press.

Calancie L, J. Leeman S. B. Jilcott Pitts, L. K. Khan, S. Fleischhacker, and K. R. Evenson. 2015. "Nutrition-Related Policy and Environmental Strategies to Prevent Obesity in Rural Communities: A Systematic Review of the Literature, 2002–2013." *Preventative Chronic Disease,* 12, E57.

Center for Disease Control. 2018. "Early Release of Selected Estimates Based on Data from January–June 2018 National Health Interview Survey." Retrieved from https://www.cdc.gov/nchs/nhis/releases/released201812.htm

Chambers, R. 2017. *Can We Know Better? Reflections for Development.* Rugby, UK: Practical Action.

Chantarat, S., A. G. Mude, C. B. Barrett, and M. R. Carter, M. R. 2013. "Designing Index Based Livestock Insurance for Managing Asset Risk in Northern Kenya." *Journal of Risk and Insurance,* 80, 205–237.

Chapple, K. 2009. Mapping Susceptibility to Gentrification: The Early Warning Toolkit. Berkeley, CA: Center for Community Innovation.

Cleland, V, C. Hughes, L. Thornton, K. Squibb, A. Venn, and K. Ball. 2015. "Environmental Barriers and Enablers to Physical Activity Participation among Rural Adults: A Qualitative Study." *Health Promotion Journal of Australia,* 26, 99–104.

Dabla-Norris, E., K. Kochhar, F. Ricka, N. Suphaphiphat, and E. Tsounta. 2015. "Causes and Consequences of Income Inequality: A Global Perspective." IMP Staff Discussion Note 15/13.

Democracy Collaborative. n.d. "Overview: Community Land Trusts (CLTs)." Retrieved from http://community-wealth.org/strategies/panel/clts/index.html

del Castillo, A. D., O. L. Sarmiento, R. S. Reis, and R. C. Brownson. 2011. "Translating Evidence to Policy: Urban Interventions and Physical Activity Promotion in Bogotá, Colombia and Curitiba, Brazil." *Translational Behavioral Medicine,* 1, 350–360.

Ding, D., J. F. Sallis, T. L. Conway, B. E. Saelens, L. D. Frank, K. L. Cain, and D. J. Slymen. 2012. "Interactive Effects of Built Environment and Psychosocial Attributes on Physical Activity: A Test of Ecological Models." *Annals of Behavioral Medicine,* 44, 365–374.

Eberhardt, M. S., and E. R. Pamuk. 2004. "The Importance of Place of Residence: Examining Health in Rural and Nonrural Areas." *American Journal of Public Health,* 94, 1682–1686.

Egli, V., M. Oliver, and E. Tautolo. 2016. "The Development of a Model of Community Garden Benefits to Wellbeing." *Preventive Medicine Reports,* 3, 348–352.

Escobar, A. 2015. "Degrowth, Postdevelopment, and Transitions: A Preliminary Conversation." *Sustainability Science,* 10, 451–462. https://doi.org/10.1007/s11625-015-0297-5

Fan J.X., M. Wen, L. Kowaleski-Jones. 2014. "Rural–Urban Differences in Objective and Subjective Measures of Physical Activity: Findings from the National Health and Nutrition Examination Survey (NHANES) 2003–2006." *Preventative Chronic Disease,* 11, E141.

Frieden T.R., W. Dietz, and J. Collins. 2010. "Reducing Childhood Obesity Through Policy Change: Acting Now to Prevent Obesity." *Health Affairs,* 29, 357–363.

Frost, S. S., R. T. Goins, R. H. Hunter, S. P. Hooker, L. L. Bryant, J. Kruger, and D. Pluto. 2010. "Effects of the Built Environment on Physical Activity of Adults Living in Rural Settings." *American Journal of Health Promotion,* 24, 267–283.

Garcia, M. C. 2017. "Reducing Potentially Excess Deaths from the Five Leading Causes of Death in the Rural United States." *MMWR Surveillance Summaries,* 66. Retrieved from https://www.cdc.gov/mmwr/volumes/66/ss/ss6602a1.htm

Gaventa, J. 2011. Towards Participatory Local Governance: Six Propositions for Discussion. *The Participation Reader.* Edited A. Cornwall. London: Zed books, pp. 253–264.

Glickman D., L. Parker, L. J. Sim, H. Del Valle Cook, E. A. Miller. 2012. "Accelerating progress in obesity prevention: solving the weight of the nation." *Institute of Medicine.* Retrieved from http://mncanceralliance.org/wp-content/uploads/2013/09/IOM-Accelerating-Progress-inObesity-Prevention.pdf

Gomez, L. F. 2015. "Urban Environment Interventions Linked to the Promotion of Physical Activity: A Mixed Methods Study Applied to the Urban Context of Latin America." *Social Science Medicine*, 131, 18–30.

Greenberg, M. H. 2009. "It's Time for a Better Poverty Measure." *Counterpoise*, 13, 21–24.

Hanlon, J., A. Barrientos, and D. Hulme. 2010. *Just Give Money to the Poor: The Development Revolution from the Global South*. Sterling, VA: Kumarian Press.

Heath G. W., D. C. Parra, and O. L. Sarmiento. 2012. "Evidence-Based Intervention in Physical Activity: Lessons from Around the World." *Lancet*, 380, 272–281.

Iannotti, L., and C. Lesorogol. 2014. "Animal Milk Sustains Micronutrient Nutrition and Child Anthropometry Among Pastoralists in Samburu, Kenya." *American Journal of Physical Anthropology*, 155, 66–76.

Imai, K. and B. Maleb. 2015. "Rural and Urban Poverty Estimates for Developing Countries: Methodologies." Kobe University Discussion Paper DP2015-07.

ISSC, IDS, and UNESCO. Eds. 2016. *World Social Science Report 2016: Challenging Inequalities: Pathways to a Just World*. Paris: UNESCO.

Jacobus, R. 2015. "Inclusionary Housing: Creating and Maintaining Equitable Communities." *Lincoln Institute of Land Policy*. Retrieved from https://www.lincolninst.edu/publications/policy-focus-reports/inclusionary-housing

Kabeer, N. 2000. "Social Exclusion, Poverty and Discrimination Towards an Analytical Framework." *IDS Bulletin*, 31, 83–97.

Kabeer, N. 2016. "'Leaving No One Behind': The Challenge of Intersecting Inequalities." *Challenging Inequalities: Pathways to a Just World, World Social Science Report*. Edited by ISSC, IDS, and UNESCO. Paris: UNESCO, pp. 55–58.

Kazoora, C., C. Tondo, and B. Kazungu. 2005. "Routes to Justice: Institutionalising Participation in Forest Law Enforcement." *Participatory Learning and Action*, 53, 61–68.

Khan, L. K., K. Sobush, D. Keener, K. Goodman, A. Lowry, J. Kakietek, and S. Zaro, 2009. "Recommended Community Strategies and Measurements to Prevent Obesity in the United States." *MMWR: Recommendations and Reports*, 58, 1–29.

Kim, Y., S. Lee, H. Jung, J. Jaime, and C. Cubbin. 2018. "Is Neighborhood Poverty Harmful to Every Child? Neighborhood Poverty, Family Poverty, and Behavioral Problems among Young Children." *Journal of Community Psychology*, 47, 594–610.

Kontakosta, C. E. 2014. "Mixed Income Housing and Neighbourhood Integration: Evidence from Inclusionary Zoning Programs." *Journal of Urban Affairs*, 36, 716–741.

Krause, A. L., and C. Bitter. 2012. "Spatial Econometrics, Land Values, and Sustainability: Trends in Real Estate Valuation Research." *Cities*, 29, S19–S25.

Lemoine, P. D., O. L. Sarmiento, J. D. Pinzón, J. D. Meisel, F. Montes, D. Hidalgo, and R. Zarama. 2016. "TransMilenio, a Scalable Bus Rapid Transit System for Promoting Physical Activity." *Journal of Urban Health*, 93, 256–270.

Lubell, J. 2016. "Preserving and Expanding Affordability in Neighborhoods Experiencing Rising Rents and Property Values." *Cityscape*, 18, 131–150.

Lutfiyya, M. N., L. F. Chang, and M. S. Lipsky. 2012. "A Cross-Sectional Study of US Rural Adults' Consumption of Fruits and Vegetables: Do They Consume at Least Five Servings Daily?" *BMC Public Health*, 12, 280.

MacMillan, S. 2017. "Record Payouts Being Made by Kenya Government and Insurers to Protect Herders Facing Historic Drought." *ILRI News*. Retrieved from https://news.ilri.org/2017/02/21/record-payouts-being-made-by-kenya-government-and-insurers-to-protect-herders-facing-historic-drought

Mamdani, M. 1996. *Citizen and Subject: Contemporary Africa and the Legacy of Late Colonialism*. Princeton, NJ: Princeton University Press.

Martin S. L., G. J. Kirkner, K. Mayo, C. E. Matthews, J. L. Durstine, and J. R. Hebert. 2005. "Urban, Rural, and Regional Variations in Physical Activity." *Journal of Rural Health*, 21, 239–244.

McGuire, S. 2012. "Accelerating Progress in Obesity Prevention: Solving the Weight of the Nation." *Advances in Nutrition*, 3, 708–709.

Mezuk, B., X. Li, K. Cederin, K. Rice, J. Sundquist, and K. Sundquist. 2016. "Beyond Access: Characteristics of the Food Environment and Risk of Diabetes." *American Journal of Epidemiology*, 183, 1129–1137.

Mohamoud, Y. A., R. S. Kirby, and D. B. Ehrenthal. 2019. "Poverty, Urban–Rural Classification and Term Infant Mortality: A Population-Based Multilevel Analysis." *BMC Pregnancy and Childbirth*, 19, 40.

Molina-Millan, T., T. Barham, K. Macours, J. A. Maluccio, and M. Stampini, M. 2016. "Long-Term Impacts of Conditional Cash Transfers in Latin America: Review of the Evidence." Inter-American Development Bank.

Muller, C. 1993. "Parent Involvement and Academic Achievement: An Analysis of Family Resources Available to the Child." *Parents, Their Children, and Schools*. Edited by J. Coleman. New York: Routledge, pp. 77–114.

Nau, C., B. S. Schwartz, K. Bandeen Roche, A. Liu, J. Pollak, A. Hirsch, and T. A. Glass. 2015. "Community Socioeconomic Deprivation and Obesity Trajectories in Children Using Electronic Health Records." *Obesity*, 23, 207–212.

Parks, S. E., R. A. Housemann, and R. C. Brownson. 2003. "Differential Correlates of Physical Activity in Urban and Rural Adults of Various Socioeconomic Backgrounds in the United States." *Journal of Epidemiology and Community Health*, 57, 29–35.

Pinard, C. A., C. B. Shanks, S. M. Harden, and A. L. Yaroch. 2016. "An Integrative Literature Review of Small Food Store Research Across Urban and Rural Communities in the US." *Preventive Medicine Reports*, 3, 324–332.

Rawlings, L., and G. M. Rubio. 2005. *Evaluating the Impact of Conditional Cash Transfer Programs*. New York: Oxford University Press.

Reinikka, R., and J. Svensson, J. 2011. "The Power of Information in Public Services: Evidence from Education in Uganda." *Journal of Public Economics*, 95, 956–966.

Reis, R. S., P. C. Hallal, D. C. Parra, I. C. Ribeiro, R. C. Brownson, M. Pratt, and L. Ramos. 2010. "Promoting Physical Activity through Community-Wide Policies and Planning: Findings from Curitiba, Brazil." *Journal of Physical Activity and Health*, 7, S137–S145.

Reis, R. S., A. A. F. Hino, D. K. Cruz, L. E. da Silva Filho, D. C. Malta, M. R. Domingues, and R. C. Hallal. 2014. "Promoting Physical Activity and Quality of Life in Vitoria, Brazil: Evaluation of the Exercise Orientation Service (EOS) Program." *Journal of Physical Activity and Health*, 11, 38–44.

Reis, R. S., D. Salvo, D. Ogilvie, E. V. Lambert, S. Goenka, R. C. Brownson, and Lancet Physical Activity Series 2 Executive Committee. 2016. "Scaling Up Physical Activity Interventions Worldwide: Stepping Up to Larger and Smarter Approaches to Get People Moving." *The Lancet*, 388, 1337–1348.

Richardson, A. S., G. P. Hunter, M. Ghosh-Dastidar, N. Colabianchi, R. L. Collins, R. Beckman, and W. M. Troxel. 2017. "Pathways Through Which Higher Neighborhood Crime is Longitudinally Associated with Greater Body Mass Index." *International Journal of Behavioral Nutrition and Physical Activity*, 14, 155.

Rothstein, R. 2017. *The Color of Law: A Forgotten History of How Our Government Segregated America*. New York: W. W. Norton.

Sallis, J. F., F. Bull, R. Guthold, G. W. Heath, G. S. Inoue, P. Kelly, and Lancet Physical Activity Series 2 Executive Committee. 2016. "Progress in Physical Activity over the Olympic Quadrennium." *The Lancet*, 388, 1325–1336.

Sallis, J. F., E. Cerin, T. L. Conway, M. A. Adams, L. D. Frank, M. Pratt, and R. Davey. 2016. "Physical Activity in Relation to Urban Environments in 14 Cities Worldwide: A Cross-Sectional Study." *The Lancet*, 387, 2207–2217.

Sallis J. F., M. F. Floyd, D. A. Rodríguez, and B. E. Saelens. 2012. "The Role of Built Environments in Physical Activity, Obesity, and CVD." *Circulation*, 125, 729–737.

Sarmiento, O. L., A. D. del Castillo, C. A. Trina, M. J. Acevedo, S. A. Gonzalez, and M. Pratt. 2016. "Reclaiming the Streets for People: Insights from Ciclovias Recreativas in Latin America." *Preventive Medicine*, 103, s34–s40.

Sarmiento, O., A. Torres, E. Jacoby, M. Pratt, T. L. Schmid, and G. Stierling. 2010. "The Ciclovía-Recreativa: A Mass-Recreational Program with Public Health Potential." *Journal of Physical Activity and Health*, 7, S163–S180.

Sen, A. 1981. *Poverty and Famines: An Essay on Entitlement and Deprivation*. Oxford, UK: Oxford University Press.

Sen, A. 1999. *Development as Freedom*. New York: Knopf.

Simoes, E. J., P. Hallal, F. Siqueira, C. Schmaltz, D. Menor, D. Malta, H. Duarte, A. Hino, G. Mielke, M. Pratt, and R. Reis. 2017. "Effectiveness of a Scaled Up Physical Activity Intervention in Brazil: A Natural Experiment." *Preventative Medicine*, 103S, S66–S72.

Siqueira Reis R, A. A. Hino C. Ricardo Rech, J. Kerr, and P. Curi Hallal. 2013. "Walkability and Physical Activity: Findings from Curitiba, Brazil." *American Journal of Preventative Medicine*, 45, 269–275.

Smith, M. 2017. "Systematic Literature Review of Built Environment Effects on Physical Activity and Active Transport: An Update and New Findings on Health Equity." *International Journal of Behavioral Nutrition and Physical Activity*, 14, 158.

Thompson, C., D. Smith, and S. Cummins. 2019. "Food Banking and Emergency Food Aid: Expanding the Definition of Local Food Environments and Systems." *International Journal of Behavioral Nutrition and Physical Activity*, 16, 2.

Thurlow, J., P. Dorosh, and B. Davis. 2019. "Demographic Change, Agriculture, and Rural Poverty." *Sustainable Food and Agriculture*. Edited by C. Campanhola, and S. Pandey. Rome: Academic Press, pp. 31–53

Torres, A., O. Sarmiento, C. Stauber, and R. Zarama. 2013. "The Ciclovia and Cicloruta Programs: Promising Interventions to Promote Physical Activity and Social Capital in Bogotá, Colombia." *American Journal of Public Health*, 103, E23–E30.

Umstattd Meyer, M. R., C. K. Perry, and J. C. Sumrall. 2016. "Physical Activity-Related Policy and Environmental Strategies to Prevent Obesity in Rural Communities: A Systematic Review of the Literature." *Preventative Chronic Disease*, 13, E03.

United Nations Department of Economic and Social Affairs Population Division. 2012. *World Urbanization Prospects: The 2011 Revision. Data Tables and Highlights*. New York: United Nations.

United Nations Development Programme. 2016a. "Human Development Report. Multidimensional Poverty Index." Retrieved from http://hdr.undp.org/sites/default/files/hdr2016_technical_notes.pdf

United Nations Development Programme. 2016b. "Human Development Report: Statistical Annex." Retrieved from http://hdr.undp.org/sites/default/files/hdr_2016_statistical_annex.pdf

United Nations Population Fund. 2011. *State of World Population*. New York: Author.

United Nations Population Fund. 2012. *State of World Population*. New York: Author.

United Nations. n.d. "Sustainable Development Goals." Retrieved from https://sustainabledevelopment.un.org

Upadhyay, S. 2005. "Law for the People: Interaction Approaches to Legal Literacy in India." *Participatory Learning and Action*, 53, 23–30.

U.S. Census Bureau. 2018. *Income and Poverty in the United States: 2017*. Report No. P60-263. Washington DC: U.S. Government Printing Office.

U.S. Central Intelligence Agency. 2014. *CIA World Factbook*. Washington, DC: Author.

Vartanian, T. P., and J. M. McNamara. 2004. The Welfare Myth: Disentangling the Long-Term Effects of Poverty and Welfare Receipt for Young Single Mothers. *Journal of Sociology and Social Welfare*, 31, 105.

Vermeulen, S. 2005. "Power Tools for Participatory Learning and Action." *Participatory Learning and Action*, 53, 9–15.

Vibert, E. 2016. "Gender, Resilience and Resistance: South Africa's Hleketani Community Garden." *Journal of Contemporary African Studies*, 34, 252–267.

Ward B, J. Schiller, M. Freeman, and T. Clarke. 2015. *Early Release of Selected Estimates Based on Data from the 2014 National Health Interview Survey.* Hyattsville, MD: National Center for Health Statistics, Division of Health Interview Statistics.

Wilcox S, C. Castro, A. C. King, R. Housemann, and R. C. Brownson. 2000. "Determinants of Leisure Time Physical Activity in Rural Compared with Urban Older and Ethnically Diverse Women in the United States." *Journal of Epidemiological Community Health*, 54, 667–672.

Wilson, W. J. 1996. *When Work Disappears: The World of the New Poor.* New York: Vintage Books.

World Bank. 2015. "Poverty and Equity Data Portal." Retrieved from http://povertydata.worldbank.org/poverty/home/

YouthSave Initiative. 2015. "YouthSave 2010–2015: Findings from a Global Financial Inclusion Partnership." A Report of the YouthSave Consortium.

10

Achieving Environmental Justice

LISA REYES MASON

Ellen lives in Montgomery Village, a public housing community in Knoxville, Tennessee (all first names are pseudonyms). Locally, Montgomery Village is known for high poverty and crime. The tenant association meets monthly, but its members are few. The Boys and Girls Club on site provides activities for youth, but attendance is unpredictable, and parent engagement is low. As Ellen and I talk about the quality of life in the neighborhood, she also describes a nearby business, "And this junkyard over here kills me. . . . They burn stuff or something. . . . Some days it is really bad over here, and it smothers me to death. I can't come outside sometimes. And I can smell it inside the house."

Angela is from Baguio City, an urban area of 350,000 people in northern Philippines. Water from the local utility company is piped to her home three days per week, for about four hours per day. Like many other women, who are the "water managers" for their families, Angela worries about whether she will have enough water for her family's needs—cooking, drinking, bathing, and cleaning. Figuring out how to store and conserve water is always on her mind. She says, "We conserve water . . . because if you do not, what will you use the next day? . . . Because if it's Monday, [water] comes at night. Tuesday, there's no water." Some families have enough money to purchase extra stores of water. Many others, who work in the informal economy and live on meager budgets, do not.

Air pollution and water insecurity are just two examples of environmental risks that disproportionately affect some groups of people more so than others. These, and many other issues at the nexus of the environment, society, and inequality, are examples of environmental injustice that must be addressed if we are to ensure livable lives for all people.

This chapter overviews the origins and evolution of environmental justice and how it resonates with social work. Air pollution and water insecurity, along with climate change, are discussed as examples of environmental injustice. Finally, an agenda for social work to achieve environmental justice through recommendations for conducting meaningful research, training social workers, and influencing policy change is reviewed.

Origins and Evolution of Environmental Justice

In 1982, protests erupted in Warren County, North Carolina. The U.S. Environmental Protection Agency had approved a permit for a new landfill to hold toxic waste. Residents of Warren County, however, were primarily African American. Protestors decried the decision as discriminatory. Hundreds of protestors were arrested. Ultimately, the landfill proceeded, but with it emerged a new term for the kind of activism seen in Warren County—environmental justice (Agyeman et al., 2016; McGurty, 1997).

Early Efforts

For two decades prior to the Warren County protests, public concern about the environment had been mounting in the United States (McGurty, 1997). In the 1960s, publication of Rachel Carson's *Silent Spring*, frequent smog alerts in Los Angeles, and water pollution in cities like Cleveland helped set the stage for major environmental legislation such as the Clean Air Act, Clean Water Act, and National Environmental Protection Act. However, these efforts largely ignored the unequal and disproportionate impacts of environmental hazards on racial minorities in particular. With the protests in Warren County, environmental racism gained national attention (McGurty, 1997).

In 1983, a study by the U.S. General Accounting Office found that hazardous waste sites were disproportionately located in predominantly African American communities in the southern United States. In 1987, the seminal United Church of Christ's Commission for Racial Justice's study reached a similar conclusion (Agyeman et al., 2016). As a solution for such environmental racism, Robert Bullard described environmental justice as the pursuit of a principle that "all people and communities are entitled to equal protection of environmental and public health laws and regulations," (Mohai, Pellow, and Roberts, 2009: 407). Over the next decade, environmental justice grew as both a grassroots movement and an area of academic study, with initial emphasis on the unequal distribution and impact of pollution (Mohai, Pellow, and Roberts, 2009).

Expanding the Concept

The environmental justice movement's early emphasis on race and pollution, and hazardous waste specifically, expanded to an array of topics and groups of people over the next three decades. In part, this resulted from a wider concept of "environment" as not just the natural environment, but the places where we live, work, and play—a concept that resonates with social work's holistic lens of person-in-environment. This evolution also came from a globalization of environmental justice efforts in many other countries, addressing concerns such as deforestation, natural resource extraction, energy production, and indigenous rights (Agyeman et al., 2016; Schlosberg and Collins, 2014).

Today, environmental justice is both wide in the variety of issues that fall under the term and deep in the diversity of contexts where it is pursued. As defined by the U.S. Environmental Protection Agency, the concept includes both fair and equal protection from hazards and participation in environmental decision-making:

> Environmental justice is the fair treatment and meaningful involvement of all people regardless of race, color, national origin, or income, with respect to the development, implementation, and enforcement of environmental laws, regulations, and policies. This goal will be achieved when everyone enjoys:
> - the same degree of protection from environmental and health hazards, and
> - equal access to the decision-making process to have a healthy environment in which to live, learn, and work. (U.S. Environmental Protection Agency, 2019)

In his book, *Blessed Unrest*, Pawl Hawken (2007) describes a flourishing global effort to address issues at the nexus of environment and social justice. Although impossible to define as a single "movement" with one leader, ideology, or structure, this effort addresses a myriad of environmental hazards and risks that threaten well-being and basic human rights of people in communities worldwide. In a rough attempt to number the organizations (often small, often community-based) working on these issues, Hawken estimates over 1 million focused on "ecological sustainability and social justice." Issues being confronted are as diverse as indigenous Nigerian groups facing pollution in the Niger River delta from oil and gas production,

Achieving Environmental Justice

Hondurans protesting luxury resort development on contested lands, and the birth of "slow food" in Italy as a challenge to large-scale agribusiness and environmental degradation.

As these efforts have expanded globally, so has the emphasis on different types of social inequalities in addition to race, such as gender, age, and income, among others. In urban Bolivia, for example, one study found that 19 percent of women reported losing income as a result of water scarcity, compared to 2 percent of men (Wutich, 2009). In rural Ghana, during a period of drought, another study found that women's workload increased by 33 percent, while men's decreased by 50 percent (Arku and Arku, 2010). Both children and older adults can experience worse physical health impacts from environmental risks, due to developing immune and physiological systems of the former and greater incidence of chronic disease or illness susceptibility among the latter (Anderson, Thundiyil, and Stolbach, 2012). During the 1995 heat wave in Chicago, Illinois, many older adults with low incomes felt unsafe going outdoors to keep cool and instead perished alone inside their own apartments (Klinenberg, 2002). Intersecting inequalities, like this last example, have also become critical in efforts to understand environmental injustice.

Resonance with Social Work

In social work, environmental justice concerns have emerged over several decades and under multiple names, such as environmental social work, green social work, and ecosocial work. Since the 1970s, "social work pioneers" in this area called on the profession to engage in environmental issues, confront environmental crises, and expand our signature person-in-environment perspective to include the natural environment as a critical context that we need to understand about people's lives (Coates and Gray, 2012).

Globally, the profession has responded with formal statements and professional policies. In the United States, the Council on Social Work Education (CSWE) added environmental justice to its core competencies for bachelor's and master's education and included the following definition:

> Environmental justice occurs when all people equally experience high levels of environmental protection and no group or community is excluded from the environmental policy decision-making process, nor is affected by a disproportionate impact from environmental hazards. Environmental justice affirms the ecological unity and the interdependence of all species, respect for cultural and biological diversity, and the right to be free from ecological destruction. This includes responsible

use of ecological resources, including the land, water, air, and food. (2015: 20)

Britain and Australia expanded their codes of ethics to address the natural environment, and the International Federation of Social Workers produced statements about issues at the nexus of the environment, globalization, and indigenous people's rights (Mason et al., 2017). In the United States, "create social responses to a changing environment" was one of 12 grand challenges set forth by the American Academy of Social Work and Social Welfare.

Fundamentally, our social work profession helps people address problems, access resources and opportunities, and lead healthy and productive lives. For these to be livable lives, in which people reach their full capacity and potential, they must have access to healthy and supportive environments—home, school, work, and neighborhood, to name a few. As social work calls for engagement with environmental justice have grown, so has our professional understanding of "environment" to include the built and natural environments as well. Social workers in public housing see how lead exposure and indoor air pollution impact early childhood development on a routine basis. At local community action offices, social workers see the effects of extreme heat or cold on people's ability to pay their rising utility costs and thus stay healthy and safe inside their own homes.

Environmental problems are social problems with multiple and overlapping consequences for people. Physical and mental health, social support, financial security, and basic access to food, water, and clean air are all impacted by environmental problems—and when a problem is an injustice, social work must respond from its concern for groups who are unfairly or unequally hurt more so than others. As a profession dedicated to enhancing well-being and quality of life, and one focused especially on people from vulnerable or marginalized groups, we are obligated to address environmental injustice to realize our larger vision of social justice and livable lives for all.

Understanding Environmental Injustice

In this section, three examples of environmental injustice are described— outdoor air pollution, household water insecurity, and climate change. The scope and impact of each problem and some of its underlying causes as a form of injustice are also discussed. Across these examples, themes of social vulnerability and structural inequality pervade. As Jesse Ribot once wrote, "vulnerability does not fall from the sky" (2010: 47). In other words, although environmental hazards or risks might sometimes be thought of as "natural" and "occurring anywhere," who is most vulnerable to the impacts of such hazards, and why, can often be traced to root issues of social, economic, and political inequality.

Outdoor Air Pollution

Scope and Impact

The World Health Organization describes air pollution as the "biggest environmental risk to health" (2016: 11). Outdoor (ambient) air pollution, in particular, is responsible for an estimated 3 to 5 million deaths per year, globally. In the United States, the six primary pollutants monitored by the National Ambient Air Quality Standards are carbon monoxide, lead, nitrogen oxide, ozone, sulfur dioxide, and particulate matter (e.g., $PM_{2.5}$ and PM_{10}). Exposure to these pollutants has been associated with higher rates of respiratory cancer, cardiovascular problems, asthma, and low birth weight (Anderson, Thundiyil, and Stolbach, 2012; Enders et al., 2019). Children, older adults, and people with pre-existing health conditions are especially susceptible to the health impacts of outdoor air pollution (Anderson, Thundiyil, and Stolbach, 2012). In places where air quality data and alerts are available, these groups are often cautioned to limit their activity outdoors on poor air quality days.

Urbanization, industrialization, and population growth are major drivers of outdoor air pollution in the United States and globally, with industrial processes and vehicle emissions being two primary sources of pollutants (Kumar et al., 2015). While lower- and middle-income countries in Africa, Asia, and the Middle East tend to have worse outdoor air pollution than other countries (World Health Organization, 2016), socioeconomic disparities in exposure to outdoor air pollutants are also found, and most often researched to date, within higher-income countries such as the United States.

Indeed, numerous U.S. studies have found that racial minorities and people with lower economic status tend to have higher exposure to particulate matter and other outdoor air pollutants. In an effort to compare production versus consumption of air pollution by race, a 2019 study (Tessum et al., 2019) found that non-Hispanic whites in the United States consume about 17 percent less air pollution than they effectively produce (via their consumption of goods and services), and that blacks in the United States consume about 56 percent more air pollution than they produce. Another 2019 study (Enders et al., 2019) focused on the impacts of air pollution early in life—on low birth weight among infants born at term (at least 37 weeks of gestation)—and found that high-risk groups included infants born to black mothers or to fathers with less than a college education.

Underlying Causes

Outdoor air pollution knows no boundaries. Pollutants produced in one locale may disperse to another. But the disparities observed in where pollution is produced, and thus where there is greater chance of direct exposure, have raised the question in the environmental justice literature of whether people or pollution "came first." As Paul Mohai and Robin Saha summarize the debate, is the fundamental cause of industrial air pollution especially "disparate siting" or "post-siting demographic change" (2015: 2)? Although longitudinal studies of air pollution to effectively answer this are few, there is evidence supporting both arguments, depending on the local context and history. In either case, larger structural forces and inequalities are at play and must be challenged as part of ensuring safe air quality for all.

With disparate siting, pollutant industries choose their location based on economic factors (e.g., cheaper property and local labor costs in lower income neighborhoods), sociopolitical factors (e.g., people from lower-income and/ or racial minority groups are seen by industry as less politically connected to oppose change and, therefore, as the path of least resistance), and/or as an act of racial discrimination (e.g., overt racism, or unintended racism but resulting from broader racist practices such as redlining, through which racial minority homeowners are concentrated in areas with lower property values) (Mohai and Sana, 2015).

With post-siting demographic change, the decision of a pollutant industry to locate itself in a particular area leads to the movement of some groups out of the area and thus resulting in a concentration of lower income or racial minority groups "left behind" (Mohai and Sana, 2015). Economically, wealthier families can more easily relocate to healthier neighborhoods. Sociopolitically, as wealthier families move away, less wealthy families who are already politically marginalized experience a "vicious cycle" of inability to effect change and prevent conditions from further declining. Regarding racial discrimination, even if local and wealthy families are black or Hispanic, historic redlining or current discrimination in the housing market may hinder their ability to relocate.

In our own research in Knoxville, Tennessee, we found that residents of a mixed income neighborhood expressed concern about a long-standing, nearby factory perceived to pollute (Mason, Ellis, and Hathaway, 2017). At the same time, however, social and economic dynamics lend tension to the problem and must be understood. The neighborhood has had an influx of Latinx immigrants in recent years, who may feel politically less empowered to advocate for change. In addition, the nearby factory is also positively seen as an investor in the neighborhood—hiring local residents and providing backpacks and holiday gifts to children at the local elementary school. One resident's comments reflected this tension:

> I'm definitely not anti-industry, but we do have . . . some odors in the air every once in a while. Such as that. And there's some concern about elevated lead levels in the air occasionally. But it's monitored, and they've never gone into the danger zone. They've just been up high enough to cause an alert to watch. So yeah. That's the down side. At the same time, I'm definitely not anti-industry in the community.

To fully understand outdoor air pollution in this, or any community, analyses of cause and environmental injustice must be highly localized, contextualized, and inclusive of multiple, diverse, and even conflicting experiences and views (e.g., Driver et al., 2019).

Household Water Insecurity

Scope and Impact

Water is fundamental to survival and has been recognized as a human right. We need clean, affordable, and reliable water for our most basic needs of drinking, preparing food, and personal hygiene to stay healthy and well. Today, about 2 billion people live in countries that are water stressed, and an estimated 30 percent of the world population does not have access to safe drinking water (UNESCO, 2019). Seasonal water shortage is also a growing concern, with at least 1.3 billion people projected to experience this problem annually by 2050 (McDonald et al., 2011).

Meanwhile, in some global or national reports, we have seen progress on ensuring water as a basic right (e.g., UNICEF and World Health Organization, 2012). In 2010, for example, the Millennium Development Goal for expanding access to improved water (e.g., water piped into a home, a public tap, a protected well, a protected spring, or rainwater) was ahead of schedule. Yet, global or national reports like this often miss or underestimate actual lived experiences of water insecurity (Bradley and Bartram, 2013). Although water from an improved source might be available to a household, it may still be unequally distributed, irregularly supplied, unclean, or expensive to obtain. As Wendy Jepson and colleagues discuss in their Wiley review article, a more comprehensive concept of water security must be used and operationalized if we are to better understand and address actual water insecurity at the household level. In their conceptualization, water security must be seen multidimensionally as "the ability to access and benefit from affordable, adequate, reliable, and safe water for wellbeing and a healthy life" (Jepson et al., 2017: 3).

In household or community studies that look more closely at water security, and especially those with a focus on equity, disparities, or justice, several groups who are most vulnerable to water insecurity or its impacts emerge. Women and girls in many lower- and middle-income countries, for example, tend to experience worse burdens or impacts of water insecurity than men and boys, due to gendered norms surrounding water collection responsibilities and norms that may prioritize distributing the scarce water that is available to male family members over females (UNESCO, 2019).

In many urban and peri-urban areas of the Global South, water insecurity is closely tied to income. Wealthier households with access to piped water in their homes often pay substantially less for water than lower-income households with no piped water, who then purchase clean water from kiosks, delivery trucks, or other water vendors in the private market. In a study (Adams, 2018) in Lilongwe, Malawi, residents of informal urban settlements, or "slums," paid twice as much per unit of water as higher income residents in the city. In our study (Mason, 2014) in a Baguio City neighborhood, in the Philippines, 17 percent of households spent over 10 percent of their monthly income on water, which is much higher than a United Nations recommendation that no more than 3 percent of household income should go toward water for it to be considered affordable.

Household water insecurity, in its multidimensional form, is also an issue in higher-income, or Global North, countries. The water crisis in Flint, Michigan, and its impacts on children's lead exposure and health illustrated how inequitable access to safe water can be in the United States. In Flint, a city with a high poverty rate and a majority of African American residents, a change in the city's water source from Lake Huron to the Flint River had immediate and disastrous consequences. As Amy Krings and her co-authors write, "Residents immediately noticed discolored and foul-smelling liquid coming from their taps. Reports of rashes, hair loss, and respiratory illnesses soon followed, and later blood lead levels in children spiked," (2018: 2). Despite numerous complaints from residents, it took 18 months for the city to switch its water source back to Lake Huron, but, nonetheless, many residents have still been left with pipes that are corroded and ongoing concerns about the health consequences of lead exposure for their children and themselves.

Underlying Causes

Population growth, urbanization, and consumption patterns are causing increased water use globally. Since 1980, global demand has increased by about 1 percent per year (UNESCO, 2019). At the same time, climate change is driving decreased or irregular water supply in many parts of the world, and as discussed in the next section, climate change itself is an issue rife with environmental justice concerns.

While in most U.S. households, accessing affordable and plentiful water is still as simple as turning on a faucet in one's home, in many other countries around the world such access is nonexistent, irregular, or not affordable for underlying reasons related to governance and resource inequalities (Bradley and Bartram, 2013; Mason, 2015). With rapid growth of many cities as rural populations have migrated for work, governments have historically seen investments in water infrastructure as a solution. However, such investments and the water services provided by governmental or quasigovernmental utilities tend to, at least initially, overlook people with the least income and consequently the least political power (Bradley and Bartram, 2013).

Furthermore, problems caused by a lack of infrastructure investment are compounded by households' inequitable access to resources that could help them secure water in other ways, such as on private water markets that are now common in many countries. Applying an assets or capitals framework to household water security can reveal how deep inequities in social, financial, and physical resources further exacerbate water insecurity for some families more so than others. In our Baguio City work (Mason, 2014), for example, we found that a household's volume of water storage—in the form of 50-gallon drums or high-volume tanks—was an important predictor of water security. For wealthier families, purchasing such storage is relatively easy. For lower-income families, such a purchase could take several months or even a year of dedicated saving, when having the money to save anything at all is already unlikely.

In the United States, meanwhile, underlying causes of water inequities are also related to inadequate investment or unfair practices, in ways that marginalize particular groups (Jepson and Vandewalle, 2016). Rural Appalachia, for example, still lacks critical water infrastructure—in part due to governance choices to not invest in expensive efforts to pipe water through difficult and remote terrain and in part due to deep and chronic poverty that prevents some households from installing modern plumbing in their own homes (Arcipowski et al., 2017). In some rural or otherwise marginalized communities, violations of safe drinking water codes have occurred, with little political enforcement of regulations intended to protect all. Affected groups have included rural residents, American Indian groups, and residents of *colonias* along the U.S.–Mexico border (Jepson and Vandewalle, 2016). In Flint, Michigan, evidence that the local government largely ignored resident concerns about water quality until those residents formed broader partnerships, including with scientists, medical professionals, and the media, is widely seen as another example of political marginalization grounded in economic and racial discrimination, as affected residents were primarily from lower income groups or were African American (Krings, Kornberg, and Lane, 2018).

Climate Change

Scope and Impact

Climate change is often described as the most pressing environmental and public health threat of our time and, potentially, an existential threat to humanity. Since the 1800s, average global surface temperatures have increased by about 0.85° C (Intergovernmental Panel on Climate Change, 2014b). Without major global action on climate change mitigation (i.e., reduction of greenhouse gas emissions), this increase is projected to reach at least 1.5° C as soon as 2030 and quite likely by 2050 (Intergovernmental Panel on Climate Change, 2018). To prevent crossing of this threshold, global greenhouse gas emissions would need to be lower than their 2010 levels by 45 percent by 2030 and lower by 100 percent by 2050 (Intergovernmental Panel on Climate Change, 2018).

The environmental consequences of climate change include sea level rise, flooding, drought, land cover change, species migration, and weather extremes that vary widely in every region of the world (Intergovernmental Panel on Climate Change, 2014a). In sub-Saharan Africa, temperatures are expected to increase much more rapidly than other parts of the world. In many parts of Asia, increased rainfall extremes will likely occur, with a more intense monsoon season. Australia has already experienced unprecedented drought and water scarcity. In North America and Europe, temperature extremes and coastal flooding impacting millions of people are concerns. In many Central and South American countries, much less precipitation in dry seasons, but much heavier precipitation in rainy seasons are problematic. Critically, these and other environmental consequences of climate change intersect with and amplify numerous other environmental justice issues, including outdoor air pollution, household water insecurity, food production and security, loss of communal or tribal lands, subsistence livelihoods, and more.

The negative human impacts of climate change are already unfolding in communities around the world—and often inequitably so, with the most vulnerable or marginalized groups either most impacted or least able to "bounce back" and recover (Mason and Rigg, 2019). For example, in coastal Louisiana in the United States, for example, United Houma tribal members are struggling with loss of ancestral lands and forced relocation in the face of rising sea levels due to climate change (Billiot and Parfait, 2019). In the Philippines, already a hotspot for natural disasters, hurricane frequency and intensity are increasing; in 2013, Typhoon Haiyan resulted in 6,000 fatalities, with millions of already impoverished Filipinos left without homes, basic water, and sanitation or livelihoods. In coastal Cameroon, gendered differences in employment, income, and access to credit have left female-headed households less able to protect their homes from severe weather than male-headed households (Molua, 2009). In Jamaica, rural water security is threatened by both climate change and governmental policies that prioritize water for the tourist economy (Hayward and Joseph, 2018). In Barbados, an invasive seaweed species, thought to be on the rise with increasing sea temperatures, is disrupting the local fishing industry on which many people depend for survival (Hayward and Joseph, 2018).

These human impacts of climate change include intersections across physical health, mental health, financial security, and social connection. Our mixed methods research (Mason, Ellis, and Hathaway, 2017; Mason et al., 2018) into people's experiences with weather extremes—summer heat and extreme winter weather, both of which are projected to increase with climate change—in Knoxville, Tennessee, illustrates this. One resident of a mixed-income neighborhood described how many of her neighbors struggle with paying their energy bills, sometimes foregoing air conditioning or heating even though they need it or would like to use it:

> There's several people . . . in this neighborhood, they have a hard time, so they ration themselves [with energy use]. Because . . . they're on a fixed income . . . and a lot of them fall into the category of "I've got just enough that I can't get help, but not enough that I can be comfortable."

She also expressed particular concern about older adults in her neighborhood, who may jeopardize health as they struggle to pay their utility bills. Meanwhile, other residents described how social isolation during winter extremes can affect their mental health, such as depression from having to stay indoors. Indeed, in our survey of lower- and moderate-income households in Knoxville, we found that at least two-thirds of participants reported some kind of impact to their physical health from weather extremes, over half reported a mental health impact, and over two-thirds reported a financial impact.

Underlying Causes

Climate change is caused by human activity—the production of greenhouse gas emissions released into the atmosphere and which have a "blanket" effect around our planet. Globally, there is tremendous inequity in which countries have contributed most to climate change (primarily higher-income countries), which will be impacted the most and which will be the least able to recover as quickly or at all (lower- and middle-income countries) (Mason and Rigg, 2019). Through international efforts such as the United Nations Framework Convention on Climate Change, there are global discussions of attempting to address, if not remedy, this disparity by having countries that emit more greenhouse gases help finance adaptation efforts in countries with lower emissions (Intergovernmental Panel on Climate Change, 2014b).

Meanwhile, within countries, regions, and communities, there are great inequities in who is and will be impacted by climate change. The concept of vulnerability is regularly used to analyze these inequities, and an integrated, three-part approach to conceptualizing the concept typically includes the following (Adger, 2006; Gallopín, 2006):

1. *Exposure* or the degree and duration of the system's direct contact with a hazard,
2. *Sensitivity* or the degree of change the system will experience if exposed, and
3. *Adaptive capacity* or the ability of the system to absorb or recover from change.

With each component, we can consider how structural systems might have created the underlying inequity. Although exposure to some hazards (e.g., earthquakes, unrelated to climate change) might be indiscriminate, in other cases, greater exposure results from legacies of racial or economic discrimination, such as African American communities in the southeastern United States often being relegated to former swampland post–Civil War and thus still subject to greater flood exposure than other communities today (e.g., Morse, 2008). Sensitivity is often applied to understanding some groups' greater degree of impact than others, perhaps for biological reasons (such as children or older adults and their inherent illness susceptibilities) or for cultural reasons (such as gendered roles and responsibilities that may disadvantage women and girls). Adaptive capacity, meanwhile, can often be understood from an assets or capitals framework, as previously mentioned, which in a system or society has greater or more expedient access to the resources needed to recover from the human impacts of climate change. Examples here are numerous and especially privilege people with higher incomes, access to credit, and the social or political capital to advocate for investment in their communities or their own households.

As awareness of climate change as an environmental justice issue—increasingly called "climate justice" (e.g., Schlosberg and Collins, 2014)—continues to emerge, it is important to remember that climate change is not the underlying cause of inequality per se. Rather, it can and should be seen as a potentially devastating threat multiplier, one that exacerbates already deeply rooted inequities in society. As Margaret Alston, a prolific social work scholar on climate change, writes,

> those most vulnerable and therefore most affected tend to be living in poverty, in unstable conditions, with limited livelihood options,

existing food and water security issues, poor services and supports and low levels of political power. Implying that climate change causes these problems may be politically expedient, but is factually incorrect. However, climate change adds a significant, and sometimes overwhelming, additional burden to vulnerable populations across the world. (2015: 356)

An Agenda for Social Work

As social workers, once we call attention to a deeply inequitable problem, and once we have sought to understand it, we must also work to try and solve it. For our profession, three ways forward on achieving environmental justice are conducting meaningful research, training social workers, and influencing policy change.

Conducting Meaningful Research

As an evidence-based profession, empirical research is foundational to successful intervention. Both a scoping review (Mason et al., 2017) and scientometric analysis (Krings et al., 2018) found that the professional research on issues at the nexus of society and the environment is increasing. Although not necessarily outpacing social work research on other critical areas of the human condition, there has still been promising growth in studies of environmental issues as social problems and that call attention to socioeconomic disparities. At the same time, this research has (1) rarely focused on deep analysis of underlying causes of the disparities observed; (2) primarily been conducted in the United States, Canada, or select Asian countries; and (3) to date, generated few empirically based implications for practice. A notable exception is social work research on response and recovery to natural disasters. Key recommendations of the scoping review (Mason et al., 2017) are to diversify where and when (e.g., not just postevent or postdisaster and not just cross-sectionally) new research is conducted, seek to understand underlying causes, use more rigorous research methods, and ask questions and design studies that can inform evidence-based interventions.

For meaningful research in this area—research that has application and impact on achieving environmental justice—community-engaged, locally focused research is key and is a way to conduct research that social work excels in relative to many other disciplines. As the previous examples of outdoor air pollution, household water insecurity, and climate change exemplify, environmental justice problems are deeply rooted in both broader structural forces and local social, economic, political, and environmental conditions. Context matters tremendously for understanding environmental justice problems and thus for solving them. Over the last several years, both the U.S. Environmental Protection Agency and National Institutes of Health have invested in community-based participatory research (CBPR) and other kinds of university-community partnerships to address environmental health and environmental justice. Social work research should pursue these funding mechanisms, conduct longitudinal and community-partnered research to understand and solve environmental justice problems locally, and then disseminate research more widely (beyond solely academic outlets) to translate local research into the broader public and policy arena.

Another direction for social work research on environmental justice is to pursue transdisciplinary science with other disciplines. The diversity of disciplines to partner with on these issues is vast, including engineering, climatology, geography, public health, nursing, psychology, philosophy, nutrition, agricultural extension, and more. Social work skills of team-building, collaboration, systems thinking, and conflict resolution are vital to the success of transdisciplinary teams, as are our professional values such as social justice, dignity and worth of the person, and importance of human relationships. Since social work scholarship is still little known by many of these disciplines, transdisciplinary science also provides an opportunity to further elevate the profession.

What would examples of this kind of research look like? Felicia Mitchell worked in partnership with American Indian tribal members to understand water insecurity and reservation life using a CBPR approach. As she writes on practical implications of the work, "the study's findings . . . support the tribe in their legal and political activities to address water concerns in their community," (2018: 286). In Knoxville, Tennessee, findings from our survey (Mason et al., 2018) that deliberately focused on lower- and moderate-income residents—and conducted by a social work, engineering, and climatology collaboration—were used by the City Sustainability Officer to inform an updated hazard mitigation plan. In their work on food security, Michelle Kaiser and colleagues (2016) have built successful, transdisciplinary teams and developed a multiyear community partnership to conduct food mapping, promote and study urban community gardening, and connect her research with service-learning opportunities for students.

Training Social Workers

With environmental justice as a relatively new area for social work practice, there is a need to train both current and future social workers in how to understand and address such problems across the micro, mezzo, and macro spectrum. For training future social workers, in the United States, CSWE's (2015) inclusion of environmental justice in its core competencies is noteworthy. As many social work programs strive to address these competencies, CSWE's Committee on Environmental Justice has been collating teaching resources and conducting workshops to infuse these topics across the social work curriculum. In addition, social work scholars have written about modules or case studies they have used to teach about environmental justice, such as examining climate change in a Contemporary Debates in Social Work Practice course or considering indigenous groups' experiences with environmental injustice in a unit Responding to Trauma, Grief, and Loss (Boddy, Macfarlane, and Greenslade, 2018).

A demand for hands-on environmental problem-solving, through service-learning courses and field placements, is also on the rise among future social workers. Course-based examples of how to provide this are Washington University's Sustainability Exchange and Interdisciplinary Environmental Law Clinic. Both bring diverse teams of students together to address real world environmental issues, such as a citywide greenhouse gas inventory, a sustainable transportation analysis, and regional environmental health concerns. Potential field placements for social work students interested in environmental justice include city or county sustainability offices, nonprofits that focus on energy efficiency for low-income residents, urban gardening collectives, and clean water or other environmental advocacy organizations. As another example, some social work programs have taken on department- or school-wide efforts to respond to environmentally unjust, natural disasters in their communities, such as posthurricane recovery.

For training current social workers, we need efforts that continue to raise awareness of the natural and built environments as part of our fundamental person-in-environment perspective, and continuing education in hands-on, practical ways to address environmental injustices with individuals and families, groups, and communities or larger-scale organizations. Surveys of current practitioners have examined their environmental awareness and integration of environmental issues in their practice. In a 2013 survey of National Association of Social Work (NASW) members (Shaw, 2013), over two-thirds had no social work training in environmental content, but 90 percent thought it should be provided. When conducting a client assessment, 13 percent of respondents said they assess pollution and 22 percent reported doing so for clean water, compared to much higher rates for assessing health care (82 percent), violence in the home (78 percent), and medications (58 percent). In a 2015 survey (Nesmith and Smyth, 2015), social workers saw food deserts, unsafe places to play, weather extremes and natural disasters, and air pollution as "the most critical environmental hazards" (p. 492) for their clients, but also agreed that they themselves had inadequate training from their social work programs to address these problems.

To reach current social workers, social work association chapters (such as NASW and its state and city chapters in the United States) can provide continuing education webinars or in-person trainings that bring together both social work scholars of environmental justice and practitioners from the field. Postcertificate programs (such as ones focused on political advocacy, trauma-informed care, or special populations such as older adults) can include modules on environmental justice and practice. Doctorate of Social Work programs, which tend to focus on advanced clinical practice or leadership, continue to grow and can explicitly infuse environmental justice training for advanced practitioners as well.

Influencing Policy Change

With the underlying causes of environmental injustice rooted in structural inequalities and historically or currently discriminatory policies, achievement of environmental justice will be elusive without significant policy change across local, state, and national levels. Social work is experiencing a resurgence of interest and commitment to macro social work practice, which includes explicit attention to policy advocacy. With what often feels like another environmental crisis in the news at every turn, the time for social work to pursue policy change for environmental justice is now.

What specific policy changes are needed? With the scope of environmental justice wide, and the number of topics that fall under this umbrella many, the list is long. In addition, as previously emphasized, contextual factors must be considered—whether for conducting research that informs policy, crafting policy language, or organizing practitioners and the public in advocacy efforts. For just the three examples described in this chapter (outdoor air pollution, household water insecurity, and climate change), Table 10.1 provides a sampling of policies to pursue at different scales. Not intended to be comprehensive, these examples are meant to illustrate some of the potential for social work to pursue policy action and change in these areas.

To be effective policy advocates, social work must think strategically about partnerships, such as with NASW and its chapters, the Congressional Research Institute for Social Work and Policy, and the National Association for the Advancement of Colored People's Environmental and Climate Justice Initiative. In addition, social work should also anticipate and prevent unintended, harmful consequences for the communities we work with (i.e., the greening of neighborhoods that leads to gentrification; Wolch, Byrne, and Newell, 2014) as environmental justice is pursued.

Table 10.1. **Policy Changes to Pursue**

Environmental Justice Problem	*Sample Policy Change*
Outdoor air pollution	• Local development that invests equitably in public transportation and walkable communities to decrease local automobile pollution • State policies that address inequitable access to health care, such as Medicaid expansion related to the Affordable Care Act in the United States to address the need for respiratory health care among vulnerable groups • National creation of outdoor air pollution standards, if nonexistent
Household water insecurity	• Local utility policies that make household connection to piped water affordable or equally accessible • State enforcement of clean water policy violations • National creation of clean water policies, if nonexistent
Climate change	• Local adaptation and resilience planning that engages and considers the view of marginalized groups • State policy that prevents utility companies from disconnecting clients for financial reasons during life-threatening weather extremes • National policies that invest in clean and renewable energy, energy efficiency, and also reduced energy consumption

Conclusion

Back in Montgomery Village, I speak with Charles on the sidewalk near the Boys and Girls Club. We look up at a weather monitor that our research team installed on an electric pole. The monitor tracks local temperature to look at whether neighborhoods like Montgomery Village experience an urban heat island effect. When we first installed the monitor, some residents asked if it was a camera, joking that it might be a "good thing" if it could help fight drugs or crime in the neighborhood. But talking with Charles about life in Montgomery Village and specifically about environmental issues like summer heat, air pollution, and green space, he expressed another sentiment about our research, "Made me thrilled. . . . Because some people don't even come around and ask about that. . . . This is the first time I've ever seen it. . . . When you're talking to somebody, it ain't all about crime and drugs and all that."

To ensure livable lives for Charles—and millions of people globally—social work must urgently pursue and achieve environmental justice. We must learn from and with people about how and why environmental injustice affects their lives and use that knowledge to develop solutions that address underlying inequities. We must train current and new social workers to see the larger environment as an essential part of the fabric of people's lives and then how to effectively intervene with this larger context in mind. Finally, we must achieve major policy change to protect both people and the planet. By doing so, we begin to ensure a safe and healthy home for generations to come, which is a cornerstone for livable lives.

References

Adams, E. A. 2018. "Thirsty Slums in African Cities: Household Water Insecurity in Urban Informal Settlements of Lilongwe, Malawi." *International Journal of Water Resources Development*, 34, 869–887.

Adger, W. N. 2006. "Vulnerability." *Global Environmental Change*, 16(3), 268–281.

Agyeman, J., D. Schlosberg, L. Craven, and C. Matthews. 2016. "Trends and Directions in Environmental Justice: From Inequity to Everyday Life, Community, and Just Sustainabilities." *Annual Review of Environment and Resources*, 41, 321–340.

Alston, M. 2015. "Social Work, Climate Change and Global Cooperation." *International Social Work*, 58, 355–363.

Anderson, J. O., J. G. Thundiyil, and A. Stolbach. 2012. "Clearing the Air: A Review of the Effects of Particulate Matter Air Pollution on Human Health." *Journal of Medical Toxicology*, 8, 166–175.

Arcipowski, E., J. Schwartz, L. Davenport, M. Hayes, and T. Nolan. 2017. "Clean Water, Clean Life: Promoting Healthier, Accessible Water in Rural Appalachia." *Journal of Contemporary Water Research & Education*, 161, 1–18.

Arku, F. S., and C. Arku. 2010. "I Cannot Drink Water on an Empty Stomach: A Gender Perspective on Living with Drought." *Gender and Development*, 18, 115–124.

Billiot, S., and J. Parfait. 2019. "Reclaiming Land: Adaptation Activities and Global Environmental Change Challenges Within Indigenous Communities." *People and Climate Change: Vulnerability, Adaptation, and Social Justice*. Edited by L. R. Mason and J. Rigg. New York: Oxford University Press, pp. 108–121.

Boddy, J., S. Macfarlane, and L. Greenslade. 2018. "Social Work and the Natural Environment: Embedding Content across Curricula." *Australian Social Work*, 71, 367–375.

Bradley, D. J., and J. Bartram. 2013. "Domestic Water and Sanitation as Water Security: Monitoring, Concepts and Strategy." *Philosophical Transactions of the Royal Society A*, 371, 20120420.

Coates, J., and M. Gray. 2012. "The Environment and Social Work: An Overview and Introduction." *International Journal of Social Welfare*, 21, 230–238.

Council on Social Work Education. 2015. *2015 Educational Policy and Accreditation Standards for Baccalaureate and Master's Social Work Programs*. Alexandria, VA: Author.

Driver, A., C. Mehdizadeh, S. Bara-Garcia, C. Bodenreider, J. Lewis, and S. Wilson. 2019. "Utilization of the Maryland Environmental Justice Screening Tool: A Bladensburg, Maryland Case Study." *International Journal of Environmental Research and Public Health*, 16, 348.

Enders, C., D. Pearson, K. Harley, and K. Ebisu. 2019. "Exposure to Coarse Particulate Matter During Gestation and Term Low Birthweight in California: Variation in Exposure and Risk Across Region and Socioeconomic Subgroup." *Science of the Total Environment*, 653, 1435–1444.

Gallopín, G. C. 2006. "Linkages between Vulnerability, Resilience, and Adaptive Capacity." *Global Environmental Change*, 16(3), 293–303.

Hawken, P. 2007. *Blessed Unrest.* New York: Viking Penguin.

Hayward, R. A., and D. D. Joseph. 2018. "Social Work Perspectives on Climate Change and Vulnerable Populations in the Caribbean: Environmental Justice and Health." *Environmental Justice*, 11, 192–197.

Intergovernmental Panel on Climate Change. 2014a. "Climate Change 2014: Impacts, Adaptation, and Vulnerability." Retrieved from https://www.ipcc.ch/report/ar5/wg2/

Intergovernmental Panel on Climate Change. 2014b. "Climate Change 2014: Synthesis Report." Retrieved from https://www.ipcc.ch/report/ar5/syr/

Intergovernmental Panel on Climate Change. 2018. "Global Warming of 1.5° Celsius: Summary for Policymakers." Retrieved from https://report.ipcc.ch/sr15/pdf/sr15_spm_final.pdf

Jepson, W., and E. Vandewalle. 2016. "Household Water Insecurity in the Global North: A Study of Rural and Periurban Settlements on the Texas–Mexico Border." *The Professional Geographer*, 68, 66–81.

Jepson, W. E., A. Wutich, S. M. Colllins, G. O. Boateng, and S. L. Young. 2017. "Progress in Household Water Insecurity Metrics: A Cross-Disciplinary Approach." *Wiley Interdisciplinary Reviews: Water*, 4, e1214.

Kaiser, M. L., C. Rogers, M. D. Hand, C. Hoy, and N. Stanich. 2016. "Finding Our Direction: The Process of Building A Community-University Food Mapping Team." *Journal of Community Engagement & Scholarship*, 9, 19–33.

Klinenberg E. 2002. *Heat Wave: A Social Autopsy of Disaster in Chicago.* Chicago: University of Chicago Press.

Krings, A., D. Kornberg, and E. Lane. 2018. "Organizing Under Austerity: How Residents' Concerns Became the Flint Water Crisis." *Critical Sociology*, 45, 583–597.

Krings, A., B. G. Victor, J. Mathias, and B. E. Perron. 2018. "Environmental Social Work in the Disciplinary Literature, 1991–2015." *International Social Work*. Online Ahead of Publication. doi: 0020872818788397.

Kumar, P., L. Morawska, C. Martani, G. Biskos, M. Neophytou, S. Di Sabatino, M. Bell, L. Norford, and R. Britter. 2015. "The Rise of Low-Cost Sensing for Managing Air Pollution in Cities." *Environment International*, 75, 199–205.

Mason, L. R. 2014. "Examining Relationships Between Household Resources and Water Security in an Urban Philippine Community." *Journal of the Society for Social Work and Research*, 5, 489–512.

Mason, L. R. 2015. "Beyond Improved Access: Seasonal and Multidimensional Water Security in Urban Philippines." *Global Social Welfare*, 2, 119–128.

Mason, L. R., K. N. Ellis, and J. M. Hathaway. 2017. "Experiences of Urban Environmental Conditions in Socially and Economically Diverse Neighborhoods." *Journal of Community Practice*, 25, 48–67.

Mason, L. R., J. Erwin, A. Brown, K. N. Ellis, and J. M. Hathaway. 2018. "Health Impacts of Extreme Weather Events: Exploring Protective Factors with a Capitals Framework." *Journal of Evidence-Informed Social Work*, 15, 579–593.

Mason, L. R., M. K. Shires, C. Arwood, and A. Borst. 2017. "Social Work Research and Global Environmental Change." *Journal of the Society for Social Work and Research*, 8, 645–672.

Mason, L. R., and J. Rigg. eds. 2019. *People and Climate Change: Vulnerability, Adaptation, and Social Justice*. New York: Oxford University Press.

McDonald, R. I., P. Green, D. Balk, B. M. Fekete, C. Revenga, M. Todd, and M. Montgomery. 2011. "Urban Growth, Climate Change, and Freshwater Availability." *Proceedings of the National Academies of Sciences*, 108, 6312–6317.

McGurty, M. M. 1997. "From NIMBY to Civil Rights: The Origins of the Environmental Justice Movement." *Environmental History*, 2, 301–323.

Mitchell, F. M. 2018 "'Water Is Life': Using Photovoice to Document American Indian Perspectives on Water and Health." *Social Work Research*, 42, 277–289.

Mohai, P., D. Pellow, and J. T. Roberts. 2009. "Environmental Justice." *Annual Review of Environment and Resources*, 34, 405–430.

Mohai, P., and R. Saha. 2015. "Which Came First, People or Pollution? Assessing the Disparate Siting and Post-Siting Demographic Change Hypotheses of Environmental Injustice." *Environmental Research Letters*, 10, 115008.

Molua, E. L. 2009. "Accommodation of Climate Change in Coastal Areas of Cameroon: Selection of Household-Level Protection Options." *Mitigation & Adaptation Strategies for Global Change*, 14, 721–735.

Morse, R. 2008. *Environmental Justice Through the Eye of Hurricane Katrina*. Washington, DC: Joint Center for Political and Economic Studies, Health Policy Institute.

Nesmith, A., and N. Smyth. 2015. "Environmental Justice and Social Work Education: Social Workers' Professional Perspectives." *Social Work Education*, 34, 484–501.

Ribot, J. 2010. "Vulnerability Does Not Fall from the Sky: Toward Multiscale, Pro-Poor Climate Policy. *Social Dimensions of Climate Change: Equity and Vulnerability in a Warming World*. Edited by R. Mearns and A. Norton. Washington, DC: World Bank, pp. 47–74.

Schlosberg, D., and L. B. Collins. 2014. "From Environmental to Climate Justice: Climate Change and the Discourse of Environmental Justice." *Wiley Interdisciplinary Reviews: Climate Change*, 5, 359–374.

Shaw, T. V. 2013. "Is Social Work a Green Profession? An Examination of Environmental Beliefs." *Journal of Social Work*, 13, 3–29.

Tessum, C. W., J. S. Apte, A. L. Goodkind, N. Z. Muller, K. A. Mullins, D. A. Paolella, S. Polasky, N. P. Springer, S. K. Thakrar, J. D. Marshall, and J. D. Hill. 2019. "Inequity in Consumption of Goods and Services Adds to Racial–Ethnic Disparities in Air Pollution Exposure." *Proceedings of the National Academy of Sciences*, 116, 6001–6006.

UNICEF and World Health Organization. 2012. *Progress on Drinking Water and Sanitation: 2012 Update*. New York: WHO/UNICEF Joint Monitoring Programme for Water Supply and Sanitation.

UNESCO. 2019. *Leaving No One Behind: Executive Summary*. Paris: Author.

U.S. Environmental Protection Agency. 2019. "Environmental Justice." Retrieved from https://www.epa.gov/environmentaljustice

Wolch, J. R., J. Byrne, and J. P. Newell. 2014. "Urban Green Space, Public Health, and Environmental Justice: The Challenge of Making Cities 'Just Green Enough.'" Landscape and Urban Planning, 125, 234–244.

World Health Organization. 2016. *Ambient Air Pollution: A Global Assessment of Exposure and Burden of Disease*. Geneva: Author.

Wutich, A. A. 2009. "Intrahousehold Disparities in Women and Men's Experiences of Water Insecurity and Emotional Distress in Urban Bolivia." *Medical Anthropology Quarterly*, 23, 436–454.

11

Engaging Older Adults

SOJUNG PARK AND NANCY MORROW-HOWELL

The productive engagement of older adults is an emerging solution to the demands of aging populations around the globe. This engagement includes a wide array of activities ranging from working longer, to civic participation, to volunteer work (Morrow-Howell, Gonzales, Matz-Costa, and Greenfield, 2015). The premise of productive aging is that by engaging older adults in meaningful roles, society benefits through the contributions of these valued activities, and older adults themselves benefit, given that higher levels of well-being are created (e.g., increased financial, physical, psychological, and cognitive health). Indeed, productive engagement fosters livable lives for older adults via financial, health, and social pathways. Positive societal outcomes, including less reliance on public and private income support systems, increased intergenerational reciprocity, and more experienced labor supplies, have also been documented (Morrow-Howell and Greenfield, 2016). The productive engagement of older adults as workers, volunteers, and caregivers has been viewed as a virtuous cycle of health-producing engagement, for both the individuals and their communities.

Nevertheless, it is also the case that ageist attitudes, outdated social structures, and inadequate programs/policies lag behind the demographic shifts in populations. These have limited the potential of older adults to remain vitally involved in productive roles. Such social conditions, often based on the foundation of age segregation, lead to the exclusion of many people over the age of 60 or 65 years. Furthermore, the most economically and socially disadvantaged older adults are the most vulnerable to exclusion. Indeed, the concept of cumulative disadvantage across the life course highlights the fact that people who have struggled during their adulthood will be particularly disadvantaged in later life as they seek to work longer, participate in the civic life of their community, or provide vital assistance to family members in need (for an extended discussion of cumulative disadvantage, see Chapter 5 of this volume).

The motivation for focusing on productive engagement in later life is to ensure that the development and utilization of people's capacity is not unnecessarily cut short by social conditions that are out of step with the reality of longer lives. The desire for purpose, meaning, and reciprocity is universal and continues throughout the life course; yet, our societies have not made it possible for everyone to remain engaged in ongoing meaningful ways (Krause, 2003; Carstensen, 1992). Older adults are at risk of being underutilized in productive roles due to a lack of fit between community, organizational, and policy environments and individuals' physical, cognitive, and mental health abilities. Furthermore, a significant segment of the older adult population, usually the most disadvantaged in terms of health and socioeconomic status, has to date been largely excluded from efforts to ensure productive engagement.

In addition, older adults with low income and education have limited access to health care, transportation, and housing options, which provide the context for productive engagement. These conditions increase the risk for social isolation, which in turn can lead to a lack of meaningful social engagement and a loss of sense of purpose and well-being (Morrow-Howell and Gehlert, 2012; Taylor, Wang, and Morrow-Howell, 2018). Such older adults are often judged poorly for not contributing to society, and yet because of a lack of person/environment fit, they possess limited opportunities to contribute.

The ultimate goal of the research and practice discussed in this chapter is to facilitate more livable lives for the older population by ensuring that all older individuals have the opportunity to be engaged and productive to the extent they desire. This engagement is vital to the concept of livable lives as outlined in the introductory chapter. Perspectives on aging often posit that older individuals—even those who have limited resources and capability—can age optimally if environmental characteristics support them in ways that compensates for their limitations or lack of resources. To increase vulnerable older adults' productive engagement, the profession of social work should identify levels of need and resources for both the person and the environment through practice and applied research. The field itself can improve the capacities of individuals through policy innovations and other approaches. It can intentionally match individuals with organizational environments conducive to productive engagement. By finding an optimal fit between vulnerable older adults' needs and environmental resources, their productive engagement will be maximized, which in turn benefits society as a whole.

In this chapter, we focus on these issues and draw upon the person/environment fit framework to understand the underlying causes and potential ways to address older adults' exclusion from productive roles and lack of optimal outcomes (see Chapter 4 of this volume for a greater discussion of social exclusion). The person/environment fit perspective suggests that unique combinations of personal needs and resources, together with characteristics of their environment, determine an individual's adaptation (Lewin, 1936; Lawton and Nahemow, 1973). The "fit" between an individual's attributes (i.e., health needs, psychological resources, social supports), and the demands and/or resources of their shifting environments is critical in achieving positive outcomes (Lawton and Nahemow, 1973). A good fit between a person and his or her environment should lead to greater well-being than a less optimal fit (Thomése and Groenou, 2006). Guided by this perspective, we review a range of personal characteristics such as ill health, low income, and education that create vulnerabilities, which may prevent optimal engagement in productive activities (specifically work, volunteering, and caregiving). Environmental characteristics include organizational, community, and policy factors that facilitate and increase feasible opportunities for vulnerable older adults' productive aging.

The issue of facilitating the productive engagement of older adults has become a pressing challenge. With the near doubling between 2015 and 2050 of the world's older adult population proportion from 12 to 22 percent, the number of vulnerable older adults continues to increase (Administration on Aging, 2018). This is particularly the case in many high-economy countries such as Japan, Italy, Germany, and France, where the percentage of the population over the age of 65 will approach 40 percent in the years ahead. In the United States, 15 percent of the population is currently 65 years and older; by 2040, this will rise to over 22 percent. Further, the fastest growth is the 85 years and older age group; and the number of African Americans, Hispanic, American Indian/Native Alaskan, and Asian older adults is growing more quickly than non-Hispanic whites (Administration on Aging, 2018). These demographic realities reiterate the importance of focusing on later life in social work's efforts to ensure livable lives.

Finally, we should note that in the research literature there are no consistent definitions as to when older adulthood begins. In general, 65 years of age is often used in the U.S. context to identify the older population; but in studies of the workforce, people over the age 50 years are often considered older workers. Throughout our chapter, several different delineations of older adults will be used.

Causes of the Under-Engagement of Older Adults

The exclusion of older adults from productive roles of working and volunteering and the lack of facilitation of caregiving roles stem from a variety of factors, including ageist attitudes, outdated social structures, and inadequate programs/ policies that are inconsistent with the new demographic realities. We focus on the current state of participation of older adults in productive roles and discuss some factors that led to the under-engagement of older adults in working, volunteering, and caregiving activities.

Working

Increases in life expectancy have led to the reality that older adults often live 20 years beyond the traditional retirement age of 65. This longer period of separation from the workforce can lead to insufficient income as well as fewer sources of meaningful engagement and social connection. In response, the average age of retirement has increased over time and the percentage of the workforce over the age of 60 has grown (Berkman, Boersch-Supan, and Avendano, 2015). Older adults are both working longer and/or returning to the workforce in greater numbers. Working has been associated with improved economic status, decreased mortality, better mental health, and better cognitive function (Rohwedder and Willis, 2010; Schmitz, 2011). However, the nature of the work, attributes of the workplace, and the level of choice involved in retirement decisions affects those outcomes (Calvo, Haverstick, and Sass, 2009; Carolan, Gonzales, Lee and Harootyan, 2018).

Some of the challenges of remaining engaged in work are individual level factors, such as declining health and out-of-date skills. The problem for low-income and/or other vulnerable subgroups of older adults is often that employment opportunities are limited by a wide variety of factors, including lower levels of education, fewer skills, a lack of a job network, and negative stereotypes (Taylor and Geldhauser, 2007). In regards to barriers in the workplace, the physical demands of certain jobs, unaccommodating work spaces, and ageism were cited as reducing the possibility of working (Carolan et al, 2018). The adverse effects of neighborhood poverty have also been linked to systemic disparities in health and well-being. In poor neighborhoods, there are fewer job-related environmental resources such as stable housing and public transportation, while social networks tend to be more tenuous due to residents' limited education and/or work history (see Chapter 9 of this volume). Although the desire for a longer work life may be common, vulnerable older individuals are less likely to have job training and workforce development opportunities, due to cost, access, and ageist attitudes.

Volunteering

In 2015, 24 percent of adults over the age of 65 volunteered for an organization, which represents a drop in participation from younger cohorts. Rates also vary among older adults by ethnicity, with whites volunteering at higher rates than African Americans, Hispanics, and Asian older adults (Bureau of Labor Statistics, 2016). A large body of research documents that older adults with more education, higher incomes, better health, social integration, and religious involvement are more likely to volunteer (Morrow-Howell and Greenfield, 2016), and that low-resourced individuals are less likely to volunteer with formal organizations (Martinez et al., 2011; Sundeen, Raskoff, and Garcia, 2007; Warburton, Paynter, and Petriwskyj, 2007; Burr, Mutchler, and Caro, 2007). Older adults who are excluded from volunteer roles are deprived of the opportunity to receive the numerous benefits that have been associated with volunteering, including lower rates of mortality, enhanced well-being, higher levels of life satisfaction, and decreased physical dependency (Piliavin and Siegl, 2015; Guiney and Machado, 2017).

One explanation for lower rates of volunteering among older adults is the fact that they are disconnected from work and educational institutions that facilitate engagement. Older adults who have been marginalized in terms of employment and education early in life are also less likely to have established patterns of volunteering that continue in later life (Morrow-Howell and Greenfield, 2016). This reality highlights the prominent role of social organizations in engaging individuals in volunteer roles. Institutional arrangements regarding outreach, training, reimbursement for expenses, and ongoing support are important to ensure the involvement of lower-resources older adults (Tang, Choi, and Morrow-Howell, 2010). Organizational supports for volunteering, such as stipends and/or recognition for service, are shown to be more important for ethnic older adults (McBride et al., 2011). Vulnerable older adults who are unable to be actively engaged and cannot contribute to their communities and society are likely to experience greater feelings of social exclusion.

Caregiving

Family caregivers provide the majority of care for disabled and older adults in need of assistance. Given demographic changes, it is increasingly the case that there are more persons who need care and fewer family members to provide such care (Pavalko and Wolfe, 2015). Approximately 60 percent of caregivers are female; half of caregivers are over the age of 50 years, with 20 percent being over the age of 65. There are larger numbers of Hispanic, African American, and Asian caregivers than white caregivers. Older caregivers are less financially stable and have poorer health than their non-caregiving counterparts or younger caregivers. Approximately 60 percent of family caregivers are employed at a paying job, with half working full time (National Alliance for Caregiving and AARP, 2015).

An increasing need for informal, unpaid care, along with rising female labor market participation (Boushey, 2011; Ness, 2011), leaves middle-aged and older women faced with balancing work and family responsibilities. Women are more likely to reduce their hours or leave their formal jobs (Dentinger and Clarkberg, 2002; Pavalko and Artis, 1997), and unstable employment or early retirement may put them at a greater risk of poverty in later life (Colombo et al., 2011; Nepal et al., 2011; Schneider et al., 2013). Employed women, less educated workers, and first-generation immigrant caregivers were more likely to report that caregiving tasks led to negative employment outcomes such as the reduction of income, job loss, or leaving their job (Lahaie, Earle, and Heymann, 2012). Women disproportionately remain in low-wage jobs that offer few benefits and workplace protection (Hegewisch et al., 2010). Women in jobs with lower skills/status encounter the greatest difficulty in finding flexible work that can accommodate health and caregiving demands (Austen and Ong, 2013).

A large body of research has documented the negative outcomes of caregiving on financial, health, and emotional well-being (Hooyman, Kawamoto, and Kyak, 2017). Furthermore, the high psychological burden of caregiving caused by an imbalance between job and caregiving tasks is well-documented (Freedman, Cornman, and Carr, 2014; MetLife Mature Market Institute, 2011). The engagement of older adults in caregiving roles is increasingly important due to the aging of the population, yet too often caregivers face negative outcomes. Thus, the challenge is to optimize caregiving engagement through organizational and policy initiatives.

In sum, there are many reasons older adults are not optimally engaged as workers, volunteers, or caregivers. Barriers at the individual level, including low income and education, affect the potential for engagement. Environmental factors play a major role in determining levels of participation as well. Age-limited opportunities, outdated organizational arrangements, a scarcity of programs, and inadequate policies all pose barriers to productive engagement. In the remainder of this chapter, we focus on environmental supports that can be improved to optimize the productive engagement of vulnerable older adults at two points: (1) the organizational and policy level and (2) the neighborhood/community level.

Organizational and Policy Solutions

Promoting Employment

The idea of social enterprise is gaining momentum in many business sectors in the U.S. and global economies. Social enterprise is defined as an organization or venture within an organization that advances a social mission through market-based strategies, including earned income in direct exchange for a product, service, or privilege (Community Wealth Ventures, Social Enterprise Alliance, and Center for the Advancement of Social Entrepreneurship, 2010). Social enterprise's mission is to foster social change, care for underserved and disadvantaged populations, and return social benefits in the form of improving people's quality of life and building the capacity of a community (Morrow-Howell and Mui, 2014). Successful social enterprise can generate financial and psychosocial well-being for vulnerable individuals (e.g., people with disabilities, ex-offenders, and/or low-income women), but it can also create significant social change in the community (Austin, Stevenson, and Wei-Skillern, 2006; Morrow-Howell and Mui, 2014). In the United States, the number of social enterprises has grown steadily since the 1970s, with the most rapid growth occurring during the 1990s and early 2000s.

Notably, social enterprises were not necessarily targeted at vulnerable older adults. Nevertheless, the increase of social enterprise in community service organizations suggests that various subgroups of older people who have barriers to employment (e.g., those with disabilities and/or substance abuse problems, the homeless, etc.) may easily be included as potential workers. Outside of the United States, an example of social enterprises that explicitly target vulnerable older workers is found in Europe. For example, several countries in the European Union (Scotland, Sweden, Finland, and Northern Ireland) launched the Older People for Older People (O4O) project to strengthen the capacity of and provide benefits for vulnerable older individuals and their communities. Within this project, social enterprises have been created to produce services identified as needed by older individuals. The project has a particular focus on older adults in rural areas because such communities often face difficulties in providing services due to high costs along with the difficulties of recruiting and retaining staff (Northern Periphery Programme, 2013). The research findings from these projects demonstrated that the majority of new older employees had physical or emotional health issues and/or long-term unemployment or homelessness. While the specific business model varied substantially depending on existing community resources, key success factors were identified. These included taking a business-minded approach undergirded with an organizational structure (e.g., planning, management, shared workload), leadership, and political and financial support. In contrast, no large-scale social enterprises for vulnerable older adults in the United States exists. However, the importance of public and private partnerships and political commitments from local, state, and federal government has been emphasized in developing and expanding sustainable social enterprises (Social Enterprise Alliance, 2011).

The only federal job program for disadvantaged older adults in the United States is the Senior Community Service Employment Program (SCSEP), Title V of the Older American's Act. Through this program, part-time community service employment is provided to individuals aged 55 and older who are unemployed and with a household income below 125 percent of the federal poverty line. The program focuses on racial/ethnic minorities, those with limited English proficiency, individuals older than 60, and/or those with the greatest economic need. Community-based agencies such as local governments or nonprofit organizations serve as training sites for job-related training, such as job search assistance, computer skills, and employment counseling along with supportive services such as transportation assistance. Participants work in a variety of community-based nonprofit organizations and government agencies as nurse's aides, librarians, day care workers, and teacher's aides. The typical participant is a nonwhite woman in her 60s, who has a relatively low level of education and lives in a rural area. Approximately 20 percent have a disability, and 13 percent are veterans or spouses of veterans (National Council on Aging, 2017). Periodic evaluations have found both program participants and agencies to be very satisfied (Charter Oak Group, 2003, 2007). Participants added close to $9 million worth of work to their host agencies and communities, with an 89 percent return on investments in the program (Independent Sector, n.d.). In addition to the economic and social benefit of SCSEP to low-income older adults, it is important to consider its potential role in addressing racial/ethnic disparities. Among adults 55 and older, blacks and Hispanics have higher rates of unemployment than non-Hispanic whites, the largest disparity being between that of Hispanic men aged 55 to 64 and non-Hispanic white men of the same age (Johnson and Mommaerts, 2010). In 2006–2007, almost half of SCSEP participants were low-income, racial/ethnic minority individuals. Although program participants are a racially diverse group, a higher percentage of blacks, American Indians, and Pacific Islanders were enrolled in the program than their prevalence in the U.S. population. On the other hand, Asians and Hispanic were under-enrolled (Washko et al., 2011).

Findings regarding the racial/ethnic disparities in program enrollment and employment outcome in SCSEP provide important information to target areas for increased federal investment. Identification of policy target groups is particularly important when the financing of existing programs is uncertain amid the changing nature of the political landscape. At the time of writing, SCSEP is expected to be eliminated from the federal budget for the 2018 fiscal year. The future of the program is of grave concern since for millions of low-income older adults, working is not a choice but an essential prerequisite for a livable life.

Promoting Volunteering

From the person/environment perspective, vulnerable low-income older adults are able to actively engage in volunteering when programs provide a good match between personal capabilities and available resources in the community. For example, the Experience Corps program relies heavily on community infrastructure (i.e., schools) to recruit and retain older volunteers. Experience Corps was first launched as a pilot in 1996 in five U.S. cities as a community-based volunteer program to promote health among older adults. The program provides $200 per month to help older adults living on modest fixed incomes cover their bus fare and other expenses of volunteering. Volunteers work 15 hours per week as tutors at public elementary schools for kindergarten to third-grade students. The program was later expanded to 23 cities. This program may be the most robustly studied volunteer program (Carr, Fried, and Rowe, 2015). Research has found that high-intensity volunteering activities combined with systematic training and a stipend were successful in recruiting and retaining diverse groups of older adults. In addition, it has generated robust benefits including higher levels of social integration and improved physical and mental health (Hong et al., 2008; Carr et al., 2015).

Research findings demonstrated that the key factor for facilitating full engagement in volunteering depends on finding the right fit between an individual's skills and experiences and the resources of their community. To increase vulnerable older adult volunteer opportunities and participation, we can more intentionally match individuals with organizational environments conducive to volunteering. For example, volunteer sites and senior housing organizations in low-income communities can intentionally match community-dwelling and senior-housing residents' abilities with needed tasks to increase productive engagement and contribute to a sense of purpose. They can also provide or arrange various community-based social and health services to meet residents' evolving needs so that volunteer engagement can be extended. These housing environments help provide older adults with appropriate volunteering opportunities in the community by utilizing transportation services and various training opportunities. Access to volunteer sites can be improved through street and sidewalk designs that facilitate use by older adults with mobility, hearing, vision, and cognitive impairments. This would include the provision of elements such as unobstructed sidewalks with even surfaces, auditory and visual crosswalk signals, and clear way-finding signs.

Limited research on senior housing environments has indicated that low-income older adults living in senior housing were likely to have better outcomes in terms of health and well-being and also were more likely to volunteer compared to their peers in conventional homes (Park, Kim, and Han, 2018; Park at al., 2017; Park, Kim, and Cho, 2017). With long-term care facilities, where highly centralized and controlled management is a norm for the sake of safety of patients, organizational schemes to encourage volunteering of residents are possible. Limited research has shown increased autonomy and well-being of long-term care residents involved in volunteering activities, such as mentoring students taking English as a second language (Yuen-Tsang and Wang, 2008) or creating flower arrangement and greeting cards for local hospice patients (Cipriani et al., 2010).

The federal government supports several volunteer programs. Among them, two well-known programs target low-income older people—the Foster Grandparent Program and Senior Companion Program. Originally created in mid-1960s and early 1970s, they have been administered since 1993 by the Corporation for National and Community Service (CNCS, 2017), the federal agency that improves lives, strengthens communities, and fosters civic engagement through service and volunteering. These programs target adults 55 and older with incomes at or below 200 percent of the poverty line. In the Foster Grandparent Program, volunteers work as tutors and mentors to children and youth with special needs, serving 15 to 40 hours a week in schools, hospitals, drug treatment centers, correctional institutions, and children's centers (CNCS, 2017). Within the Senior Companion Program, volunteers help frail seniors and other adults maintain independence, usually in the client's own home. Senior Companions work 15 to 40 hours a week to provide physical and emotional assistance to those who are frail, homebound, and live alone. In 2017, there were 182 senior companion projects across the nation. The majority of the Senior Companions are women (83 percent); approximately 40 percent of the volunteers are from minority groups (Wacker and Roberto, 2018). In both programs, volunteers receive a stipend of $2.65 an hour and other benefits including monthly training, reimbursement for transportation, and meals while on duty.

Despite the long history of these programs, there is fairly limited information about their effectiveness in meeting the service needs of the community and benefiting the older volunteers. Tan and colleagues (2016) examined the programs by comparing national data on program participants to a sample of older adults from the nationally representative Health and Retirement Study. They found that the two programs engaged racial/ethnically diverse groups of older volunteers: Foster Grandparent Program (FGP) and Senior Companion Program participants were 42 percent and 38 percent African American (non-Latino), respectively, compared with 26 percent of Health and Retirement Study volunteers (in other programs) and 22 percent of nonvolunteers. The two programs were also able to engage individuals with mobility limitations, suggesting that these programs can facilitate low-income volunteers with physical disabilities (Tan et al., 2016). Reflecting the importance of engaging older minorities, the CNCS committed $2.65 million in new Senior Corps grants to federally recognized Indian tribes and tribal organizations for the needs in Native American communities (Wacker and Roberto, 2018).

One notable subgroup in the inclusive policy efforts for productive engagement is LGBT older adults. Many LGBT aging organizations were founded and built to a significant degree by LGBT older adults. Recognizing the value of sustaining and building such involvement, a handful of LGBT groups have launched programs to formally encourage civic engagement among older adults. Several non-LGBT organizations have likewise made targeted efforts to involve LGBT older adults as volunteers in initiatives that reach beyond the LGBT community. For example, the Leadership Academy of Lavender Seniors of the East Bay in San Leandro, California, provides an annual day-long training on how older adults can get involved in local government advisory boards. Existing national programs need to reach out and include LGBT elders, who may feel they would not be welcome (Movement Advancement Project and Services and Advocacy for Gay, Lesbian, Bisexual and Transgender Elders, 2010). To achieve their full potential, these initiatives must provide a culturally competent welcome to LGBT elders, whose experience, wisdom, and skills stand to benefit not only the LGBT community but also the community as a whole (Grant, 2010).

Supporting Caregivers

Combining care and work is especially difficult for those who already lack adequate financial resources and for whom welfare supports are not available or accessible (Sarasa, 2008; Saraceno, 2010). Existing evidence on caregiving and work has centered around the importance of workplace flexibility that can accommodate caregiving responsibilities (Berecki et al., 2007; Carney, 2009; Larsen, 2010). Yet women disproportionately work in low-wage jobs that offer few benefits and workplace protections (Hegewisch et al., 2010), and women in jobs with lower skills/status encounter the greatest difficulty with inflexible arrangements, suggesting an important role for paid sick leave and holiday leave in boosting employment retention (Austen and Ong, 2013).

The United States is the only advanced industrialized country without a national law providing family caregivers with paid sick leave. The Family and Medical Leave Act (FMLA) ensures job protection and health benefits when workers take family and medical leave. Although job protection is the defining feature of this policy, it covers only certain employees and their spouse, parents, and children with serious health conditions. Only 59 percent of the workforce is covered, and among those eligible, the most common reason for not taking leave was the inability to forego pay (Klerman, Daley, and Pozniak, 2012). A majority of family caregivers are working women and those with lower levels of education (Estes and Williams, 2013). Consequently, they are less likely to have paid sick leave and supportive resources, especially since low-wage employees are more likely to work for employers not covered by the FMLA. In taking the leave, many would face financial burdens, a reduction of income, and negative employment consequences.

A paid family leave (PFL) program has been fully implemented in three states—California, New Jersey, and Rhode Island. In these states, family caregivers can take paid leave for up to six weeks each year. In 2004, California was the first state to implement the program. The program provides up to six weeks of compensation based on a percentage of the individual's weekly pay capped at $987 per week. Unlike FMLA, almost all private sector workers are eligible and wage replacement is 55 percent, up to a ceiling based on the state's average weekly wage. In 2009, New Jersey implemented a similar paid leave program. Washington State also passed a more limited paid leave programs in 2012. Currently, there are ongoing efforts at both the state and federal levels to enact similar laws (Baum and Ruhm, 2016).

There is little direct empirical evidence on the effects of paid leave programs on employment outcomes among middle-aged female caregivers. Studies of paid sick leave or other employee benefits, however, provide relevant insights into the potential benefits of programs like California Paid Family Leave. One study with a sample of women caring for an ill or disabled family member found a significant positive difference in the likelihood of staying in the labor force associated with access to paid sick leave or vacation leave (Pavalko and Henderson, 2006). Using Current Population Survey data from 1999 to 2010, Rossin-Slater, Ruhm, and Waldfogel (2013) examined the effect of accessibility to PFL in California on employment outcomes among mothers following childbirth. They found that with access to PFL, mothers with infants were more likely to use maternity leave. A similar study (Baum and Ruhm, 2016) also found positive midterm employment outcomes from the California Paid Family Leave. Under the program, mothers were 18 percent more likely to be working a year after the birth and to work more hours and earn higher wages. Despite evidence of the positive effect among mothers on employment outcomes, this knowledge cannot necessarily be generalized to older family caregivers experiencing caregiving squeeze.

Given the socioeconomic disparity in access to the Family Medical Leave Act and California Paid Family Leave, it is important to examine the potential benefits of PFL for less advantaged family caregivers. Rossin-Slater et al (2013) found a particularly large growth in the use of paid leave among less advantaged mothers, suggesting the program had an effect for disadvantaged workers. Similarly, Hill (2013) found that the positive effects of paid sick leave on job stability were strongest for workers without paid vacation leave. To date, there is little empirical knowledge about the effect of PFL on employment outcomes among family caregivers with lower socioeconomic status. As a rare example, Kang et al. (2018) examined the effect of the PFL program in California on employment among older female caregivers using multiple years (2000–2014) of the Current Population Survey. The findings showed that even without job protection features, PFL may increase employment stability by allowing family caregiver workers to accumulate human capital in general. Importantly, this study did not find any positive effect of California's PFL for those with less education and among the poor.

Neighborhood/Community Level Solutions

Developing age-friendly environments that meet the needs of older people is a recent social policy focus in many countries because they recognize that adaptive, responsive environments may help older adults to productively engage in the community and receive health and well-being benefits (Buffel, Phillipson, and Scharf, 2012). An age-friendly environment generally refers to a community in which older adults are valued, involved, and supported (Alley et al., 2007). From the person/environment fit perspective, an age-friendly environment refers to a community that has goodness of fit between resources and their older residents' needs and resources (Menec et al., 2011; Keating, Eales, and Phillips, 2013). As a multidimensional concept, an age-friendly environment includes the physical and social infrastructure that supports daily activities through transportation; local amenities; safe and accessible housing, neighborhoods, and communities; access to social support; and opportunities to engage in meaningful activities (Plouffe and Kalache, 2011; Scharlach and Lehning, 2013). During the past decade, a number of government and international organizations have launched age-friendly initiatives in the United States and across the world.

The most well-known initiative is the World Health Organization's (WHO, 2007, 2010) age-friendly Cities and Communities. This initiative targets eight areas of livability—outdoor space and buildings; transportation; housing; social participation; respect and social inclusion; civic participation and employment; communication and information; and community and health services. In the United States, more than 40 towns, cities, and counties enrolled in age-friendly networks (AARP, 2015). Portland, Oregon, became the first city in the United States to be accepted into the WHO Global Network of Age-Friendly Cities project in 2010. The Age-Friendly Portland initiative is coordinated by the Institute on Aging at Portland State University. What is unique about the Portland initiative is that it uses a city–university–community model that takes advantage of existing relationships between the institute and local community and government agencies in developing and updating the initiatives across ten domains adapted from the checklist of the WHO initiative (Neal, DeLaTorre, and Carder, 2014). Age-Friendly Portland is working to improve the city's public transportation system for older adults and individuals with disabilities, focusing on increasing services during nights and weekends and improving safety measures (Scharlach and Lehning, 2016).

Another prominent example is Age-Friendly Philadelphia, launched in 2009 by the nonprofit Philadelphia Corporation for Aging. Building on the U.S. Environmental Protection Agency's (EPA) Aging Initiative, Age-Friendly Philadelphia focused on four areas: social capital, flexible and accessible housing, mobility, and eating healthy (Clark and Glicksman, 2012). Examples of Philadelphia's aging-friendly initiative include a multisector collaboration among government and nongovernmental organizations to revise the city's zoning codes to include accessible dwelling units (Clark and Glicksman, 2012).

Common across these various programs/initiatives is an emphasis on older people's participation, empowering them, and cultivating their capacities to enhance their neighborhoods and communities (Lui et al., 2009). Despite expanding interest in and adoption of an age-friendly environment as part of aging policy, some concerns have been noted. From the person/environment fit perspective, the emphasis on social participation and inclusion for all (which is a common stated goal of various programs/initiatives) raises concern.

First, there has been a lack of attention to vulnerable subgroups of older adults. Although age-friendly environmental characteristics can benefit older adults in general, there may be subgroups at risk because they lack the necessary resources to take advantage of these initiatives (Scharlach, 2012). The AdvantAge initiative has a specific focus on economic disparity in developing age-friendly communities (Scharlach and Lehning, 2016). Started by the Center for Home Care Policy and Research of the Visiting Nurse Service of New York, the initiative developed 33 indicators in four key areas of an age-friendly community: (1) addressing older adults' basic needs; (2) promoting and protecting older adults' mental and physical health; (3) facilitating independence; and (4) encouraging civic and social participation (Hanson and Emlet, 2006). Results from national surveys of the initiative showed the vulnerable subgroup referred to as the "Frail Fraction" (those living below 200 percent of the federal poverty line) were more likely to be African American or Latino and highly likely to be socially excluded (Feldman, Sussman, and Zigler, 2004). The findings highlighted that explicit program efforts are needed to target vulnerable older people in the development and implementation of interventions.

Second, little attention has been paid to rural areas (Menec et al., 2014). This is not surprising since the initial impetus for age-friendly environments lay in the concomitant phenomena of the rapid growth of the older population, urbanization that often entails decay, and the well-known tendency to remain in familiar homes regardless of declining functioning and health. The problem is that socioeconomically depressed rural communities, in which the majority of residents are lower-income older adults, are limited in their ability to develop and implement sustainable age-friendly communities. In addition, commonly known components of urban age-friendly communities are not necessarily applicable to rural areas (Golant, 2014). In a number of developed countries, the population is aging faster in rural areas. The Canadian age-friendly project offers a good starting point. Drawing on the same methodology and checklist as the WHO age-friendly initiative, researchers in ten rural areas in Canada found that specific age-friendly factors were different. For example, physical environment issues included prompt snow removal, and the main mode of communication about community events and activities was the "gossip mill," perhaps reflecting a close/narrow physical and social environment in rural areas (Keating et al., 2013).

It is notable that an employment-related environment for older adults has not been considered in existing programs despite being one of the eight domains of the WHO initiative. To ensure the development and promotion of job opportunities, there should be focused efforts to identify who may be at risk of noninvolvement among subgroups of older adults. For example, the findings from the AARP's Age-Friendly Community Survey showed that in Atlanta, Georgia, there was an absence of relevant policy efforts and funding allocated to job opportunities (Binette, Harrison, and Thorpe, 2016). On the other hand, the District of Columbia made job creation a strategic goal in pursuing age-friendly community development by establishing an interagency work group to increase coordination and spread awareness of employment services for residents over age 50, including phased retirement (Government of the District of Columbia, Office of the Deputy Mayor for Health & Human Services [DMHHS], 2018).

Age-friendly community development in the United States has not been an official part of federal or state governments' aging policies, resulting in limited funding (Grantmakers in Aging, 2014). In contrast, Canada has seen the development of age-friendly community's development that has been adopted federally and locally, with funding and support for implementation provided. There are 316 age-friendly communities in eight provinces that have participated in the program (Plouffe and Kalache, 2011). We would argue that given limited funding and competing demands for resources in the United States, it is important to prioritize the development of age-friendly environments.

Summary and Future Directions

The productive engagement perspective focuses on policies and programs to optimally engage older adults in roles that benefit individuals, families, communities, and society. In contrast to the successful aging perspective, where the focus is more on individual health behavior, in this chapter we have focused on the environmental contexts that maximize the fit of individual older adults as workers, volunteers, and caregivers. Indeed, we propose that programs and policies are easier to modify than individual behavior and that these macro changes have wider effects. Furthermore, we focus on vulnerable older adults (those experiencing economic and social disadvantage) who may have been marginalized across their lives and who face risk of exclusion or lack of support for productive engagement in later life.

We have reviewed the current state of engagement of vulnerable older adults and highlighted barriers to participation in working, volunteering, and caregiving. We also described organizational and policy efforts to support productive engagement. The conclusion of this review is that as a society we are not responding as strongly as needed in the face of significant demographic shifts. It is particularly discouraging that the current federal government is weakening programs, like the Senior Community Service Employment and Senior Corps, which facilitate involvement of low-income older adults in work and volunteer roles. Efforts to support family caregiving have advanced unevenly between states and local organizations. In the absence of incentives and stronger evidence of benefits to the organization, employer organizations have been slow to adapt policies to attract and retain older workers. In sum, the challenge of ensuring that all older adults have opportunities and supports to be engaged and productive remains pressing, while older adults with limited resources and capability remain at higher risk for exclusion. The failure to optimize the productive engagement of older adults reduces the possibility of livable lives for individuals, families, and communities.

As we have emphasized throughout this chapter, expectations to be productively engaged in later life may lead to the devaluation of lower-income, less-educated older adults who are denied equal access or necessary supports to be engaged. Ethnic and lower-income older adults will continue to be marginalized if efforts to ensure inclusion are not strong. Caregivers are vulnerable to negative financial, health, and mental health outcomes as a result of their caregiving efforts. We must support caregiving as the critically important productive activity that it is, as well as not penalizing caregivers. Failure to support transitions between working and caregiving, in both directions, weakens our families' abilities to take care of one another.

Even as we recommend ways to maximize productive engagement of older adults by improving the fit between individual capacity and environmental characteristics, there are some overarching issues that require serious attention. Age discrimination and age bias undercut the full engagement of older adults and prevent the accurate recognition of the capability and potential in older populations. There is a viscous cycle between devaluing older individuals and excluding them from vital involvement in their communities. Exclusion perpetuates negative stereotypes that not only leads to further age segregation but also harms the older individual and society more generally (Levy, 2009). A virtuous cycle where inclusion and support of older adults in workplaces, colleges and universities, and community organizations may lead to more positive views of aging (Morrow-Howell et al., 2017). To begin addressing the challenge of age bias, we must take a life course perspective in understanding and intervening to optimize productive engagement in later life. As young children and adults age across the life course, they need to develop the resources (e.g., education, life skills, good health) necessary for later engagement. Interventions at each stage of life are necessary to prevent the accumulation of disadvantage which may not be fully expressed until the retirement years (see Chapter 5 of this volume).

Knowledge-building remains important in supporting the development of programs and policies to optimize productive engagement. In terms of working, we need more evidence about the organizational cost and benefits of recruiting and retaining older adults so that employers are more incentivized to transform workplaces. Greater understanding is needed about what type of work and work arrangements allow longer working lives for those who need and want to remain in the workforce. From a life course perspective, we need to test institutional interventions to increase retirement savings.

In regards to volunteering, much is known about who volunteers and why, but we do not know how to incentivize and transform organizations to maximally involve older adults. Successful demonstration programs exist at the local level around the country (such as property tax exemptions for serving in the local elementary school) but the wider implementation of evidence-based programs has remained limited.

In addition, more knowledge is needed about attitudes regarding older adults in national service programs. These programs have been traditionally youth focused. Increasing age-diversity appears limited by ageist ideas on the part of both the organizations and potential participants. Although there is a great deal of knowledge about effective caregiving support programs aimed at the individual caregiver, knowledge about the effects of policy interventions or potential policy initiatives remains limited. The necessity of lifelong education and training to enable productive engagement in later life is evident, but again, knowledge to guide innovation of educational institutions is nascent.

Taking a life course approach to education and training may begin to address the deep-rooted ageist social and cultural structures in a fundamental way. At the same time, to accomplish the ultimate goal of achieving more livable lives for the older population across the full socioeconomic spectrum, it is important to find the optimal fit between personal vulnerability and environmental resources. This entails matching individuals with resources at the organizational, community, and policy level. Equally important, the profession of social work can identify levels of need and resources in both the person and the environment to increase vulnerable older adults' productive engagement.

As discussed in the introductory chapter and throughout this book, a livable life is achieved when people can flourish over their life course, exert agency over their lives, and reach their full potential. The gains in longevity attained over the last 100 years of human history create enormous potential for added years of flourishing and contribution. Yet as the number and capacity of the older population has increased, there has not been the necessary increase in organizational and policy supports to maximize this human potential. In fact, the gains in human and social capital associated with longer lives are thrown away in the face of ageist attitudes, old expectations, and outdated policy and programs. The promise of the productive engagement perspective is that as we increase the person–environment fit and remove the barriers to participation, older adults will be empowered to engage in productive roles that bring them meaning and bring benefits to society. Whether that be through volunteering, working longer, or providing caregiving to family and friends, it is essential that we use the capacity and experience of older adults to ensure livable lives for them, their families, and their communities.

References

Administration on Aging. 2018. *A Profile of Older Americans, 2017*. Washington, DC: Administration on Aging.

Alley, D., P. Liebig, J. Pynoos, T. Banerjee, and I. H. Choi. 2007. "Creating Elder-Friendly Communities." *Journal of Gerontological Social Work*, 49, 1–18.

Austen, S., and R. Ong. 2013. "The Effects of Ill Health and Informal Care Roles on the Employment Retention of Mid-Life Women: Does the Workplace Matter?" *Journal of Industrial Relations*, 55, 663–680.

Austin, J., H. Stevenson, and J. Wei-Skillern. 2006. "Social and Commercial Entrepreneurship: Same, Different, or Both?" *Entrepreneurship Theory and Practice*, 30, 1–22.

Baum, C. L., and C. J. Ruhm. 2016. "The Effects of Paid Family Leave in California on Labor Market Outcomes." *Journal of Policy Analysis and Management*, 35, 333–356.

Berecki, J., J. Lucke, M. R. Hockeye, and A. Dobson. 2007. *Changes in Caring Roles and Employment in Mid-Life: Findings from the Australian Longitudinal Study on Women's Health*. Callaghan, Australia: Department of Health and Ageing.

Berkman, L. F., A. Boersch-Supan, and M. Avendano. 2015. "Labor-Force Participation, Policies & Practices in an Aging America: Adaptation Essential for a Healthy & Resilient Population." *Daedalus*, 144, 41–54.

Binette, J., E. Y. Harrison, and K. Thorpe. 2016. *Livability for All: The 2016 AARP Age-Friendly Community Survey of Southeast and Southwest Atlanta, Georgia AARP Members Age 50-Plus*. Washington, DC: AARP Research.

Boushey, H. 2011. "The Role of the Government in Work-Family Conflict." *The Future of Children*, 21, 163–190.

Buffel, T., C. Phillipson, and T. Scharf. 2012. "Ageing in Urban Environments: Developing 'Age-Friendly' Cities." *Critical Social Policy*, 32, 597–617.

Burr, J. A., J. E. Mutchler, and F. G. Caro. 2007. "Productive Activity Clusters Among Middle-Aged and Older Adults: Intersecting Forms and Time Commitments." *The Journals of Gerontology Series B: Psychological Sciences and Social Sciences*, 62, 267–275

Calvo, E., K. Haverstick, and S. A. Sass. 2009. "Gradual Retirement, Sense of Control, and Retirees' Happiness." *Research on Aging*, 31, 112–135.

Carney, T. 2009. "The Employment Disadvantage of Mothers: Evidence for Systemic Discrimination." *Journal of Industrial Relations*, 51, 113–130.

Carolan, K., E. Gonzales, K. Lee, and R. A. Harootyan. 2018. "Institutional and Individual Factors Affecting Health and Employment for Low-Income Women with Chronic Health Conditions." *The Journals of Gerontology Series B: Psychological Science and Social Sciences*, XX, 1–10. https://www.doi.org/10.1093/geronb/gby149

Carr, D. C., L. P. Fried, and J. W. Rowe. 2015. "Productivity and Engagement in an Aging America: The Role of Volunteerism." *Daedalus*, 144, 55–67.

Carstensen, L. L. 1992. "Social and Emotional Patterns in Adulthood: Support for Socioemotional Selectivity Theory." *Psychology and Aging*, 7, 331–338.

Charter Oak Group LLC. 2003. *Final Report: Pilot Project to Assess Customer Satisfaction in the Senior Community Service Employment Program*. Glastonbury, CT: Author.

Charter Oak Group, LLC. 2007. *The SCSEP Performance Story: Preliminary Results for Program Years 2004 and 2005*. Glastonbury, CT: Author.

Cipriani, J., R. Haley, E. Moravec, and H. Young. 2010. "Experience and Meaning of Group Altruistic Activities Among Long-Term Care Residents." *British Journal of Occupational Therapy*, 73, 269–276.

Clark, K., and A. Glicksman. 2012. "Age-Friendly Philadelphia: Bringing Diverse Networks Together Around Aging Issues." *Journal of Housing for the Elderly*, 26, 121–136.

Colombo, F., J. Llena-Nozal, J. Mercier, and F. Tjadens. 2011. *Help Wanted? Providing and Paying for Long-Term Care*. Paris: OECD.

Community Wealth Ventures. 2010. *Social Enterprise: A Portrait of the Field*. Washington, DC: Author.

Corporation for National and Community Service. 2017, May. "Senior Corps Fact Sheet." Retrieved from https://www.nationalservice.gov/sites/default/files/documents/CNCS-Fact-Sheet-2017-SeniorCorps_2.pdf

Dentinger, E., and M. Clarkberg. 2002. "Informal Caregiving and Retirement Timing among Men and Women: Gender and Caregiving Relationships in Late Midlife." *Journal of Family Issues*, 23, 857–879.

Estes, C. L., and E. Williams. 2013. *Health Policy: Crisis and Reform*. Burlington, MA: Jones and Bartlett Learning.

Feldman, R., A. L. Sussman, and E. Zigler. 2004. "Parental Leave and Work Adaptation at the Transition to Parenthood: Individual, Marital, and Social Correlates." *Journal of Applied Developmental Psychology*, 25, 459–479.

Freedman, V. A., J. C. Cornman, and D. Carr. 2014. "Is Spousal Caregiving Associated With Enhanced Well-Being? New Evidence from the Panel Study of Income Dynamics." *The Journals of Gerontology Series B: Psychological Sciences and Social Sciences*, 69, 861–869.

Golant, S. M. 2014. *Age-Friendly Communities: Are We Expecting too Much?* Montreal: Institute for Research on Public Policy.

Government of the District of Columbia, Office of the Deputy Mayor for Health & Human Services. 2018. *Age-Friendly 2023 Strategic Plan*. Washington, DC: Author.

Grant, J. 2010. *Outing Age 2010: Public Policy Issues Affecting Lesbian, Gay, Bisexual and Transgender Elders*. Washington, DC: National Gay and Lesbian Task Force Policy Institute.

Grantmakers in Aging. 2014. *Community Agenda: Q and A*. Arlington, VA: Grantmakers in Aging.

Guiney, H., and L. Machado. 2017. "Volunteering in the Community: Potential Benefits for Cognitive Aging." *The Journals of Gerontology Series B: Psychological Sciences and Social Sciences*, 73, 399–408.

Hanson, D., & C. A. Emlet. 2006. "Assessing a Community's Elder Friendliness." *Family and Community Health*, 29, 266–278.

Hegewisch, A., H. Liepmann, J. Hayes, and H. Hartmann. 2010. *Separate and Not Equal? Gender Segregation in the Labor Market and the Gender Wage Gap*. Washington, DC: Institute for Women's Policy Research.

Hill, H. D. 2013. "Paid Sick Leave and Job Stability." *Work and Occupations*, 40, 143–173.

Hong, S., N. Morrow-Howell, F. Tang, and J. Hinterlong. 2008. "Engaging Older Adults in Volunteering." *Nonprofit and Voluntary Sector Quarterly*, 38, 200–219.

Hooyman, N., K. Kawamoto, and H. Kyak. 2017. *Social Gerontology: A Multidisciplinary Perspective*. New York, NY: Pearson Education.

Independent Sector. n.d. *Value of Volunteer Time*. Washington, DC: Author.

Johnson, R. W., and C. Mommaerts. 2010. *Age Differences in Job Displacement, Job Search, and Reemployment*. Chestnut Hill, MA: Boston College Center for Retirement Research.

Kang, J. Y., S. Park, B. Kim, E. Kwon, and J. Cho. 2018. "The Effect of California's Paid Family Leave Program on Employment among Middle-Aged Female Caregivers." *The Gerontologist*. https://www.doi.org/10.1093/geront/gny105

Keating, N., J. Eales, and J. E. Phillips. 2013. "Age-Friendly Rural Communities: Conceptualizing 'Best-Fit.'" *Canadian Journal on Aging/La Revue Canadienne Du Vieillissement*, 32, 319–332.

Klerman, J., K. Daley, and A. Pozniak. 2012. *Family and Medical Leave in 2012: Technical Report*. Cambridge, MA: Abt Associates.

Krause, N. 2003. "Neighborhoods, Health, and Well-Being in Late Life." *Annual Review of Gerontology and Geriatrics*, 23, 223–249.

Lahaie, C., A. Earle, and J. Heymann. 2012. "An Uneven Burden: Social Disparities in Adult Caregiving Responsibilities, Working Conditions, and Caregiver Outcomes." *Research on Aging*, 35, 243–274.

Larsen, T. P. 2010. "Flexicurity from the Individual's Work-Life Balance Perspective: Coping with the Flaws in European Child- and Eldercare Provision." *Journal of Industrial Relations*, 52, 575–593.

Lawton, M. P., and L. Nahemow. 1973. "Ecology and the Aging Process." *The Psychology of Adult Development and Aging*. Edited by C. Eisdorfer and M. P. Lawton. Washington, DC: American Psychological Association, pp. 619–674.

Levy, H. 2009. *Income, Material Hardship, and the Use of Public Programs Among the Elderly*. Ann Arbor, MI: Michigan Retirement and Disability Research Center.

Lewin, K. 1936. *Principles of Topological Psychology*. New York: McGraw-Hill.

Lui, C., J. Everingham, J. Warburton, M. Cuthill, and H. Bartlett. 2009. "What Makes a Community Age-Friendly: A Review of International Literature." *Australasian Journal on Ageing*, 28, 116–121.

Martinez, I. L., D. Crooks, K. S. Kim, and E. Tanner. 2011. "Invisible Civic Engagement among Older Adults: Valuing the Contributions of Informal Volunteering." *Journal of Cross-Cultural Gerontology*, 26, 23–37.

Mcbride, A. M., E. Gonzales, N. Morrow-Howell, and S. Mccrary. 2011. "Stipends in Volunteer Civic Service: Inclusion, Retention, and Volunteer Benefits." *Public Administration Review*, 71, 850–858.

Menec, V., R. Means, N. Keating, G. Parkhurst, and J. Eales. 2011. "Conceptualizing Age-Friendly Communities." *Canadian Journal on Aging/La Revue Canadienne Du Vieillissement*, 30, 479–493.

Menec, V. H., S. Novek, D. Veselyuk, and J. Mcarthur. 2014. "Lessons Learned from a Canadian Province-Wide Age-Friendly Initiative: The Age-Friendly Manitoba Initiative." *Journal of Aging & Social Policy*, 26, 33–51.

MetLife Mature Market Institute. 2011. *The MetLife Study of Caregiving Costs to Working Caregivers: Double Jeopardy for Baby Boomers Caring for Their Parents*. New York: MetLife Mature Market Institute.

Morrow-Howell, N., and S. Gehlert. 2012. "Social Engagement and a Healthy Aging Society." *Public Health for an Aging Society*. Edited by T. Prohaska, L. Anderson, and R. Binstock. Baltimore, MD: Johns Hopkins University Press, pp. 205–227.

Morrow-Howell, N., E. Gonzales, C. Matz-Costa, and E. A. Greenfield. 2015. "Increasing Productive Engagement in Later Life." Grand Challenges for Social Work Initiative Working Paper No. 8. Cleveland, OH: American Academy of Social Work and Social Welfare.

Morrow-Howell, N., and E. A. Greenfield. 2016. "Productive Engagement in Later Life." *Handbook of Aging and the Social Sciences*. Edited by K. Ferraro and L. George. Cambridge, MA: Academic Press, pp. 293–313.

Morrow-Howell, N., C. J. Halvorsen, P. Hovmand, C. Lee, and E. Ballard. 2017. "Conceptualizing Productive Engagement in a System Dynamics Framework." *Innovation in Aging*, 1(1), igx018.

Morrow-Howell, N., and A. C. Mui. 2014. *Productive Engagement in Later Life: A Global Perspective*. London: Routledge.

Movement Advancement Project, and Services and Advocacy for Gay, Lesbian, Bisexual and Transgender Elders. 2010. *Improving the Lives of LGBT Older Adults*. Boulder, CO: Movement Advancement Project.

National Alliance for Caregiving and AARP. 2015. *Caregiving in the U.S.* Washington, DC: AARP Public Policy Institute.

National Council on Aging. 2017. *Senior Community Service Employment Program (SCSEP)*. Arlington, VA: Author.

Neal, M. B., A. K. DeLaTorre, and P. C. Carder. 2014. "Age-Friendly Portland: A University–City–Community Partnership." *Journal of Aging & Social Policy*, 26, 88–101.

Nepal, B., L. Brown, G. Ranmuthugala, and R. Percival. 2011. "A Comparison of the Lifetime Economic Prospects of Women Informal Carers and Non-Carers." *Australian Journal of Social Issues*, 46, 91–108.

Ness, D. L. 2011. "Women, Caregivers, Families, and the Affordable Care Act's Bright Promise of Better Care." *Generations*, 35, 38–44.

Northern Periphery Programme. 2013. *O4O: Older People for Older People Final Report*. Copenhagen, Denmark: Author.

Park, S., B. Kim, and J. Cho. 2017. "Formal Volunteering among Vulnerable Older Adult from the Environmental perspective: Does Senior Housing Matter?" *Journal of Housing for the Elderly*, 31, 334–350.

Park, S., B. Kim, and Y. Han. 2018. "Differential Aging-in-Place and Depressive Symptoms: Interplay Among Time, Income, and Senior Housing." *Research on Aging*, 40, 207–231.

Park, S., J. Smith, R. Dunkle, B. Ingersoll-Dayton, and T. Antonucci. 2017. "Health and Social-Physical Environment Profiles Among Older Adults Living Alone: Associations with Depressive Symptoms." *Journals of Gerontology Series B: Psychological Sciences and Social Sciences*, 74, 675–684.

Pavalko, E. K., and J. E. Artis. 1997. "Women's Caregiving and Paid Work: Causal Relationships in Late Midlife." *The Journals of Gerontology Series B: Psychological Sciences and Social Sciences*, 52, 170–179.

Pavalko, E. K., and K. A. Henderson. 2006. "Combining Care Work and Paid Work." *Research on Aging*, 28, 359–374.

Pavalko, E. K., and J. D. Wolfe. 2015. "Do Women Still Care? Cohort Changes in US Women's Care for the Ill or Disabled." *Social Forces*, 94, 1359–1384.

Piliavin, J., and E. Siegl. 2015. "Health and Well-Being Consequences of Formal Volunteering." *The Oxford Handbook of Prosocial Behavior*. Edited by D. Schroeder and W. Graziano. New York, NY: Oxford University Press, pp. 494–523.

Plouffe, L. A., and A. Kalache. 2011. "Making Communities Age Friendly: State and Municipal Initiatives in Canada and Other Countries." *Gaceta Sanitaria*, 25, 131–137.

Rohwedder, S., and R. J. Willis. 2010. "Mental Retirement." *Journal of Economic Perspectives*, 24, 119–138.

Rossin-Slater, M., C. J. Ruhm, and J. Waldfogel. 2013. "The Effects of California's Paid Family Leave Program on Mothers' Leave-Taking and Subsequent Labor Market Outcomes." *Journal of Policy Analysis and Management*, 32, 224–245.

Saraceno, C. 2010. "Social Inequalities in Facing Old-Age Dependency: A Bi-Generational Perspective." *Journal of European Social Policy*, 20, 32–44.

Sarasa, S. 2008. "Do Welfare Benefits Affect Women's Choices of Adult Care Giving?" *European Sociological Review*, 24, 37–51.

Scharlach, A. 2012. "Creating Aging-Friendly Communities in the United States." *Ageing International*, 37, 25–38.

Scharlach, A. E., and A. J. Lehning. 2013. "Ageing-Friendly Communities and Social Inclusion in the United States of America." *Ageing and Society*, 33, 110–136.

Scharlach, A. E., and A. J. Lehning. 2016. *Creating Aging-Friendly Communities*. New York, NY: Oxford University Press.

Schmitz, H. 2011. "Why Are the Unemployed in Worse Health? The Causal Effect of Unemployment on Health." *Labour Economics*, 18, 71–78.

Schneider, U., B. Trukeschitz, R. Mühlmann, and I. Ponocny. 2013. "Do I Stay or Do I Go? Job Change And Labor Market Exit Intentions of Employees Providing Informal Care to Older Adults." *Health Economics*, 22, 1230–1249.

Social Enterprise Alliance. 2011. *State Policy Toolkit*. Washington, DC: Social Enterprise Alliance.

Sundeen, R. A., S. A. Raskoff, and M. C. Garcia. 2007. "Differences in Perceived Barriers to Volunteering to Formal Organizations: Lack of Time Versus Lack of Interest." *Nonprofit Management and Leadership*, 17, 279–300.

Tan, E. J., A. Georges, S. M. Gabbard, D. J. Pratt, A. Nerino, A. S. Roberts, S. M. Wrightsman, and M. Hyde. 2016. "The 2013–2014 Senior Corps Study: Foster Grandparents and Senior Companions." *Public Policy & Aging Report*, 26, 88–95.

Tang, F., E. Choi, and N. Morrow-Howell. 2010. "Organizational Support and Volunteering Benefits for Older Adults." *The Gerontologist*, 50, 603–612.

Taylor, M. A., and H. A. Geldhauser. 2007. "Low-Income Older Workers." *Aging and Work in the 21st Century*. Mahwah, NJ: Erlbaum, pp. 49–74.

Taylor, H. O., Y. Wang, and N. Morrow-Howell. 2018. "Loneliness in Senior Housing Communities." *Journal of Gerontological Social Work*, 61, 623–639.

Thomése, F., and M. B. Groenou. 2006. "Adaptive Strategies after Health Decline in Later Life: Increasing the Person–Environment Fit by Adjusting the Social and Physical Environment." *European Journal of Ageing*, 3, 169–177.

U.S. Bureau of Labor Statistics. 2016, February 25. "Volunteering in the United States, 2015." Retrieved from https://www.bls.gov/news.release/volun.nr0.htm

Wacker, R. R., and K. A. Roberto. 2018. *Community Resources for Older Adults: Programs and Services in an Era of Change*. Thousand Oaks, CA: SAGE.

Warburton, J., J. Paynter, and A. Petriwskyj. 2007. "Volunteering as a Productive Aging Activity: Incentives and Barriers to Volunteering by Australian Seniors." *Journal of Applied Gerontology*, 26, 333–354.

Washko, M. M., R. W. Schack, B. A. Goff, and B. Pudlin. 2011. "Title V of the Older Americans Act, the Senior Community Service Employment Program: Participant Demographics and Service to Racially/Ethnically Diverse Populations." *Journal of Aging & Social Policy*, 23, 182–197.

World Health Organization. 2007. *Global Age-Friendly Cities: A Guide*. Geneva, Switzerland: Author.

World Health Organization. 2010. *Other Participating Cities Announced*. Geneva, Switzerland: Author.

Yuen Tsang, A. W. K., and S. Wang. 2008. "Revitalization of Social Work in China: The Significance of Human Agency in Institutional Transformation and Structural Change." *China Journal of Social Work*, 1, 5–22.

12

Generating Effective Demand and Use of Social Services

MELISSA JONSON-REID, MATTHEW W. KREUTER, EDWARD F. LAWLOR,
DAVID A. PATTERSON SILVER WOLF, AND VETTA L. SANDERS THOMPSON

Despite a growing understanding of the services and programs that might better serve vulnerable populations, many of the most significant economic, health, and social problems remain. Prior thinking had suggested that needs predict services, and while services are rarely provided to those without need, the idea that need results in services has turned out to be false (Jonson-Reid, 2011; McGorry, Bates, and Birchwood, 2013; Walters et al., 2016). Even when access does occur, retention, quality, and the siloed nature of services remain barriers to creating effective change. Although social work has made important advances in addressing barriers to access, reducing stigma, and improving cultural acceptability, these efforts have remained largely focused on single problem areas or particular populations (Stiffman, Pescosolido, and Cabassa, 2004; Tovar, Patterson Silver Wolf, and Stevenson, 2015). Furthermore, improving access and acceptability does not guarantee availability of appropriate services and/or sufficient quality.

Health, mental health, safety, education and/or vocational preparation, and material needs impact the day-to-day functioning of individuals and families. When these needs go unmet, the ability to achieve a livable life is severely compromised. The various chapters throughout this book have illustrated the many ways in which livable lives are undermined by serious problems that have been left unaddressed. The practice of social work is intimately tied to the necessity of ensuring that human needs are addressed through effective and comprehensive services. This is particularly the case for those most vulnerable and disadvantaged. In this chapter we explore the gap between needs and services, and how that divide can best be bridged.

The Disconnect Between Services and Need

Social services for children and youth (e.g., child welfare, education, and juvenile justice) are a prime example of how a patchwork of services hampers access and limits preventive impact. Only in the case of K–12 public education has there been an explicit attempt to provide universal services for achieving the goal of an educated and productive citizenry (Jonson-Reid, 2015). Within this system, however, services are often reactive and disjointed. For example, special education programs designed to help students struggling with cognitive, emotional, or serious health conditions are accessed only after a certain level of failure is demonstrated. Recent studies indicate that minority group students are under-identified controlling for similar socioeconomic, behavioral, and academic achievement factors. This is due to issues of stigma, as well as a lack of access to health care and other providers to diagnose disabilities and inform parents of services, along with a higher likelihood of attending low-performing schools, which are less likely to identify disabilities to avoid cost of providing services (Morgan et al., 2015). Barriers to access, however, do not resolve issues of quality of intervention. Specific forms of disability, particularly emotional disturbance, receive few services even after eligibility is determined (Jonson-Reid, 2011; Lee and Jonson-Reid, 2009). It is perhaps unsurprising that youth who are deemed eligible for special education due to emotional disturbances experience high rates of adult negative behavioral and economic outcomes (such as unemployment or criminal arrests) in adulthood (Wagner and Newman, 2012).

Another example of a disconnect between services and need can be found in the response to juvenile status and delinquency offenses. The juvenile court was developed in the early 20th century to move from a more punitive adult model to a more protective and rehabilitative model (Trattner, 1984). This intent would seem to imply a service heavy early intervention approach. Despite some promising programs for first-time or less serious offenders (e.g., Bouffard, Cooper, and Bergseth, 2016; Ryon, Early, and Kosloski, 2017) as well as some regional examples of comprehensive services such as the Redeployment Program in Illinois (State of Illinois Department of Human Services, 2014), such interventions are not the norm. Peter Greenwood (2008) argues that only 5 percent of youth who should be eligible to participate in delinquency prevention programming do so, largely because implementation of these programs is not widespread. A similar figure was given for the percentage of high-risk juvenile justice involved youth that were provided with evidence-based treatment (Henggeler and Schoenwald, 2011). Similarly, while promise is noted in reducing recidivism for first-time offenders when referred to appropriate mental health care, effective screening and referral is far from universally available (Spinney et al., 2016; Zeola, Guina, and Nahhas, 2017). Across most jurisdictions, the juvenile court is severely under-resourced, providing services only after a youth's behaviors become serious enough to warrant more intensive supervision. Understanding the true extent of the problem is complicated by the limited scope of surveillance. National statistics on juvenile offenders only track formal assignment to probation, detention, or other out-of-home placement (Puzzanchera, Adams, and Sickmund, 2010). As might be expected, research indicates that long-term outcomes are worse for youth with court contact preventive services (e.g., Bright, Kohl, and Jonson-Reid, 2014). A meta-analysis concluded that doing nothing might be slightly better than official processing of less serious offenders, yet both are worse than when offenders are diverted from formal adjudication but still provided services (Petrosino, Turpin-Petrosino, and Guckenburg, 2013).

For most children served in education and juvenile justice, readers might be quick to blame the failure of parents to insist on services. Yet information about available services may be difficult to obtain because there are often disincentives for agencies with limited resources to advertise services (Lipsky, 2010). Considerable research points to the difficulties parents have in navigating service systems even if system contact has already been made (e.g., Burke, 2013; Cusworth et al., 2015; Khanlou et al., 2015; Morgan et al., 2015). For example, while parent advocacy for services is arguably a key part of assuring that a child with a disability receives the best care in the educational system, research indicates that the reading skill level required to understand available parent handbooks often exceeds that of many of the parents (Fitzgerald and Watkins, 2006).

Processing or system outcomes are also not always linked to client health or well-being (Bradley and Taylor, 2013; Lipsky, 2010). In part this may be because a given outcome is often only achieved through services across multiple systems (Jonson-Reid et al., 2017; Bradley and Taylor, 2013). While the basic tenants of permanency and safety outcomes in child welfare has existed since the mid-1980s, it was nearly 20 years before policy evolved requiring attention to health and well-being outcomes (Jonson-Reid and Drake, 2016). Of course, how such an outcome was to be achieved was not clear, and research attempting to link outcomes to various collaborative efforts to achieve health and well-being are not common. Although a 2008 policy requiring coordination between health and child welfare was enacted, we still have little understanding of the success of the models being implemented in response (Jaudes et al., 2012; Jee et al., 2010).

A similar disconnect between system perception, individual need, and actual services exists in adult social service sectors. In health care, the United States has been singled out for its relatively low investment in social services overall, as well as its disconnect between services and health (Bradley and Taylor, 2013).

For example, untreated substance abuse disorders continue to be a major health problem in the United States (Bouchery et al., 2011; National Drug Intelligence Center, 2011). Tens of thousands of Americans die prematurely from this illness each year, while the financial costs to our economy extend beyond $200 billion annually (Harris, Edlund, and Larson, 2005). Furthermore, the rate of unmet need for both mental health and substance use disorder is consistently higher among ethnic minority populations (Wells et al., 2001; Walker et al., 2015). Structural barriers such as the lack of sufficient health insurance remains significant for these populations (Wen, Druss, and Cummings, 2015). While the Affordable Care Act held considerable promise in remedying this barrier to access, not all states implemented the Medicaid expansion required for low-income populations to realize this benefit (Missouri Medicaid, 2016; Patterson Silver Wolf, 2015).

Many persons in need of health or mental health care also have substantial social and material needs (Bradley and Taylor, 2013). As a result of the Affordable Care Act, significant attention has been paid to the integration of social services and health, particularly housing services, transportation, behavioral health, and substance abuse treatment. New forms of payment, incentives, and penalties have caused many health care providers to either partner or develop on their own new service approaches. For example, Medicare financial penalties on hospitals for high rates of readmission encouraged development of case management, transportation, and other out-of-hospital community-based services. A number of states have experimented with models of service integration in their Medicaid programs, often in the context of producing Medical Homes for beneficiaries that attempt to coordinate primary care and community-based clinics with social services. Outcomes research on such models is still emerging, but studies indicate promising results (Berkowitz et al., 2017; Garg et al., 2015; Gottlieb et al., 2016; Gottlieb, Wind, and Adler, 2017). One randomized control study of integration of screening for material needs into community health clinics for mothers of infants found that when formal screening was conducted, it was associated with a significantly higher rate of referral as well as a higher rate of mothers contacting referral sources (Garg, et al., 2015). Another randomized control study found similar benefits in regard to parent-reported global child health when screening was paired with assistance in navigating resources for family social needs (Gottlieb et al., 2016). Additional studies have focused on the development of care management programs for patients with complex medical and social service needs, finding some evidence for decreased hospital admissions and in some cases improved health behaviors and quality of care (Berkowitz et al., 2017; Hong, Siegel, and Ferris, 2014).

Reducing structural barriers, however, does not guarantee adequate services. Many adults with behavioral health or substance use disorder needs report a lack of adequate care (Wen et al., 2015). Frontline substance use disorder therapists in the United States base their services mainly on intuition rather than hard data or scientific evidence (Patterson Silver Wolf et al., 2014). Indeed, over the many years of research experience related to substance abuse treatment, one of the authors of this chapter has observed that there is a rather pervasive and long-held belief that well-educated and highly trained therapists are adequately meeting the needs of their patients without any performance measures supporting this notion (Patterson Silver Wolf, personal communication, December 15, 2017). Similar challenges to assuring that adults receive evidence-based treatments for mental health care exist in public and private systems (Keller et al., 2014).

The fact that it is often persons of color and the poor who are most in need of these hard to access services is in stark contrast to the mission of social work to "enhance human well-being and help meet the basic needs of all people, with particular attention to the needs and empowerment of the people who are vulnerable, oppressed and living in poverty" (National Association of Social Workers, 2008). Social work has long supported the use of an ecological approach that acknowledges the complex interactions between needs, risks, and protective factors upon services and policies. The crisis orientation and siloed nature of services often hinders the mission of social work to enhance human well-being.

Addressing the gap between the need for services, and the receipt of effective services, requires understanding the barriers to both access and provision of evidence-based, high-quality services. This ultimately requires action on a number of fronts. At the policy level, resources must be adequate and provided consistently to help persons receiving services achieve optimal functioning. As currently provided, many services are nested within separate policy and organizational structures, making integration and coordination of services a priority when multiple needs are present. At the programmatic level, even if evidence-based approaches are embraced, services must also be perceived as relevant and culturally appropriate for the target audience. At the individual level, persons need to be aware of the resources available and how to access them. To support a livable life over time, services should be able to evolve to meet new or changing demand. All of these areas are well suited to social work research and practice.

Barrier to Service Delivery and Access

At the policy level, the continual use of the word "system" can lead those that control regulation and funding to believe that a fully functional approach to addressing a need exists. When outcomes at the so-called system level are poor, system reform is called for without attention to whether or not there was ever a fully constructed system designed to produce the outcomes in question (Jonson-Reid and Drake, 2018; Jonson-Reid, 2015). A system is defined as "regularly interacting or interdependent group of items forming a unified whole" (Merriam Webster, 2017). Few would argue that there is a unified approach to providing the health and social services needed.

Most organizations tasked with services addressing health, mental health, and economic needs typically deliver very limited services that are unequally available across regions and population characteristics such as socioeconomic status. For example, a national study of youth with mental health disorders reported that only slightly over one third received services and that for black and Hispanic youth the rate was much lower (Merikangas et al., 2011). Oftentimes what we refer to as "systems" is more like a patchwork of crisis responses designed only for the most serious and short-term concerns (e.g. the so-called child welfare system; Jonson-Reid and Drake, 2018). Individuals living from one crisis to the next cannot effectively attend to their roles in the family, at work, or in the community, preventing them from reaching their full potential. Nor is the success of one service necessarily independent of the provision of another service in a different sector of care, as discussed by Bradley and Taylor (2013) in regard to poor health outcomes in the United States. Some research indicates that even within a system specializing in serving a given need, there is significant variation in the awareness of agency service providers as to what assistance may be available to their clients (Khanlou et al., 2015; Stahlschmidt et al., 2018). Addressing the complexity of problems like child maltreatment, improving health care outcomes, substance abuse, or poverty requires a move away from linear models gated by narrow diagnostic categories and sectorial funding toward integration of programming and policy initiatives built on expertise from a variety of disciplinary perspectives (Bradley and Taylor, 2013; Head and Alfird, 2015; Rigotti and Wallace, 2015; Dowding et al., 2015).

Such a movement requires transparency and the availability of data that goes beyond counting how many persons have a given problem, to what is being done in response across the sectors they engage (e.g., education, health, social services). Often it is nearly impossible to tell who actually received services within a system and what exactly was included in such services when received. This creates a reactive approach to policy based on the latest "failure" instead of being able to identify gaps and integrate what is known about the complex needs associated with various behavioral, health, and economic problems. This lack of knowledge grounded in data also complicates the process of advocating for effective, needed, and sustainable resources.

Financing and Incentives

A root cause of this crisis-driven, reactive, and fragmented system is the absence of a coherent and stable financing approach to social services. Most service organizations are funded through a patchwork of public sector grants and contracts, private philanthropy, and small amounts of fee-for-service. Some services, such as youth development programs in low-income communities, have no dedicated source of funding, resulting in providers being forced to cobble together financing from United Way or other philanthropic sources, individual gifts, and episodic grants and contracts. Very few of these financing sources cover overhead, general operations, or agency infrastructure. Furthermore, the relentless pursuit of grants and contracts consumes considerable staff time and energy and often causes agencies to lurch off mission to keep their doors open (i.e., competing with peer organizations for a limited pool or resources, which may not be conducive to integration).

In addition, major sources of program funding for services have been declining in recent years, causing agencies to close, merge, or reduce staff. Nationally, United Way fundraising has declined, leading to reductions in scarce general operating support for member agencies. The rapid ascendance of donor-advised funds may slow the distribution of philanthropic resources and almost certainly will benefit some programs more than others, in ways that are still evolving. Budget problems and fiscal crises in many states have led to dramatic reductions in support for services, in some cases producing long delays in payment or even failure to reimburse service already rendered. For example, the inability of the State of Illinois to pass a budget for two consecutive years, and its resulting failure to pay agencies for a broad array of social services, resulted in agencies experiencing substantial financial losses, reducing services, and laying off staff. Lutheran Social Services, the second-largest provider of social services in the state, illustrates these effects. It was forced to cut services in 30 of its programs—from senior services to alcohol and drug treatment—and terminate more than 750 employees, 43 percent of its workforce (Kapos, 2016).

The wider implication of this systemic funding challenge is that service organizations underinvest in infrastructure, including technology, skills and performance improvement of staff, and physical facilities. This problem has been described as the "nonprofit starvation cycle," and it impedes the ability of organizations to address the modern imperative to implement evidence-based services, manage data, use technology appropriately, evaluate and assess services (see the following discussion), and otherwise innovate and implement organizational change (Coggins and Howard, 2009; Lecy and Sterling, 2014). Social service organizations simply lack the capital to upgrade their information technology and management systems, invest in skills improvement for staff, and pursue organizational growth and change. In particular, the absence of modern and uniform technology systems across the social service sector is a crippling limitation that often prevents meaningful integration across services and providers.

Stigma, Relevance, and Access

Recognizing significant advances in social work, efforts remain siloed by problem area and population. Identifying common elements that can be infused across service sectors is imperative. Clear processes are essential to identify when adaptations are needed and how they are made for specific populations (Jones and Wells, 2007; Tovar et al., 2015) Access issues should move beyond agencies to the environment, such as the integration of social work and urban planning, to reduce barriers such as poor public transportation.

To fully comprehend system barriers, the changes needed, and resources required to meet such challenges, community engagement as operationalized through partnerships, collaborations, and coalitions are required (International Association for Public Participation, n.d.). The calls for community engagement and community-based participatory research represent efforts to reduce the stigma associated with accessing a variety of social services. At the heart of all public participation and community engagement strategies is an acknowledgment that those most affected by social issues and concerns should have a voice in how their needs will be addressed (Zakus and Lysack, 1998).

As existing programs are reviewed, communities may shed light on aspects of social service efforts that are objectionable because they fail to address gaps in knowledge or linguistic and literacy concerns, conflict with values and cultural beliefs and/or involve implementation plans that overlook structural, emotional, and psychological barriers. Castro, Barrera, and Martinez suggest that the aim of cultural adaptations should be "to generate a culturally equivalent version of a model prevention program" when elements in the original intervention/program produce resistance to program activities or are in conflict with cultural attitudes and beliefs (2004: 43). Nevertheless, to be effective, it is essential to understand the when and how to adapt services and service delivery systems (Chaffin et al., 2012; Jones and Wells, 2007).

Effective Demand

Access can also be influenced by demand, although it is not clear if this is specific to particular service needs. The terminology "effective demand" is used more frequently in international work (Ensor and Cooper, 2004; Srihari et al., 2014) and refers to whether the intended recipient of services is asking for or seeking out that service. By definition, effective demand requires that the recipient have knowledge of the service and its purpose. When services are gated to immediate crises, such as the need for medical care for a broken arm, there is little opportunity for discussion of broader access to preventive health care services. While this may be fine for intervention, and certainly appropriate to address crisis needs, it may not optimal for preventive or early intervention approaches. For example, there is increasing concern that by focusing on clinical care following a problem, we may continue to fail to address the social determinants of those problems to begin with (Bayer and Galea, 2015). This seems unlikely to be resolved without assuring that the public is informed about the structural changes needed to achieve population health.

Although models of collaboration and efforts to improve evidence-based care exist, endeavors are often not paired with community engagement and education. This leads to a lack of understanding into the menu of possible supports that could be used to systematically address the underlying issues that maintain individuals, families, and communities in a vulnerable status. This lack of outreach to educate the public about the range of possible services also presents a missed opportunity to address issues of stigma that may be associated with seeking care or system involvement (Devaney and Spratt, 2009; Wen, Druss, and Cummings, 2015). Further, lack of understanding of what persons in need can and should expect precludes client participation in advocating for system improvement and responsiveness (Keller et al., 2014; Lipsky, 2010). However, as Michael Lipsky (2010) points out, the dissemination of information regarding services is sometimes curtailed out of concern for driving up demand for those services when there are insufficient resources to meet the needs of those already being served.

How Can We Address and Potentially Solve the Problem?

A multisector problem such as what we have been reviewing in this chapter will require a multifaceted solution. Such an approach includes innovation and action at the policy and agency levels. It also requires integrating new resources, such as advancing technology, to help improve the reach of information about services. The foundation for these improvements should be social work's ownership of the social service sector and its problems. As noted at the beginning of this chapter, this is clearly central to the mission of social work. A recent leadership essay has argued:

> Significant changes in the organization of services, payment and finance, and information and accountability for services are underway. As social work as a profession operates within the social services environment, it is important to respond to these trends in the formulation of our educational content, in articulating an evidence-based research agenda, and in strategic planning. (Lein et al., 2017: 68)

Ownership does not mean that social work should act alone in resolving complex needs, as obviated by the need for collaboration argued earlier. However, this lack of ownership as a barrier to advancing the social work profession moves beyond the critique of Harry Specht and Mark Courtney (1995) who worried that social work would merely become another form of psychotherapy. Instead, it points to having a sense of professional pride and identity related to the services and systems that form the bulk of the workplace environment for social work. Such professional pride is noted as key for long-term performance and avoidance of burnout across several professions (Butler and Constantine, 2005; Nilsson et al., 2005). Even Abraham Flexner's (2001) early critique of the field of social work suggested that having a professional spirit is the foremost trait needed to be a professional. Social workers must embrace the complexity of the issues that impede successful and socially just outcomes to effect change from the individual to the macro level of policy advocacy.

Critical to this agenda will be research, education, and advocacy for improved organization and financing of the social services sector. This sector needs the next generation of leadership from our graduates. The sector also needs the organizational and financial wherewithal to adopt new technology, implement evidence-based practices, and innovation in the uses of big data and other modern tools of management and evaluation (see Chapter 14 of this volume). It requires the ability to understand and work with policymakers and service providers outside the social services sector, and a commitment to working collaboratively with partner agencies.

Improved Use of Technology

Advancing technology has created new potential for outreach, access to data to guide practice and policy decisions, and increasing use of systems science tools. Use of such tools may help advance our understanding of a path forward.

Treatment Planning and Evaluation

While therapists continuously collect large amounts of key patient health data that are entered into electronic health record systems (e.g., bio-social-psycho assessment, treatment plan, individual/group, and other ongoing data), technologies such as a performance dashboard can return key clinical performance and patient health indicators back to the therapist and patient in a visually pleasing, easy-to-digest format that will facilitate real-time adjustments and decisions (Pauwels et al., 2009). According to Ruben Amarasingham and colleagues (2009), higher levels of information automation in hospital-based care (as measured by physician ratings on the Clinical Information Technology Tool) are associated with lower mortality rates, lower rates of complications, and lower overall costs. For every 10-point increase in information automation, fatal hospitalizations decreased by 15 percent ($56.3 billion), while the risk of complications fell by 16 percent ($60.1 billion). The result was a savings of $116.4 billion (Amarasingham et al., 2009).

Clinical practices should be based in empiricism, responsive to client needs, and outcomes-focused (Rosen, 2003). Clinical service providers/organizations often represent the first point of contact and will maintain an ongoing interaction with patients. Any failures to provide the highest quality of care using the best information available primarily rests with organizations and the professional therapists within these systems. Better integration of technology with clinical care provides the opportunities to measure in real-time the impacts of services.

For example, a next step in the substance use disorders social services industry would be to develop a fully functional, HIPAA (Health Insurance Portability and Accountability Act of 1996) compliant performance dashboard that pulls key performance indicators from electronic health record systems. Informed by the contextualized technology adaptation process, the performance dashboard tool would be integrated into established substance use disorders treatment monitoring systems (Ramsey et al., 2015). Therapists will be able to view up-to-date patient data as they are entered into the electronic health record system, enabling them to monitor their patients' progress toward meeting treatment plan goals during usual care timetables as well as monitoring their own performance data over time (e.g., patient demographics, retention, completion). A similar approach could be used for clinical services in mental health care more broadly.

Similarly, in child welfare and education, data are increasingly being used for near real-time performance reviews and identification of families at risk to better target preventive services (Florida Department of Education, n.d.; Lery, Putnam-Hornstein, Wiegmann, and King, 2015). The National Social Work Grand Challenges on family violence highlights a program called Birth Match as an example of how data are used to find families with newborns in which there had been prior child maltreatment with an older sibling. The program then provides a home visit with voluntary services to offset risk to the infant as well as to support the family (Kulkarni, Barth, and Messing, 2016). Data systems, properly aligned and supported by information sharing protocols, have the capacity to allow multiple organizations serving the same clients to see what each other are doing in near real time to better coordinate efforts for helping clients reach their goals.

Assessment and Service Provision

Phone and computer technologies are being used to facilitate accessing services as well as providing information to potential consumers of services. Implementation of a telehealth program for veterans provided additional case management and care coordination resulting in a reduction in hospital stays and was well received by the participants (Darkins et al., 2008; Luxton et al., 2011). The use of smartphones as tools to enhance clinical mental health practice is growing with the use of apps that can assess symptoms, provide education, and help in locating resources (Krishna, Boren, and Balas, 2009). Other applications in health care, including prevention education, are also being developed and tested (Purnell et al., 2014). Phone-based engagement protocols have also been tested in regard to parent engagement in child mental health services (McKay and Bannon, 2004). Internet support groups have been developed for special populations such as parents of children with special health care needs (Baum, 2004). Some computer-based mental health treatments have also been found to be quite effective in addressing issues like social anxiety (Amir et al., 2009) and are touted for their ability to address issues of access and efficiency (Griffiths and Christenson, 2006).

Policymaking and Program Planning

Finally, there is the need to more effectively use technology in program planning and policymaking. Big data can be leveraged to address everything from monitoring prevalence of need, to cross-sector system participation, to laying the foundation for monitoring of interventions to improve outcomes (Coulton et al., 2015). This topic is discussed in much greater detail in Chapter 14 of this volume, but here we discuss the issue in the context of service systems.

As noted earlier, services and information from multiple sectors are often needed to address the needs of populations with whom social workers and health providers routinely interact (Bradley and Taylor, 2013; Jonson-Reid et al., 2017). The use of such linked data to inform both the consumer and policy is much more advanced in other countries (Lyons et al., 2009; Sadana and Harper, 2011; Thygesen et al., 2011). Indeed, the United Kingdom has moved toward empowering the general public through the use of linked data to understand conditions in their region (Shadbolt et al., 2012). A similar approach, called For the Sake of All, was launched by Washington University faculty to empower communities with data to improve health disparities in the St. Louis region (Purnell et al., 2018). This has the potential of encouraging effective demand (discussed earlier) as well as what Bovaird (2007) describes as the coproduction of public services. In the United States, the use of big data to inform policy and programming is gaining increasing traction. There is a growing network of researchers using linked data and a wider movement toward leveraging such data for social good that holds promise for accelerating the appropriate use of linked data in the United States (e.g., Data Science for Social Good, University of Chicago; Los Angeles Children's Data Network). On the other hand, some research indicates that such linked approaches like Collective Impact do not necessarily result in good collaborative application of big data (Fink, 2018). In other words, gathering more data is only a tool that can increase impact if it is effectively and collaboratively applied.

Along with the need for linked data, however, is the need for the application of nonlinear approaches that can account for complex system interactions (Bradley and Taylor, 2013; Jonson-Reid et al., 2018; Vaithianathan et al., 2013). There are a variety of systems science and machine-learning approaches appearing in the health and social sciences. One example is the increasing discussion of the use of predictive risk modeling (long used in health care) in social service sectors like child protection to better target preventive services (Vaithiainathan et al., 2013). Another example is the use of microsimulation for modeling possible impacts of policy shifts. Microsimulation methods are part of a family of models sometimes described as systems science models, which are widely used to model the effects of policy and systems change on people, organizations, and populations. Microsimulation models use large numbers of "micro" units (usually individuals or families drawn from real samples or administrative data) to quantitatively measure the impacts of social policy or program changes (Levy, 2014).

In the past, large microprocessors were required for estimating microsimulation models, particularly if the models used large populations, required many iterations to estimate, or relied on sophisticated dynamic models. With the rapid development of computing power, microsimulation models are now easily handled on most personal computers. A prior barrier to preventing the widespread use of such approaches was the technical expertise required in computer science. In the past, models were built using older computer languages (e.g., FORTRAN, COBOL), but currently a variety of software packages can be used for this process including SAS or SPSS, which are commonly used in social work research (Goldhaber-Fiebert et al., 2012). A microsimulation approach can be useful not only for informing policy (the more typical use for this method) but also for researchers seeking implementation of new practices for children reported to child protective services (Aarons et al., 2012).

Another systems science approach is the use of group model building that allows group members trying to address a given problem to develop a shared understanding over time (Hovmand et al., 2012; Hovmand, 2014; Munar et al., 2015). The approach uses visual formal causal maps and computer models within a structured approach (Black and Anderson, 2012; Hovmand, 2014) that provides a powerful tool for designing effective transdisciplinary collaborations and learning collaboratives for identifying intervention or strategies.

Finally, techniques like network analyses provide understanding into complex interrelationships (Luke et al., 2013) as well as collaborative networks designed to support program and policy (Harris et al., 2017). While individual-linked data help us understand the flow of service consumers through systems, analysis at the social network level can help us understand the collaboration between providers, researchers, and policy networks.

Linking Policy to Performance

Systems should be developed with complete logic models and clear connections between the populations, needs, services, and outcomes. These models should be linked across sectors. Such models can support flexibility to redirect resources among social service providers based on need and consolidate (or coordinate) services to reduce inefficiency. Such a framework also supports advocacy by clearly illustrating gaps between outcomes desired and services available.

Financial Innovations and System Reform

Because payment systems in health care are rapidly moving to forms of accountable health care organizations, strong incentives are emerging that emphasize social service providers in health care delivery. A burgeoning literature has indicated improved health outcomes and cost savings from these efforts to integrate health and social services (Hong et al., 2014; Taylor et al., 2016). While the change of federal administration and policy leadership casts some uncertainty over this health and service integration movement, it is clear that service integration with health, especially in behavioral health and substance abuse treatment, will present important opportunities for social work and social service organizations.

Alternative models of funding for services with financing problems have received a great deal of attention in the literature, along with interest from foundations and government. Social entrepreneurship has been seen as one pathway out of financial distress by some organizations. Globally, various forms of "pay for performance" or "pay for success" have been proposed, and a number of projects have been implemented, although little outcome data are available (Iovan, Lantz, and Shapiro, 2018). In many ways, these new pay for success initiatives are extensions of a long tradition of performance based contracting in social services. The most dramatic of these new models are Social Impact Bonds, which tie private investment to measurable service outcome targets and, if met, provide investors with financial returns. The earliest of these Social Impact Bonds in the United States attempted to reduce juvenile offender recidivism at Rikers Island in New York City. The project attracted investment capital from Bloomberg Philanthropies and Goldman Sachs, but because the recidivism targets were not met, the investor repayments were not made (Cohen and Zelnick, 2015). Despite this early unsuccessful experience, the federal government, state governments, and numerous foundations have been developing Social Impact Bonds projects in child welfare, public health, homelessness, early childhood education, and many other applications. Recent work points out that the viability of this approach may well depend on the availability of experts to identify the appropriate cost basis for outcomes, whether payments are based on expected short- or long-term outcomes, and the participation of organizations capable of handling the extensive administrative responsibilities of these programs (Temple and Reynolds, 2015). The successful use of this approach for bolstering social work programming and policy must also rely on the availability of evidence-based approaches with sufficient effect sizes to engage investors (Bafford, 2014). Empirical evidence for the use of this approach in improving social problems remains elusive (Fraser et al., 2018).

Another collaborative finance approach deals with the "collective impact" movement. This approach for solving social issues encourages cross-sector collaboration around an agreed upon issue with significant attention to coordination effort and outcome assessment (Wolff, 2016). These include unified foundation led approaches. Experts caution, however, that funders must not drive the effort but rather support the development of the collaboration needed to impact change, which often takes several years (Easterbrook, 2013). Other critics of the approach point to the fact that it lacks the depth of community engagement and willingness to address structural/policy changes needed to achieve goals found in more grassroots community organizing efforts (Christens and Inzeo, 2015). It is not clear if this tendency toward less community engagement may impact the longer-range financial support of such approaches.

While these new financing arrangements have many agendas, they are fundamentally about changing the incentives for services, encouraging new forms of collaboration and service delivery, and increasing program and financial accountability. It is still too early to say whether these new financing and organizational models will actually leverage significant new financial capital into services, lead to innovations in service delivery, or break down the many siloes amongst organizations (Gustafsson-Wright, Gardiner, and Putcha, 2015).

Research and Program Planning

There is a need to map out the desired (or understood) relationship of a given policy against real data on the provision of services and outcomes achieved. For example, a service system may hold on to an erroneous idea about how a given policy is related to service provision. In national reports as well as some state policy, substantiation is used as an indicator of whether or not maltreatment actually occurred and if a child should be labeled as a "victim." This designation can then drive practice in relation to which children and families need services. Drake and Jonson-Reid (2000) identified a disconnect between the use of substantiation as a case disposition and the need for services among families reported for abuse or neglect. In subsequent work, an additional disconnect was made clear between the use of substantiation and a variety of child outcomes (Drake et al., 2003; Hussey et al., 2005; Kohl, Jonson-Reid, and Drake, 2009). Evidence indicates that substantiation is a poor proxy for both service needs and maltreatment outcomes. In other words, a child may have experienced maltreatment but not receive a designation of substantiation. Unfortunately, the term "substantiation" remains conflated with the term "victim" in policy. When the federal government reports summary data from states on child maltreatment reports, details are only provided on "victims" (cases that were substantiated; U.S. Department of Health and Human Services, 2019). This creates a much lower prevalence rate for maltreatment. This lower number, in turn, often guides consumption of other policy relevant research like the recent Centers for Disease Control–sponsored effort to estimate the cost of maltreatment (Fang et al., 2012). The cost of $124 billion that is most frequently repeated is actually only the cost for substantiated cases.

As Michael Lipsky (2010) points out, it is important to not only be aware of the intended meaning of a given policy or process but also the practical application. Not understanding this can lead to erroneous decisions about the function of a system or categorization of a case as in the previous example. Another example lies in the reforms to address the overrepresentation of ethnic minority children in special education that was based on inaccurate analyses of participation rates (Morgan et al., 2015). The unintended consequence of incentives to prevent the enrollment of ethnic minority children appears to be the under-representation and service of this group.

System reform is arguably different than system creation or completion. However, neither can be effectively achieved without careful examination of what exists in policy and how it is executed (Jonson-Reid, 2011; Jonson-Reid et al., 2017; Lipsky, 2010). There are often significant gaps in our understanding of the characteristics of people served, the services provided, and outcomes. For example, despite the creation of the Indian Child Welfare Act over 30 years ago (Fletcher, Singel, and Fort, 2009), we know relatively little about how services are provided. Furthermore, tribal child welfare data are often not reported to state child welfare agencies (Fox, 2003). This results in reports that American Indian/Native Alaskan children have lower rates of maltreatment reports than black, white, or Hispanic groups (Kim et al., 2017) despite overwhelming evidence of the high rate of trauma exposure among native children (Bubar, 2010; Dorgan et al., 2014; Ehlers et al., 2013; U.S. Census Bureau, 2011). Not clearly understanding the characteristics of a population to be served and what services are being provided can lead to a mismatch of funding allocation as well as problems of culturally relevant intervention. Integrated data (or big data), which is the topic of Chapter 14 of this volume, also has the potential to better assist us in conducting policy relevant research as well as targeting populations most in need of services (Comer et al., 2011; Jonson-Reid and Drake, 2008; Putnam-Hornstein, Needell, and Rhodes, 2013).

Michael Lipsky (2010) notes that there is also a need to understand the provider and organizational context that may alter the actual execution of a given policy due to resource constraints, training, or both. Concerns about costs in the health care system may lead to impossible caseloads and decreased time with patients. On the other hand, demand for services and fears of reprisals if these demands are not met may result in overprescribing medical intervention (Bradley and Taylor, 2013). In public social services, there are often instances of competing demands between policy mandates and the reality of the practice environment. In child welfare, for example, workers are often called upon to make difficult decisions in the context of low resources and constrained time (Jonson-Reid and Drake, 2018).

While social work has long embraced the ecological or person-in-environment model, the complex interplay of service consumer characteristics and needs, available services, and the context of service provision requires professionals to not only think about nested influences but also the complex and dynamic interactions between them. When goals are or are not achieved, social workers must be able to think through the many competing explanations for these outcomes to best identify the leverage points for change.

New Integrated Models of Practice

In health care, the Centers for Medicare and Medicaid Services (2017) has sponsored a large number of innovation demonstration projects designed to develop and test new models of service and health care integration. These models leverage existing community services to address social determinants of health and produce crosswalks to adjacent social and health needs such as behavioral health and long term care. For example, the State of Minnesota created an Accountable Communities for Health program that integrates medical care with behavioral health services, public health, long-term care, social services, and other forms of care. Operationally, this model includes community care teams that combine health care providers (e.g., physician groups, hospitals) with behavioral health, public health, social services, and community-based economic development organizations.

Collaborative planning and service integration can be a complex task. In addition to traditional approaches for developing logic models in planning and evaluation (Julian, 1997; Monette et al., 2013), there are innovative means of using technology to bridge the gap between policy and practice. As discussed earlier, advances in technologies make use of available data to guide practice from the policy level down to the individual client assessment and outcome level. Better mining and use of existing data linked between sectors of care provide opportunities to address disparity and improve outcomes by understanding how individuals or families are or are not accessing services provided through different organizations and sectors of care (Hall et al., 2012; Krahnet al., 2010). The aforementioned approaches such as network analyses can also be a powerful tool in understanding the process of collaboration among organizations (Luke and Harris, 2007). For example, this process can assist in identifying areas for strengthening collaboration among partners (Harris, et al., 2017). As social and health services data are increasingly automated, the creation of complex computational models to simulate (as well as evaluate) practice may lead to differing models of care for addressing what seemed intractable before.

Building Effective Demand

The issue of access to care across domains of need can be linked to demand. In other words, in addition to advocacy by social or health services providers and organizations, some argue that demand should also come from the consumer. This is similar to the idea that once individuals become aware of the value of a given product (i.e., a new cereal), they will begin to demand that local stores carry that product. While this is more commonly thought of in terms of demand for a given higher-quality intervention, it has also been applied more broadly for demand of services that support areas of functioning that are not tied to a particular crisis. For example, this approach has been used to influence the availability and use of contraception in international settings (Belaid et al., 2016). While social service providers can and should proactively identify and address challenges faced by clients beyond the needs that brought them to their service (Thompson, Kreuter and Boyum, 2015), there is also a need for broader public education.

Marketing the availability of services across multiple demands as compared to a specific topic does not easily lend itself to public education campaigns. There are, however, other approaches such as community resource fairs (a recommended child abuse prevention strategy in the 2016 Children's Bureau of Prevention Resource Guide) or various information dissemination strategies based in community centers (Children's Bureau, 2016; Broeckling et al., 2015). Actual outcome research on such approaches remains limited, while informational efforts are often grouped as one aspect of a larger programmatic effort (Beals-Erickson and Roberts, 2016; Worthy and Beaulieu, 2016). Hypothetically, these efforts offer a means of providing attendees with a menu of services and resources that may be needed now or in future local forums. It is not known how such approaches in and of themselves may change help-seeking behavior. More recently, at least one community has attempted to offer an electronic version of a menu-driven resource information guide (Fleefler et al., 2016). Nevertheless, research on building knowledge related to social services opportunities is relatively scant although the use of some form of public education approach is found in the international health literature and in at least one U.S. study of preventive mental health intervention (Boyum et al., 2016).

Other avenues to improve awareness in communities exist. Community-engaged strategies, variously called community-based participatory or community action research, have led to the development and assessment of educational strategies designed to increase knowledge among community members in critical areas. These efforts and the community response to them may provide information and knowledge relevant to attempts intended to increase awareness of social services resources and their use. Guided by the Children's Bureau of Prevention Resource Guide principles, the Program for the Elimination of Cancer Disparities researchers implemented a community training initiative that increased community research literacy, confidence, and willingness to engage as equals with practitioners and academic researchers. The Community Research Fellows Training program (D'Agostino McGowan et al., 2015) has trained community members, with participants now engaging in diverse activities that include partnership participation, research project coordination, research review, community interventions, and advisory board service (Thompson et al., 2015). Other approaches have included the use of community educators who are lay persons trained to deliver information about the need for and availability of care (Srihari et al., 2014). Efforts of the type described may be useful in increasing demand for existing and additional services developed through engaged strategies.

When the right to self-determination by members of marginalized and vulnerable groups is recognized (in conjunction with input from important stakeholders, including community organizations, social service agencies, political leaders, and community advocates), there is an opportunity to establish mutually agreed upon goals (International Association for Public Participation, n.d.; Zakus and Lysack, 1998). In the atmosphere of collaborative problem-solving, there is a greater likelihood of resource commitments and development of strategies and interventions that operate at multiple levels (Castro, Barrera, and Martinez, 2004). More recently, this idea has been extended beyond mere input from stakeholders to realizing the community as co-producers of services (Bovaird, 2007). In some ways, this is akin to the intent and operation of grassroots community organizing principles (Christens and Inzeo, 2015) but applied to the development and delivery of services. The results of public participation and community engagement serve as catalysts for changing policies, programs, and practices.

Social work, with its emphasis on client self-determination and advocacy for social justice, is ideally positioned to improve the participation of communities in the development and oversight of services. On the other hand, there are limiting system constraints that argue against increased information because of the inability to respond (Lipsky, 2010; Morgan et al., 2015). Social work must be willing to work across levels and professions to advocate for the system level resources needed to match the demand so that stakeholder involvement can be fully realized and lead to impactful change.

Adapting Intervention to Enhance Acceptability and Reduce Stigma

While it is generally accepted that the highest-quality evidence-based interventions should be used, the existence of an intervention that is not acceptable or culturally sensitive to a given population can be a significant barrier to participation. Castro, Barrera, and Steiker (2010) identified steps that should guide decisions to culturally adapt evidence-based interventions. First, the time and effort required to complete a cultural adaptation must be justified. This may be based on prior failure to reach or engage members of low income, impoverished, and/or other marginalized populations, program failure, and/or the presence of unique cultural risk factors or symptoms. Once cultural adaptation has been justified, an evidence-based intervention is selected and cultural adaptations can be made in program content and delivery. Manuel Barrera and colleagues (2013) report five stages of cultural adaptation that represent a refinement of earlier recommendations: information gathering, preliminary design, preliminary testing, refinement, and final trials for diabetes interventions. Their review suggests that interventions involving the inclusion of cultural elements in an adaptation are more effective than control or usual care conditions. However, there is little evidence to suggest that all or most adaptations of this type incorporate this or earlier recommended strategies (Thompson Sanders et al., 2015).

Frameworks for cultural adaptations have emerged in two forms (Thompson Sanders et al., 2015). The first involves modification within content categories (Kreuter et al., 2003; Resnicow et al., 1999; Sosa, Biedeger-Friedman, and Yin, 2013). The second relates to the creation of approaches to intervention with the community at the onset. Most prominent among the first form was Resnicow et al.'s (1999) reference to "deep structure," which recognizes, reinforces. and builds upon a group's cultural values, beliefs, and behaviors to provide context and meaning to important components of the intervention.

Further efforts to specify the elements discussed by Resnicow have moved toward the second form. Matthew Kreuter and colleagues (2003) focused on the use of data specific to a group (e.g., testimonials, narratives, stories, and statistics) to raise awareness and/or perceived vulnerability to issues and constituent-involving strategies, including hiring group members who are indigenous to the population, training paraprofessionals from within the community, and extensive community engagement (Aguilar-Gaxiola et al., 2002). Through designing interventions around cultural constituents, their insider knowledge regarding the community's perceptions increased acceptability and relevance at the community level (Aguilar-Gaxiola et al., 2002; Satterfield et al., 2014; Sosa et al., 2013).

It is important to note that while much of the literature on adaptation and stigma may focus on ethnic culture, similar issues may arise when attempting to serve vulnerable populations beyond ethnicity. For example, some of the same elements noted in the adaptation and stigma literature are also strategies recommended in the engagement literature for vulnerable populations such as parents involved with child welfare, LGBT youth, HIV prevention, rural populations, military families, and others (Boyce et al., 2018; Cigrang et al., 2016; Kemp et al., 2009; Vance, 2017). The idea of adaptation based on a given context to reduce stigma and enhance access to and engagement with services is consistent with the long history of reliance on an ecological model of social work (Ungar, 2002).

Building the Research Infrastructure

The ability to address the complex issues behind access and participation in effective services requires ongoing research. Rowena Fong (2012) suggests that social work education, particularly at the doctoral level, needs to move from viewing social work as solely professional practice to one of science. Resolving system barriers through research requires a complex understanding of the populations served, utilization of community engaged research, and effective use of advancing technologies. Analytic models must embrace the complexity of factors, from the client, to the line worker, to the organization, to policy, to assure that barriers and inefficiencies are identified and the proper target level for intervention is set in place. Rigorous measurement of outcomes achieved when changes are implemented must identify the practical significance to justify cost. The complexity of the issues addressed and the systems engaged call for an interdisciplinary or transdisciplinary approach for this training (Tucker, 2008).

Advancing in scientific rigor, of course, does not imply the absence of applied and community-engaged approaches. Many schools of social work specifically embrace community-engaged research approaches while methodology texts have been designed to support this emphasis (Padgett, 2008; Soska and Butterfield, 2013). Research also exists to guide the process of partnership development to support these efforts (Begun et al., 2010). In addition to U.S. based efforts, schools of social work around the globe are increasingly teaching research skills. Such immersion in community and various cultures is evidenced by the work done at the University of Texas at Austin to create a research practicum in a military setting for preparing doctoral candidates interested in working with this population (Dumars et al., 2015). Recognizing the specific time limitations of faculty and students addressing the range of needs to build evidence among community partners, the George Warren Brown School of Social Work has invested in an Evaluation Center that provides training for community partners as well as brokering evaluation opportunities and assisting with evaluation efforts.

Increasingly, schools of social work are also embracing the training of future researchers in advanced uses of data and analytic approaches. For example, at Washington University, the Center for Public Health Systems Science sponsors an interest group in network science to share information about related techniques and applications among students and established scholars (http://networkscience.wustl.edu/). The Social System Design Lab offers coursework and project-based learning for graduate students and faculty interest in systems science approaches to solving social problems (https://sites.wustl.edu/ssdl/research-and-training/). The Center for Innovation in Child Maltreatment Policy, Research and Training includes a large project focused on development of cross-state data programming and analysis infrastructure. It not only provides training opportunities for students but is also ultimately designed to offer a programming and analysis toolkit that will be available for researchers as well as state agency organizations (Child Welfare Data SMART; https://cicm.wustl.edu/about-us/projects-2/).

Application of technology is not limited to analytic approaches that lend themselves to systems problems. Doctoral students must also be prepared for advanced applications of data as well as use of technology in research. Pennsylvania State University has recently launched an integrative graduate education program aimed at training researchers in social data analytics (http://bdss.psu.edu/soda). A number of universities now offer specialized programming to support the development of and use of data for social good (Zheng, 2018). The University of Southern California School of Social Work houses and partially supports the Los Angeles Children's Data Network providing a range of opportunities for fellows and students and well as faculty. Washington University has begun a new doctoral program in Computational and Data Sciences that blends expertise in an applied social science area (including social work) with advanced methodological training in computational and statistical methods.

Transdisciplinary and translational work is also key to working on complex problems and developing high-impact research products (Nurius, 2016). While examples exist of truly interdisciplinary doctoral programs that require joint degrees across disciplines such as at the University of Michigan; most are not. There is also a role for postdoctoral interdisciplinary and transdisciplinary education to assist with this process (James et al., 2015). Finally, transdisciplinary approaches must apply to both team science and the dissemination of information (Jonson-Reid et al., 2013). The most efficacious model for developing researchers capable of thinking across systems and disciplines is not yet clear, but the need to innovate in the area remains critical.

Training Effective Practitioners

Graduate-level education must also keep pace with the need to work across systems and disciplines along with the need for access to data and technology. While the acceptance of evidence-based practice preparation across schools of social work has grown, the need for a transdisciplinary approach is also becoming evident (Bellamy et al., 2013; Stanhope et al., 2015). The common comorbid existence of problems and needs stands in stark contrast with the siloed nature of our service systems. Calls for better collaboration and coordination are unlikely to succeed without a workforce that is prepared to operate in this space. For example, the call for integration of behavioral health and health care not only provides an opportunity for social work but also requires an approach to training that integrates knowledge of complex issues as well as the sometimes divergent service systems (Croft and Parish, 2013; Patel et al., 2013).

Students must also be prepared to use data and technology in practice. As innovations like clinical dashboards and performance-based system feedback (Dowding et al., 2015; Florida Dept of Education, n.d.) are increasingly implemented, students must enter the field literate in their use (Lery et al., 2015). Further, there is increasing use of technology such as apps and telehealth to complement in-person services (Ramsey and Montgomery, 2014). The skills needed for effective and ethical client engagement and practice in such models may differ from the way in which direct practice skills are traditionally taught (Dombo, Kays, and Weller, 2014; Mishna, Fantus, and McInroy, 2016).

Finally, similar to the education of future researchers, the education of future practitioners must include attention to effective practice within diverse communities. While this is generally an area of strength in social work, methods of training such as immersion in diverse settings continue to evolve (Dumars et al., 2015). Indeed, the understanding of culture and community is deeply important for practice innovations such as the use of information and communication technology in social services (Bryant et al., 2018). As culture and community are not static, it is important that the understanding of these constructs is continually updated and appropriate material infused throughout the curriculum.

For example, computerization of training is being tested both in terms of ongoing professional development to advance practice (Patterson Silver Wolf et al., 1997), as well as treatment and outreach for service users (Amir et al., 2009; Mishna et al., 2014; Hughes et al., 2017). While the social justice aspects of reaching underserved and vulnerable populations are many, training for practitioners on the best practices in technology use will be an important aspect of professional development in social work (Bryant et al., 2018; Lee and Harathi, 2016). This is a continually evolving area that requires both improvements to graduate education along with outreach to alumni for them to engage in professional development as new technologies or use of technologies are developed and tested.

As improved practice frameworks for interorganizational and community collaboration are developed, they must be effectively communicated to the practice community. For example, literature suggests that collaborative models should be supported in strategic planning efforts to assure maximum effort in place-based initiatives (Dupre et al., 2016). Partnerships with academic institutions that can provide consultation to address these needs using tools like network analyses or systems dynamics are warranted. This requires graduates to remain connected to the research world whether at the clinical, management, or policy levels. The School of Social Work at Washington University has cultivated such partnerships around systems analytic approaches through the Social Systems Dynamics Lab trainings and the Center for Public Health Systems Network Research Interest Group. The school's Clark-Fox Institute Graduate Policy Scholars Program helps connect students with opportunities for working with leadership to engage in policy analysis, communication strategies, and advocacy efforts. Additionally, the institute convenes forums and assists with advocacy outreach for key issues that continue to engage alumni and other community members in policy advocacy. The Brown School Professional Development program provides outreaches to the broader community that provides ongoing training in evidence-based clinical and management approaches.

At the policy advocacy level, future practitioners should be able to use or develop empirical data that helps to articulate where there are gaps in services or poor quality. They must be skilled in effectively sharing knowledge with policymakers and the community, ideally being aware of both the potential solutions and costs.

Related to issues of effective demand and culturally acceptable and appropriate services, social work practitioners must be a part of the process of disseminating information to communities and individuals about the types of supports available to them. In this way, social work advocates engagement with vulnerable communities to develop effective demand as well as encouraging participation in policy advocacy work. Finally, there is a need to advocate for earlier connection to the supports that provide better opportunities for ameliorating potential economic, educational, health, and mental health difficulties in the long-term.

Conclusion

A livable life means accessing effective services when needed across the lifespan rather than waiting until problems worsen and become increasingly impossible to overcome. This requires a fundamentally different mindset toward how we view supportive services. Rather than discussions focused narrowly on one silo as illustrated by the current debate about health care, service functions should be guided by an ecodevelopmental frame. We need to ask what services are necessary across what sectors and during what periods of life to support an individual's ability to function in relationships, families, the workplace, and their community. We also must have the capacity to deliver services across regions and populations at consistent rather than episodic crisis-oriented levels. Services should also be accessible and acceptable to the population in need. In addition, they must be data driven such that services adapt to changing needs.

Social work, by its very nature takes a multidisciplinary and ecological perspective on the world. Given this, the profession should focus on building systems to support positive development rather than reacting within siloed systems of care. A social justice approach to services may help advance this work. In other words, if we view services as a public good that is necessary to a livable life, then access to effective services (including assurance that the public is adequately informed about best practices and resources available) is an integral part of advancing social justice. Reaching this goal will also require more than efforts within social work. Clearly, this is a transdisciplinary problem that will require the willingness and the literacy needed to effectively collaborate at the practice, policy, and research levels.

References

Aarons, G. A., A. E. Green, L. A. Palinkas, S. Self-Brown, D. J. Whitaker, J. R. Lutzker, and M. J. Chaffin. 2012. "Dynamic Adaptation Process to Implement an Evidence-Based Child Maltreatment Intervention." *Implementation Science*, 7, 1–9.

Aguilar-Gaxiola, S. A., L. Zelezny, B. Garcia, C. Edmondson, C., Alejo-Garcia, and W. Vega. 2002. "Mental Health Care for Latinos: Translating Research into Action: Reducing Disparities in Mental Health Care for Mexican Americans." *Psychiatric Services*, 53, 1563–1568.

Amarasingham, R., L. Plantinga, M. Diener-West, D. J. Gaskin, and N. R. Powe. 2009. "Clinical Information Technologies and Inpatient Outcomes: A Multiple Hospital Study." *Archives of Internal Medicine*, 169, 108–114.

Amir, N., C. Beard, C. T. Taylor, H. Klumpp, J. Elias, M. Burns, and X. Chen. 2009. "Attention Training in Individuals with Generalized Social Phobia: A Randomized Controlled Trial." *Journal of Consulting and Clinical Psychology*, 77, 961–973.

Bafford, B. 2014. "The Feasibility and Future of Social Impact Bonds in the United States." *Sanford Journal of Public Policy*, 3, 12–19.

Barrera, M., F. G. Castro, L. A. Stryker, and D. J. Toobert. 2013. "Cultural Adaptations of Behavioral Health Interventions: A Progress Report." *Journal of Consulting and Clinical Psychology*, 81, 196–205.

Baum, L. S. 2004. "Internet Parent Support Groups for Primary Caregivers of a Child with Special Health Care Needs." *Pediatric Nursing*, 30, 381–390.

Bayer, R., and S. Galea. 2015. "Public Health in the Precision-Medicine Era." *New England Journal of Medicine*, 373, 499–501.

Beals-Erickson, S. E., and M. C. Roberts. 2016. "Youth Development Program Participation and Changes in Help-Seeking Intentions," *Journal of Child and Family Studies*, 25, 1634–1645.

Begun, A. L., L. K. Berger, L. L. Otto-Salaj, and S. J. Rose. 2010. "Developing Effective Social Work University-Community Research Collaborations." *Social Work*, 55, 54–62.

Belaid, L., A. Dumont, N. Chaillet, A. Zertal, D. V. Brouwere, S. Hounton, and V. Ridde. 2016. "Effectiveness of Demand Generation Interventions on Use of Modern Contraceptives in Low and Middle Income Countries." *Tropical Medicine and International Health*, 21, 1240–1254.

Bellamy, J. L., E. J. Mullen, J. M. Satterfield, R. P. Newhouse, M. Ferguson, R. C. Brownson, and B. Spring. 2013. "Implementing Evidence-Based Practice Education in Social Work a Transdisciplinary Approach." *Research on Social Work Practice*, 23, 426–436.

Berkowitz, S. A., A. C. Hulberg, S. Standish, G. Reznor, and S. J. Atlas. 2017. "Addressing Unmet Basic Resource Needs as Part of Chronic Cardiometabolic Disease Management." *JAMA Internal Medicine*, 177, 244–252.

Bingley P., and I. Walker. 1997. "The Labour Supply, Unemployment and Participation of Lone Mothers in In-Work Transfer Programmes." *The Economic Journal*, 107, 1375–1390.

Black, L., and D. Andersen. 2012. "Using Visual Representations as Boundary Objects to Resolve Conflict in Collaborative Model-Building Applications." *Systems Research and Behavioral Science*, 29, 194–208

Bouchery, E. E., H. J. Harwood, J. J Sacks, C. J. Simon, and R. D. Brewer. 2011. "Economic Costs of Excessive Alcohol Consumption in the U.S., 2006." *American Journal of Preventive Medicine*, 41, 516–524.

Bouffard, J., M. Cooper, and K. Bergseth. 2016. "The Effectiveness of Various Restorative Justice Interventions on Recidivism Outcomes Among Juvenile Offenders." *Youth Violence and Juvenile Justice*, 15, 465–480.

Bovaird, T. 2007. "Beyond Engagement and Participation: User and Community Coproduction of Public Services." *Public Administration Review*, 67(5), 846–860.

Boyce, K. S., M. Travers, B. Rothbart, V. Santiago, and J. Bedell. 2018. "Adapting Evidence-Based Teen Pregnancy Programs to Be LGBT-Inclusive: Lessons Learned." *Health Promotion Practice*, 19, 445–454.

Boyum, S., M. W. Kreuter, A. McQueen, T. Thompson, and R. Greer. 2016. "Getting Help from 2-1-1: A Statewide Study of Referral Outcomes." *Journal of Social Service Research*, 42, 402–411.

Bradley, E. H., and L. A. Taylor. 2013. *The American Health Care Paradox: Why Spending More Is Getting Us Less*. New York: PublicAffairs.

Broeckling, J., L. Pinsoneault, A. Dahlquist, and M. Van Hoorn. 2015. "Using Authentic Engagement to Improve Health Outcomes: Community Center Practices and Values (at the Agency)." *Families in Society*, 96, 165–174.

Bryant, L., B., Garnham, D. Tedmanson, and S. Diamandi. 2018. "Tele-Social Work and Mental Health in Rural and Remote Communities in Australia." *International Social Work*, 61, 143–155.

Bubar, R. 2010. "Cultural Competence, Justice, and Supervision: Sexual Assault Against Native Women." *Women and Therapy*, 33, 55–72.

Burke, M. M. 2013. "Improving Parental Involvement: Training Special Education Advocates." *Journal of Disability Policy Studies*, 23, 225–234.

Butler, S., and M. Constantine. 2005. "Collective Self-Esteem and Burnout in Professional School Counselors." *Professional School Counseling*, 9, 55–62.

Castro, F. G., M. Barrera Jr., and C. R. Martinez Jr. 2004. "The Cultural Adaptation of Prevention Interventions: Resolving Tensions Between Fidelity and Fit." *Prevention Science*, 5, 41–45.

Castro, F. G., M. Barrera Jr., and L. K. Holleran Steiker. 2010. "Issues and Challenges in the Design of Culturally Adapted Evidence-Based Interventions." *Annual Review of Clinical Psychology*, 6, 213–239.

Centers for Medicare and Medicaid Services. 2017. "State Innovation Models Initiative: Model Test Awards Round One." Retrieved from https://innovation.cms.gov/initiatives/State-Innovations-Model-Testing/index.html

Chaffin, M., D. Bard, D. S. Bigfoot, and E. J. Maher. 2012. "Is a Structured, Manualized, Evidence-Based Treatment Protocol Culturally Competent and Equivalently Effective Among American Indian Parents in Child Welfare?" *Child Maltreatment*, 17, 242–252.

Christens, B. D., and P. T. Inzeo. 2015. "Widening the View: Situating Collective Impact Among Frameworks for Community-Led Change." *Community Development*, 46(4), 420–435.

Cigrang, J. A., J. V. Cordova, T. D. Gray, E. Najera, M. Hawrilenko, C. Pinkley, M. Nielsen, J. Tatum, and K. Redd. 2016. "The Marriage Checkup: Adapting and Implementing a Brief Relationship Intervention for Military Couples." *Cognitive and Behavioral Practice*, 23, 561–570.

Cohen, D., and J. Zelnick. 2015. "What We Learned from the Failure of the Rikers Island Social Impact Bond." *Nonprofit Quarterly*. https://nonprofitquarterly.org/2015/08/07/what-we-learned-from-the-failure-of-the-rikers-island-social-impact-bond/

Comer, K. F., S. Grannis, B. E. Dixon, D. J. Bodenhamer, and S. E. Wiehe. 2011. "Incorporating Geospatial Capacity Within Clinical Data Systems to Address Social Determinants of Health." *Public Health Reports*, 126(Supp 3), 54–61.

Coulton, C., R. George, E. Putnam-Hornstein, and B. de Haan. 2015, July. "Harnessing Big Data for Social Good: A Grand Challenge for Social Work." Working Paper No 11. Retrieved from http://aaswsw.org/wp-content/uploads/2015/12/WP11-with-cover.pdf

Croft, B., and S. L. Parish. 2013. "Care Integration in the Patient Protection and Affordable Care Act: Implications for Behavioral Health." *Administration and Policy in Mental Health and Mental Health Services Research*, 40, 258–263.

D'Agostino McGowan, L., J. Stafford, V. L Thompson, B. Johnson, and M. S. Goodman. 2015. "Quantitative Evaluation of the Community Research Fellows Training Program." *Frontiers in Public Health*, 3, 179. http://dx.doi.org/10.3389/fpubh.2015.00179

Darkins, A., P. Ryan, R. Kobb, L. Foster, E. Edmonson, B. Wakefield, and A. E. Lancaster. 2008. "Care Coordination/Home Telehealth: The Systematic Implementation of Health Informatics, Home Telehealth, and Disease Management to Support the Care of Veteran Patients with Chronic Conditions." *Telemedicine and e-Health*, 14, 1118–1126.

Devaney, J., and T. Spratt. 2009. Child Abuse as a Complex and Wicked Problem: "Reflecting on Policy Developments in the United Kingdom in Working with Children and Families with Multiple Problems." *Children and Youth Services Review*, 31, 635–641.

Dombo, E. A., L. Kays, and K. Weller. 2014. Clinical Social Work Practice and Technology: Personal, Practical, Regulatory, and Ethical Considerations for the Twenty-First Century. *Social Work in Health Care*, 53, 900–919.

Dorgan, B. L., J. Shenandoah, D. Bigfoot, E. Broderick, E. Brown, V. Davidson, A. Fineday, M. Flitcher, J. Keel, R. Whitener, and M. Zimmerman. 2014, November. "Ending Violence So American Indian Alaska Native children Can Thrive." Attorney General's Advisory Committee, U.S. Department of Justice.

Dowding, D., R. Randell, P. Gardner, G. Fitzpatrick, P. Dykes, J. Favela, S. Hamer, Z. Whitewood-Moores, N. Hardiker, E. Borycki, and L. Currie. 2015. "Dashboards for Improving Patient Care: Review of the Literature." *International Journal of Medical Informatics*, 8, 87–100.

Drake, B., and M. Jonson-Reid. 2000. "Substantiation, Risk Assessment and Involuntary Versus Voluntary Services." *Child Maltreatment*, 5, 227–235.

Drake, B., M. Jonson-Reid, I. Way, and S. Chung. 2003. "Substantiation and Recidivism." *Child Maltreatment*, 8, 248–260.

DuMars, T., K. Bolton, A. Maleku, and A. Smith-Osborne. 2015. Training MSSW Students for Military Social Work Practice and Doctoral Students in Military Resilience Research. *Journal of Social Work Education*, 51(Supp 1), S117–S127.

Dupre, M. E., J. Moody, A. Nelson, J. M. Willis, L. Fuller, A. J. Smart, D. Easterling, and M. Silberberg. 2016. "Place-Based Initiatives to Improve Health in Disadvantaged Communities: Cross-Sector Characteristics and Networks of Local Actors in North Carolina." *American Journal of Public Health*, 106, 1548–1555.

Ehlers, C. L., I. R., Gizer, D. A. Gilder, J. M. Ellingson, and R. Yehuda. 2013. "Measuring Historical Trauma in an American Indian Community Sample: Contributions of Substance Dependence, Affective Disorder, Conduct Disorder and PTSD." *Drug and Alcohol Dependence*, 133, 180–187.

Ensor, T., and S. Cooper. 2004. "Overcoming Barriers to Health Service Access: Influencing the Demand Side." *Health Policy and Planning*, 19, 69–79.

Fang, X., S. D. Brown, C. S. Florence, and J. Mercy. 2012. "The Economic Burden of Child Maltreatment in the United States and Implications for Prevention." *Child Abuse and Neglect*, 36, 156–165.

Fink, A. 2018. "Bigger Data, Less Wisdom: The Need for More Inclusive Collective Intelligence in Social Service Provision." *AI and Society*, 33, 61–70.

Fitzgerald, J. L., and M. W. Watkins. 2006. "Parents' Rights in Special Education: The Readability of Procedural Safeguards." *Exceptional Children*, 72, 497–510.

Fleegler, E. W., C. J. Bottino, A. Pikcilingis, B. Baker, E. Kistler, and A. Hassan. 2016. "Referral System Collaboration Between Public Health and Medical Systems: A Population Health Case Report." NAM Perspectives. Discussion Paper, National Academy of Medicine,

Washington, DC. Retrieved from https://nam.edu/referral-system-collaboration-between-public-health-and-medical-systems-a-population-health-case-report/

Fletcher, M., W. Singel, and K. Fort. 2009. *Facing the Future. The Indian Child Welfare Act at 30*. East Lansing: Michigan State University Press.

Flexner, A. 2001. "Is Social Work a Profession?" *Research on Social Work Practice*, 11, 152–165.

Florida Department of Education. n.d. "PK–20 Data Warehouse." Retrieved from http://www.fldoe.org/accountability/data-sys/edw/

Fong, R. 2012. "Framing Education for a Science of Social Work: Missions, Curriculum, and Doctoral Training." *Research on Social Work Practice*, 22, 529–536.

Fox, K. A. 2003. "Collecting Data on the Abuse and Neglect of American Indian Children." *Child Welfare*, 82, 707–726.

Fraser, A., S. Tan, M. Lagarde, and N. Mays. 2018. "Narratives of Promise, Narratives of Caution: A Review of the Literature on Social Impact Bonds." *Social Policy and Administration*, 52, 4–28.

Garg, A., S. Toy, Y. Tripodis, M. Silverstein, and E. Freeman. 2015. "Addressing Social Determinants of Health at Well Child Care Visits: A Cluster RCT." *Pediatrics*, 135, e296–e304.

Goggins, G. A., and D. Howard. 2009. "The Nonprofit Starvation Cycle." *Stanford Social Innovation Review*, 7 48–53.

Goldhaber-Fiebert, J. D., S. L. Bailey, M. S. Hurlburt, J. Zhang, L. R. Snowden, F. Wulczyn, J. Landsverk, and S. M. Horwitz. 2012. "Evaluating Child Welfare Policies with Decision-Analytic Simulation Models." *Administration and Policy in Mental Health and Mental Health Services Research*, 39, 466–477.

Gottlieb, L. M., D. Hessler, D. Long, E. Laves, A. R. Burns, A. Amaya, P. Sweeney, C. Schudel, and N. E. Adler. 2016. "Effects of Social Needs Screening and In-Person Service Navigation on Child Health: A Randomized Clinical Trial." *JAMA Pediatrics*, 170(11): e162521.

Gottlieb, L. M., H. Wing, and N. E. Adler. 2017. "A Systematic Review of Interventions on Patients' Social and Economic Needs." *American Journal of Preventive Medicine*, 53, 719–729.

Greenwood, P. 2008. "Prevention and Intervention Programs for Juvenile Offenders." *The Future of Children*, 18, 185–210.

Griffiths, K. M., and Christensen, H. 2006. "Review of Randomized Controlled Trials of Internet Interventions for Mental Health Disorders and Related Conditions." *Clinical Psychologist*, 10, 16–29.

Gustafsson-Wright, E., S. Gardiner, and V. Putcha. 2015. *The Potential and Limitations of Impact Bonds*. Washington, DC: Brookings Institution.

Hall, K. L., B. A. Stipelman, K. S. Eddens, M. W. Kreuter, S. I. Bame, H. I. Meissner, K. R. Yabroff, J. Q. Purnell, R. Ferrer, K. M. Ribisl, R. Glasgow, L. A. Linnan, S. Taplin, and R. Glasgow. 2012. "Advancing Collaborative Research with 2-1-1 to Reduce Health Disparities: Challenges, Opportunities, and Recommendations." *American Journal of Preventive Medicine*, 43(Supp 5), S518–S528.

Harris, J., M. Jonson-Reid, B. Carothers, and B. Castrucci. 2017. "The Composition and Structure of Multisectoral Networks for Injury and Violence Prevention Policy in 15 Large US Cities." *Public Health Reports*, 132, 381–388.

Harris, K. M., M. J. Edlund, and S. Larson. 2005. "Racial and Ethnic Differences in the Mental Health Problems and Use of Mental Health Care." *Medical Care*, 43 775–784.

Head, B. W., and J. Alford. 2015. "Wicked Problems Implications for Public Policy and Management." *Administration and Society*, 47, 711–739.

Henggeler, S. W., and S. K. Schoenwald. 2011. "Evidence-Based Interventions for Juvenile Offenders and Juvenile Justice Policies That Support Them." *Social Policy Report*, 25(1). https://eric.ed.gov/?id=ED519241

Hong, C. S., A. L. Siegel, and T. G. Ferris. 2014. "Caring for high-Need, High-Cost Patients: What Makes for a Successful Care Management Program." Commonwealth Fund Issue Brief 19, 9.

Hovmand, P. S., D. F. Andersen, E. Rouwette, G. P. Richardson, K. Rux, and A. Calhoun. 2012. "Group Model Building 'Scripts' as a Collaborative Planning Tool." *Systems Research and Behavioral Science*, 29, 179–193.

Hovmand, P. 2014. *Community Based System Dynamics.* New York: Springer.

Hughes, M., N. Maher, Y. Shen, C. Shore-Fitzgerald, Y. Wang, C. Metts, and D. A. Patterson Silver Wolf. 2017. "Computerized Behavioral Interventions: Current Products and Recommendations for Substance Use Disorder Treatment." *Journal of Social Work in the Addictions,* 4, 339–351.

Hussey, J. M., J. M. Marshall, D. J. English, E. D. Knight, A. S Lau, H. Dubowitz, and J. B. Kotch. 2005. "Defining Maltreatment According to Substantiation: Distinction Without a Difference?" *Child Abuse and Neglect,* 29, 479–492.

International Association for Public Participation. n.d. IAP2 Core Values. Retrieved from http://www.iap2.org/?page=A4

Iovan, S., P. M. Lantz, and S. Shapiro, 2018. "'Pay for Success' Projects: Financing Interventions That Address Social Determinants of Health in 20 Countries." *American Journal of Public Health,* 108, 1473–1477.

James, A. S., S. Gehlert, D. J. Bowen, and G. A. Colditz. 2015. "A Framework for Training Transdisciplinary Scholars in Cancer Prevention and Control." *Journal of Cancer Education,* 30, 664–669.

Jaudes, P. K., V. Champagne, A. Harden, J. Masterson, and L. A. Bilaver. 2012. "Expanded Medical Home Model Works for Children in Foster Care." *Child Welfare,* 91, 9–33.

Jee, S., M. Szilagyi, S. Blatt, V. Meguid, P. Auinger, and P. Szilagyi. 2010. "Timely Identification of Mental Health Problems in Two Foster Care Medical Homes." *Children and Youth Services Review,* 32, 685–690.

Jones L., and K. Wells. 2007. "Strategies for Academic and Clinician Engagement in Community-Participatory Partnered Research." *Journal of the American Medical Association,* 297, 407–10.

Jonson-Reid, M. 2011. "Disentangling System Contact and Services: A Key Pathway to Evidence-Based Children's Policy." *Children and Youth Services Review,* 33, 598–604.

Jonson-Reid, M. 2015. "Education Policy." *Encyclopedia of Social* Work Online. Edited by C. Franklin. New York: Oxford University Press.

Jonson-Reid, M., and B. Drake. 2008. "Multi-Sector Longitudinal Administrative Databases: An Indispensable Tool for Evidence-Based Policy for Maltreated Children and Their Families." *Child Maltreatment,* 13, 392–399.

Jonson-Reid, M., and B. Drake. 2016. Child Well-Being: "Where Is It in Our Data Systems?" *Journal of Public Child Welfare,* 10, 457–465.

Jonson-Reid, M., and B. Drake. 2018. *After the Cradle Falls: What Child Abuse Is, How We Respond to It and What You Can Do About It.* New York: Oxford University Press.

Jonson-Reid, M., B. Drake, P. Kohl, S. Guo, D. Brown, T. McBride, H. Kim, and E. Lewis. 2017. "Why We Should We Care About Usual Care." *Children and Youth Services Review,* 82, 222–229.

Jonson-Reid, M., P. Kohl, T. McBride, B. Drake, D. Brown, S. Guo, P. Hovmand, C. Chiang, H. Kim, and E. Lewis. 2018. "Intervening in Child Neglect: A Microsimulation Evaluation Model of Usual Care: Final Report." Administration of Children and Families 90 CA 1832.

Jonson-Reid, M., N. Weaver, B. Drake, and J. Constantino. 2013. "Violence and Injury Prevention and Treatment Among Children and Youth." *Transdisciplinary Public Health: Research, Methods, and Practice.* Edited by T. McBride and D. Haire-Joshu. San Francisco, CA: Jossey-Bass.

Julian, D. A. 1997. "The Utilization of the Logic Model as a System Level Planning and Evaluation Device." *Evaluation and Program Planning,* 20, 251–257.

Kapos, S. 2016, January 22. "Big Lutheran Social Agency Cuts 750 Jobs Amid Budget Impass." *Crain's Chicago Business.* Retrieved from http://www.chicagobusiness.com/article/20160122/NEWS07/160129931/big-lutheran-social-agency-cuts-750-jobs-amid-budget-impasse

Karlin, B. E., and G. Cross. 2014. "From the Laboratory to the Therapy Room: National Dissemination and Implementation of Evidence-Based Psychotherapies in the US Department of Veterans Affairs Health Care System." *American Psychologist,* 69, 19–33.

Keller, S. C., B. R. Yehia, F. O Momplaisir, M. G. Eberhart, A. Share, and K. A Brady. 2014. "Assessing the Overall Quality of Health Care in Persons Living with HIV in an Urban Environment." *AIDS Patient Care and STDs,* 28, 198–205.

Kemp, S. P., M. O. Marcenko, K. Hoagwood, and W. Vesneski. 2009. "Engaging Parents in Child Welfare Services: Bridging Family Needs and Child Welfare Mandates." *Child Welfare*, 88, 101–126.

Khanlou, N., N. Haque, S. Sheehan, and G. Jones. 2015. "It Is an Issue of Not Knowing Where to Go: Service Providers' Perspectives on Challenges in Accessing Social Support and Services by Immigrant Mothers of Children with Disabilities." *Journal of Immigrant and Minority Health*, 17, 1840–1847.

Kim, H., C. Wildeman, M. Jonson-Reid, and B. Drake. 2017. Lifetime Prevalence of Investigating Child Maltreatment Among US Children. *American Journal of Public Health*, 107(2), 274–280.

Kohl, P. L., M. Jonson-Reid, and B. Drake. 2009. "Time to Leave Substantiation Behind: Findings from a National Probability Study." *Child Maltreatment*, 14, 17–26.

Krahn, G., M. H. Fox, V. A. Campbell, I. Ramon, and G. Jesien. 2010. "Developing a Health Surveillance System for People with Intellectual Disabilities in the United States." *Journal of Policy and Practice in Intellectual Disabilities*, 7, 155–166.

Kreuter, M. W., S. N., Lukwago, D. C., Bucholtz, E. M., Clark, and V. Sanders-Thompson. 2003. "Achieving Cultural Appropriateness in Health Promotion Programs: Targeted and Tailored Approaches." *Health Education and Behavior*, 30, 133–146.

Krishna, S., S. A. Boren, and E. A. Balas. 2009. "Healthcare via Cell Phones: A Systematic Review." *Telemedicine and e-Health*, 15, 231–240.

Kulkarni, S. J., R. P. Barth, and J. T. Messing. 2016, September. "Policy Recommendations for Meeting the Grand Challenge to Stop Family Violence." Grand Challenges for Social Work Initiative Policy Brief No. 3. Cleveland, OH: American Academy of Social Work and Social Welfare.

Lecy, J. D., and E. A. M Searing. 2014. "Anatomy of the Nonprofit Starvation Cycle." *Nonprofit and Voluntary Sector Quarterly*, 44, 539–563.

Lee, J. Y., and S. Harathi. 2016. "Using Health in Social Work Practice with Low-Income Hispanic Patients." *Health and Social Work*, 41, 60–63.

Lee, M., and M. Jonson-Reid. 2009. "Special Education Services for Emotional Disturbance: Needs and Outcomes for Children Involved with the Child Welfare System." *Children and Youth Services Review*, 31, 722–731.

Lein, L., E. S. Uehara, E. Lightfoot, E. F. Lawlor, and J. H. Williams. 2017. "A Collaborative Framework for Envisioning the Future of Social Work Research and Education." *Social Work Research*, 41 67–71.

Lery, B., E. Putnam-Hornstein, W. Wiegmann, and B. King. 2015. "Building Analytic Capacity and Statistical Literacy Among Title IV-E MSW Students." *Journal of Public Child Welfare*, 9, 256–276.

Levy, D. 2014. "The Use of Simulation Models in Public Health with Applications to Substance Abuse and Obesity Problems." *Defining Prevention Science*. Edited by Z. Sloboda and H. Petras. New York: Springer US, pp. 405–430.

Lipsky, M. 2010. *Street-Level Bureaucracy: Dilemmas of the Individual in Public Service*. Russell Sage Foundation.

Luke, D. A., and J. K. Harris. 2007. "Network Analysis in public Health: History, Methods, and Applications." *Annual Review Public Health*, 28, 69–93.

Luke, D. A., L. M. Wald, B. J. Carothers, L. E. Bach, and J. K. Harris. 2013. "Network Influences on Dissemination of Evidence-Based Guidelines in State Tobacco Control Programs." *Health Education and Behavior*, 40, 33S–42S.

Luxton, D. D., R. A. McCann, N. E. Bush, M. C. Mishkind, and G. M. Reger. 2011. "Health for Mental Health: Integrating Smartphone Technology in Behavioral Healthcare." *Professional Psychology: Research and Practice*, 42, 505–512.

Lyons, R. A., K. H. Jones, G. John, C. J. Brooks, J. P. Verplancke, D. V. Ford, G. Brown, and K. Leake. 2009. "The SAIL Databank: Linking Multiple Health and Social Care Datasets." *BMC Medical Informatics and Decision Making*, 9, 3.

McGorry, P., T. Bates, and M. Birchwood. 2013. "Designing youth Mental Health Services for the 21st Century: Examples from Australia, Ireland and the UK." *The British Journal of Psychiatry*, 202, s30–s35.

McKay, M. M., and W. M. Bannon Jr. 2004. "Engaging Families in Child Mental Health Services." *Child and Adolescent Psychiatric Clinics*, 13, 905–921.

Merikangas, K. R., J. P. He, M. Burstein, J. Swendsen, S. Avenevoli, B. Case, K. Georgiades, L. Heaton, S. Swanson, and M. Olfson. 2011. "Service Utilization for Lifetime Mental Disorders in US Adolescents: Results of the National Comorbidity Survey–Adolescent Supplement (NCS-A)." *Journal of the American Academy of Child and Adolescent Psychiatry*, 50, 32–45.

Merriam-Webster. 2017. "System." Retrieved from https://www.merriam-webster.com/dictionary/system

Mishna, F., M. Bogo, J. Root, and S. Fantus. 2014. "Here to Stay: Cyber Communication as a Complement in Social Work Practice." *Families in Society*, 95, 179–186.

Mishna, F., S. Fantus, and L. B. McInroy. 2016. "Informal Use of Information and Communication Technology: Adjunct to Traditional Face-to-Face Social Work Practice." *Clinical Social Work Journal*, 45, 49–55.

Missouri Medicaid. 2016, August. "Legislature Continues to Reject Medicaid Expansion." Retrieved from https://www.healthinsurance.org/missouri-medicaid/

Monette, D. R., T. J. Sullivan, C. R. DeJong, and T. P. Hilton. 2013. *Applied Social Research: A Tool for the Human Services*. Belmont, CA: Cengage Learning.

Morgan, P. L., G. Farkas, M. M. Hillemeier, R. Mattison, S. Maczuga, H. Li, and M. Cook. 2015. "Minorities Are Disproportionately Underrepresented in Special Education: Longitudinal Evidence Across Five Disability Conditions." *Educational Researcher*, 44, 278–292.

Munar, W., P. S. Hovmand, C. Fleming, and G. L. Darmstadt. 2015. "Scaling-Up Impact in Perinatology Through Systems Science: Bridging the Collaboration and Translational Divides in Cross-Disciplinary Research and Public Policy." *Seminars in Perinatology*, 39, 416–423.

National Association of Social Workers. 2008. "Code of Ethics." Retrieved from https://www.socialworkers.org/pubs/code/code.asp

National Drug Intelligence Center. 2011. "The Economic Impact of Illicit Drug Use on American Society." Washington, DC: U.S. Department of Justice. Retrieved from http://www.justice.gov/archive/ndic/pubs44/44731/44731p.pdf

Nilsson, K., A. Hertting, I. L., Petterson, and T. Theorell. 2005. "Pride and Confidence at Work: Potential Predictors of Occupational Health in a Hospital Setting." *BMC Public Health*, 5, 92.

Nurius, P. S. 2016. "Social Work Preparation to Compete in Today's Scientific Marketplace." *Research on Social Work Practice*, 27, 169–174.

Padgett, D. K. 2008. Qualitative Methods in Social Work Research. 2nd ed. Thousand Oaks, CA: SAGE.

Patel, V., G. S. Belkin, A. Chockalingam, J. Cooper, S. Saxena, and J. Unützer. 2013. "Grand Challenges: Integrating Mental Health Services into Priority Health Care Platforms." *PLoS Med*, 10(5), e1001448.

Patterson Silver Wolf, D. A. 2015. "Factors Influencing the Implementation of a Brief Alcohol Screening and Educational Intervention in Social Settings Not Specializing in Addiction Services." *Social Work in Health Care*, 54, 345–364.

Patterson Silver Wolf, D. A., E. Maguin, A. Ramsey, and E. Stringfellow. 2014. "Measuring Attitudes Toward Empirically Supported Treatment in Real-World Addiction Services." *Journal of Social Work Practice in the Addictions*, 14, 141–154.

Patterson Silver Wolf, D. A., L. Pullen, E. Evers, D. L. Champlin, and R. Ralson. 1997. "An Experimental Evaluation of HyperCDTX: Multimedia Substance Abuse Treatment Education Software." *Computers in Human Services*, 14, 21–38.

Pauwels, K., T. Ambler, B. H. Clark, P. LaPointe, D. Reibstein, B. Skiera, and T. Wiesel. 2009. "Dashboards as a Service: Why, What, How, and What Research Is Needed?" *Journal of Service Research*, 12, 175–189.

Petrosino, A., C. Turpin-Petrosino, and S. Guckenburg. 2013. "Formal System Processing of Juveniles: Effects on Delinquency." Crime Prevention Research Review No. 9 Washington, DC: U.S. Department of Justice, Office of Community Oriented Policing Services.

Purnell, J. Q., M. Goodman, W. F. Tate, K. M. Harris, D. L. Hudson, B. D. Jones, and K. Gilbert. 2018. "For the Sake of All: Civic Education on the Social Determinants of Health and Health Disparities in St. Louis." *Urban Education*, 53, 711–743.

Purnell, J. Q., J. Griffith, K. S. Eddens, and M. W. Kreuter. 2014. "Mobile Technology, Cancer Prevention, and Health Status Among Diverse, Low-Income Adults." *American Journal of Health Promotion*, 28, 397–402.

Putnam-Hornstein, E., B. Needell, and A. E. Rhodes. 2013. "Understanding Risk and Protective Factors for Child Maltreatment: The Value of Integrated, Population-Based Data." *Child Abuse and Neglect*, 37, 116–119.

Puzzanchera, C., B. Adams, and M. Sickmund. 2010. "Juvenile Court Statistics 2006–2007." Pittsburgh, PA: National Center for Juvenile Justice. Retrieved from https://www.ojjdp.gov/ojstatbb/njcda/pdf/jcs2007.pdf

Ramsey, A. T., A. Baumann, B., Cooper, and D. A. Patterson Silver Wolf. 2015, December. "Informing the Development of an Electronic Clinical Dashboard in Addiction Services." Poster Presentation at the 8th Annual Conference on the Science of Dissemination and Implementation, Washington, DC.

Ramsey, A. T., and K. Montgomery. 2014. "Technology-Based Interventions in Social Work Practice: A Systematic Review of Mental Health Interventions." *Social Work in Health Care*, 53, 883–899.

Resnicow, K., T. Baranowski, J. S. Ahluwalia, and R. L. Braithwaite. 1999. "Cultural Sensitivity in Public Health: Defined and Demystified." *Ethnicity and Disease*, 9, 10–21.

Rigotti, N. A., and R. B. Wallace. 2015. "Using Agent-Based Models to Address 'Wicked Problems' Like Tobacco Use: A Report from the Institute of Medicine." *Annals of Internal Medicine*, 163, 469–471.

Rosen, A. 2003. "Evidence-Based Social Work Practice: Challenges and Promise." *Social Work Research*, 27, 197–208.

Ryon, S. B., K. W. Early, and A. E. Kosloski. 2017. "Community-Based and Family-Focused Alternatives to Incarceration: A Quasi-Experimental Evaluation of Interventions for delinquent youth." *Journal of Criminal Justice*, 51, 59–66.

Sadana, R., and S. Harper, 2011. "Data Systems Linking Social Determinants of Health with Health Outcomes: Advancing Public Goods to Support Research and Evidence-Based Policy and Programs." *Public Health Reports*, 125(Supp 3), 6–13.

Sanders Thompson, V. L. S., B. Drake, A. S. James, M. Norfolk, M. Goodman, L. Ashford, and G. Colditz. 2015. "A Community Coalition to Address Cancer Disparities: Transitions, Successes and Challenges." Journal of Cancer Education, 30, 616–622.

Sanders Thompson, V. L., M. Johnson-Jennings, A. A. Bauman, and E. Proctor. 2015. "Use of Culturally Focused Theoretical Frameworks for Adaptations of Diabetes Prevention Programs: A Qualitative Review." Preventing Chronic Disease, 12, 140–42.

Satterfield, D., L. DeBruyn, C. D. Francis, and A. Allen. 2014. "A Stream Is Always Giving Life: Communities Reclaim Native Science and Traditional Ways to Prevent Diabetes and Promote Health." *American Indian Culture and Research Journal*, 38, 157–190.

Shadbolt, N., K. O'Hara, T. Berners-Lee, N. Gibbins, H. Glaser, and W. Hall. 2012. "Linked Open Government Data: Lessons from data.gov.uk." *IEEE Intelligent Systems*, 27, 16–24.

Sosa, E. T., L. Biediger-Friedman, and Z. Yin. 2013. "Lessons Learned from Training of Promotores de Salud For Obesity and Diabetes Prevention." *Journal of Health Disparities Research and Practice*, 6, 1–13.

Soska, T., and A. K. J. Butterfield. 2013. *University-Community Partnerships: Universities in Civic Engagement*. London: Routledge.

Specht, H., and M. E. Courtney. 1995. *Unfaithful Angels: How Social Work Has Abandoned Its Mission*. New York: Simon and Schuster.

Spinney, E., M. Yeide, W. Feyerherm, M. Cohen, R. Stephenson, and C. Thomas. 2016. "Racial Disparities in Referrals to Mental Health and Substance Abuse Services from the Juvenile Justice System: A Review of the Literature." *Journal of Crime and Justice*, 39, 153–173

Srihari, V. H., C. Tek, J. Pollard, S. Zimmet, J. Keat, J. D. Cahill, S. Kucukgoncu, B. C. Walsh, F. Li, R. Gueorguieva, N. Levine, R. Mesholam-Gately, M. Friedman-Yakoobian, L. J. Seidman, M. S. Keshavan, T. H. McGlashan, and S. W. Woods. 2014. "Reducing the Duration of Untreated Psychosis and Its Impact in the US: the STEP-ED Study." *BMC Psychiatry*, 14, 335.

Stahlschmidt, M. J., M. Jonson-Reid, L. Pons, J. Constantino, P. L. Kohl, B. Drake, and W. Auslander. 2018. "Trying to Bridge the Worlds of Home Visitation and Child Welfare: Lessons Learned from a Formative Evaluation." *Evaluation and Program Planning*, 66, 133–140.

Stanhope, V., L. Videka, H. Thorning, and M. McKay. 2015. "Moving Toward Integrated Health: An Opportunity for Social Work." *Social Work in Health Care*, 54, 383–407.

State of Illinois, Department of Human Services. 2014, March 26. "Redeploy Illinois Annual Report 2012–2013." Retrieved from https://www.dhs.state.il.us/page.aspx?item=70551

Stiffman, A. R., B. Pescosolido, and L. J. Cabassa. 2004. "Building a Model to Understand Youth Service Access: The Gateway Provider Model." *Mental Health Services Research*, 6, 189–198.

Taylor L. A., A. X. Tan. C. E, Coyle, C. Ndumele E. Rogan M. Canavan, L. A. Curry, and E. H. Bradley. 2016. "Leveraging the Social Determinants of Health: What Works?" *PLoS ONE*, 11(8), e0160217.

Temple, J. A., and A. J. Reynolds. 2015. "Using Benefit–Cost Analysis to Scale Up Early Childhood Programs Through Pay-for-Success Financing." *Journal of Benefit-Cost Analysis*, 6, 628–653.

Thompson, T., M. W. Kreuter, and S. Boyum. 2015. "Promoting Health by Addressing Basic Needs Effect of Problem Resolution on Contacting Health Referrals." *Health Education and Behavior*, 30, 616–622.

Thygesen, L. C., C. Daasnes, I. Thaulow, and H. Brønnum-Hansen. 2011. "Introduction to Danish (Nationwide) Registers on Health and Social Issues: structure, Access, Legislation, and Archiving." *Scandinavian Journal of Public Health*, 39, 12–16.

Tovar, M., D. A. Patterson Silver Wolf, and J. Stevenson. 2015. "Toward a Culturally Informed Rehabilitation Treatment Model for American Indian/Alaska Native Veterans." *Journal of Social Work in Disability and Rehabilitation*, 14, 163–175.

Trattner, W. 1984. *From Poor Law to Welfare State*. 3rd ed. New York: Free Press.

Tucker, D. J. 2008. "Interdisciplinarity in Doctoral Social Work Education: Does It Make a Difference?" *Journal of Social Work Education*, 44, 115–138.

Ungar, M. 2002. "A Deeper, More Social Ecological Social Work Practice." *Social Service Review*, 76, 480–497.

U.S. Census Bureau. 2011. "Current Population Survey, 2011." Annual Social and Economic Supplement, POV46, Poverty Status by State.

U.S. Department of Health and Human Services, Administration of Children and Families, Children's Bureau. 2019. "Child Maltreatment 2017." Retrieved from https://www.acf.hhs. gov/sites/default/files/cb/cm2017.pdf

Vaithianathan, R., T., Maloney, E. Putnam-Hornstein, and N. Jiang. 2013. "Children in the Public Benefit System at Risk of Maltreatment: Identification via Predictive Modeling." *American Journal of Preventive Medicine*, 45, 354–359.

Vance, C. 2017. "Toward a Radical Model of Social Work in Rural Communities." *Journal of Progressive Human Services*, 28, 2–5.

Wagner, M., and L. Newman. 2012. "Longitudinal Transition Outcomes of Youth with Emotional Disturbances." *Psychiatric Rehabilitation Journal*, 35, 199–208.

Walker, E. R., J. R. Cummings, J. M., Hockenberry, and B. G Druss. 2015. "Insurance Status, Use of Mental Health Services, and Unmet Need for Mental Health Care in the United States." *Psychiatric Services*, 66, 578–584.

Walker, S. C., A. S. Bishop, M. D. Pullmann, and G. Bauer. 2015. "A Research Framework for Understanding the Practical Impact of Family Involvement in the Juvenile Justice System: The Juvenile Justice Family Involvement Model." *American Journal of Community Psychology*, 56, 408–421.

Walters, K. L., M. S. Spencer, M. Smukler, H. L. Allen, C. Andrews, T. Browne, P. Maramaldi, D. P. Wheeler, B. Zebrack, and E. Uehara. 2016. "Health Equity: Eradicating Health Inequalities for Future Generations." Grand Challenges for Social Work Initiative Working paper No. 19. Retrieved from http://grandchallengesforsocialwork.org/wp-content/uploads/2016/01/WP19-with-cover2.pdf

Wells, K., R. Klap, A. Koike, and C. Sherbourne. 2001. "Ethnic Disparities in Unmet Need for Alcoholism, Drug Abuse, and Mental Health Care." *American Journal of Psychiatry*, 158, 2027–2032.

Wen, H., B. G. Druss, and J. R. Cummings. 2015. "Effect of Medicaid Expansions on Health Insurance Coverage and Access to Care Among Low Income Adults with Behavioral Health Conditions." *Health Services Research*, 50, 1787–1809.

Wolff, T. 2016. "Ten Places Where Collective Impact Gets it Wrong." *Global Journal of Community Psychology Practice*, 7(1), 1–13.

Worthy, S. L., and L. J. Beaulieu. 2016. "Turning the Tide on Poverty: Strategies and Challenges Related to Tackling Poverty in Rural Communities in the South." *Community Development*, 47, 403–410,

Zakus, J. D. L., and C. L. Lysack. 1998. "Revisiting Community Participation." *Health Policy and Planning*, 13, 1–12.

Zeola, M. P., J. Guina, and R. W. Nahhas. 2017. "Mental Health Referrals Reduce Recidivism in First-Time Juvenile Offenders, But How Do We Determine Who Is Referred?" *Psychiatric Quarterly*, 88, 167–183.

Zheng, J. 2018. Using data science for social good. Towards Data Science.com Available online: https://towardsdatascience.com/using-data-science-for-social-good-c654a6580484

13

Designing and Implementing Policy and Program Innovations

BARRY ROSENBERG, PATRICK J. FOWLER, AND ROSS C. BROWNSON

A livable life depends on programs and policies that effectively address the needs of all, particularly the most marginalized. These programs and policies are implemented on the ground level to those in need of services. The profession of social work has played an important role across the decades in the delivery of these human services. Yet, despite considerable advances in promoting a healthier society, intractable social problems continue to challenge the provision of services that facilitate livable lives. A clear need exists for a broad application of novel approaches that address the complex systems driving inequities in society.

Advances in social innovation represent promising avenues for introducing systematic changes. Nevertheless, a number of barriers prevent social work from paving the way to broad-scale applications that encourage livable lives. This chapter articulates some of the key challenges facing human services and proposes a framework to retool social work for future innovation. Rooted in strong capacities for promoting social justice and social good, the braided approach that we develop emphasizes the integration of methods that foster both continuous and discontinuous innovations with human services. These strategies can prepare future leaders to leverage opportunities for promoting livable lives.

This ambitious call to action requires the profession to rise to the challenge of designing and testing complex solutions to complex social problems. We attempt to illuminate ways forward for the field from the perspective of academics working within an institutional setting. We recognize the implementation and dissemination of a braided approach requires input from partners outside of the academy. This chapter provides an initial step for an evolving process of reshaping human services that facilitate livable lives.

The Problem and Importance: Stalled Changes for Livable Lives

Social work has provided leadership in the use of evidence-based practices to promote livable lives. Researchers have identified effective interventions in mental health services, health care delivery, educational practices, and human services management. The field continues to drive groundbreaking research on implementation and dissemination of interventions that work (Brownson, Colditz, and Proctor, 2012). Simultaneously, social work training models now center around the use of evidence, with accreditation requiring competency in research-informed practice and approaches for social interventions (Council on Social Work Education, n.d.). Professional development and licensing requirements further expose practitioners to advancements in empirically informed practices. Mobilization of the sizable workforce toward evidence-based approaches represents a seismic shift in coordinated efforts toward livable lives.

Unfortunately, the promulgation of evidence-based practice and policy has yet to eradicate social problems. Despite the advances in research and training over the past century, intractable social problems continue to challenge the provision of services that facilitate livable lives in our society. Poverty and social exclusion threatens the well-being of families and individuals across the world (see Chapter 5 of this volume). Racism and discrimination occur locally and globally in our increasingly interconnected societies (see Chapter 4 of this volume). Marginalization and exposure to toxic environments produce devastating effects on the development of healthy people and communities (see Chapters 2 and 10 of this volume). The complex conditions that diminish livable lives have adapted and resisted widespread use of evidence-based practices. Social work needs to consider alternative strategies for promoting well-being.

The Challenge: Complexity in Promoting Livable Lives

A number of challenges inhibit social work from leading in delivering broad-scale strategies to foster livable lives. Barriers range from the wicked nature of social and racial inequities to educational approaches that unintendedly perpetuate the status quo. Moreover, the absence of social work as a leader in social entrepreneurship threatens future leadership in human service, as well as failing to contribute a much-needed perspective on responsible innovative practices that balance social justice and the social good.

Complexity and Evidence-Based Approaches

The complexity of social problems make them quite difficult to address. Firmly entrenched and dynamic processes foster oppression and marginalization. Effective approaches that promote livable lives need to be multilevel, adaptable, and scalable, as well as sustainable. This requires complex interventions that coordinate multiple components delivered across various settings and times with fidelity. These initiatives often require extensive collaboration that further challenges effective delivery, especially in the context of constrained resources. Growing demand for services, competing tangible needs, and limits in terms of funding, time, organizational capacity, and competencies force difficult decisions about whom and what to serve. Thus, complexity impedes the design and implementation of evidence-based initiatives that advance livable lives (Fowler et al., 2019; Kube, Das, and Flower, 2019).

Concerns about the impact of many programs and the speed of new program development further complicate reliance on evidence-based interventions. Traditional evidence-based interventions develop across a linear set of stages (Landsverk et al., 2012). After extensive research on the epidemiology and determinants of social problems, interventions are designed to target key mechanisms that promote well-being. These are piloted and tested in controlled settings to isolate efficient components. Demonstration of success warrants subsequent testing through effectiveness studies that apply the intervention across intended settings. Finally, the few interventions that show promise through the development process get tailored for widespread implementation through the development of strategies to train and deliver interventions. Research shows this process is resource intensive with considerable delays in knowledge transfer; estimates suggest the pipeline from research to practice averages 17 years (Balas, 1998; Grant et al., 2000). Consequently, social work professionals must continually wait for guidance from research.

Delays inherent to evidence-based practices provide a poor fit with the complex reality facing social work professionals. Human services respond to dynamic conditions that continually shift the demand for and supply of available resources. Rarely do the contexts match those upon which evidence was generated. As they wait for better evidence, social work professionals are trained to improvise with best practices. Although better than doing nothing, this stopgap approach threatens to introduce and further entrench inefficient practices and policies. Moreover, focus on best practices and improvisation does little to address the root problem of delays in knowledge generation and transfer.

Scale up presents a related barrier for widespread promotion of livable lives through evidence-based policies and practices. Scale up refers to a process for sustainable implementation of programs that provide the greatest good to the largest number (Fowler et al., 2017; Larson, Dearing and Backer, 2017: v). Few examples exist of widely scalable initiatives led by social workers (Hoagwood et al., 2014; McHugh and Barlow, 2010; Milat, Bauman, and Redman, 2015). Numerous obstacles exist to achieving scale, including time, cost, resistance, and the need to align multiple players around new solutions. Insights on key processes, such as adoption, adaptation, and de-adoption, inform improvements in the efficiency of services and policies that facilitate livable lives. However, incremental gains in efficiency continue to encounter systematic shortages in capacities to meet broad demand for supports.

The complexity of social problems and interventions undermines the broad utility of evidence-based approaches. Time and resources are needed for research to define the problem, develop and test responses, and assure broad implementation and dissemination. As researchers look for evidence-based solutions, social problems worsen and adapt. For example, small problems grow exponentially in scope and complexity, while policy and programmatic responses introduce unintended consequences that perpetuate inefficiencies. A sizable workforce trained in evidence-based approaches is necessary but not sufficient in designing and implementing social interventions that broadly enable livable lives.

What Is Innovation?

Innovations may refer to a process or a product. Innovation, whether social or otherwise, is presumed to result in some improvement through the introduction of new products, services, public policies, processes, technologies, institutions, organizational structures, systems of collaboration, and methods of interacting with organizational members (Cajaiba-Santana, 2014; Damanpour, 1991). Innovations may be designed to address the effectiveness of programs and policies or their efficiency (Osborne, 1998). Some may achieve both. Several scholars (Light, 2009a; Osborne, 1998) limit the definition of innovation to discontinuous changes. Others (Seelos et al., 2012; Prange and Schlegelmilch, 2010) suggest that innovation may result in minor or major discontinuities. Herein, we consider innovations that may be either discontinuous or continuous, or even incremental, such as those comprising modest alteration through continuous quality improvement. Disruptive innovations introduce entirely new products, technologies, or services that eventually displace existing ones (Christensen, 2011). All innovations contain an element of novelty and change. However, innovations need not be original; they may be new for only a particular user, context, or application (Damanpour, 1987; Phills, Deiglmeier, and Miller, 2008).

Social Innovation and Entrepreneurship Gaps
in Human Service

Under-representation in the emerging domains of social entrepreneurship and social innovation represent another challenge for social work. Developed from an extensive set of strategies used in business, innovation and entrepreneurship offer processes for generating, testing, and scaling novel solutions that meet consumer demands with greater speed and effectiveness. Although too elaborate to detail here, the procedures follow a general structure (Christensen, 2011). Data typically are leveraged to gain insights into unobserved demand for products, technologies, and procedures. Solution generation focuses on the potential experiences of end users to design better options. Initial design and testing usually involves multiple prototypes that address demand in different ways. Options are selected for further development through structured decision-making procedures that consider multiple data sources, such as feedback, rapid cycle testing, development costs, and so on. Success and subsequent decisions about scaling depend on multiple metrics collected from sales and added value.

The availability and use of evidence throughout the planning process differs from typical human service development. Continuous collection of timely and accurate data on key metrics offer opportunities for ongoing adjustments. Data on human services and policies, on the other hand, tend to be incomplete and difficult to access for real-time decision-making. For instance, administrative records on service provision represent self-selected segments of the population who are able and willing to engage with services and, thus, provide little information on unobserved demand. Social workers learn workarounds for program planning and evaluation that require additional resources to collect needed information, such as community assessments. However, the absence of live data combined with the dominant evidence-based framework may further delay course corrections for human service delivery.

Responding to calls for innovation in human services, there has been a dramatic growth in the attraction of discontinuous and especially entrepreneurial methods of innovation. The concept emerged in the 1980s from the work of Ashoka helping to fund entrepreneurs as well as new ventures identifying different sources of revenue for organizations (Dees, 2007). The driving forces emanated from a growing complexity and scope of human service needs, declining government support, and under-resourced human service organizations (Dees, 1998, 2007; Gauss, 2015; Gray, Healy, and Crofts, 2003; Light, 2009a; Nandan and Scott, 2013; Skoll, and Osberg, 2013; Seelos, and Mair, 2012). Sectoral blurring and the growth of socially conscious business, the cultural elevation of the entrepreneur, and the allure of the "new" have also fueled the movements (Berzin and Pitt-Catsouphes, 2015; Phills, Deiglmeier, and Miller, 2008).

Social entrepreneurship, as well as social intrapreneurship, often function outside of social work to generate more timely responses to community health threats. Social entrepreneurs recognize, respond, and adapt to the complexity of changing and emerging population needs, shifts in the environmental context, and desires to improve organizational and program effectiveness, efficiency, and sustainability. Social innovations occur "when a new idea establishes a different way of thinking and acting that changes existing paradigms" and entails social action oriented toward social change (Cajaiba-Santana, 2014: 44). Some view social innovations as "more just" than prevailing approaches (Salamon, Geller, and Mengel, 2010: 2) because the value created accrues primarily to society as a whole rather than private individuals (Phills et al., 2008: 36).

Social entrepreneurs approach innovation through the creation of new organizations, programs, and organizational relationships. If effective, replicated, and/or translated into social policy, they achieve widespread scale. Some choose market-based social enterprise models, socially responsible for-profit businesses, or corporate responsibility approaches, while others do so through nonprofit structures. Others develop blended or hybrid organizational structures and funding strategies (Phills et al., 2008). Social entrepreneurship incubators, accelerators, venture capital, impact investing, and program-related investments by foundations are prevalent strategies for supporting entrepreneurial efforts.

Social intrapreneurs embody many of the characteristics and skills of entrepreneurs but work within existing organizations to develop new programs, interventions, and processes (Nandan, London, and Bent-Goodley, 2015). There is also substantial research on the characteristics and conditions for organizations to be innovative and what some term an entrepreneurial orientation, which incorporates innovativeness, risk-taking, proactiveness, and the alignment of multiple actors including the governing board, top management, and key staff (Beekman, Steiner, and Wasserman, 2012).

Social work has been slow to adopt the methods of social entrepreneurship and innovation in practice and training (Center for the Advancement of Social Entrepreneurship at Duke University, 2008; Westley and Antadze, 2010). Despite recognition of the potential value for human service, too few professionals are exposed to structured educational models (Berzin, 2012; Berzin, and Pitt-Catsouphes, 2015; Berzin, Pitt-Catsouphes, and Gaitan-Rossi, 2016; Germak, and Singh, 2009; Gray, Healy, and Crofts, 2003; Nandan, London, and Bent-Goodley, 2015). New students remain unlikely to receive adequate exposure to concepts, while little push has been made by the field to retool through professional development. Delays miss key opportunities to shape and guide responsible applications for human service. The absence of a pipeline of prepared leaders also bodes poorly for the future.

Limitations of Social Innovation and Social Entrepreneurship

Although entrepreneurial methods remain underutilized in human service and policy design, critiques of existing applications warn that entrepreneurial methods of social innovation are insufficient for generating livable lives. Popular depictions frequently romanticize the entrepreneur as singular genius or super-hero for social impact, while ignoring the interdependence of collectives working toward livable lives (Andersson, April 11, 2012; Andersson and McCambridge, 2017; Berzin and Pitt-Catsouphes, 2015). Social entrepreneurs (as sometimes contrasted with legacy human service managers) are characterized as visionary, creative, optimistic, transformative, driven, courageous, relentless actors, disrupters and risk-takers who not only wish to alleviate suffering, but achieve sustainable, scalable, social transformation (Bornstein, 2004; Dees, 1998; Light, 2009b; Martin and Osberg, 2007; Skoll Foundation, n.d.). This focus may mask the reality that entrepreneurship generally occurs within organizations—even nascent ones—and that multiple actors are involved in its implementation (Andersson and McCambridge, 2017; Cnaan and Vinokur-Kaplan, 2015; Light, 2009b).

Among criticisms leveled at social entrepreneurship are that the movement has spawned many often duplicative, poorly resourced, start-up efforts; that many represent ideas that lack an evidence base; that they elevate the individual in relation to the organization (Edgington, June 24, 2011); that entrepreneurs often fail to transition to sound management of their initiatives and are weak on governance and transparency (Light, 2009a); that the great majority of start-ups fail; and that too few reach meaningful scale (Ross, 2014). Another common critique of social entrepreneurship and social innovation concerns change only for the sake of change. Cnaan and Vinokur-Kaplan (2015) make the point that there may be no reason to focus on innovation when stable, mature organizations are providing effective services that meet a well-defined need. Others argue that the emphasis on discontinuous innovation and disruption detracts from the potential beneficial impact of incremental innovation (Osborne, Chew, and McLaughlin, 2008; Osborne, and Flynn, 1997; Seelos and Mair, 2012; Seelos et al., 2012). The absence of coordinated professional values fails to curb haphazard applications of social innovation and entrepreneurship.

The limitations of social innovation and entrepreneurship signal an unmet demand for community-driven applications. Too frequently, innovations poorly align with stakeholder needs and resources. Misalignment reflects, at least in part, inadequate engagement with the social problem, which is a common challenge in human services. Poor engagement misses opportunities for change and, more insidiously, threatens to perpetuate ongoing disparities. Social work can mitigate these risks through reflective and responsive practice rooted in social justice; strategies refined over 100 years of education and training. The absence of professional standards to guide social innovation and entrepreneurship raise concerns for the future.

Management and Policy Challenges for Innovation

A ubiquitous challenge for livable lives concerns the uncertainty involved in managing responses to complex social problems. As a result of the dynamic nature of problems, responses remain constantly in flux and small shifts can undermine effectiveness of existing interventions while simultaneously creating opportunities for novel solutions. For instance, the success of local policies to promote equitable access to fair housing diminishes as communities grow increasingly racialized. However, the context creates disruptive opportunities for placed-based strategies of community development. Motivating action toward novel solutions proves incredibly difficult given the inertia created by existing responses. The feedback processes create exceedingly complex contexts for managers and policymakers to navigate, as any social work professional knows.

The tensions faced in innovation are readily apparent when considering the allocation of scarce resources. Managers and policymakers at all levels constantly determine the best use of time, energy, and capital. Scarcity means that investments in one area take away from another. Solutions generated by social entrepreneurial and social innovative methods often represent risky investments requiring longer-term considerations. The prototyping and iteration processes necessary for designing novel solutions requires more time and energy than adapting an existing intervention. However, pressures to respond to current demands incentivize investments in existing solutions, regardless if the solutions maintain the status quo or are degrading in utility. A trap emerges for managers and policymakers who are compelled to shift resources away from innovation to address short-term needs. This is especially true at pivotal moments when doubling down on potential breakthrough innovations (Fowler, Wright et al., 2019; Lyneis and Sterman, 2016). Thus, sustainable innovation requires considerable managerial capacities.

There is a growing body of theory, research, and commentary focused on the antecedents, methods, prerequisites, contributing and inhibiting factors, and priorities related to the skill sets needed by innovators and organizations

(Phills et al., 2008). Exploration and exploitation represent two strategies that organizations use to adapt to changing contexts and remain competitive. Each represents an alternative strategic orientation to the use and development of knowledge to achieve impact (March, 1991). Exploration describes a process of discontinuous change and includes things such as search, variation, risk taking, experimentation, flexibility, discovery, or innovation. Exploitation involves such things as refinement, choice, production, efficiency, selection, implementation, and execution. These, in turn, can produce a process of incremental change. Such processes are self-reinforcing, and organizations generally show a propensity to one or the other (Prange and Schlegelmilch, 2010). Although challenging, what are known as ambidextrous organizations are capable of doing both (March, 1991; O'Reilly and Tushman, 2013; Tushman and O'Reilly, 1996).

The emphasis on leadership and organizational capacities contrasts with common conceptions of the social entrepreneur. Innovation processes require coordination of multistaged and multilevel processes that involve a host of people with a variety of skills. Although challenging to develop and maintain, the resulting networks create a system of checks and balances that improve the value of emerging ideas and products. Innovation embedded within networks organized around social change also helps ensure productivity.

Diminishing Value of Human Service Leadership

The diminishing presence of social work professionals in leadership roles represents another barrier for human service that enables livable lives. Numerous scholars document the declining ability of social workers to obtain top leadership positions in human service organizations, within which they can shape and influence innovation (Friedman, 2008; Hoefer, 2009; Perlmutter, 2006; Rosenberg and McBride, 2015; Sullivan, 2016; Wuenschel, 2006). For example, a recent study of 12 large national nonprofit networks (e.g., Boy Scouts, Boys and Girls Clubs, Catholic Charities, YMCA) finds half of the chief executives of local branches held graduate degrees; a third had MBAs; and 20 percent had MSWs (Norris-Tirrell, Rinella, and Pham, 2017). Thus, only 10 percent of some of the most significant human service organizations are actually led by social work professionals.

Factors attributed to such declines focus largely on training gaps (Ezell, Chernesky, and Healy, 2004; Nesoff, 2007). Human service professionals are increasingly perceived as less prepared to handle management and leadership challenges of complex service delivery. This coincides with increasing competition from individuals with training in business, public administration, and nonprofit management (Hoefer, Watson, and Preble, 2013; Mirabella, 2007; Milton, 2016). The absence implies that other professions with different values are moving into and owning social change practice. Thus, solutions may or may not attend to principles of social justice and the greatest good for the greatest number. A failure of social work to engage in innovative practices not only threatens professional value but also the quality of responses to major social problems.

Challenges Summary

As summarized in Table 13.1, a number of barriers face the social work profession for leading innovations in policies and practices that promote livable lives. Overreliance on evidence-based practices, combined with delays and inefficiencies inherent in their use, fail to address the complexity of social problems and miss opportunities to apply innovative methods that better respond to complex social problems. The growing fields of social entrepreneurship and social intrapraneurship have produced important innovations. However, social work has been largely absent from this movement. Although there are limitations to social entrepreneurship, social work's absence threatens the profession's leadership of human services as other professions fill the gap. Moreover, failure to incorporate the social work perspective in social innovations threatens core considerations of fair and equitable human service.

The Solution: A Braided Approach for Transformative Human Service and Policy

Call for Innovation

Weaknesses and limitations of both evidence-based practice and social entrepreneurship argue against the field's overreliance on either. It appears likely that social work will continue to emphasize the importance of evidence-based interventions based on high-quality research and a growing body of dissemination and implementation science. However, the profession thus far has exhibited limited engagement in processes of discontinuous innovation and social entrepreneurship. By incorporating these tools into traditional research and policy practice, the next generation of social work professionals will be more prepared to move the livable lives agenda forward.

Echoing the call of other scholars (Berzin, 2012; Berzin and Pitt-Catsouphes, 2015; Berzin, Pitt-Catsouphes, and Gaitan-Rossi, 2016; Germak and Singh,

Designing and Implementing Policy

Table 13.1. Key Barriers and Opportunities Facing Social Work and Public Health for Promoting Livable Lives Through Practice and Policy

Problem	Strengths	Challenges	Responses
Complexity of social problems	• Long histories and extensive experience in social change • Rooted in values of social justice and social good	• Entrenched and enduring inequities • Resistant to standard policies and best practice approaches • Require adaptive responses	• Continue to foster values of social justice and social good • Build research and training capacities for complex systems change
Overreliance on evidence-based practices	• Values evidence in decision-making • Considerable infrastructure for education • Competitive advantage for workforce	• Delays and inefficiencies in development • Barriers for broad implementation and dissemination • Incompatibility with complexity • Narrows definitions of credible evidence • Tension with demands for social change	• Encourage flexible research designs • Value multiple approaches for generating evidence • Promote complex systems thinking
Lack of entrepreneurship and innovation in human service	• Unique professional capacity for ambiguity • Competitive advantage for integrating practice-based evidence • Infrastructure for retooling	• Innovation requires balancing discovery with efficiency • Difficult to manage competing demands for scarce resources • Mismanagement perpetuates status quo or leads to failure • Lack of examples discourages practices	• Promote braided practice that integrates continuous and discontinuous change • Train professionals and leaders in ambidexterity

continued

Table 13.1. **Continued**

Problem	Strengths	Challenges	Responses
Diminishing leadership in human service	• Tradition of leadership in human service • Considerable experience addressing complex social problems	• Fewer CEOs trained in human service • Innovators currently trained outside of human service • Social innovation not necessarily rooted in public good • Limits influence on current practices • Risks losing values of social justice and social good in human service	• Provide opportunities for retooling • Prepare future leaders to integrate innovation into practice

2009; Gray, Healy, and Crofts, 2003; Nandan, London, and Bent-Goodley, 2015), we submit that human service professionals must embrace both continuous and discontinuous innovation methods that better respond to complexity and the need for scale. Tying these two strands together, professionals need to obtain the knowledge and skills to draw from a broader toolkit incorporating not only empirical research, but also skills in exploitation, exploration, social entrepreneurship, and intrapraneurship that can be employed across the entire spectrum of innovation processes to develop, implement, and bring to scale policy and program innovations that contribute to a livable life.

We argue that what we are labeling a "braided approach" is fully congruent with social work values and practice. Innovation strategies and skills are consistent with emphasis on macro practice, while entrepreneurship integrates macro practice principles and business activities (Germak and Singh, 2009; Pitt-Catsouphes and Berzin, 2015; Nandan et al., 2015). A shift in integrating human service can respond to calls for social work to claim its place within the social entrepreneurship movement and for the field to develop and intensify educational models that will prepare professionals to innovate (Center for the Advancement of Social Entrepreneurship at Duke University, 2008; Westley and Antadze, 2010). The braided approach forwards the practice of systems change necessary to livable lives.

A Braided Toolbox

We advocate for the profession to develop a broad toolbox that can be employed across the spectrum of innovation processes from the most incremental to the most disruptive. This toolbox should also be compatible with those needed to effectively lead and manage human service organizations. In addition, these skills may be useful in identifying interventions that are ripe for de-adoption. The development of entrepreneurial skills calls for specific training in techniques such as design thinking (Brown and Wyatt, 2010), lean start-up (Ries, 2011; Blank, 2013), Agile project management tools, rapid testing cycles, and participatory planning, as well as general skills in organizational management and human resource administration (Pitt-Catsouphes and Berzin, 2015; Nandan et al, 2015). Other skills that exploit existing capacities for change such as continuous quality improvement, performance management, and program evaluation are central to incremental innovation. Innovators also need management and leadership skills to create change or sustain staff fidelity to evidence-based protocols. Moreover, leaders need to understand strategies used to minimize the challenge of organizational ambidexterity and to be aware and understand the management implications of each type of innovative strategy (Damanpour, 1987; Osborne and Flynn, 1997). Likewise, the imperative to impact social policy at all levels requires skills in advocacy, policy practice, and dissemination strategies.

Fostering Ambidexterity

Implementing a braided approach requires promoting ambidextrous leadership and organizational capacities. Ambidexterity refers to the process of balancing exploration and exploitation, for both continuous and discontinuous adaptation (Lavie, Stettner, and Tushman, 2010; O'Reilly and Tushman, 2004). Organizations typically exhibit a propensity to one or another strategy (Prange and Schlegelmilch, 2010). Continuous and discontinuous change, exploitation, and exploration processes reflect different organizational strategies, compete for resources, and require different skill sets (March, 1991). Ambidextrous organizations have the ability to be aligned and efficient in the management of today's business demands, while simultaneously being adaptive to changes in the environment (Raisch and Birkinshaw, 2008). The positive impact of ambidexterity has been supported empirically (He and Wong, 2004) and undergirds some theory on leadership (Rosing, Frese, and Bausch, 2011).

The dynamics of ambidexterity are especially important for sustainability (Bryson, Boal, and Rainey, 2008; O'Reilly and Tushman, 2004; Tushman and O'Reilly 1996). James March (1991) observed that the results of exploitation are clearer, more immediate, and certain than those of exploration. They have immediate payoffs, result in quicker improvements, reduce variation, and contribute to stability. These self-reinforcing qualities may lead to path-dependency that blocks exploration. Moreover, they can result in what Levinthal and March (1993) termed a "success trap," where exploitation drives out exploration.

Achieving ambidexterity may be particularly challenging for traditional, mature, and currently successful organizations. Clayton Christensen highlighted this problem in his work on disruptive innovations with the concept of a value network, represented by "the context within which a firm identifies and responds to customers' needs, solves problems, procures input, reacts to competitors, and strives for profit" (2011, p. 36). To compete successfully with existing products and services, companies develop and refine an integrated network of structures, capabilities, resource allocations, and relationships, which hamper the ability to respond to disruptive changes in technology or the environment. Berzin and Pitt-Catsouphes (2015) note that intrapreneurial efforts face competing demands and resistance to change.

A similar constraint is explained by institutional theory, which suggests that to obtain legitimacy, organizational behavior is shaped by the relevant institutional environment and dominant institutions such as government and funders (Schmid, 2009). Coule and Patmore (2013) discuss how assumptions about the organization's role in the institutional field impact organization decisions to innovate or maintain service stability. Media scrutiny and expectations of funders and stakeholders may raise cautions that discourage organizational innovation because of the diversion of resources and risk of failure (Jaskyte, 2010).

Nonetheless, acknowledging the challenges, older and more traditional organizations can develop an entrepreneurial orientation to innovation (Light, 2009b). Several strategies and typologies for achieving organizational ambidexterity and balancing exploitation and exploration processes are outlined in the literature. These include assigning exploration activities to a separate operating unit, alternating periods of exploration and exploitation within the same organization or operating unit, and developing a strategic context for doing both simultaneously. Interorganizational alliances might also be an option for balancing exploitation and exploration (Lavie and Rosenkopf, 2006). Managers need to develop skills to manage the organizational tradeoffs and implications (for an overview, see Lavie, Stettner, and Tushman, 2010). It would be wise to explore more fully how funders, accrediting agencies, professional associations, and governing boards shape human service organization's willingness and freedom to innovate.

Illustrations

Mary Jane Rotheram-Borus and colleagues (2012) advocate strategies that illustrate a braided approach to therapeutic and preventive interventions to address drawbacks and limitations of the existing paradigm for developing, implementing, and the scaling up of evidence-based interventions. They seek disruptive innovations that provide, "a simpler and less expensive alternative that meets most of the same needs for a majority of consumers" (467). As one example, they cite Minute Clinics, which provide less robust and specialized services than do physicians, but which are more accessible, less expensive, and are able to satisfy the majority of common health care needs.

Rotheram-Borus et al. (2012) call for new research agendas that identify and synthesize the common elements and robust features of evidence-based practices. They then advocate experimentation with novel delivery formats such as consumer-controlled diagnostics, paraprofessional delivery, and the use of technology that can serve more people in less time and at less cost. These have sometimes been termed "good-enough" interventions (Christensen et al., 2006). A related approach is found in international development through "task shifting," where programs are unbundled and nonprofessionals are trained to provide specific, limited, but evidence-based services at costs less than those delivered by highly trained practitioners (World Health Organization, 2007). The authors suggest that the use of market research techniques (which are common in design thinking) can better identify factors that affect consumer and provider adoption of new interventions. They further advocate use of iterative processes of continuous quality improvement processes in contrast to insistence on replication with fidelity.

The development and evolution of the Naturally Occurring Retirement Community-Supportive Services Program (NORC-SSP) illustrates aspects of a braided approach to social innovation utilizing both exploration and exploitation processes. Initially implemented as a novel (discontinuous) innovation, the NORC-SSP model was validated through a federally funded demonstration process involving multiple prototypes that responded to varied situational conditions. Based on a developing evidence base, the NORC-SSP model expanded, receiving both government and philanthropic support. In numerous locales, the core concepts have been adapted and refined in response to evolving local conditions through continuous innovation processes. However, despite enhancing livable lives and reducing financial costs of aging, declining government funding led to the closing or scale back of many programs.

Naturally occurring retirement communities are places that "developed a high concentration of older residents, because seniors tend to either remain in or move to these communities when they retire" (Masotti et al., 2006: 1164). To enhance livable lives, NORC-SSPs provide a variety of relatively low-cost supportive interventions, such as transportation, wellness, social programming, and household repairs that promote healthy, dignified, and less costly aging in place. The first program was launched in 1985 by the United Jewish Appeal, Federation of Jewish Philanthropies of New York. Following advocacy by the

Jewish Federations of North America, congressional funding (under the Older Americans Act) supported 45 demonstration programs in 26 states (Greenfield et al., 2012). A national evaluation concluded that NORC-SSPs effectively facilitate aging in place, with residents experiencing increased socialization, decreased isolation, greater linkage to services, and more involvement in volunteerism. Participants felt healthier and more likely to remain in their own homes as a result (Bedney et al., 2007). However, despite enhancing livable lives and reducing financial costs of aging, declining government funding led to the closing or scale back of many programs.

In a program evaluation conducted for the St. Louis, Missouri NORC-SSP, participants reported greater awareness of community resources, feeling part of a strong community, making new friends, and improving or maintaining their health. Data further suggested that the NORC-SSP helped delay or reduce nursing home admittance and enable participants to remain in their own homes longer (Elbert and Neufeld, 2010). The service and activity mix evolved in response to use and participant preferences. Additionally, continuous innovation processes changed the St. Louis model over time. For example, the St. Louis model serves a suburban subdivision and low-rise apartment population, which is different than the vertical, high-rise model of the first NORC. To better identify and engage residents and stimulate socialization, the St. Louis NORC initiated a series of resident councils with monthly meetings. This process continued until natural relationships developed that reduced the need for an artificial structure. A later change involved the introduction of a membership fee. In St. Louis and other cities, the NORC-SSP model retains relevance through continuous innovation.

Leadership Development

Upper echelons theory holds that organizations are shaped by those at the top of the organizational hierarchy and that those executives act on their personalized interpretations of the strategic issues they face (Hambrick, 2007; Hambrick and Mason, 1984). These interpretations are shaped by education, prior experience in the field, and other factors. Thus, training and career path matter because they shape the manner in which executives learn to frame and evaluate issues. This ultimately shapes how they decide on courses of action. For social innovations to be designed and implemented in a manner consistent with social work knowledge, values, and ethics, social work professionals must be in positions of leadership and influence.

To maintain social work leadership of innovation and human services, the authors join calls for the expansion and intensification of management and leadership training at the master's degree, continuing education, and executive education levels. Richard Hoefer (2009) argues that social work education should position the MSW as the preferred degree for managers at all levels of human service organizations. The 2010 Social Work Congress addressed this issue. Among a series of ten Imperatives for the Next Decade, two were particularly pertinent: "infuse models of sustainable business and management practice in social work education and practice" and "integrate leadership training in social work curricula at all levels" (National Association of Social Workers, 2010). We call for increased focus, engagement, and education around policy and program innovation and human service leadership and management in general. This echoes calls for a much greater appreciation and commitment to macro practice in social work (Reisch, 2016; Rothman, 2013; Special Commission to Advance Macro Practice in Social Work, 2015).

Curricular Innovation

There is a substantial literature addressing the knowledge, competencies, and training required to develop solid management and leadership skills. Among other curricular frameworks, a comprehensive definition of human service management competencies has been developed for the Network for Social Work Management (Wimpfheimer et al., 2018). Nandan and Scott (2013) advocate interdisciplinary models of education and highlight a 12-credit social entrepreneurship specialization at Washington University's School of Social Work as an innovative model. The growth of the evidence-based management movement (Pfeffer and Sutton, 2006) reinforces an approach consistent with the social work commitment to data-driven practice.

The authors propose that graduate-level leadership and management training adopt an ambidextrous perspective. Doing so will prepare graduates to understand the full range of innovation processes, the relative strengths and weaknesses of exploitation and exploration, the conditions under which one is preferable, and the skills necessary to function effectively within either mode of innovation. Birkinshaw and Gupta (2013) emphasize that the key to organizations being able to achieve ambidexterity rests on the quality of management.

Washington University's School of Social Work offers a case example of evolving curricular innovation and development that embraces the braided model and complements its leadership in the development and teaching of evidence based practice (Rosenberg and McBride, 2015). In addition to a joint MSW/MBA option, the school has offered a 12-credit Social Work Management Specialization since 1984. In 2011, it became the first school of social work in the United States to offer a 12-credit specialization in Social Entrepreneurship partnering with the university's Olin School of Business. Since 2015, it has likewise offered a Social Policy Specialization. Each specialization is designed to integrate with every MSW concentration.

Beginning in 2014, the school has required all MSW students to complete three credits of content in management and leadership. In part to accommodate this requirement, the school complemented a full menu of three-credit management and leadership courses with a series of one-credit skill labs. These include such topics as continuous quality improvement, grant writing, strategic planning, volunteer management, and effective facilitation and meeting management to develop marketable, career-oriented skills. In 2016, the school recruited its first Kauffman Endowed Professor of Practice in Innovation and Social Entrepreneurship and now hosts the university's Social Entrepreneurship and Innovation Competition. The school has seen enrollment in these specializations grow, as well as a growing recognition of the role of policy, management, and leadership among its student body. In 2018, the school instituted a required curriculum in leadership for students across all three degree programs—MSW, MPH and its new Master in Social Policy. In 2020, the school will offer a full MSW concentration in Social Impact Leadership, incorporating a braided approach that integrates traditional management with social innovation and entrepreneurship training.

Conclusions

Social work is well-positioned to develop, leverage, and enhance social innovations that promote livable lives. The field brings considerable expertise in flexible adaptation that addresses complex societal problems. New skills in design and social innovation complement current practice, while extensive infrastructure exists for retooling.

Professional synergies also promise to address current limitations of innovation. Social innovation and entrepreneurship remain poorly coordinated with human service. Lack of integration wastes resources and introduces difficult decisions regarding how to invest in social change. Expanding applications raise pressing concerns for human service and policy. Social work must act quickly to engage and lead around social innovation that ensures livable lives for all.

The failure to implement, sustain, and scale up social innovations and social policies carries momentous implications for social work. Fundamentally, ineffective or unavailable services and policies miss opportunities to address social conditions that threaten well-being. They also diminish the role of the profession in addressing service quality and systemic injustices, which pushes the field away from its core professional values. Moreover, failure to take on leadership roles in social innovation threatens to marginalize the profession and its ability to make social change. Social innovations will develop, whether or not social workers are in the forefront. Other professions are positioned to provide leadership to the development of innovations in many areas in which these professionals are active. Although undoubtedly they will play many roles in the development and implementation of social innovations, the failure to assume leadership poses a risk of diminishing professional identity and market value. It also risks advancement of practices less rooted in the core values and ethics of social justice and social good.

Recommendations

1. *Expand the social work paradigm of how human service innovations and services should be developed and implemented.* The social work profession has successfully adopted and socialized an evidence-based model of human service design and implementation that draws its assumptions from medicine and is based on robust empirical research and implementation with strict fidelity. A fundamental step is to expand the paradigm to legitimize social entrepreneurial and social enterprise processes that support discontinuous and even disruptive innovations and what are known as "good-enough" innovations (Christensen et al., 2006) that produce speedier, more efficient, and sustainable impact.
   - An educational and attitudinal campaign within and directed to the major framing organizations of the profession: accrediting bodies, professional research and practice associations, academic and practice journals, teaching institutions (e.g., American Academy of Social Work and Social Welfare, Council on Social Work Education, Society for Social Work and Research).
     - Conferences
     - Special interest groups
     - Special journal editions
     - Recognition and awards for social innovation
   - Activism by social work academics and leading practitioners to obtain governance and advisory roles in relevant government and human service boards, commissions, and committees.
2. Increase funding and supports for research, education, and practice in entrepreneurial innovation, while maintaining and/or expanding support for evidence-based interventions and implementation and dissemination strategies.

- Professional advocacy to government bodies and philanthropic resources to expand funding criteria and increase funding to entrepreneurial ventures.
  - Creation of social innovation funds
  - Social innovation incubators and accelerators
  - Funding of strategies to scale successful innovations
- Increased university funding for faculty–community research partnerships to develop, implement, and scale social innovations.

3. Increase masters and doctoral level education in leadership, management, innovation, and entrepreneurship to prepare graduates to obtain organizational leadership positions and promote innovation in human services.
   - Collaboration and transdisciplinary teaching about innovation, entrepreneurship, leadership, and management with schools and professional associations within the fields of business, nonprofit management and public administration.
   - Increased emphasis and expanded curriculum at the Masters level in leadership, management, innovation and entrepreneurship as well as policy practice.
     - Required curricular content for all masters students, including incorporation of ambidextrous approaches to program planning and evaluation.
     - Full concentration curriculum in leadership, management, innovation and entrepreneurship emphasizing ambidexterity
     - Joint degree programs—MBA, MNPA, MPA, MPH
     - Practicum and internship opportunities with senior managers and entrepreneurs
     - Co-curricular programs such as innovation centers, competitions, student groups
   - Expansion of practice doctoral (DSW) programs with a leadership and management focus.

4. Expand professional and executive education to improve knowledge and skills of current organizational leaders in braided approaches to innovation and impact.
   - Expanded university-based professional development and executive education for social work graduates and other human service leaders in leadership, management, innovation, and entrepreneurship, as well as policy practice.
     - Postmasters certificates
     - Participation in university-based innovation centers, accelerators, innovation funds

- Education of nonprofit governing boards to improve organizational supports for innovation

5. Expand the research agenda regarding innovation processes in human services.
   - Collaboration and transdisciplinary research to expand and adapt knowledge about innovation processes with schools and professional associations within the fields of business, nonprofit management, and public administration.
   - Identification of barriers to the development, implementation, and scaling of social innovations in nonprofit and public organizations including the role of funders, accreditation bodies, professional organizations, and governing boards.
   - Assessment of the effectiveness of alternate strategies of achieving ambidexterity and the conditions for success within nonprofit and public human service organizations.
   - Assessment of the antecedent conditions, skills and strategies needed to successfully employ entrepreneurial practices such as design thinking and rapid prototyping in human service organizations.
   - Identification of key leadership and management skills and strategies for promoting social innovation in human service organizations.

Concluding Thoughts

Social work has been at the forefront of movements for social change with considerable success. Since its birth in the late 19th and early 20th centuries, the profession has played an instrumental leadership role in shaping service delivery and innovations in programs and public policy in a broad range of human services. This impact extends from early settlement house movements and disease prevention to substantial contributions in areas such as child welfare, income support, consumer protection and financial capability, mental illness, American Indian rights, veterans services, housing, community development, aging, and substance abuse. Indeed, Jane Addams could be considered social work's first innovator. These gains in population well-being demonstrate the utility of social work in addressing complex social problems.

Social work's embrace of evidence-based practices has elevated the profession and extended its considerable impact. Adoption of treatment methods such as cognitive-behavioral therapy and motivational interviewing along with social work's role in the development of program models such as the Naturally Occurring Retirement Community, Oasis Institute's Intergenerational Tutoring, or Wyman Center's Teen Outreach Program have done much to enhance livable lives for varied populations.

Likewise, the growth of social entrepreneurship has contributed important innovations and advances in human services such as the micro finance movement epitomized by the Grameen Bank, groundbreaking organizations such as the Aravind Eye Care System, and national movements such as City Year. However, the limited role of social work in these movements challenges the professions' leadership role in human services. Moreover, it challenges the ability to infuse social work values, ethics, and unwavering commitment to social justice into the widest circle of human services. Retooling social work to adopt a braided approach to innovation will significantly expand, deepen, and speed the development of social innovations that promote livable lives for all.

References

Andersson, F. O. 2012, April 11. "Social Entrepreneurship as Fetish." *Nonprofit Quarterly*. Retrieved from https://nonprofitquarterly.org/2012/04/11/social-entrepreneurship-as-fetish-2/

Andersson, F. O., and R. McCambridge, R. 2017. "Social Entrepreneurship's All-American Mind Trap." *Nonprofit Quarterly*, 24, 28–33.

Balas E. A. 1998. "From Appropriate Care to Evidence-Based Medicine." *Pediatric Annals*, 27, 581–584.

Bedney, B., D. Schimmel, R. Goldberg, I. Cotlar-Berkowitz, and D. Bursztyn. 2007. "Rethinking Aging in Place: Exploring the Impact of NORC Supportive Service Programs on Older Adult Participants." Paper presented at the 2007 Joint Conference of the American Society on Aging and the National Council on Aging. Chicago, IL.

Beekman, A. V., A. Steiner, and M. E. Wasserman. 2012. "Where Innovation Does a World of Good: Entrepreneurial Orientation and Innovative Outcomes in Nonprofit Organizations." *Journal of Strategic Innovation and Sustainability*, 8, 22–36.

Berzin, S. C. 2012. "Where Is Social Work in the Social Entrepreneurship Movement?" *Social Work*, 57, 185–188.

Berzin, S., and M. Pitt-Catsouphes. 2015. "Social Innovation from the Inside: Considering the 'Intrapreneurship' Path." *Social Work*, 60, 360–362.

Berzin, S., M. Pitt-Catsouphes, and P. Gaitan-Rossi. 2016. "Innovation and Sustainability: An Exploratory Study of Intrapreneurship Among Human Service Organizations." *Human Service Organizations: Management, Leadership and Governance*, 40, 540–552.

Blank, S. 2013. "Why the Lean Start-Up Changes Everything." *Harvard Business Review*, 91, 63–72.

Brown, T., and J. Wyatt. 2010. "Design Thinking for Social Innovation." *Development Outreach*, 12, 29–43.

Birkinshaw, J., and K. Gupta. 2013. "Clarifying the Distinctive Contribution of Ambidexterity to the Field of Organizational Studies." *The Academy of Management Perspectives*, 27, 287–298.

Bornstein, D. 2004. *How to Change the World: Social Entrepreneurs and the Power of New Ideas.* New York: Oxford University Press.

Brownson, R., G. Colditz, and E. Proctor. 2012. *Dissemination and Implementation Research in Health: Translating Science to Practice.* New York: Oxford University Press. doi:10.1093/acprof:oso/9780199751877.001.0001

Bryson, J. M., K. B. Boal, and H. G. Rainey. 2008. "Strategic Orientation and Ambidextrous Public Organizations." Paper presented at the conference on Organizational Strategy, Structure, and

Process: A Reflection on the Research Perspective of Raymond Miles and Charles Snow. Cardiff University and the Economic and Social Research Council. Cardiff, UK. Retrieved from http://kimboal.ba.ttu.edu/Selected%20writings/organizationalambidexterity.pdf

Cajaiba-Santana, G. 2014. "Social Innovation: Moving the Field forward. A Conceptual Framework." *Technological Forecasting and Social Change*, 82, 42–51.

Center for the Advancement of Social Entrepreneurship. 2008, June. "Developing the Field of Social Entrepreneurship: A Report from the Center for Advancement of Social Entrepreneurship (CASE), Duke University, the Fuqua School of Business." Durham, North Carolina: Duke University.

Christensen, C. M. 2011. *The Innovator's Dilemma: The Revolutionary Book That Will Change the Way you Do Business.* New York: Harper.

Christensen, C. M., H. Baumann, R. Ruggles, and T. M. Sadtler. 2006. "Disruptive Innovation for Social Change." *Harvard Business Review*, 84, 94–101.

Cnaan, R. A., and D. Vinokur-Kaplan. 2015. *Social Innovation: Definitions, Clarifications, and a New Model. Cases in Innovative Nonprofits: Organizations that Make a Difference.* Thousand Oaks, CA: SAGE.

Coule, T., and B. Patmore. 2013. "Institutional Logics, Institutional Work, and Public Service Innovation in Non-Profit Organizations." *Public Administration*, 91, 980–997.

Council on Social Work Education. n.d. "2015 Educational Policy and Accreditation Standards for Baccalaureate and Master's Social Work Programs." Retrieved from https://cswe.org/getattachment/Accreditation/Accreditation-Process/2015-EPAS/2015EPAS_Web_FINAL.pdf.aspx

Damanpour, F. 1987. "The Adoption of Technological, Administrative, and Ancillary Innovations: Impact of Organizational Factors." *Journal of Management*, 13, 675–688.

Damanpour, F. 1991. "Organizational Innovation: A Meta-Analysis of Effects of Determinants and Moderators." *Academy of Management Journal*, 34, 555–590.

Dees, J. G. 1998. "Enterprising Nonprofits." *Harvard Business Review*, 76, 54–69.

Dees, J. G. 2007. "Taking Social Entrepreneurship Seriously." *Society*, 44, 24–31.

Edgington, N. 2011. "The Problem with Social Entrepreneurship: Guest Post." *Social Velocity*. Retrieved from http://www.socialvelocity.net/2011/06/the-problem-with-social-entrepreneurship-guest-post/

Elbert, K. B., and P. S. Neufeld. 2010. "Indicators of a Successful Naturally Occurring Retirement Community: A Case Study." *Journal of Housing for the Elderly*, 24, 322–334.

Ezell, M., R. H. Chernesky, and L. M. Healy. 2004. "The Learning Climate for Administration Students." *Administration in Social Work*, 28, 57–76.

Fowler, P. J., A. F. Farrell, K. E. Marcal, S. Chung, and P. S. Hovmand. 2017. "Housing and Child Well-Being: Emerging Evidence and Implications for Scaling Up Services." *American Journal of Community Psychology*, 60, 134–144.

Fowler, P. J., P. S. Hovmand, K. E. Marcal, and S. Das. 2019. "Solving Homelessness from a Complex Systems Perspective: Insights for Prevention Responses." *Annual Review of Public Health*, 40, https://doi.org/10.1146/annurev-publhealth-040617-013553

Fowler, P. J., K. Wright, K. E. Marcal, E. Ballard, and P. S. Hovmand. 2019. "Capability Traps Impeding Homeless Services: A Community-Based System Dynamics Evaluation." *Journal of Social Service Research*, 45, 348–359.

Friedman, B. D. 2008. "Where Have All the Social Work Managers Gone?" *Management and Leadership in Social Work Practice and Education.* Edited by L. H. Ginsberg. Alexandria, VA: Council on Social Work Education, pp. 22–31.

Gauss, A. 2015, July 29. "Why We Love to Hate Nonprofits." *Stanford Social Innovation Review.* Retrieved from https://ssir.org/articles/entry/why_we_love_to_hate_nonprofits.

Germak, A. J., and K. K. Singh. 2009. "Social Entrepreneurship: Changing the Way Social Workers Do Business." *Administration in Social Work*, 34, 79–95.

Grant, J., R. Cottrell, F. Cluzeau, and B. Fawcett. "Evaluating 'Payback' on Biomedical Research from Papers Cited in Clinical Guidelines: Applied Bibliometric Study." *BMJ*, 320, 1107–1111.

Gray, M., K. Healy, and P. Crofts. 2003. "Social Enterprise: Is It the Business of Social Work?" *Australian Social Work*, 56, 141–154.

Greenfield, E. A., A. Scharlach, A. J. Lehning, and J. K. Davitt. 2012. "A Conceptual Framework for Examining the Promise of the NORC Program and Village Models to Promote Aging in Place." *Journal of Aging Studies*, 26, 273–284.

Hambrick, D. C. 2007. "Upper Echelons Theory: An Update." *Academy of Management Review*, 32, 334–343.

Hambrick, D. C., and P. A. Mason. 1984. "Upper Echelons: The Organization as a Reflection of Its Top Managers." *Academy of Management Review*, 9, 193–206.

He, Z., and P. Wong. 2004. "Exploration vs. Exploitation: An Empirical Test of the Ambidexterity Hypothesis." *Organizational Science*, 15, 481–494.

Hoagwood, K. E., S. S. Olin, S. Horwitz, M. McKay, A. Cleek, A. Gleacher, and M. Hogan. 2014. "Scaling Up Evidence-Based Practices for Children and Families in New York State: Toward Evidence-Based Policies on Implementation for State Mental Health Systems." *Journal of Clinical Child and Adolescent Psychology*, 43, 145–157.

Hoefer, R. 2009. "Preparing Managers for the Human Services." *The Handbook of Human Services Management*. Edited by R. J. Patti. Thousand Oaks, CA: SAGE, pp. 483–501.

Hoefer, R., L. Watson, and K. Preble. 2013. "A Mixed Methods Examination of Nonprofit Board Chair Preferences in Hiring Executive Directors." *Administration in Social Work*, 37, 437–446.

Jaskyte, K. 2010. "Innovation in Human Service Organizations." *Human Services as Complex Organizations*. Edited by Y. Hasenfeld. Thousand Oaks, CA: SAGE, pp. 481–503.

Kube, A., S. Das, and P. J. Fowler. 2019. "Allocating Interventions Based on Predicted Outcomes: A Case Study on Homelessness Services." *Proceedings of the AAAI Conference on Artificial Intelligence*, 33(July), 622–629. https://doi.org/10.1609/aaai.v33i01.3301622

Landsverk, J., C. H. Brown, P. Chamberlain, L. A. Palinkas, M. Ogihara, S. Czaja, J. D. Goldhaver-Fiebert, J. A. Rolls Reutz, and S. M. Horwitz. 2012. "Design and analysis in dissemination and implementation research. *Dissemination and Implementation Research in Health*. Edited by R. C. Brownson, G. A. Colditz, and E. K. Proctor. New York: Oxford University Press, pp. 225–260.

Larson, R. S., J. W. Dearing, and T. E. Backer. 2017. "Strategies to Scale Up Social Programs: Pathways, Partnerships and Fidelity." *Diffusion Associates*. Retrieved from http://www.wallacefoundation.org/knowledge-center/Pages/how-to-scale-up-social-programs-that-work.aspx

Lavie, D., and L. Rosenkopf. 2006. "Balancing Exploration and Exploitation in Alliance Formation." *Academy of Management Journal*, 49, 797–818.

Lavie, D., U. Stettner, and M. L. Tushman. 2010. "Exploration and Exploitation Within and Across Organizations." *The Academy of Management Annals*, 4, 109–155.

Lyneis, J., and J. Sterman. 2016. "How to Save a Leaky Ship: Capability Traps and the Failure of Win–Win Investments in Sustainability and Social Responsibility." *Academy of Management Discoveries*, 2, 7–32.

Levinthal, D. A., and J. G. March. 1993. "The Myopia of Learning." *Strategic Management Journal*, 14, 95–112.

Light, P. C. 2009a. *The Search for Social Entrepreneurship*. Washington, DC: Brookings Institution Press.

Light, P. C. 2009b. "Social Entrepreneurship Revisited." *Stanford Social Innovation Review*, 7, 21–22.

March, J. G. 1991. "Exploration and Exploitation in Organizational Learning." *Organizational Science*, 2, 71–87.

Martin, R. L., and S. Osberg. 2007. "Social Entrepreneurship: The Case for Definition." *Stanford Social Innovation Review*, 5, 28–39.

Masotti, P. J., R. Fick, A. Johnson-Masotti, and S. MacLeod. 2006. "Healthy Naturally Occurring Retirement Communities: A Low-Cost Approach to Facilitating Healthy Aging." *American Journal of Public Health*, 96, 1164–1170.

Designing and Implementing Policy

McHugh, R. K., and D. H. Barlow. 2010. "The Dissemination and Implementation of Evidence-Based Psychological Treatments: A Review of Current Efforts." *American Psychologist*, 65, 73–84.

Milat, A. J., A. Bauman, and S. Redman. 2015. "Narrative Review of Models and Success Factors for Scaling Up Public Health Interventions." *Implementation Science*, 10, 113.

Milton, V. I. 2016. "A Study of Board Members' Perceptions of Leadership Competencies That Professionally Trained Social Workers Should Possess Who Lead Nonprofit Human Service Organizations as Adopted in the Council on Social Work Education (CSWE) Strategic Plan, 1998–2000." Retrieved from http://digitalcommons.auctr.edu/cauetds/22/

Mirabella, R. M. 2007. "University-Based Educational Programs in Nonprofit Management and Philanthropic Studies: A 10-Year Review and Projections of Future Trends." *Nonprofit and Voluntary Sector Quarterly*, 36, S11–S27.

Nandan, M., and P. A. Scott. 2013. "Social Entrepreneurship and Social Work: The Need for a Transdisciplinary Educational Model." *Administration in Social Work*, 37, 257–271.

Nandan, M., M. London, and T. Bent-Goodley. 2015. "Social Workers as Social Change Agents: Social Innovation, Social Intrapreneurship, and Social Entrepreneurship." *Human Service Organizations: Management, Leadership and Governance*, 39, 38–56.

National Association of Social Workers. 2010. *2010 Social Work Congress Final Report.* Washington, DC: NASW Press.

Nesoff, I. 2007. "The Importance of Revitalizing Management Education for Social Workers." *Social Work*, 52, 283–285.

Norris-Tirrell, D., J. Rinella, and X. Pham. 2017. "Examining the Career Trajectories of Nonprofit Executive Leaders." *Nonprofit and Voluntary Sector Quarterly*, 47, 146–164.

O'Reilly, C. A., III, and M. L. Tushman. 2004. "The Ambidextrous Organization." *Harvard Business Review*, 82, 74–81.

O'Reilly, C. A., and M. L. Tushman. 2013. "Organizational Ambidexterity: Past, Present, and Future." SSRN Scholarly Paper ID 2285704. Rochester, NY: Social Science Research Network. https://papers.ssrn.com/abstract=2285704

Osborne, S. P. 1998. "Naming the Beast: Defining and Classifying Service Innovations in Social Policy." *Human Relations*, 51, 1133–1154.

Osborne, S. P., C. Chew, and K. McLaughlin. 2008. "The Once and Future Pioneers? The Innovative Capacity of Voluntary Organisations and the Provision of Public Services: A Longitudinal Approach." *Public Management Review*, 10, 51–70.

Osborne, S. P., and N. Flynn. 1997. "Strategic Alliances Managing the Innovative Capacity of Voluntary and Non-Profit Organizations in the Provision of Public Services." *Public Money and Management*, 17, 31–39.

Perlmutter, F. D. 2006. "Ensuring Social Work Administration." *Administration in Social Work*, 30, 3–10.

Pfeffer, J., and R. I. Sutton. 2006. "Evidence-Based Management." *Harvard Business Review*, 84, 62–72.

Phills, J. A., K. Deiglmeier, and D. T. Miller. 2008. "Rediscovering Social Innovation." *Stanford Social Innovation Review*, 6, 34–43.

Pitt-Catsouphes, M., and S. Cosner Berzin. 2015. "Teaching Note-Incorporating Social Innovation Content into Macro Social Work Education." *Journal of Social Work Education*, 51, 407–416.

Prange, C., and Schlegelmilch. 2010. "Heading for the Next Innovation Archetype." *Journal of Business Strategy*, 31, 46–55.

Raisch, S., and J. Birkinshaw. 2008. "Organizational Ambidexterity: Antecedents, Outcomes, and Moderators." *Journal of Management*, 34, 375–409.

Reisch, M. 2016. "Why Macro Practice Matters." *Journal of Social Work Education*, 52, 258–268.

Ries, E. 2011. *The Lean Startup: How Today's Entrepreneurs Use Continuous Innovation to Create Radically Successful Businesses.* New York: Crown Business.

Rosenberg, B., and A. M. McBride. 2015. "The Management Imperative: Displacement, Dynamics, and Directions Forward for Training Social Workers as Managers." CSD Working Paper No. 15-41. St. Louis, MO: Washington University, Center for Social Development.

Rosing, K., M. Freese, and A. Bausch. 2011. "Explaining the Heterogeneity of the Leadership-Innovation Relationship: Ambidextrous Leadership." *The Leadership Quarterly*, 22, 956–974.

Ross, R. K. 2014. "We Need More Scale, Not More Innovation." *Stanford Social Innovation Review*, 12, 1–6.

Rotheram-Borus, M. J., D. Swendeman, and B. F. Chorpita. 2012. "Disruptive Innovations for Designing and Diffusing Evidence-Based Interventions." *American Psychologist*, 67, 463.

Rothman, J. 2013. "Education for Macro Intervention: A Survey of Problems and Prospects." Report for the Association of Community Organization and Social Administration (ACOSA).

Salamon, L. M., S. L. Geller, and K. L. Mengel. 2010. "Nonprofits, Innovation, and Performance Measurement: Separating Fact from Fiction." *Listening Post Project*, 17, 1–25.

Schmid, H. 2009. "Agency-Environment Relations." *The Handbook of Human Services Management*. Edited by R. J. Patti. Thousand Oaks, CA: SAGE, pp. 411–433.

Seelos, C., and J. Mair. 2012. "Innovation Is Not the Holy Grail." *Stanford Social Innovation Review*, 10, 44–49.

Seelos, C. 2012. "What Determines the Capacity for Continuous Innovation in Social Sector Organizations?" Retrieved from https://pdfs.semanticscholar.org/f722/da82f678247806a be38794a1e87dfe1f3188.pdf

Skoll Foundation. n.d. "Approach." Retrieved from http://skoll.org/about/approach/

Skoll, J., and Osberg, S. 2013. "Social Entrepreneurs Dare to Change the World." Retrieved from http://www.cnn.com/2013/09/07/opinion/skoll-osberg-social-entrepreneurs/

Special Commission to Advance Macro Practice in Social Work. 2015. "Macro Practice in Social Work: From Learning to Action for Social Justice." Retrieved from http://files.ctctcdn.com/ de9b9b0e001/0e4f058e-1226-4f8f-b7e1-a2a4d677cbfc.pdf

Sullivan, W. P. 2016. "Leadership in Social Work: Where Are We?" *Journal of Social Work Education*, 52, S51–S61.

Tushman, M. L., and C. A. O'Reilly III. 1996. "Ambidextrous Organizations: Managing Evolutionary and Revolutionary Change." *California Management Review*, 38, 8–30.

Westley, F., and N. Antadze. 2010. "Making a Difference: Strategies for Scaling Social Innovation for Greater Impact." *The Innovation Journal*, 15, 1–19.

Wimpfheimer, S., K. Beyer, D. Coplan, B. Friedman, R. Greenberg. K. Hopkins, M. Mor Barack, and J. Tropman. 2018. "Human Services Management Competencies: A Guide for Non-Profit and For-Profit Agencies, Foundations and Academic Institutions." Los Angeles: Network for Social Work Management.

World Health Organization. 2007. "Task Shifting: Rational Redistribution of Tasks Among Health Workforce Teams: Global Recommendations and Guidelines." Retrieved from https://apps. who.int/iris/handle/10665/43821

Wuenschel, P. C. 2006. "The Diminishing Role of Social Work Administrators in Social Service Agencies." *Administration in Social Work*, 30, 75–18.

14

Leveraging Big Data Analytics and Informatics

DEREK S. BROWN, BRETT DRAKE, PATRICK J. FOWLER, JENINE K. HARRIS, AND KIMBERLY J. JOHNSON

The goal of a livable life has been explored throughout this book. The chapters have addressed a wide variety of problems and challenges preventing people from living life to its fullest. In this chapter, we discuss a relatively new medium that provides the tools and solutions to help people live better lives. That medium is big data. We will discuss what big data is, and how advances in data availability, storage, processing, and analysis make it a truly new phenomenon. We will also explore how this new phenomenon can be used as a powerful tool in improving people's lives.

The humanistic ideal of assuring people a dignified life where their needs are met, and they have opportunity for growth may seem unrelated or even antithetical to the image of billions of data elements residing antiseptically on a server farm. Nothing can be further from the truth. Knowledge, after all, is power, and big data is knowledge at its most basic and raw form.

Throughout this chapter we emphasize three underlying themes. First, the use of big data is necessary if we are to do the best job possible achieving livable lives. It is axiomatic that evidence-based policy requires the best available evidence. Much of the time this evidence lies in big data. The same applies to the tools necessary for effective practice. Big data include the information needed for the creation, testing, and use of either traditional tools (such as actuarial risk assessments) or tools that can only be created using big data (such as predictive analytics based on machine learning). Much as a surgeon will function better if they use a sharp scalpel, a social policymaker or clinician will function better if they have access to more precise tools.

The second general theme we will emphasize is our current historical context. It could be argued that big data have always existed. However, this is truer in a theoretical than a practical sense. As an example, the U.S. Census has collected data at the individual level that has been constitutionally mandated for two and a half centuries. And yet there is a big difference between riding your horse 400 miles to spend a month looking through stacks of semi-legible writing in contrast to accessing American Fact Finder to get a more accurate answer to your question in under 30 seconds. Beyond the question of access, big data are also growing exponentially in terms of available sources and our ability to interlink these sources.

The third general theme we will address includes specific ways in which big data can be used to address social problems. While we refer to big data as a tool, it might be more correct to describe it as something much broader, perhaps as a new workshop space or language. The potential ways in which big data can help people to achieve livable lives have only begun to be explored.

This new frontier of big data is no longer just technical, it is conceptual: What do we do with it and how can we analyze this new kind of data? For professionals in social work the ultimate question must be, "How can we use it to help people live better lives?" Recent attempts at redefining big data acknowledge these concerns, including operationalizing big data as cross-sector, creative, process-based, and having the potential to utilize data in motion or live data.

Social work is already a prime beneficiary of big data. Revealing patterns of service delivery and timely use is furthering community, family, and individual well-being. Big data analytics hold enormous potential to increase the speed at which some kinds of research can be done by an order of magnitude. This promotes responsivity in research. Cross-sector big data have increased the breadth of research that can be done, fostering transdisciplinarity, model building and testing, and methodological rigor. Big data can provide an alternative to the ivory tower syndrome and thereby enhance the practical relevance of the work we do. For example, agencies generally record data with high field relevance or interest to themselves, rather than data of theoretical or arcane interest.

Big data provide a practical means of meeting emerging societal expectations regarding real-time answers to social problems. We are moving into an age in which real-time data are expected by default. Big data are the only available source of information to fuel methodologically valid large-scale, real-time research. In the past 20 years, administrative data in the social sciences have moved from being seen as second rate, to commonplace, to highly desirable. In the next 20 years, big data will become either the empirical foundation (e.g., linked cross-sector databases) or an auxiliary data source (e.g., hospital records, geographical contextual variables) for virtually all methodologically sound work. As an example, try to imagine a large-scale child maltreatment prevention effectiveness study that does not use official reports of child maltreatment as one of several outcome measures—such an idea is becoming increasingly implausible.

Large amounts of data are collected in state and private social service systems on millions of clients they come in contact with. For some people, this data trail is brief and fleeting; for others, rich and protracted. Social workers must leverage these big data collected from disparate sources and at multiple levels to gain deep insights into which clients are being helped or are being failed.

This chapter will address the challenge of big data in social work. First, we cover a preliminary set of topics to help acquaint the reader with what big data are in a general sense, along with specific and emerging characteristics of big data that are particularly relevant to improving people's lives. This reflects the first two general themes identified above—the emerging need to embrace big data and how our current moment in time is making this possible. In many ways, these are inseparable issues—two sides of the same coin.

We are at the dawn of the age of big data. At the George Warren Brown School of Social Work, big data are routinely used in epidemiological work, intervention studies, disparity work, and many other kinds of research. However, we recognize that we have seen only the first rays of a new day. It is imperative that we forge transdisciplinary partnerships with data-mining and machine-learning experts in computer science who are currently developing computational algorithms. There is a need to coalesce and construct repositories of big data for informing targeted design and delivery of social services in order to raise the quality of life for marginalized and disadvantaged populations. It is also imperative that we ensure that the next generation of social work scholars are trained in the techniques that are needed to carry out this work.

Defining Big Data and Its Place in History

Big data is a commonly used term but has no consistent definition. Originally, NASA used the term "big data" to mean just that—massively large information (Press, 2014). The *Oxford English Dictionary* still espouses such a definition. This was, perhaps, mainly a naming of a then-critical limiting factor—data outstripping hardware (and software) capacity. Nowadays, a 128-gigabyte thumb drive can be had for $15 and complex data management or analysis programs using millions of records and hundreds of variables can be run in minutes or (rarely) hours on a sub $2,000 computer. The constraint posed by computer space/time has become less and less of an issue in big data applications.

Although size is implied (Ward and Barker, 2013), big data has no clear and uniform definition, having arisen as a broad concept simultaneously in academia, industry, and the media around 2011. The earliest attempt at a definition, while not specifically mentioning big data per se, is a 2001 report (Laney, 2001) that proposed volume, velocity, and variety (the three Vs) as characteristics of the changing nature of the data landscape. In the context of big data, volume refers to the size of data sets; variety refers to the data types, repositories, or domains where data originate; and velocity is the rate of data flow. More recently, the Information Technology Laboratory of the National Institute of Standards and Technology (NIST) convened a working group and reviewed proposed definitions of big data appearing in blog posts, magazine articles, the dictionary, and numerous academic sources. Ultimately, the workgroup retained the three Vs proposed in 2001 and added a fourth V, variability, which refers to change in other characteristics (NIST, 2015).

Google searches for big data increased sharply from late 2010 through 2015, although they have leveled off at a slight decrease since that peak (Google Trends, n.d.). Likewise, the Web of Science shows one publication with big data in the title in 2010, but steadily increasing over time to 2,036 by 2018. The rapid rise of both interest and research suggests that an overview of key aspects of big data and their utility in social science and social policy is warranted (Gandomi and Haider, 2015).

Challenges in Access and Limitations of Big Data

Social scientists study constructs such as community violence or depression. As we study these constructs, we generate, analyze, and interpret variables, such as numbers of violent experiences in the past year, numbers of assaults per 1,000 persons in a ZIP code, an individual's score on the Beck Depression Inventory, or whether or not a particular person has been formally diagnosed with depression. There are many potential ways to transform a general construct into an operationalized variable, and this is one of the key tasks we teach our students at the BSW, MSW and PhD levels.

Perhaps the greatest single challenge in accessing big data is privacy. Furthermore, individual-level data are almost always harder to get than aggregate level data. To obtain confidential individual data, you must generally have written consent of the person in question or have a data use agreement with the owner of the data (i.e., the data steward) such as a state or federal agency. In addition, you may also need to get Institutional Review Board (IRB) approval from both the agency holding the data and your home institution. For example, a person in a domestic violence treatment effectiveness study may give consent for you to request police or medical records specific to them personally.

Large-scale studies are often done with de-identified individual data, where all the data used in the study are from one or several big data sources. For example, many years of linkable de-identified information at the individual level on diagnosed cancer and relevant risk factors is available to researchers, and many studies have been done linking these. In such studies, the subjects are never contacted by any researcher, and, ideally, the researcher never receives any identifying data about the subject at all, except as may be necessary for initial matching between the various databases used. In this latter scenario, data use agreements are often needed, while IRB approval is typically not needed because this type of research is considered exempt.

Prior to big data, it was reasonable to think almost exclusively in terms of going out and collecting your own data or conducting a secondary analysis using data someone else had collected. For example, if you wanted to know about the levels of community violence a person was exposed to, you might ask them directly using a standardized questionnaire. Alternately, you might see how detailed the police annual reports were, hoping for aggregate counts at a neighborhood level (e.g., beats, tracts, ZIP codes). Failing this, you might send a research assistant to the local police station to abstract police files manually (one of the authors did this as an undergraduate student).

Big data offers a different option. It is perhaps more correct to say that the big data has always existed, but that there is a large practical difference between hand-coding literal walls full of manila envelopes in the basement of a police building, on the one hand, and downloading something from the Internet in minutes, on the other. Many cities, such as Austin, Texas, have electronic data going back years, making longitudinal data analyses relatively easy.

A key challenge of big data is that it is always limited by the fields it already contains. The data may not be available at all or may not be aggregated in the unit of analysis that you would prefer. You may want records on all police calls but are only be able to get data on arrests. Perhaps you want data on a particular kind of assault but can only get data on simple versus aggravated subtypes. In income maintenance data, the reasons for a given case being terminated may only be found in a series of overly broad and, therefore, not very useful categories. This is very much a half-full/half-empty issue. Social scientists are used to broad freedoms in what kinds of data they collect, constrained mainly by cost, respondent burden, and human subjects research issues. When using existing data, the question of which variables your study can include shifts from "What would I like to have and is practical to get?" to "What data already exist that will serve well enough?" For example, big data may include records of official diagnosis for depression but cannot be used to measure lower levels of depressive symptomatology that could be picked up by an instrument such as the DASS-21 (Henry and Crawford, 2005).

On the other hand, this kind of limitation can be an advantage. Social science research has a long history of testing propositions derived from theories that are academically fascinating but may be limited in practical utility. Reliance upon big data brings more practically grounded players into the game and degrades the academic hegemony on social science knowledge generation. You cannot use big data, for example, to test the effects of different kinds of toilet training on adult behavior. In this way, big data forces a kind of democratization or at least modification of the questions that can be asked and answered by academics. We see this as generally a good thing.

To consider these issues in a more applied way, let us consider two examples—one at an individual level of analysis and one at a neighborhood level of analysis—and consider what kinds of options big data might offer. In the first case, let us posit that we are interested in understanding outcomes in children who have experienced radically different forms of parenting, which were extensively catalogued using a series of measures during their first decade of life. "Outcomes" is a broad term, and we may be interested in negative behavioral outcomes such as delinquency, school drop-out, violent crime victimization, risky sexual behavior, and a range of other counterproductive behavior. All of those topics can be accessed via big data if we have the subject's permission. School records, medical records, and child protection and juvenile court records, along with other sources, can provide a rich trove of information. We also want to make sure that our models are well-controlled, particularly with regard to extra-familial environment, which can be difficult to measure. For example, we might include neighborhood (ZIP code) violent and property crime (from law enforcement websites), economic mobility, race, ethnicity, and other demographic indicators (Census American Community Survey data). These can be easily merged on to individual-level databases to provide contextual information. In some states, we can even get useful retrospective data, including parental crime/delinquency, income maintenance, child maltreatment, medical conditions, and other indicators predating the child's birth.

As a second example, let us say we are interested in looking at the degree to which high community mobility is associated with disruption at the family level. We could use Census data to get mobility rates at the block group, tract, ZIP code, county, or state levels, and we could include a vast number of control variables (e.g., income, poverty, available transportation, employment, distance traveled to work, demographic factors). We could also access a number of aggregated crime and medical factors to use as outcome variables. For example, the excellent Missouri Information for Community Assessment (MICA) online website provides detailed data on death, hospital records (including by diagnosis or mechanism), and a range of other outcomes. The database features a very strong drill-down capability. If you want to know the number of white women between the ages of 18 and 24 who started prenatal care in their first trimester between 2010 and 2012 in ZIP code 63130, you just have to hit the right keys. Multiple ZIP codes can be examined at once using a tabular feature that is captured and transferred to a spreadsheet such as Excel and, from there, to any data analysis program. The possibilities for such work using publically available data (both the Census and MICA are freely available online without any permission required) to answer long-standing questions of crucial importance to social work is nothing short of breathtaking, particularly considering the ease with which this can now be done.

Another important point is that data are not always where you first expect them to be. For example, for violence researchers, the obvious place to look is law enforcement and the courts. However, more useful information on some types of violence, especially victimization, may actually come from medical records. A number of social constructs can be explored using variables drawn from medical data, and this is becoming easier with electronic medical records. Treatment for sexually transmitted disease, gunshot wounds, and other types of information can be tremendously useful. Again, these data may not always be exactly what you want. For example, in some states, very strong data exist covering all hospital contacts, but visits to urgent care may not be included. In such cases, compromises must be made. For example, instead of attempting to measure all injuries that could potentially be due to violence, researchers might restrict their analysis to gunshot wounds, which are likely to be treated in a way and at a place that will leave an official record.

When using big data, the use of proxy measures can be a good idea. For example, medical data showing inadequate prenatal care, or lack of needed medical care, may be indicative of some forms of neglect. Similarly, school suspensions and juvenile court proceedings may suggest certain kinds of behavioral problems. It is absolutely necessary, of course, that any proxies be thoroughly discussed in relation to exactly what they can and cannot measure.

A related issue is triangulation. A study measuring a given construct such as risky sexual behavior may use self-report or parental report data but can also clearly benefit from access to medical records or even arrest data. To the degree that such radically different means of measurement agree, faith in the validity of the study is increased. Triangulation has other key uses, such as determining the validity of a given measure or approach.

The widespread use of big data in social science is an emerging issue, and there are concerns in some quarters regarding the quality of big data. In our experience, these concerns have mitigated radically over the past few decades. In the 1990s, administrative data were frequently assumed to be invalid or useless by default. The obvious recent utility of big data sources in science and in other fields, such as business, have caused a shifting of the ground in this area. It is no longer the case that administrative data are seen as "second-class" observations. The simple truth of the matter is that like a well-written or poorly written survey item, big data can be of high or low quality. The quality of big data depends on a number of factors too exhaustive to catalogue here, but let us point out several general principles.

As with many things, money can help. Data sources related to expenditures (such as income maintenance or health files) are routinely checked and audited. The utility of this "free" data checking (from the researcher's perspective) should not be underestimated. Data quality also tends to be better when the field represents something concrete (such as deaths that are captured in mortality data) than something requiring the judgment on the part of the individual entering the data (such as a psychological diagnosis). This case raises a tricky point. Perhaps the main quality problem with research data is not the data per se, but how it is used to make inferences about what is happening in the real world. All science requires sound methodology as a first principle. To return to our prior example, a record that a person received of a particular Medicare diagnosis is just that—and it is a fully reliable (or nearly so) measure of the diagnosis that was made, not of the accuracy of the diagnosis. Sometimes individuals with specific conditions are identified based on billing codes, but just because a person went to a physician to be examined for the presence of a specific condition and was billed for that visit with a code for that condition does not mean that the person actually has the health condition. Therefore, the use of administrative data to determine the population prevalence of a given health problem could be quite inappropriate and inaccurate. On the other hand, using this information to understand the frequency of diagnoses of specific health conditions and how they change over time could be very informative and valid. This can be of critical importance, such as in the use of big data to explore over-diagnosis or over-prescription within a given subpopulation (Raghavan et al., 2005).

Big data are often notable for false negatives—a person may be involved in delinquent behavior that is never captured in a data set. This problem is reduced when multiple data sources are used and when those sources are longitudinal in nature. It is easy to imagine a chronic criminal not showing up in this year's arrest records, but it is very unlikely that such a person will not show up across many databases over time.

We must also acknowledge the "compared to what" question. Those who disparage the use of administrative data a priori often advocate for the use of other sources, such as survey measures of abstract psychological constructs, in which substantial error in both reliability and validity is accepted. We do not mean to imply that administrative or big data are innately valid. On the contrary, the single most valuable skill a big data researcher can have is a suspicious mind, in which the maxim "garbage in, garbage out" is always remembered. What we do mean to say is that big data are data, and should be subjected to the same checks (such as temporal stability and criterion validity checks) that any scientist would use with other data. The best possible solution is for triangulation to be established between radically different data sources.

We would make a final comment on big data limitations before we leave this topic. It is critically important to know the process that generated the big data. Because big data are often generated for other purposes, it is essential that the researcher understands its limitations. Not knowing how the data was collected and for what purpose can lead to significant problems for the researcher down the road including incorrect interpretation of findings and even retraction. An illustrative example of this comes to us from the field of oncology regarding a study on breast cancer that used data from the National Cancer Database that collects diagnosis and treatment information on an estimated 70 percent of U.S. cancer patients. The researchers aimed to examine whether the use of radiation therapy decreased stage 1 estrogen receptor-positive breast cancer in women after a 2004 clinical trial showed no survival benefit of postoperative radiation therapy. The National Comprehensive Cancer Network (NCCN), a nonprofit that, among other things, releases guidelines for cancer treatment also publicized their support of the results of this trial when it released its national practice guidelines in 2004. The researchers included women who were diagnosed with stage 1 estrogen-receptor positive breast cancer (or at least they thought they did) from 1998 to 2012. They wished to examine trends in radiation therapy use before and after 2004 to evaluate whether the trial results and the NCCN guidelines had any effect on the clinical practice of delivering postoperative radiation therapy in this patient population. What the researchers failed to realize in their study was that the data on hormone receptor expression, a key variable used to identify their patient population, was not "reliably or consistently collected" prior to 2004 so a not inconsequential proportion of patients diagnosed from 1998 to 2004 should not have been included in their study. Although the National Cancer Database does alert researchers to variable limitations in its data, this was not fully appreciated until it was too late. The moral of the story is you must strive to become an expert on the limitations and uncertainties of the data before you start and certainly before you publish.

In conclusion, big data allows us to ask real-world questions using information collected from larger and larger segments of the population. However, it is critically important to understand the challenges of big data including access issues along with limitations of data that are collected without your research question in mind. In addition, researchers must understand how the quality of the data that is collected may impact their ability to answer their questions, as well as the degree of uncertainty in their results that is due to data quality issues. There may be a reflexive tendency for researchers to doubt the validity and utility of big data simply because it is new. This may be something of an overreaction. Big data often results in findings that are convergent with existing estimates generated from other data sources (Kim et al., 2017) or which can be

Challenges in Managing Data

"Garbage in, garbage out" is a mantra in research that applies in different ways to big data. The challenges of parameterizing the analytic model described earlier are compounded when using big data. A common challenge pertains to data structure. In social services, big data often come from either service records or accounting information. This type of information is collected for different purposes and often requires translation to be used by researchers. Differences in database management systems need to be reconciled for use in analyses. For example, administrative data are often archived in relational or object-relational databases (e.g., Microsoft Access, SQL, Oracle) that facilitate storage of hierarchal data structures. Service records may track child characteristics (i.e., demographics) and encounters (i.e., dates of services) within family units (i.e., link to head of household) across time. Relational data sets store information in separate files that can be queried for reports, which is appropriate for annual reporting and audits. However, they do not facilitate statistical analyses. Moreover, data management systems may be outdated, which adds effort to pull data.

Data linkages present another challenge. Relational databases split files to be reassembled using key identifiers or a set of identifiers that link units across files. For example, Social Security numbers or birth record numbers provide unique identifiers that could be used to match children in the child welfare system with children using homeless services. However, unique identifiers are not perfect; they may be entered incorrectly or missing in one or both systems. Moreover, the files of interest may not include a unique identifier, which requires creating a crosswalk (linking variable) between files to achieve a match.

Probabilistic matching is often necessary because unique identifiers may be missing. This is especially true for privacy regulations that prohibit collection or disclosure of unique identifiers. Probabilistic matching leverages available information to infer linkages up to a degree of certainty. For example, data may include names, dates of birth, and other basic demographics. Just looking for matches across first name, last name, and date of birth are likely to identify unique pairs for a bulk of cases. However, there will also be nonmatches due to duplicates (e.g., same name and date of birth) or missing data, and this becomes increasing more likely when trying to match across time or across populations. Models can incorporate other demographics to estimate the probability that a match exists based on available information. Researchers can set cut-offs based on the research context; a demographer examining population trends over time might be comfortable with 95 percent accuracy, whereas a researcher studying service costs of the relatively small population of homeless families in the child welfare system may want greater confidence to limit potential bias in estimates.

Once data are assembled, the research must make sense of the information collected. Data documentation is often incomplete or not available. Variable names and values may be unavailable and definitions may have changed over time. Decimal places on costs of housing services for child welfare-involved families varied by an order of 1,000 across nonconsecutive years in one state. Considerable effort is needed to make sense of data, and this is facilitated through descriptive statistics, data visualization, as well as emerging artificial intelligence approaches.

A practical consideration that quickly emerges pertains to missing data. Missing data occurs for a variety of reasons in big data sets. For example, a variable may be collected after (or before) a specific date, or variables may only be collected for a subset of participants. Patterns of missing data may be immediately discernable or obscured by layers of policies or basic programming. For example, a researcher using homeless service records may not realize that data for certain variables are omitted for domestic violence victims to ensure privacy. This may greatly influence the research questions and approaches. It also requires decisions on how to handle missing data. In addition, it highlights the need for the big data researcher to "know their data." Patterns of missing data, such as the omission of certain variables for domestic violence victims as previously discussed, must be looked for and understood. Big data researchers must be comfortable "getting their hands dirty" in the data and cannot merely accept what exists uncritically.

A related challenge concerns censoring. Censoring occurs when the observed value only provides part of the story. For example, data that include dates of homeless shelter exit may be systematically missing for people still in shelters, and, conversely, shelter entry dates collected at a specific point in time fail to include full information on those who will subsequently become homeless. Censoring can bias statistical analysis and must be considered. Inherently, big data includes information on cohorts, such as everyone in the system at a single point or those who enter or exit within a period of time. For whom the data are used depends on the system and research question. If a researcher wants to understand flow through the system, they cannot just look at enterers, but rather also needs to include those already in the system. This becomes more challenging in real-world situations when data are missing before or between key time periods. The researcher must think carefully about selection bias in the design of the study, particularly regarding areas of bias or incompleteness which can systematically, rather than randomly, bias findings.

348   TOWARD A LIVABLE LIFE

Making Sense of Big Data

Much of social science research is focused on understanding how a program or policy works to improve lives or how characteristics of individuals are related to each other so we can identify who needs what. Examples include whether children growing up in more violent neighborhoods experience greater trauma symptoms compared with similar children living in less violent neighborhoods, whether increased dosage of statins corresponds with decreases in cholesterol, or whether achievement gaps over time lead to changes in school policies. This type of information comprises our evidence base and is essential in guiding researchers and practitioners toward interventions that actually work to better the lives of people. Traditional inferential statistical methods widely used in social science to generate this evidence base often rely on p-values to determine whether results are statistically significant or not. Generally speaking, a p-value is defined as the probability of your data, given your hypothesis. Setting aside disagreements among statisticians on the practical meaning of the p-value (Aschwanden, 2016), researchers often use statistical significance as an indicator that a finding is more likely to represent a real relationship as opposed to random chance.

For example, the independent samples t-test is a widely used test to compare means on some continuous variable across two groups. A t-test might be used in a study examining minutes of exercise per week in a group living in a neighborhood with sidewalks compared to another group living in a less walking-friendly area. The test statistic, t, is computed by dividing the difference in means between the two groups by the sum of the differences in standard deviations over the sample sizes of the two groups. When sample sizes are very large, the denominator of this test statistic becomes very small, and the t-statistic becomes large. Larger values of a t-statistic are considered less likely to happen by random chance and are therefore associated with small p-values, indicating statistical significance often interpreted as the difference between the two groups having a good chance at being real. Consider what would happen in a t-test where mean number of minutes exercising in the sidewalk group was 19.2 with a standard deviation of 5.0, while a non-sidewalk group totaled 17.6 minutes per week with a standard deviation of 5.7 minutes per week. In a study where the group sample sizes were 50 per group, the t-statistic would be 1.5 with a nonsignificant p-value of 0.14. If the group sizes were increased to 500 per group, the same means and standard deviations result in a t-statistic of 4.72 and a corresponding p-value of <0.00001. The same difference in mean minutes of exercise per week becomes statistically significant when the sample size increases from 100 to 1,000. The same difference between groups contributes different results to our evidence base when we collect more data.

Consider now the size of big data. In going from 100 people to 1,000, we influenced our understanding of how sidewalks influence health, but what would happen if we collected big data on 1 million people or 10 million people? How small could the differences between groups be and still be statistically significant? Of course, the question may become simpler when full populations are used in big data studies. Inferential statistics are meant to infer from the sample to the full population. If you have the full population, there is often no need for inferential statistics. For example, if you know the weight of 100 Labradors and 100 German Shepherds, you might find the German Shepherds are, on the average, 1 pound heavier and that there is a 98 percent chance ($p \leq 0.02$) that German Shepherds are heavier than Labs. On the other hand, if you know the weight of all Labradors and all German Shepherds, you can say, "The median German Shepard weighs 1.23 pounds more than the median Labrador." This is a statement of fact, not of inference. Probabilities do not enter into it. The answer is known, not estimated (although that answer may be temporally or otherwise bounded; e.g., applying to the United States in 2017). Not surprisingly, big data is causing statisticians to reconsider traditional usage of the p-value (Wasserstein and Lazar, 2016; Ioannidis, 2018).

Simple Geometry: The Power of Cross-Sector Data

If you have two points, you can draw one line between them. If you have three points, you can draw three lines. Five points will allow you to draw up to ten lines, and 20 points will allow you to draw 190. These same figures apply to the number of bivariate relationships that can be tested between any given number of variables. If you know median household income and units of mental health service provision, you can check the correlation between them—two variables allow you to explore one relationship. If you add in family structure, number of contacts with law enforcement, and the educational level of the head of household, you can look at up to ten different bivariate relationships and can also utilize multivariate or other advanced methods. This brings us to cross-sector data. Cross-sector data can pre-exist—many states will link data from different agencies such as income maintenance, child maltreatment, and juvenile court records. The advantages of such linked data are obvious. An analysis of juvenile court trajectories can be substantially improved by the inclusion of income and maltreatment data. Such data can be used as predictors, controls, grouping variables, or even as censoring variables (you may not want to track delinquency among children who are in residential out-of-home care). Various academic studies have used massively cross-sector data, including administrative records from income maintenance, education, crime, juvenile justice, medicine, and child maltreatment. Such studies have literally thousands of usable variables and are often longitudinal in nature (Jonson-Reid, Kohl, and Drake, 2012). Even these studies constitute only a small example of the potential of cross-sector data. Among the most comprehensive cross-sector resources in the country, South Carolina's Integrated Data System includes linked data from virtually every conceivable government program and a wide range of medical, educational, and other sources. There are thousands of different ways (at a bare minimum) in which the data from this one source could be used for research or to support policy or practice.

For the researcher, cross-sector data also provides one of the best sources of triangulation and a superior means of checking the validity of measures. Few researchers are uninterested in having more data or in having multiple variables that relate to the same construct and can be compared to one another. Cross-sector data can also be used in unexpected but simple ways. One study (Drake et al., 2011) used data from a range of sources (medical, child welfare, vital statistics) to attempt to determine the degree to which child maltreatment data could be racially biased. There had been concern that racial disparities in child maltreatment report rates might be due to reporter bias, and it was a simple matter to check racial disparities in child maltreatment rates against disparities in other existing child safety and well-being measures that were not as subject to bias (e.g. mortality, low birth weight, prematurity).

Fast, Faster, Fastest: Data in Motion

Electronic databases and computers obviously confer the ability to store and analyze data in ways never before possible. What may be less apparent is that there are fundamentally new applications and uses of data that can be completely automated, with no person in the loop at all. Data can be used "live" to change people's experiences. Readers will recognize that Internet pages customize advertisements based on your prior browsing history and other information. This is an example of data in motion. As you make different choices, your data changes and you are treated differently. We can start with a very simple and basic, but potentially lifesaving application—Maryland's Birth Match system (Shaw et al., 2013). This system draws upon two different data sets, one showing parents who have given birth that day and one containing a list of parents who have previously had both a result from child protective services and who have also had a termination of parental rights (TPR) for a child in the last five years (Child Welfare Information Gateway, 2013). For those unfamiliar with what a TPR is, it is a very high bar requiring a series of court hearings and represents the view of a judge that the parent is not able to safely care for a child, resulting in the effective severing of parental rights. Drawing upon data showing that new children born to parents with a previous TPR faced a high risk of serious maltreatment, the State of Maryland decided to create a system that checked a list of parents who had just given birth that day against a list of parents who had been TPR'd in the past five years. This check is done daily, and each day the state child welfare agency is provided a list of the prior day's matches. The state then sends a worker out to assess the situation. Depending on what is found, further action may or may not ensue.

Birth match is in place in several states now and is among the simplest possible examples of "live" data impacting social work practice. It is easy to see how this general approach could be utilized in a number of ways. Staying with the field of child welfare, let us consider a situation where two different parents bring a young child to an emergency room with an injury that may or may not suggest abuse. In both cases, no report is made. The next week, a similar injury occurs, and the parents of the first child return to the same emergency room. At that time a pattern is noted by the hospital, and a call to child protective services is made. The second family, however, goes to a different emergency room, no call is made, and therefore no investigation ensues and the child remains at risk. This is an information issue. If a shared database existed between emergency departments at various hospitals (or if the hospitals had live access to state-level databases, which already exist in many states), the outcome of the second case would likely be different. However, this case is subtly, but importantly different from Birth Match in that the data would be most valuable if it were provided to the participating emergency room in real time. Data provided the next day (which is perfectly suitable for purposes of Birth Match) would be too late. We move from "almost live" to "fully live" data. Of course, these are still extremely preliminary applications. Nevertheless, we hope we have conveyed the main point—data can be an active "now" tool, not just an entry in a ledger.

Yesterday, Today, and Tomorrow: Longitudinal Data

Individuals conducting research or evaluating their practice understand the advantages that longitudinal data confer. Many questions can only be answered with longitudinal data. If you want to know about treatment effectiveness, how risks manifest, effects of cumulative exposure, trajectory over time, or a host of other factors, then longitudinal data provide the best means for addressing your questions.

In many cases, the longitudinal nature of a study or a program evaluation is forward-facing. If you are researching the effectiveness of a given intervention, you will probably go back to the subjects for follow-up measurements at some time (a year is common) after treatment. This is generally done through a visit or through the mail or perhaps via electronic communication. In any case, it is something that must be done by the researcher and something that will generally require funding or at least substantial effort.

In other cases, such as risk assessment or when examining the current outcomes for something that has happened in the past, backwards-facing longitudinal data are required. This is often the case when attempting to isolate the causes of current problems, such as mental health issues (Scott et al., 2012). Retrospective measures are often used when asking the person about their past, with the respondent being asked to recall things that happened decades ago.

Big data are innately longitudinal. Arrest records, for example, can be either collected from the past as a means to quantify the subject's prior experiences, or as a means of quantifying the subject's parent's experiences. Similarly, such data will continue to accrue, and researchers can plan to collect future data without ever contacting the subject again, so long as they have permission to access the appropriate database at the appropriate time. Obviously, both approaches can be done at the same time for triangulation purposes. Studies where a dependent measure leaves a mark in the big data system is appropriate for such a strategy. Whether you want to reduce hospital admissions for heart disease, prevent child abuse, or improve a family's financial stability, big data may already exist providing detailed information about the past, about what is happening now, and, if you can wait a bit, about what will happen in the future.

A rather arcane but critically important point associated with longitudinal data is the issue of reducing false negatives. If you have information from a given week, month, or year, you may well find no record of a particular issue in big data. For example, a person who is subject to committing acts of violence may have no data within the past year that would point to such a trait. If there are data reaching back years or decades, however, it is far more likely that some indication will be present. If longitudinal data are available across multiple databases (e.g., medical, criminal, child welfare, adult protection, domestic violence), then the chances of missing something important becomes ever more unlikely. For example, try to imagine a person who is prone to frequent acts of serious violence but leaves no traces of said propensity in any health, social services, educational, justice, or any other data system. Such a thing could happen, but not very often.

Ethical Concerns

There are many ethical considerations involving the use of big data. Ethical concerns often represent a primary limiting factor. Many of these issues have yet to be fully framed, let alone clarified or resolved. Perhaps surprisingly, a number of big data applications actually do not involve ethical concerns because much of big data is either (1) public domain, (2) already held by the agency seeking to use it, or (3) available from other agencies with certain safeguards. Viewed from this perspective, many big data applications have no ethical issues whatsoever—there is no reason for agencies not to use big data approaches to harness data that they already have or are already entitled to get.

Public Domain Data

It is easy to forget that many very useful big data sources are public domain. This is particularly true of geographically aggregated data, such as the U.S. Census or the U.S. Department of Agriculture food desert maps, lead exposure risk maps, local crime maps, or the data that can be found on state public information portals such as the California Child Welfare Indicators Project. Practitioners, policymakers, and researchers using such sources can understand what is going on in particular areas by accessing these locations. For example, in many areas all you need to know is a given address, and you have instant access to full local crime, economic, demographic, food availability, child welfare, and social service resource availability data. None of these things are secret or subject to confidentiality concerns, and many of them can be of help to social workers. As a very simple example, an automatic system that notes if the clients' address is in a food desert could be useful information to many agencies. Some individual-level data are also publicly available, including arrest, conviction, incarceration, and sexual offender data.

Internal Agency Data

Does the agency in question use the data it has? While this question applies to all agencies, it may be most critical for public agencies, which tend to have large amounts of available data. For example, if a state's Department of Human Services receives a child protective services hotline call, is all of the relevant agency information about that family added to the report? Again, to pick a very simple and obvious example, let us imagine that a family is undergoing a child abuse investigation for neglect, but the worker is never made aware that the Temporary Assistance for Needy Families (TANF) funding for the family will be discontinued in a week's time. Although the person working the family's TANF case may work in the same building as the response worker, the data are never shared, and the worker remains uninformed of a looming new risk factor and is deprived of the chance to intervene around the issue in a timely manner. Another example can be found in risk assessment tools, which are often used in child welfare practice. Workers are sent out to the field with pencil and paper checklists that ask questions like "Is the family receiving public assistance?" and "Has there been a prior CPS report?" when the agency's computers already know the answers to these questions. A basic risk assessment could be created live and automatically by the agency computer as the hotline call is coming in (the screener could see it in real time), with no need for the worker to drive to the home, sit down, pull out their pencil, fill out a form, and have that form be entered later (if at all) into a file, which might never be read. This is but one example. Dozens of other kinds of information exist that the state has and that the worker has no access to.

Shared Agency Data

Different states vary in the degree to which data can be legally shared between state agencies. However, to the degree to which such data are available, they should be used. For example, state birth records include a number of measures of risk factors associated with child maltreatment. One recent study (Putnam-Hornstein and Needell, 2011) found that among the very small set of children with a high number of risk indicators on their birth record, 89.5 percent of them would have a child abuse report within the next five years. If the state is legally able to talk to itself with regard to these data, then these data could be used to inform targeted, voluntary, and preventative services. Of course, the ethical questions are serious and manifold, but ethical risks ensue whether the state chooses to act or not to act. Does the child welfare agency have the right to see birth records of families who have not been reported? Is it morally acceptable for the state to possess near-certain knowledge of a child maltreatment report before it happens and *not* take action? While taking such action may seem morally suspect from the perspective of the parent's right to privacy, not taking action would be equally suspect from the perspective of the child's safety rights. If the state has information that could serve as a spur to protecting a child's safety, which is, after all, the primary purpose of child protection, and fails to act on those data, is that a form of negligence? Certainly, if a state ignored a serious report or failed to monitor a foster home, that would be considered negligent, but ignoring data could also be a form of negligence. This links back to the prior discussion of the Birth Match policy. A case can be made that the state incurs ethical risk if either it institutes such a program or if it fails to institute such a program.

The degree to which data from various state agencies could inform and improve practice at a given agency is large and requires only a small amount of imagination to appreciate. Many social problems leave footprints across state or private agencies, and sometimes, these agencies can freely share data with the worker. For example, is it ethically desirable or undesirable for should not a state social worker investigating the abuse of a mentally incapacitated elder have access to that elder's medical records? What about access to data from other state agencies that may be relevant, such as a history of domestic violence or child abuse? Many of these questions are as yet unanswered, but they will have to be faced in the near future.

Conclusion

It is said that the more things change, the more they stay the same. In our case, what is staying the same is the simple reality that the more we know, the better able we are to help our clients. It has always been easier for social workers to help people when they possess sound empirical data upon which to base their actions. Big data merely represent a new stream of data to permit us to better fulfil our core purpose of helping people to live better lives. In our view, big data will be an especially important arrow in our evidentiary quiver as it promises rapid responsivity, general applicability, and the opportunity to gain increasing confidence in what we know using other methods.

Looking a little further forward, it is reasonable to expect a future where social workers are far more embedded in the information universe than they are now, and where we take for granted the ability to access a far larger amount of "live" information that can help clients in the moment. It is important that child welfare workers can return to their office and request the arrest history of a family member and have that information within a day or so. It would be better if that information self-populated instantly whenever a new family member's name was entered by the social worker into their laptop. It is important that social workers might know about local domestic violence shelters and have contact numbers allowing them to contact those agencies to check for availability. It would be better if the social worker could immediately access a map with available spaces as they exist in the moment. We see big data as not only an asset to the researcher and the policy maker, but also, increasingly, to the caseworker.

References

Aschwanden, C. 2016. "Statisticians Found One Thing They Can Agree On: It's Time to Stop Misusing p values." *Five Thirty Eight.* Retrieved from http://fivethirtyeight.com/features/statisticians-found-one-thing-they-can-agree-on-its-time-to-stop-misusing-p-values/

Child Welfare Information Gateway. 2013. "Grounds for Involuntary Termination of Parental Rights." Washington, DC: Author.

Drake, B., J. M. Jolley, P. Lanier, J. Fluke, R. P. Barth, and M. Jonson-Reid. 2011. "Racial Bias in Child Protection? A Comparison of Competing Explanations using National Data." *Pediatrics,* 127, 471–478.

Gandomi, A., and M. Haider. 2015. "Beyond the Hype: Big Data Concepts, Methods, and Analytics." *International Journal of Information Management,* 35, 137–144.

Google Trends. (n.d.). "Search for term 'Big Data.'" Available from https://trends.google.com/trends/explore?date=allandq=big%20data

Henry, J. D., and J. R. Crawford. 2005. "The Short Form Version of the Depression Anxiety Stress Scales: Construct Validity and Normative Data in a Large Nonclinical Sample." *British Journal of Clinical Psychology*, 44, 227–239.

Ioannidis, J. P. A. 2018. "The Proposal to Lower P Value Thresholds to .005." *Journal of the American Medical Association*, 319, 1429–1430.

Jonson-Reid, M., P. L. Kohl, and B. Drake. 2012. "Child and Adult Outcomes of Chronic Child Maltreatment." *Pediatrics*, 129, 839–845.

Kim, H., C. Wildeman, M. Jonson-Reid, and B. Drake. 2017. "Lifetime Prevalence of Investigating Child Maltreatment among US Children." *American Journal of Public Health*, 107, 274–280.

Laney, D. 2001. "3D Data Management: Controlling Data Volume, Velocity, and Variety." Technical Report, META Group.

National Institutes of Standards and Technology. 2015. "NIST Big Data Interoperability Framework: Volume 1, Definitions." NIST Special Publication 1500-1. Available online at http://nvlpubs.nist.gov/nistpubs/SpecialPublications/NIST.SP.1500-1.pdf

Press, G. 2014, September 3. "12 Big Data Definitions: What's Yours?" *Forbes*. Available from http://www.forbes.com/sites/gilpress/2014/09/03/12-big-data-definitions-whats-yours/

Putnam-Hornstein, E., and B. Needell. 2011. "Predictors of Child Protective Service Contact between Birth and Age Five: An Examination of California's 2002 Birth Cohort." *Children and Youth Services Review*, 33, 1337–1344.

Raghavan, R., B. T. Zima, R. M. Andersen, A. A. Leibowitz, M. A. Schuster, and J. Landsverk. 2005. "Psychotropic Medication Use in a National Probability Sample of Children in the Child Welfare System." *Journal of Child and Adolescent Psychopharmacology*, 15, 97–106.

Scott, K. M., K. A. McLaughlin, D. A. Smith, and P. M. Ellis. 2012. "Childhood Maltreatment and DSM-IV Adult Mental Disorders: Comparison of Prospective and Retrospective Findings." *The British Journal of Psychiatry*, 200, 469–475.

Shaw, T. V., R. P. Barth, J. Mattingly, D. Ayer, and S. Berry, S. 2013. "Child Welfare Birth Match: Timely Use of Child Welfare Administrative Data to Protect Newborns." *Journal of Public Child Welfare*, 7, 217–234.

Vaithianathan, R., T. Maloney, E. Putnam-Hornstein, and N. Jiang, N. 2013. "Children in the Public Benefit System at Risk of Maltreatment: Identification via Predictive Modeling." *American Journal of Preventive Medicine*, 45, 354–359.

Ward J. S., and A. Barker. 2013. "Undefined by Data: A Survey of Big Data Definitions." *arXiv*, 1309.5821.

Wasserstein, R. L., and N. A. Lazar. 2016. "The ASA's Statement on P-Values: Context, Process, and Purpose." *The American Statistician*, 70, 129–133.

15

Looking Back, Looking Ahead

EDWARD F. LAWLOR, MARY M. MCKAY, SHANTI K. KHINDUKA,
AND MARK ROBERT RANK

The field of social work is at a crossroads in the United States. At a societal level, numerous indicators demonstrate that the quality of life may be in decline . For example, life expectancy has fallen during the past several years. This unprecedented drop reflects the impact of many of the social problems dealt with throughout this book. Economic inequality has been growing steadily since the mid-1970s. Political polarization and disaffection of multiple groups has also increased and hardened, especially during the last decade. Racial injustice, reflected in the disproportionate burden experienced by people of color with respect to the criminal justice system, voting suppression, and obstacles to educational and employment opportunities, persists and threatens the progress that had been made since the 1960s. Locally, the protests in Ferguson, Missouri, as a result of the tragic death of Michael Brown, challenges our profession to engage in effective activism and create new solutions via research contributions, student education, and community collaboration.

Many of the historical supports and underpinnings of the social service system, from public sector social assistance programs to funding stalwarts like the United Way, are also in retrenchment if not all-out elimination. Sentinel events, such as the closing of the Hull House Association in Chicago, an original settlement house, reveal the underlying weakness of funding streams, leadership, and public support for the safety net and its associated human service providers.

Around the globe, we are also seeing increasing social and economic problems. In many countries, there has been a retrenchment of both the social contract and the safety nets that governments had once provided. Racial, ethnic, and religious tensions have also been on the rise. And of course, global warming will have a disproportionate negative impact upon those in lower-income countries.

These challenges to the profession are intellectual, pragmatic, and political. Social work has historically provided important leadership in research, teaching, policy development, and advocacy. Social workers continue to provide the principal leadership and workforce in fields such as community mental health and social development, but the visibility and impact of our profession and research is admittedly insufficient. Across the profession, there is a clear need to re-energize and reassert our leadership role in social policy and social safety net service networks.

The chapters in this book have provided an understanding into the myriad of problems facing the profession, and they have outlined various ways in which social workers can begin to alleviate such problems. Social workers are in a unique position to take up this challenge. They have the skills and experience essential to act as change agents, coupled with their on-the-ground knowledge of the ways in which these problems harm individuals, families, and communities.

The School of Social Work at Washington University in St. Louis has repeatedly tackled these challenges at many points throughout its history (O'Connor, 2008). Most recently, in the aftermath of Ferguson in 2014, its faculty came together to consider how they might better connect the academic and professional work of the school to the challenges of the nation. These discussions paralleled the efforts by many social work organizations to frame and tackle its Grand Challenges. These have largely revolved around the most significant social, economic, and health equity issues that could be solved in a generation. The goal of the Brown School faculty's efforts was to help in reframing this agenda by summarizing the state-of-the art in research and professional action, building on expertise and work at the school itself.

Relying on the school's long-standing commitment to evidence-based practice and social action, a group of faculty outlined a set of priority issues where considerable expertise was found, as well as recommendations for reform and implementation. Professors Mark Rank and Gautam Yadama took leadership of this effort, looking to identify key policy challenges that would be informed by particular faculty expertise and research. The priority areas identified by the faculty constitute the chapters of this volume.

Looking Back

The George Warren Brown School of Social Work has had a long and distinguished history. Its beginnings at Washington University can be traced back to the fall of 1909. One of its founding members was Roger Baldwin, who would later go on to start the American Civil Liberties Union (ACLU) in 1920. In 1937, it became the first social work program in the nation to have constructed its own building designed exclusively for teaching students and conducting research in the fledgling discipline. A generous gift from Betty Bofinger Brown in memory of her husband, George Warren Brown, gave the school its namesake.

As discussed in the introduction, the three pillars of social work have been well represented throughout the school's history. Those pillars are characterized by (1) striving for a more socially just world; (2) understanding problems and situations through the person-in-environment perspective (which incorporates an interdisciplinary and international focus); and (3) evaluating and designing solutions by means of research-based evidence. The school has largely been defined by its emphasis upon these three seminal ideas.

From its inception, the school has emphasized a commitment to social justice. Its origins (in its predecessor organizations—Provident, The St. Louis School of Philanthropy, and the St. Louis School of Social Economy) were motivated by observed injustice and poverty among immigrants, African Americans, children, the elderly, and disabled persons, including those with mental illness. From the outset, the problems and concerns of the school and its faculty included a range of social justice issues such as child labor, public health, and low wages. While social work methods and casework have varied over time, the fundamental values and concerns of the school have remained remarkably consistent. Dean Shanti Khinduka expressed this commitment as a key test for the future of the school: "This School will not justify its existence if it does not remain the champion of equality, fairness, and social justice" (cited in O'Connor, 2008: 151). Dean Mary McKay, reiterated these values in her 2017 report on the school's initiatives to advance equity:

> The Brown School is committed to adding our voice, our science and our resources to the ever-growing chorus demanding social justice.... The common thread that ties this work together is a sharp focus on advancing equity. Unless we specifically target structural racism and systemic oppression in our studies, projects, teaching and advocacy, social change is likely to be stalled or incremental. (2017: 1)

Throughout its history, the school has also pursued research leadership, interdisciplinary studies, and evidence-based applications to practice and policy. As early as Dean Benjamin Youngdahl's term in the 1950s, the school sought to bring science to bear on applied problems of social service and social policy. Dean Youngdahl recruited William Gordon, a quantitative ecologist, to build rigorous research and a high-quality doctoral program at the school. In addition, Gordon was instrumental in introducing the person-in-environment framework to the field. His 1990 obituary read, "He was among the first scholars to introduce the ecological framework into social work thinking, believing that the central focus in social work should be the interaction between the person and the environment" (O'Connor, 2008: 76).

Youngdahl and Gordon both emphasized that social work deserved an evidence-based approach that was equal to that of other sciences and professions, that doctoral education should embody the methods and rigors of science, and that this research should be guided by an ecological perspective.

This pursuit of rigorous, evidence based scholarship continued under Dean Khinduka's stewardship, as the school made significant faculty appointments, launched bold scholarly initiatives, founded new centers of inquiry and instruction, and successfully pursued and won coveted national awards and grants. In 1976, the school recruited Martha Ozawa, an expert on social security, who was one of the first scholars in the profession to undertake research-based analysis of the impact of social welfare programs on women and children.

One year later, the school lunched the *Journal of Social Service Research,* one of the earliest journals in the profession of social work to publish only those scholarly papers that would be based on sound empirical research. During a ten-year span, between 1990 and 2000, the school established the Kathryn Buder Center for American Indian Studies, the Center for Mental Health Services Research, the Center for Social Development, and the Co-Morbidity and Addictions Center. In addition, in 1991, the school created a dedicated research office and infrastructure under the leadership of Enola Proctor, the first such capacity in a School of Social Work.

For over 40 years, the school has also brought a global perspective to social work and social welfare. Dean Khinduka and his faculty partner, Professor Richard Parvis, opened up access to international students, built numerous international partnerships, and infused global content into the curriculum and culture of the School. The Center for Social Development pursued an international agenda on asset building from its inception. This work has been extended up to the present with the development of global joint degrees, the recruitment of McDonnell Academy international scholars, and the creation of new research centers on global social work and public health. This global perspective was further reinforced recently by Dean McKay establishing Khinduka Fellowships for students working toward global impact. Importantly, this global influence has fed back into ideas and models for social research and policy in the U.S. context.

The school has also sought to build a faculty from many different disciplines in seeking to understand social problems from a broader person-in-environment perspective. In addition, it has encouraged its students to extend their focus beyond social work by exposing them to ideas and research from other academic fields. Following its tradition of creating joint degrees in social work and law, social work and architecture, and social work and business, Dean Edward Lawlor launched the first joint degrees in social policy with partner universities in China.

Under the leadership of Dean Lawlor, the school extended this emphasis on interdisciplinary research and training by launching in 2008 a program in public health. A key idea in public health faculty recruitment and program design was the production of "transdisciplinary" research and education (Lawlor et al., 2015). For example, in the Masters of Public Health program, the goal is to educate a new type of professional, one who could tackle difficult applied problems of public health with the full armament of biological science, social science, social work, and public health professional training; as well as understandings of ethics, diversity, and community context. Key features of the curriculum are transdisciplinary problem-solving courses. The school also led in the creation of an interdisciplinary Institute for Public Health, incorporating all seven schools at Washington University.

To take advantage of these interdisciplinary opportunities presented by the wide range of academic backgrounds represented by the faculty, the school committed to a "One School" approach. Instead of creating silos between methods, disciplines, and professions, the school emphasized the intermixing of faculty in research and education. This disciplinary mix was extensive: An early analysis of faculty backgrounds identified 35 separate disciplines among 51 faculty. A network analysis of faculty working together documented significant collaboration in grants and papers, often crossing substantive and professional backgrounds (Luke, 2013). The collaborations between faculty in this book are an intellectual testament to the success of this One School model.

The school's commitment to social policy also extends back to its early history. In 2007, reflecting on Dean Youngdahl's 1952 talk entitled, "What We Believe," Dean Lawlor noted,

> Youngdahl believed that social work must be grounded in a deep commitment to individual freedom, and he was passionate that it should inform social policy. While some of the language has changed, the School's current emphases on economic opportunity, evidence-based practice, civic engagement, public health, social policy, and international development all resonate with these fundamental beliefs and priorities (O'Connor, 2008: 162–164).

Dean McKay has continued this evolution in social policy, organizing and elevating the Clark Fox Policy Institute and expanding the school's master's degree in social policy to include students from new countries, as well as domestic

Looking Ahead

As three long-serving deans, we believe the analyses and recommendations of this book are exemplars for how we might restructure our social work institutions and social policy—via professional organizations and research and education in social work schools, as well as through community and policy partnerships. The work captured in these chapters represent the long lines of the school's commitments to social justice and equity, to rigorous interdisciplinary research, to a global perspective, and to policy impact.

As we are asked to look into the next decades of the 21st century, we reiterate the importance placed upon these commitments. The answers to many of the problems that we will face in the years ahead will undoubtedly involve bringing these values and skills to bear.

But solving the problems of the 21st century will also involve a new appreciation into our interconnection to each other and to the wider social systems. Many of the nation's problems are embedded in a fundamental misunderstanding of the nature of these problems. The social work approach of understanding the ecological context and person-in-environment, we believe, is one of the keys to creating social change in the future. Our students, practitioners, and researchers are well positioned to apply this perspective to the most pressing issues of the 21st century.

The root causes of many, if not most, of the problems dealt with in this book are to be found at a systemic level. They include long standing systems of oppression, exclusion, and privilege. The recognition and resolve to change and alter these systems will be essential for moving the country and the globe toward a more humane and sustainable world.

Dean Khinduka summarized these sentiments in a 2001 lecture entitled, "Musings on Social Work and Social Work Education." In that lecture he noted,

> By the very nature of our mission, social workers challenge many of society's widely held priorities. . . . When others blame the downtrodden themselves for their misfortunes, we point to the unfairness of our dominant institutions. When others celebrate the unprecedented prosperity of this nation, we draw attention to the unconscionable poverty in our midst. . . . Social workers can thus aspire to become the conscience of a society, but hardly ever its cheerleader. Our psychic

income comes not from being counted among the elite, the powerful, the popular, or the glamorous set. It comes from knowing that we have done our bit in wiping a human tear, in serving a child or frail elderly, in organizing people for empowerment, in fighting injustice, in occasionally winning a skirmish or two on behalf of human dignity. (O'Connor, 2008: 149–150)

We also believe that the fundamental goal of a livable life for all succinctly captures what our profession should be striving for in the 21st century. Many of the issues that social work grapples with on a daily basis revolve around this goal. We would encourage our professional social work organizations to rally and advocate around this objective. Likewise, schools of social work should consider how their training of students, and the academic research of their faculty can help facilitate a movement toward this goal.

On a more targeted level, new solutions will require innovation in research and education. As the chapters on program design, social services, and big data demonstrate, we are entering a new world of social service systems, finance, and accountability. Total reliance on the traditional solutions of the welfare state are no longer feasible or necessarily desirable.

We also need to rededicate our schools of social work around the country and globe to connecting and engaging with communities in order to break down the distrust and divide that is unfortunately so pervasive. This work requires commitment and capability for dealing with the hard issues of race and diversity. Running through the discussion of a livable life are observable disparities in health and social opportunity that have deep roots in history and discrimination. Breaking down these structural and cultural barriers is integral to making progress in services and policy. We believe that new professionals in social work will be necessary change agents in breaking down these barriers.

Finally, we need to create new bridges to policy-making, including new methods for translation of research to service design and policy. Great potential exists in communities, local and state governments, and service delivery systems such as healthcare. The field of dissemination and implementation pioneered at the school, is one intellectual toolkit for this translation.

Concluding Note

During our tenures, we have seen hundreds of students and dozens of faculty and staff pass through our hallways. The energy, innovation, and commitment of these members of our academic family have left us inspired and filled with promise for the future. They encompass the best of what social work offers, and they will certainly play a key role in helping to shape a more socially just world in the future.

In addition, recent data indicate that the profession itself is on the upswing. According to U.S. Census data, in 2015 there were 850,000 self-defined social workers, 650,000 with social work degrees, and 350,000 who were licensed (Marsh and Bunn, 2018). These numbers have been steadily increasing over recent decades.

Moreover, during the past 15 years there has been a noticeable increase in students entering social work programs. As Jeanne Marsh and Mary Bunn note, between 2005 and 2015, "the number of master's degrees in social work (MSWs) awarded grew from 16,956 to 26,329, an increase of 55.3 percent. Over the same period, the number of bachelor's degrees of social work (BSWs) awarded grew from 13,939 to 21,164, an increase of 51.8 percent" (2018: 669). Furthermore, it would appear that there is a greater range of fields and areas of practice that social workers are entering. Altogether, the profession is experiencing considerable momentum as we enter the future. It is a field that we believe will be very much in demand and of importance in the years ahead.

But perhaps the last word should be given to our predecessor Benjamin Youngdahl, the former dean and groundbreaking leader, who remarked in his "What We Believe" 1952 speech,

> Our philosophy and approach in social work is essentially an optimistic one. We think that it is worth doing something about given situations. We believe that progress can be made toward our goals by the intelligent application of knowledge. We are a dynamic profession, refusing to accept the cynicism and pessimism of some of our contemporaries.

As we look into future, these words ring as true today as they did nearly 70 years ago. We believe we are on the verge of enormous economic, social, political, and environmental changes. Never before have the challenges been as great. And yet, never before have the opportunities and need for social workers been as essential. We are indeed a "dynamic profession," and one that is eager, informed, and well trained to work for a better world in the 21st century. Such a world will undoubtedly be one in which the dream of a livable life has become the reality that every child can look forward to.

References

Lawlor, E. F., M. W. Kreuter, A. K. Sebert-Kuhlman, and T. D. McBride. 2015. "Methodological Innovations in Public Health Education: Transdisciplinary Problem Solving." *American Journal of Public Health*, 105, S99–S103.

Luke, D. 2013. "The Science Behind Collaboration: And What It Means for Brown." Center for Public Health Science, George Warren Brown School of Social Work.

Marsh, J. C., and M. Bunn. 2018. "Social Work's Contribution to Direct Practice with Individuals, Families, and Groups: An Institutionalist Perspective." *Social Service Review*, 92, 647–692.

McKay, M. M. 2017. *Commitment to Equity.* St. Louis, MO: Washington University.

O'Connor, C. 2008. *What We Believe: A History of the George Warren Brown School of Social Work, 1909–2007.* St. Louis, MO: Washington University George Warren Brown School of Social Work.

INDEX

For the benefit of digital users, indexed terms that span two pages (e.g., 52–53) may, on occasion, appear on only one of those pages.

Tables are indicated by *t* following the page number.

AARP Age-Friendly Community Survey, 267
abuse. *See* child maltreatment
Accountable Communities for Health program, Minnesota, 293
Acorns app, 144
Addams, Jane, 4, 65, 331
Adjepong, Anima, 77
administrative data, 343–44
AdvantAge initiative, 266
advocacy-oriented civic engagement, 194
affordable banking services, access to, 128
Affordable Care Act (ACA), 34, 278–79
African Americans. *See also* race/ethnicity
    environmental racism, 233–34
    health effects of defensive othering, 79–80
    racial wealth gap, 130–32
age
    environmental injustice and, 235
    as factor leading to child maltreatment, 163
    relation to civic engagement, 197–98
"Age of Extremes, The" (Massey), 97–98
Age-Friendly Community Survey, AARP, 267
age-friendly environment, 265–67
agency, and livable life concept, 10
agricultural insurance, index-based, 219–20
Aid to Families with Dependent Children (AFDC), 219
air pollution, 232
    policy changes to pursue, 249*t*
    scope and impact, 237
    underlying causes, 238
Allen, H., 5–6
allostatic load, 29
Allport, Gordon, 73

Alston, Margaret, 244–45
alternative financial services, 128
Amarasingham, Ruben, 286
ambidexterity, in braided approach to social work, 323
ambient air pollution. *See* air pollution
American Academy of Social Work and Social Welfare, 236
American Dream and the Public Schools, The (Hochschild and Scovronick), 100–1
analytics. *See* big data
apps, financial capability, 144
Aristotle, 9–10
Aristotle's Way (Hall), 9–10
Arnstein, Sherry, 194–95
ASPIRE Act, 135–36
assessment, technology use in, 287
asset accumulation, 31–32, 220–21
    causes of wealth inequality
        economic barriers to asset building, 126
        institutional barriers to asset building, 127–32
        overview, 125–26
    financial benefits of
        educational attainment, 119
        homeownership, 118
        overview, 117
        protecting against emergencies and meeting basic needs, 117
        retirement and intergenerational wealth transfers, 120
    general discussion, 145–46
    importance to livable lives, 115–17
    nonmonetary benefits of

asset accumulation (*cont.*)
    avoiding scarcity mindset, 123
    building expectations and future
      orientation, 122
    overview, 122
    physical and mental health, 124
  overview, 114–15
  potential solutions
    Child Development Accounts, 135
    emerging solutions, 142–45
    Individual Development Accounts, 136
    overview, 133, 135
    reforming policies and programs, 141
    reframing understanding of inequality, 133
    tax policies, 137
    universal retirement accounts, 138
    using research to enhance impact, 139
  as strategy to alleviate poverty, 64
Assets for Independence IDA program, 136–37
auto title loans, 129–30
awareness, relation to civic engagement, 202

Baguio City, Philippines, 232, 240, 241
Baldwin, Roger, 358–59
Bandura, Albert, 72
bank account ownership, 128
banking services, access to, 128
Barrera, M., 283, 295–96
Bartlett, Jessica, 163
basic needs
  effect of poverty on satisfaction of, 50
  meeting through asset accumulation, 117
behavioral economics interventions, 143
beliefs, relation to civic engagement, 201–2
Berry, Jeffrey, 201
Bertrand, Marianne, 103
Berzin, S., 324
big data, 176
  challenges in access and limitations of, 340–46
  challenges in managing data, 346–47
  defining, 339–40
  ethical considerations
    internal agency data, 353
    overview, 352–53
    public domain data, 353
    shared agency data, 354
  general discussion, 355
  making sense of
    cross-sector data, 349
    data in motion, 350
    longitudinal data, 351
    overview, 348–49
  overview, 337–39
  using to inform policy and
    programming, 287–88
Bill and Melinda Gates Foundation, 35
Birkinshaw, J., 327

Birth Match program, 165–66, 286–87, 350–51
birth-related complications, deaths related
  to, 24–25
blacks. *See* African Americans; race/ethnicity
blaming the victim, 86
Blank, Rebecca, 62
Blessed Unrest (Hawken), 234–35
Bourdieu, Pierre, 75–76
Bradley, E. H., 281
braided approach to social work
  call for innovation, 320
  curricular innovation, 327
  fostering ambidexterity, 323
  general discussion, 328–32
  illustrations, 324
  leadership development, 326
  toolbox for, 323
Bristol Social Exclusion Matrix, 75
Bronfenbrenner, Urie, 72
Brookings Institution, 138–39
Brown, Betty Bofinger, 358–59
Brown, George Warren, 358–59
Brown School. *See* George Warren Brown School
  of Social Work
budget priorities, role in addressing cumulative
  inequality, 109
built environment, 215, 216, 221
Bullard, Robert, 233–34
Bunn, Mary, 7, 364
Bureau of Labor Statistics, 196

Cabassa, Leopoldo, 29
California Paid Family Leave, 264–65
Canadian age-friendly project, 267
capabilities, and livable life concept, 10–11, 211
capability depreciation, 75
capability development, in communities, 218
careers, and cumulative inequality, 102. *See*
  also jobs
caregivers
  child maltreatment prevention focused on
    poverty, 167–68
  engagement of older adults in, 257
  impaired capacity of, and child
    maltreatment, 161
  organizational and policy support for older, 263
  services for, in prevention of child
    maltreatment, 168
  support for, in prevention of child
    maltreatment, 170–71
Castro, F. G., 283, 295–96
censoring, 347
Census data, 342–43
Center for Innovation in Child Maltreatment
  Policy, Research and Training, 297–98
Center for Public Health Systems
  Science, 297–98

INDEX

Centers for Disease Control and Prevention (CDC), 153, 157, 161
Centers for Medicare and Medicaid Services, 293
Checkoway, Barry, 206
Chetty, Raj, 98
child care, 107, 172
Child Development Accounts (CDAs)
  economic benefits of, 146
  optimizing programs, 139–40, 142
  overview, 135
  promoting to reduce poverty, 64, 220–21
  role in making higher education affordable, 107
  and social determinants of health, 31–32
child maltreatment
  as barrier to livable life, 155
  defining, 152–53
  factors leading to
    child age and vulnerability, 163
    impaired caregiver capacity, 161
    overview, 158–59
    poverty, 159
  general discussion, 177
  overview, 152
  prevalence, 153
  prevention
    addressing child trauma, 172
    addressing intimate partner violence, 169
    addressing poverty, 167
    creating complete support system, 173
    improving services for caregivers, 168
    overview, 165
    preparing research pipeline, 175
    professionalism, 174
    providing parenting support, 170
    surveillance for, 165
  social work implications, 157
  substantiation, 291
child marriage, 25–26
child protection system
  creating complete, 173
  data in motion use in, 350–51
  inefficacy of related to child maltreatment prevention, 164–65
  professionalism in, 174–75
  technology use in, 286–87
children
  addressing cumulative inequality for, 106–7
  economic cost of poverty among, 53
  effect of poverty on health of, 49
  health effects of defensive othering, 80–81
  poverty as stunting growth, 51
  social services for, 277–78
Children's Bureau of Prevention Resource Guide, 294–95
Children's Defense Fund, 53
Christensen, Clayton, 324
chronic stress exposure, 29–30

civic engagement
  barriers to, 198
  defining, 193–94
  general discussion, 205–7
  overview, 193
  patterns of, 196
  promoting, 203–5
  scope and importance of, 193–95
climate change
  policy changes to pursue, 249t
  scope and impact, 242
  underlying causes, 243
clinical practices, technology use in, 286
Cnaan, R. A., 317
CNCS (Corporation for National and Community Service), 262–63
Code of Ethics, NASW, 45, 204
collaborative finance approaches, in social services, 289–90
collective action, in thriving communities, 211
collective impact movement, 290
colonialism, 214
Commission for Racial Justice, United Church of Christ, 233–34
Commission on Social Determinants of Health (CSDH), 18, 20, 31
communities. *See also* neighborhoods
  achieving thriving
    overview, 217–18
    physical activity and healthy eating, 223
    poverty reduction and capability development, 218
    urban design, 221
  building assets in, 64–65
  building effective demand for social services, 293
  and child maltreatment, 159–61
  child maltreatment prevention focused on, 167–68
  creating intervention approaches with, 296
  engaging to improve social services access, 283
  environmental justice research in, 245–46
  general discussion, 224–26
  importance of thriving, 211
  poverty and inequality in, 211–13
  solutions for productive engagement of older adults, 265–67
  stakeholders in, partnerships with, 33–34
  training of effective practitioners related to, 299–300
  underlying causes of problems in, 213–17
  volunteer opportunities for older adults in, 261
community land trusts, 222–23
community participation. *See* civic engagement
Community Research Fellows Training program, 205, 294–95
community service employment for older adults, 260

complexity of social problems, 313, 321t
computer technologies, in social service
    provision, 287
conditional cash transfers, 32, 218–19
consumption support, 133, 219
continuing education in environmental
    justice, 247–48
continuous innovation. *See* innovation
Corporation for National and Community Service
    (CNCS), 262–63
costs
    of child maltreatment, 155
    of cumulative inequality, 105–6
    of poverty, 52
Coule, T., 324
Council on Social Work Education (CSWE), 45,
    235–36, 246–47
Courtney, Mark, 4, 8, 285
CPS Civic Engagement Supplement, 196
credit access, lack of, 128
credit builder loans, 143
credit scores, 130
critical reflectivity, need for in social work, 84–87
cross-sector data, 349
CSDH (Commission on Social Determinants of
    Health), 18, 20, 31
cultural adaptation of interventions, 295
culturally tailored health programs, 35–36
culture
    practitioner understanding of, 299
    as social determinant of health, 25
cumulative inequality, 16–17, 52, 253
    addressing, 106–9
    general discussion, 109–10
    overview, 94–96
    process and dynamics of
        geography of disadvantage, 96
        health disparities, 103
        jobs and careers, 102
        older adults, 104
        schools and education, 99
    reasons to be concerned about, 105–6
curricular innovation, 327
Curriculum Policy Statement, CSWE, 45

Darity, W., 31–32, 130–31
data in motion, 350. *See also* big data
decision-making, effect of asset accumulation
    on, 123
deep structure, 296
defensive othering
    critical reflectivity and structural social
        work, 84–87
    expanded conceptualization of, 75–78
    general discussion, 87–89
    and livable lives
        economic well-being, 81
        overview, 78

physical and mental health, 78
    overview, 70
    related concepts, 71–75
de-identified individual data, 340–41
delivery of social services. *See* social services
demand, effective, 283, 293
Department of Agriculture, 20–21
Department of Education, 100
Department of Health and Human Services
    (DHHS), 21
Detroit REACH project, 29
development
    child maltreatment impact on, 155
    personal, in livable life concept, 10
    poverty as stunting, 51
    without displacement, 222–23
diet
    effect of poverty on, 49
    social context as determinant of health, 30–31
    in thriving communities, 223
Digit app, 144
direct cash transfers, 219
discontinuous innovation. *See* innovation
discrimination
    addressing cumulative inequality related to, 108
    conceptualizations of, 71, 73, 88
    critical reflectivity and structural social
        work, 84–87
    expanded conceptualization of defensive
        othering, 75–78
    general discussion, 87–89
    in labor market based on race/ethnicity, 103
    and livable lives
        economic well-being, 81
        overview, 78
        physical and mental health, 78
    overview, 70
disparate siting, 238
doing without, as barrier to livable life, 48
Dovidio, J. F., 73–74, 88
Drake, B., 291
Duncan, Greg, 101–2
Durlauf, Steven, 98–99

early childhood interventions, in prevention of
    child maltreatment, 170
early parenting intervention, in prevention of child
    maltreatment, 172
Earned Income Tax Credit (EITC), 59–60, 108,
    137–38, 146
earnings. *See* income; wealth inequality
ecological approach
    child maltreatment in, 156
    in social work, 5
economic barriers. *See also* poverty; wealth
    inequality
    to asset building, 126
    to livable life, 11–12

INDEX

economic costs
of child maltreatment, 155
of poverty, 52
economic determinants of health. *See*
social determinants of health;
socioeconomic status
economic fluctuations, vulnerability to, 127
economic policy, stimulating job growth
through, 60–61
economic structures, role in poverty, 54–57
economic vulnerability, in US, 9
economic well-being, 81, 99. *See also* asset
accumulation; wealth inequality
education
addressing cumulative inequality, 107
asset accumulation and expectations
for, 122–23
in braided approach to social work, 327, 330–31
and cumulative inequality, 99
and disparities in health outcomes, 20
interdisciplinary, 298, 361
link between asset accumulation and, 119
in prevention of child maltreatment, 171–72
relation to civic engagement, 197–98, 202
relation to jobs and careers, 102–3
relation to neighborhood, 98–99
training effective practitioners, 298
effective demand for social services, 283, 293
EITC (Earned Income Tax Credit), 59–60,
108, 137–38, 146
elderly. *See* older adults
Ellwood, D. T., 61
embodiment, of stress, 24, 29
emergencies
asset accumulation as protecting against, 117
impact of for persons without assets, 115–16
programs promoting saving for, 140–41
racial wealth gap, 131–32
vulnerability to, 127
employer-based financial wellness programs, 143
employer-sponsored retirement programs, 130
employment. *See* work
empowerment, 10
enacted stigma, 79–81
engagement of older adults. *See* productive
engagement of older adults
English Poor Laws, 82
enlightened self-interest, 53, 105–6
entrepreneurship, social, 321t
in braided approach to social work, 323, 328–32
braided toolbox, 323
curricular innovation, 327
fostering ambidexterity, 323
gaps in human services, 315
leadership development, 326
limitations of, 317
management and policy challenges for, 318
recommendations for, 329

environmental factors, in social work approach, 5
environmental health hazards, relation to
neighborhood, 98
environmental justice
agenda for social work
conducting meaningful research, 245
influencing policy change, 248
overview, 245
training social workers, 246
general discussion, 249–50
origins and evolution of, 233–35
overview, 232–33
resonance with social work, 235–36
understanding environmental injustice
climate change, 242–45
household water insecurity, 239–41
outdoor air pollution, 237–39
overview, 236–37
Environmental Protection Agency, 234, 245–46
environmental racism, 233–34, 241
Esping-Andersen, Gosta, 107
ethical considerations related to big data
internal agency data, 353
overview, 352–53
public domain data, 353
shared agency data, 354
ethnicity. *See* race/ethnicity
Europe
access to key social and public goods
in, 63–64
labor market in, 57–58
social enterprise in, 259
social safety net in, 62–63
evaluation, technology use in, 286
evidence-based practices, 7, 312, 313, 321t
exclusion, social. *See* social exclusion
expectations, asset accumulation as building, 122
Experience Corps program, 261
exploitation strategy, 318–19, 323–24, 325
exploration strategy, 318–19, 323–24, 325
Ezzell, Matthew, 77

Fabbre, Vanessa, 85–86
Faith, E., 174–75
false negatives, in big data, 344, 352
family
background of, and cumulative inequality, 101
child maltreatment prevention focused on
poverty, 167–68
poverty in, relation to child maltreatment, 161
Family and Medical Leave Act (FMLA), 263–64
Family First Prevention Services Act, 173–74
family support system
creating complete, 173
current lack of, 164–65
fathers. *See* parents
felt stigma, 79–81
Fight for 15, 110

372 INDEX

financial benefits of asset accumulation
  educational attainment, 119
  homeownership, 118
  overview, 117
  protecting against emergencies and meeting
    basic needs, 117
  retirement and intergenerational wealth
    transfers, 120
financial capability apps, 144
financial emergencies
  asset accumulation as protecting against, 117
  impact of for persons without assets, 115–16
  programs promoting saving for, 140–41
  racial wealth gap, 131–32
  vulnerability to, 127
Financial Security Credit, 137
financial stress, 115–16, 124. *See also* poverty
financial wellness programs, employer-based, 143
financing, for social services, 282, 289
Flanagan, C., 198
Flexner, Abraham, 285
Flint, Michigan, 240, 241
FMLA (Family and Medical Leave Act), 263–64
Fong, Rowena, 297
food deserts, 20–21
food stamps (SNAP), 132, 133–34, 141–42
For the Sake of All initiative, 287–88
Ford, C. L., 26–27
Foster Grandparent Program (FGP), 262–63
Framework Convention on Tobacco Control
    (FCTC), 35
freedoms essential to human flourishing, 213–14
fundamental causes of health, 22, 23
funding
  in braided approach to social work, 329–30
  for social services, 282
future orientation, asset accumulation as
    encouraging, 122

"garbage in, garbage out", 344, 346
Garfinkel, I., 5
Gee, G. C., 26–27
Gehlert, Sarah, 28–29
gender. *See also* women
  environmental injustice and, 235, 240
  as social determinant of health, 24
General Accounting Office, 233–34
gentrification, 222–23
George Warren Brown School of Social Work,
    13, 175–76
  big data, 339
  collaborative models at, 299–300
  community partners, 297
  curricular innovation at, 327–28
  focus on livable life, 1–2
  future directions for social work, 362–63
  global perspective of, 360

history of, 358–62
  priority areas identified by, 358
Geronimus, A. T., 29
Gini Index, 212
girl child marriage, 25–26
Givens, J., 79–80
global perspective, Brown School, 360. *See also*
    international aspects of livable life
God Bless the Child (Holiday and Herzog), 96
Goffman, Erving, 71
"good-enough" interventions, 325
Gordon, William, 359–60
Government Accountability Office, 199
governments
  importance of civic engagement to, 195
  role in creating and addressing poverty and
    inequality, 216–17
  role in environmental injustice, 241
Greenwood, Peter, 277–78
group model building, 289
growth, stunted, related to poverty, 51
Gupta, K., 327

Hall, Edith, 9–10
Hamilton, D., 31–32, 130–31
hands-on environmental problem-solving, 247
Hatzenbuehler, M. L., 78–79, 81
Hawken, Pawl, 234–35
HDI (Human Development Index), UN, 212
health
  as benefit of asset accumulation, 124
  and cumulative inequality, 103
  defensive othering and, 78
  disconnect between social services and, 278–80
  effect of poverty on, 49
  relation to neighborhood, 98
  social determinants of
    addressing, 31–36
    consequences of social policies and
      practices, 27
    defining, 18–19
    gender, 24
    health as cornerstone of livable life, 17–18
    health disparities as affecting livable
      lives, 19–22
    overview, 16–17
    race/ethnicity, 26
    social context, 30
    socioeconomic status, 23
    stress, 28
    tradition/culture, 25
    underlying causes, overview of, 22–23
  status of in US, 9
Health Affairs journal, 22
health care
  and defensive othering, 79–81
  effect of poverty on access to, 49

INDEX

evidence-based care, 35
expanding access to, 34
integrating social services with, 289, 293
role in addressing cumulative inequality, 108–9
socioeconomic status and, 19, 23–24
women's unequal access to, 25
health equity, 21, 31–36
healthy eating, in thriving communities, 223
Healthy People 2020, 34
"heat or eat" dilemma, 50, 123–24
helping profession, social work as, 4–5
Herzog, Arthur, Jr., 96
high-cost short-term loans, 128
Hill, H. D., 264–65
Hochschild, Jennifer, 100–1
Hoefer, Richard, 326–27
Holiday, Billie, 96
Holleran Steiker, L. K., 295–96
Holosko, M. J., 174–75
home loans, low-interest, 27–28
Home Owners Loan Corporation
    (HOLC), 27–28
home visitation, to prevent child
    maltreatment, 170–71
homeownership, link between asset accumulation
    and, 118
hospital social work. *See* social determinants
    of health
hospital-based care, information automation
    in, 286
household water insecurity, 232
    policy changes to pursue, 249*t*
    scope and impact, 239
    underlying causes, 240
housing
    consequences of policies, 27
    in thriving communities, 221
How the Other Half Lives (Riis), 65
Hull House, 65
Human Development Index (HDI), UN, 212
human services. *See* social services; social work
humanism, radical, 86–87
Humphreys, N. R., 203

ID laws, voter, 200
Illinois, funding for social services in, 282
impaired caregiver capacity, and child
    maltreatment, 161
incentives for social services, 282
inclusionary zoning, 223
income. *See also* poverty; wealth inequality
    alleviating poverty through adjustments to, 58–59
    environmental injustice and, 232, 237, 240, 241
    inequality in, in US, 8–9
    relation to civic engagement, 197–98, 199–200
    relation to education, 102
    role in addressing cumulative inequality, 108–9

income stagnation, 126
income support, 133
independent samples *t*-test, 348
index-based agricultural insurance, 219–20
individual civic engagement, 194
Individual Development Accounts (IDAs),
    136, 146
individual level of stigma, 72
individualistic view of poverty, 54, 82–83, 84
inequality. *See also* cumulative inequality;
        environmental justice; wealth inequality
    in communities
        overview, 211–13
        underlying causes of, 213–17
    intersecting types of, 235
    structural causes of, 213–14
Inequality Adjusted Human Development Index
    (HDI), UN, 212
inferential statistical methods, 348–49
inflation, indexing minimum wage to, 58–59
informatics. *See* big data
information automation, 286
Information Technology Laboratory,
    NIST, 339–40
injustice. *See* environmental justice; *specific forms
    of injustice*
innovation, 321*t*
    in braided approach to social work, 320, 328–32
    braided toolbox, 323
    curricular, 327
    defining, 314
    fostering ambidexterity, 323
    gaps in human services, 315
    leadership development, 326
    limitations of, 317
    management and policy challenges for, 318
    recommendations for, 329
Institute of Medicine, 175
Institute on Assets and Social Policy, 131–32
institutional barriers to asset building, 127–32
institutional theory, 324
insurance, index-based agricultural, 219–20
Integrated Data System, South Carolina, 349–50
integrated models of practice, 293
interaction discrimination, 74
interdisciplinary education, 298, 361
Interdisciplinary Environmental Law Clinic, 247
intergenerational paradox, 101
intergenerational wealth transfers, 120, 130–31
Intergovernmental Panel on Climate Change, 244
intermittent voters, 202–3
internal agency data, 353
internalization of defensive othering, 79–81
international aspects of livable life
    access to key social and public goods, 63–64
    availability of decent paying jobs, 57–58
    causes of problems in communities, 216

374 INDEX

international aspects of livable life (*cont.*)
  CDA programs, 64, 135–36
  child maltreatment prevalence, 154
  deaths related to birth-related
    complications, 24–25
  engagement of older adults, 255
  environmental justice
    climate change, 242–43
    as global movement, 234–35
    household water insecurity, 232, 239–41
    outdoor air pollution, 237
  initiatives to improve health equity, 35
  overview, 13–14, 357
  poverty rates and inequality, 212–13
  social enterprise, 259
  social safety net, 62–63
International Federation of Social Workers, 236
Internet-based civic engagement, 197
interpersonal level of stigma, 72
intersectional identities, 72–73
interventions
  adapting to enhance acceptability and reduce
    stigma, 295
  braided approach to, 325
  complexity of social problems, effect on, 313
intimate partner violence, 162, 169
intrapreneurship, social, 316
investments, economic barriers to, 126
Israel, CDA program in, 135–36

Jargowsky, Paul, 96–97
Jefferson, Thomas, 201–2
Jepson, Wendy, 239
jobs
  addressing cumulative inequality, 108–9
  in age-friendly community development, 267
  and cumulative inequality, 102
  ensuring availability of decent paying, 57
  lack of sufficient good paying, 55
  need for further research on older adults
    and, 269
  promoting work for older adults, 258
  under-engagement of older adults, 256
Johnson, W., 79–80
Jonson-Reid, M., 291
Jouriles, Ernest, 162
Journal of Social Service Research, 360
justice, social. *See* social justice
juvenile court, 277–78

Kahne, J., 198
Kaiser, Michelle, 246
Kalleberg, Arne, 102, 103
Kang, J. Y., 264–65
Kaye, Deborah, 97
Kennedy, John F., 10

key social goods, providing access to, 61
Khinduka, Shanti, 359, 360, 362–63
King, Martin Luther, Jr., 10, 14
knowledge, relation to civic engagement, 201–2
Knoxville, Tennessee, 232, 238–39, 243, 249–50
Kohl, Jurgen, 62–63
Kondrat, Mary, 6–7, 85
Kozal, Jonathan, 100
Kreuter, M. W., 296
Krieger, N., 24, 29
Krings, Amy, 240

labor market. *See also* jobs
  cumulative inequality in, 102
  ensuring availability of decent paying jobs, 57
  structural failings leading to poverty, 54–57
Lane, S. R., 203
language, relation to civic engagement, 200
Lawlor, Edward, 360–61
leadership
  development of, in braided approach to social
    work, 326
  diminishing value of human service, 319, 321*t*
Leidenfrost, Nancy, 49
Levinthal, D. A., 323–24
Levitas, Ruth, 75
LGBT older adults, 263
life course perspective on poverty, 47–48
Link, B. G., 22, 71, 73–74, 75–76, 78–79, 88
Lipsky, Michael, 284, 291–92
literacy, relation to civic engagement, 202
livable life
  asset accumulation, importance to, 115–17
  background of goal, 8
  barriers to, 11
  book organization, 13–14
  challenges to promotion of in social work, 321*t*
    complexity and evidence-based
      approaches, 313
    diminishing value of human service
      leadership, 319
    general discussion, 320
    innovation, defining, 314
    limitations of social innovation and
      entrepreneurship, 317
    management and policy challenges for
      innovation, 318
    overview, 312
    social innovation and entrepreneurship
      gaps, 315
  child maltreatment as barrier to, 155
  defensive othering and
    economic well-being, 81
    overview, 78
    physical and mental health, 78
  as fundamental goal of social work, 363

health as cornerstone of, 17–18
health disparities as affecting, 19–22
meaning of, 9
overview, 1–2
poverty as barrier to
doing without, 48
overview, 48
stress, 50
stunted growth, 51
productive engagement of older adults and, 254
relation to environmental justice, 236
role of social services in, 276, 300
role of thriving community in, 211
live data, 350
livestock, programs providing, 220
Living on the Edge (Rank), 82–83
loans from alternative financial services, 129–30
longitudinal data, 351
long-term care facilities, 261–62
long-term investments
inability to save for, 126
unequal access to, 130
low-income households. *See* asset accumulation;
poverty; wealth inequality
low-interest home loans, 27–28
Lum, Doman, 73
Lutheran Social Services, 282

mainstream banking services, access to, 128
mainstream credit access, lack of, 128
maltreatment. *See* child maltreatment
management
challenges for innovation in social work, 318
curricular innovation in braided approach, 327
March, J. G., 323–24
Marmame, Richard, 101–2
marriage
effect of poverty on, 50–51
girl child, 25–26
Marsh, Jeanne, 7, 364
Martinez, C. R., Jr., 283
Maryland Birth Match system, 350–51
Maslow, Abraham, 78, 157, 177
Massey, Douglas, 97–98
material needs, in child maltreatment
prevention, 167
Maternal, Infant, and Early Childhood Home
Visiting Program (MIECHV), 170
maternal deaths, 24–25
Matthew Effect, 95
McClure, Amy, 77
McEwen, Bruce, 29
McIntosh, Peggy, 77
McKay, Mary, 359, 360, 361–62
McLaughlin, M., 53–54, 106
McLeod, Jane, 52

McMurrer, Daniel, 101
media sources, relation to civic engagement, 202
medical social work. *See* social determinants of health
mental health
as benefit of asset accumulation, 124
of caregivers, relation to child
maltreatment, 161
defensive othering and, 78
effect of poverty on, 52
improving services for, to prevent child
maltreatment, 168
Merton, Robert, 95
Mezuk, B., 30–31
microsimulation, 288–89
Middaugh, E., 198
Mikulski, Barbara, 204
Miller, Jean, 76
minimum wages
alleviating poverty through adjustments to, 58–59
in efforts to reduce wealth inequality, 133
role in addressing cumulative inequality, 108
struggle for as reciprocal process, 6
Minnesota Accountable Communities for Health
program, 293
Minsky, Hyman, 61–62
Mint app, 144–45
Minute Clinics, 324–25
missing data, 347
Missouri Information for Community Assessment
(MICA) website, 342–43
Mitchell, Felicia, 246
mixed-methods approach, 8
Mohai, Paul, 238
Montgomery Village, Tennessee, 232, 249–50
Morgan, C., 88
mothers. *See* parents
Mt. Sinai Hospital, 29
Mullainathan, Sendhil, 103
Mullaly, Bob, 86–87
Multidimensional Poverty Index, 213
multilevel approach for reducing health
disparities, 31–36
multilevel perspective on stigma, 71–72
"Musings on Social Work and Social Work
Education" (Khinduka), 362–63
myRA program, 138

Nandan, M., 327
National Association of Social Workers (NASW),
45, 204, 247–48
National Cancer Database, 345
National Center for Charitable Statistics, 201
National Comprehensive Cancer Network
(NCCN), 345
National Institute of Standards and Technology
(NIST), 339–40

National Institutes of Health, 19–20, 245–46
National Research Council, 175
Naturally Occurring Retirement Community-Supportive Services Program (NORC-SSP), 325–26
needs
effect of poverty on satisfaction of, 50
hierarchy of, 157, 177
meeting basic, through asset accumulation, 117
Neger, E. N., 169
neglect. *See* child maltreatment
neighborhood disorder, 160
neighborhoods. *See also* communities
addressing cumulative inequality in, 108
assets embedded in, 34
and poverty as barrier to livable life, 50
process and dynamics of cumulative inequality, 96
role in engagement of older adults, 256
schools and education as related to, 99
as social determinant of health, 20–21, 30
solutions for productive engagement of older adults, 265–67
network analyses, 289
Network for Social Work Management, 327
New Deal policies, 27–28
new structural social work, 86–87
Noble, Charles, 62
nonprofit starvation cycle, 282–83
nonprofits, civic engagement through, 201
North Carolina, environmental justice movement in, 233
Nurse Family Partnership model, 170–71
Nussbaum, Martha, 11

older adults
civic engagement of, 197–98, 201
and cumulative inequality, 104
productive engagement of
causes of under-engagement, 255–56
general discussion, 268–70
neighborhood/community level solutions, 265–67
overview, 253–55
promoting employment, 258
promoting volunteering, 261
supporting caregivers, 263
Older People for Older People (O4O) project, 259
Oliver, Melvin, 130–31
One School model, Brown School, 361
online civic engagement, 197
organizations
civic engagement through, 201
promoting productive engagement of older adults, 258–65
outdoor air pollution, 232
policy changes to pursue, 249*t*

scope and impact, 237
underlying causes, 238
Ozawa, Martha, 360

Pachankis, J. E., 72
paid leave programs, 263–65
Panel Study of Income Dynamics, 130–31
parents
advocacy for child social services by, 278
child maltreatment prevention focused on poverty, 167–68
impaired capacity of, and child maltreatment, 161
services for, in prevention of child maltreatment, 168
support for, in prevention of child maltreatment, 170
participatory civic engagement, 194
partnerships, role in improving health equity, 33–34
Parvis, Richard, 360
Pate, D. J., 79–80
Patmore, B., 324
pay for success initiatives, 290
payday loans, 129–30
payment streams, building savings into, 143
Pennsylvania State University, 298
performance dashboards, 286
person/environment fit perspective, 254–55, 261, 265, 266–67
person-in-environment perspective, 5
person-to-person discrimination, 74
Pew survey on civic engagement, 196
Phelan, J. C., 22, 71, 73–74, 75–76, 78–79, 88
Philadelphia, Pennsylvania, 266
phone technologies, in social service provision, 287
photo identification laws for voting, 199
physical activity, in thriving communities, 223
physical barriers to livable life, 12
physical health. *See* health
Pitt-Catsouphes, M., 324
policy
braided approach
call for innovation, 320
curricular innovation, 327
fostering ambidexterity, 323
general discussion, 328–32
illustrations, 324
leadership development, 326
toolbox for, 323
challenges for innovation in social work, 318
economic, stimulating job growth through, 60–61
influencing change for environmental justice, 248, 249*t*
to promote asset accumulation, 135–39

promoting productive engagement of older
adults, 258–65
reforming to spread wealth, 141
science, and social determinants of health
lens, 36
serving as barriers to wealth building, 132
social services, linking to performance
financial innovations and system reform, 289
new integrated models of practice, 293
overview, 289
research and program planning, 291
technology use in making of, 287
as underlying cause of social determinants of
health, 27
PolicyLink, 33
political barriers to livable life, 12
political social work, 203–4
political structures, role in poverty, 54–57
pollution, outdoor air, 232
policy changes to pursue, 249t
scope and impact, 237
underlying causes, 238
Poor Laws, English, 82
Portland, Oregon, 265–66
post-siting demographic change, 238
potential
fulfilling, in livable life concept, 10
poverty as stunting achievement of, 51
poverty. *See also* asset accumulation
addressing, in prevention of child
maltreatment, 167
as barrier to livable life
doing without, 48
overview, 11–12, 48
stress, 50
stunted growth, 51
and barriers to civic engagement, 199–200
in communities
overview, 211–13
reducing, 218
underlying causes of, 213–17
and cumulative inequality, 96, 99, 103–4
and defensive othering, 81
economic cost of, 52
education as related to, 99, 102
efforts to provide health equity despite, 31–32
environmental injustice and, 232, 237, 240, 241
as factor leading to child maltreatment, 159
general discussion, 65–66
health, relation to, 103–4
mechanisms behind, 54–57
person-in-environment perspective on, 6
scope of, 46–48
social work emphasis on alleviating, 45–46
strategies to alleviate
building assets, 64
ensuring availability of decent paying jobs, 57

overview, 57
social safety net and access to key social
goods, 61
power, stigma, 75–76, 78
predictive analytic models, in child maltreatment
prevention, 165–67
prejudice, conceptualizations of, 73. *See also*
discrimination
prevention of child maltreatment. *See* child
maltreatment
Prinz, R. J., 169
privacy, as challenge to accessing big data, 340–41
privilege, and defensive othering, 77–78
probabilistic matching, 346–47
Proctor, Enola, 360
productive assets, programs providing, 220
productive engagement of older adults
causes of under-engagement
caregiving, 257
overview, 255–56
volunteering, 256
working, 256
organizational and policy solutions
general discussion, 268–70
neighborhood/community level
solutions, 265–67
promoting employment, 258
promoting volunteering, 261
supporting caregivers, 263
overview, 253–55
professionalism, 174, 285
Program for the Elimination of Cancer
Disparities, 294–95
program planning
linking policy to performance in social
services, 291
technology use in, 287
proxy measures, 343
public domain data, 353
public education, 98–99, 120, 277
public education approaches for social
services, 293–95
public goods, providing access to key, 61
public health approach for reducing health
disparities, 31–36
public service employment programs, 61
public stigma, 72
Putnam, Robert, 195, 196
p-values, 348–49

Qapital app, 144
Queer Aging (Fabbre), 85–86
Quillian, Lincoln, 98

race/ethnicity
addressing cumulative inequality related to, 108
and barriers to civic engagement, 199–200

race/ethnicity (*cont.*)
  and discrimination in job market, 103
  and employment as older adults, 260
  and exposure to air pollution, 237
  housing policies, consequences of, 28
  neighborhood context of cumulative
    inequality, 97, 98
  and poverty, relation to child
    maltreatment, 160–61
  racial wealth gap, 130
  schools and education as related to, 100–1
  as social determinant of health, 20–21,
    26, 103–4
racism
  environmental, 233–34, 241
  health effects of defensive othering, 79–80
  structural, 26–27
radical humanism, 86–87
radical structuralism, 87
Rainy Day EITC proposal, 137–38
Rank, Mark, 47, 53–54, 82–83, 84, 106, 358
Ravallion, Martin, 54
REACH project, Detroit, 29
Reagan, Ronald, 84
reciprocal processes, in person-in-environment
    perspective, 6–7
redlining, 28, 238
Refund to Savings Initiative, 140–41, 143–44
Reisch, Michael, 11
Reisner, S. L., 72
relational databases, 346–47
relevance, as barrier to social service delivery and
    access, 283
research
  on asset accumulation programs, 139
  in braided approach to social work, 331
  building infrastructure for, 297
  on child maltreatment and prevention, 175
  in environmental justice agenda for social
    work, 245
  linking policy to performance in social
    services, 291
residential segregation
  on basis of income, 97–98
  racial, 20–21, 26–27
Resnicow, K., 296
resource allocation, and challenges for
    innovation, 318
retirement
  and cumulative inequality, 104
  employer-sponsored programs for, 130
  financial benefits of asset accumulation, 120
  NORC-SSP, 325–26
  universal retirement accounts, 138
Ribot, Jesse, 236–37
Richmond, Mary, 7
rights-based approach to poverty reduction, 221

Riis, Jacob, 65
risk assessment tools, 353–54
risk-related poverty reduction approaches, 218–21
Robert Wood Johnson Foundation, 33–34
Rosenstock, Irwin, 201–2
Rossin-Slater, M., 264–65
Rotheram-Borus, Mary Jane, 324–25
Ruhm, C. J., 140–41, 264–65
rural communities, 215, 223, 224, 267
Ryan, William, 86

safety net programs
  changes in, relation to poverty, 56
  in efforts to reduce wealth inequality, 133–34
  providing effective, 61
Saha, Robin, 238
Sampson, Robert, 97
Save More Tomorrow program, 143–44
savings. *See also* asset accumulation; Child
    Development Accounts (CDAs)
  building into existing payment streams, 143
  economic barriers to, 126
  Individual Development Accounts, 136, 146
  policies serving as barriers to, 132
  promoting to reduce poverty, 220–21
  to protect against emergencies and meet basic
    needs, 117
  racial wealth gap, 131–32
  retirement, 120–21
  tax policies designed to promote, 137
Sawhill, Isabel, 101
scale up, 313–14
scarcity mindset, avoiding, 123
Schiller, Bradley, 49, 57
School of Social Work at Washington University.
    See George Warren Brown School of
    Social Work
schools. *See also* education
  and cumulative inequality, 99
  relation to neighborhood, 98–99
Schwalbe, M., 76, 83
science policy, incorporating social determinants
    of health lens into, 36
scientific productivity, and cumulative
    advantage, 95
Scott, P. A., 327
Scovronick, Nathan, 100–1
SDGs (Sustainable Development Goals), UN,
    35, 218
Seebohm Rowntree, Benjamin, 7
SEED for Oklahoma Kids, 31–32
segregation, residential
  on basis of income, 97–98
  racial, 20–21, 26–27
self-awareness, of social workers, 85–86
self-interest, enlightened, 53, 105–6
self-stigma, 72

Sen, Amartya, 10–11, 12, 75, 83, 211, 213–14
Senior Community Service Employment Program
  (SCSEP), 260
Senior Companion Program, 262–63
senior housing organizations, 261–62
service opportunities, and civic engagement, 204–5
service organizations. *See* social services
settlement house movement, 65
sexual minorities
  health effects of structural stigma, 81
  LGBT older adults, 263
  need for social worker self-awareness related
    to, 85–86
Shanahan, Michael, 52
Shapiro, Thomas, 130–31
shared agency data, 354
Sharkey, Patrick, 98
short-term loans, 128
Simon, Barbara, 45
single-parent families, effect of poverty on, 51
small livestock, programs providing, 220
Smeeding, T. M., 57–58
Smith, Judith, 51–52
SNAP (Supplemental Nutrition Assistance
    Program), 132, 133–34, 141–42
social barriers to livable life, 12
social cognitive model, 71–72
social connectedness, 34
social determinants of health
  addressing, 31–36
  defining, 18–19
  health as cornerstone of livable life, 17–18
  health disparities as affecting livable lives, 19–22
  overview, 16–17
  underlying causes of
    consequences of social policies and
      practices, 27
    gender, 24
    overview, 22–23
    race/ethnicity, 26
    social context, 30
    socioeconomic status, 23
    stress, 28
    tradition/culture, 25
social ecological approach, 71–72, 217–18, 224–25
social enterprise, 258–59
social entrepreneurship, 321t
  in braided approach to social work, 320, 328–32
  braided toolbox, 323
  curricular innovation, 327
  fostering ambidexterity, 323
  gaps in human services, 315
  leadership development, 326
  limitations of, 317
  management and policy challenges for, 318
  pay for success initiatives, 290
  recommendations for, 329

social exclusion
  conceptualizations of, 71, 74, 88
  critical reflectivity and structural social
    work, 84–87
  expanded conceptualization of defensive
    othering, 75–78
  general discussion, 87–89
  and livable lives
    economic well-being, 81
    overview, 78
    physical and mental health, 78
  overview, 70
social goods, providing access to key, 61
Social Impact Bonds, 290
social innovation, 321t
  in braided approach to social work, 320, 328–32
  braided toolbox, 323
  curricular innovation, 327
  fostering ambidexterity, 323
  gaps in human services, 315
  leadership development, 326
  limitations of, 317
  recommendations for, 329
social intrapreneurship, 316
social justice
  in approach to social services, 301
  Brown School commitment to, 359
  civic engagement oriented toward, 194
  in social work approach, 4
social learning theory, 72
social policies and practices, as social determinant
    of health, 27. *See also* policy
social problems. *See also specific social problems*
  complexity of, 313, 321t
  intractable, 312
social safety net
  changes in, relation to poverty, 56
  in efforts to reduce wealth inequality, 133–34
  providing effective, 61
Social Security, 120–21, 133–34
social services
  barriers to delivery and access
    effective demand, 283
    financing and incentives, 282
    overview, 280–81
    stigma, relevance, and access, 283
  disconnect between need and, 277–80
  general discussion, 300–1
  overview, 276
  potential solutions for delivery and access
    adapting interventions, 295
    building effective demand, 293–95
    building research infrastructure, 297
    improved use of technology, 285–89
    linking policy to performance, 289–93
    overview, 284–85
    training effective practitioners, 298

380 INDEX

social supports
    changes in, relation to poverty, 56
    relation to child maltreatment, 162–63
Social System Design Lab, Washington University,
    176, 297–98
social vulnerability, 244
social work. *See also* George Warren Brown School
    of Social Work
    barriers to promotion of livable lives
        complexity and evidence-based
            approaches, 313
        diminishing value of human service
            leadership, 319
        general discussion, 320
        innovation, defining, 314
        limitations of social innovation and
            entrepreneurship, 317
        management and policy challenges for
            innovation, 318
        overview, 312
        social innovation and entrepreneurship
            gaps, 315
    book organization, 13–14
    braided approach
        call for innovation, 320
        curricular innovation, 327
        fostering ambidexterity, 323
        general discussion, 328–32
        illustrations, 324
        leadership development, 326
        toolbox for, 323
    and child maltreatment prevention
        addressing child trauma, 172
        creating complete child protection/family
            support system, 173
        overview, 157
        professionalism, 174
        surveillance, 165–67
    community focus, 225–26
    current challenges to, 357–58
    emphasis on alleviating poverty, 45–46
    environmental justice agenda for
        conducting meaningful research, 245
        influencing policy change, 248
        overview, 245
        training social workers, 246
    environmental justice concerns in, 235–36
    future directions for, 362–63
    general discussion, 331
    as helping profession, 4–5
    intractable social problems faced by, 312
    need for novel approaches in, 311
    optimistic outlook on future of, 363–64
    overview, 1–2
    ownership of social service sector and its
        problems, 284–85
    promoting civic engagement, 203–5

    recommendations for, 329
    structural, critical reflectivity and, 84–87
    unique approach of
        evidence based, 7
        overview, 3
        person-in-environment perspective, 5
        social justice, 4
Social Work Congress, 326–27
Social Work Grand Challenges report, 165–66
societal institutions, importance of civic
    engagement to, 195
socioeconomic status. *See also* poverty; wealth
    inequality
    improving, 31–32
    as social determinant of health, 18, 20–21,
        23, 103–4
sociology, relation to social work, 3
South Carolina Integrated Data System, 349–50
Specht, Harry, 8, 285
special education programs, 277, 291–92
special needs, maltreatment of children with, 164
Spencer, Michael, 29
stagnant incomes, 126
state shared agency data, 354
statistical significance, 348–49
stigma
    adapting interventions to reduce, 295
    as barrier to social service delivery and access, 283
    conceptualizations of, 71, 88
    critical reflectivity and structural social
        work, 84–87
    enacted and felt, 79–81
    expanded conceptualization of defensive
        othering, 75–78
    general discussion, 87–89
    and livable lives
        economic well-being, 81
        overview, 78
        physical and mental health, 78
    multilevel perspective on, 71–72
    overlap with discrimination, 73–74
    overview, 70
    public, 72
    self, 72
    structural, 81
Stigma (Goffman), 71
stigma power, 75–76, 78
stigmatized person, discrimination operating
    through, 74
stress
    coping with through poor health
        behaviors, 30–31
    financial, health effects of, 124
    related to lack of assets, 115–16
    related to poverty, as barrier to livable life, 50
    as social determinant of health, 28
    socioeconomic status and, 24

structural barriers to civic engagement, 198
structural causes
    of poverty and inequality, 213–14
    of social vulnerability, 244
structural discrimination, 74
structural level of stigma, 72
structural racism, 26–27
structural social work, 84–87
structural stigma, 81
structuralism, radical, 87
student loan debt, 119–20
stunted growth, related to poverty, 51
substance abuse
    by caregivers, relation to child maltreatment, 161
    disconnect between social services and
        need, 278–80
    improving services for, to prevent child
        maltreatment, 168
    technology use in treatment of, 286
substantiation of child maltreatment, 291
success trap, 323–24
Supplemental Nutrition Assistance Program (SNAP
    or food stamps), 132, 133–34, 141–42
surveillance, for prevention of child maltreatment,
    165, 174
Survey of Household Economics and
    Decision-Making, 131–32
Susser, Mervyn, 26
Sustainability Exchange, Washington University, 247
Sustainable Development Goals (SDGs), UN,
    35, 218
Syme, Leonard, 22
systemic level causes of social problems, 362–63
systems, social service, 280–81, 289. *See also*
    social services
systems dynamic approaches, 176
systems science, 288–89

Tan, E. J., 262–63
task shifting, 325
tax policies
    alleviating poverty through, 58, 59–60
    to promote asset accumulation, 137
    role in addressing cumulative inequality, 108, 109
Taylor, L. A., 281
technology
    building research infrastructure, 297–98
    training effective practitioners in, 299
    using to close gap between services and needs
        assessment and service provision, 287
        integrated models of practice, 293
        overview, 285
        policymaking and program planning, 287
        treatment planning and evaluation, 286
Temporary Assistance for Needy Families (TANF
    or welfare assistance), 132, 133–34,
    141–42, 219

termination of parental rights (TPR), 350–51
thriving communities
    achieving
        overview, 217–18
        physical activity and healthy eating, 223
        poverty reduction and capability
            development, 218
        urban design, 221
    importance of, 211
tradition, as social determinant of health, 25
training
    and diminishing value of human service
        leadership, 319–20
    for effective practitioners, 298
    in environmental justice agenda for social
        work, 246
transdisciplinary education, 298, 361
transdisciplinary science, 246
transgender people, effects of defensive othering
    on, 80–81
trauma, child, 172. *See also* child maltreatment
treatment planning and evaluation, technology use
    in, 286
triangulation, 343
Triple P program, 171–72
t-test, 348
tunneling, 123
Turner, Margery, 97

unbanked status, 128
underbanked status, 128
under-engagement of older adults
    caregiving, 257
    overview, 255–56
    volunteering, 256
    working, 256
unemployment, 55. *See also* poverty; work
unique identifiers, 346–47
United Church of Christ Commission for Racial
    Justice, 233–34
United Nations
    Inequality Adjusted Human Development
        Index, 212
    Sustainable Development Goals, 35, 218
United Nations Population Fund (UNFPA), 25, 26
universal retirement accounts, 138
University of Chicago, 298
University of Southern California School of Social
    Work, 298
University of Texas at Austin, 297
upper echelons theory, 326
upward mobility, 98
urban communities. *See also* communities
    built environment in, 221–23
    causes of problems in, 215–16
urban design, 221
U.S. Department of Agriculture, 20–21

U.S. Department of Education, 100
U.S. Department of Health and Human Services (DHHS), 21
U.S. Environmental Protection Agency, 234, 245–46
U.S. General Accounting Office, 233–34

value network, 324
Vinokur-Kaplan, D., 317
volunteering. *See also* civic engagement
  need for further research on older adults and, 269
  patterns of, 196–97
  promoting for older adults, 261
  under-engagement of older adults in, 256
voting. *See also* civic engagement
  barriers to, 198–200, 202–3
  improving participation, 204
  need for further research on, 206
  patterns of, 196, 197
vulnerability, as factor leading to child maltreatment, 163. *See also specific vulnerable groups*

wage subsidies, 61
Waldfogel, J., 5, 140–41, 264–65
Warren County, North Carolina, 233
Washington University. *See also* George Warren Brown School of Social Work
  hands-on environmental problem-solving at, 247
  Social System Design Lab, 176, 297–98
  training in data and analytic procedures at, 297–98
water insecurity, 232
  policy changes to pursue, 249t
  scope and impact, 239
  underlying causes, 240
Watts, R. J., 198
wealth inequality. *See also* asset accumulation; cumulative inequality; poverty
  causes of

economic barriers to asset building, 126
  institutional barriers to asset building, 127–32
  overview, 125–26
  current status of, 109–10
  racial wealth gap, 130
  reframing understanding of, 133
  schools and education and, 99
  in US, 8–9
weathering, 29
Web of Science, 340
welfare assistance (TANF), 132, 133–34, 141–42, 219
Welty, E. D., 61
"What We Believe" (Youngdahl), 364
White-Hughto, J. M., 72
Whitehead, Margaret, 21
Who Is the "Self" in Self-Aware (Kondrat), 85
Wilson, William Julius, 97
women
  as caregivers, 258, 264
  environmental injustice and, 235, 240
  gender as social determinant of health, 24
  girl child marriage, 25–26
work
  addressing cumulative inequality, 108–9
  in age-friendly community development, 267
  and cumulative inequality, 102
  ensuring availability of decent paying jobs, 57
  lack of sufficient good paying jobs, 55
  need for further research on older adults and, 269
  promoting for older adults, 258
  under-engagement of older adults in, 256
World Health Organization (WHO), 17–18, 35, 152, 237, 265–66

Yadama, Gautam, 358
Youngdahl, Benjamin, 359–60, 361, 364
youth
  civic engagement in, 197, 198, 204–5
  social services for, 277–78